BEATRICE'S LAST SMILE

BEATRICE'S
LAST SMILE

A NEW HISTORY OF THE MIDDLE AGES

MARK GREGORY PEGG

OXFORD
UNIVERSITY PRESS

OXFORD
UNIVERSITY PRESS

Oxford University Press is a department of the University of Oxford. It furthers the University's objective of excellence in research, scholarship, and education by publishing worldwide. Oxford is a registered trade mark of Oxford University Press in the UK and certain other countries.

Published in the United States of America by Oxford University Press
198 Madison Avenue, New York, NY 10016, United States of America.

CIP data is on file at the Library of Congress

ISBN 978-0-19-976648-2

DOI: 10.1093/oso/9780199766482.001.0001

Printed by Sheridan Books, Inc., United States of America

To Margaret, Veronica, and Eva

Contents

Preface

After climbing down through the circles of hell, then ascending the mountain of purgatory, Dante the Pilgrim stands alone at the summit (which is the Garden of Eden). Virgil, his guide until then, has left. Beatrice, a young woman whom he once loved, appears to take him to paradise. She shames him by saying that after her early death he quickly forgot her. He confesses his guilt.

Then Beatrice lifts her veil. No longer stern and forbidding, she is smiling. He is transformed. They fly off together through the stars, soaring through one heavenly sphere after another until reaching the final sphere encircling all the others. During their flight Beatrice becomes more and more beautiful, but stops smiling. Dante wonders why. She answers that as they approach the Eternal Fountain her smile would incinerate him with its divinity. He shuts his eyes.

As soon as they are in the presence of Christ and the Virgin Mary, Beatrice tells Dante to look at her face, as he can now survive her smile. He feels as if the whole cosmos is smiling. The white rose of paradise, whose petals are the souls of the just, surrounds him like a vast Roman amphitheater. Suddenly he realizes Beatrice is gone. He looks up and sees her in the rose's distant third tier. She smiles at him one final time before turning away. Yet, far from being sad, Dante (Pilgrim and poet, his fictional and real selves merging) is joyful—he finally understands love, himself, and the universe, indeed all existence that ever was and ever will be. Because of Beatrice's last smile.

All this occurs at the end of Dante's early fourteenth-century *Comedy*. Jorge Luis Borges thought Beatrice's last smile the most moving image ever achieved in Western literature.[1] For me it encapsulates the history of the Middle Ages because it evokes the ebb and flow of holiness and humanity in the living of a life, whether on earth or in heaven (or in hell or in purgatory), that shaped the medieval world.

This book follows these fluctuations between the divine and the human through an interweaving of stories about men, women, and children living and dying between the third and the fifteenth centuries. It opens and closes with the martyrdom of two young women: a twenty-two-year-old mother in Carthage in 203, Vibia Perpetua, and a nineteen-year-old girl in Rouen in 1431, Jeanne la Pucelle (or Jeanne d'Arc). Their deaths, while horrible and heartrending, nevertheless shine with the density of life. But these lives were in the past, and whatever we may wish—and such wishes are worthy—there is nothing at all similar between us and them. The past has never been another country; it has always been another universe. Yet trying to evoke lives long gone, such as Perpetua's and Jeanne's, and maybe capturing some part of their incandescent reality, is what is so wonderful about being a historian.

Historical thinking is a profound gift. It is the foundation of all knowledge, humanistic and scientific. And so if the ten chapters of this book do nothing else, I trust they will give the reader an appreciation of change over time, of seeing that nothing is written in stone, that nothing is inherent, obvious, or natural. This might sound like cynicism. Far from it. Rather, it is a reminder that we must think hard about the whys and wherefores of the past (and of the present) and that we must always be ready to defend ideas and behavior we take for granted because societies really do forget as easily as they remember.

This book is not a religious history, despite my emphasis on holiness as a connective thread throughout the Middle Ages. Or to be more precise, this is not a history written by a religious person who assumes that religion in and of itself has some meaning outside of time and space. The great seductive achievement of religion is the denial of history. Religion was and is a way of understanding the world, and so any explanation of it in the past or the present must take into account the specific world that gives a religion meaning at a particular time and place. Religion is merely one manifestation of holiness. To argue over the holy is to argue over the very nature of what it means to be human, from the most mundane daily activity to the most sublime act of the imagination. It is to argue over how politics, economics, art, philosophy, and literature are realized in a society.

Although not a religious history, this book can be read as a history of medieval Christianity, for that is inescapable in any history of the Middle Ages. Nevertheless, there is a long and learned historiographic tradition in medieval history, especially in America, that assumes that anything defined as religion—which usually means "I know it when I see it"—can never be studied objectively and so the sensible thing is to ignore it. I was trained in this tradition and admire it.

This book is not a history of medieval Europe. Of course, I am well aware of the geographical region where much of my narrative occurs. Yet I have never thought of myself as a historian of Europe. (Perhaps this is because I am Australian.) Either way, no man, woman, or child before the fifteenth century would have recognized themselves as "European." Jeanne la Pucelle did—which is one of the reasons the book concludes with her.

Having said what the book is not, I should say what it is: a history of the "West." That term is a convenient shorthand for the lands and peoples that constituted the Western Roman Empire before and after its fall. But even in these centuries the West means more than just what was the Respublica—including, for instance, Irish monks freezing in the Inner Hebrides or the Prophet Muhammad in the Arabian peninsula receiving messages from the Highest God. By 700, though, the term usefully designates the developing religious and social distinctiveness of the regions between the Mediterranean and the North Sea that were not part of the East Roman (or Byzantine) Empire or Muslim Islamicate (or Islamdom). This difference only became more accentuated during the later centuries.

Indeed, what is commonly assumed to be the defining characteristics of Western civilization, especially a particular sense of the self, were formed in the twelfth and thirteenth centuries of Latin Christendom. To talk of the "West" should not be to engage in any form of cultural triumphalism. History is not a metaphysical discipline; it is an epistemological one. It is not about how the world could have been or could be; it is about what can be known of the actual world, as it is and was. I believe in historical truth, even if that truth is always beyond my reach, even if it can never be grasped. Searching for it must be enough.

"The old dictum is always true," the great French medieval historian Marc Bloch observed almost a hundred years ago, "years of analysis for a day of synthesis."[2] A famous aphorism, less often quoted with what he went on to say: a good historian knows that their specific analytic research is always shaped and guided by the grand narrative syntheses written by other historians. When this self-awareness is lacking, it is all too easy to repeat hypotheses, historiographies, and narratives that are either shopworn, misguided, or just wrong.

What was crucial for Bloch was that historians need syntheses, whether we like it or not, as they are the inescapable background music to our research and writing, and whether we wrote them or not, grand narratives are what we should always be imagining we would go on to write. In an ever-expanding universe of unwritten books, the curse of all scholars, our own unwritten sweeping syntheses actually matter, as they are constantly shaping the analytic research we do publish.

Moreover, big narrative histories for Bloch are exercises in collective public knowledge, helping form the ideas of all readers about the past. Such histories help societies define what was and is truth.

This book is the background music that I have been privately listening to for more than twenty years about the Middle Ages. Attentive readers will easily pick up melodies and themes from others. This is the unwritten book that has shaped so much of my life, finally written down.

Christmas Day, 2022
Wamberal
New South Wales
Australia

List of Maps

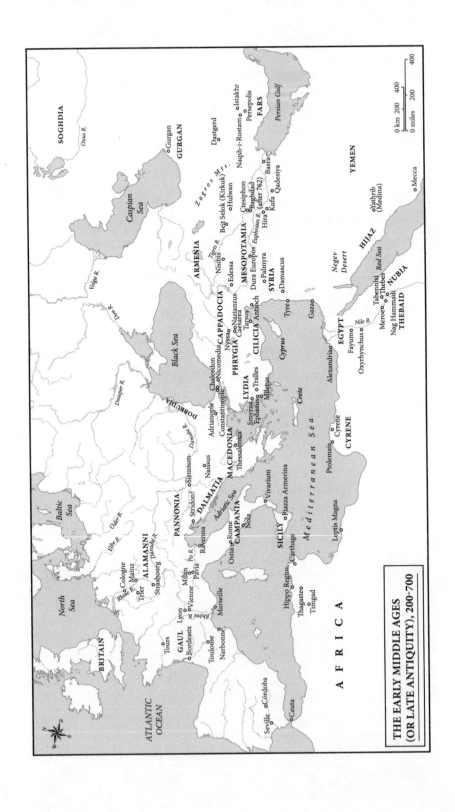

THE EARLY MIDDLE AGES
(OR LATE ANTIQUITY), 200-700

SOGHDIA

Oxus R.

GURGAN
Gurgan

Caspian Sea

Dastgerd

Naqsh-i-Rustam Istakhr
Persepolis
FARS

Persian Gulf

YEMEN

Mecca

Zagros Mts.

Tigris R.
Beg Selok (Kirkuk)
Hulwan
Ctesiphon
Baghdad
Euphrates R. (after 762)
Hira Kufa Qadesiya
Basra

Dvin?

MESOPOTAMIA
Dura Europos

ARMENIA
Nisibis
Edessa

HIJAZ
Yathrib
(Medina)

Red Sea

Negev Desert

Palmyra

SYRIA
Damascus

NUBIA
Tabennisi
Meroe Thebes
Nag Hammadi THEBAID

Nile R.

EGYPT

Fayumo
Oxyrhynchus

Alexandria

Gaza

Tyre

Cyprus

Crete

Ptolemais
Cyrene
CYRENE

Black Sea

Dnieper R.

Volga R.

Don R.

CAPPADOCIA
Caesarea
Nazianzus
Nyssa
PHRYGIA

CILICIA
Tarsus
Antioch

LYDIA
Tralles
Smyrna Ephesus
Miletus

Chalcedon
Nicomedia

Adrianople
Constantinople

DOBRUDJA

Danube R.

MACEDONIA
Thessalonica

Naissus

Sirmium
Stridon?

PANNONIA

DALMATIA

Adriatic Sea

Vivarium

Piazza Armerina

SICILY
Carthage

Leptis Magna

Mediterranean Sea

AFRICA

Baltic Sea

Oder R.

Elbe R.

North Sea

ALAMANNI
Cologne
Mainz
Trier
Strasbourg
Danube R.

Rhône R.

Milan
Pavia
Po R.
Ravenna

Rome
Ostia
CAMPANIA
Nola

Vienne
Lyon

GAUL
Tours
Bordeaux
Toulouse
Narbonne
Marseille

BRITAIN

ATLANTIC OCEAN

Seville Córdoba

Ceuta

Thagaste
Timgad

Hippo Regius

N
W E
S

0 km 200 400
0 miles 200 400

I

What God?

203–337

1 A Hairpin for Disheveled Hair

In early March 203, Vibia Perpetua, a twenty-two-year-old noble Roman mother, was arrested in Thuburbo Minus—a small town on the North African coast—for being Christian, along with three men and a pregnant slave girl named Felicity. She and the other Christians were imprisoned in Carthage. Her dungeon was dark, crowded, and stiflingly hot. "Above all," she wrote in a journal later smuggled out, "I was tormented by anxiety for my baby." For a price, Perpetua was moved to another cell to nurse her newborn son. "Prison suddenly became a palace, so that I didn't want to be anywhere else."

Perpetua asked God for a vision about her future, whether "martyrdom or freedom." He replied that evening with a dream in which she climbed a great bronze ladder to a garden in the sky and, surrounded by thousands of people clothed in white, an old shepherd gave her a mouthful of cheese. She awoke, "still chewing on something sweet," with martyrdom as her answer. Soon after, the procurator Hilarianus sentenced the Christians from Thuburbo Minus to fight wild animals in the amphitheater of Carthage.

Perpetua's dead little brother then visited her in two other dreams. In the first, "coming out of a place of shadows," he was thirsty and filthy, and his face was disfigured with the weeping sores that had killed him. In the second, he playfully drank from a low basin in spotless clothing with only a small scar on his face. His sister knew that he had been "released from his toils." A day before the games Perpetua dreamed she was a naked young man, glistening in olive oil like an athlete, stomping on the head of an Egyptian gladiator. "I knew that I was going to be fighting not with animals but with Satan! I knew victory was mine!"

A week after her arrest, Perpetua was led to the amphitheater. She greeted the other Christians from Thuburbo Minus, discovering that Felicity had given birth to a daughter three days earlier. (The babies of both women were taken away and raised by their families.) Before entering the arena, the men were costumed as priests of Saturn and the women as priestesses of Ceres. Perpetua—"noble to the end," according to one witness—refused to wear such regalia. "The point of deliberately going this far was not to have our freedom taken away; the point of taking our lives was to avoid doing this kind of thing," she told the tribune choreographing the games. "That was our pact with you." The tribune agreed—instead of religious fancy dress, he stripped Perpetua and Felicity and draped fishing nets over their naked bodies.

Perpetua entered the amphitheater singing, indifferent to her nakedness, already victorious over Satan, "already stepping on the Egyptian's head." Her reverie was cut short when the Christian men started yelling threats at the spectators (as many as thirty thousand) in the stands. "What you do to us," they even shouted at Hilarianus, "God will do to you!" The crowd cried out for *venatores* (gladiators who fought wild animals) to whip them. After being scourged, the Christian men were mauled by leopards, wild pigs, and bears. (One slow-witted *venator* was himself torn apart by a swift boar.)

Perpetua and Felicity, in another part of the arena, waited for a wild cow to gore them. The tribune was mocking them as new mothers with this specially chosen beast. The crowd, suddenly aware that the condemned had recently given birth, shuddered and screamed at the sight of exposed maternal flesh, especially Felicity's postpartum "dripping breasts." (Only a few moments earlier these same spectators had cheered, "Had a great bath! Had a great bath!" as blood spurted from one of the Christian men when a leopard ripped him open.) Stagehands quickly wrapped the women in loose robes. After this brief interruption, the show resumed. Perpetua, when first hurled by the cow, nonchalantly requested a hairpin for her disheveled hair, "so that no one might think she grieved in her glory." Finally, the bloody and mutilated women were ritually murdered by gladiators with swords.

Perpetua, initially stabbed in the collarbone by her nervous and inept executioner, steadied his hand and, already living in her garden in the sky, joyfully, wantonly, embraced death as she helped him slice her throat.[1]

2 An Empty Pageant

"In the life of a man," observed the Roman emperor Marcus Aurelius around 175, three decades before Vibia Perpetua's death, "his time is but a moment, his being an incessant flux, his senses a dim rushlight, his body a prey for worms, his soul an unquiet eddy, his fortune dark, and his fame doubtful."[2]

When Marcus Aurelius wrote these quick-fire exhortations to himself— less end-of-day meditations than sleepless inner tirades—he was in his late forties ruling over an empire that was 2,500 miles from east to west and 2,300 miles from north to south, with a population of 50 to 60 million, that is, somewhere between a fifth and a sixth of the world's population.[3] Of that number, 5 million (perhaps as many as 9 million) men, women, and children were slaves, and somewhere around 250,000 individuals were born into slavery each year.[4] The Roman imperium extended from the North Sea to the Mediterranean, from the Danube River to the Euphrates, and from the Black Sea to the Upper Nile, embracing three continents and what are now roughly sixty modern nation-states. The population of Rome was close to 1 million, with Alexandria and Antioch each approaching 300,000, and many ancient Hellenistic poleis in Asia Minor exceeding 100,000. Most cities, especially in the western provinces, such as London or Cologne, had populations of no more than 20,000. Carthage (in what is now northern Tunisia) was the largest city in Roman Africa, with over 100,000 residents, capital of the wealthy grain-growing province of Proconsularis (or Zeugitania).[5]

Marcus Aurelius described (in the vivid if moody vocabulary his Stoic philosophy reveled in) the teeming humanity within his empire as "an empty pageant, a stage play," no more than "flocks of sheep, herds of cattle; a tussle of spearmen; a bone flung amongst a pack of curs; a crumb tossed in a fishpond; ants, loaded and laboring; mice, scared and scampering; puppets, jerking on their strings."[6]

Marcus Aurelius epitomized *Romanitas* blended with *paideia*, that is, the martial vigor of "Romanness" constrained by the poise of the Hellenistic philosopher. He was acutely aware that existence was transient—"like warfare, a brief sojourn in an alien land"—and yet for all his cosmic fatalism, he would never think of chasing death.[7] A wise man might commit suicide, but chasing after death for no other reason than an inability to compromise, as he felt was the case with Christians, was offensive "stage heroics."[8] There was no garden in the sky awaiting him when he died, only oblivion. Philosophy and the manners of the philosopher were his warm existential comforts. He sought well-being by accommodating himself to the jangling way of the world, by performing correctly and seriously in the puppet show of life. Philosophers were experts in the art of living, practicing a rhetoric of mind and body whose affectations, apart from being a language understood by all Roman elites, helped individuals transcend the "dim rushlight" of routine reality for transcendent ethical clarity.

Such studious composure meant that any person of *paideia* should be able to stand unmoved when threatened with death.[9] Perpetua, while consciously emulating such self-possession—she was, after all, "noble to the end"—embraced her execution with almost sensual pleasure. Life was ephemeral for her too, but she wanted to die as a joyous martyr and "bride of Christ." Unlike emperors or millions of other Romans worshipping the old gods or even most other Christians throughout the empire, Perpetua knew without a doubt that death was merely a journey (specifically a climb) to everlasting divinity with her high-dwelling God.

3 Sacred Threads

The dreadful knowledge that to die was to lose whatever divinity a person had in life, and that living without death was the prerogative of the immortal gods, underscored the religious attitudes and habits of the civilizations around the Mediterranean Sea for more than a thousand years.

The act of worshipping the gods was, in no small part, an exercise in envy. Individuals felt no need to imitate the Homeric gods, whose excitable, savage, and unpredictable behavior was no model for living day to day. "Strangely violent is the grace of gods who sit enthroned in holiness," warned the Greek playwright Aeschylus in the middle of the fifth century BC.[10] As a bulwark against the cosmic capriciousness of the gods, human worship was consistent, predictable, and intensely local. This communal and familial worshipfulness, where every sacrifice, prayer, swirl of incense, or knee-bend before a statue was specific to each town and household in the Roman Empire, celebrated custom, continuity, and tradition. Such wonderfully varied and parochial rituals, whose scrupulous performance was frequently more important than the god so honored, evoked the experience of timelessness and immortality denied the individual.[11]

Romans thought of the world and their lives as intersected by an infinite number of holy powers. Poets and priests called them *numina*, while a specific sacred thread (speck, segment, particle) or a singular numinous bundle (suffusing a person or thing) was a *numen*. The gods were embodiments of these powers, greater or lesser swaths of divinity woven into anthropomorphic form. Everything and anything—door hinges, cooking pots, cloudy skies, weeping sores, magnificent temples—was infused with these prodigious forces. Holiness was forever keeping step with Romans, dogging them, getting under their feet, either wrapping them in lustrous sheaths or leaving them exposed to misfortune. Emperors were cocooned in the sacred stuff.

The proper and correct function of *religio* was the public and pious orchestration of these holy powers through traditional rites. Piety involved choreographing holiness through ritual so as to bring about good fortune. Tragedy existed, and with it all the large and small cruelties and sorrows that tear lives apart, but a morally specific notion of evil—tangible and quantifiable—did not. Religion was not about abstract morality—that was for philosophy and philosophers—but about maintaining the established rhythms and conventions of holiness through respect, ritual, and repetition. "The very power of *numina* stirs our hearts," observed the Roman poet Ovid at the beginning of the first century, before adding, "And there is nothing disgraceful in yielding to such credulity."[12]

Romans found it easy to absorb other gods and cults into a universe splintered by holiness. A cosmos so fragmented required (and therefore was always producing) a diversity of gods, beliefs, and practices. A universal set of religious habits and routines was unimaginable to a follower of the old gods. A traveler to a city or shrine might understand the local religion, even participate in a ceremony, but he or she knew that the specific holy powers of one place were not transferable to another. Of course, the cult of the emperor possessed similar attributes throughout the empire, with all Romans honoring his divinity, although even these rites varied when woven into local ritual calendars.

Radical Christians rejected this worship of the emperor. Two decades before Vibia Perpetua's martyrdom, twelve Christians (seven men, five women) in Carthage were rebuked for impiety by the proconsul Vigellius Saturninus when they refused to pray for Marcus Aurelius. "We too are a religious people, and our religion is a simple one," he informed them. "We swear by the genius of our lord the emperor and we offer prayers for his health—as you should too!"[13] The proconsul put the sacrilegious Christians to death. Perpetua belonged to a radical prophetic sect as well—overly zealous and hence impious even to other Christians—that was consciously disrespectful to the emperor and the public rituals maintaining the right and proper flow of holiness in the world.

4 The Hidden Mystery

In the city of Edessa around 215, a decade after Vibia Perpetua's death, the Christian nobleman and philosopher Bardaisan observed in conversation with friends (at least in a Platonic dialogue written by his student Philippus) that as regards Christians, "wherever they may find themselves, the local laws cannot force them to give up the law of the Messiah."[14] Everyone else was trapped by custom, as "the laws of men are stronger than Fate," and so, whether they wished it or not, Persian men married their daughters and sisters, Parthian men were polygamous, mobs of British men shared one wife, all Hindus were burned in death, no Edessene was chaste, the Greeks never stopped doing gymnastics, and the Romans were "always conquering new lands."[15] Edessa was then the capital of the kingdom of Osrhoene, on the Balih River (a branch of the Euphrates), a fertile Syriac-speaking corridor in Upper Mesopotamia between the Roman Empire and the Arsacid Parthian kingdom.

Bardaisan was not talking about Christians like Perpetua, who, despite denying local laws, was still so ensnared by custom that she chose to die like a noble Roman. His Christianity was a religion of the great caravan routes across Eurasia, a way of living untouched by the specificity of place, the vicious whims of princelings, or the mundane necessities of survival; and which, having no need for physical or ecclesiastical structures, or even visions of an afterlife, was imbued with a Platonic lightness of being, escaping the clutches of the world. It was a Christianity of Hellenistic philosophers and Eastern wanderers, neither welcoming death nor embracing violence, and so temperamentally closer to Stoic emperors than Carthaginian martyrs. It was a "universal" religion, in that Christians were to be found from the North Sea to the Asian steppes. On this point, Perpetua and other Roman Christians in the third century would have agreed with Bardaisan. None of them, however, assumed that the universe was exclusively Christian or even should be.

Bardaisan died around 222, two years before the last Arsacid Parthian king, Artabanos IV, was killed by the Sasanian Persian king Ardasir I at the Battle of Hormozgan on the Persian Gulf.[16] Although the Arsacids sometimes claimed they were the heirs of the Persian Achaemenids, defending themselves against one Roman emperor after another who imagined he was Alexander the Great, Ardasir I boasted that his new Sasanian Empire would, according to the Roman historian Dio Cassius, "win back everything that the ancient Persians had once held as far as the Grecian Sea."[17] Roman Syria and Mesopotamia (as well as provisional kingdoms like Osrhoene) were "his rightful inheritance from his forefathers," stolen after the death of the last Achaemenid king of kings, Darius Codomannus III, five hundred years earlier in 330 BC.[18] Ardasir I and his son, Sapur I, while never quite conquering Roman Asia Minor, did expand the old Parthian realm into a formidable empire whose ambitions and identity were defined in opposition to Rome. For the next four hundred years the Roman and Sasanian Empires repeatedly clashed, incinerating cities and enslaving populations, until the latter was destroyed during the great "Muslim" holy wars of the seventh century.

Amidst this Persian reformation, a twenty-four-year-old named Mani, whose mother was perhaps a royal Arsacid, received a divine revelation after wandering the Iranian plateau and the Hindu Kush in search of it. In 240, the same year Ardasir I died, either the Syzygos (his unsleeping divine twin or "pair-comrade," who never left his side) or the Paraclete ("comforter" or "Spirit of Truth," also his divine twin, forever whispering to him in Syriac about Jesus) "unveiled to me the hidden mystery, the one that is hidden from worlds and the generations . . . the mystery of light and darkness, the mystery of the calamity of conflict and war."[19] Mani was impelled to explain these mysteries in a new religion that would be explicitly universal. "The Lord Zoroaster came to Persia. . . . The Lord Buddha, the wise, the blessed one, came to the land of India. . . . Jesus the Christ, in the western lands of the

Romans, came to the West," and now Mani, superseding all of them, was a prophet to all these lands.[20] A pure "elect" living in "blessed poverty" recited his enlightenment, which was collected in codices, to aspiring "hearers."[21]

The core of this knowledge was a dualist vision of the cosmos that we call Manichaeism. Unlike the dualism of Zoroastrianism, which celebrated the tension between light and darkness, existence and nonexistence, in a world made by the wise god Ahura Mazda, and where the flickering flame (light, dark, light, dark . . .) was its symbol, Manichaeism loathed dark matter as an entrapment of the bright spirit. Bardaisan's Christian Platonism possessed similarities to Mani's mystery of light and dark. (In the early fourth century the Syrian Christian theologian Ephrem insulted Bardaisan's memory by calling him a "teacher of Mani.")[22] Manichaeism swiftly spread throughout the Sasanian, Roman, and even Chinese empires. As far as Mani was concerned, the universe belonged exclusively to his followers, for only they could escape the crushing weight of earthly darkness for effervescent spiritual light.

As the third century progressed, Roman emperors increasingly saw the universe as belonging only to them and their gods too, and so while the *numina* were still without limit, pernicious threads like Manichaeans or Christians were now systematically picked out and destroyed.

5 Not All Emperors Were Blunderers

The emperor Caracalla modeled himself on Alexander the Great and, apart from hoping to conquer Asia with the same blazing sense of destiny, piously granted, in a grand gesture worthy of the Macedonian monarch and "as an honor to the gods," Roman citizenship to all or almost all the free inhabitants of the empire in 212 or early 213. This innovation, far from being the obvious outcome of previous imperial enfranchisements, was unexpected and seemingly popular, if the number of new citizens who adopted Caracalla's official name, Aurelius, is anything to go by.[23] Although Caracalla's Alexandrine dreams collapsed two years later when his expedition against Parthia failed miserably, prompting his bodyguard to murder him (as he relieved himself by the roadside) near Edessa in 217, his radical vision of Rome was a demonstration of imperial confidence. The empire needed reforming, and while his father, Emperor Septimius Severus, retrospectively had his family adopted by the great Marcus Aurelius (hence

Caracalla's official name), he recognized that the "classical" empire of his adoptive ancestor was fracturing and that, unless something dramatic was done, it might collapse altogether.[24]

Less than two decades later—after the murder of two mediocre emperors, Macrinus and the teenage Elagabalus, whose frenzy at making the Syrian god Elagabal the supreme deity throughout the empire was a harbinger of further imperial religious experiments—the empire did fall apart. After the emperor Alexander Severus was brutally killed (along with his mother) by soldiers at Mainz in 235, the empire barely survived a half century of calamity and crisis, including no fewer than twenty-two emperors, almost all of whom died violent deaths, until the ascension of the emperor Diocletian in 284.

In many ways it seems more surprising—although perhaps not to Caracalla—that these decades of imperial crisis were so late in coming. The Roman Empire, far from being a tightly centralized state, was a loose-limbed entity, a mighty regional federation governed by local urban elites, whose close and immediate authority was sanctioned by the distant and awesome power of the emperor. The empire was a galaxy of thousands upon thousands of cities and towns, major and minor stars all glistening with civic works (baths, statues, temples, fora, amphitheaters) and honorable town councils, all emulating in their own way the great sun of Rome. In central Italy, Sicily, southern Spain, and northeastern Africa (125 miles inland from Carthage to the barren hinterland), cities were no more than ten miles apart, which was a half a day's journey on foot, slightly longer with a loaded donkey.[25] Such urban density was commonplace throughout most of the Roman East, including Egypt and Syria, lessening near the Arabian peninsula and the borderlands with Sasanian Persia. In northern Italy and parts of the south, the Dalmatian coast, Mediterranean Gaul, northern Spain, and a sixty-mile-wide littoral strip along the northwest African coast, cities were around twenty-five miles apart.

Outside this bright constellation—less Plato's sullen frogs squatting around the Mediterranean pond than ebullient fireflies—cities were few and far between, particularly in northern Gaul, Britain, and the Danubian riverine frontier.[26] Local urban elites, around sixty-five thousand in the Roman West and almost three times as many in the East by the early third century, were, as town councilors or *curiales*, responsible for religious festivals, maintaining law and order, and, most crucially, collecting imperial taxes, which were low for so vast an empire—somewhere between 5 and 10 percent of the agrarian surplus.[27] This pliant system, where an elite few maintained the imperium over millions, stopped working in the third century when the empire was threatened by external enemies, civil wars, economic disintegration, and a chorus line of inept emperors.

Throughout the empire, urban rhythms, from worshipping the old gods to gathering taxes, were largely local anticipations of and responses to harvest time, when prosperity was hopefully guaranteed for another year. Almost all wealth in the empire, more than 60 percent, derived from agriculture. More than 80 percent of the population, free or slave, were engaged in the labor of farming or animal husbandry. The suspense and satisfaction accompanying the harvest lasted from early spring to late summer for grain, late autumn to early winter for grapes and olives. Hailstorms and tempests, whose probability cruelly coincided with the Mediterranean harvest, could lacerate and flatten wheat, olives, or vines in a matter of minutes. Extended droughts caused famines. Variations in temperature could reduce yields by half. Olive trees, which take eighteen years or even more to mature, wither and die after a severe night frost.

In the third century, the flood of the Nile between June and September was consistently disappointing—fewer fields were covered with rich mud, with only a sterile slurry washing the majority, leading to wretched or failed harvests. The yearly cereal shipments to Rome were less bountiful.[28] Around 300 an Egyptian schoolboy copied on a wax tablet a poem to the "divine Nile" in Greek, which, more than anything, was a song about the widespread worry every summer awaiting the flood:

> Children singing all together the annual hymn
> in prayer inviting you to manifest yourself most perfect,
> for through hopes of you the life of mortals is sweeter . . .
> When you are rising, blessed one, our fatherland has glory.[29]

All of this anxiety about crops was only amplified by the damage from rampaging legions and brigands. Since all wealth for the next thirteen centuries was overwhelmingly tied to the land, who owned it, and who worked it, similar fears and worries lasted until the end of the Middle Ages.

Not all third-century emperors were blunderers; quite a few never reigned long enough to do much, and a handful were just catastrophically unlucky. All of them understood that the empire was in crisis, often trying extraordinary remedies. Almost immediately upon coming to the throne in

249, the emperor Trajan Decius issued a formal edict to all citizens of the empire (apart from Jews) demanding they sacrifice to "all the gods," eat the meat of the "sacred victims," and swear that they had always sacrificed.[30] Local *curiales* were to witness these sacrifices and issue certificates of their performance. Anyone refusing to sacrifice would be punished, from exile to loss of property to torture and death. What was so unusual about the edict was that it made what had once been public and parochial now individual and universal. Sacrifices were normally great sacred barbecues before large audiences in cities and towns, where the rising smoke, the smell of burning flesh and gristle, and mouthfuls of cooked meat engulfed humans and gods in shared fumes, aromas, and palates. They followed regional calendars, they celebrated the specificity of place, and they confirmed the prestige of local elites as patrons of *religiones*.

The mandate of Decius, while not disavowing such civic or cult festivals, demanded individual sacrifices and the pouring of libations in the same way as taxes were individually exacted—each one involved certification by *curiales*, each one guaranteed the security of the empire. It was a blunt acknowledgment that public works, whether communal sacrifices, baths, or temples, were disappearing from cities. Wealthy elites, especially in the West, preferred spending money on walls and fortifications. (Rome itself was ringed with walls in the 270s.) Decius was trying to unify a fractious and fearful empire. Christians, while not specifically the target of the edict, suffered the most if they refused to sacrifice to the gods. For the first time they were punished systematically throughout the empire; nevertheless, perhaps surprisingly, there was no widespread or official animosity against them, as there would be under Diocletian.[31] Whatever Decius hoped his edict would accomplish was cut short when it lapsed after he died fighting against invading Goths in Moesia Inferior (northern Bulgaria) in 251. As much as Caracalla's general enfranchisement had signaled the end of the classical empire, the edict of Decius confirmed its expiration.

If further confirmation were needed that this was no longer the empire of Trajan or Marcus Aurelius, the emperor Valerian was crushed in battle by Sapur I outside Edessa and taken prisoner in 260. "I, the Mazda-worshipping 'god' Sapur, king of kings of Iran and non-Iran," proclaimed the trilingual (Middle Persian, Parthian, Greek) inscription on the Ka'Ba-i Zarduct (Cube of Zarathustra) in Naqs-i Rustam near Persepolis by the river Pulvar, "captured the emperor Valerian with our own hands and . . . the praetorian prefect and senators and officials . . . and we made them all prisoners and deported them to Persis."[32] These words were carved soon after the death of Sapur I in 272 on the massive ruins of a Zoroastrian fire temple built by the Achaemenid Darius the Great eight centuries earlier and destroyed when Alexander the Great incinerated Persepolis in 330 BC.[33] They testified to Sasanian glory and Roman disaster, commemorating the destruction of a large Roman army ("a force of 70,000 men"), the desolation of Syria, and the ransacking of Antioch for a second time. They framed the conflict between the empires as a holy war. There was no mention of what happened to Valerian in captivity. There were Roman rumors that he died an old man somewhere in Persia after years of humiliation, even being dishonored in death with his skin flayed, dyed red, and displayed in a Zoroastrian sanctuary.[34]

Despite military catastrophes and the empire breaking apart into autonomous entities under self-proclaimed rulers such as Odaenathus, lord of Palmyra in Syria, some Roman regions, if not quite thriving, were on a day-to-day level largely untouched by imperial turmoil. Egypt was such a province, and it was here, a decade after Valerian's capture and seven years before Mani's death, that an unhappy Christian youth had a revelation and went to live amongst the dead and the demonic.

6 The Lonely One

Antony, a prosperous farmer of the Fayum in the Nile delta of northern Egypt, walked into his village church sometime around 270 and heard someone repeat the words of Jesus to the rich man: "If you would be perfect, go and sell everything you possess and give it to the poor and come, follow me, and you will have treasure in heaven." This was divine advice for the despondent adolescent (he was not yet twenty), who, ever since his parents had died six months earlier, felt overwhelmed by possessions and responsibility for his little sister. Immediately, he divided his farm (two hundred acres) amongst his neighbors, sold everything he owned (including at least two slaves), gave his profit to the poor, and entrusted his sister to faithful Christian virgins after setting aside income for her. He then walked to the edge of his village, where he lived and prayed upon a rush mat. He stopped oiling and perfuming his body like other young Egyptian men. He only ate bread and salt once a day, then every two, then every four. Antony replaced all memories of his family with the words of Christ (or at least those he recalled, as his memory was his only book).

The devil took an interest in Antony and started chatting with him at night. They talked about sisters, delicious food, money, good weather, the pleasure of laziness, and the difficulty of virtue. One offered temptations, while the other numbed himself with prayers. The devil, giving up his bon vivant persona, metamorphosed into a beautiful girl and, through tender caresses, aroused the young loner. Antony, disgusted by his bodily desire, fought off the wicked slut by thinking of agonizing fire and ravenous worms. After this, so as to smother his living flesh, he went to the desolate area just beyond the village where the dead were buried, locking himself inside an ancient tomb. The devil chased after Antony and, with a gang of thuggish demons, smashed in the door and beat him senseless.

"Look, here I am," Antony taunted the devil when he regained consciousness, even as he lay splayed out in rippling pain. "I do not run away from your fights!" The devil was amazed and furious that neither lust nor injury deterred the youth from living amongst the dead. "Take up your weapons," he commanded his demons, "we must attack with greater force!" The tomb began to shake violently. Demonic hordes in the form of lions, bulls, wolves, vipers, serpents, scorpions, leopards, and bears poured through holes in the crumbling walls. Roaring and hissing, they attacked their supine prey. "Look, here I am," Antony mocked the beasts as they mauled and gored him, "devour me!"

Antony endured the feeding frenzy, staring upward, his body in bloody agony, until the roof of the tomb suddenly burst open and a shaft of light swept over him. All his pain disappeared, all the demons vanished. Antony reprimanded the light: "Where were you, good Jesus? Where were you? Why were you not here from the beginning to heal my wounds?" A voice, mildly amused at being scolded, replied, "Antony, I was here, but I was waiting to watch your fight. But now, since you have bravely held your own in this struggle, I will always help you and I will make you famous throughout the world." Antony rose to his feet, strong and unscathed.

Antony was about thirty-five when Jesus promised to make him famous. Diocletian had been emperor for a year. Yet what was happening in the empire was irrelevant to Antony; indeed, in an effort to escape even further from the realm of the living, he went off to the "mountain" (Greek *oros*, Coptic *toou*)—that is, the desolate desert escarpment of the Nile valley.

Antony had been walking no more than a day when he found an abandoned stone fort (more likely Ptolemaic than Roman) with a small spring. None of the physical distances he traveled were great, whether to the tombs separating his village from the desert or now in the desert itself, but in terms of the Egyptian imagination, Christian or not, it was a heroic enterprise, one in which all traces of his humanity were gradually lost—first amongst the dead, and now in the "mountain" where only demons, barbarians, and wild beasts lived.

When Antony first entered the fort "a huge number of snakes fled as if they had been chased out." He blocked the entrance with stones, storing enough bread for six months (and arranging for more bread to be delivered twice a year). Inside he argued and fought with demons. Soon hundreds of other men (and some women) began living amongst the ancient ruins and caves in the desert near Antony, imitating his way (or what they thought was his way) of accruing treasure in heaven. After twenty years of emulating a man they never saw and rarely heard—and then only when he loudly clashed with demons—their exasperation erupted in the hysterical destruction (clawing, scratching, bashing) of the fort's wooden gates. Antony walked outside in an "aura of holiness" like one of the old gods emerging from a divine sanctuary. He was beautiful: his body was not flabby, despite no exercise, and his face was not pale, despite fasting and fighting demons. It was as if no time had passed. Except now he was famous throughout the world, as Jesus had promised. He was the indomitable "man of the mountain," *erémétikos*; he was the courageous "lonely one," *monachos*. [35]

Antony would become the enduring model of a Christian hermit and monk for the medieval world.

7 Dance of Immortal Love

Antony died in 356, and what we know of his life was written in Greek sometime in the next decade by Athanasius, bishop of Alexandria, and soon translated into Latin by Evagrius of Antioch. [36] The bishop was Antony's friend and disciple, and his biography was written in a Roman Empire no longer in crisis and, even more astoundingly, where the emperor himself and much of his court were now Christian. Athanasius was also a theological rabble-rouser in an empire where debates about the humanity of Christ could incite riots, so his portrait of the first *erémétikos* was as much political pamphlet as spiritual history. The outcome of Antony's holy struggle in the last decades of the third century was never in any doubt for Athanasius—and yet it so clearly had been when the young Egyptian first gave away all his earthly wealth so as to gain heavenly riches. Antony's journey away from the living into the desert was an experiment with the divine, a rigorous inquiry in which he tested the limits of the world with his own shameful flesh.

Antony's experiment in the desert was similar to what many Romans who believed in the old gods wanted to inflict upon their own bodies in the third century. The philosopher Plotinus, who died in 269—the same year, as it happens, as Antony's parents—was another Egyptian famously ashamed of his body. He despised his flesh for hindering his quest for the holy. According to his student Porphyry, who edited his Greek writings (now known as *The Enneads*) and prefaced them with a biography sometime before 300, "Plotinus did everything to be released and escape from the bitter waves of the blood-drinking life here"—except, that is, live amongst the dead or chase after death.[37]

Indeed, Plotinus lived comfortably in Rome in the houses of wealthy patrons or in his own academic palazzo surrounded by students, noble widows, and orphaned children, even as he disciplined his body by refusing medical treatments (especially enemas) and eating very little ("he would not even touch bread"). He saw himself as different from the humanity around him. He had much more in common with the One, a singular transcendent principle, which he sometimes called God (*theos*), "who has neither shape nor any form; who is enthroned above mentality and all intelligible things." Plotinus was a "god-like man."

Porphyry even recalled an incident when an Egyptian priest who was visiting Rome called up the personal daemon of Plotinus. Instead of a daemon, a god appeared. "You are blessed for you have a god as your daemon and not a companion of the subordinate type," said the priest with admiration. Daemons were usually manifestations of the perfect forms of individual selves (and so were time-traveling visitors from the future perfection of men and women after death). They were guardian spirits helping souls on earth through "the troubled seas of life." They were not sublime enough for Plotinus. When he walked through the streets of Rome, a god kept pace with him. The *numina* shaped themselves around him, rather than the other way around.[38]

Intriguingly, while Plotinus praised and taught *paideia*, as a Roman philosopher should, Porphyry stressed that he was sometimes imperfect in speech (particularly long words) and manner (slightly sweaty, rumbling bowels), and so while he was always "beautiful to behold," his body denied him perfection. Philosophy derived from Plato was his compensation—for to wrestle with an idea, let alone understand it, was in a profound sense to wrestle with the divine, and so understand the universal qualities of God or the One. Plotinus tested the limits of the cosmos with his mind, that is, his soul. "For him the end and goal was to be united to and draw near to God who is above all things." According to Porphyry, he achieved this four times in life. In death, Plotinus achieved this goal forever, finally joining "Plato, Pythagoras, and as many others who are set upon the dance of immortal love."[39]

Plotinus and Porphyry were leading figures of a third-century Roman philosophical renaissance that we call Neoplatonism. Plato had been rediscovered by educated men and women throughout the empire, including Jews and Christians. His *Timaeus*—a majestic dialogue about the creation of the universe by a Demiurge or Creator God and written in the decade before he died in 347 BC—was especially influential. His notion that the world around us (the world of Becoming) was merely an ugly and corrupted memory of a more beautiful and incorruptible world (the world of Being) was, not surprisingly, comforting for many Roman intellectuals during the decades of imperial crisis. This Platonic revival extended beyond the empire, inspiring, as we have already seen, individuals like Bardaisan in Edessa and (to a lesser extent) Mani on the Iranian plateau.

Porphyry thought Plato lived again in Plotinus. He and his teacher proudly referred to themselves as Platonici (Platonists)—as did many other philosophers and theologians for the next thirteen centuries in the West, even when such intellectuals were overwhelmingly Christian.[40] Some of the most controversial and important ideas in the Middle Ages, especially about the nature of Christ, were inspired by Neoplatonism.

Porphyry would have been appalled. He sincerely disliked Christians, even if he had briefly flirted with their religion when young. He viewed them as arrogant and lacking in respect for traditional beliefs, such as their refusal to sacrifice to the old gods (which, for his own transcendent reasons, Plotinus refused to do as well). He even wrote a treatise known as *Against the Christians* (*Contra Christianos*) before his death in 310. Although this polemic is lost, fragments survive in the many books written by medieval Christian intellectuals attacking it for over a millennium (often respectfully, as they were usually Platonici themselves). Plotinus in his godlike detachment from the world seemingly had no opinions about Christianity.[41]

Antony's "escape from the bitter waves of the blood-drinking life" into the desert was a deliberate rebuke of the philosophical pursuit of holiness as exemplified by a Plotinus or even a Christian like Bardaisan. He rejected *paideia*, which required, apart from oiling and grooming one's body with rhetoric, an audience, much the way the old gods had. He exaggerated his lack of an education (which Athanasius embellished even further), arguing that all he needed were God's words to know God, and that these words were in everyday Coptic and not learned Greek. This anti-intellectualism underscored Antony's rejection of civilized society for the desolate community of demons.

Paradoxically, this desolate community was the very embodiment of urbane Roman civilization, in which Antony's demons were the *numina* reconfigured as manifestations of evil. In the desert the *numina* were severed from the public rituals and processions that gave them power and meaning, and with only Antony watching and listening, those that had been holy companions for a philosopher in Rome were transformed into maleficent demons for a monk in an empty fort. Much as Plotinus always had a lesser god beside him, Antony always had the devil. The old gods never went away for Antony. They remained vivid presences, long shadows trailing humanity, except now they were cruel and immoral entities. The universe was, as it had been for Vibia Perpetua almost a century earlier, not entirely Christian.

This was a reality harshly confirmed when Diocletian issued an edict at Nicomedia (modern Izmit in Turkey) on Wednesday, February 24, 303—the same year Antony walked out of his fort to present himself to his followers—that all Christian churches be destroyed, all Christian scriptures burned, all Christians in imperial service removed, all Christian freedmen enslaved, and all legal protections for Christians revoked.[42]

8 An All-Embracing Authoritarianism

Nineteen years earlier, when Diocletian became emperor, it had seemed more than likely that the routine assassination of rivals, betrayal of friends, and mercurial acclamation of soldiers that had swiftly elevated him would just as quickly replace him with someone else. Instead, rather than attempting to rule by himself an immense empire fractured with pretenders and rebels, he raised a soldier named Maximian to the rank of Caesar to govern with him as deputy. The new Caesar quickly subdued a rebellion in Gaul and fought off marauders along the Rhine. In recognition of this achievement, Diocletian elevated Maximian to Augustus (co-emperor) in 286. The empire was divided between the two Augusti, with Maximian overseeing the Latin-speaking western regions and Diocletian focusing upon the Greek-speaking eastern provinces. They were partners, Jupiter and Hercules, even if it was understood that Diocletian was senior.

Seven years later, in 293, Maximian, acknowledging that even half an empire still troubled with renegade legions and imperial claimants was too much for one individual, appointed the soldier Constantius (who was husband to his stepdaughter Theodora) as his Caesar. In less than a month Diocletian added to his household a Caesar named Maximianus Galerius (to whom he married his daughter Valeria). This tetrarchy, with four imperial courts constantly moving around the western and eastern provinces and building elaborate palaces in strategic cities (such as Trier and Sirmium), was a powerful demonstration that the classical empire held together by local Roman elites was gone. Imperial authority was no longer enforced and reflected in each town and city through an urban-dwelling squire-archy. It was now selfishly guarded as the awesome property of the four imperial courts and their attendant soldiers and bureaucrats. Emperors and their Caesars aspired to be authoritarian and universal, shaping all aspects of life within the empire.

In April 297 Diocletian issued an edict in Alexandria ordering the proconsul of Africa, Julianus, to punish Manichaeans, a "superfluous pestilence" from Persia, "by burning them in the flames together with their abominable writings." All property of this "infamous sect" was to be confiscated by the imperial treasury. Their crime was trying "to replace the old religions with new and unknown creeds." As Diocletian had purged the empire of imperial pretenders, he now cleansed it of religious renegades, "for it is the greatest crime to open to debate what was once decided upon and defined by the forefathers."[43] This was radical persecution in the guise of sober traditionalism.

Diocletian's edict was also part of the war effort against the Sasanian king of kings Narse, who, wishing to emulate Sapur I in a grand campaign of conquest, was threatening Roman Syria. A Manichaean, even if he or she was a Roman citizen (as most of them were in Egypt), was irremediably poisoned by Persian religious nonsense against Rome. (Julianus, who compiled the initial report on the Manichaeans for Diocletian, was seemingly unaware that when Mani died a prisoner of the Sasanian monarchy and Zoroastrian priesthood in 276 or 277, he was accused, amongst other things, of not acting like a Persian.)[44] It is unclear how widespread (or even effective) was the edict against the Manichaeans. Antony in his desert solitude vehemently thought they deserved punishment. Much of the imperial zeal undoubtedly abated when a year later Galerius attacked Narse near the Armenian city of Satala and annihilated the Sasanian army. (The Augustus, so it was whispered, deliberately avoided campaigning with his Caesar, so as not to end up as a skinned vermilion trophy like Valerian.) Now that the eastern frontier was calm, Diocletian focused upon everything volatile and unsound in the empire, from coinage (too debased) to food prices (too high) to the size of provinces (too large) and, finally, to Christians (too dangerous).

The imperial assault against Christians beginning in 303, and known to later Christian writers as the "Great Persecution," while possessing similarities to the attack on the Manichaeans, such as "purifying" the *numina* of persons denigrating the old religions, was different more than just in scope. Christianity was not an "unknown creed" from another empire. Christians, while perhaps no more than 10 percent of the Roman population, had been for three centuries familiar individuals, mostly concentrated around the Mediterranean, especially North Africa, Egypt, Syria, and Palestine. Few were as radical as Vibia Perpetua and Antony; most were rather commonplace persons from the middling stratum of Roman society—neither virile slaves nor the doe-eyed debutantes of old Hollywood movies—living easily amongst neighbors who walked with daemons.[45]

By the beginning of the fourth century a Christian church was a modest structure usually in a side street, often overshadowed by a large, elegant synagogue. Despite such architectural modesty, those gathered inside—fifty or so men, women, and children—were, like the Jews whom they imitated in this regard, ostentatiously worshipping in a way antithetical to a believer in the old gods, whose religion was manifested in the public spectacle outside a temple. (The hidden, often exquisite interiors of temples were for deities and not humans.) It was not so much that Christian worship was secret, although depending on the town or city it sometimes was, only that the Christian religious sense of self was not geared to local holy rhythms. Instead, it was, with increasing intensity throughout the third century, a sensibility overwhelmed by the universal nature of humanity confronting the universality of an omnipresent God. The numinous specificity of time and place as the vital mechanism in keeping a cosmos of many gods functioning, of holiness anchored in parochial smoke, sculpture, and sacrifice, melted away before a God worshipped the same way everywhere, or so it was imagined by Christians. Inside a church, however small, the infinite vastness of God was asserted; amongst worshippers, however few, the commonality of all human experience was affirmed.

This all-encompassing Christian vision was remarkably similar to how Diocletian and other believers in the old gods, especially imperial courtiers, understood themselves and their relationship to the holy at the beginning of the fourth century. An all-embracing authoritarianism had gradually extinguished the relative autonomy of towns and cities; the sublime patchwork of gods and goddesses across the empire had slowly mutated into a more unified religious organism, one exemplifying the ubiquity of imperial power and the subservience of all citizens before such transcendent majesty. Distinctive cults and mythologies still played out across the empire, but rather than being a sacred cacophony whose very disharmony was comforting to Marcus Aurelius, they were now part of a divine symphony, which, while a dance of immortal love for a soul like Plotinus, was a martial anthem of conformity for Diocletian. Believers in the old gods saw themselves as worshippers within a polytheistic system as universal and coherent as that of monotheistic Christianity. The gods were imagined, at least by educated elites, as varying expressions of a singular godhead who possessed no form. This new polytheism—whose worshippers, if they called themselves anything, preferred "Hellenes"—was the religious culmination of the improvised edicts and impromptu solutions to third-century turmoil generated by successive emperors and their officials. By the time of Diocletian, the excessive claims of Christianity (and Manichaeism) were irreconcilable with such an imperious religion.

In 304 an imperial amnesty momentarily halted the campaign against Christians. Over the previous eighteen months the ferocity and efficiency of the assault had varied throughout the empire. Some officials did no more than announce the decree, while others chased down papyrus scriptures and recalcitrant worshippers for incineration. Overall, there were few deaths. For example, in Palestine, where many Christians lived and the bureaucrats were vigorous, seven individuals were executed in 303.[46] There were limits to tetrarchic absolutism. The amnesty, ostensibly an act of benevolence from Diocletian celebrating his elevation as emperor two decades earlier, was also an acknowledgment that the harrying of Christians had achieved some of its purpose. Although Christianity had not been eliminated—if that was ever the goal in any case—how Christians understood their relationship to the empire and to each other was profoundly altered.

To be Christian and Roman now seemed incompatible. *Romanitas* clashed with *Christianitas*. Where formerly many Christians had participated in celebrations glorifying local divinities, or even attended games in honor of emperors, they did so knowing that it did not affect their own sacred sense of themselves. Now they had to make a choice. They were, like all citizens, compelled (albeit more harshly than à la mode polytheists) to reevaluate what it meant to be Roman in the revived empire. Both the edict against Christians and the munificence of the amnesty demonstrated the exalted and violent power of the state for all Romans. To Diocletian this projection of authority was more important than erasing (for now) a vainglorious cult worshipping a crucified Jew.

9 By This Conquer

"What God," an elderly Gallic orator asked Constantine, the son of Constantius, at Trier in August 313, "encouraged you when almost all of your comrades and commanders were not only silently muttering but even openly fearful?" What God, "against the counsels of men, against the warnings of soothsayers," had revealed "that the time had come to liberate the City?" The answer, as the orator well knew, was the divine culmination of a series of events that had begun with the death of Constantius seven years earlier at York, Constantine's swift acclamation as emperor by the British legions, his conquest of the western provinces from other imperial pretenders until, before the walls of Rome in October 312, he defeated Maxentius, the son of Maximian, at the Milvian Bridge over the swift-flowing Tiber, liberating the city in the name of the Christian God.

Constantine becoming a follower of this God was momentous, yet precisely when and why it happened is unclear. When Diocletian abdicated in 305, satisfied that the empire was secure, he never assumed that the elevation of Constantius to Augustus in the West (with Galerius ruling in the East) was, even if indirectly, promoting Christianity. He retired to a vast palace at Split on the Dalmatian coast and, Jupiter masquerading as Pan, pottered about his private Arcadia growing cabbages, seemingly indifferent as his tetrachic system fell apart (except for a tepid effort at repair in 308), dying two months after the Battle of the Milvian Bridge.

Although the Gallic orator knew all this recent history, as a believer in the old gods he struggled to elucidate what it meant for an emperor to favor the Christian God. "You," he directly addressed Constantine's God, "supreme creator of things—whose names you wished to be as many as the tongues of nations, for what you yourself wished to be called we cannot know—whether you are some kind of force and divine mind spread over the whole world, mingled with all the elements, moving of your own accord," or whether "you are some power above all heaven" looking down upon us, "surely there is supreme goodness and potency in you." There were many Romans like the orator, who were still baffled by the question "What God?"[47]

Amongst those perplexed Romans was Constantine himself, at least before the victory of the Milvian Bridge, if not throughout most of his life. Eusebius, bishop of Caesarea in Palestine, in his *Life* of Constantine, composed before 339, recalled the emperor telling him many years later of a vision he had had while campaigning in Britain or Gaul. "About the time of the midday sun, when the day was just turning, he said he saw with his own eyes, up in the sky and resting over the sun, a cross-shaped trophy formed from light, and a text attached to it which said, 'By this conquer.'"[48] In a dream the night before Constantine's attack on Rome the "Highest God" (*summus Deus*) told him to copy what he had once seen silhouetted against the northern sun as a talisman against his enemies.[49] When his soldiers massed before the Milvian Bridge their shields were emblazoned with this new solar symbol, along with the Greek letters *chi* and *rho*, which referred either to Christ or to *chrestos*, "good luck."[50] What is often called Constantine's "conversion"—an anachronistic concept suggesting modern notions of individuality, sincerity, and spiritual awakening (with distinctly Protestant overtones)—was initially a revelatory insight into the singular divinity shimmering within, and so ultimately orchestrating, the infinite *numina*.

In this Constantine was like other emperors before him in the late third century, including his father, who worshipped the "Invincible Sun" (Sol Invictus), linking his martial exploits and imperial legitimacy to an exalted deity in the numinous pantheon that spoke to him directly and exclusively. Constantine's Highest God was sublimely violent, associated with the sun, and reassuringly authoritarian. A God of war; a God who traversed the boundless heavens; a God for an emperor. Ironically, as well, a God with most of the qualities Diocletian celebrated in the old gods, apart from this new God's unique superiority to all other divine pretenders. Although Constantine soon understood that his Highest God was the same deity as that of the Christians, it did not necessarily make him a Christian. A long reign and hindsight would do that.

10 A Golden Age

Five months before the Gallic orator wondered aloud about the nature of the divine mind guiding imperial decisions, Constantine was in Milan discussing his all-conquering God and the oppression of Christians with another imperial claimant, Licinius, whose legions had recently acclaimed him Augustus. Both emperors acknowledged the divinity of the Christian God as well as their reverence for the old gods. In June 313 Licinius (who married Constantine's half sister Constantia) issued an edict at Nicomedia to all the eastern provinces recalling what the two Augusti had discussed in Milan. (There was no actual "Edict of Milan," even if what was proclaimed in the East was initially drafted in the West.) As the Highest God protected Rome and Christians, the edict stated unequivocally, the latter were no longer to be persecuted; indeed, there was to be no more religious persecution at all in the empire, so that any Roman "may have a free opportunity to engage in whatever worship he has chosen."[51]

Constantine himself had already stopped all assaults on Christians before meeting with Licinius (which was why he saw no need to issue his own edict). After capturing Rome he rewarded the bishops and priests of the Christians, "commonly known as clergy," specifically excusing them from the onerous responsibilities of local civil government and from paying some taxes, although not the land tax.[52] He did not reward Christians as a group, apart from ending their persecution, or see himself as a member of their small sect of mostly mediocre persons; rather, he honored their ritual experts, who maintained the proper *religio* praising the Highest God.

A bishop in the first and second centuries was a relatively humble person amongst Christians who had come together for spiritual and material support in a "church"—*ekklesia* in Greek, meaning "gathering" or "assembly," and adopted into Latin as *ecclesia*. Although his title designated him as an "overseer"—Greek *episkopos*, rendered into Latin as *episcopus*—what holiness he possessed was neither more nor less than that of anyone else in his small group, as communion with God was achieved collectively rather than being guided by him. His most important episcopal duty was as an intermediary between his church and the often hostile (or just contemptuous and condescending) local town councilors and imperial officials. Vibia Perpetua, though, lived and died as a Christian in a visionary fellowship neither having nor wanting even a modest "overseer."

By the third century the position of bishop had developed into an exalted rank within Christian communities. Churches, while never completely egalitarian, had become much more hierarchical, more obviously reflecting the society of which they were a part. A bishop was chosen by his community as a superior Christian and an outstanding Roman. He usually had been a priest, deacon (Greek *diakonos*, "servant"), or presbyter (Greek *presbyteros*, "elder" or "old man," and specifically one learned in theology). He interpreted the scriptures and explained the mysteries of Christianity (which was why presbyters in some churches were his equals). He administered property and gifts bequeathed by his congregation for supporting the clergy and helping destitute Christians. For example, in 251 the church in Rome funded 154 clerics (52 were exorcists) and comforted more than 1,500 widows, orphans, and indigents.[53]

A bishop passed judgment in his own ecclesiastical court on disagreements within his flock. He sometimes convened councils with neighboring bishops in difficult cases. Around 300 such an episcopal council in Elvira in southern Spain debated the issue of slaves dying from beatings ordered by their Christian mistress.[54] A bishop was a *papa* (father) to his church—at first a general honorific for all western bishops in the early third century before belonging almost exclusively to the bishop of Rome as "pope" after 300. (The earliest surviving reference to the *papa* in Rome is from a funerary inscription in the catacombs when Marcellinus was bishop between 296 and 304.) The early responsibility of bishops as mediators between Christians and the imperial government was even more important. Such public accountability resulted in some bishops dying as martyrs during Diocletian's "Great Persecution." By the early fourth century Christianity was viewed by the Respublica—the Roman state—as a sect organized by and around its bishops.[55]

This was why Constantine honored the bishops and, as they were usually accomplished local administrators who knew their place in society, enlisted them into helping him govern his reformed empire. Most of them, surprised and pleased they were no longer being persecuted, enthusiastically complied. The emperor and his officials now intervened in the choosing of bishops, as they did with any civilian functionaries. Sometimes a Christian congregation presented a list of names (usually three) to an imperial bureaucrat for vetting; more often than not, they just accepted whoever was picked for them. Monks were now often chosen as bishops—a stark change from three generations earlier when Antony and other "lonely ones" vehemently opposed all offers of episcopal rank, with one monk even cutting off his ears so as not to hear some Christians begging for his leadership. (Of course, Antony's *Life* was written by the bishop of Alexandria, and so his antipathy to men like his biographer was conveniently forgotten.)[56]

Some western congregations succeeded in outmaneuvering emperors and imperial bureaucrats by electing men who were already elite servants of the Respublica, men embodying Romanness more than they did Christianity. The most famous example of such a man, even at the time, was Ambrose (Ambrosius), who when acclaimed as bishop of Milan in 374 was not even a baptized Christian but was the local "consular" governor of Aemilia-Liguria. He was as surprised as the imperial court by his election. And yet he swiftly transformed himself—after a life honed by philosophy (especially the Platonism of Cicero), the scriptures, public service, and the confidence of being an immensely wealthy noble of senatorial rank (he even preferred dressing like a noble as bishop)—into a formidable preacher and pugnacious player in the high politics of empire. Ambrose was the first aristocratic bishop in the West.[57]

Six decades earlier, Constantine would have thought it inconceivable that such a grand Roman as Ambrose could be (or would even want to be) a bishop. Indeed, he believed that the evident mediocrity of Christians had caused them to misunderstand the overwhelming power of their deity, or at least that they had never possessed the wisdom and resources to properly harness it. Constantine's God governed a universe that was simultaneously Christian and non-Christian. Apart from being an assertion of His sovereignty over all other gods and daemons, it was an affirmation that whenever a Roman worshipped any divinity, it was ultimately an act of piety toward Him. In such a cosmos Constantine could honor the old gods in Rome, establish a cult to his genius, and show fulsome respect to influential senatorial families, who were overwhelmingly polytheists, without in any way contradicting or angering his Highest God. Traditional Roman religion was actually endorsed, if not reinvigorated, by the all-pervasive undercurrents of this deity.

Constantine erected a triumphant arch (or rather repurposed one already under construction by Maxentius) in the valley of the Colosseum in Rome, celebrating his victory "at the prompting of the divinity." The arch's elaborate sculptural tableaux, most of which were remodeled from monuments to Trajan and Marcus Aurelius, along with a new frieze of the emperor escorting the goddess Roma, recalling the baroque grandeur of the Antonines while celebrating conventional non-Christian piety (and a traditional aesthetic) as a hallmark of the Highest God.[58]

In the decade after 313 Constantine secured and reformed his western imperium. He stabilized the economy with the gold solidus, a coin whose purity—seventy-two were minted from a pound of gold—and eventual ubiquity confirmed that his reign was indeed a "golden age," *aurea aetas*.[59] All imperial servants, even the most humble soldier or bureaucrat, were paid in these dazzling coins. Diocletian's debased and nasty bronze pennies were the neglected small change of the rural poor, and even respectable silver slowly faded from most transactions. All taxes were now collected in solidi, or, if collected in grain, livestock, or other produce, their worth computed in gold specie. The solidus became a marker of who was favored by the emperor and his officials and who was not. It signified the godlike generosity of imperial benevolence, the unwavering severity when such kindness was withdrawn, and, without stretching the imagination too far, a precious glimmer of the heavenly treasure of the Highest God.

Significantly, when Constantine radically expanded the ranks of the Roman Senate with provincial elites (Rhenish grandees, propertied Lyonnais) and with his own courtiers (hard-bitten generals, unyielding administrators), with each one granted the senatorial title *vir clarissimus*, "most brilliant man," these individuals judged themselves and each other as worthy of their new status by accumulating and generously spending great oceans (or at least deep lagoons) of solidi.[60] As the ambition of this new "golden age" flashed across the Mediterranean, the inevitable war between Constantine and Licinius finally erupted in 324. After a series of summer battles (Adrianople, Chrysopolis, Byzantium), where the former's victorious legions marched under the same cross-shaped standards as at the Milvian Bridge, the latter surrendered at Nicomedia in December (and, after a short exile, was executed). One emperor now ruled the Roman Empire for the first time since 286.

11 Pagans and Christians

Around the beginning of the fourth century some unsophisticated Christians began referring to individuals who were outside their religious community as *pagani*, "pagans." They had adopted the term from the legions in the Western Empire. *Pagani* was the slang of tough military men whose blunt sense of noncombatant outsiders was synonymous with city-dwelling civilians. A soldier calling someone (tavern-keeper, merchant, senator visiting the front lines) a *paganus* was boorish, even a bit showy, and not necessarily (if at all) a Christian. After Constantine's victory at the Milvian Bridge, the legions, following their commander, now honored the God of the Christians, and so *pagani* as barrack-room lingo now encompassed urban civilians who worshipped the old gods. Educated Latin-speaking Christians snobbishly preferred "gentile" (adapted from Greek-speaking Jews) as the label for an individual not believing in their God. By the end of the fourth century, however, "pagan" had shed its uncouth martial origins and was now commonly used as the epithet for non-Christians by emperors, bishops, and monks throughout the Roman West.[61]

Antony in his wilderness, at least when Evagrius translated Athanasius' late fourth-century Greek phrase *eis hellenismon* as Latin *ad paganismum*, saw himself as superior to "paganism."[62] In this instance, "pagans" was a straightforward translation of "Hellenes," specifically referring to philosophers like Plotinus, professors like the Gallic orator oozing *paideia*, or any civvy highbrow who sauntered about town with daemons. Using the term *pagani* was in keeping with the studious anti-intellectualism of the "monk of the mountain." Some fifth-century Latin Christian wits punning on *pagani*—men of the *pagus* (rural settlement or village)—continued this mockery of elite bookish Romans enamored of philosophy or the old ways, even if such men and women were now overwhelmingly Christian, by asserting that such individuals as pagans were no better than unlettered rustics or hicks. Less than a century later, most monks and bishops in the West no longer got the joke (which was hardly a rib-tickler in the first place) and took this etymology literally. Paganism for them was associated with so-called *rustici*—common people or peasants—supposedly worshipping the old gods in dark woods and hidden springs in the countryside.[63]

The broader point is that "paganism" in the fourth and fifth centuries does not refer to a coherent religion different from Christianity, and while the majority of the men, women, and children in the Roman Empire were now classified as "pagans," this was an accusation by followers of the Christian deity and not a form of self-identification by those who still knelt before the old gods.

Many Christians in an empire no longer hounding them were less interested in slandering intellectual dilettanti by calling them "pagans" than in denouncing fellow believers as impious and morally craven, and therefore "outside" their churches. North African Christians in the aftermath of Diocletian's persecution were torn apart by the question of whether a man or woman who lapsed in faith during the tyranny (such as pouring libations to a daemon or surrendering the scriptures to be burnt) could or even should be forgiven, and if such absolution could be offered, who possessed the prerogative to do so.

What is known as the Donatist schism (after Donatus, a Carthaginian bishop whom unforgiving hard-liners rallied behind) fractured the North African churches until the Muslim holy wars in the seventh century. Constantine, although frustrated at the ingratitude of these

Christian separatists, did not apply his heavy imperial hand against them. Instead, he convened two councils of bishops (Rome and Arles) in 313, delegating to these religious journeymen a portion of his judicial power so they might achieve a solution. On the Donatist schism the bishops failed to arrive at a consensus, but the precedent of ecclesiastical councils broadly determining Christian doctrine and the assumption by bishops throughout the empire that they shared imperial authority with the emperor was established—a largely illusionary premise in the East, but with profound consequences for bishops (like Ambrose) and the Respublica in the West.

12 We Believe in One God

Another fourth-century Christian dispute involved an Alexandrian priest named Arius, a charismatic street-corner preacher who wanted a philosophically cogent solution to the question "What God?" He was particularly sympathetic to the confusion amongst pagans—and quite a few Christians—regarding the relationship of Jesus Christ and the Highest God. He answered by drawing upon Plato's notion of the Demiurge or Creator God in the *Timaeus*. If God is eternal, always existing, having no beginning or end, and so ultimately beyond the comprehension of humans trapped in the transient here and now, then Christ cannot be God, since He lived and died like a mortal man. Christ therefore came into existence after the Highest God, but before the formation of the world. If God is perfect, indivisible, and immutable, then He cannot have fashioned a Son out of Himself, so Christ, created before all creation, was formed from nothing. Christ was inferior and below His Creator. He was not human, even if He resembled a man. Christ being neither God nor man was, according to Arius, a sublunary echo or recollection of the Highest God. As memory was the profound Platonic reservoir of truth, the ability to know the Son was, however imperfectly, a souvenir of the seemingly unknowable Father.

Around 318, Alexander, bishop of Alexandria, denounced Arius for being too clever by half, accusing him of heresy. Arius countered by damning his opponents as fools and heretics, complaining that they deliberately misconstrued him as "saying that the Son is a belch, or that He is a projection, or that He is unbegotten."[64] This disagreement on the nature of Christ caused riots amongst Christians in Alexandria, eventually spreading turmoil throughout the churches in the eastern Mediterranean. Soon after defeating Licinius, Constantine decided to resolve this Christological mayhem.

In early June 325—after two false starts—more than three hundred bishops from the eastern and western provinces of the empire (and one or two from Sasanian Persia) gathered at Nicaea (modern Iznik in Turkey), a town with a pleasant climate and vista near the imperial palace at Nicomedia on the eastern end of Lake Ascanius. This was the first time that Christians and their churches were indisputably demonstrated—especially to one another—as existing throughout the *oikoumene*, the "inhabited world." The *oikoumene* for Greek-speaking intellectuals had once been shaped by the conquests of Alexander the Great and the Hellenistic kingdoms of his Diadochoi (Successors), such as Ptolemy I Soter in Egypt or Antigonus One-Eye's vast realm from Asia Minor to the Iranian uplands. But with the ascendency of Rome from the first century BC onward, the "inhabited world" was understood as corresponding to the Roman Empire by the millions living within it.[65] Christians, though, having long imagined themselves as members of a faith unconstrained by empires and kingdoms, envisioned the "inhabited world" as wherever they existed. Bardaisan had thought this a century earlier in Edessa. Christianity was an "ecumenical" religion. Nicaea confirmed for the bishops and their churches that they really were part of a "universal Church."

And a "Catholic Church." The Greek adjective *katholikos*—"general," "whole," or "universal"—had been used as early as the second century by Ignatius, bishop of the church in Antioch, as a way of comforting a small group of Christians in Smyrna (on the Aegean coast of Anatolia) that all churches were part of the "whole [*katholike*] Church." (The Christians in Smyrna seemingly lacked a bishop in their church.) By the third century "Catholic Church" was being used more frequently by bishops, especially in the western provinces, where it was expressed in Latin as *ecclesia catholica*. The term still possessed the consoling assumption that however isolated or persecuted a Christian congregation may have felt, they were in fact, like a pointillist dot, part of a vivid and luminous whole. But now it also demarcated what a bishop had determined was correct Christian doctrine and ritual within their own and other churches. During the third century when a bishop accused Christian individuals or groups of not being "Catholic," he was implicitly accusing them of heresy. By the fourth century the accusation was explicit, and it stayed that way for the next millennium within the Catholic Church in the West.[66]

More prosaically, Nicaea affirmed that however much the bishops thought of themselves as overseeing a Catholic and ecumenical Church, they were in fact the servants of an imperial Church ruled by a Roman emperor who in the thirteen years since his victory at the Milvian Bridge had developed a clearer sense of what it meant to worship the Christian God.

"I may be present as a spectator and participant," Constantine informed the bishops when he initially called them to Nicaea.[67] He was much more than that. As ruler of a newly unified empire so obviously protected by his Highest God, he knew exactly what were the proper and pious verdicts on the problems confronting the council. The emperor did not ignore the opinions of his bishops—and they were definitely "his" bishops now—but he expected agreement with his vision of the Church, and in agreeing with him they were, whether they liked it or not, reconciling with one another. This is why the statement of faith adopted by the council was, despite whatever drafts were written by Eusebius of Caesarea and a Cappadocian priest named Hermogenes, a holy prayer (in Latin and Greek) from Constantine to his God.

"We believe in one God, the Father Almighty, Creator of all things visible and invisible—one Lord Jesus Christ, the Son of God, the only begotten of the Father, who is of the same substance [homoousios] of the Father," this statement of faith or creed began (and still begins).[68] This invocation was all the more remarkable in that Constantine was at first receptive to "Arian" doctrine, and yet what was more important was oneness, "in heaven and earth," in holiness and empire. Arius and his philosophy of "before He was begotten He was not" were condemned as blasphemous. Constantine, buoyed by martial success, prompted by controversy, now recognized himself as a Christian emperor and so, as it were, substantially a Christian.

13 No Blood-Dripping Sacrifices

On Sunday, May 22, 337, when the sun was at its highest point around midday, Constantine died aged sixty-five at Achyron, an imperial villa not far from Nicomedia. Shortly before his death, Eusebius, bishop of Nicomedia, baptized him. (This was a different Eusebius from the emperor's biographer;

indeed, he had been anathematized at Nicaea for his "Arian" views, then forgiven two years later when both he and Arius recanted.)

Baptism at the end of life was not so unusual, especially as the emperor supposedly delayed the ceremony over the years, never finding the right moment to visit the river Jordan and immerse himself like Christ. It also exemplified how Constantine, while gradually accepting the spiritual consequences of being a ruler worshipping the Christian God, neither expected nor wished for himself or his empire to be entirely Christian. Again, there remains the risk of anachronism, reading backward with not just modern presuppositions but views from even later in the fourth century, and certainly later in the Middle Ages, on what constituted a Christian emperor. Constantine's conviction after capturing Rome that the superiority of his deity was affirmed by the presence of the old gods never wavered. It was a politically convenient view in an empire where most Romans were still not Christian, but no less sincere for being that.

Constantine's belief in the enduring presence of the old gods in a universe ruled by his One God was enacted on an epic scale when he chose Byzantium as the new eastern imperial capital in 324, renaming it after himself as Constantinople. When he dedicated this "second Rome" on Monday, May 11, 330, its streets, docks, covered porticos, baths, forum, circus, churches, and palaces were ostentatiously decorated with ancient monumental treasures (gifts from city councils, art requisitioned by official connoisseurs) honoring the old gods. Far from being an overstuffed museum of soulless grandeur, the obelisks, friezes, bronzes, and statues retained their awesome sacred dignity. Constantine even dedicated a new goddess to his city, Anthousa, symbolizing Tyche (Fortune, Chance). The old gods in Constantinople, as the pagan epigrammatist Palladas wittily and perceptively observed, "having become Christian, dwell here unharmed."[69]

As "Christians," the old gods (even Anthousa) received no blood-dripping sacrifices in Constantinople. Constantine may have welcomed them into his city, but as he observed to the Sasanian king of kings Sapur II around 325, while he worshipped his God upon bended knee, he shunned "all abominable blood and foul hateful odors" redolent of pagan sacrifice.[70] He was not opposed to human blood flowing as entertainment; the Gallic orator praised him for the sport of executing "barbarian" Franks in the amphitheater at Trier. He warned Sapur II that bloody warfare was sanctioned by his God, "whose sign my army, dedicated to Him, carries on its shoulders."[71] What he opposed were those great Homeric hecatombs of the classical imagination, those holy barbecues of animal blood, sizzling fat, and sweet smoke. It did not matter that old believers rarely (if at all) practiced such rituals. It did not matter that in his empire such public rites, if they were ever to be performed, needed gold solidi from the imperial treasury. What he shunned was what he thought unnecessary for the adoration of any god, including the Zoroastrian Ahura Mazda. It was a trenchant statement about proper *religio*, public finances, urban planning, holiness, and empire, old Rome and new.

Around 326 Constantine commanded Macarius, bishop of Jerusalem, to destroy a temple to Aphrodite above Christ's tomb. All the ancient masonry, rocks, and dirt around the tomb were to be excavated and carted far away, removing all traces of sacrificial blood and smoky miasma that had leached down from the temple. Upon this site was to be built at public expense a church of the Holy Sepulcher, "to outshine the finest buildings in the city, more beautiful than any basilica anywhere."[72] He wanted a dazzling interior—marble columns, deep-hued mosaic floors, beautiful wall paintings, and a gilded ceiling. He wanted an imperial palace for his God, a basilica for the emperor of the universe. It was to be the very opposite of a pagan temple sanctified by blood sacrifice. Constantine was carving out a holy province for Christians around Jerusalem, "kept clear of every defilement and restored to its ancient holy state," which by default excised anything Jewish as well as pagan.[73] Unlike Constantinople, only the Highest God could dwell in Jerusalem.

14 The Beginning of the Middle Ages

Vibia Perpetua was unquestionably an ancient noble Roman woman and an ancient Roman Christian, but her early martyrdom foreshadows that defining medieval phenomenon of redemption through holy violence, either to oneself or to others. Like Marcus Aurelius, she embodied a more "classical" civilization that had disappeared by the end of the third century. As this world faded away, certain contours and outlines remained, which metamorphosed into what is known as Late Antiquity or the beginning of the Middle Ages. So much of this shift can be discerned in the way the old gods and the Christian God were understood to interact with one another. It is this distinct change in the relationship of humanity to holiness that inaugurates a sensibility amongst some individuals that has more in common with a man or woman in, say, seventh-century Jarrow or fifteenth-century Paris.

The Roman Empire did not collapse in the third century, and in many ways it arose stronger under a Christian emperor, even if that strength was less secure than it initially seemed. What Constantine, Perpetua, and even Antony of Egypt did share was a conviction that the universe was not nor should be wholly Christian.

This belief endured for at least another two centuries, both on the chilly Irish Sea and under the North African sun.

II

Swan Songs

337–476

1 Why Not Now?

In late summer 386 a thirty-two-year-old professor of rhetoric named Augustine (Aurelius Augustinus) was lounging with his younger friend Alypius in a stylish house they shared in Milan. Both were from the same modest North African town of Thagaste (modern Souk Ahras in hilly eastern Algeria). Another African, Ponticianus, surprised them with a visit. They engaged in small talk. Ponticianus picked up a book lying on a table and discovered it contained the writings of the Apostle Paul. As a baptized Christian, he was astonished. "When I indicated to him that those scriptures were the subject of deep study for me," Augustine recalled more than a decade later, "a conversation began in which he told the story of Antony the Egyptian monk." Augustine and Alypius had never heard of him. Ponticianus, amazed by such ignorance, lectured excitedly on the greatness of Antony. "He developed the theme and talked on while we listened with rapt silence."

Ponticianus suddenly digressed in the middle of his lecture, remembering when he and three friends had strolled through the imperial gardens outside the walls of Trier. At one point the foursome divided, with each couple wandering in different directions. When Ponticianus and his companion reunited with the other two around sunset, their friends had been reborn as Christian monks. What had caused this whirlwind transformation was the chance discovery of Evagrius' Latin translation of Athanasius' biography of Antony in a house in which lived some men modeling their lives on the Egyptian *monachos*. One friend began reading the book and was "set on fire," experiencing a furious inner conversion visible only to God. Purely because of hearing what was in the book, the other friend converted as well. When they met up again, Ponticianus and his companion, while deeply moved by what they heard, would not copy their friends, despite being begged to do so. They returned to the imperial palace "dragging their hearts along the ground," while their friends, returning to the simple house and the marvelous book, "fixed their hearts on heaven."

At the end of this convoluted tale of memories within memories, Augustine abruptly noted that he had stopped listening while Ponticianus was talking, because, "Lord, You turned my attention back to myself." He looked within himself and was appalled; violently overcome by a sense of shame. All his memories gnawed at his inner self. He remembered praying as an adolescent, "Grant me chastity and continence, but not yet." He remembered reading Cicero's *Hortensius* at nineteen, where searching for wisdom was preferred over discovering it. He remembered wanting more than worldly success, but doing nothing about it.[1]

Augustine's conscience soon complained that it had had enough of regret: "Where is your tongue?"

This shocked Augustine back into the present, and after mutely watching Ponticianus finally depart, he cried out to Alypius, "What is wrong with us?" His friend stared in astonished silence. How was it, wondered Augustine, that uneducated men like Antony were capturing heaven, yet men of *paideia* like themselves rolled in mud and blood? "Do we feel no shame at making not even an attempt to follow?"

Augustine was trembling, his voice strange, his face flushed. He ran out into the garden. Alypius quietly kept pace. Augustine berated himself for his lack of will, for being unable to cast off his past. "Inwardly I said to myself: Let it be now!" He hesitated. Vanity and desire, "my old loves," coquettishly whispered, "Are you getting rid of us?" He blushed and wept. His past gripped him, bewailing, "How long, how long is it to be?" Augustine yelled at his past, "Why not now?"[2]

Suddenly the voice of a boy or a girl from a nearby house started singing, "Pick up and read, pick up and read." Augustine interpreted the child's song as a divine command to read the Gospels at random, as Antony had once randomly heard them. He raced across the garden, picked up the Apostle Paul, and, finding Alypius, flung open the book. "Not in riots and drunken parties," he silently read, "not in eroticism and indecencies, not in strife and rivalry, but put on the Lord Jesus Christ and make no provision for the flesh in its lusts." All doubt was gone. Augustine would be celibate and a baptized Christian.[3]

This overwrought melodrama, lasting perhaps no more than a few minutes, was a pivotal memory within Augustine's *Confessions*, written soon after he became Catholic bishop of Hippo Regius (later Bône, now Annaba on the Algerian coast) around 396. A number of factors provoked him into writing. One was local animosity by Catholic Christians who distrusted his obvious brilliance, for he never erased the intellectual panache and eloquence of the cosmopolitan (and so possibly pagan) professor. And, as Augustine had once been a Manichaean, there were accusations of heresy against the ascetic group (not quite monks, more like chaste gentlemen scholars) who gathered around him in Thagaste after he left Milan in 388. It did not help that in Hippo the schismatic Donatists were the majority, delighting in any opportunity to attack a Catholic bishop. (The Donatists, while also thinking of themselves as part of the "universal Church," nevertheless differentiated their Christianity from that of "Catholic Christians," whom they viewed as participating in an impure imperial Church that had never shaken off the stigma of Diocletian's persecution.)

The more benign provocation came from Alypius, who was now bishop of Thagaste. He had been asked to describe his own conversion into Christian asceticism by Pontius Meropius Paulinus (better known as Paulinus of Nola), a senator from Bordeaux who had renounced his immense wealth to become a priest in Campania. Alypius mentioned this request to Augustine. Whatever Alypius composed is lost, if indeed he drafted anything, but his friend was inspired into writing an extraordinary Platonic autobiography in the form of a long prayer to God.[4]

Like a great luminous wave curling over and over, seemingly in forward motion yet never breaking on the shore, Augustine narrated his life as a series of radiant concentric memories spiraling within one another. "The power of memory is great, very great, my God. It is a vast and infinite profundity. Who has fathomed its depth?"[5] It was from Plotinus that he derived his understanding of Plato and the importance of memory in discovering the truth about himself and God. Everything Augustine knew or would know was already present in his memory, albeit dispersed. All his erudition was the recollection of knowledge scattered in the secret caverns of his mind. What happened to him in the Milan garden all those years earlier was the revelation that deep in his memory he had already succumbed to God. A past without Christ was just forgetfulness.

The other crucial reminiscence in the *Confessions* involved Augustine and his mother, Monica, as they waited at Ostia, the port near Rome, for a ship to Carthage in 388. She had been a Christian for many years, he for less than two. "Alone together," standing by a window overlooking a garden, "we talked very intimately." They discussed the eternal life of saints and immortal truth. "Our minds were lifted up by an ardent affection towards eternal being itself. Step by step we climbed beyond all corporal objects and heaven itself, where sun, moon, and stars shed light on the earth." They ascended even further through inner reflection to a plane of bountiful wisdom, "where there is no past and future." In a sudden electrifying jolt they touched this truth before the noise of their talking ("where a sentence has both a beginning and an end") brought them back to earth. "That is how it was when at that moment we extended our reach and in a flash of mental energy attained the eternal wisdom which abides beyond all things. If only it could last!"

Although this holy shock was like the "dance of immortal love" that Plotinus had achieved four times in life and finally in death, it was different as mother and son shared their ecstasy. For the philosopher this rare achievement was about the individual being absorbed into the eternal wisdom of the godhead or the One; for the two Christians it was about absorbing the immortal love of God within themselves. This was a radical change in perspective. The infinite immortality of the universe no longer lay outside humans; it lay within them.[6]

"My son," observed Monica after their mutual joy, "I now find no pleasure in life." Five days later she collapsed in a fever, and nine days after that she died. She was fifty-six. "Bury my body anywhere," she said.[7] Augustine lived another forty-two years, writing incessantly (even his friend and biographer Possidius complained no one could read all of him), never forgetting those gardens in Milan and Ostia, dying as Hippo was besieged by the Vandals in 430.[8]

2 As if His Neck Were in a Vise

After Constantine's death in 377 his three sons shared the empire. The oldest and youngest sons, Constantine II and Constans, carved up the West, while the middle son, Constantius II, grabbed the East. Men descended from Constantine's stepmother, Theodora, were also intended to rule, but they were all swiftly slaughtered, apart from two young half brothers, Julian and Gallus. Less than three years later Constantine II died in battle attempting to eliminate Constans. A decade later Constans was overthrown and killed in a coup by one of his generals, Magnentius. Constantius, preoccupied with his eastern campaigns against the Sasanian king of kings Sapur II, had turned a blind eye to the surprise elevation of his little brother as sole sovereign over two-thirds of the empire; now, though, with a lull in the Persian conflict and his sibling murdered by a usurper, he launched a western war in 351.

Julian remembered this campaign of Constantius as a "truly sacred war." The West itself was not "sacred territory," he stressed; rather, his cousin was waging a holy war, avenging "the laws and the constitution and the slaughter of countless citizens." What further exalted this conflict for him was that Magnentius was "a miserable remnant saved from the spoils of Germany," a "genuine barbarian," a Frank from across the Rhine pretending to be a Roman.[9] By summer 353 Constantius was victorious. Two years later the military commander in Gaul rebelled, proclaiming himself Augustus. He was killed within three weeks by his own soldiers. Significantly, like Magnentius, the commander was of Frankish descent.

Constantius was a deeply suspicious autocrat, seeing, with some justification, threats and conspiracies everywhere. The system bequeathed to him by his father fostered such anxiety. After promoting Gallus as his Caesar, he executed him in 354, fearing competition. Nevertheless, he spared Julian; a member of the imperial family in Gaul and along the Rhine frontier might temporarily dissuade pretenders. It was a risk worth taking (or a sacrifice worth making). In 355 Constantius summoned Julian from his studies in Athens, marrying him to his sister and appointing him his Caesar.

Around Easter 357, Constantius visited Rome. The pagan historian Ammianus Marcellinus, writing forty years later, vividly remembered the arrival of the emperor: "As if he were contriving to terrify the Euphrates or the Rhine . . . he sat alone upon a golden chariot in the resplendent blaze of shimmering stones, whose mingled glitter seemed to form a sort of shifting light." The glistening chariot was surrounded by purple banners woven in the form of dragons mounted on golden spears, whose gaping mouths hissed in the breeze, "as if aroused by anger," and whose tails danced in the wind. On either side marched twin lines of infantrymen with shields, shining in mail shirts. Amongst these foot soldiers were heavily armored cavalry known as *clibanarii* (oven-wearers), "fully masked, girt with iron belts, and furnished with protecting breastplates, so that you might have supposed them statues polished by the hand of Praxiteles, not living men." Thousands of citizens shouted their salutations to the Augustus, while he, despite the roar and spectacle, never stirred, showing himself as "calm and imperturbable, as he was commonly seen in his provinces." Constantius gazed straight ahead, "as if his neck were in a vise," turning neither to the left nor right, never moving even if the carriage jolted, as if he were not human, only the "image of a man."

While Ammianus dismissed this performance as "affectation," he admitted it also showed "endurance."[10] More than just posturing or stamina, Constantius II was heralding himself as the highest representative of the Highest God on earth. He was not imitating a statue of an old god swaddled in *numina*; he was imitating Christ as envisioned by the priest Arius. As the Son was neither God nor man, so too was the emperor. As the Son was the radiant memory of the Creator, so too was the emperor. Divinity was always reverberating through the emperor from on high, and his inhuman self-discipline ensured that everyone remembered it. Although Ammianus was unmoved by Constantius as Christ, and while many Romans, Christian or not, saw nothing unusual in such an affectation, there were Christians appalled at the emperor's rejection of what had been agreed upon three decades earlier at Nicaea—that Jesus is of the same substance as the Father and that He and God are One.

One of these Christians was Athanasius, intermittent bishop of Alexandria, and, as we have seen, the biographer of Antony of Egypt. He was a young cleric at Nicaea and a zealous opponent of Arius. This zealotry only became more extreme over the decades. He accused anyone he disagreed with or who disagreed with him of "Arianism." Occasionally the individuals he denounced were sympathetic to Arius' views, which, despite Nicaea, were persuasive to many elite Romans, whatever their religion, especially in an intellectual milieu immersed in the Neoplatonism of Plotinus. A pious authoritarian like Constantius II was persuaded—and yet he would never have called himself an Arian.

So many individuals and groups for the next millennium, particularly in the sixth and seventh centuries in the West, were accused by Catholic bishops and monks of being Arians. There never were any actual Arians, just the accusation by Catholic clergy. What complicates this is that there were some "barbarian" groups like the Goths (and probably the Franks) who when they converted to Christianity adopted the views of an emperor like Constantius about the relationship of Christ to the Highest God. This

specific kind of imperial Christianity in which the divinity of God reson-
ated though an autocratic Christlike ruler remained a vital belief for later
Gothic kings and their followers. Again, they never labeled themselves as
Arians—if anything, they saw themselves as proper Catholic Christians, unlike their fervid accusers.

Most of those Athanasius attacked in the fourth century, however, were
indifferent to Arius, and yet such apathy was worse than outright heresy,
as it signaled calamitous disregard for the universal power of the Nicene
Creed. Also, of course, hatred of Athanasius was proof of Arianism.

And Athanasius was easy to hate. Constantius loathed him, expelling him
from Egypt. "A man who came from the lowest depths of infamy," he reminded Alexandrians about their troublesome bishop.[11] Overall, Athanasius
was exiled five times by four different emperors before his death in 373.
Only by audacious political maneuvering across the empire whenever he
was a refugee did he repeatedly claw his way back to Alexandria. For every
imperial official or bishop who despised him, others found him deeply
charismatic. Some of this charisma was evident in his life of Antony, which
was as much about him as the monk. By the end of the fourth century
Athanasius' fierce and undeniably swashbuckling advocacy of Nicaean
orthodoxy was the heroic story promoted by other boldly confident bishops, particularly in the West. It was a narrative of Catholic Christianity
righteously vanquishing (if not now, then in the future) Roman emperors
and barbarian kings poisoned by Arianism.

3 Gaudy Trousers

In late winter 356 bands of Alamanni (men united) departed the Rhine
and Danube frontiers to raid towns and farms along the Rhône and Seine
valleys. Julian, as Caesar, was in Vienne (a town on the Rhône) when he
heard how these "barbarians had made a surprise attack upon the ancient
city of Autun, whose walls were of great extent but crumbling with age."[12]
He slowly moved his court and legions to the city, "intending like a sea-
soned commander of proven strength and sagacity to attack the barbarians,
who were scattered all over the countryside."[13] He finally arrived at the end
of June. Eager for action after months of sluggish movement, he swiftly
marched to Auxerre with a small company of *clibanarii* and foot soldiers.

Again, trusting in speed over preparation, he hastened to Troyes with his company. It was a perilous journey through thick woods, with Alamanni repeatedly ambushing the Romans. Julian survived by closing ranks, steadfast as his foes exhausted themselves in chaotic assaults. He never pursued the barbarians, as his cavalry were too encumbered by their heavy armor. He finally reached Troyes, only to be refused entry, as the frightened citizens were unable to tell the difference between weary Roman soldiers and rampaging Alamanni fighters. Barbarians, as Ammianus Marcellinus observed, while readily attacking towns and cities, never settled in them, regarding them as lifeless prisons, as "tombs surrounded by nets."[14] Julian and his men, although looking like barbarians to nervous eyes, relished the comforts and protection of Roman urbanity, even if in the mid-fourth century it was somewhat tarnished in the West. After much pleading, the gates of Troyes reluctantly opened to the young Caesar and his companions.

Mistaking Roman soldiers for barbarians was hardly surprising. At least since Diocletian the uniforms worn by the Roman legions were stylized versions of barbarian fashions. The Roman soldier cut a flashy figure: brightly colored trousers and ankle boots, a short slim-fitting long-sleeved tunic fastened about the waist by a *cingulum militiae*, a thick belt whose ornate buckle signified rank; and, framing all this like a lush theatrical curtain, a heavy great cloak (decorated in stripes, embroidery, or fur) fastened at the shoulder by a golden fibula (brooch), whose design also expressed rank. Apart from genuine utility—there is a lot to be said for trousers—such clothing marked out the army as separate from civilian habits and values. The flamboyant *cingulum militiae* by itself identified a soldier in a gathering of noncombatants.[15]

Augusti and Caesars in the fourth century were frequently encamped with their legions along the *limites*, the militarized border zones defining the end of civilization and the beginning of the *barbaricum*, that is, all lands outside of the empire, which by default were populated by barbarians. (In this sense, even the Sasanian Empire was part of the *barbaricum*.) The "wild people" beyond the Rhine and Danube were never going to destroy Rome—another cycle of civil wars was more likely to do that—but there was no lasting glory (or sense of security) in Roman fighting Roman, whereas there was honor in Roman fighting barbarian.

Romans genuinely feared unchecked barbarism. A vital part of the divine majesty of an emperor was in allaying, and so justifying, these fears through battlefield victories and strong fortifications. For much of the fourth and fifth centuries the political hub of the empire actually lay on the periphery, especially northern Gaul and Roman Germany, where emperors, soldiers, and courtiers defended and redefined *Romanitas*.[16] Gaudy trousers and swinging great cloaks brought the exoticism, danger, and raw power of the frontier into the heart of the empire whenever a soldier wandered through the streets of Constantinople or Milan. Such barbaric clothing emphasized why Romanness mattered and why the martial authoritarianism established by Diocletian and Constantine was necessary.

Apart from the Alamanni, Roman emperors worried about five other barbarian groups in the mid-fourth century: the Goths, along the lower Danube (at uneasy peace with the empire since 332); the Burgundians, along the upper Danube and Rhine frontier (largely sharing the same lands as the Alamanni); the Vandals, to the east of the Burgundians and Alamanni; the Franks, "the fierce people," amongst the islands and estuaries of the Rhine-Meuse delta (although they raided as far south as Worms); and the Saxons, further along the North Sea coast near Jutland.[17] None of these Germanic groups were ethnically, linguistically, or culturally that distinct from one another. What distinguished one group from another was the talent of individual warlords or kings in protecting followers from the raids of other barbarians and, crucially, being honored as "big men" by Romans across the frontier.

These barbarian groups were in constant flux, breaking apart and re-forming around more successful leaders, then settling down before fracturing again. Roman writers recycled names for these various groupings (and regroupings), giving the impression of continuity and stability. Whatever coherence was achieved was on account of Roman emperors and generals making alliances with one king over another, by rewarding one warlord with more gifts (and so prestige) than another. Roman goods (buckles, brooches, weapons, gold solidi as jewelry, wine), language (Latin), and religion (Christ, the old gods, Sol Invictus) crossed over the Rhine and Danube, while military recruits flowed back the other way. Even the extravagant dress of Roman soldiers was adopted by elite men and women living inside the *barbaricum*.[18] When the gifts stopped or were too slow in coming, rulers attacked Roman towns and farms, not to destroy Rome but to reestablish the flow of honor. That was why around three thousand Alamanni were charging about the Seine valley under a warrior king named Chnodomar in 356. A year later Julian crushed this motley confederacy at the Battle of Strasbourg, reestablishing the status quo.

All peoples living in the *barbaricum* were inescapably caught within the gravitational pull of the Roman Empire. Despite indulging in ethnographic clichés about barbarians going all way back to Herodotus, Roman emperors, soldiers, bureaucrats, and historians, whether Christian or pagan, recognized that the people across the frontier were formed as much by *Romanitas* as they themselves were. This is not to underestimate the genuine violence of the Roman borderlands, but there were conventions, mostly followed by either side, keeping a tense equilibrium. All this came to an end in 378.

4 The Axeman

On Thursday, June 26, 363, Julian was killed when a spear pierced his ribs as he recklessly charged Persian skirmishers at Samarra (about fifty miles north of modern Baghdad). Two years earlier he had become sole Augustus when Constantius II unexpectedly died just as civil war was erupting between them. Although raised a Christian, Julian had started secretly worshipping the old gods as a youth, and as emperor he ordered their temples opened and sacrifices made upon their altars. He intended to cleanse Rome of the pollution of Christianity and the regime established by Constantine honoring the "Galilean." He told the Eastern bishops to set aside their schisms, believing they would soon tear each other apart, as toleration was anathema to them; as Ammianus Marcellinus noted, "No wild beasts are such dangerous enemies to man as Christians are to one another."[19] (Not surprisingly, Julian despised Athanasius, exiling him from Alexandria.)

Julian's paganism (or rather Hellenism) was an intellectual mix of Neoplatonism and romanticism about the Roman past—the religion of a bookish boy growing up in fear. He was deeply sincere and wildly enthusiastic: growing a beard like Marcus Aurelius (a sign of a pagan philosopher), banning Christians from teaching Homer or any book mentioning the old gods, and sacrificing so many bulls and other animals that the altars flowed with blood, earning him the mocking nickname Victimarius, "slaughterer" or "axeman."[20] Unfortunately, the *numina* resisted being remade into a fairy-tale version of what the cosmos had been like two centuries earlier.

Christianity, even if halfheartedly practiced or understood, was ingrained in the imperial martial and bureaucratic elite. Even most Hellenes were unsympathetic to Julian's new-old religion. Even if the young emperor had reigned longer, it is doubtful how permanent his holy revanchism would have been.

As Julian lay dying, an East Roman Christian writing two centuries later had him declaim in a melodramatic gasp: "You have won, Christ! Take your fill, Galilean!"[21]

5 The Goths

In spring 376 thousands of terrified Goths known as the Tervingi gathered on the northern bank of the southern Danube in Thrace (modern Bulgaria). They were fleeing, according to Ammianus Marcellinus, a previously unknown people who, "like a whirlwind descending from high mountains," were destroying everything in their path. They were hoping for safety in the Roman Empire from these Huns.

Ammianus described the Huns with horror, wonder, and fantasy. "From the moment of birth, they make deep gashes in their children's cheeks, so that when in due course hair appears, its growth is checked by the wrinkled scars," giving them the appearance of beardless eunuchs as men. "They have squat bodies, strong limbs, and thick necks, and are so prodigiously ugly and bent that they might be two-legged beasts." Although they were human in form, "however disagreeable," their way of life was not considered at all human. They never cooked their food or used spices, "but live on the roots of wild plants and the half-raw flesh of any sort of animal, which they warm a little by placing it between their thighs and the backs of their horses." They avoided all buildings, "as we avoid living in the neighborhood of tombs." They wore grubby linen clothing "or the skins of field-mice." The men rarely got off their horses, "hardy but ugly beasts," eating, drinking, buying, selling, and sleeping upon them. When they did dismount, they jumped onto wagons, where their women and children lived. In battle they rode in packs, yelling war cries, before suddenly darting here and there, fearlessly charging ramparts or pillaging camps; this made them moving targets, too swift and nimble to be killed. "What makes them the most formidable of all warriors is that they shoot from a distance arrows tipped with sharp splinters of bone." There was no overall leader, only improvised councils of warlords expressing the will of their men. "They are totally ignorant of the distinction between right and wrong, their speech is shifty and obscure, and they are under no restraint from religion or superstition." Perpetually on the move, the Huns were like fugitives from nowhere.[22]

The Huns, while unfamiliar to Romans, had been known to the Tervingi for at least a decade. Around 370 these nomadic warriors crossed the Volga River, shifting the sweep of their kinetic and bellicose existence from the Alati region (modern Kazakhstan and Mongolia) to the Transdanubian plains. During the middle decades of the fourth century there was a devastating drought across Central Asia, and while this was not the only motivation for the Hunnic host moving westward, searching for new pastures, it certainly confirmed an orientation already adopted by some outrider war bands.[23] Once again, reports of the Huns owed as much to barbarian stereotypes as to reality, although in this case some of the invention was as much Gothic as Roman. Two centuries later, Jordanes, an imperial secretary in Constantinople, noted in his short and fanciful history of the Goths that the Huns were descended from the swamp-dwelling offspring of exiled Gothic sorceresses and unclean spirits.[24] This occult genealogy was possibly a story told by aristocratic Goths in sixth-century Italy. If so, then in hindsight the heirs of the Tervingi saw the Huns as a kindred people whose onslaught was vengeance on behalf of their long-dead supernatural mothers. Either way, such fabulous tales were not the concern of the men, women, and children mobbing the Danube, whose society of small farms and villages, already destabilized by recent Roman campaigns, was fatally shattered by the Huns.

Two Gothic warlords, Alavivus and Fritigern, promised the emperor Valens that if the Tervingi were permitted to flee the *barbaricum* and live in the Roman Empire, they would supply his army with thousands of soldiers. The emperor was preparing for another war with Persia and this pool of supplicant warriors seemed providential, so he agreed, offering fertile land in Thrace. "With these high hopes various officials were sent to transport this wild host, and the greatest care was taken to ensure that, even if an individual were suffering from a mortal illness," wrote Ammianus with a suave sneer, "none of those destined to overthrow the Roman Empire should be left behind."[25]

Despite such disdain ex post facto, the emperor's decision was based on precedent—other barbarian groups had peacefully settled in the empire—and on pragmatism: his soldiers could massacre the Goths if necessary. Further, most of the Tervingi were Christian and sympathetic to Arianism, as was Valens. Day and night, somewhere between twenty thousand and forty thousand people were ferried over the Danube. This "eruption of armed men from the barbarian lands, like lava from Etna," required capable local Roman commanders, to say the least. Sadly, this entire operation was overseen by rapacious fools.[26] No one had given any thought to feeding or sheltering the refugees. Roman officers exploited this situation by selling dog meat to the Goths in exchange for men and boys as slaves. Soon enough, as these same hustlers had also forgotten to disarm most of the warriors, there was the threat of insurgency. As a stopgap, large numbers of Goths were escorted from the frontier by Roman soldiers, and in so doing other Goths, known as the Greuthungi, sailed over the unwatched Danube. One Roman general tried and failed to kill Alavivus and Fritigern at a banquet. Not surprisingly, the Tervingi rebelled and, joined by the Greuthungi, ravaged the Balkan provinces.[27]

Two years later, Valens, during an interlude in his Persian war, marched the elite Eastern field army against the Goths. Fritigern appealed to the emperor, saying he wanted nothing more than peace and the Thracian farmland of their earlier agreement. The customary cycle of frontier violence ultimately leading to a restoration of what each side had previously enjoyed, or, in this case, hoped to enjoy, was still his working assumption. The last thing he and his followers wished was the destruction (or even the weakening) of Rome. Valens dismissed the appeal. As his Persian campaigns were ineffectual, he was desperate for martial glory, and so, supremely confident of an easy victory, he rashly attacked what he thought was an insignificant barbarian war band near the city of Adrianople (Edirne in modern Turkey) on Thursday, August 9, 378. Instead, what greeted him was the massed Gothic host, which, outnumbering and outmaneuvering their assailants, slaughtered the Romans. The field of battle was "one dark pool of blood." Valens died during the fighting, his body lost amongst the dead. One story had it that an arrow felled him; another said he was burned alive as the Goths set ablaze a farmhouse in which he lay wounded. Two-thirds of the Roman army, between ten thousand and twenty thousand men, were killed by the Goths. "No battle in our history except Cannae," exclaimed Ammianus, "was such a massacre."[28]

6 Our Old, Sober Morality

Ammianus Marcellinus blamed the catastrophe of Adrianople on the retreat of the old gods from the Roman Empire. Yet, just as Rome had rebounded from the shattering defeat at Cannae by Hannibal Barca almost six hundred years earlier, he hoped the empire might rally once again. He recalled that even under Marcus Aurelius the empire suffered disasters from barbarians and was quickly restored. But that was then, when "our old, sober morality had not yet been undermined by the temptations of a laxer and more effeminate way of life." This was now, when the great and the wealthy craved only "ostentatious banquets and ill-gotten gain." For Ammianus, Adrianople was the terrible consequence of Constantine and Christianity, of the ancient deities being shunted aside for the Galilean, so that high and low were no longer of one mind, "eager to meet a glorious death for the state as if it were a peaceful and quiet harbor."[29] The Gothic crisis was a symptom of the corruption, incompetence, and selfishness of imperial courtiers, senatorial elites, and military leaders as Christian fops. Ammianus appealed to his rich and powerful readers, especially cursory Christians and listless pagans, to openly embrace the gods of the past as the only remedy for saving the present.

Such an appeal was a wistful cry in the wilderness when Ammianus made it around 390. And he knew it. The emperor in Constantinople, Theodosius, was a strident Catholic Christian who loathed pagans and Arians alike and who, according to imperial propaganda, had triumphantly revived the empire after Adrianople. This revival was much less secure than it seemed and hardly the result of any coherent strategy. The panicked responses in late 378 included mass executions of Gothic troops in the Eastern legions, Bishop Ambrose in Milan melting down church plate ("useful gold") for refugees from the Balkans, and the Western emperor, Gratian, turning his back on the whole problem.[30] Theodosius was a plodding general from Spain before being proclaimed Augustus in 379, and another three years of unwavering martial mediocrity ended only when he negotiated a "peace" with the Goths. The terms and conditions of this agreement are unknown. Why the emperor offered an armistice is perhaps explainable—he was achieving very little—but why the Goths agreed is not.

All that is known is that the Gothic crisis was over in 382. More than anything, the Gothic wildfire simply burned itself out. It was never an invasion, never an attempt at overthrowing Rome. All that the frightened individuals who had gathered on the Danube four years earlier ever wanted was accommodation within the empire. They only wanted to be Roman. This seems to have happened, as the Goths disappear for more than a decade after 382, absorbed into the army or settled in taxpaying villages in Thrace and Lower Moesia. Even leaders like Fritigern were never mentioned again. Nevertheless, a shift between Romans and barbarians had happened. Until 378 the Goths had been one of many groups outside the Roman frontier; now they were inescapably part of the internal tempo of the empire.[31] When the Goths reappeared in 395 under a young Roman general of Gothic descent named Alaric, the consequences were even more apocalyptic than Adrianople.

7 The One Great God

In the same year Ammianus Marcellinus lamented the old gods being displaced by Christianity, the pagan grammarian Maximus of Madauros (a city in Roman Numidia) jocularly argued otherwise in a letter to his friend Augustine in Hippo: "There is a Greek myth of uncertain authenticity that Mount Olympus is the dwelling place of the gods. But we have the evidence of our eyes that the forum of our own town is occupied by a throng of beneficent deities [*salutarium numinum*]. Yet who would be so foolish, so touched in the head, as to deny that there is one highest God, without beginning, without natural offspring, the great and magnificent Father, as it were?"

Like many Romans, Christian or pagan (including Ammianus himself), Maximus saw no contradiction between a world crowded with gods and a singular supreme God, whose powers, "scattered throughout the material world, we call upon under various names, since (of course) none of us knows His true name." All religions used the name "god," and in so doing invoked the one God. "And so it is that, while we as supplicants grasp certain of His members, as it were, piece by piece, in various supplications, we seem to worship Him as whole." Leaving aside the North African martyrs, whom he thought stupid for chasing after death, along with their ugly names (Namphamo, Mygdo, Lucitas) and the even uglier veneration of their tombs, Christian worship was just another form of prayer amongst a multitude of non-Christian prayers, all honoring the same Highest God. Such religious diversity was common sense to Maximus, being no more than a variation of Constantine's own sacred revelation eight decades earlier.[32]

Annianus, son of Matutina, modestly exemplified this religious common sense when, after his purse of six silver coins was stolen in the valley of the river Avon in southwest Britain, he visited the sacred spring of Sulis Minerva in Bath. On a lead curse tablet he implored the "Lady Goddess" to catch the thief, "whether gentile or Christian, whomsoever, whether man or woman, whether boy or girl, whether slave or free."[33] By the middle of the fourth century, the customary legal and religious formula classifying all possible suspects (and recited in thousands of holy sites throughout the empire by other petitioners) now included followers of the Christian God. Annianus, who was probably a Christian himself (especially as he used the genteel "gentile" for a believer in the old gods), took it for granted that the power of Sulis Minerva was no less potent or encompassing in an empire with Christian emperors or in a universe ruled by one Highest God. The infinite elasticity of the *numina* was still a forensic fact for him, even if, as for Maximus, cursing in the name of a goddess was implicitly understood as cursing in the name of the great and magnificent Father.

Ammianus was nevertheless correct in viewing Adrianople as hastening a shift—more acrimonious, less commonsensical—already under way in the relationship between Christians and believers in the old gods. If nothing else, it facilitated the ascendancy of the zealous Theodosius.

Augustine himself, in the opening sentence of his reply to Maximus, captured the increasingly intolerant tone of this debate on the holy: "Are we carrying on a serious conversation, or do you want to joke?" He knew his friend was teasing him, but he was in no mood for urbane wit (unless he did it himself). Maximus was wrong, and his humor was dangerously impious and unlawful. "If, nonetheless, you want to laugh, you have lots of material for laughing in your own religion: a god of manuring, a god of the toilet, bald Venus, the god Fear, the god Pallor, the goddess Fever, and countless others of this sort for whom the ancient Romans, worshippers of images, constructed temples." The biggest joke for Augustine was that if these images and temples perished through neglect, then the gods of Rome expired with them.

This was one of many reasons worshipping the one and true God was not the same as adoring a nude statue or dancing through the streets inebriated. The Christian God did not vanish if no one saw a Christian pray. This was why Christians did not worship dead bodies in tombs, and even if they did, it was not the idolatry of the old religion. God was not a pagan punch line, so, as one African to another, Augustine curtly told Maximus not to write again, "unless I know you want to have a serious conversation."[34]

Soon after Augustine warned Maximus that religion was no laughing matter, Theodosius banned the worship of the old gods throughout the empire in 392. Sacrifices were strictly forbidden. Trees tied with ribbons or altars of sod, "no matter how humble," were an "outrage against religion."[35] A year earlier he had told the prefect of Rome to shutter all temples and stop all sacrifices. A decade before these harsh statutes, when he was clumsily chasing allegedly Arian Goths around Thrace, he had banned the theology of Arius throughout the Church and reaffirmed, or rather reformulated without any hint of ambiguity, the creed from Nicaea.

Theodosius was already a Catholic dogmatist before becoming emperor, but radical bishops in the West, especially Ambrose, flattered and bullied him into even greater pious intensity. In 388 a Catholic mob wrecked the synagogue and "Arian" church in Callinicum, on the Euphrates frontier. Theodosius ordered the local bishop to fix the buildings and punish the rioters. Ambrose preached that this was wrongheaded, as Jews and heretics deserved such violence. The emperor acquiesced. That same year Theodosius banned marriage between Jews and Christians.[36]

Constantine was a severe autocrat, more than willing to punish any citizen, city, or province with the full terror of his majesty, yet he never assumed that what he did on earth altered the curvature of the cosmos or interrupted the immortal souls dancing in the Milky Way. By contrast, the divine stringency imposed by Theodosius throughout the empire against heretics and pagans was a deliberate effort at imposing his religious absolutism in the celestial realm. The *numina* were to be legislated into extinction, this boundless and ancient coral reef of brilliant variegations and religious wonder bleached into petrification by imperial diktat.

Of course, enacting grim laws, even with the power of the Roman Empire behind them, did not mean the old gods and their worshippers disappeared overnight, or even that their disappearance was necessarily inevitable. However, as Augustine dismissively pointed out to Maximus, pagan

deities needed their temples and all of the rituals associated with such institutions to exist. Without material structures erected by mortals and the
movement of physical bodies honoring them, the undying gods would not
so much pass away as fade from the memories and routines of humanity.

This certainly was the militant Christian theory (and an undeniably sophisticated one) of Western bishops like Augustine and Ambrose, put into
law by Theodosius. This was also without doubt what the noble pagan
Symmachus had feared when, as prefect of Rome in 384, he composed
his *relatio* (memorandum) to the emperor Valentinian II requesting the restoration of the tax and dole privileges of the college of the Vestal Virgins,
which imperial penny-pinchers had recently cut. "The Divine Intellect
has assigned to different cities different religions to be their guardians," he
wrote, and so the Vestals (seven noble virgins), as guardians of Rome and as
exemplifications of the religious diversity that held the universe together,
deserved to be supported by the public purse. Whether an individual was
Christian or not, "we all look up at the same stars," we all search for the
One in the same cosmos. "Not by one avenue exclusively can we arrive at
so tremendous a secret." To stop funding the Vestals was to close down a
vital path to the holy. No man or god had a right to do that.[37]

Ambrose, always ready to grab any chance at maligning believers in the old
gods, deliberately misrepresented the *relatio* of Symmachus as a cri de coeur
for paganism, denouncing it as reprehensible and obscene.[38] (Augustine was
more circumspect; Symmachus was an early patron.) Although Valentinian
did not restore to them their privileges, the Vestals continued praying for
Rome and for him—they even prayed for Theodosius, who, not surprisingly, was indifferent to their devotion.

In the end, though, what happened to ancient Roman *religiones* at the
end of the fourth century was the result of the imperial reforms undertaken by Diocletian and Constantine almost a century earlier. The slow
and steady erasure of the unique civic and pious calendars orchestrating
the yearly rhythms in thousands of towns and cities throughout the empire,
and the replacement of this urban cacophony with a common totalitarian
thud, was largely complete by then. The venerable tradition of Roman
elites lavishing their wealth on their beloved cities gradually stopped. The
maintenance of temples, baths, holiday rituals, and games now relied on
funds from the emperor or his officials. Only the continued munificence
of Christian emperors allowed the old gods and their sacred role in the life

of a city to continue as they had always done. It was a tenuous covenant, easily broken.

8 Let Her Think the World Has Always Been What It Is Now

In 413 the Christian priest Jerome sent a letter from Bethlehem to three-year-old Pacatula and her noble father, Gaudentius, with advice about raising a girl in Rome. "It is hard," he acknowledged, "to write to a little girl who cannot understand what you say, of whose mind you know nothing, and of whose inclinations it would be reckless to predict." Jerome had lived in Rome three decades earlier as a protégé of Pope Damasus, and, like Plotinus in the third century, he was a spiritually and intellectually flamboyant figure (intensely austere, ferociously learned, sarcastically witty), at home in the salons of elite Christian women, frequently lecturing on the education and religious guidance of little girls and widows.

Back then, and now with Pacatula, he advocated lifelong ascetic virginity for girls. Despite making this vow, some mothers, he lamented, allowed their daughters to enjoy pretty clothes and parties before renouncing such pleasures. They thought it better for their daughters to know what they must eventually despise, rather than perpetually yearn for what they never knew. Jerome thought otherwise, explaining himself to Pacatula and Gaudentius with a foreskin metaphor. The circumcised, that is, virgins, cannot become uncircumcised, that is, "seek the coat of marriage given to Adam on his expulsion from the paradise of virginity." The uncircumcised, "enveloped in the skin of matrimony," lost their chance for raw and naked "eternal chastity."[39] In other words, cutting children off from society was wiser than pretending that, once experienced, they could be unsheathed of its values. Jerome's phallic drollery was as archly amusing as it was serious. Pacatula must live in her own paradise of virginity, raw and naked, just like a monk. "The desert loves those stripped to the bone" was Jerome's aphorism for such asceticism—*nudos amat eremus*.[40]

"All Pacatula's pleasure should be in her *cubiculum*," her inner room in the palace of Gaudentius, advised Jerome. This guarded room, where she slept, worshipped, and was educated, should become, like the fort in which Antony of Egypt had locked himself away, a hidden garden of spiritual delight. (Evagrius of Antioch, who translated Athanasius' biography of Antony into Latin, was an early patron of Jerome.) "She must never look at young men or turn her eyes on curled dandies." She must never hear girls singing sweet songs. Nothing must "contaminate our secluded Danaë." She should commit to memory "the psalter and books of Solomon, the Gospels, the Apostles and prophets should be the treasure of her heart."[41] In elite Christian circles such meditation upon the scriptures was as beautiful and arousing as contemplating Plato and Plotinus on the beguiling allure of the One. The sensual shock of the holy shared by Augustine and Monica at Ostia was what Pacatula should feel every day.

Jerome did not deny a girl's sexuality, which he thought began when she was seven, but he argued that it must be enclosed in her *cubiculum*, removed from the social whirl of Rome, and only enjoyed in ecstatic memories of the scriptures. When he lived in Rome he translated an up-to-date Latin version of the Gospels for the pope, more concerned with capturing divinely rapturous truth than prosaic historical veracity. The Vulgate Bible of the Middle Ages derived from his translation.[42]

Jerome radically reimagined the mansions of the rich, so that instead of being elegant courtyards and reception rooms open to the world, every space was now an architectural expression of a girl's private bedroom. A house should be closed to the world, emulating the inhospitable desert of the monks.[43] Jerome acknowledged that not all elite Christian women agreed with his monastic formula for girls and palaces, and that scandalous gossip from such women had chased him from Rome. However, these women were not "daughters of peace," punning on Pacatula's name, which meant "Little Peace."[44]

Jerome abruptly ended his letter by recalling a devastating tragedy, one that still paralyzed him with grief and overwhelmingly demonstrated why Pacatula must dwell in sacred and sexual isolation. Three years earlier the Roman general and Gothic *rex* (king) Alaric had sacked Rome. "All the world sinks into ruin," he reminded Gaudentius (who needed no reminding). "Such are the times in which our little Pacatula is born. Such are the swaddling clothes in which she draws her first breath. She is destined to know of tears before laughter and to feel sorrow sooner than joy." Pacatula's salvation lay in exiting the stage before being able to walk upon it. She would live in her *cubiculum* as if each day were her last, delighting in the life after death. "Let her think the world has always been what it is now.

Let her know nothing of the past, let her shun the present, and let her long for the future."[45]

9 City of God

Alaric's pillaging of Rome for three days in late August 410 was the dismal endgame of the all-too-familiar scenario of a Roman general swept up in a maelstrom of civil war, campaigning from one end of the empire to another, desperately chasing after gold, imperial honors, and a lost status quo, only to be disappointed time and time again by broken promises, ephemeral victories, and squandered opportunities. Although the legions that had initially rebelled with Alaric in the Balkans fifteen years earlier were mostly troops of Gothic origin, neither they nor he ever thought of themselves as anything other than Roman soldiers. Even the title *rex* that Alaric seemingly adopted was only one of many epitaphs he claimed as he fought for the legitimacy of his demands. When camped outside Rome in 408 (and starving the city by blocking all shipping along the Tiber) he demanded the rank of *magister utriusque militiae* (master of both infantry and cavalry, the highest military command in the West), four provinces, 5,000 pounds of gold, 30,000 pounds of silver, 4,000 silk tunics, 3,000 vermilion-dyed skins, and 3,000 pounds of pepper.

The emperor Honorius and his court in Ravenna refused the rank and provinces, but the Roman Senate delivered the luxury goods. However, all the opulence in the world was pointless to Alaric without cities and farms upon which to lavish it and lawful Roman authority guaranteeing his possessions. So, in an act of violent frustration, hoping the imperial government would finally compromise, he did the unimaginable: he ransacked Rome. It was no slaughterhouse, although many neighborhoods were set alight. Anything precious, beautiful, and portable, including Honorius' sister, Galla Placida, was snatched and carried away. Alaric died soon after from fever in southern Italy, with his wife's brother, Athaulf, becoming the new king of his homeless Roman army and its overstuffed baggage train.[46]

While inevitable given the circumstances, Alaric's looting of Rome was still a cataclysmic shock to the Roman world. Although the city was no longer the political capital of the empire, it still represented the eternal and imperishable magnificence of *Romanitas*, a transcendent Romanness claimed by both Christians and pagans. The city symbolized an entire civilization. The imaginative foundations of what it meant to be Roman, at least amongst elites in the early fifth century, were ripped apart. It appeared as though the old gods were exacting their revenge for being forgotten, for being swept aside for the High God of the Christians. Paganism, which had been limping along amongst donnish Platonici, deracinated urban festivals, and half-remembered household rituals, suddenly revived. In this darkest hour the nearly extinguished *numina* seemed to glow again like luminescence in a cave, offering light and hope. Fair-weather Christians momentarily expressed spiritual regret. This pagan awakening, while brief and never really more than upper-class intellectuals pondering counterfactual what-ifs, was enough to arouse Christian writers into a rhetorical frenzy of downplaying recent history to the point of absurdity. Around 417 the Spanish priest Orosius drafted a *History Against the Pagans (Historiarum adversum paganos)*, which, apart from arguing that Rome's destiny was always to be a Christian empire, pretended that Alaric's troops, while a bit rough, mostly behaved admirably, especially toward churches. If one listened to Romans themselves, what one heard amongst the smoldering ruins was that "nothing had happened."[47]

Refugees from Rome disagreed, none more so than the wealthy families and their hangers-on fleeing to cities and villas in North Africa. One young man in particular, Rufius Agrynius Volusianus, thought that a great deal had happened, all of it tragic, all of it due to the idiocy of Christianity. His father, Albinus, was pagan and a friend of Symmachus; his mother, Albina, was a devout Christian and a friend of Augustine. More than likely, Volusianus had once nominally been Christian, having perhaps occasional doubts in his library after reading Porphyry, but a willing enough worshipper in the religion of the emperors.

After 410 Volusianus embraced his seminar-room skepticism. What he believed about the old gods all came from the books he studied, as all public pagan worship in Rome was (with a few skittish exceptions during Alaric's siege) only a memory. Religion and philosophy were indistinguishable for him; the literary salon was his ritual space. The *Saturnalia* of Macrobius, a series of Platonic dialogues involving men like his father and Symmachus, was a holy text. Virgil's *Aeneid* was more redemptive than the Bible. There was salvation and splendor in such a learned tradition. His soul ached for the immortal blessedness of Plotinus, for dissolution in the Milky Way. Volusianus swanned about the garden parties and symposia of

Carthage, advocating not so much for a Rome without Christ—he knew that was impossible—as for an empire where Christianity was recognized as the parvenu religion it so obviously was, and where the old gods returned in triumph to help guide humanity.[48]

Augustine was determined to crush such wishful thinking. After some hesitation, he began a *magnum opus et arduum*—"a great and arduous work"—entitled *The City of God* (*De civitate Dei*), circulating the first three books amongst the African literati in 413. Thirteen years and another twenty-two volumes later, he finished his "giant of a book."[49] It was more than just an epic Christian apologia on the fall of Rome; it was a magisterial (and mischievous) retelling of all Roman history, religion, and philosophy for the last millennium, and an exposition of why what seemed a glorious past to pagan intellectuals was in fact nothing but one shabby century after another disgraced by hollow gods and human greed.

The City of God was no pedestrian pamphlet such as Orosius had written (and which he dedicated to a slightly embarrassed Augustine). At first glance, it seemingly lacks the literary innovation of the *Confessions*, as it was deliberately written in the highly mannered style favored by bookish antiquarians like Volusianus. Yet Augustine was not only demolishing everything his pagan readers believed, and the foundations upon which those beliefs rested, but doing so in a masterly parody of their rhetorical sophistication, of the cultured chic he had once aspired to himself. His pastiche was so accomplished that many readers admired its ornate mannerism and florid erudition, not fully grasping how serious and cutting was his satire in form and content. Augustine (mostly) spared Porphyry and Plotinus the sarcasm he lavished on other philosophers, as their Platonic search for freeing the soul still moved and inspired him. They were wrong, but their errors were magnificent.

The "earthly city," *civitas terrena*, which encompassed all humans after the Fall, was transient and evil, mendaciously idolized by pagans and unwise Christians. All that mattered was the "most glorious city of God," eternal and heavenly, where humanity, rendered equal by shared sin, was equally granted citizenship as Catholic Christians. *The City of God* was ultimately a dissertation on the blatantly obvious for Augustine—whatever pagans and their fellow travelers might think, they were just delaying the inevitable, because in the time to come, everyone, apart from the Jews, would be Christian.[50]

Augustine did not want individuals like Volusianus (of whom he was very fond) punished for their foolish ideas, but he thought it right and proper that the coercive power of the Roman state, which still functioned in North Africa, should be applied in all its terrible might against anyone thinking they still had a choice about being a Catholic Christian. The imperial laws condemning heresy and paganism were just. Individuals needed to be forcefully reminded of (or harshly inspired by) the inevitability of their Catholicism. As there was no choice in heaven, there should be no choice on earth. Free will was an illusion.

Another refugee from Rome, Pelagius, a Christian layman originally from Britain, vehemently disagreed with Augustine (even walking out of a reading of *The City of God* in Carthage). As humans had never lost their original good nature, he argued, they should be free to choose the good that was within them, and given that goodness and self-rule were what God wished for His children, individuals would willingly seek out baptism and perfection in Christ.

This was utter nonsense to Augustine. No one could make themselves good whenever they felt like it, as everyone was deeply flawed and sinful, forever depending upon the grace of God for guidance and loving coercion. Sin was the day-to-day reality of every man, woman, and child.[51] Christians (and so potentially all persons) were like hedgehogs, he suggested in a sermon from 403, covered from head to foot in tiny little sins, *peccata minutissima*, requiring the daily penance of prayer.[52] Somewhat surprisingly, at least from a modern perspective, this was a prickly virtue for Augustine. The wonderful thing about sin was that by making Christians always focus on a future without it, past and present tragedies were only momentarily sad when compared with the eternal happiness to come—even events as devastating as the death of a mother or the fall of an empire.

10 Treasure in Heaven

Rich senatorial refugees slowly returned to Rome after Alaric's sack, but other citizens returned more swiftly, if in reduced numbers. By 412 the *annona* (the free grain, oil, and pork given to the *populus Romanus*) was insufficient for all the mouths demanding to be fed (around 120,000).[53] This resilient civic continuity of tens of thousands expecting the dole and the urban prefect knowing it was his job to satisfy them, while undeniably impressive, nevertheless highlights how provisioning the city would become more and more difficult from now on. Within two decades the grain shipments from North Africa ceased, and within four decades the surrounding farmland was largely uncultivated wilderness. As a consequence of these escalating administrative and agricultural troubles, the population of Rome slowly but inexorably dropped in the fifth and sixth centuries to less than 50,000 by 700, never again even coming close to the approximately 500,000 residents before the Gothic sack.[54]

The architectural fabric of the city never fully recovered either. It was now a landscape of deserted gardens, waterless fountains, broken paving stones, crumbling tenements, burned-out mansions, and forlorn statues overlooking empty streets. Remarkably, though, amidst these ruins the surviving palaces of the senatorial nobility stood out like bright flowers in a field of ashes. Roman nobles were still immensely wealthy despite all the disorder, with annual income in rents between 120,000 and 300,000 solidi (2,000 to 5,000 pounds of gold).[55] They restored and repaired their grand houses with the same studious antiquarianism that Volusianus and his circle expended on Virgil, except these buildings were not expressions of last-gasp paganism but aristocratic affirmations that the city still belonged to them. Gilded palazzi were the focal points around which islands of habitation developed for the wealthy and their impoverished clients.[56]

Little Pacatula lived inside such a mansion. Jerome in his 413 letter to her even complained about such palatial refurbishing in a bleak and dismal Rome: "We live as though as we are going to die tomorrow, yet we build as though we are always going to live in this world." Walls, ceilings, and capitals shone with new gold leaf, "yet Christ dies before our doors naked and hungry in the persons of His poor."[57] What so upset Jerome was that wealthy Romans had not listened closely enough to what he and other Christian intellectuals, especially Western bishops like Augustine and Ambrose, had been admonishing them to do for more three decades. Instead of the traditional elite model of open-handed spending upon their local towns and cities, particularly the extravagant underwriting of games and festivals, such munificence should be spent upon the poor. The irony of such Christian lecturing of the rich was that, for the most part, the emperors and their bureaucrats had effectively taken over such civic spending themselves since the fourth century.

Again, like so much about Roman elites, especially in the unraveling Western Empire, what Christian intellectuals were assaulting was a self-image more idealistic than actual. The senatorial nobility in Rome, while rebuilding their own urban enclaves within the city, did come together to mend the Senate House. They also erected façades for hiding decaying buildings. This allowed them to parade through Rome in front of Potemkin palaces, giving the illusion of continuing urban grandeur. Either way, their focus was upon themselves and their own families, rather than fellow citizens. This was still an intense localism, but one devoid of the old civic euergetism, even if it gave lip service to ancient customs. This phenomenon was occurring throughout the cities and towns in the West and seemed misguided to Jerome and hundreds of less well-known preachers. The rich should not invest in themselves or their cities; they should invest in the poor as an earthly down payment on everlasting "treasure in heaven."[58]

11 Like an Endless River

Slaves, however, were not part of the holy and amorphous poor for Christians. They were precisely defined individuals, accepted, with little or no regret, as an inescapable part of Roman society. "Why do you have so many slaves?" the youthful priest John Chrysostom ("Golden Mouth," on account of his great rhetorical skill) asked his audience in the Great Church in Antioch at the end of the fourth century. "What need is there for them? There's none at all. For one master should need only one slave, or really two or three masters, one slave." Slavery did not bother him; rich Christians followed by a "herd of slaves" did. "The wealthy go around to the baths, to the market, as though they were shepherds or slave-traders."[59] Such ostentatiousness was shameful. Amongst the less well-off, in the narrow streets where shopkeepers and craftsmen lived in Antioch, the screams of slave girls being savagely beaten by their mistresses were all too common. "What's going on there?" neighbors would wonder about the racket from a nearby house. "So-and-so," someone replied, "is beating her own slave." "What could ever be more shameful than to hear this shrieking?" sighed John. "What is most disgraceful of all, some mistresses are so ruthless and harsh that when they lash their slaves, the stripes don't dissipate within the day." Some even displayed wounded girls naked to their husbands. "And you don't think it shameful?" he fumed. "Should this happen in Christian houses?"

"But slaves are an evil tribe!" retorted the matrons of Antioch. Slave girls needed to be disciplined! "Yes, I know this," John conceded. "But there are other ways to maintain order—fear, threats, words—which are more effective and rescue you from shame." He was saying this not for the sake of the enslaved "but for you the free, so that you do nothing indecent or shameful." Slaves were not inherently evil; only an ungodly master or mistress made them so. "Why are you all blushing?" John teased his audience.[60] There was no shame in a Christian owning slaves, only shame in allowing such dominion to bring out the worst in you.

Augustine in the last years of his life worried deeply about individual freedom and the shamefulness of the slave trade in North Africa. The sack of Rome, and the continuing turmoil devastating senatorial estates and yeoman farms on the Italian peninsula and in southern Gaul, had resulted in a dearth of slaves (killed, stolen, or escaped). Galatian slavers, colloquially known as *mangones* (from a Greek root meaning "to deceive"), were now kidnapping African peasants for this ravenous market. "With ululating war-cries, dressed up as soldiers and barbarians to inspire fear, they invade sparsely populated and remote rural areas," Augustine wrote to his old friend Alypius about the marauding gangs of slavers in 428. All the men in villages were killed and the women and children carted off. Free Romans, especially from Numidia, were being captured and marched in columns, "like an endless river," to the slave ships at the docks in Hippo. Local Catholic Christians (unlike the Donatist Christian majority) ransomed 120 victims. What was so shocking was that the merchants organizing the raids were protected by imperial officials, through bribes and indifference. They even sued Augustine and his staff for damages for interfering in legal trade.

This was why Augustine wrote to Alypius, who was visiting the imperial court in Ravenna as bishop of Thagaste. He requested that Alypius look in libraries in Rome for legal precedents and to appeal directly to the emperor. He even told Alypius what to say: "But who resists these traders who are found everywhere, who traffick, not in animals but in human beings, not in barbarians but in loyal Romans?" Like John Chrysostom, he did not oppose slavery on principle, only the sinful illegality of seizing and selling free Romans. "Who will resist, in the name of Roman freedom—I do not say the common freedom of the Roman state but of their very own."[61]

An archdeacon named Felix had views about freedom and slavery in the second half of the fifth century. He was from either Rome or Sardinia, and he owned a slave who wore a copper or bronze collar three-quarters of an inch wide and roughly sixteen inches in overall length. (The collar was later unearthed in Sardinia, but such bands were more common in Rome.) Inscribed on the collar was: "I am the slave of Felix the archdeacon. Retain me lest I flee."[62] Despite the cascading crises in the Western Empire, the market for slaves thrived, and for all their rhetorical brilliance and disgust at what slavery could do to a free Roman Christian, John Chrysostom and Augustine were no different from the obscure Felix in accepting the enslavement of some human beings as a fact of life.

12 A Great Invasion

In late 405 a large group of Siling and Hasding Vandals, Sueves, and Alans crossed an undefended stretch of the northern Rhine near Mainz. What likely began as an opportunistic foray became, by default, a "great invasion." Apart from a spirited but short-lived defense by Frankish auxiliaries, no legions stopped the barbarians, as all imperial troops had recently evacuated northwestern Gaul for the Italian peninsula. As had happened three decades earlier with the Goths on the Danube, this was another mass of men, women, and children fleeing the Huns. While it seems there were "kings" amongst these various peoples, nothing about this incursion suggests coordination or farsighted purpose; it was merely a headlong rush into the security of the Roman Empire.

Unfortunately, instead of the protective and negotiated embrace of *Romanitas*, however inconstant and incompetent that embrace had become, a gaping political and martial emptiness greeted the refugees. They exploited this void—what else could they do?—spreading throughout the land as raiders and settlers. In Britain the collapse of northern Gaul was so alarming that a general named Constantine proclaimed himself Augustus, promising to reestablish imperial rule along the Rhine. In 406 he crossed the Channel with all of the British field army, quickly defeating and scattering the invaders. A band of Vandals, Sueves, and Alans escaped over the Pyrenees into northern Spain. Almost all of Gaul and

Spain, despite those obdurate barbarian guerrillas, were soon under the rule of this general, who called himself Constantine III. This empire within the empire disintegrated five years later with the British pretender's beheading at the hand of a Gallic pretender, who was himself beheaded a year later.

It was into this transalpine shambles that Athaulf marched the surviving Goths of Alaric's army in 412.[63] Like Alaric, he petitioned the imperial court in Ravenna for a title and land, only to be rebuffed. Angry and running low on grain, he seized Narbonne, Toulouse, and Bordeaux. Emperor Honorius now demanded the return of his sister Galla Placida, whom Alaric had taken as a prize a year earlier. Athaulf married her instead in a lavish ceremony (even using some stunning silverware looted from Rome). The emperor was outraged, sending his new *magister utriusque militiae*, a man named Constantius, to eliminate the Goths once and for all. Athaulf retreated over the Pyrenees, and although he captured Barcelona, his army was starving and mutinous, leading to his assassination in 415. After a few weeks of internecine mayhem, the new Gothic king, Wallia, returned Galla Placida to her brother, who then promptly married her to Constantius.

At this point the Goths, who never stopped acting and thinking of themselves as a Roman army, agreed to fight for the emperor in Spain against the Vandals, Sueves, and Alans. In less than three years they had largely destroyed the barbarians. In 418 (or 419) Constantius ordered the Gothic army (perhaps ten thousand strong) to leave the Iberian peninsula and settle in southern Gaul, occupying Toulouse and the Garonne valley. He was not establishing an independent kingdom; quite the contrary, he was affirming and stabilizing imperial rule below the Loire with interim battle-hardened garrisons under his command, so that he could campaign in northern Gaul. This was not Alaric's dream of a permanent settlement of small farms with his heirs as Roman high officials. Constantius, rather pleased with himself, announced he was co-emperor in 421; alas, he died shortly afterward. Honorius, whose remarkable survival on the throne for thirty years is all the more exceptional because he was an incomparable mediocrity, died in 423. After two years of the usual cycle of pretenders and civil war, Valentinian, the six-year-old son of Constantius and Galla Placida, became Augustus with help from the Eastern emperor, Theodosius II.[64]

13 The Nature of Christ

The Syrian monk and priest Nestorius was chosen by Theodosius II as bishop of Constantinople in 428. Polemical and austere, he considered it blasphemous to think that God had suffered as a man upon the cross. The majesty and divinity of the Father were untouched by the crucifixion of His human Son and servant. Christ, while uniquely blessed by God in world history, was nevertheless like other prophets of monotheism before Him. Nestorius mocked the idea of the Virgin Mary as Theotokos, "she who gave birth to God." Such views, widespread in Constantinople, were to him little better than worshipping a pagan mother-goddess. God, as the Creator of time, could not be created in time, so it was nonsense to think an immortal godhead could be born of a mortal woman.[65] Nestorius was no Arian either, as his Christ was not a Platonic echo of the Highest God.

Cyril, the bishop of Alexandria, was horrified by Nestorius. He saw himself as another Athanasius, zealously fighting paganism and heresy. In 415 he incited a Christian mob into attacking and killing the Neoplatonist philosopher Hypatia on the streets of Alexandria.[66] In 431 he goaded Theodosius II into holding a council at Ephesus to debate—really, to sabotage—the theology of Nestorius. For Cyril the humanity and divinity of Christ were indissoluble, a perfect fusion into a single "nature." (He and his militant followers came to be known as Monophysites, from *monos,* "single," and *physis,* "nature.") When God walked upon the earth as His Son, He experienced what it meant to be human, even what it meant to suffer and die. Christians did not have to reflect on the ineffable to meld with God. All they had to do was look at the mundane world around them and recall that Christ had once lived like them. Theodosius II, while not totally affirming what Cyril believed, succumbed to the outrage (and shrewd politicking) of the Alexandrian, condemning Nestorius as a heretic and exiling him first to a monastery in Antioch, then to a more isolated one in Egypt.[67]

Theodosius II, although sympathetic to Nestorius, was nevertheless more concerned with moral and civic order, and the bishop of Constantinople had (perhaps unfairly) become a figure of dissension. Like his grandfather Theodosius I, he was obsessed with legislating the relationship between heaven and earth, between God and empire, so that every Roman, especially the elite, would know what was religiously, politically, and legally correct. Two years before his condemnation of Nestorius, he commissioned twenty-two lawyers in Constantinople to collect, edit, and arrange chronologically every law since Constantine in a codex, that is, a bound book. The *Theodosian Code*—sixteen volumes, 2,700 laws—was published (in a series of ritual acclamations) by the Senate in Rome in 438.[68] It was a revolutionary testament by an emperor who, for all the ongoing fracturing of the West, could still envision from the "new Rome" of Constantinople an empire of sublime coherence and organization.

Yet within the *Theodosian Code*, numerous laws acknowledged the breakdown of the western provinces and the barbarian threat, even if they were more about what should be than what was. For example, any person wearing boots, trousers, long hair, or shaggy hides in Rome would be exiled.[69] This was less about banning barbarism than about warning ambitious generals and their soldiers, as such fashions had been à la mode for the military (and many Roman nobles) for almost a century. Senators were similarly banned from wearing the "awe-inspiring military cloak" within the Sacred City.[70] Ultimately, though, the *Theodosian Code* was a monument to an empire that was now resolutely Christian and Catholic, where the *numina* no longer existed, except perhaps as the literary residue of "the error of stupid paganism," and where Jews, schismatics, and heretics were as much civil criminals as religious ones.[71]

In 450, after forty-nine years as Augustus, Theodosius II died when he fell from a horse. A year later the new Eastern emperor, Marcian, summoned six hundred bishops to a council at Chalcedon, a town across the water from Constantinople near the mouth of the Bosphorus (now modern Kadikoy, a suburb of Istanbul), to definitively affirm the true nature of Christ. Despite marrying the late emperor's sister Pulcheria—or perhaps because of her, as it was widely assumed she picked him as a biddable weakling—he wanted a spectacular show of strength and discipline. Instead, he approved an earlier middle-of-the-road "Tome" from Pope Leo I that gave equal weight to the divine and the human in Christ. This seemed theologically straightforward to Latin Christian intellectuals in the West, simultaneously dismissing Arius and Nestorius. Unfortunately, as far as the followers of Bishop Cyril of Alexandria were concerned, Leo's doctrinal equilibrium suggested that the divinity and humanity of Christ could be separated in the first place, and so was no better than the Nestorian heresy.[72] Even burning all the works of Nestorius and requiring that all children with his name be rebaptized with new names did not calm the zealots.[73] (It was after the Council of Chalcedon that the important and influential bishops of Alexandria, Antioch, Jerusalem, Constantinople, and Rome became commonly known as "patriarchs." The bishop of Rome, though, rarely used this title, preferring "pope.")

Nevertheless, the Leonine compromise prevailed, even if the controversy surrounding the nature of Christ never subsided in the East or the West. This was more than just a debate amongst Christian intellectuals. To know how the human and the divine were constituted in Christ was to know how body and spirit were potentially constituted within all men, women, and children, whether they were Christians or Jews, Romans or barbarians.

14 Knees Without Wrinkles

In May 427 or 429 the Vandals under their king, Gaiseric, sailed from the Iberian peninsula to North Africa. They routed an African Roman army sent against them. Valentinian III and his *magister utriusque militiae*, Aëtius, hoping to halt their advance, formally surrendered Numidia and the Mauretanian provinces in 434. Five years later, with the court in Ravenna focused on Gaul and Spain, the Vandals seized Carthage in a lightning attack. This shocking development, much more materially consequential than Alaric's sack of Rome, cut off the richest provinces from the troubled Western Empire, severing strong, healthy limbs from an ailing torso. Tax revenues were now 50 percent lower than in 400.[74]

The repercussions were immediate. Since 432 the Goths had been prodding and poking the emperor and his generals, raiding Narbonne, threatening Arles, for more leverage within Gaul. A few months after the fall of Carthage, Aëtius concluded a treaty with the Gothic king, Theodoric I. What had been a temporary billet when Constantius settled the Goths around Toulouse two decades earlier was now a largely autonomous kingdom within the empire. Theodoric still recognized imperial authority, but only insofar as it underpinned his own kingliness.

Elsewhere in Gaul and Spain, the so-called Bacaudae (or Bagaudae) rebelled and were suppressed "with much slaughter," as an anonymous Marseille chronicler approvingly noted.[75] We do not know who these dissenters were, or what their insurrection was specifically against, or if their revolts were connected; all we know is that they were considered Romans and not barbarians by the Roman soldiers killing them. If anything, the Bacaudae were symptomatic of a viral separatism spreading throughout the West, one in which an expansive *Romanitas* no longer held sway and what it meant to be Roman was devolving into myriad local identities worth defending against other communities claiming to be Roman.

In this sense, the Goths and the mysterious Bacaudae each used Romanness as they defined it for their own ends, and while the latter disappeared, the former became a new and distinct "people" at once Gothic, Gallic, and Roman. By 450 the only regions directly controlled by Valentinian III and Aëtius—that is, the Respublica of the legitimate Roman Empire—were Italy, Provence, and the southern valley of the Rhône, from Lyon to Arles to Marseille.[76]

In 451 Attila, king of the Huns, crossed the Rhine. More famous than he has any right to be, this epitome of what many modern people think of when they imagine a "barbarian" only rampaged about Gaul and Italy for two years before dying in his sleep from a nosebleed induced by excessive boozing. For a few years before invading the Rhineland, he had successfully extorted the Danubian provinces and Constantinople itself; now, though, he justified his western offensive on the grounds of a marriage proposal. Honoria, the older sister of Valentinian III, had petulantly offered herself as wife to the Hunnic king after her brother executed her lover. It is doubtful that Attila thought the offer anything other than the folly of a sulking princess; nevertheless, he demanded his bride and half the Western Empire as dowry from the emperor.

Obviously, this was not going to happen. A coalition of Roman soldiers from what was left of the old British field army and the Rhine frontier guard, Gothic legions led by Theodoric I, some miscellaneous Franks, and former Bacaudae (as vaguely defined in the sources as ever) from northern Gaul, all under the command of Aëtius, clashed with the Hunnic host between Troyes and Châlons-sur-Marne. This Battle of the Catalaunian Fields (or of the Campus Mauriacus) was, as Jordanes wrote in his history a century later, "horrible, fickle, fierce, and long-lasting—antiquity has never recorded anything like it."[77] Aëtius was victorious, Theodoric was dead, and Attila withdrew to the southern Danube.

A year later the Huns took their revenge upon northern Italy, sacking cities along the Adriatic coast, even marching on Rome, before abruptly returning to their Danubian lands. After Attila's death in 453 his Hunnic "kingdom" quickly dissolved, with some factions following other barbarian kings, while quite a few, somewhat ironically, petitioned the Eastern emperor to settle within the empire.[78]

The new Gothic king, Theodoric II, who killed his elder brother in the aftermath of the Battle of the Catalaunian Fields so as to succeed their father, was apparently a ruler whose palatial villas in the Garonne valley evoked "Greek elegance, Gallic plenty, Italian briskness, the dignity of state, the attentiveness of a private home, the ordered discipline of royalty."[79] This flattering (indeed fawning) description was by a Roman noble from Lyon, Sidonius Apollinaris, in a letter to his brother-in-law Agricola. It is unclear when Sidonius visited Theodoric's court, as apart from two trips to Italy he spent all of his life in the imperial enclaves of the Auvergne and the Rhône valley, dying in 490 as bishop of Clermont. More than likely, he stayed with the king when he was in his early twenties, probably as an emissary from the imperial government in Arles, so it would have been around 455.

Why this matters is that as he got older, Sidonius, in his many letters to his friends, stressed more and more the differences between Romans and barbarians. *Romanitas* became like a family heirloom that only he and his friends possessed, celebrated, and eulogized. Consequently, his Romanness came to have a quality to it as if nothing had changed since the early fourth century (or even the late second); like a faux cameo of Constantine (or Marcus Aurelius) set in purple amethyst, it was bijou, fusty, and exquisitely mannered—and not very Christian. Yet in his portrait of Theodoric, the overwhelming impression he wished to convey was that the Gothic king was as much a Roman as anyone in his own circle. Sidonius called him a perfect creation of God and nature: strong, sincerely Christian (and, while an "Arian," only a halfhearted one), wise in administering justice, moderate in drink, hirsute but groomed, and possessing a flat stomach, sturdy calves, small feet, and "knees completely free from wrinkles."[80] Theodoric was just another version of what it meant to be a Roman aristocrat in Gaul, which, for the most part, was the reality of the mid-fifth century. It was what happened over the next thirty years that changed the views of Sidonius (and men like him) regarding Romans and barbarians.

15 The Little (and Last) Emperor

In 474 the *magister militum* (master of soldiers) Orestes assumed overall authority in Italy, ruling in the name of his young son, Romulus, whom he named as Western emperor. (Fascinatingly, Orestes had formerly been an official at the court of Attila.) Two decades of turmoil in the already fracturing Respublica in the West—Vandals had sacked Rome after sailing into Ostia, Goths now occupied most of the Rhône valley, and seven dismal emperors (one of whom was the father of Sidonius Apollinaris' friend Agricola) barely wore the purple long enough before either being shunted aside or assassinated—had led to this masquerade by a puppetmaster father and his marionette son.

Odoacer, another general in the army of Italy, ended this farce by killing the father and deposing and exiling the "Little Emperor," the Augustulus, in 476. He then appealed to the Eastern emperor Zeno, saying there was no need for an emperor in the West, as just one ruler in Constantinople was enough, and so, as compensation for making all this possible, he should be given the rank of patrician (and so govern Italy unhindered). Zeno was furious, dismissing the request out of hand. Odoacer shrugged and named himself *rex*.[81]

16 The Dwindled Tiber

In 477 a glum Sidonius Apollinaris was in Bordeaux hoping for an audience with the Gothic king Euric. He was the exiled bishop of Clermont (an ancient Roman town in the Auvergne) after the Goths had captured his city two years earlier. Aside from one brief acknowledgment of his existence, Euric had ignored him for two months. This was one more humiliation in the many he had suffered in the last eight years. In 469 he had been banished from the rump Respublica in Arles, having been accused of consorting with a traitor (an easy accusation to make of any noble Roman in the late fifth century). It broke his heart. Sidonius' consecration as bishop of Clermont the next year was a comedown from serving the Roman state, even one so diminished as it was in the West.[82]

Sidonius in Bordeaux—which was like being in prison for him—sent a letter to a friend, Lampridius, who lived in the city and was contentedly reconciled with having a Gothic overlord. It contained a melancholy poem ostensibly about the splendor of their Gothic "lord and master" and which he hoped that Euric might somehow hear. He worried that his personal troubles and the general sadness weighing upon the world affected his "silly trifles," but perhaps, just perhaps, there might be a pleasing melody in his verse, "like the songs of swans, whose cry is more tuneful in moments of agony."

Unlike his praise (in prose) for Theodoric two decades earlier for being just like a Roman, Sidonius sighed (in verse) that Euric neither wished nor needed to be Roman, as all peoples, even Romans, now emulated the Gothic king and his "warrior-settlers" beside the Garonne. "I feel no envy, but rather wonder," he wrote. Sidonius, while unaware of all that had recently happened in Italy, knew enough to conclude that the "dwindled Tiber" would never be powerful and majestic again, that imperial Rome was no longer the stuff of barbarian dreams—or, rather, the imperial Rome of which Sidonius dreamed.[83]

When Sidonius died sometime between 480 and 490 as bishop of Clermont—he had returned from exile soon after his letter to Lampridius—he had made no arrangements to describe himself as an *episcopus* on his sarcophagus; instead, he had chosen to have it proudly list his literary works and his long-ago offices in the long-lost Respublica. As would be the case for any elite Roman man or woman, Sidonius' death was dated by the regnal year of the Roman emperor, which for him was Emperor Zeno in Constantinople—the Rome of his dreams had fallen in the West.[84]

17 Crumpling into Pointlessness

The Roman Empire did not so much fall as crumple in the West. After the torrent of catastrophes and emergencies of the fifth century, its moral and political rationale dissipated in the eyes of soldiers and peasants, bishops and nobles, Romans and barbarians. *Romanitas* still had some persuasive purpose, but it was now a distinctly local miscellany of abstractions and practicalities, differing from region to region, deserted city to empty town, barbarian ruler to Roman official, divorced from universal imperial ideals and realities—most especially the necessity of an emperor.

The imperial collapse into irrelevancy was also not the result of barbarians rushing over the Rhine and Danubian frontiers inflamed with a hatred of civilization—if for no other reason than that, even when killing an emperor at Adrianople or sacking Rome, the various barbarian groups only ever wanted to be Romans themselves. The barbarian migrations and invasions (and only a fine line sometimes separates one from the other) were as much a consequence as a cause of Western woes. The formation of the barbarian kingdoms directly resulted from emperors and senators failing to supply the honor, security, and treasure that went with *Romanitas*. Barbarian identity was do-it-yourself Romanness.

Almost to the bitter end, there were serious attempts at reversing the loss of one western province after another, but through a mix of bad luck, incompetence, and the powerful centrifugal forces unleased by a cavalcade of competing pretenders, wandering Roman armies, and selfish generals, the remarkable recovery after the crisis of the third century was impossible in the fifth. The divine oneness and universalism that the Christian God conferred upon the martial authoritarianism of Constantine, while still efficacious in the East, had, like everything else crumpled into a sacred parochialism in the West.

ITALY IN THE EARLY
MIDDLE AGES

---·-·-· Boundaries around 700
○ City
⚔ Monastery
◆ Settlement

III

The Flutter of Blackbirds

440–613

1 A Holy Boy

Patricius, a sixteen-year-old Christian lad living with his father, Calpornius, in a small, run-down Roman villa in northwestern Britain, was kidnapped by Irish raiders and sold into slavery in northwestern Ireland around 440. Half a century later, with Patricius now an elderly bishop traversing the Irish Sea, his memories of abduction, captivity, and escape (twice over) were the unreliable threads holding together his fragile and heartfelt *Confession*. He had been abducted "with so many thousands—and we deserved it!" Only by "losing family and homeland," by being stolen and enslaved, was he given the "gift of knowing and loving God." Only through suffering was Patricius "reformed by the Lord."

As a lonely slave pasturing sheep, Patricius prayed a hundred times every day and every night. After six years he ran away when a voice in his sleep said: "See, your ship is ready." He wandered east for days until he finally found a ship. The crew—pagan pirates—were friendly, welcoming him aboard. He was wary, "so I refused to suck their nipples because of the fear of God." Three days later the shallow-draft ship was dragged ashore on the British coast, but there were no humans anywhere, just wilderness. Patricius and his shipmates trudged for twenty-eight days, hungry and lost. "What about it, Christian?" said the captain. "You say your God is great and powerful. Well, then, why can you not pray for us? We are in danger of starving." Patricius prayed and, "lo and behold, a herd of pigs appeared."

The next morning just before dawn, as everyone slumbered, Satan attacked Patricius. He felt as if a huge rock was crushing him. "And meanwhile I saw the sun rising in the sky and on shouting 'Helias, Helias' with all my might, see, the brilliance of the sun fell on me and at once shook me free of all the weight." He was unsure why he called upon Helias (the Latin name for Elijah, although he clearly fused the Jewish prophet with the sun god Sol or Helios); no matter, he knew it was Christ who helped him. Patricius eventually found his family, and he immediately decided to leave them after another night vision told him to go back to Ireland.[1]

In this vision a man named Victoricus arrived from Ireland with "countless letters," and he gave one to Patricius. "I read the heading of the letter, 'The Voice of the Irish,' and as I read these opening words aloud" he imagined (in his dream) hearing British slaves in Ireland crying: "We beg you, holy boy, to come and walk again amongst us." "I was stung with remorse in my heart and could not read on, and so I awoke." Patricius resolved there and then to be a holy man preaching the Gospel in Ireland to Roman Christian exiles, especially the women, and to Irish pagans.

"Why is this fellow walking into danger amongst enemies who do not know God?" haughtily wondered other British Romans. Patricius ignored such disdain, dismissing all doubts about him as resulting from "my lack of education." He worried repeatedly in his *Confession* that his Latin was poor, as he had not spoken it when enslaved. He was embarrassed about his learning when compared to other British men whose adolescent studies were not interrupted by kidnapping. Yet none of this stopped him from traveling "where no-one had ever penetrated to baptize or ordain clergy or confirm people." Each day "I expect to be killed, betrayed, reduced to slavery, or whatever." It was his zealous enthusiasm for risking body and soul (awake and asleep) that demonstrated his holiness. He saw himself as God's envoy, a sacred plenipotentiary equal to (if not above) the hundreds of petty rulers whose authority pockmarked Ireland. Some of these rulers imprisoned him, others he bribed with gifts to let him pass unscathed, and more than a few welcomed him and his God. Patricius eventually surrounded himself with the sons of these kings (usually by paying them) as symbols of his "diplomatic immunity."

Over the course of five decades, Patricius created his own "kingdom of God" in Ireland and northwestern Britain, separate from and superior to all earthly realms, and populated with monks, priests, and holy virgins loyal to him. He was a "Roman" living in a world where almost everything associated with Romanness, apart from Christianity, had collapsed by the time he was born, and so his "kingdom of God" was, for all its vulnerability, an attempt at establishing order amongst the ruins.[2]

It seems breathtaking how quickly Britain fell apart when most of the Roman field army—roughly forty thousand soldiers, an eighth of all imperial forces, soaking up one-sixteenth of the annual budget of the Western Empire—departed within the first decade of the fifth century. Facets of Romanness were already fading away in the fourth century. Iron production in the Weald (woodland in southeast Britain) fell by a quarter around 350 and stopped altogether in 410. Nails completely disappeared by 390 (no more hobnailed boots, sturdy coffins, or thick-planked ships and boats). The great kilns of the New Forest and Oxfordshire declined so precipitously after 370 that by the beginning of the fifth century no one in Britain was making pots anymore, with large areas becoming aceramic. The temples in Bath, such as Sulis Minerva, were not being repaired by 400 (even if the streets were recobbled six times between the mid-fourth century and the early fifth). In Canterbury the sewers were clogged, foul-smelling, and broken for half a century before the legions left. York reverted back to marshland, becoming home to a menagerie of wetland creatures such as mice, water voles, weasels, and shrews. All of Britain's towns and cities ceased to exist by 420.[3]

Anyone still living in the urban detritus risked attack from animals and, most especially, other Romans. In the early fifth century a father, mother, and two children were violently killed (a heavy blow crushed the skull of one child) in Canterbury. Other Romans solicitously buried them in a grass-lined pit within the city walls. The parents were seated and dressed in silver Roman jewelry. One child sat on the mother's lap, the other at her feet, while two dogs rested upon the father.[4] Everything about this funeral would have shocked Romans (whether pagan, Jew, or Christian) elsewhere in the empire, but more than anything, they would have been horrified that the dead were interred within the city, as for thousands of years this had been the great taboo of all ancient Mediterranean religions. As Britain's temples, fora, sewers, walls, and factories collapsed, so too did the old urban piety. And all of this physical and spiritual ruination occurred without the presence of any "barbarians."

Around 420 boat people from the northern Rhine, Jutland, and southern Scandinavia began settling in eastern Britain. They were not an organized invasion. They were rough-and-ready opportunists braving the North Sea in small animal-skin vessels. Some were like the "blue-eyed Saxon" pirates in the poetry of Sidonius Apollinaris, "afraid of the land, accustomed to the sea."[5] Others were fleeing their cold, hardscrabble communities, searching for new lands. The disintegration of Roman Britain was a lucky chance. Unlike the Goths, Vandals, or Franks, none of these "Germanic" settlers were formerly Roman soldiers or even all that familiar with *Romanitas*. Undoubtedly, they experienced some of the gravitational pull of the empire, but it was a faint tidal ripple, barely affecting their societies. Certainly, none of them were Christian. By the time Patricius composed his *Confession*, the few seafaring chancers of his youth had become a torrential flow of immigrants, none of them with any knowledge of Rome or Christ.

Yet Patricius never mentioned the new settlers in Britain. He only referred to other Roman Britons like himself in his *Confession*, living amongst the debris of a half-remembered empire. The greatest threat, as far as he was concerned, was not even pagan Irish slavers but, as with the family buried in Canterbury around the time he was born, other Romans. A late fifth-century letter survives from Patricius condemning a Roman *rex* (king) named Coroticus who murdered, robbed, and kidnapped Roman Christians. Patricius called him a patricide, a fratricide, a ravening wolf "devouring God's people like so much bread." Unlike in Gaul, he lamented, where at least holy men like himself ransomed Roman Christians captured by the Franks, Coroticus would "kill or sell them," and not to other Romans, but as slaves for the Picts and the Irish.

In western and northern Britain hundreds of "blood-thirsty men" and "rebels of Christ" like Coroticus established themselves in ancient hill forts or run-down Roman fortifications (like the gatehouses and towers of Hadrian's Wall), giving shelter and protection to anyone (Romans, Irish, North Sea immigrants) willing to follow them. Patricius hated this thuggish reality and how too many Romans sheepishly accepted it. "I am resented," he sighed. "I am very much despised" for denouncing wolves and sheep alike. Patricius ended his letter with an appeal for some "servant of God" to read out his carefully crafted Latin in the presence of Coroticus before his words were censured or, much worse, simply forgotten, like smoke scattered by the wind.[6]

Patricius was tormented by what other Romans thought or said about him. His *Confession* had in fact been prompted by British "elders" accusing him of something he had done as a boy (not yet fifteen, "in the space of an hour") before his kidnapping and which he long ago confessed to a friend "in a depressed and worried state of mind." Although he wrote it in Ireland, he hoped Roman Christians in northwest Britain might see or hear "my declaration before I die."[7] We have no idea if they did. If, like his letter to Coroticus, his *Confession* was in the end never read by anyone apart from himself, or perhaps only a small circle of Irish and British companions, it is, nonetheless, still an extraordinary document—not least for its existence when, like so much else associated with *Romanitas* in fifth-century Britain, reading and writing had largely disappeared as skills and as cultural necessities. Yet Patricius assumed there were men and even women who had been educated after a late Roman fashion and who, while perhaps lacking new pots or glassware or iron nails, kept alive, if only in a snobbish and spiteful way, facility with Latin and an awareness of Jerome's Bible (especially the Old Testament) and Virgil's *Aeneid*.

Patricius defended his life in the *Confession* in a skittish stream of consciousness. Memories overlap and interrupt one another; time abruptly flows backward, then suddenly jumps forward. Like Augustine in his *Confessions*, Patricius portrayed himself as a man and a Christian within a nonlinear narrative. But, lacking the tightly wound coil of Platonic memories, the almost limitless imperial imagination, and the literary gifts (as well as the humor) of the African, he sketched in nervy naive prose his anxiety at how body and soul, earth and heaven, were unstable at the "ends of the world." He was never sure whether the voices he heard every night "were within me or beside me." He worried about what he had done being forgotten, not just by others but even by himself.

What ultimately gave Patricius his sense of identity, apart from his lasting bitterness at the condescension of some Romans and his horror at the violence of others, was his slavery in Ireland, where he was first given "God's gift." Whenever he felt himself dissolving in existential doubt, "His Spirit dwelling within me," this divinity within and around him, this past and future holiness, afforded clarity, if only for a moment, in a precarious world.[8]

2 That Is What You Did to My Ewer

Clovis, son of Childeric, was "king" of what had been the Roman army of the Loire when Patricius praised him and his soldiers for at least ransoming the Romans they had captured to Christian holy men. This army, while still including many Romans (sons of British veterans, demobbed Parisian legionnaires, senatorial scions in search of glory), was by the beginning of the sixth century more "Frankish" than Roman. It was an identity not at all defined by ethnicity; rather, it was shorthand for the new post-Roman "kingdom" that, beginning in the Paris basin and expanding south along the Rhône and eastward across the Rhine, encompassed much of what had been Roman Gaul and even territory (settled by the Alamanni) beyond the old imperial *limites* by 507. Initially, though, Clovis was, like his father, a "barbarian" Roman general of the familiar late fifth-century type in the shattered Western Empire when he became king in 486 (or 491) and probably an "Arian" Christian.[9]

Unfortunately, so much of our image of Clovis is shaped by what Gregory (Georgius Florentius Gregorius), bishop of Tours, wrote a century later in his *Books of Histories* (*Libri historiarum*), an erratic if engaging ten-book blend of history, fabrication, hagiography, and episcopal memoir. The bishop depicted the Frankish king and his warriors as buccaneering barbarians and idolatrous pagans. "I put it to you my lusty freebooters," said Clovis to his army in a famous anecdote about a great silver ewer (a jug for pouring wine into the Eucharistic chalice) stolen from a church, "that you should agree here and now to grant me that ewer over and above my normal share." He wanted to return the ewer to its Catholic bishop. His followers all agreed, apart from one "feckless fellow, greedy, and prompt to anger," who, raising his battle-axe, sliced the ewer in half, shouting, "You shall have none of this booty . . . except your fair share!" Clovis sighed, hiding his fury. A few months later, while inspecting his army, he paused before the same fellow. "Your javelin is in a shocking condition," he wryly observed, "and so are your sword and your axe." He grabbed the offending axe and threw it on the ground. As the soldier stooped to pick up his weapon, Clovis swiftly raised his own battle-axe and split the man's skull. "That is what you did to my ewer," he shouted.

Gregory played up (as well as made up) the "Frankishness" and paganism of Clovis and his army as a way of emphasizing just how lacking in Romanness they were—only barbarians, for example, shared spoils. Thus when the king eventually converted to Catholic Christianity, it was a transformation of cosmic importance, signifying not just the special holiness of the ruler and his family but also the special holiness of the land over which they ruled. Gaul was more than just a kingdom, a *regnum*—it was Christendom itself.[10]

The conversion of Clovis, according to Gregory, occurred during a brutal battle with the Alamanni around 496 (or 506). The Frankish army was being annihilated and, moved to tears, the king raised his eyes to heaven and begged, "Jesus Christ . . . if you give me victory over my enemies . . . then I will believe in you and I will be baptized in your name." Immediately the Alamanni stopped fighting and ran away. Even more miraculously, a few weeks later in Reims, all the Frankish warriors, assembled before their king, shouted in unison without any prompting: "We will give up worshipping our mortal gods . . . to follow the immortal God." Clovis smiled; his wife, Clotid, who was already a Catholic Christian, smiled; and Remigius, bishop of Reims, arranged a royal baptism. "The public squares were draped with colored cloths, the churches were adorned with white hangings," and the baptistry was a "perfumed paradise" with sweet-smelling candles glowing in a delicious fog of incense. "Like some new Constantine," Gregory eulogized, Clovis stepped toward the baptismal font, "ready to wash away the sores of his old leprosy and to be cleansed in flowing water from the sordid stains which he had borne so long." "Bow your head in meekness," said Remigius. "Worship what you have burnt, burn what you have been wont to worship."[11]

Like the story of the silver ewer, the tale of the conversion of Clovis was another fiction by Gregory. His looking up in the sky and asking Christ for victory was inspired by Eusebius describing Constantine seeing a cross outlined in the midday sun as a sign to follow the Highest God. The disease metaphor for the baptism of Clovis was borrowed from the fanciful *Actus Sylvestri*, written in fifth-century Rome, where the pagan emperor was afflicted with leprosy until his baptism by Pope Sylvester.[12] Remarkably, despite Gregory comparing Clovis to the first Christian emperor, and Gregory's own overweening pride in being descended from a Gallo-Roman senatorial family, the history of Rome itself was recalled with no consistency or even obvious interest in the *Histories*. Emperors functioned as walk-ons, doing little, saying even less, vaguely suggesting the passage of time. By contrast, the *Histories* overflowed with thrilling stories about the post-Roman Church in Gaul and its marvelous supply of holy martyrs and saintly bishops like himself. In the late sixth century, at least for a man like Gregory, *Christianitas* had so totally absorbed *Romanitas*, and both had so fractured into intensely local phenomena, that even the story of imperial collapse in the West was secondary, if not irrelevant, to the much more important history of *virtutes sanctorum*, "the deeds of the saints," such as Saint Remigius baptizing a barbarian pagan king.

Of course, Clovis did actually convert to Catholic Christianity sometime between 496 and 507 (probably closer to the later date) and was baptized by Remigius at Reims. It was a savvy decision. For his new Roman subjects, Clovis showed esteem for the old Christian emperors, the current emperor in Constantinople, and the established Church in Gaul. For his Frankish warriors, it added one more path they must follow, if they were not already Catholic, in identifying their physical and spiritual well-being with their king. By becoming a Catholic, Clovis sharply differentiated himself from the Arian Gothic kings in Italy and Spain. Unlike these heretics, he and his kingdom could claim to be the rightful heirs of the emperors and their empire in the West—at least in Gaul, which was all that mattered to him. This supposed continuity with the past was important to Clovis and his family, as they were arrivistes in the post-imperial chaos. This was why they called themselves "Merovingians," that is, the descendants of Merovech, who was apparently the father of Childeric, suggesting a lineage as far back as Emperor Theodosius II.

Even if being baptized a Catholic was a useful way of unifying his Roman and Frankish subjects, especially as those identities already overlapped in his army, and of proclaiming his legitimacy as a ruler, none of this utility denies religious conviction on the part of Clovis. If anything, it demonstrates that utilitarianism was (and is) as meaningful a reason for conversion as a prayer answered in battle.

The importance of legitimacy for Clovis was highlighted when, around the time of his conversion, he commissioned Roman lawyers from the schools in Lyon or Reims to make a Latin law code for the Franks and Romans (and miscellaneous *barbari*) in his lands between the Loire and the Ardennes. This *Lex Salica*, as it is known, was legislative *spolia*, a collation of old and new laws, inspired by the majestic legal compendium of Theodosius II. Clovis never intended for these laws to be enacted. It was the fact that he could commission such a code that was important. New kings, like old emperors, had laws, and such laws were organized and, where possible, written in codices. This might be *Romanitas* at its shallowest, but there was august symbolism in the very existence of the legal hodgepodge cobbled together by the Roman lawyers. The overwhelming impression of the code was a world of small, insecure villages threatened by thieving warbands and refugee strangers, a lawless world of rough justice. The *Lex Salica* was copied, edited, and supplemented by later Merovingians, an heirloom passed down as a symbol of kingship.[13]

Clovis, "who believed in the Trinity, crushed the heretics with divine help and enlarged his dominion to include all Gaul," died in 512.[14] He was buried in Paris. Despite the effort at establishing a sense of historical continuity, lawfulness, and religious orthodoxy, the centrifugal forces fracturing the Western Empire in the late fifth century, and which Clovis so successfully exploited in conquering Gaul, were unleashed again at his death. The kingdom was split between his four sons, as none of them acknowledged the superiority of one over another (especially as the mother of the eldest was not the same as the mother of the younger three). This recurring tendency for fragmenting and internecine violence remained a characteristic of the Merovingians, and then the Carolingians, for the next four centuries, transforming the ad hoc partible inheritance of the sons of Clovis into a customary practice amongst the Franks.

Gregory of Tours so loathed these "civil wars" between the sons, queens, brothers, nephews, and uncles of Merovingian kings, and the recurring damage to Gaul, that in his final anecdote about Clovis a brutal remedy was outlined (and implicitly recommended by the bishop). "How sad a thing it is that I live among strangers like some solitary pilgrim," the king lamented before a group of followers just before his death, "and that I have none of my own relations left to help me when disaster threatens!" Clovis said this not because he grieved that all his relatives were dead but, according to Gregory, "because in his cunning way he hoped to find some relative still in the land of the living whom he could kill."[15]

3 The Consolation of Philosophy

Philosophy floats down from heaven in 524. She is very old and her robe, while made of imperishable material, has been ripped by violent hands. Her eyes glow, however, and vitality flushes her face; a little disconcertingly, her size fluctuates from the human to a colossus whose head crashes through the clouds. She has come to comfort Ancius Manlius Severinus Boethius as he glumly awaits his execution in Pavia (a town on the Ticino River in Lombardy). Or so he imagined in his *Consolation of Philosophy*, a Platonic dialogue between himself and "my nurse Philosophy" written during his imprisonment.

Boethius had been *magister officiorum* (master of offices) for the Arian Gothic king of Italy, Theodoric, until the monarch accused him (unfairly) of treason. His *consolatio*, while imbued with the same Platonism by way of Plotinus as Augustine's *Confessions* a century earlier, was, despite its mix of poetry and prose modeled on Menippean satire, neither a conscious effort at literary innovation nor even a seemingly Christian salve. It was gallows meditation as philosophical autobiography, exemplifying Samuel Johnson's quip about how the prospect of being hanged in a fortnight concentrates the mind wonderfully.[16]

"You have forgotten your own identity," Philosophy scolds Boethius as he wallows in self-pity. "I emphatically agree with Plato," he tells her, "the contamination of the body made me lose my memory." He has forgotten that he is, like all humans, essentially happy, "and every happy person is God." Crucially, God knows all things, says Philosophy, "not as a sort of foreknowledge of the future, but as knowledge of the unceasingly present moment." Everything that has happened and that was to happen exists as synchronous divine awareness. In this eternal simultaneity, Philosophy concludes, "man's freedom of will remains intact." Boethius now faces his execution happily, like Socrates or Cicero, knowing that as he remembers the divinity within himself, his death is nothing to fear, as it is no more than one event amongst many in an unceasing present in which he is already inseparable from God, the One and the Good.[17]

Boethius was from one of the oldest families of Rome, and perhaps one of the last Romans schooled with *paideia*, even if it was now imbued with Catholic Christianity and a démodé ethos confined to only a few men and women like himself. He not only translated Porphyry and Aristotle from Greek into Latin but wrote a Latin treatise attacking the theology of Nestorius. His library in Rome was expensively stocked with books and beautifully glazed with alabaster windows. It was the memory of these books and their comforting universal knowledge that shaped his *consolatio*. Christianity, while seemingly absent from his conversation with Philosophy, was implicit in every dialogue and poem. *Romanitas* and *Christianitas* were one for Boethius, and in the divine unceasing present of the philosopher and the theologian, both worse-for-wear Philosophy and inviolable Christianity existed as part of God. The *numina* still surrounded him as imperishably ancient and sempiternally Christian. As much as the maudlin Boethius in the *Consolation of Philosophy* identifies with pagan philosophical martyrs like Socrates and Cicero, the Boethius scribbling in his prison was also a Catholic martyr persecuted by an Arian heretic.

Boethius was tortured and killed soon after finishing the *Consolation of Philosophy*—"a cord bound about his forehead so tightly that his eyes cracked in their sockets," and finally, blind and bloody, "he was beaten to death with a cudgel."[18]

4 The Talented Goth Imitates the Roman

In the late fifth century, four decades before the death of Boethius, Theodoric and his Gothic army, after threatening Constantinople, were bribed by the emperor Zeno with the spectacular prize of Italy, which, as far as the imperial court was concerned, had been stolen by the usurper Odoacer. These Goths, or Ostrogoths as they are also known—tempted by the wealth (real and imagined) of Rome and Ravenna, and, despite being Arians, blessed (albeit reluctantly) by Zeno—crossed the Julian Alps in 489. Four years later Theodoric was the new strongman of Italy, ruling for thirty-three years, an emperor in all but name.[19]

Theodoric's *regnum* as Respublica went no further than the Italian peninsula—apart from a few pockets in Sicily, southern Gaul, and the Balkans into which his Goths had punched their way—but within his kingdom he encouraged Romanness, even if it was now diminished in scope and ambiguous (if not confused) in meaning. He and his Goths dreamed of being Romans. "The talented Goth imitates the Roman," Theodoric supposedly said, "whereas the poor Roman imitates the Goth."[20]

Theodoric restored crumbling public buildings throughout his kingdom, especially in Ravenna (his capital), Pavia, and Rome. He erected statues of himself, when new statuary had almost completely disappeared in the Western Empire after 410.[21] He distributed 8,500 *modii* of grain to the poor gathered around the shrine of Saint Peter in Rome (roughly a year's supply for three hundred people) in 500.[22] His Gothic generals lived in rural palaces outside Ravenna in the same grand manner as any Roman noble. On gold coins celebrating his *tricennalia* (thirty-year jubilee) he was dressed as a sixth-century Roman soldier—which, of course, was the same as showing him dressed as a sixth-century Gothic warrior.[23]

Flavius Magnus Aurelius Cassiodorus, who became master of offices after the arrest of Boethius, nevertheless termed what Theodoric was doing as *modernus* (modern); that is, it was Romanness inspired by, and yet very different from, the old *Romanitas*.[24] As absolute monarch, Theodoric flattered senatorial elites like Boethius and Cassiodorus, enlisting them as bureaucrats, Catholic collaborationists undermining papal authority, courtiers, and panegyrists, until inevitably they disappointed him by being "Roman" in ways he condemned.

After Theodoric died in 526, his charismatic if menacing patronage of Romanness fractured and frayed, and Ostrogothic Italy, while hardly becoming the badlands of what had been Roman Britain, did, at least for some Romans and Goths, seem a place more haunted by past ruin than future renovation. "It is evident how great was the population of the city of Rome," reflected Cassiodorus around 533. "Never could a people that ruled the world be small in number. For the vast extent of the walls bears witness to the throngs of citizens, as do the swollen capacity of the buildings of entertainment, the wonderful size of the baths," and the great number of derelict water mills that so obviously once fed thousands.[25] Roughly fifty thousand people lived amongst these ruins, and, give or take a few thousand, that remained the population for the next five centuries.[26] Rome, while still impressive, was a vast empty stage littered with decaying operatic scenery of past glory. It was no longer even a city occasionally pampered by a "modern" Gothic despot, as Theodoric's grandson, King Athalaric, was young, debauched, and mostly drunk.

Yet, far away in the "New Rome" of Constantinople, shabby old Rome was not forgotten. The same year Cassiodorus was waxing nostalgic about the once prodigious (and prodigiously hungry) *populus Romanus*, the emperor Justinian (Petrus Sabbatius Justinianus) dispatched an East Roman fleet and army on a grand holy war of Western reconquest and cleansing of heresy. Three years later, after capturing Vandal North Africa in a dazzling four months, then the equally swift subjugation of Sicily and southern Italy, a triumphant East Roman army under the brilliant general Flavius Belisarius marched unopposed into Rome in early December 536.[27]

5   Nika!

Four years earlier a firestorm had raged through Constantinople. What started it was a riot of the sporting social clubs known as the Blues and the Greens in the great hippodrome. In every city of the East Roman Empire these two social clubs faced each other as frenzied factions on the grandstands of lesser hippodromes, yelling insults, getting into deadly fights, cheering *"Nika!"* (win) as the charioteers raced. Apart from the racetracks, these social clubs crowded the urban theaters, even sponsoring their own troupes of actors, dancers, acrobats, prostitutes, and wild animal shows.

The young male members of these social clubs were fanatical ultras, hooligan show-offs with "Hunnish" haircuts (a kind of mullet), extravagantly long beards and mustaches, and flamboyant clothes like sails flapping in the wind.[28] When not brawling with each other in the racetrack grandstands and theater stalls, they paraded about the cities, day and night, getting into street fights and committing crimes (petty and serious).[29] They cared for nothing, "divine or human," except loyalty to their club. "They fight against the rival faction without knowing why they are putting themselves at such risk," observed Procopius of Caesaria, historian and military secretary to Belisarius, after witnessing these bully boys. "So that I, for my part, do not know what to call this if not a mental disorder."[30]

Imperial officials mostly ignored this club madness as long as they only fought amongst themselves. In January 532, though, the urban prefect of Constantinople sentenced to death seven particularly violent thugs from the Blues and the Greens for sedition. Astonishingly, the social clubs called a truce and jointly appealed to Justinian to release the condemned. The emperor ignored them. The ultras were enraged and set fire to the city. The Church of Hagia Sophia (Holy Wisdom), the exquisite baths of Zeuxippos, thousands of ancient sculptures, the Senate house, and parts of the imperial palace were all destroyed. As Constantinople burned, the young men and women of the Blues and the Greens cried, *"Nika!"*[31]

In their righteous and murderous euphoria, the rioters hunted for corrupt or hated imperial bureaucrats to kill. One of these officials was Tribonian, a talented (and possibly venal) lawyer commissioned by Justinian with overhauling and reforming all Roman law in 528. (Tribonian and his research assistants cast aside the less-than-a-century-old *Theodosian Code* as unworthy and amateurish, quickly publishing a revised and more professional *Justinianic Code*. In 533 they issued a hefty legal *Digest* and a new textbook, the *Institutes*, for the Beirut law schools.)[32] After braying for the death of the imperial lawyer, the mob roared for the overthrow of Justinian himself. They crowded into the hippodrome, their usual playground, waiting for news. In the imperial palace next to the hippodrome, the emperor was frightened and unsure what to do, especially as he had always favored the

Blues, manipulating their ultras against anyone he disliked. He did not know whether to stay or flee.

The empress Theodora, herself once an actress (and probably a prostitute) in the Blues social club, was disgusted by her husband. She advised against flight. "May I *never* be parted from the purple! May I *never* live to see the day when I will not be addressed as Mistress by all in my presence!" Of course, the emperor could cut and run like a coward. "But consider whether, after you have saved yourself, you would then gladly exchange safety for death. For my part, I like the old saying, namely that kingship is a good burial shroud."[33]

Justinian regained his nerve, sending Belisarius and another general named Mundo into the hippodrome with ruthless army veterans. Thirty thousand Blues and Greens were slaughtered in the grandstands and on the racetrack. Although much of Constantinople was still an inferno, the *Nika* revolt was over.[34]

Justinian had been in his early forties when he came to the throne in 527 and, despite his having lived in Constantinople for almost three decades as the adopted son of his uncle Justin (an up-from-the-ranks army officer and the late emperor), many East Roman nobles still thought of him as nothing more than a Latin-speaking peasant parvenu from a backwater Thracian village (Tauresium, southeast of modern Skopje in North Macedonia).[35] He quickly put them in their place. In 529 he decreed that all "abominable pagans" and their families must be baptized within three months. If not, their properties would be forfeited and they would be exiled. He also banned all knowledge taught by "persons diseased with the insanity of the unholy pagans" as soul-destroying. The imperial treasury would no longer fund public professorships of such profanity.[36] A separate decree silenced the privately endowed Neoplatonic faculty at the Academy in Athens. (Many of the Athenian dons fled to the Persian court.)[37]

Justinian may have been a zealous Christian, but he was no fool or anti-intellectual. He knew there really were no more pagans like a fourth-century Symmachus, but such an accusation was a powerful way of threatening and shaking up the old, smug elites. He encouraged public denunciations of supposedly pagan officials. Many noble families were still schooled in *paideia*, and now such learning and mannerisms were a liability. Almost all of them were sincere Christians, but that was no protection with Plotinus on the bookshelf. (Some professors, though, did think of themselves as intellectually "pagan" on account of their adulation of the Platonic canon.)

These laws against "unholy" knowledge and behavior signaled an aggressive and revolutionary vision of imperial patronage and Christianity. Justinian in the aftermath of the *Nika* revolt—which was partially provoked by his new cultural and religious puritanism—was even more convinced that God had singled him out as the divine reformer of the Roman Empire.

Justinian immediately began rebuilding the Church of Hagia Sophia as a stupendous monument to himself as pious imperial patron. It was also a less-than-subtle reminder that a revolt against him was a revolt against God. Most of the massive building was finished in five years. Its nave was about 260 feet long and its great dome more than 180 feet high. It dominated the skyline of Constantinople (as it still does in Istanbul). It was the largest vaulted interior in the world for more than a millennium.

Inside this impossibly heavy structure of stone, marble, and tesserae, the architects Anthemius of Tralles and Isidore of Miletus evoked an eternal springtime of heavenly wonder. "One might imagine that you had come upon a meadow with its flowers in full bloom," wrote Procopius about the interior marble columns and walls in an architectural panegyric to Justinian. "For you would surely marvel at the purple of some, the green tint of others, and at those on which the crimson glows and those from which the white flashes."[38] The nave floor of interlocking white and gray-flecked Proconnesian marble elicited the feeling that one was weightless and floating, like "walking on water."[39] When Justinian dedicated the new Church of Hagia Sophia on Sunday, December 27, 537, he supposedly exclaimed, "Solomon, I have outdone you!"[40]

Another consequence of the *Nika* revolt was the armada dispatched for the conquest of North Africa and Italy. In 536 (the same year Belisarius marched into Rome) Justinian confidently hoped "that God will grant us to rule over the rest of what, subject to the ancient Romans to the limits of both seas, they later lost through their easy-going ways."[41] The Western Roman Empire had fallen, that was obvious to him, but its loss was only temporary. Like other radical affirmations of his sacred authority since becoming emperor in 527, and especially after 532, he would reclaim what was rightfully the patrimony of all Romans and purify these former provinces of heresies and unholy "easy-going ways."

Although the "Gothic War" in Italy was far from over in 536—it would last almost another two decades—the great entrance hall known as the Chalkê in the imperial palace was redecorated with shimmering mosaic propaganda. According to Procopius, these tiny colored cubes of stone showed "many cities being captured, some in Italy, some in Libya [North Africa]." Belisarius and the imperial army stood out as unscathed, rewarding the emperor with "spoils, both kings and kingdoms." The emperor and empress, encircled by the Roman Senate, glowed with "exultation on their very countenances." The senators, smiling proudly, offered Justinian, "because of the magnitude of his achievements, honors equal to those of God."[42]

6   Plague

"During those times there was a plague that came close to wiping out the whole of humanity," wrote Procopius in his *Wars*, a military and political history of Justinian's reign written in the style of Thucydides. "It originated amongst the Egyptians who live in Pelousion" in 541, arriving in Constantinople "in the middle of the spring of its second year, where I happened to be at the time." Some people saw demons in the city streets before succumbing to the disease. Others dreamed of demons before falling ill. "Most people, however, were taken ill without the advance warning of a waking vision or a dream."

The initial symptoms were tepid fevers, easily ignored, quickly followed by buboes, swellings in the groin, upper thighs, and armpits. "Up to this point the symptoms of the disease were more or less the same for everyone," but then some collapsed into a deep coma, while others ran amok with acute dementia. The comatose starved to death, while the demented threw themselves off buildings. Everyone else suffered and died in lucid pain. "Some died immediately, others after many days." If the sick vomited blood or their bodies "blossomed with dark pustules about the size of a lentil," they died instantly.

There was seemingly no cure or comfort. Everyone was "holed up in their homes," too frightened to go outside. There was famine, despite food in the shops. Even the dregs of the Blues and Greens stopped fighting each other. (The social clubs had returned to their usual animosity after the *Nika* massacre.) Anyone in the streets was "either tending to the sick or mourning for the dead." Funeral rites were haphazard or ignored. The dead were heaped in alleys or thrown in deep trenches. The city choked on the stench of rotting corpses. Justinian himself survived painful buboes. The plague ravaged Constantinople for four months, according to Procopius, "until the toll in deaths reached five thousand a day, and after that, it reached ten thousand, and then even more."[43]

This plague, while horrible and deadly in specific places, was perhaps not as broadly devastating as suggested by Procopius. His recollection of charnel-house Constantinople deliberately mimicked the description by Thucydides of plague in Athens at the beginning of the Peloponnesian Wars in 430 BC. In his *Secret History*, a tale of tabloid palace gossip, priggish porn, conspiracy theories, and a blazing hatred of Justinian and Theodora—and which he apparently never published, as it was only discovered in the Vatican archives in 1623—the plague was just one of the earthly calamities (earthquakes, floods) by which Tyche cruelly favored the demons in human form that were the emperor and empress. Just like the pestilence killing all humanity, the imperial couple "visited disaster upon the entire inhabited world."[44] Procopius was a man of wildly divergent literary mood swings, from Thucydidean objectivity to court panegyric to salacious yellow journalism, and yet, when it comes to his descriptions of plague, he is frequently read as if he were an epidemiologist taking clinical notes. The plague certainly infected villages and cities around the Mediterranean, such as Constantinople or Arles, and even reached some scattered settlements around the North Sea, but the number of deaths was not as high as tallied by Procopius or the equally sensational 50 to 60 percent of the total sixth-century population calculated by some modern historians.[45]

This "Justinianic plague" is often understood by comparing it to what is commonly known as the "Black Death" from the middle of the fourteenth century. As tens of millions died between 1347 and 1351, the analogy goes, a similar number must have died between 541 and 543. Yet the textual, archeological, and artistic remnants of the sixth-century plague are almost nonexistent compared to the formidable evidence of a catastrophic pandemic eight hundred years later.[46] This is why the accounts of Procopius carry so much weight, as very few of his contemporaries mentioned the plague.[47]

As for *Yersinia pestis*, the bacterium associated with bubonic plague, its DNA has been found in no archeological sites in the eastern Mediterranean and in only five sites in what are now Bavaria (Aschheim, Altenerding) and France (Vienne, Sens, Poitiers).[48] Although recent research has shown that *Yersinia pestis* can be transmitted to humans through other insect vectors (cat flea, human flea, human body louse, human hair louse) and not just the fleas (*Xenopsylla cheopis*) of common black rats (*Rattus rattus*), few rats (and so their fleas) lived around the Mediterranean until well after the sixth century.[49] There just were not that many rats in the Roman Empire. The plague, of course, might have been spread by ectoparasites other than rat fleas or in some pneumonic form.

All this is to say that while there seems to have been a disease like the bubonic plague in the sixth century, its immediate and long-term effects were mostly negligible. Indeed, rural regions of the empire barely suffered at all. Whatever depopulation occurred in the eastern Mediterranean, it was not dramatic and was remedied within a generation.[50] The Justinianic plague was not a natural disaster changing, as some have argued, the course of history.[51]

7 You Are Mine, Man, for I Made You

Around 490, Caesarius, a twenty-year-old from minor Roman nobility in Chalon-sur-Saône, fled the "shackles of the world" by journeying south to the tiny Mediterranean island monastery of Lérins, just off the coast from Cannes.[52] Another Roman noble, Honoratus, had established the monastery at the beginning of the fifth century because the hot and squalid island suggested the deserts of Egypt. Laboring at least six hours a day, he, his well-to-do monks, and their "brother" slaves set about transforming the foulness of Lérins into a small, lush estate resembling the Gallic villas they had left behind—and the nearby palatial estates on the Côte d'Azur. Elite Western Roman men and women adopting Christian asceticism in the fourth and fifth centuries did so within their (or their friends') villas, completely dependent upon these estates functioning normally around them. Such leisurely pious seclusion by the wealthy required the crushing cycles of agricultural labor by peasants and slaves to keep on spinning. An indifference to wealth was not the same as having no wealth.[53]

The barbarian invasions and civil wars of the fifth century fractured such pretensions. Lérins was a refuge from such chaos and a rebuke to rich aristocrats languidly playacting as monks and nuns on their estates. The authentic monk was "a refugee immigrant in this world, a landless man," the enigmatic ascetic John Cassian had said in Marseille around 420.[54] This was a good thing. As landless men, monks were stripped of the wealth that once defined their sense of self, "so that, apart from the will of the abbot, hardly any will should be alive."[55] The Lerinian monks were not quite as severely "Egyptian" as Cassian might have wished, but they were close enough (and he even dedicated a series of sermons on being a monk to Honoratus).[56] Although refugees from a turbulent Gaul, many of the abbots of Lérin sailed back to the mainland (no more than twenty minutes, yet imaginatively a vast sea journey) as bishops, beginning with Honoratus himself, who became bishop of Arles in 426.

Lérins was indisputably an "island of saints" when Caesarius stepped ashore in 490, yet even amongst the *sancti* he stood out, judging many of the monks as weak and greedy. Left alone, he "afflicted himself with what he loved, ceaseless reading, recitation of the Psalms, prayer, and vigils." Boiled herbs and gruel were his only nourishment. After a year or so, he was curled over with searing stomach pain and shivering with fevers, his young body broken and bent. His maladies were too much for the Lerinians—and, honestly, he was too much for them too—so he was sent to Arles to recover with a devout noble family. There, his aguish sanctity was noticed by the bishop, who, while not from Lérins, was from Chalon-sur-Saône. "My son, you are my fellow citizen and relation," he told Caesarius, and so the young man should be one of the bishop's priests. When Caesarius was better— although the shivers and gripes never really abated—his abbot handed him over to the bishop. Nevertheless, "he remained a monk by humility, charity, obedience, and mortification." In 503 the old bishop died after a long illness, but not before he nominated Caesarius as his successor. Arles needed the discipline of a febrile holy man.[57]

The city of Arles was rich, and so was its church, yet its bishops, especially those who were former monks from Lérins, struggled to reconcile being "landless men" with administering great swaths of land, ostentatiously indifferent to wealth while carefully overseeing ecclesiastical assets. Caesarius, "imitating the Apostles, calling God to witness," delegated the management of episcopal properties to subordinates so that he could "free himself entirely for the Word of God." By freeing himself from being an earthly accountant—even if he regularly preached against the late payment of tithes owed to him—he focused on heavenly capital. He spent lavishly on feeding the poor and caring for the sick, as these material transactions rewarded everyone with spiritual dividends. "What we advance the poor in the world, we entrust to Christ as a deposit on earth what we will receive in heaven."

Caesarius also spent vast amounts on ransoming prisoners of war. In the early sixth century, the Franks under Clovis, then the Goths under Theodoric, then the Franks again under Theudebert (grandson of Clovis) rampaged throughout the lower Rhône, repeatedly attacking and capturing Arles. Caesarius was bishop of a war zone. Refugees sheltered in his basilica, homeless and starving. Hundreds of men, women, and children were scooped up by Arian Goths and Catholic Franks as prizes to be redeemed. Caesarius always found the cash to buy them back. And if he was short, he chopped up silver chalices with axes and ripped out gold baubles from churches. What else could he do? Especially when Christ was always nagging him about what should be done. It was impossible for Caesarius not to hear Him—"He begs, persuades, warns, and calls all to witness."[58]

In Arles it was impossible not to hear Caesarius too. He preached relentlessly, begging, persuading, warning, calling everyone to affirm their faith. What troubled him deeply were "pagan" habits that Christians unthinkingly—or worse, enjoyably—did as common sense. He adapted (often ad-libbing from memory) many of Augustine's sermons from a century earlier. Except whereas the bishop of Hippo really was surrounded by paganism, even if it was highly mannered and bookish, the bishop of Arles was acutely aware that the paganism he attacked was not the worship of the old gods. What Caesarius mocked and attacked was a grab bag of nervous tics, old sayings, silly customs, honest but erroneous fears, holiday fun and games, and frankly embarrassing *rusticitas* (hick-like or boorish attitudes and behavior), which, whether petty or profound, were all symptoms of the devil to him.

For example, Caesarius decried Christians wearing charms or magical words when sick as diabolical, and even if these trinkets were given by priests or monks, these clerics were the "devil's helpers." It did not matter if anyone was healed, which he acknowledged was often the case, as this was just devilish cunning: "Sometimes the devil has taken away bodily infirmity, because he has already killed the soul." Or the ringing of bells and the blowing of trumpets during an eclipse of the moon: "If the substance of this heavenly body is inferior to you, why do you fear to offend it by your silence? If it is superior, why do you think it needs your help?" What happened in the sky was up to God, and no human cacophony changed that. Or on the Kalends of January (the first day of the month and of the new year) when men, wrapped in sheepskins or crowned with animal heads or dolled up in women's clothes (especially shocking when bearded butch soldiers did it), danced drunkenly in the streets, because the devil tricked them into celebrating the birth of a pagan new year with more joy than the birth of Christ. Or predicting the future from sneezes, when only God knows what will happen a day, a month, a year from now. Or women who, after two or three children, drank abortifacient draughts because they worried about feeding more infants: "For, what else must they think when they do this, except that God will not be able to feed or direct those He has commanded to be born?" Despite warning such women that they would have to plead before Christ's tribunal at the Last Judgment with the children they killed in the womb watching and listening, Caesarius was, for him, vaguely sympathetic to wives forced into unwanted pregnancies, even if his solution was strict: "You do not want to have a child?" You and your husband agree to holy chastity.[59]

Just like Caesarius himself, ordinary Christians must erase every demonic idea and practice resonating with the presumption of individual will—which was a deceit of the devil—so that all that was left was the will of God.

Caesarius looked out on a world that manifestly belonged to God and to God alone. "Of course, you are Mine, man, for I made you," he imagined God saying. "Mine is the earth which you cultivate. Mine the seeds you sow. Mine are the animals you work. Mine are the rain and the showers. Mine are the blasts of wind. Mine is the heat of the sun."[60] Too many Christians failed to grasp that they were the property of God, that they were inherently "landless," refugees permitted to live in a world owned and ruled by Him. Earthly existence added up to nothing unless it was disciplined preparation for the Last Judgment, for only then did the Christian émigré finally find a home, good or bad. "*Duo sunt, nihil est medium,*" Caesarius was remembered shouting in his sleep. "There are two places. There is nothing in between. Either one goes up to heaven or down to hell."[61]

Boethius worrying about free will as he faced death would have been pagan posturing to the bishop of Arles, no different from yelling at the moon or joyfully dancing in drag on a cold winter's day. Caesarius monasticized the universe, with God as a severe but loving abbot. It was a close-fitting and hermetic vision, precise and parochial, relentless and proscriptive. Caesarius may have been loyal to the memory of Augustine, but he lacked, or rather simply could not conceive of, the almost infinite intellectual and sacred horizons of the bishop of Hippo.

The sermons of Caesarius were harsh and uncomfortable to listen to, especially as everything he damned as "pagan" would not have been thought of as such by the Christians (or Jews) of Arles. Some men once tried sneaking out of church just before he began preaching. "What are you doing, my sons?" he shouted after them. "Where are you going, led by some evil idea? Stay here! Listen to the sermon for the good of your souls and listen carefully! You will not be able to do this at Judgment Day!" Caesarius from then on locked all doors until he was finished speaking.[62]

8 The Walls of His Thought

Around the time Caesarius became bishop of Arles in 503, an adolescent from the Umbrian gentry named Benedict ran away to live in seclusion as a Christian holy man in a mountain cave fifty miles from Rome, a grim place named Subiaco (Sub Lacum, "under the lake," or rather below a reservoir built for Emperor Nero). The lad, however, was rarely alone, as a kindly monk from a nearby monastery soon gave him bread and advice, and within three years, after two shepherds discovered him dressed in animal skins, hundreds of people journeyed to his grotto, bringing him food in exchange for the "food of life in their hearts" of his words. He never shunned visitors, male or female, Roman or Goth, Catholic or Arian.

Not surprisingly, the devil was paying attention. According to a *Life* of Benedict written by Pope Gregory I (known as "the Great") in 593 or 594, the devil fluttered about the saintly recluse in the form of a little blackbird, which, in a curious bit of erotic ornithology, elicited passionate memories of a girl. Benedict, flushed with sensual pleasure, quickly cast off his animal skins and rolled around naked in sharp thorns and nettles. The bloody sores and scratches "allowed him to remove the mental wound from his body by turning the pleasure to pain." Gregory, who framed his *Life* as a Platonic dialogue with his young deacon Peter, observed that the flutter of black-birds was why monks must exhaust themselves in "works of obedience," as the "heat of temptation" only receded when a man turned fifty. Benedict, while admiring monks, did not yet really think of himself as one in his cave-dwelling years, "as he lived with himself, alone in the sight of Him," content within the "walls of his thought."[63]

Benedict's bush seclusion was very different from the wealthy ascetic Romans living in their villas or the monks in the monasteries above and below him on the mountain. He did not work for his own subsistence or rely on slaves working around him; he survived on the kindness of strangers. He did not even beg, as some monks did in Egypt or Syria. He embraced poverty, but it was the deprivation of an animal in nature or an old god in a sacred grove. It is easy to forget that there were many men and women like Benedict, purposely not monks or nuns as understood by a John Cassian (who would have loathed Benedict in his cave) or a Caesarius (who would have mocked Benedict and his animal-skin *rusticitas*), choosing overtly feral existences, and so eliminating everything human about themselves apart from their innermost thoughts, as they searched for holiness. Eventually, many of these wilderness saints did become monks or nuns, persuaded by acolytes or censure or maturity or hunger into entering or founding monasteries.

Around 520, with dozens of men and boys camping out in the Subiaco scrub, serving the holy cave-dweller food and listening to his words, Benedict stepped outside the "walls of his thought" and organized these hangers-on into twelve monasteries, each with twelve monks and one abbot. Gregory's *Life* treated this seemingly instantaneous transition from bestial loner to blessed administrator as divinely predestined, even if it was a plan long contemplated and an intractable problem that could no longer be ignored. After a few years, with the Subiaco escarpment crowded with monasteries (which would have looked like rough-hewn shepherd huts), Benedict decided to leave and establish another monas-tery farther away. He and some monks, after traveling south for seventy miles, squatted inside an abandoned stone fort known as Monte Cassino, high up a rugged mountain overlooking the road from Rome to Naples.

In a copse next to the fort was an ancient shrine to Apollo, whom local villagers still honored with gifts of food. Benedict demolished it—he was done with groves and grottos—building over the rubble a small church dedicated to Saints Martin and John. ("Benedict, Benedict," the devil whined, identifying with Apollo. "Why are you persecuting me?") In the decade before Benedict died in 543 (or 545), he composed a *Rule* (*regula*) for his monks at Monte Cassino, which was eventually adopted (and corrupted and reformed) by all monasteries in the medieval West for the next millennium.[64]

"Listen, my son, to the master's instructions and take them to heart. These are the instructions of a loving father," began Benedict's *Rule*. "It is to you that my words are now addressed, if you are ready to take the powerful and glorious weapons of obedience, renouncing your will with the intention of fighting for the true king, Christ the Lord." Benedict's monastery was a "school [*scola*] for the Lord's service" and his *Rule* was its syllabus, time-table, and manifesto in plain everyday Latin.[65] He was deeply influenced by Cassian (which was acknowledged), especially on the importance of stripping away the individual will, and by the anonymous *Rule of the Master* (which was unacknowledged), a monastic rule in the form of a Platonic dialogue written in Rome in the early sixth century. Benedict's monastery, though, was no postgraduate institution; it was a rigorous boarding school for beginners, where elite men cast off their adult selves for reeducation on the path of salvation.[66]

Benedict was strict about the erasure of all social status still clinging to the monk. Inside the monastery there was no personal property, including gifts or letters from family. The abbot was to regularly check beds for private goods. All monks were to be dressed in the same robe and cowl (two of each) in whatever cloth was the cheapest in their region, whatever the color or scratchiness.[67] The distinctive "religious" clothing of medieval monks—which, in later centuries, often led to fiery debates about what color or coarseness it should be—was initially just the thrifty commonplace garb of peasants or slaves in the sixth-century Valle Latina.

All monks were to be silent, never speaking unless given permission. There was to be no gossip or witticisms for the purpose of making anyone laugh. The urbane speech habits of a Roman upper-class education were rendered mute.[68] In overwhelming silence, all monks labored on their scrappy fields and read their sacred texts, their individual wills subsumed in "unhesitating obedience" to the abbot. Benedict emphasized that the abbot was "Christ's representative in the monastery," as this title was also given to Him. "As is clear from the words of the Apostle"—Paul in his Epistle to the Romans—"You have received the spirit of adoption of sons by which we call out, *Abba* [in Aramaic], Father!"[69]

It is worth noting that Benedict in his *Rule* did not completely approve of what he himself did as a young man. (Gregory in his *Life* observed that the *Rule* was like a partial memoir by Benedict.) "Anchorites, that is, hermits"—which was to say, monks hiding out in caves or copses—were only permitted such seclusion as older men, "trained by a lengthy period of probation in the monastery," learning how to fight against the devil. "Well armed, they go out from the ranks of the brothers to the single combat of the desert." Indeed, Benedict as a youth was very close to being like one of the "sarabaites," which the *Rule* described as the "most detestable kind of monks," living in twos or threes or alone, doing whatever they wanted, "calling their every whim holy." At least he was never one of the "gyrovagues," who were wandering monks and even worse than the sarabaites. According to the *Rule*, the only true and faithful monks were "cenobites" living in monasteries under a rule with a mature *abba* like Benedict.[70]

9 Splendid Deeds of Power

In 543—the same year that both Caesarius and Benedict died—there was, according to Gregory of Tours in his *Histories*, a plague in various parts of Gaul, especially Arles, "causing great swellings in the groin." Gallus, the bishop of Clermont and Gregory's uncle, prayed night and day to the Lord so that his diocese might not be destroyed. One night the angel of the Lord, "whose hair as well as his robe shone white as snow," visited him in a dream. "Divine piety looks kindly upon you, O bishop," said the angel, "on account of your supplication for your people. Therefore do not fear, for your prayer has been heard. You and your people will indeed be rescued from this illness; while you are alive no one will perish from its devastation. So don't be afraid this time." The angel then added a caveat: "After eight years, however, do be afraid!"

Gallus awoke, joyous and confident, even if he now knew the year of his death. He immediately "instituted the prayers and processions called Rogations in the middle of Lent, when people go on foot to the basilica of the blessed Julian in Brioude," forty miles away. As the people walked they saw tau-like crosses shimmer on buildings. "I regard his grace as by no means small," commented Gregory on Gallus, "since he as their shepherd merited not to see his sheep being devoured, for they were protected by the Lord."[71]

Gregory told the same story about his uncle, almost word for word, in his *Seven Books of Miracles* (*Libri septem miraculorum*), which he wrote at the same time as his *Histories*, insisting that the two books be read together. Except the Gallus in the *Miracles*, dying when the angel said he would in 551, had metamorphosed into a dead holy man—he had become a saint. He was sixty-five when he died, and as his corpse waited in church for other bishops to attend his funeral, "the faithful put earth over his blessed body, as is the custom of common people [*rustici*], so that it not be swollen by the heat."

When Gallus was carried to the basilica of Saint Lawrence for burial, throngs of people, Christians and Jews, followed his body, dressed in mourning as if for a dead spouse, "wailing and carrying lighted lamps." After the funeral a virgin named Meratina used the discarded corpse-cooling earth as topsoil in her garden, and after frequent watering "she made it come alive with plants, for the Lord made them grow." The sick recovered after drinking drafts made with these plants, while "the faithful who said a prayer over them merited to be heard." And these miracles were just from Gallus' postmortem dirt!

"At his tomb many powerful deeds have been manifested," boasted Gregory. "Remember me," a priest shivering with quartan fever once prayed to Gallus at his tomb. "For it was you who raised me, taught me, and called me to office. Now remember me, your foster son, whom you cherished with your special love, and rescue me from the fever that clutches me!" After eating some small plants scattered around the sepulcher, the priest was cured. "It cannot be doubted that it is through the power of the One who called forth Lazarus from his tomb," observed Gregory about the miracles of Saint Gallus, "that deeds of power are brought forth from the tombs of His servants."[72]

The miracles of Gallus at his tomb were only a few of the many wonders occurring throughout Gaul because of other dead holy men (and some women) throughout the sixth century. Gregory collected such stories of the "deeds of saints," compelled to broadcast them in writing. He was especially concerned with the tomb and miracles of Martin, bishop of Tours in the late fourth century, who was his predecessor and holy *patronus*, protector and patron. "I once saw in a dream vision, in the middle of the day, that many ill people who were oppressed by various diseases were being healed in the church of the lord Martin." Gregory was lost in his daydream until his mother, who was watching him, said: "Why are you so slow to write about what you see?" Flustered, he replied that he lacked the artistry and skill for such a commission. "And do you not know," she encouraged him, ignoring his false modesty, "that if someone speaks to us in a way the people understand, as you do so well, he will therefore be regarded as more brilliant? Therefore don't hesitate, and don't delay doing this, because you will be faulted if you are silent."

Gregory's Latin was, as he himself (and his mother) described it, a literary experiment in *rusticitas*—ordinary speech for describing the extraordinary. As Christ "chose not orators but fisherman, not philosophers but common men [*rustici*]," Gregory, like a new apostle, would spread news of "splendid deeds of power."[73]

As these saints were almost always former bishops or abbots, the holiness, authority, and esteem they commanded while alive were affirmed by their miracles after death. That was why the angel of the Lord told Gallus "Do be afraid!" in death, not because dying itself was awful—although his was particularly painful—but because he would be judged by God when his last breath was taken, and if he was found wanting, he would be punished. The path to heaven was frightening, even for a saint. In celebrating "the deeds of the saints," Gregory, who had been a bishop since 573, when he was thirty-four, was also promising that he too in death might be embraced by God as one of them, and so his possible future in heaven was an affirmation that the things he had done in the past and the things he was doing in the present were likewise "deeds of power."

Gregory in his *Histories* has a vivid vignette of himself as a "man of power," a *potens*, in a confrontation with Chilperic, king of Neustria (the Seine basin and lands west and south of Paris), in 577. He was summoned to a meeting outside Paris after defending the bishop of Rouen, whom the king had accused of bribery and treason. "When I arrived the king was standing outside a little arbor made of the branches of trees." There was also a table with bread and soup, and on either side of the king were two lickspittle bishops. "As a bishop," complained Chilperic, "you are supposed to administer justice to all men. You are now behaving most unjustly towards me." "My lord king," Gregory answered, "if any one of our number has attempted to overstep the path of justice, it is for you to correct him. If, on the other hand, it is you who act unjustly, who can correct you? We can say what we think to you. If you wish to do so, you listen to us. If you refuse to listen, who can condemn you for it, except Him who has promised eternal justice." "All other men treat me fairly," the infuriated Chilperic yelled. "You are unjust to me!" "It is not for you to say whether or not I am unjust," Gregory calmly replied. "God alone, to whom the secret places of the heart are open, knows what is in my conscience."

Such sanctimony enraged the king even further, but before he could speak, the bishop of Tours interrupted him. "I'm wasting my breath on you," sniffed Gregory. "You will soon come to realize that the judgement of God hangs over your head." Chilperic's mood abruptly changed after this divine threat and, sulking beneath feigned bonhomie, he offered his guest acquiescence and soup: "There is nothing in it except chicken and some peas." Gregory may have overplayed his bravado in winning this contest of wills, but he was expected to act as a bishop and as a bold *potens* in the hazardous politics between the powerful men and women, the *potentes*, of Merovingian Gaul.[74]

By the late sixth century the aristocracy of Gaul, or Francia as it can now be called, was an amalgam of individuals and families descended from Franks and Romans that was becoming a unified ruling class, one defined by their affluence and secular "deeds of power." Despite Gregory's relentless tales of civil war and violence in his *Histories*, the Frankish kingdoms were not ripped apart or destroyed. Merovingian Francia was the most coherent political entity in the post-Roman West, even if it was a ragged patchwork of parochial power brokers firmly tied to their rural estates or farms (numbering in the tens or thirties). The holding of land and its local exploitation was now, more or less, the sole basis of wealth. Even King Chilperic rarely traveled farther than forty miles from Paris, as this was the extent of the properties he held directly and the terrain upon which he was most secure militarily and financially.[75]

Taxation, which, apart from slavery, had been the very definition of the economy of the Roman Respublica—*homo oeconomicus* collected and paid

taxes—had all but disappeared in much of the West by 600. Curiously, accruing exceptions for taxes (in wine or grain) that had not been levied for
decades was a demonstration of power, and Gregory boasted about getting
them for the churches of Tours. Similarly, forgoing the collection of taxes
that were never going to be collected was the grand gesture of a monarch. "Let us set light to these iniquitous tax registers!" exclaimed Queen
Fredegund, Chilperic's wife, in a frenzy of grief when her children were
sick during a dysentery epidemic. "What are you waiting for?" she yelled at
the king. "We may still lose our children, but we shall at least escape eternal
damnation!" Chilperic tossed the tax registers in the fire. Gregory scripted
this little melodrama by way of explaining why there was no longer any
royal taxation in Neustria.[76] Even without a tax system, the kings and lords
of Francia were the richest elites between the Mediterranean and the
North Sea.

The 110 bishops of Francia were part of this new nobility. Yet many of
them, while always freeborn, were from the lower rungs of the gentry. Or
they were refugee clerics from Justinian's wars in Italy and North Africa.
Of course, there were exceptions, like Bertram, bishop of Le Mans, who,
largely on account of family connections (Frankish noble father and Gallo-
Roman mother) and royal patronage (Chlotar II, king of the Franks after
613) left a fortune of 740,000 acres (one hundred estates around seventeen
cities, roughly just over 0.5 percent of all Francia) when he died in 616.[77]

Rich or middling, these bishops were very different from bishops of a
century earlier, when men like Caesarius of Arles either were from or defined themselves in relation to the immense fortunes (and the comfortable
asceticism this allowed) of the Roman senatorial nobility. (There was still a
Western emperor when Caesarius was born.) Gregory, while no Bertram
of Le Mans, was socially superior to many of his colleagues, although
his wealth and reputation ultimately derived from his family being high
churchmen for three generations rather than being Roman senators once
upon a time. As a bishop and a Frankish *potens*, though, his ongoing prosperity and status came from being the lord and servant of Saint Martin of
Tours. This afforded Gregory a share in heaven's treasure, which, in a world
nervously awaiting the Last Judgment, was a fungible resource of infinite
possibilities.[78]

The decline of the Western Roman city had been going on since at
least the late fourth century, but the final flight of urban populations into

the countryside definitively occurred during the sixth century. This did not mean that cities ceased to exist, although that was certainly the case in Britain, and they had never existed in Ireland, but the kind of civic existence that once defined so much of the West would not return in any recognizably similar form until the twelfth century. Cities were now largely the *mise-en-scène* for rituals honoring the very special dead. It cannot be stressed enough how extraordinary this transformation of urban space was. The burial of individuals within cities—and the role of their corpses as part of an ever-expanding "cult of the saints"—is one of the more significant signs that we are now fully within a Latin Christian medieval universe. (The murdered family buried within the walls of Canterbury in the early fifth century already showed this civilizational change happening in Britain, although we do not know if those dead Cantuarians were in any sense purveyors of miracles.) As so many miracles involved the use of soil accumulating around the tombs of saints or the plants growing in nearby crevices, these wonders justified urban decay by sacralizing the rampant "greening" of towns and cities. Bishops like Gregory still lived in their cities, orchestrating the ceremonial rhythms of pilgrims, supplicants, and endowments given at the shrine of a saint like Martin.

Dead holy men like Gallus and Martin joined heaven and earth at their tombs. Their corpses were like high-energy conduits, humming with and radiating the power of God from on high, as well as relaying prayers up to heaven from supplicants. They were at once lifeless in their tombs and brilliantly alive in paradise. "No funeral urn confines him, but he is embraced in the arms of God," sang Gregory's Italian friend Venantius Fortunatus in a poem about Gallus. "So you too who dwell in the heavens, Martin, on behalf of Fortunatus convey to God holy words of prayer," ended another poem.[79] As men, women, and children approached the tomb of a saint, their flesh tingled. It was this necessity for the body of the saint to be physically present for miracles to happen that led to the chopping up of their bodily parts. Bones and slices of flesh, no matter how small or distant they were from the saintly corpse, still functioned as if part of the whole. A paralyzed man walked again after he kissed the cloth over a box holding relics of Martin that Gregory gave to the bishop of Avanches.[80] The devil even appeared once as "Martin" to a woman named Leubella in Berry, giving her bits of his fake body so that she could heal the sick during an outbreak of the plague in 571. The hermit Patroclus and the Holy Spirit made these ersatz relics and the devil disappear.[81]

These saints were inimitable on earth; no human could or should be like them. A young monk named Wulfolaic discovered this the hard way. He was inspired to go and become a living saint by some miraculous dust—which, like dough rising in an oven, kept expanding inside a box, breaking it apart—from Martin's tomb. The trouble with this plan was that such earthly holy men only existed, and should only exist as far as bishops like Gregory were concerned, in the East Roman Empire. Wulfolaic, unperturbed by this small detail, decided to copy Simeon Stylites—who a century earlier had prayed atop a column for thirty-seven years in Syria—by standing barefoot on an old Roman column near the banks of the Moselle outside Trier. "When winter came in its season," he told Gregory years later, "it so froze me with its icy frost that the bitter cold made my toenails fall off, not once but several times, and the rain turned to ice and hung from my beard like wax which melts from candles." His body ended up being covered with sores, which only oil from Martin's shrine cured. Eventually, local bishops told him this was ridiculous, particularly in such a climate—where did he think he was, Antioch?—and to get down and stop being a fool. As soon he climbed down, the bishops smashed his column. Wulfolaic learned his lesson, returning to his monastery and praising the endless miracles (especially involving dust and oil) of Martin's tomb.[82]

Another story about a column from Gregory: "If you wish to see the world, here is a column," an angel said to the hermit Patroclus in a dream. The dreamer climbed to the top and "saw murders, thefts, slaughter, adulteries, fornications, and all the perverse things done in the world." He quickly climbed down, exclaiming, "Lord, let me not return to the perversities which I had forgotten about since I devoted myself to you." "So stop seeking the world, lest you perish with it," the angel rebuked him. Columns were profane and dangerous; nothing good came of them or what they symbolized. Unlike the sign of the cross, which was easily found if you just looked around you—as Patroclus immediately did when he awoke and discovered a clay tile engraved with a cross at his feet.[83]

The cult of the saints reconfigured every miraculous event throughout Gaul as a manifestation of one of these very special dead persons (or a relic of them), so that, at least for Gregory, there was no longer any paganism or *rusticitas* to be mocked, just a lack of awareness of who really caused wonder and redemption in the world.[84]

10 Holy Commonwealth

One morning in early summer 552, the Gothic king Totila and his soldiers faced an East Roman army under Justinian's eunuch general Narses at Busta Gallorum, an undulating Umbrian plain of grassy mounds supposedly covering the ancient tombs of cremated Gauls. The Gothic army was waiting upon two thousand reinforcements, so their king galloped out between the two armies and, as a delaying tactic, engaged in an astonishing martial ballet. Totila was armored in gold and dressed in purple, sitting upon a massive horse, which he raced around the field in circles. "As he rode he hurled his javelin into the air and caught it again as it quivered above him, then passed it rapidly from hand to hand, shifting it with consummate skill, and he gloried in his practice of the art, falling back on his shoulders, spreading his legs and leaning from side to side, like one who has been instructed with precision in the art of dancing from childhood."

Totila's mesmerizing performance lasted most of the morning, until his reserves arrived. After changing into the uniform of an ordinary soldier, he attacked during the midday meal, hoping to surprise the East Romans. Narses, suspicious of (even if entertained by) the royal dressage, was ready. The battle lasted until nightfall, when suddenly the Gothic army, "filled with terror as if ghosts had fallen upon them or heaven were warring against them," panicked and fled. Totila was mortally wounded as he escaped. A few months later, in early autumn, the new (and last) Gothic king, Theia, and his remaining warriors were cut to pieces by a fusillade of East Roman arrows and javelins at the Milky Mountain, a jagged peak below Vesuvius. Twenty-six years after the death of Theodoric, the Ostrogothic kingdom was erased by Justinian, and Italy below the Alps was once again part of the Roman Empire.[85]

In November 565 Justinian died aged eighty-three and his Holy Commonwealth (*sancta res publica*) from Constantinople to Ravenna, while hardly on its knees, was nevertheless exhausted and dispirited. Three years earlier peace had finally been concluded with the Sasanian king of kings Khusro I Anoshirwan after two devastating decades of warfare. "I become dizzy as I write about such a great calamity," wrote Procopius as he recalled the shocking capture of Antioch by the Persians in 540.[86] Khusro even constructed next to his capital, Ctesiphon, a new city he sarcastically named Veh-Antiok-Khusro, "Khusro made this city better than Antioch."[87]

The Gothic War was longer than it needed to be—even taking into account Totila's outmaneuvering of imperial armies for a decade before Busta Gallorum—because of the head-spinning calamities in Syria devouring men and matériel. The winding down of the wars on the western front amidst the ongoing conflict with Persia inspired Justinian into a misbegotten attempt at appeasing Syrian Monophysites who never accepted the Council of Chalcedon. In 553 at a council in Constantinople he issued an edict known as the Three Chapters, condemning three long-dead Syrian bishops who had once disagreed with Cyril of Alexandria on the nature of Christ. This wishy-washy rewriting of Chalcedon required shunting aside the "Tome" of Pope Leo I and dismissing all opinion from bishops in the West. Pope Vigilius was even dragged from Rome to Constantinople, knocked about a bit until he approved what he did not really understand, then unceremoniously shipped back.[88] Justinian's mix of halfhearted cajolery and outright bullying failed miserably in both the East and the West. Monophysite Syrians were scornful, while Western Latin Christian (and so Chalcedonian) bishops were offended, forever distrustful of "Greek" machinations.

After the sixth century, what was the East Roman Empire is commonly called by modern scholars the Byzantine Empire (from Byzantium, the old name for the town over which Constantinople was built). This marks it as "medieval" and so distinct from the Late Antique empire of Constantine the Great. Perhaps more usefully, it distinguishes the Byzantine Empire from the numerous small and parochial Latin "Christendoms" coming into play between the sixth and eleventh centuries in the West. Of course, no medieval person, whether in the eastern or western Mediterranean, ever spoke of "Byzantines" or a "Byzantine Empire." As for East Romans themselves, at least from the sixth century until the fifteenth, they understood themselves as living in an imperial Romanía, that is, "Romanland."[89]

In 568, three years after Justinian died—and almost as if Tyche were posthumously mocking the grand illusions of the old despot in Constantinople—the Lombards (another barbarian group) under their king, Albion, crossed the Alps from the lower Danube and, meeting little to no resistance, established a kingdom north of the Po River and two duchies around Spoleto and Benevento.[90] Italy, after only fourteen years as a unified polity within the renewed Roman Empire, slipped away into fractiousness lasting more than a millennium.

11 The Conversion of Reccared

In May 589 the Gothic king in Spain, Reccared, converted to Catholic Christianity from the "error of the Arians" at a council in Toledo.[91] The Gothic, or Visigothic as it is also known, kingdom in the Iberian peninsula was even more prone to assassinations and civil wars than the Frankish *regnum* in Gaul, which, even taking into account the exaggerations of Gregory of Tours, is saying something. It did not help that after Busta Gallorum, Justinian's fleet seized a strip of the southeastern peninsula as the new "Roman" province of Spania.[92] This "Roman" outcrop of Christian "orthodoxy" challenged both Catholics (mostly of Roman descent) and Arians (mostly of Gothic descent). It explicitly demanded loyalty from the former as it castigated the latter as heretics. It added even more volatility to the Spanish civil wars.

Reccared, like Clovis nine decades earlier, adopted Catholicism as a way of unifying at least his Gothic and Roman elites in opposition to the constant threat of religious sabotage from the neighboring "Romans." His aristocracy, while not as homogenous as that developing in Francia, was nevertheless no longer separated by their Christianity. Officially, Arianism no longer existed in Spain. As to whether any of the canons of the Toledo council were, or even could be, enforced—and the punishments for not obeying them were severe (excommunication, fines, or exile)—no one seemingly challenged the sincerity or, more importantly, the obligations entailed by Reccared's conversion.

12 The Greater Pilgrimage

"Flee young man!" a hermit nun living in a hut near the river Liffey admonished an angry Irish youth named Columbanus around 560. The adolescent was furiously hiking through the countryside tortured by the devil with a "lust for sluts" when he discovered the nun. He berated her for being a woman, obviously tempting him. "Flee!" she scolded. "Escape damnation into which, as you know, many have fallen. Forsake the way that leads to the gates of Hell."

As Columbanus could apparently never be around women and not be seduced, he needed to seek out a place of *peregrinatio*, "pilgrimage," exiling himself far away as a monk. "Touched by these words," wrote Jonas of Bobbio seven decades later in his *Life* of Columbanus, "and frightened more than you would expect a young man to be, he thanks her for criticizing him." The flustered lad raced home, informing everyone he was leaving "his native land, which the inhabitants call Leinster." His mother, "overcome with sorrow, pleads with him not to leave." Lying on the floor, she blocked the door with her body. Columbanus skipped over her, wishing her happiness, never seeing her again.

Columbanus traveled north to Lough Erne, where an abbot named Sinilis presided over a tiny island monastery. As he was only home-schooled in grammar, he had much to learn, especially scripture, so the abbot tutored him. After a few years he fled farther north to the monastery of Bangor on the shores of the Lough of Belfast. He lived there for almost two decades until his longing for the blazing sanctity of supreme exile overwhelmed him. The nun near the Liffey had told him that the greater *peregrinatio*, a much greater pilgrimage than exile from family and home, and which only men could do, was crossing the sea and leaving Ireland forever. With twelve companions from Bangor, Columbanus "set out through the straits into the uncertain sea-lanes," eventually landing upon the coast of Brittany. Seemingly with no plan in mind, apart from the "spirit of the all-merciful Judge" guiding them, they walked into Gaul in 590.[93]

Columbanus and his companions "from the far end of the ocean" were pioneers of a more northern orientation in Latin Christianity than that found in the Mediterranean. As they wandered throughout Neustria and Burgundy as perpetual exiles proudly indifferent to local customs, self-conscious expatriates never giving up personas from the old country, their heroic if undeniably eccentric spirituality was deeply appealing to Frankish kings and aristocrats. A Burgundian king persuaded Columbanus to journey into the heavily forested (with conifers and beech) low mountains of the Vosges in search of wilderness for a monastery. The Irishman and his followers initially camped in an old fort, living on tree bark and herbs, before moving further into the upland woods and building a monastery next to the ruins of "pagan" hot baths in an old Roman town named Luxeuil.

The monastery was soon crowded with noble Franks submitting themselves to Hibernian "medicines of penance" (*paenitentiae medicamenta*). Columbanus frequently escaped into his own exile from Luxeuil—a *peregrinatio* from *peregrinatio*—by hiking through the valleys with a book satchel on his shoulder, reading and fasting in caves or under trees. He liked nature, especially its dangerous bestiality, because where there was no humanity, there was only God. His thoughts ran to questions such as whether it was better to "fall into the snares of men or to be mauled by wild beasts." (Obviously, mauled by wild beasts.)[94] In these years he composed a severe and flinty *Rule*, in which the former selves of his monks were ground down into serene nothingness by unwavering obedience, two hours of sleep, and daily confession. What filled this human void was the immense love of God.[95]

Columbanus, unlike Gregory of Tours, shunned "deeds of power," whether by himself or by the Frankish elite. He was an exile and the machinations of Merovingian *potentes* were irrelevant. Inevitably, his stubborn tone-deafness to all political politesse, refusing to say soothing words to a monarch or mouthing agreement with bishops, was too foreign to be tolerated, and he and his surviving Irish companions were expelled from Burgundy in 610. As Columbanus was being escorted by soldiers to the Atlantic coast for deportation to Ireland, there was an assassination attempt, a night at the tomb of Saint Martin in Tours (Gregory, who would have been very suspicious of the Irishman, had died in 594), conversations with a Syrian woman in Orléans, exorcisms of the possessed, and other assorted miracles until finally, at the Bay of Biscay, his prison ship, unable to row past the surf, was tossed back on the beach. By now, no one seemed to care what happened to Columbanus, so he escaped to Austrasia (northeastern Francia around the Moselle and the Rhine).

The wanderlust of perpetual *peregrinatio* and the turmoil of the Merovingian civil wars soon led Columbanus to the Lombard court in Milan, where the king, Agilulf, welcomed him. He was still the charismatic stranger amongst strangers, if now a bit more willing to play by local rules. He preached against the "deceits of the Arians, with the cauterizing blade of the Gospel," and while it is unclear if he was accusing leftover Goths or seditious Lombards or both, his outsider fury was a useful moral cudgel against the rivals of his new royal patron. Columbanus was even sympathetic to Justinian's pallid compromise of the Three Chapters, as he knew this was also the view of the Lombard queen.

In 613 Agilulf endowed the politic holy man with land in the foothills of the Apennines at a place named Bobbio (and where Jonas as a monk wrote his *Vita Columbani* between 639 and 643) near the river Trebbia, "on the banks of which Hannibal once, while passing the winter here, suffered severe loss of men, horses, and elephants."[96] Columbanus died later that year during the first snowfall in his new monastery, far from home, forever the fleeing exile.[97]

13 The End of Late Antiquity

The swift, cataclysmic disintegration of Roman Britain in the fifth century is one of the most stunning societal breakdowns in world history. What happened in other regions of the former Western Roman Empire were hardly "soft landings," but for all the upheaval from Paris to Rome to Carthage, there were some continuities that only finally disappeared by the end of the sixth century. The so-called barbarian successor kingdoms in North Africa, Spain, Italy, and Gaul were surprisingly effective in co-opting, or coercing, elite Romans into the new governing entourages gathering around these Vandal, Visigothic, Ostrogothic, and Frankish kings. These kingdoms were relatively stable, despite a marked tendency for civil war.

What shattered them was Justinian's great campaign of reconquest. In Italy, for instance, not only was the kingdom established by Theodoric destroyed, but so too were the old Roman senatorial families. As much as the Mediterranean was once again almost completely dominated by Constantinople, the cultural and religious contours of the West were moving away from southern and eastern influences. It is an irony that Justinian's ambition at reestablishing and reforming the Roman Empire as a Holy Commonwealth was the very thing that ultimately fractured the Christian East and West.

As we move from Patricius to Columbanus, from an Ireland that was never part of the Roman Empire to an Ireland now defining many of the religious rhythms of the post-Roman West, we are moving, without any caveats or asides or qualifications, into the Middle Ages.

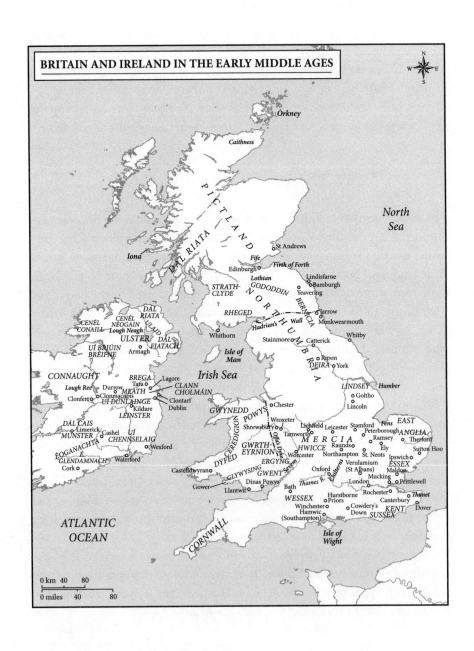

BRITAIN AND IRELAND IN THE EARLY MIDDLE AGES

Orkney

Caithness

PICTLAND

DÁL RIATA

Iona

St Andrews
Fife
Edinburgh *Firth of Forth*
Lothian
STRATH-
CLYDE
GODODDIN
Lindisfarne
Bamburgh
Yeavering

*North
Sea*

RHEGED

NORTHUMBRIA

BERNICIA

Jarrow
Monkwearmouth

Hadrian's Wall

DÁL
RIATA

CENÉL
NÉOGAIN

CENÉL
CONAILL

CENÉL
CONAILL

ULAID

Lough Neagh

ULSTER
DÁL
FIATACH

UÍ BRIÚIN
BRÉIFNE

Armagh

Whithorn

Stainmore
Catterick
Whitby

*Isle of
Man*

DEIRA
Ripon
York

CONNAUGHT

Lough Ree

BREGA
Tara
Durrow
Clonmacnois
UÍ DÚNLAINGE
Clonfert
Kildare
Lagore
CLANN
CHOLMÁIN
Clontarf
Dublin

Irish Sea

LINDSEY
Humber
Goltho
Lincoln

LEINSTER

DÁL CAIS
Limerick
MUNSTER
Cashel
EÓGANACHTA
GLENDAMNACH
Cork
Waterford
UÍ
CHENNSELAIG
Wexford

GWYNEDD
POWYS
Chester
Wroxeter
Shrewsbury
CEREDIGION
DYFED
GWRTH-
EYRNION
ERGYNG
CASTELLDWYRAN
GLYWYSING
GWENT
Gower
Llantwit
Dinas Powys
Bath
Lichfield
Tamworth
MERCIA
HWICCE
Worcester
Raunds
Northampton
St. Neots
Verulamium
(St Albans)
Oxford
Thames
Leicester
Stamford
Fens
Peterborough
Ramsey
Ely
Ipswich
ESSEX
Maldon
Mucking
London
Chilterns
Rochester
Hurstborne
Priors
Cowdery's
Down
Canterbury
Thanet
Dover
KENT
SUSSEX

EAST
ANGLIA
Therford
Sutton Hoo

Severn

WESSEX
Winchester
Hamwic
(Southampton)

*Isle of
Wight*

CORNWALL

ATLANTIC
OCEAN

0 km 40 80
0 miles 40 80

IV

Mad Poets

597–735

1 Old Beliefs

In 597 an Italian abbot named Augustine and forty monks landed on the island of Thanet, separated by the Wantsum Channel from southeastern Britain. He had been dispatched a year earlier from Rome by Pope Gregory I with the gift of Christianity for the "pagan" king of Kent, Æthelbert. It was a long, terrifying journey to the end of the world, and Augustine almost abandoned the mission, fearful of barbarous Britain. He was no Columbanus, embracing far-off horizons.

According to the Northumbrian monk Bede (known later as the Venerable Bede) in his *Ecclesiastical History of the English People* (*Historica ecclesiastica gentis Anglorum*), finished in 731, Augustine announced (through interpreters acquired in Francia) that "he had come from Rome bearing the best news, namely the sure and certain promise of eternal joys in heaven and an endless kingdom with the living and true God to those who received it." This news was too much all at once for Æthelbert, so he ordered the Italian monks to stay on the island until he decided what should be done with them. He already had a fair idea of the "living and true God," as his Frankish wife, Bertha, was Christian and most of western Britain was Christian—after an older Patrician and Irish fashion. He was certainly sympathetic to Christianity, if not already indulging in it piecemeal, but this "exotic" version from Rome needed quarantining first.

After a few days Augustine and Æthelbert met in the open air on the island. The king was superstitious about magic deceiving him if they met inside a building. He listened attentively as Augustine preached (through the Frankish translators), and then concluded: "The words and promises you bring are fair enough, but because they are new to us and doubtful, I cannot accept them and abandon the age-old beliefs." Nevertheless, Æthelbert gave Augustine a wooden house and provisions in the tumbledown and largely empty city of Canterbury and allowed him to preach.[1]

In Canterbury Augustine and his monks settled into the routines of Benedict's *Rule*. On one of the city streets was a decrepit old Roman church honoring Saint Martin, and here, along with the Frankish queen, the Italians "assembled to sing the psalms, to pray, to say Mass, to preach, and to baptize." Æthelbert soon converted, along with many of his followers, giving Augustine "greater liberty to preach everywhere and to build or restore churches." Bede rather disingenuously observed that the king "compelled no one to accept Christianity; though none the less he showed greater affection for believers since they were his fellow citizens in the kingdom of heaven."[2]

2 Giants Groan Beneath the Waters

Pope Gregory I was a papal anomaly before the eleventh century; unlike almost every other early medieval pope, his influence and imagination went slightly further than the courtyards of the Lateran Palace. Although as a twenty-six-year-old Roman aristocrat in 575, and only two years after engaging in Rome's faded civic glitter as urban prefect, he retreated from the world by transforming his father's palace on the Clivus Scauri into a monastery dedicated to Saint Andrew with himself as abbot. His monks were all young men like himself, pious sons of the long-standing Christian nobility whose antiquated palazzi crowded the Aventine and Caelian hills. This palatial hilltop enclave overlooked the rotting heart of the classical city, a desolate panorama where, as Gregory himself said, "we see walls crumbling, houses demolished, the churches destroyed by a whirlwind, and buildings, weakened by great age, lying on the ground in spreading ruins."[3]

The posh monastery on the Clivus Scauri did not follow any discernable rule. Gregory was not yet an impresario of Benedict's *Rule*, and his monastery was explicitly not a huddle of huts on a scrubby mountain. His monks were more like the chaste gentlemen scholars who had gathered around Augustine of Hippo in Thagaste two centuries earlier. Or, rather, they were like little Pacatulas, living lives as dictated by Jerome, retreating within rooms within rooms, never leaving the cool marble of their mansion, devoting all their ascetic energies to ecstatic reading. Gregory devoured Augustine so obsessively that he harmed his health (painful bowels, asthmatic fevers) with study. His sojourn as a monk ended before it really began when the pope made him a deacon and sent him to Constantinople as a diplomat in 579. Yet he never stopped thinking of himself as a monk, as only participating in the world under duress, as an exile from paradise. Soon after he returned to Rome from Constantinople, this burden only got worse when Gregory was unexpectedly elected pope in 590.[4]

A phrase from the Book of Job summed up how Gregory now saw his life as pope: "Behold, the giants groan beneath the waters."[5] He was caught in the great swell of what it meant to be the bishop of Rome, whose towering responsibilities, like immense waves rising and falling, might at any moment pull him under. He fed the urban poor starving amongst the ruins (from papal estates in Sicily), mollified the Lombard warlords (who destroyed monasteries like Monte Cassino), and supported (financially and morally) the bored and largely irrelevant East Roman garrisons in Italy.[6] Gregory also provided spiritual life rafts for Christian elites in two books he wrote within his first twelve months as pope.

The first book, the *Moralia in Job*, was an allegorical exegesis of one book of the Bible. It was the summation of years of "table talk" between Gregory, his monks in Clivus Scauri, and his friends in Constantinople. It was spiritual autobiography as holy parlor game, where every word of the Book of Job was analyzed for clues to the secret meanings of God. Like such games, it is convoluted, repetitive, tedious, and achingly arcane, and yet, for those who enjoy such play—and there were enough of those in the late sixth century—it was a revelation. The *Moralia in Job* revealed that God was everywhere and in everything, if only you looked and thought hard enough. All human existence was exile from paradise, but if you solved His puzzles, you might just get there again.[7]

The other book was the *Regula Pastoralis* (*Rule for Pastors*), which, inspired by Benedict's *Rule* for monks, was Gregory's *Rule* for bishops. It would end the amateurishness, as he saw it, of so much episcopal care of souls. It was a law code for salvation. Gregory even listed thirty-nine different spiritual types and antitypes, with the proper disciplining for each one.[8] (This typology replicated the thirty-nine strokes of the rod for a disobedient monk—an oddly important number for monks in Italy and Gaul. Caesarius of Arles, for example, benevolently only thrashed slaves this amount.) The *Regula Pastoralis* was even adopted by some kings and lords as a guide on the dutifulness of power. When Gregory sent Augustine and his companions, all of whom were Clivus Scauri monks, to Britain, copies of the *Moralia in Job* and the *Regula Pastoralis* accompanied the missionaries.

3 Gold Under Gravel

When Augustine landed off the Kentish coast there were at least thirteen "kingdoms" in eastern Britain. In the century since the arrival of the first Frisian, north Rhenish, and Scandinavian boat people, thousands of colonists and their descendants had settled in fields, hills, river valleys, and abandoned towns. These squatters were constantly joining other settler communities, then breaking off to form different alliances before again rupturing in search of more secure coalitions. It was a world in constant flux, achieving some sense of stability only in the sixth century when immigrant families and their dependents offered (willingly, reluctantly) their loyalty and tribute to "kings." These kingdoms ran the gamut from a few modest farms clustered around a hill to ambitious congeries of farming hamlets, mills, malting ovens, cattle pastures, pigsties, hay meadows, and isolated fields worked by slaves.

All of these kingdoms, however small, were focused upon the king's household and, specifically, upon his wooden royal hall. All goods and services flowed into the royal residences, where kings distributed them amongst their followers. Successful rulers built bigger halls, developed more elaborate rituals around themselves, entertained more lavishly, and triumphed over weaker and hungrier kings. In a world where everyone, high and low, repeatedly experienced starvation, the ability to offer food and drink, or take it away, was a mighty demonstration of sovereignty. Slap-up showmanship as much as martial strength defined power amongst the various settler communities from the river Medway to the Humber estuary, whom we may call the English or Anglo-Saxons.[9]

An extraordinary example of this showmanship was the barrow funeral mounds of English rulers and their followers in the sixth and seventh centuries. Most of these barrows were repurposed Bronze Age monumental mounds. Or if they were new, they were constructed to appear ancient. They marked out the boundaries of kingdoms; they signaled the wealth and authority of nouveau riche aristocrats; they showed that the land had always belonged to those now inhumed beneath it. Inside these barrows were chambers of turf and wood requiring the work of a hundred or more men (who, when not building burial rooms, were farmers). In these "earth galleries" recycled Roman ceramic pots, or occasionally wildly lavish bronze vessels imported from the Mediterranean, held the ashes of cremated elites. Sometimes a body was not incinerated. For example, in the early seventh century on Swallowcliffe Down, in Wiltshire, a young, elegantly dressed woman lying on an ornate wooden bed was placed within an ancient barrow. Around the dead were arrayed costly grave goods. Weapons (swords, spears, and axes) were common in the early sixth century, even for children and women.

By 600 this practice was fading away, apart from a few deliberately archaizing and profligate barrow burials in the seventh century. Sides of beef, pork, grain, and cider were frequently placed in the tombs. The "sleeping princess" beneath Swallowcliffe Down was accompanied by delicate jewelry of gold and silver foil and blown-glass palm cups. Famous, and spectacular, was the over-the-top faux-traditional ship burial at Sutton Hoo in Suffolk.[10] There was an unmistakable element of potlatch to all this mortuary display. In a world where famine was a constant, even in a good year, the extravagant wastefulness of resources in things and labor exemplified by a barrow burial was heroic, compelling, and not easily forgotten. It was an exclamation of triumph, not so much over death but over what it meant to be human.

An anonymous Christian poet singing in English in the eighth or ninth century ended his song (at least in the version written down around 1000) of the "fabled warrior" Beowulf, king of the Geats, with the cremation and barrow burial of his hero, who dies from wounds incurred while killing a fifty-foot fire dragon, itself the "mound-guard" of an ancient barrow hoarded with treasure hidden for a "thousand winters underground":

> The Geat people built a pyre for Beowulf
> stacked and decked it until it stood four-square,
> hung with helmets, heavy war-shields
> and shining armour, just as he had ordered, just as he had ordered.
> Then his warriors laid him in the middle of it,
> mourning a lord far-famed and beloved.
> On a height they kindled the hugest of all
> funeral fires; fumes of woodsmoke

billowed darkly up, the blaze roared
and drowned out their weeping, wind died down
and flames wrought havoc in the hot bone-house,
burning it to the core. They were disconsolate
and wailed aloud for their lord's decease . . .
      . . . Heaven swallowed the smoke.
Then the Geat people began to construct
a mound on a headland, high and imposing,
a marker that sailors could see from far away,
and in ten days they had done the work.
It was their hero's memorial; what remained from the fire
they housed inside it, behind a wall
as worthy of him as their workmanship could make it.
And they buried torques in the barrow, and jewels
and a trove of such things as trespassing men
had once dared to drag from the hoard.
They let the ground keep that ancestral treasure,
gold under gravel, gone to earth,
as useless to men now as it ever was.[11]

No elite man, woman, or child had been buried in a barrow for more than a century, perhaps two centuries, when the poet of *Beowulf* was singing, and yet these monumental mounds scattered throughout the countryside were still celebrated as memorials to the danger and grandeur of "days gone by," *in gear-dagum*.

In sixth-century western Britain (what is now Cornwall, the West Country, the West Midlands, Wales, and western Scotland) there were numerous petty "kings," some of whom were descended from Romans like the "blood-thirsty" Coroticus, whom Patricius loathed. In these "kingdoms" a vibrant Christianity existed alongside the residue of a half-remembered *Romanitas*. There were no barrows rising up by the Irish Sea, there were no buried weapons or treasure (or dragons under the earth). Indeed, following late Roman habits, almost nothing was buried with the dead, who, for the most part, were inhumed in old Roman cemeteries alongside old Roman roads. Dozens of inscribed cemetery stones suggest the continued use of everyday Latin. Written on a sixth-century cemetery stone, the text *Cantiori hic iacit [v]enedotis cive fvit [c]onsobrino ma[g]li magistrati* (Of Cantiorix, here he lies. He was a citizen of Gwynedd and cousin of Maglos the magistrate) even suggests that Roman notions of citizenship and public office boastfully lingered amongst small groups of Britons.[12]

Similarly, Roman schooling in Latin grammar and rhetoric survived in some British families. The cleric Gildas in his *On the Ruin of Britain*, written sometime in the sixth century, marshaled a rambling rococo style reminiscent of Sidonius Apollinaris in a jeremiad against sinful "stiff-necked and haughty" Britons. Despite the British living "in an island numb with chill ice and far removed, as in a remote nook of the world, from the visible sun, Christ made a present of his rays."[13] Only "Christ the true sun" could dispel the shadows amongst the ruins. What caused this ruination were barbarian invasions, the indifference of Rome, local tyrants, and "Arians" (which was just a synonym for all heretics). The British were "Israelites" lost and forlorn in the "desert." Gildas, in his eccentric, cranky, and rare pamphlet (there are no other British Latin texts surviving from the sixth century), assumed he was not alone in being disgusted at the state of Britain.

There were many Irish immigrants in western Britain. The number of cemetery stones inscribed with ogham, a script of Irish elites, either alone or bilingually alongside Latin, reveals that in some communities, like Devon and Cornwall, a new aristocracy of mixed Irish and British Christian families was emerging in the fifth and sixth centuries.[14] (Cantiorix and Maglos, for example, were Irish names.) The most famous Irishman to settle on the British west coast was Columba, a descendant of the former high king of Ireland, Niall of the Nine Hostages. In 563 he sailed away from Ireland as a penitential exile to the blowy, almost treeless metamorphic island of Iona in the Inner Hebrides, "the spine of Britain," off the western coast of Scotland. Why he left is unclear, although his life, written a century later by his kinsman Adomnán, abbot of Iona, linked his *peregrinatio* with the bloody battle of Cúl Drebene in northwest Ireland between his family and their cousins in 561.[15] Two years later—the same year Justinian died—he established a monastery on his "desert" island for English and Irish warrior aristocrats. Columba was a young deacon and not a warrior before coming to Iona, but Irish warfare and savage clannish violence were always on his mind (and, crucially, on Adomnán's).

Unlike Columbanus three decades later, Columba never assumed he was leaving Ireland forever, or really even leaving what was culturally familiar to him; rather, he was removing himself from the murderous petty loyalties of kinship so as to cast over the North Atlantic a broad holy net in which the only loyalty was to God. This divine fealty, though, was shaped by the same obligations, especially "terrible vengeance upon enemies," as any English or Irish king expected from their spearmen.[16]

There were discernable cultural differences between western and eastern Britain before the seventh century. Yet they were not razor sharp. British, Irish, and English elites commonly intermingled and intermarried. Aristocratic warriors across the British Isles shifted their allegiances between all the various kings and kinglets. All of the kingdoms attacked one another, enslaving men, women, and children from different regions and traditions. The English word for "slaves" was *wealas*, which also meant "foreigners" or "outsiders"—although who was "foreign" or "outside" a kingdom sometimes only meant families living beyond the next hill. After the seventh century, though, *wealas* was used as a catchall term defining some communities in western Britain as "Welsh."[17]

Interestingly, *wealas* was not a synonym for "Christians," despite most British and Irish elites (and probably everyone else west of the Cambrian mountains) following various forms of Christianity. There were clearly Christians descended from fifth-century Romans living under English kings, perhaps as "slaves" or "outsiders," although many were probably just tribute-paying farmers; a few must have been warriors in royal households. Nothing about English burial mounds necessarily suggests an incompatibility with Christianity; then again, neither do they suggest some overarching commitment to "paganism."

Yet if the English were not Christians, at least not in any form recognizable to a Gildas or Columba, what was their religion? Bede certainly wanted his eighth-century English readers to think that their ancestors were sincere, thoughtful, and even good-looking pagans. "I must relate here a story, handed down to us by tradition, which explains Gregory's deep desire for the salvation of our nation." This famous and fanciful story from the *Ecclesiastical History* opens with Gregory, before he was pope, descending from the palatial Clivus Scauri to shop in the slave markets of Rome. He saw some boys exposed for sale. "These had fair complexions, fine-cut features, and beautiful hair." He asked where they came from. "They come from the island of Britain," a slave merchant replied, "where all the people have this appearance." He asked if they were Christians or still ignorant heathens. "They are pagans." "Alas!" sighed Gregory, distressed that behind such pretty faces were minds lacking God's grace. "What is the name of these people?" he inquired. "They are called Angles [*Angli*]." "That is appropriate," he punned, "for they have angelic faces, and it is right that they should become joint-heirs with the angels in heaven." Bede then had

Gregory make two more excruciating puns before observing that the not-yet pope wished to immediately rush off to Britain as a missionary himself. Of course, Gregory did not, but the memory of the angelic boys eventually led to Augustine's expedition.[18]

Another story from Bede concerned the conversion of Edwin, king of Northumbria, in 627. Twenty-four years earlier, Edwin tramped Britain as a young exile, outrunning the murderous rage of a king named Æthefrid. One night, when he was frightened and lost, "tormented by inward fires that brought no light," an odd-looking man suddenly appeared. The stranger asked why Edwin was sitting alone in the murk on a cold stone. The youth said that was his business. "Don't think that I am unaware why you are sad and sleepless," replied the stranger.

He then asked Edwin three questions: What reward would you give the man who delivered you from your troubles? What if this man crushed your enemies and made you the most powerful king amongst the English? What if this man offered guidance and salvation unknown to your parents and kinfolk? To the first question, Edwin answered that he would give anything and everything; to the second question, he said that he would promise his undying gratitude; and to the third question, he replied that he would faithfully follow the man who erased his troubles and raised him to a throne. The stranger placed his right hand on the young exile's head, saying, "When you receive this sign, remember this occasion and our conversation, and do not delay the fulfilment of your promise." The odd-looking man instantly vanished, for he was a spirit.[19]

Soon after that night, Edwin fortuitously killed Æthefrid in battle beside the river Idle and, without assassins hunting him, eventually succeeded the sonless king of Northumbria. He married Æthelburga of Kent, the daughter of Æthelbert, and in her entourage was Paulinus, an Italian monk from Augustine's monastery in Canterbury (and Clivus Scauri before that). The Christian holy man preached every day, causing Edwin to sit alone for hours debating with himself "what religion should he follow." After one lengthy sermon, Paulinus audaciously laid his right hand on the king's head, asking if he remembered this sign. Edwin fell to his knees, trembling. "Remember the third promise that you made, and hesitate no longer," said the Italian in a friendly voice. "If you will henceforth obey His will, which He reveals to you through me, He will save you." The king, always aware, even if he never wanted to admit it, that the spirit who had spoken to him so long ago was a messenger of God, told Paulinus he would become a Christian. First, though, so that all Edwin's aristocratic followers, his "ealdormen" and "thegns," would be "cleansed together in Christ" with him, he summoned them to the royal wooden hall at Yeavering beside the river Glen to hear their opinions on what was inevitable.[20]

"Your Majesty," said Coifi, the chief pagan priest, "I frankly admit that, in my experience, the religion that we have hitherto professed seems valueless and powerless." The reason for this swift and complete dismissal of everything he had believed all his life, he argued with awe-inspiring selfishness, was that if the pagan gods really had any power, then he would be richer and showered in greater honors. A tough act to follow, but one man did, saying:

> When we compare the present life of man on earth with that time of which we have no knowledge, it seems to me like the swift flight of a single sparrow through the banqueting-hall where you are sitting at dinner on a winter's day with your ealdormen and thegns. In the midst there is a comforting fire to warm the hall; outside, the storms of winter rain or snow are raging. The sparrow flies swiftly in through one door of the hall, and out through another. While he is inside, he is safe from the winter storms; but after a few moments of comfort, he vanishes from sight into the wintry world from which he came. Even so, man appears on earth for a little while; but of what went before this life or what follows, we know nothing. Therefore, if this new teaching has brought any more certain knowledge, it seems only right we should follow it.

This affecting speech, more so than Coifi's complaint, convinced everyone present of what Edwin willed. Paulinus then baptized hundreds of people for thirty-six continuous days in the chilly waters of the river Glen.[21]

What Bede did not explicitly mention was that the royal wooden hall at Yeavering was built beneath a large Iron Age hill fort, known as Yeavering Bell, at the end of a small valley already crowded with a henge (an ancient stone circle) and a ring barrow. There were no recent barrow burials, but underfoot, and perhaps unknown in the seventh century, were vast archaic burial pits full of ox skulls and even a human buried with a goat head.[22] It was holy ground from "days gone by" specifically chosen by Edwin for his hall, and while none of this suggests what his system of belief was before or even after becoming a Christian, it does show a serious royal effort at recycling a monumental landscape known to be sacred. Pope Gregory would have applauded the king, for in 601 he informed Augustine (replicating laws in the *Theodosian Code*) that pagan temples in Britain should not be destroyed, only the idols within them. "When the people themselves see that these temples are not destroyed," they will easily worship God "with more familiarity to the places they have been accustomed to."[23]

Bede seemingly disagreed with (even as he quoted) the pope a century later, as well as implicitly acknowledging what surrounded Yeavering, when he inflamed the former chief priest with the almost parodic iconoclastic zeal of a new convert. After begging Edwin for arms and a stallion—the pagan chief priest was normally forbidden weapons and could only ride a mare—Coifi galloped throughout the countryside, spearing idols, burning temples, and knocking over henges. "Inspired by the true God, he desecrated and destroyed the altars that he had himself dedicated."[24]

4 Singing the Law

In 616 Æthelbert died, and amongst his accomplishments, such as being the first English king "to enter the kingdom of heaven," was, according to Bede, "a code of law inspired by the example of the Romans, which was written in English."[25] Monks in the decade after the arrival of Augustine—most likely Italian or Frankish, although they could easily have been British or Irish—transformed a Germanic dialect spoken in Kent into a written language that, with some variation here and there, was eventually adopted throughout much of eastern Britain. Like Clovis and the *Lex Salica* a century earlier, Æthelbert was convinced, or had convinced himself, that a law code in the Roman manner was a dazzling artifact of a king and a Christian. Except unlike the *Lex Salica*, these ninety laws were not written in Latin. Æthelbert may have wanted written laws like a Roman, or at least like Roman monks and their monastic rule, but in wanting them in the day-to-day language of his aristocratic followers, he stressed that writing, while decorative and impressive like silver spoons from the Mediterranean, did not supplant vernacular memories of the "lore of the past." A law code in English was like a song in which the singer extemporized from the memory of other songs what was pragmatically necessary for a specific situation. In the same way, after Beowulf kills the magnificent and cruel monster Grendel,

> a thane
> of the king's household, a carrier of tales,
> a traditional singer deeply schooled
> in the lore of the past, linked a new theme
> to a strict metre. The man started
> to recite with skill, rehearsing Beowulf's
> triumphs and feats in well-fashioned lines,
> entwining his words.[26]

Æthelbert's laws functioned in a fundamentally oral culture, where literacy, that is, the written word, served no practical purpose in commonplace royal governance. Laws, like songs, were locked away in the "word-hoards" of individuals schooled in tradition and were skillfully recited along "well-fashioned lines" whenever needed. As the poet of *Beowulf* assumed know-ledge of at least twenty other songs in his listeners (including different versions of *Beowulf*), Æthelbert's laws assumed an awareness of other laws apart from what was written out.

A few of Æthelbert's laws transcribed (or even invented) by the monks were: thumbnail knocked off, 3 shillings; any of the four front teeth knocked out, 6 shillings a tooth; a mouth or eye disfigured, 12 shillings; one man kills another in the king's hall, 50 shillings to the king; lying with a serving maid, 6 shillings; if one man slays another man, 20 shillings before the grave is closed, then 80 shillings within forty days; a bruise, 1 shilling; a foot cut off, 50 shillings; and if a freeborn woman with long hair acts unseemly, 30 shillings.[27] (As no one used coins in Britain, and certainly no kings were minting them, the damages in "shillings" was monkish shorthand for . . . stuff worth something.)

What comes through in Æthelbert's laws, like in so much English poetry, is the sheer smallness of the communities that made up his kingdom, and that the constant anticipation and frustration of inter-necine violence provoked by a little bruising or the tiniest spillage of blood was an existential necessity if these communities were not to be torn apart by feuding and "terrible vengeance." There was always com-pensation, there was always a song that could be sung, no matter the crime, ensuring collective peace and communal absolution if not forget-fulness. It was a legal and moral ethos echoed in the hopeful yet pensive refrain of the anonymous English poem known as "Deor": "That went by: this may too."[28]

5 Messenger and Prophet

In 610 a forty-year-old man named Muhammad ibn 'Abdullah was all alone amongst the drift sand and basalt pebbles of the Hijaz in the western Arabian peninsula, perhaps just before the meager November rains, when he suddenly collapsed, shivering and trembling, as a thunderous and unfathomable noise reverberated through him, and which, once his body attuned to the great roar, miraculously revealed itself as the mellifluous, skin-tingling, soul-quaking voice of the One God Himself.

After Muhammad's first solitary revelation in the desert, the terrifying sound of the King of the Day of Judgment shocked and jolted him again and again, whether in crowded oases or leading camel-men into battle, until he died in 632. He instinctively (sometimes assisted by the archangel Gabriel) translated this unearthly music into Arabic, singing the *ayas* (verses, signs) of the greatest of all sacred songs as the Messenger and Prophet of the One God and which, decades after his death, were finally written down and edited in 114 *surats* (chapters) in what came to be known as the Qur'an. A century after Muhammad's death, avowed followers of his received revelations, now known as Muslims, had conquered most of the Iberian peninsula, North Africa, Egypt, Syria, and the vast Iranian plateau as far as the Indus River, all in the name of a new monotheistic religion, Islam.[29]

Unfortunately, how we get from the voice of the One God pummeling His Messenger in a stony desert to a mighty Islamic empire four generations later is not at all clear-cut. Everything we know about Muhammad was written decades, if not centuries, later by Muslim and Christian authors. These biographical stories, often no more than a snippet, and rarely less than implausible, were a hodgepodge of myth, artfulness, piety, and contradiction.

The traditional biography of Muhammad woven out of these tales begins with his birth and early orphaning in Mecca, a small pagan cultic town stranded in a dried-up basin (two miles long, half a mile wide) surrounded by desolate high mountains in the Hijaz. He was of the Hashim clan within the dominant tribe of Quraysh. In the middle of Mecca was the Ka'ba, a boxy temple to the old gods, particularly Hubal, with a sacred black stone glistening like a large eggplant in one corner. The stone was the focus of local pilgrimages of varying ritual intensity and sacrifice, the lesser *'umra* and the much greater *hajj*. Mecca was a *haram*, a holy place where violence and the shedding of blood were forbidden.

Muhammad was a young agnostic orphan in this pagan clannish town. He married an older wealthy widow named Khadija; years later, when he told her what was revealed to him in the desert, she was his first believer. After 610 he preached of the One God in the streets of Mecca, infuriating worshippers of the old gods, especially the Quraysh. A few men believed him, such as his cousin 'Ali ibn Abi Talib, Abu Bakr (of the Yaym clan), and 'Uthman ibn 'Affan (of the Umayya clan). Despite Mecca being a *haram*, threats against Muhammad from the Quraysh escalated until, soon after Khadija died, he and his followers escaped on their *hijra* ("emigration" or "taking refuge") to a cluster of date-palm oases two hundred miles north in 622. These watering holes were collectively known as Yathrib, later renamed Medina (from *madinat al-nabi*, "city of the prophet").

Muhammad soon enforced a pact between his Meccan refugees, the *muhajirun* or "Emigrants," his Yathribi supporters, *ansar* or "Helpers," and sympathetic Yathribi Jewish clans, making them into one *umma*, a singular community or tribe under the One God. Over the next decade what began as raids by the Emigrants against Quraysh caravans spiraled into all-out warfare (battles, sieges) between polytheistic Mecca and the monotheistic *umma*. Finally, after crippling the Quraysh by audacious military and religious gamesmanship, Muhammad occupied Mecca in 630, everyone submitting to the One God and His Messenger.[30]

Most of this biography, perhaps all of it, is a pious falsehood. It is even possible that Muhammad never existed. Two Syrian Monophysite Christians from the middle of the seventh century, however, do mention him, or at least a "Muhammad," and warrior nomadic followers from the Arabian peninsula. An anonymous, barely legible scribble on the flyleaf of a Bible noted that a "Muhammad" and some "nomads [Syriac *tayyaye*]" destroyed many villages and slaughtered an East Roman army in southern Syria in 636.[31] Around 640 Thomas the Presbyter remembered the "nomads [*tayyaye*] of Muhammad" routing East Roman troops four years earlier near Gaza in Palestine; then "the nomads invaded all Syria and went down to Persia and conquered it."[32] If this was Muhammad before all the later mythological accretions, then the faded flyleaf scrawl suggests he lived beyond 632. Either way, these two references do not really add up to much.

Unfortunately, there are no Arabic records nor archeological evidence from the Hijaz mentioning Muhammad or his followers in the early seventh century, with the notable exception of the Qur'an. And even with this text there are serious historical problems. Leaving aside modern theories that the Qur'an coalesced over two hundred years mostly outside Arabia—and which, while very far from foolish, are more thought-provoking than convincing—the fact remains that the book was only knitted together around 660 at the earliest, and more likely closer to 700.[33] It is a composite of different texts, some more poetic, some much older, some much longer. It is coherent neither in style nor in content, with many passages resolutely enigmatic in language or meaning (as perhaps is the case with anything God says). It also presupposes knowledge of many other holy songs, especially Christian, sung across Syria and Arabia. Yet with these reservations in mind, and understanding that approaching the Qu'ran in this way is rather like studying *Beowulf* to learn what the English believed before the arrival of Augustine—that is, something one must do very warily—some insights into Muhammad and the One God in the early seventh century can be derived from the Qur'an.

God in the Qur'an relentlessly calls out (over a thousand times) to His "Believers," *mu'minun*, rather than (just seventy-five times) to His *muslimun*, "Muslims" (literally "those who submit"). Only in the eighth century did individuals now self-consciously identifying as Muslims stress that all the followers of the Prophet in the early seventh century were Muslims too. Sometimes a person in the Qur'an is both a *mu'min* and a *muslim*, and while the designations are related, they are not synonyms. "The bedouin say, 'We Believe,'" observes God dismissively in Surat al-Hujurat ("Apartments"). "Say [to them]: 'You do not Believe'; but rather say 'we submit,' for Belief has not yet entered your hearts." "Belief" is more than just words; it must be heartfelt. Until an individual understands this, there can only be "submission."[34]

If we accept that this *surat* reflects something of the early seventh century, then a Muslim aspired to be a Believer, and might one day achieve this status. "Abraham," explains Surat al-Imran ("The Family of Imran"), "was neither a Jew nor a Christian, rather he was a *muslim hanif* and not one of the *mushrikun*." When Abraham "submitted" himself to God in the distant past, with *hanif* being an earlier if imperfectly understood version of the revelation eventually given to Muhammad, the ancient prophet exemplified how being a *muslim* was a stage on the path of becoming a Believer. A religious hierarchy existed amongst the prophetic antecedents and contemporary followers of Muhammad, probably established after 622, in which Muslims, lacking the necessary (and perhaps never to be achieved) inner "belief," were inferior and subservient to the Believers. Abraham, as a Muslim prophet, was lesser than the Prophet. Muhammad, paradoxically, was not a Muslim.

The *mushrikun* were not pagans or believers in the old gods; rather, as the Qur'an constantly affirms, they worshipped Muhammad's God, whose two names were Allah and al-Rahman. They were not especially idolatrous, and Mecca, the Ka'ba, and the black stone are not mentioned in the Qur'an. (It is not even certain Mecca existed as a town in the early seventh century.) What the *mushrikun* were guilty of was falsely ascribing things to God, *iftira' 'ala llah*. They assumed that there were lesser gods and angels beneath (and sometimes on the same level as) the Highest God, even if they identified Him with the biblical God of Jews and Christians. Or at least they understood Him in the sense that Constantine initially understood Him and the *numina* three centuries earlier. Or as many East Roman Christians undoubtedly did in the sixth and seventh centuries. The *mushrikun* stupidly thought God had children. "Jews say: 'Uzayr is the son of God'; Christians say: 'Christ is the son of God'"—nothing but old nonsense from the *mushrikun*, according to Surat al-Tawba ("Repentance"). "They say: 'God has begotten a son,'" He laughs in Surat Maryam ("Mary") about Jesus as Him. "You have uttered a grievous thing, which would split open the skies, rip apart the earth, and cleave mountains." In Surat al-Najm ("The Star") some *mushrikun* even believed that God has daughters named al-Lat, al-Uzza, and Manat. God was particularly scornful of anything suggesting feminine divinity. (The word "goddess" never appears in the Qur'an.) "Those who do not believe in the hereafter call the angels by female names," He scolds in Surat an-Najim. Gods and angels are interchangeable in the Qur'an, and while most are reconfigured as demons, as *ginn*, some angelic beings are approved by Him. "Are we to abandon our gods for a mad poet?" say the *mushrikun* in Surat as-Saffat ("Who Stand Arrayed in Rows"), dismissing the God-given verses of the Messenger.[35]

"When We made the covenant with the prophets," recalls God in Surat al-Ahzab ("The Allied Troops"), "with Noah and Abraham, Moses and

Jesus son of Mary," He was testing their sincerity and truthfulness, but now such trials end with Muhammad as the last "apostle of God and seal of the prophets." No more revelations would be "sent down" to other prophets. Muhammad was the final apostle or messenger (*rasul*) and ultimate prophet (*nabi*) of the One God.

Why? The world was coming to an end. An apocalyptic and millennial urgency surges through the Qur'an, requiring all Believers to ready themselves for "the Hour" of destruction. "When what is to happen comes to pass," says God in Surat al-Waqi'ah ("The Inevitable") about the impending Last Day, "the earth is shaken up convulsively, the mountains bruised and crushed, turned to dust, floating in the air." "Truly We have warned you of a punishment near," implores God in Surat an-Naba ("The Announcement"), "a day on which a man shall see what his hand has done before, and [on that day] the unbeliever says, 'I wish I were dead!'" Fear of the apocalypse and Last Judgment motivated Muhammad and his Believers—"O Prophet Fear God."

By preparing themselves for the Last Judgment—which, in itself, might possibly save the world from God's destruction—Muhammad and the Believers were, as He commands in Surat al-Tawba, "to strive against the unbelievers and hypocrites and to treat them roughly, as their final resting place is hell." The Qur'anic term meaning "to strive" is *jihad*. Although sometimes a striving Believer was an individual grappling with achieving heartfelt inner belief, *jihad* overwhelmingly meant confronting and violently cleansing the world of unbelievers, of the *mushrikun*. "Those Believers," clarifies God in Surat an-Nisa ("The Women"), "who remain passive, other than those who are injured, are not on the plane with those who strive in the way of God [*fi sabil allah*] with their property and their selves." In Surat al-Tawba God admonishes any Believer who mistakenly thought giving water to pilgrims or even visiting a place of prayer, a *masjid* or mosque, was the same as "believing in God and the Last Day and striving in the way of God." "O Prophet, incite the Believers to fight," instructs God in Surat an-Anfal ("Spoils of War"), and even if there are only twenty or a hundred Believers, "make great slaughter in the earth," as He will help you triumph over two hundred or a thousand unbelievers. "Kill the *mushrikun* wherever you find them," orders God in Surat al-Tawba. "It is not for the Prophet and those who Believe to ask forgiveness for the *mushrikun*, even if they are close relatives." "Seize them, besiege them, ambush them in every way," says God—and then, seemingly contradicting Himself, he adds, "Nevertheless, if they repent . . . let them go their way."

The Qur'an frequently likens *hijra* to *jihad*, giving more nuanced and broader meanings to both "striving" and "emigration." "Truly," observes God in Surat an-Anfal, "those who have Believed and made *hijra* and strive in God's way . . . and those who gave asylum and aided [them]—those shall be mutual helpers of one another." *Jihad*, then, was simultaneously a striving to cleanse the earth of unbelief and a refuge from that corruption, a transcendent liminal existence in which sanctified violence was righteous sanctuary for the Believer.[36]

"We destroyed generations before you when they acted oppressively while their messengers brought them proofs, yet they did not Believe," remembers God in Surat Maryam. "Thus do we repay a guilty people. Then we made you successors in the land after them, so we may see how you behave." Sometimes in the Qur'an the earlier messengers were Believers rather than Muslims; unfortunately, no one in the past believed them, or rather no one fully understood what God was saying through them. In Surat Maryam it also seems the Hour might actually be forestalled by the piety of the Believers. As the Hour was terrifyingly close, Muhammad urgently preached for a reformation of belief in the One God. It was a fiercely puritanical vision, one stripped of all that was superficial, pointless, and nonsensical. In Surat al-Ahqaf ("The Wind-Curved Sand Hills") God tells His Messenger, "Say: I am no innovator amongst the messengers . . . I am only a clear warner." Muhammad was not the prophet of a new religion; he was the purifying prophet of an old religion in the Last Day.

At Easter 622, when traditionally Muhammad and the Emigrants made their *hijra* from Mecca to Yathrib, the East Roman emperor Heraclius departed Constantinople on the first campaign of a great holy war against the Sasanian Empire. Twelve years earlier the soldiers of King of Kings Khusro II Parvez had captured Jerusalem, seizing a piece of the True Cross (and the patriarch Zacharias) and sending it (and him) all the way back to the Zoroastrian priests at the royal palace at Dastkart. It all seemed so catastrophic and grim for the Eastern Empire, a harrowing of the Holy Commonwealth topped off by the Persians securing Alexandria and occupying Egypt in 619.

Surprisingly, Heraclius quickly regained Syria in 623, then, after four years of hard slog through the Caucasus into northern Mesopotamia, crushed the Persian army at the ancient ruins of Nineveh. He then marched back to Jerusalem (now wearing the *tzaggia*, the red knee-high boots of Persian monarchs) with the True Cross as his standard.[37]

Three decades earlier, Khusro II Parvez, far from hating the East Romans, had offered the emperor Maurice this cosmic flattery: "God effected that the whole world should be illumined from the very beginning by two eyes, namely the most powerful kingdom of the Romans and by the most prudent sceptre of the Persian state."[38] By 628 not only had the Persian king been overthrown and executed but the Sasanian Empire had collapsed into chaos from which it never recovered.

"The Romans have been conquered," says God in the Qur'an in the Surat al-Rum ("The Romans"), seemingly referring to the Persian victories over Syria and Egypt. "But having been conquered they will conquer in a few years, less than ten"—a prediction (or recollection) by Him of what did happen. "On that day the Believers will rejoice in the help of God." Although Muhammad was certainly aware of the two resplendent eyes glowing in Constantinople and Ctesiphon, he lauded only the Romans and their "striving" in the name of the One God.

Muhammad's messages from God were sophisticated if often enigmatic responses to the tumultuous debates on the holy that had convulsed the eastern Mediterranean since at least the fourth century. These debates, involving believers in the old gods, Jews, and Christians (and to some extent Manichaeans and Zoroastrians), were shaped by the intensifying militant orthodoxy of a Christian Roman Empire. The great holy wars of the East Roman and Sasanian empires in the early seventh century were the blazing endpoints of these long-running controversies for Muhammad, penultimate conflagrations heralding the approaching Hour. His revelations were meant to sum up and conclude these centuries of eschatological wrangling.

In traditional biographies of (and occasionally modern scholarship on) Muhammad, the Arabian peninsula, especially the Hijaz, is terra incognita, a moonscape cut off from the wider world. What God reveals to His Messenger occurs in a religious and political no-man's-land. Sometimes a biographer even made Muhammad illiterate, knowing nothing until God informs him. This is all pious fiction. Even the Qur'an itself situates the Messenger's activities not in the inhospitable Hijaz but in the more agricultural northwest of the Arabian peninsula, toward the Dead Sea. Muhammad was no religious outsider in the Middle East, and neither was Arabia.

So was Muhammad a Jew or a Christian before his revelations? He was probably a Christian.[39] The *mushrikun* were also Jews and Christians. Yet not all Jews and Christians were unbelievers; some were in the category of *ahl al-kitab*, "people of the book." That is, neither *mushrikun* nor Believers; perhaps initially, like Abraham, they were "Muslims" on the path to becoming Believers. Indeed, some Jews and Christians were already Believers, ready for Muhammad's warnings. "There are amongst the people of the book," God informs His Messenger in Surat al-Imran, "those who Believe in God and what was sent down to you and was sent down to them."

The Qur'an, or what there was of it in the early sixth century, was a nonlinear autobiographical poem composed over many years by Muhammad, a series of sibylline sound bites he heard from God about himself as the last Messenger in the Last Day. It was a swirl of memories of what had happened in the past and what would happen in the future. It was a work in constant progress—revised, erased, revised again, to be finished only at the coming of the Hour. It was by its very apocalyptic impulse an ephemeral message, never intended to be written down, like any urgent warning. And yet it was as much a literary and spiritual innovation (despite what God told His Messenger to tell his audience) as Augustine of Hippo's *Confessions*. Muhammad was not a parochial tub-thumper only for Arabs; he preached in a world primed for his message. He was never a lonely mad poet singing songs no one wanted to hear.

The Believers were swept up in an apocalyptic movement in which by purifying the world they purified themselves. They committed themselves to lasting "emigration" and "striving," to perpetual *hijra* and *jihad* as "nomads" chasing *umm qastal*, the "Mother of Dust" (that is, the dust of battle), fulfilling or postponing the Last Day.[40] As most Arabs were town-dwellers and the Qur'an was explicitly for an urban audience, the adoption of this nomadic warrior status as *muhajirun* was a powerful sign of becoming a Believer. In some ways it was a liminal existence similar to what Columbanus undertook in his *peregrinatio*, a casting aside of past habits and habitats to live as holy exiles or emigrants in expectation of the Day of Judgment. A Believer was still a nomadic refugee even if he barracked within a town or city. He was also a foot soldier rather than cavalry or camel-man.

Moreover, if Muhammad's revelations and early activities actually occurred near the Dead Sea, as the Qur'an suggests, then he likely intended
purging Syrian unbelievers first before even contemplating slaughtering
mushrikun in the Hijaz or southern Arabia. It is even probable that some
East Roman Christians in southern Syria were already Believers before the
nomads arrived, having heard the Messenger's verses in Arabic or in translation. What this means is that whether Muhammad died in 632 or a few
years later, he and his Believers were always going to spread out northward
into Syria from the Arabian peninsula in their "striving" in the name (or
names) of the One God.

All this is to say that the extraordinary conquests after Muhammad's
death under a series of *amir al-mu'minins*, "commanders of the Believers,"
while unexpected in their lightning achievement, such as occupying most
of Syria by 637 and eliminating the Sasanian Empire by 650, were an inevitable consequence of the driving holy-war apocalypticism of the Messenger.
Yet, as with all apocalyptic movements when the world does not come to
an end and the Last Day recedes as a pressing reality, disillusion and dissension took over. In 656 'Ali ibn Abi Talib, Muhammad's cousin and husband
of his daughter Fatima, was acclaimed *amir al-mu'minin* in Medina after the
assassination of the previous commander. He was opposed by Mu'awiya
ibn Abi Sufyan, who named himself *amir al-mu'minin* in Syria. A civil war
ensued, which only ended when one of the Kharijites (zealous schismatics
from *shi'at 'Ali*, "the party of Ali") killed Ali in 661. ("Shi'a" or "Shi'ites"
derived from *shi'at 'Ali* and was, as it still is, the name for Muslims revering
the Prophet's cousin; whereas "Sunni," signifying the majority of other
Muslims, only appeared in the ninth century.) In 692, after another civil war
amongst the Believers, 'Abd al-Malik, claiming descent from the Meccan
Umayya clan, established himself first as *khalifat allah*, "God's deputy," and
then as *khalifa*, "caliph," with his capital in Damascus.[41]

Famously, 'Abd al-Malik built the sumptuous Dome of the Rock in
Jerusalem before 700, a puzzling structure that, though modeled on East
Roman Christian basilicas, was neither church nor mosque, despite being
decorated with Qur'anic verses. These verses are almost illegible from the
ground, suggesting they were not meant to be read; rather, they were poetic
motifs already known to any pious viewer. The Qur'an was still a song, with
all the variant possibilities of individual memory and orality; nevertheless,
these just-out-of-sight ornamental verses signal a shift to more textual and

established sacred habits. The Dome of the Rock was, if nothing else, a shimmering monument to religious change and metamorphosis, signaling that the Believers no longer existed and that Muhammad's revelations four generations earlier had only ever been about and for Muslims.[42]

6 Casting a Net over Past Wisdom

"Those whom the pagan world calls 'bards' we call 'prophets,' as if they were 'predictors,' because indeed they speak and make true predictions about the future," begins the entry *"De prophetis"* ("The Prophets") in the *Etymologies* of Isidore, bishop of Seville, published by his friends soon after his death in 636. Seven kinds of prophecy are listed: ecstasy, vision, dream, "through a cloud," filled with the Holy Spirit, oracle, and "a voice from heaven."[43]

The *Etymologies*, consisting of twenty books, is a bowerbird-like compendium of Latin bits and bobs by an omnivorous bibliophile. There are entries on all sorts of things: front doors; red gems; parchment; the Ganges; ropes (long, short, twisted); heresy; Plato; nouns; licorice; Europe ("a third of the globe," beginning with the river Don, "passing to the west along the northern ocean as far as the border of Spain, and its eastern and southern parts rise from the Pontus [Black Sea] and are bordered the whole way by the Mediterranean"); eyebrows; war (four types: "just, unjust, civil," and "more than civil," when citizens and families fight); white hair; parsley; the seven terms and attributes of the soul; Augustine of Hippo (who "wrote so much that not only could no one, working by day and night, copy his books, but no one could even read them"); penance (which, when perfect, "is to weep for past sins and not allow future ones"); and "Saracens" (who live in a "very large deserted region," and were so named because they claim descent from Abraham's wife Sarah, and whom "Genesis teaches us" can also be called "Ishmaelites" from their ancestor Ishmael).[44]

Isidore worked on the *Etymologies* for more than twenty years, constantly fending off letters from friends asking when it would be done. (Although around 620, he did send a draft with a dedication to Sisebut, the Visigothic king in Toledo, who had asked for a copy.)[45] As he was trying to cast an all-encompassing net over past wisdom, giving coherence to what seemed overwhelmingly disparate, it was a vision without end. Isidore was no prophet in the *Etymologies*, even if, beneath the confident erudition, he was motivated by a sense of urgency about the inevitable fragility of the world, especially in Spain, and so a future where, if knowledge was forgotten, then so would be God.

Seven decades after Isidore died, Christian Spain was conquered by Saracens. Muslim Arab and Berber warriors (no more than seven thousand) under the command of Tariq ibn Ziyad, governor of Tangier for the Umayyad caliph al-Walid, crossed the narrow straits of Gibraltar into southern Spain in the spring of 711. The Visigothic king, Witiza, had died a year earlier, and while an aristocrat named Roderick was elected the new monarch, some nobles (including the late king's sons) immediately fomented rebellion. This was entirely predictable. Despite seventeen great councils in Toledo between 589 and 694, at which kings, nobles, and bishops issued laws with all the "Roman" grandiosity of Theodosius II or Justinian, so that no aspect of living in a Christian realm was seemingly untouched, from the proper way of singing psalms to increasingly shrill prohibitions on Jews, internecine violence was always one royal death or aristocratic feud away. Legal pomp and circumstance merely cloaked raw volatility.

Tariq was perhaps encouraged by the Visigothic rebels to intervene as a distraction (later Arabic sources suggested that Witiza's sons invited him); more likely, he saw an opportunity in the rumbling Spanish chaos. By the end of summer he defeated and killed Roderick in battle near the city of Sidon (renamed Medina-Sidon) on the far southern Atlantic coast of the Iberian peninsula. In less than five years, after two more Umayyad armies invaded, the Visigothic kingdom was erased. All of Spain, apart from some isolated valleys in the Pyrenees, especially the western hilly country of the Basques, now belonged to followers of the Prophet Muhammad and was known in Arabic as al-Andalus.[46]

Far away in Northumbria, Bede, around 717 or 718, read prophecy in "He will be a wild man, his hand will be against all men, and all men's hands against him" from Genesis (16:12), linking it to what he had heard of the heretical Saracens.

> *This means that Ishmael's seed was to dwell in the desert, and without fixed habita-*
> *tions. These are the nomadic Saracens who raid all the peoples on the edge of the desert,*
> *and who are attacked by all.* But this was long ago. Now, however, his *hand* is
> *against all men, and all men's hands* are *against him,* to such an extent that the
> Saracens hold the whole breadth of Africa in their sway, and they also hold
> the greatest part of Asia and some part of Europe, hateful and hostile to all.[47]

7 Barontus in Paradise

"Glory to you, God! Glory to you, God! Glory to you, God!" abruptly yelled the Frankish monk Barontus at cockcrow on Friday, March 25, 679, after lying half dead for a day and a night in the monastery of Saint Peter the Apostle in Longoretum (now Saint-Cyran, west of Bourges). The monks who had been singing psalms over his body stopped in shock.

A bright-eyed Barontus sat up and told them a terrifying and marvelous story. "When last you saw me return to my cell after I had sung Christ's praises with you at Matins [between 2:30 and 3:00 a.m.], I at once fell heavily asleep." Immediately two hideous demons strangled him, "trying to swallow me down and so carry me off to hell." They attacked Barontus for seven hours until the archangel Raphael, "shining in splendor of light," flew down from heaven and ordered them to stop. "If God's glory does not take him from us, you cannot do so," scoffed the demons. "If this is as you say," replied Raphael, "let us go together before God's judgment throne," where the demons' claim would be heard. "I'm taking this soul," he finally said at sunset. The demons howled they would never let go. The archangel placed a finger on Barontus' throat. "At once I felt my soul plucked out of my body." It was surprisingly little, "as small as a hen's chick when it comes out of the egg." Tiny as it was, "it took with it my head, eyes and the rest, sight, hearing, taste, smell and touch." As the bantam Barontus was lifted up by Raphael, one demon hung on tight, while the other kicked his buttocks, furiously flapping its wings, screaming, "I have already had you in my power once and done you great harm. Now you will be tormented in hell forever."[48]

All four of them, Barontus, Raphael, and the demons, floated above the woods, marshes, and ponds surrounding the monastery. "Go away, go away, you cruel beasts," cried Raphael, "you can no longer hurt this little soul." The demons grabbed Barontus even tighter and, as a reminder that his soul still felt physical pain, punched his ribs. In the "twinkling of an eye" this unearthly gaggle flew twelve miles, briefly hovering over the monastery of Méobecq, which, unfortunately, was long enough for four more demons to swoop in, gnashing and clawing Barontus. Raphael, curiously incompetent in battle, only triumphed when two sweet-smelling angels in white darted out of the night sky and, swinging from his feet like acrobats, sang a psalm that promptly sent the new demons crashing to the ground. The first two demons were impervious to the song and, now shadowed by the angels, continued gripping and punching Barontus on the flight to heaven.[49]

This aerial caravan, after passing by the doorway to hell (close enough to see the guards), swiftly winged its way through the first three gates of paradise. Barontus spoke with five monks from his monastery who happened to be milling around the first gate waiting for the Day of Judgment; they were appalled to hear that one of their brethren was in the clutches of demons. "I do not deny that all I suffer is due to my sins," he said shamefacedly. "A soul is going to judgment!" squealed a vast throng of white-clothed children and virgins at the second gate. "Conquer, thou warrior Christ, conquer," they giddily cried, "and let not the devil take him down to hell." Inside the third gate, a translucent portal seemingly made of glass, was a great city of countless gold mansions inhabited by enthroned saints. Other palaces were being constructed for future tenants, one of whom Barontus discovered would be his abbot back on earth, a charming if sickly man, whose reward of eternal joy was on account of his excellent land management, education of noble boys, care of pilgrims, and fear of God. "Conquer, O strong warrior Christ, who has redeemed us by shedding Thy blood" echoed throughout the mansions and palaces as Barontus approached the fourth gate of paradise. "Let not the devil take this soul down to hell."[50]

"Why, brother Raphael, have you sent for me?" asked Saint Peter at the fourth gate. "The demons accuse one of your little monks and are not willing to let go of him," replied the archangel. "What crime do you have against this monk?" Peter politely asked the demons. "Big sins," they said. "Recount them!" "He had three wives, which was not permitted. He also committed other adulteries and many other sins which we convinced him to do." (Barontus sighed in his narration to the monks around his bed, "And the demons went over in detail all the sins I had committed from infancy onwards, including those which I had totally forgotten.")

"Is this true, brother?" Peter asked. "Yes, Lord," said Barontus. The apostle then calmly explained to the demons that even if the little monk had done some bad things in the past, he had since given alms, confessed his sins to priests, undertaken penance, bestowed his hair (by tonsure) to the monastery, and given up all his possessions in the service of Christ. "These good deeds outweigh all the evil actions you recount. You cannot take him from me now." "Unless God's glory takes him from us, you cannot do so," they resisted. "Begone, evil spirits, begone, enemies of God," Peter angrily commanded, "let him go!" The two demons defiantly refused. In farcical frustration, the apostle lashed out with one of the three keys in his hand, trying to whack the demons on their heads. They dodged the key and, spreading their black wings, turned to flee back through the heavenly gates, except Peter roared, "You have no permission, you foul spirits, to go that way!" The crestfallen demons soared high above the fourth gate, disappearing into the celestial air.[51]

"Ransom yourself, brother!" Peter sternly told Barontus. "O good shepherd, what can I give? I have nothing here at hand." The apostle testily pointed out that as he had wrongfully hidden twelve gold solidi when he became a monk, he had enough to give a poor man one solidus every month for a year. Barontus accepted this penance. "Lord, if he gives all this, are his sins forgiven him?" asked a saintly old man who appeared as if out of nowhere. "If he gives what I told him to give, his evil deeds are forgiven him at once," answered Peter.

And with that penitential resolution (and convenient exposition), it was time to leave heaven. Raphael having already flown away, two beautiful boys in white stoles escorted Barontus to his monastic brethren at the first gate, where one of them was to take him to his body, "to my transitory fatherland, to my own place of pilgrimage." Framnoaldus, who had died as a boy and was buried near the monastery church, agreed to guide the little soul.

Peter, though, was not quite done with the little soul, stipulating that on the journey to earth he must view the torments of hell.[52] "As we were traveling between paradise and hell," recalled Barontus, he saw Abraham, "an old man of most beautiful appearance, with a long beard," on a throne overseeing this transitional space. When he and Framnoaldus reached the gate of hell, it was shrouded in thick dirty fog and great plumes of steam. "But I will expound what God allowed me to see through the guard posts watched over by demons." What was revealed to him were infinite hordes of men and women, bound and fettered, moaning and lamenting, swarming as a mass of misery, "like bees returning to their hives." Elsewhere, demons herded kindred souls "entangled in sins" into circles where, sitting on hot lead chairs, "the proud were grouped with the proud, the lascivious with their peers, perjurers and their like, homicides with other murderers."

Barontus was not surprised to see a lot of clerics in hell, especially those who had "defiled themselves with women." He even saw the late bishops of Bourges and Poitiers, well-known sinners, with the former dressed in grubby beggarly rags. Miraculously, every midday in hell white-robed beings who looked like deacons held dew-like manna from heaven in front of the mouths and noses of all sinners who had done some good in the world, refreshing them. All the other sinners watched in envy, calling out, "Woe to us wretches, who did nothing good when we could have!"[53]

Framnoaldus and Barontus floated back down to the monastery of Saint Peter the Apostle in Longoretum. The boy went to his tomb and was upset to see it filthy with soil and leaves. "Here, brother, is where my body lies!" After Barontus promised to keep the grave clean, his ability to fly was taken away. He fell to the ground in a heap. "I began to drag myself along the ground and hasten back to my body." His chick-sized soul was actually as light as a feather, just not to him. A God-sent gust of wind wafted Barontus in the "twinkling of an eye" into the mouth of his comatose body, and he awakened, exclaiming, "Glory to you, God! Glory to you, God! Glory to you, God!"[54]

Barontus' trip to heaven and hell was recorded in a short book by an anonymous monk, or perhaps even by himself, soon after it happened. "I, who have dared to write down these things, have done so not by hearsay but according to what I myself have experienced up to now."[55] He wrote nothing but the truth, even if he worried that his Latin suffered from *rusticitas*. Despite such clichéd modesty, his Latin was genuinely plain and awkward, rather than the accomplished "rustic" experimentation of Gregory of Tours a century earlier. For all its stylistic simplicity, though, his narrative was a revolutionary visionary achievement. The fantastic flight of Barontus' little soul signals, or rather confirms, a decisive and distinctive shift during the middle decades of the seventh century in the medieval West.

Barontus was no saint, as he was the first to admit, but his soul still ascended into heaven while his body remained on earth. An Irish monk named Fursey had a similar near-death vision three decades earlier, except his journey into a blazing valley of fire confirmed his saintliness. (Bede recalled an old brother of his monastery who knew a man who once met Fursey on a bitter wintry day in East Anglia. The Irishman, though thinly dressed, "was sweating profusely as though it was summer," haunted by memories of demons and flames.)[56] Although Barontus only visited paradise for a night, his otherworldly tourism revealed that such excursions could now happen unexpectedly to any living human. The distance between heaven and earth still existed, but it could be crossed over before death. It was still the monasticized universe of Caesarius of Arles, with a God so distant that Barontus never even met Him, but it was now explicitly humanized, and far from being close-fitting and hermetic, it was vast and infinite. This seeming paradox of a cosmos at once intimately human and majestically limitless was exemplified in the penitential salvation of Barontus.

As Saint Peter told the ancient bit player unexpectedly appearing stage left inside the fourth gate of paradise, if Barontus did his rather undemanding penance with the twelve solidi, then all his sins would be forgiven. Of course, this was the penitential medicine that Columbanus and his monks had introduced into Francia four generations earlier, and the monastery at Longoretum was a Columbanian foundation, so penance and confession were part of its *Rule*. Yet in the vision of Barontus, such penitential medicine was now the framework within which all humans, inside and outside the monastery, in heaven and on earth, were to understand themselves as persons awaiting the judgment of God. An individual life was a collection of public and private (or at least unseen) sins going back to childhood, as Barontus discovered to his dismay, but all of them could be erased with the right public penance. All lives were full of gaps where sinful actions and thoughts had been deleted. The last thing an individual wanted was an uninterrupted biographical narrative, where evil was interwoven with virtue, where the recollection of wrongdoing never disappeared. A good life was a sequence of jump cuts, abrupt transitions from one penitential act to another. It was a sense of the self in which all traces and memories of sinfulness were to be eliminated in preparation for death. The perfect soul in heaven, while unquestionably human, was surprisingly bland.

Jonas of Bobbio in his *Life* of Columbanus even has a story about a young nun named Gibitrudis from the monastery of Faremoutiers (east of Paris near Meaux, on the edge of the Marne valley) who, having died from a fever, had her soul carried by angels into the sky before the "tribunal of the Eternal Judge." Once there, though, a voice from the throne said, "Go back, for you have not completely left the world behind." In death Gibitrudis still remembered insults from three other nuns because, when alive, she had not forgiven them. She still possessed a "feeling of resentment," a wound only healed by the penitential "remedy of forgiveness." Back in her body and alive again, "she recounted with sad cries the sentence that had been passed, confesses her crime, calls her companions against whom she had borne hostile feelings, and asks their pardon lest, due to this silent deceit, she might incur the loss of eternal life." Six months later, gripped by another fever, Gibitrudis, having erased the bitter memory of nunnish backbiting, "achieved a happy death."[57]

Barontus was probably around forty, perhaps a bit older, and had only just become a monk when he was whisked off to heaven and hell. Yet for most of his adult life as a Merovingian noble, despite the three wives and miscellaneous mistresses, he would have emulated the ritual decorum of monks (if not the tonsure or celibacy). The upper-class violence of the Merovingian nobility still existed, although seemingly much less than a century earlier, but this noble ferocity was powerfully tempered by a new aristocratic ethos modeled on the Columbanian monastery. By adopting a penitential way of viewing oneself and others, Frankish noble men and women consciously monasticized their day-to-day existence in a received code of behavior. They were a serious and ceremonious lot, addressing each other as *peccator*, "fellow sinner."[58] By imitating the community of monks and nuns in their own lives, they brought a touch of paradise into every social interaction. They wished, more than anything, for the virtuous sexless blandness of a soul in heaven. What Barontus and so many men and women like him dreamed of achieving on earth were happy lives ending in happy deaths.

Not surprisingly, if the Frankish kingdom was imagined as a great monastery by its aristocracy, much of its land was given away by noble men and women as gifts to monasteries. When Gregory of Tours died in 594 there were around 220 monasteries in Francia, whereas by the beginning of the eighth century there were around 550, with at least 230 established in the central and northern regions like Longoretum (whose ailing abbot was promised a heavenly palace in part because of his proprietorial skills). Perhaps as much as 30 percent of the kingdom belonged to monasteries.[59] This is an extraordinary transformation of the post-Roman landscape, replicated in varying degrees throughout the early medieval West.

It was during the 670s, when Barontus flew to heaven, that the Merovingian kings became, if not quite irrelevant, then certainly spectral figures within their kingdom. They still possessed symbolic authority, conferring legitimacy on the actions of the noble families now largely ignoring them, like authorizing the monastic bequests eating away at their realm.

They were definitely not the abbots of their monasticized kingdoms. They were, if anything, rather like the distant God Barontus never met, but from whom all judgments by celestial and demonic beings derived legality. In such a universe, the words and deeds of Saint Peter were pragmatically the most important. In Francia, the Petrine equivalent were the *maiores domus*, "mayors of the palace," powerful aristocrats who, while never overthrowing the Merovingian monarchy, were strongmen acting in the royal name—coercing, threatening, and dominating all other nobles and so the kingdom by the end of the eighth century. After 687 Pippin of Herstal (whose family came from the Ardennes) was the unchallenged *maior* of the kingdom of Austrasia, and after 714 it was his son Charles Martel, that is, Charles "the Hammer."[60]

It would be too much to say that Barontus' specific vision of paradise was now the common view amongst all Christians in the West, as such otherworldly uniformity was impossible in the patchwork of "micro-Christendoms" developing between the Mediterranean and the North Sea.[61] Yet, however vaguely articulated here and there, an assumption that ordinary humans journeyed to heaven and hell was widespread—or, at least for Barontus, that only noble Christians might embark on these flights. He certainly thought that nobility and Christianity went hand in hand, and by implication that anyone not a noble would always be less than Christian. Even if the penitential culture shaping Barontus' life was resolutely aristocratic, such a culture of redemptive finesse and precision was easily and inevitably extrapolated onto the infinite variety of human existence, from a tiny village to a great wooden hall.

8 Theodore's Penitential

In 668 a Syrian monk named Theodore was living in Rome when, un-expectedly, Pope Vitalian sent him off to "Great Britain" as archbishop of Canterbury. He was sixty-six and one of the many East Roman refugees scattered throughout the western Mediterranean fleeing the "nomads of Muhammad." He was born in Tarsus, on the eastern coast of what is now Turkey, and as a youth had witnessed the Persian armies sweep into Palestine. In Rome he busied himself like other East Roman émigrés, showing off his Greek, being unusually literal in his reading of the Bible (none of those

allegorical parlor games of Gregory the Great for him), and flinging theological insults against the imperial fools in Ravenna and Constantinople.

Three decades earlier, Heraclius, soon after Syria was overrun by the
Believers, and by way of rallying Monophysite Christians under occupation, proclaimed that Christ had a unified "single will" (*monos*, "single"
and *theléma*, "will") transcending His human and divine natures. This
"Monothelite" compromise was relatively popular in northern Syria,
Palestine, and Anatolia, but not with the exiles in Carthage or Rome. When
the emperor Constans began an Italian campaign against the Lombards in
662—hoping to build a western bulwark from which to reclaim Syria and
Egypt—Vitalian decided to send troublemakers like Theodore as far away
as possible.[62]

On Sunday, May 27, 689, Theodore arrived in Canterbury after traveling via Arles and Paris. He was accompanied by Hadrian, an East Roman
from North Africa and formerly an abbot in Campania. "Theodore was the
first archbishop whom the entire Church of the English obeyed," wrote
Bede rather grandly, stressing how the Syrian traveled throughout Britain
teaching the "Christian way of life" and, even more importantly, the correct "Roman" method of keeping Easter, which was a serious and lingering
issue in the north.

In 664, the king of Northumbria, Oswy, had summoned a council at
his royal monastery (for both men and women) of Streanaeshalch, more
commonly known as Whitby, to establish the proper dating of the death
and resurrection of Christ. What he really wanted to do was redraw the
lines of sacred authority across his kingdom, all but erasing the prestige of
the Columban warrior Christianity emanating from Iona across northern
Britain and the Irish abbots his Northumbrian nobility were often more
willing to obey than him.

A Roman Christianity like that in Kent was the solution. The difference
between Ionan and Roman Easter—the former overlapped with Jewish
Passover, the latter did not—was profound in a society where such festivals, and this holiday in particular, defined the whole ritual cycle for the
year. Roman Easter, like Mediterranean glass, was also an exotic luxury
good, a magnificent gift from across the sea given by Oswy to his followers.
Only "stupid" Picts, Britons, and Irishmen on "two uttermost islands of the
ocean" would not want such largesse. Equally, the monks of Iona were pa-
rochially tonsured, shaving and hacking their hair at the front, disfiguring

what should have been the long tresses of Irish or English warriors. The Council of Streanaeshalch sorted this out too. From now on, only the Roman "tonsure of Peter" with a "crown" on the very top of the head was allowed in Northumbria. Theodore was so "crowned" when he arrived in Canterbury—after first growing out the buzz cut of a Syrian monk.[63]

As Theodore and Hadrian were learned in Greek and Latin, sacred and secular texts, "they attracted a large number of students, into whose minds they poured the waters of wholesome knowledge day by day." Bede still knew some former students, now old men, "as proficient in Latin and Greek as in their native tongue." In ramshackle Canterbury Theodore described the almost unimaginable wonders of Antioch and Constantinople, as the English, while not quite living in a "world of wood," rarely built with stone, and then only with Frankish masons. As one English poet sang of the mighty Roman ruins throughout Britain, they must have been "the work of the Giants."[64]

Theodore frequently explained the customs of Greek Christians in the shattered East Roman empire. He obviously discussed the Saracens or Ishmaelites—they were, after all, what caused the series of events that led him to Canterbury—and yet none of his English students had any lasting impression about what the archbishop thought of these nomads from the desert, especially their beliefs. Bede, such an assiduous collector of memories and religious anecdotes, would have written something down if he had heard anything unusual in what anyone remembered the old Syrian saying about the Saracens. There was only one reference to the nomads in the *Ecclesiastical History*, when a "swarm of Saracens ravaged Gaul with horrible slaughter" as two comets soared across the sun in 729, and, as was prophesied in Genesis, these new Ishmaelites were heretics, which, while appalling, was neither strange nor exceptional.[65]

Irish and English "medicines of penance," though, were exceptional religious innovations for a Greek-speaking East Roman like Theodore. Fortunately, he adapted surprisingly well. Although perhaps never quite approving of this way of cleansing the soul, he was a willing sounding board, discussing and adjudicating an array of questions about penances asked by local priests, monks, and laypeople as he traveled throughout Britain. An anonymous Northumbrian monk collected many of the opinions of Theodore on penitential remedies in a small guide for "physicians of the soul." Many of these remedies were responses to questions asked by a priest named Eoda, some were answers to the crowds of men and women constantly asking for advice about their sins, and quite a few the archbishop just recycled from an Irish penitential book when he was stumped. The anonymous collator probably composed his little book after Theodore died in 690, as he was particularly worried that these laws would, "on account of the age or negligence of copyists, be perpetuated in a confused and corrupted state, as is usual." Yet at the same time he knew these laws were not, and should not be, rigid and unchanging. The anonymous Northumbrian monk concluded by accepting and even recommending that, where necessary, his list of penances should be amended or even suppressed as circumstances, customs, and disagreements about what was acceptable changed over the years.[66]

The penitential remedies of Theodore were, in a sense, already out of date when written down, almost all of them being one-off answers to very specific questions from specific English communities, sometimes a monastery, sometimes a hamlet. More often there was only the duration of the penance, leaving the actual "medicine" up to the "physician." Many of the queries were about sex, either what a man, woman, or child had done or would do or what other people were imagined as having done or would do. Penances were listed for "fornication" between men and men (four years for a first time, ten years for more than that), men and animals (ten years, and the animal killed), men and boys (two years for a boy's first time, four years for repeats), women and women (three years), between son and mother (fifteen years, or seven years with "perpetual pilgrimage"), brother and sister (fifteen years), brother and brother (fifteen years without meat), and boys and boys (just a flogging).

Related to these sins were penances regarding pollution by blood and semen. Ejaculating in the mouth of a man or woman was "the worst of evils," with "penance to the end of life" or twelve years. The penance for male masturbation was forty days, though if a priest masturbated, it was three weeks; female masturbation carried a penance of three years. Drinking blood or semen demanded a penance of three years; however, it was not a sin to unknowingly ingest blood in saliva, although it was if a wife tasted her husband's blood as a cure for illness, in which case the penance was forty days fasting. And menstruating women could not enter churches.[67]

When Theodore was not being asked about sex and bodily fluids, his answers ranged widely, often having nothing to do with penance, as his questioners just worried about getting the details of living as Christians right. Wood for a church could only be used for a church. Men could marry again if enemies kidnapped their wives. Only God judges a suicide caused by despair or fear. Beware of the Arian heresy. Fathers could sell sons into slavery up to age seven. If a mouse fell into a liquid and lived, the drink could still be drunk after a sprinkle of holy water; if the mouse drowned, the liquid should be thrown away. Greek monks did not have slaves, whereas Latin monks did. A fetus was not alive before forty days in the womb, although abortion was still wrong. A girl's body was her property after seventeen. Horsemeat could be eaten if necessary (still, really, follow the Irish and do not). And, as always in Northumbria, a tonsure was cut this way and Easter was on this date.[68]

This miniature exactitude was the hallmark of penitentials, and, like little slide rules of the holy, they allowed for the resolution of all spiritual abnormalities with no recriminations or lasting guilt (as we saw with Barontus in paradise). English law codes like Æthelbert's in Kent were influenced by penitentials in their style and content as much as by Roman legal precedents, if not more so. Some priests remembered and extemporized from long lists of penances in similar songful ways like law codes. Penitentials were pragmatic hymns about God's judgment and forgiveness.

All too often when studying the medieval world, what individuals believed below the level of nobles or other elites is difficult to fathom, and yet in Theodore's little book of "penitential remedies" we hear, however faintly, some of these voices.

9 Saint Patrick

The Irish monk Muirchú moccu Machtheni read the *Confession* of Patricius and the letter to Coroticus around 690. He then wrote a *Life* of the British holy man and, in an act of hagiographic legerdemain, transformed the nervy and idiosyncratic Roman struggling with being human and Christian into the resplendently brutal and "Christ-like" Saint Patrick.

The coming of this sacred prizefighter, "who was also called Sochet," and his miraculous religion "from afar across the seas" to Ireland is, according to Muirchú, prophesied in song by two pagan sorcerers. "So when these things happen, our kingdom, which is heathen, shall not stand," they sing to the Irish king at Tara. Soon enough, Patrick arrives during Easter (Roman dating) ready to drive an "invincible wedge" into the "head of all idolatry" (although Muirchú makes him first go on a *peregrinatio* through Francia and into the Alps, following in the footsteps of Columbanus). After a series of violent miracles by the saint, where one of the sorcerers, after being hurled in the air, is "smashed to pieces" on the ground, while the other burns alive in a magic act gone wrong, the king at Tara says, "It is better for me to believe than to die." A fierce and terrifying Patrick then preaches Christianity throughout Ireland.

Muirchú ended his life of Saint Patrick with one last miracle against the "cruel tyrant" Coroticus, who, after hearing a singer foretell his downfall, suddenly turns into a fox, "and from that day and that hour, like a passing stream of water, he was never seen anywhere again."[69]

10 Sing Me a Song

Caedmon hated singing. When he feasted in his lord's hall and it was decided (as it always was after enough drink) that everyone should sing a song, he would get up from the table and go home before the harp reached him. One night, as usual, he left the festivities before it was his turn to sing, going into the nearby stables to look after the cattle. He soon fell asleep and dreamed of a mysterious man talking to him. "Caedmon," said this man, "sing me a song." "I don't know how to sing," replied the dreamer. "It is because I don't know how to sing that I left the feast and came here." "But you shall sing to me," commanded the man. "What should I sing about?" "Sing about the creation of all things." Caedmon in his dream instantly sang this song in a Northumbrian dialect of English:

> Praise now to the keeper of the kingdom of heaven
> the power of the Creator, the profound mind
> of the glorious Father, who fashioned the beginning
> of very wonder, the eternal Lord.
> For the children of men He made first
> heaven as a roof, the holy Creator.
> The Lord of mankind, the everlasting Shepherd,
> ordained in the midst as a dwelling place,
> Almighty Lord, the earth for men.

When Caedmon woke up he remembered his dream song; even more as-tonishingly, he discovered he could now sing songs of his own composition while awake.[70]

Caedmon was in his fifties and, having only ever known husbandry as a tenant farmer, his new poetic skill was obviously "a free gift from God." His reeve (farm supervisor) allowed him to become a monk at Streanaeshalch. When other monks and nuns told him stories from the Bible or explained Christian doctrine, within a few hours he had reconfigured what he heard into moving and wondrous songs. "So Caedmon stored up in his memory all that he learned, and like one of the clean animals chewing the cud, turned it into melodious verse that his delightful renderings turned his instructors into auditors." He composed more than a hundred songs and hymns (on Genesis, the Crucifixion, the terrors of the Last Judgment, the horrors of hell and the joys of heaven) in the decade or so before he died around 700. He even devised practical songs of God's judgments and pen-ances. He never sang whimsical or bawdy songs, as his gift muzzled him from doing so. None of Caedmon's poems survive, apart from the verses dreamed in the stable.[71]

An anonymous poem from these years, known as "Dream of the Rood," gives a sense of what was so admired about Caedmon's vernacular religious art. "Listen!" begins the song. "A dream came to me at deep midnight," and in that vision the singer sees "the Tree itself," that is, the Rood or Cross of the Crucifixion. It is sheathed in "overlapping gold, glancing gems fair at its foot, and five stones set in a crux flashed from the crosstree." All these shining stones and yellow metal were like a warrior's "mail-coat." Yet the golden armor does not hide the Rood's terrible wound, as "it bled from the right side," all "slicked in sweat, spangled with spilling blood." As the dreamer stares in sorrow, the Tree breaks the silence, talking and reminis-cing, until at one point it recalls the Crucifixion:

> They drove me through with dark nails
>   on me are the deep wounds manifest,
> wide-mouthed hate-dents.
>   I durst not harm any of them.
> How they mocked at us both!
>   I was all moist with blood
> sprung from the Man's side
>   after He sent forth His soul.

In this extraordinary poem the great hero of the Crucifixion was not Christ but the cross of wood. "On me the Son of God spent a time suffering," says the Rood, and from that burden "I have the power to save every man who fears me." The Tree was martyred, buried by enemies, and then, like the body of a saint or a "fabled warrior," unearthed and adorned in silver and gold. The Rood's confessional song within the larger framework of the dreamer's song is an anthropomorphic and hagiographic wonder, a rare and vividly imagined poetic autobiography in which the Rood has more humanity than the Son. As He ascends into the kingdom of Heaven surrounded by angels, the Rood remains on earth with the Crucifixion (hate-dents and blood) seared into its memory and the very fiber of its being. Like any human sinner, the Rood says of itself, "Formerly, I was the worst of punishments, the most hateful to the peoples," before following and so becoming "the right way to life."

The Cross was a sign that all sins were forgivable. It was a symbol of penance. By around 700 much of the Rood's speech was carved in runes on an impressively "Roman" stone cross erected in Ruthwell (in Dumfriesshire, Scotland). "But every soul on earth who intends to dwell with the Lord," the Rood says, majestically ending its *confessio* within the poem, "shall come to the kingdom through the Rood."[72]

Caedmon lived in a northern world where so much was remembered, communicated, and understood by song. Poetry was a sacred gift, and while not all singers were endowed with insight and beauty, the rare few were, like Muhammad in the Arabian peninsula, prophets, messengers, and visionaries of God.

11 No One Is Wiser than He Needs to Be

Bede was fifty-nine when he finished his *Ecclesiastical History* in 731. It was a narrative of how those Rhenish and Scandinavian boat people colonizing eastern Britain in the fifth century had, "258 years after coming," become not only Christian but also a holy *gens Anglorum*, "nation of the English." This was not an ethnic or racial category—Britain was not the Promised Land and the English were not new Israelites.[73] Rather, it was a redemptive classification encompassing more than just the descendants of those post-Roman squatters; it included any inhabitant of Britain adopting Roman

Christianity and, crucially, the proper dating of Easter. British or Irish Christians were equally "English" as long they celebrated the Crucifixion correctly.

According to Bede, those early proto-English settlers arriving as the Roman armies departed were the divine catalyst setting in motion a cycle of sinfulness and penance in which almost all pagan and Christian errors were erased from the British Isles. He had written a penitential history in which the English were judged and then cleansed of their sins by God. Every story and anecdote, whether about a king like Æthelbert of Kent or a farmer like Caedmon, was a lesson in how individuals, by acknowledging past sins, no matter how petty or horrible, expunged such errors as penitent Christians. The vividness of Bede's anecdotes and his obvious amusement and delight at what he sometimes wrote are not diminished by how many of them end with the necessary blandness of penitential redemption. Perhaps, though, the long-term consequences of this virtuous monotony did worry him. For at the very end of the *Ecclesiastical History*, after applauding how many Northumbrians, "noble and simple," had given up weapons and warfare, so that they and their children could be tonsured as monks, Bede wryly concluded, "What the result of this will be, a later generation will discover."[74]

Bede was pleased with what he had accomplished in the *Ecclesiastical History*, adding a precious autobiographical endnote conveying his joy. "I was born on the lands of this monastery," he wrote—that is, at Wearmouth and Jarrow in Northumbria—"and on reaching seven years of age" was entrusted by his family to the abbot to be educated. "I have spent all the remainder of my life in this monastery and devoted myself entirely to the study of the scriptures." He had always done what was required of a monk; nevertheless, "my chief pleasure has always been in study, teaching, and writing." Bede then listed more than thirty books and compilations that he had written or edited. These books were who he was and what he wished to be remembered by. It was autobiography as bibliography. Bede felt there was no need to say any more about himself.[75]

Books were marvelous artifacts. More than just demonstrations of knowledge, they were monuments involving the labor of hundreds. A total of 1,545 animal skins of good quality (no wounds or scars) were used in making three pandects (complete volumes) of the Bible at Wearmouth and Jarrow between 688 and 716.[76] (One of these pandects weighed seventy-seven pounds and was carried all the way to Rome as a gift for the tomb of Saint Peter.)[77] Perhaps around five hundred skins would make a copy of the *Ecclesiastical History*. Great flocks of sheep and herds of cattle grazed around monasteries as the raw material for books.

One did not need to know how to read to instantly see the immense coercive authority required in the making of a book. The scraping, preparing, and writing of a book on parchment required as much skill, expense, and effort as the construction of a stone church. For the Irish and the English in particular, there was a miraculous physical intimacy between holy men and books. Adomnán in his *Life* of Columba even once had the saint immediately know without even opening a newly copied psalter that every word on every leaf was perfect, "except a vowel *I*, which alone is missing."[78] Skillful editing was a sacred act. Bede never pretended to such stupendous holiness, but in identifying himself with his books, he was explicitly saying, like Gregory of Tours, whom he closely read, that he was a man of "splendid deeds of power."

Four years after finishing the *Ecclesiastical History*, Bede lay dying in his cell, feet swollen and lungs congested, and yet he was still dictating a book chapter to a worried student who thought it was too much effort for him. "It's easy," Bede said with a smile. "Take your pen and prepare it and write quickly." To be alive was knowing Latin and studying and writing, always writing. In his last days, though, Bede comforted himself (and calmed his students) by singing songs in his Northumbrian dialect. Another student and friend, Cuthbert, even transcribed one of these songs.

> Before that sudden journey
> no one is wiser in thought than he needs to be,
> In considering, before his departure,
> what will be adjudged to his soul, of good or evil
> after his death-day.[79]

12 A Penitential Culture

By the beginning of the eighth century a penitential culture now defined much of the early medieval West. This was a new understanding of what it meant to be human, to be Christian, and to be judged by God and His servants. Of course, there was great variation in how this culture was realized in day-to-day existence between the Mediterranean and the North Sea, but within this patchwork of Christendoms there were distinctive similarities. It was now a very different world from the East Roman and the Islamic worlds. At the end of the sixth century this had not so clearly been the case. Muhammad and Caesarius of Arles, for example, looked at the universe in ways that were much more similar to each other than to those of Barontus and Bede. Despite the British Isles and the Arabian peninsula being equally crisscrossed by songlines, whatever resemblances these regions seemingly possessed, especially in their understanding of the holy, had disappeared by 700. Finally, unlike persons in Constantinople or Damascus, when men, women, and children looked up at the night sky over Tours or Canterbury, they knew that other humans were flying over them on marvelous and frightening journeys to heaven or hell.

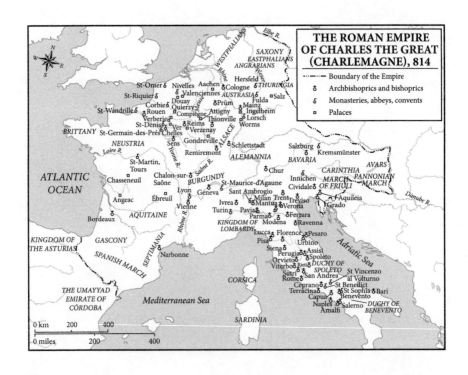

**THE ROMAN EMPIRE
OF CHARLES THE GREAT
(CHARLEMAGNE), 814**

- - - - - Boundary of the Empire

☦ Archbishoprics and bishoprics

☦ Monasteries, abbeys, convents

◻ Palaces

Elbe R.

WESTPHALIANS

SAXONY
EASTPHALIANS
ANGRARIANS

Hersfeld
THURINGIA

St-Omer Nivelles Aachen Cologne
St-Riquier Valenciennes *AUSTRASIA* Salz
Douay Prüm Fulda
Corbie Quierzy Mainz
St-Wandrille Rouen Compiègne Attigny Ingelheim
Verberie Thionville Lorsch
St-Denis Reims Worms
BRITTANY St-Germain-des-Prés Chelles Ver Verzenay
Loire R. *NEUSTRIA* Sens Gondreville *ALSACE*
Remiremont Schlettstadt Salzburg Kremsmünster
St-Martin, *ALEMANNIA* *BAVARIA*
Tours Chur *AVARS*
ATLANTIC Chalon-sur- *CARINTHIA* *PANNONIAN*
OCEAN Chasseneuil Saône *BURGUNDY* St-Maurice-d'Agaune Innichen *MARCH* *MARCH*
Angeac Ébreuil Lyon Geneva Sant Ambrogio Cividale *OF FRIULI*
AQUITAINE Vienne Milan Trent Treviso Aquileia *Danube R.*
Bordeaux Ivrea Mantua Verona Grado
Turin Pavia Ferrara
KINGDOM OF Parma Modena Ravenna
KINGDOM OF *GASCONY* *LOMBARDY* Lucca Florence Pesaro
THE ASTURIAS Pisa Urbino *Adriatic Sea*
SPANISH MARCH Siena Assisi
Narbonne Perugia Spoleto
Viterbo Rieti *DUCHY OF*
CORSICA Orvieto *SPOLETO* St Vincenzo
Sutri San Andrea al Volturno
THE UMAYYAD Rome Ceprano St Benedict
EMIRATE OF *Mediterranean Sea* Terracina St Sophia Bari
CÓRDOBA Capua Benevento
Naples Salerno *DUCHY OF*
Amalfi *BENEVENTO*

SARDINIA

0 km 200 400

0 miles 200 400

V

An Everlasting Star

722–824

1 A Restless Battler

On Tuesday, June 22, 778, Huneberc, a young English nun in the monastery of Heidenheim (north of the Danube in Bavaria), transcribed what her kinsman Willibald, a monk and bishop in his late seventies, told her about the extraordinary travels of his youth in the eastern Mediterranean. The day was hot (it was just before the summer solstice) and she took copious notes. Soon afterward, she started writing a *Life* of her esteemed relative—"I have flowered from the same root . . . albeit from the lowest stalks of its branches"—which she called a *hodoeporicon*, "relation of a voyage." When Huneberc was finished, she observed that what she had written on parchment was, in a florid metaphor that obviously amused her, "black tracks plowed by a pen in a furrowed path on the white plains of these fields."[1]

Huneberc began by waxing about what "a loveable little creature" Willibald had been as a baby, greatly loved by his noble parents, until at the age of three "he was suddenly attacked by a severe illness," leading him to the "doors of death." The parents, "in great anxiety of mind," placed the barely breathing child at the foot of a great stone cross—like the one in Ruthwell with "Dream of the Rood" carved on it—on their lands in the kingdom of Wessex in southwest Britain. (Huneberc helpfully informed her Frankish readers that, more so than churches, English noble families throughout Britain erected such grand eye-catching crosses for their daily prayers.) Willibald's parents promised God that if their child lived they would tonsure him and place him "under the discipline of monastic life."

The boy survived and, two years later, he became a novice at Waltham monastery near the river Hamble (in Hampshire). After fifteen or so years of "obedience and meekness," assiduous study, and reflection day and night about what made a perfect monk, and having survived the "disturbing period of adolescence," Willibald resolved that he must journey to lands unknown to him on a long *peregrinatio*. Pilgrimage was the only way in which perfection was truly achieved for a monk, the only way in which the fleeting pleasures of this world were truly despised and renounced, particularly "homeland, parents, and relatives."[2]

As soon as Willibald decided to "brave the perils of the pathless sea he went immediately to his father and opened his heart to him." The monastery at Waltham, being neither Benedictine nor Columbanian, possessed a decidedly flexible *Rule*, allowing monks to visit their families whenever they liked (especially if those families were powerful enough to build monumental crosses on their estates). Willibald begged his father for permission to travel to the shrine of Saint Peter in Rome; once that was given, he begged him to come along too. "At first his father declined, excusing himself from the journey on the plea that he could not leave his wife and young children." It was "cruel and unchristian" to abandon them. Willibald would not listen to such excuses, berating his father, "now with fearful threats of damnation, now with bland promises of eternal life." His father soon succumbed, as did a younger unmarried brother named Wynnebald.

In late summer 722, father and sons sailed excitedly across the English Channel, landing in northern Francia. Their joyful exile as a family only lasted six weeks, as the father was dead by autumn, struck down by illness in the Italian city of Lucca. After burying him, the brothers continued on foot "through the vast land of Italy, through the deep valleys, over the craggy mountains, across the level plains, climbing upward toward the peaks of the Apennines." Eventually, they reached Rome, where, using the remaining funds their father had carried with him, they followed their own private "monastic discipline" as exiles. Wynnebald was not a monk and was not tonsured, but he lived for six months as if he was a "soldier of Christ" like his brother. Such shared holiness by the brothers ended just before Easter when, suddenly, "at one moment they were shivering with cold, the next burning with heat." They had the "black plague." The brothers survived, but whereas a sickly Wynnebald stayed in Rome, Willibald decided to go on the most austere, dangerous, and beautiful *peregrinatio* he could imagine—"to the city of Jerusalem and gaze upon its pleasant and hallowed walls."[3]

In 723, a few days after Easter Sunday, Willibald, "this restless battler," began his pilgrimage from Rome to Jerusalem, accompanied by two English monks, one of whom was named Tidbercht. They hopped, skipped, and jumped from one fortuitous ship to another, landing first in Naples, then Catania and Syracuse in Sicily, before crossing the Adriatic to Monembasia at the tip of the Peloponnese, until finally, after briefly sheltering on the Aegean island of Chios, stepping ashore at Ephesus on the East Roman Anatolian coast. This journey had taken them almost two months, whereas two centuries earlier it would have taken less than two weeks.

The Englishmen walked south away from Ephesus, reaching the small town of Phygela, where they begged for some bread, dipping what they were given in a fountain to soften it. After a "bitter and icy winter" huddled together starving, the emaciated trio hitched a boat ride to Miletus. There they discovered two men living on towering columns like Simeon Stylites (or Wulfolaic on the Moselle), except these columns were in the rushing waters of the Meander River (which, clogged with sediment and changing course over the centuries, had overwhelmed an ancient temple). Once more, despite being weak from hunger, they cadged a trip via Cyprus on their way to Tartus on the coast of Syria. It was Easter and a year since Willibald had left Rome, except now Huneberc counted seven companions, as five men had joined the English exiles since Tartus. Most likely these new individuals were a mix of indigent Syrian monks and some of the English and Irish holy flotsam drifting about the world on perpetual pilgrimage. The members of this ragtag fellowship were soon arrested as spies by the Umayyad authorities in Hims (formerly Emesa) and imprisoned.[4]

A wealthy and curious old Muslim man from Hims questioned Willibald and his companions in prison. They told him everything about their journey so far. "I have often seen men coming from those parts of the world, fellow countrymen of theirs," announced the old man, "they cause no mischief and are merely anxious to fulfill their law." The Umayyad governor in Hims, which was the capital of one of the four administrative districts of Syria, was not convinced, and the pilgrims remained imprisoned. A Christian (or possibly Muslim) merchant, though, stepped forward—a "wonderful dispensation of Almighty God"—offering to redeem Willibald and his friends. "But he was unable to release them." Nevertheless, he fed them twice a day, elegantly clothed them, had his son take them to a bathhouse twice a week, and on Sundays escorted them to the resplendent church in Hims, half of which was now a mosque.[5] (Huneberc noted that all the Himsis townspeople stared at Willibald and his friends every Sunday as they were so beautifully dressed, "young, and handsome.")

A Spanish Muslim now intervened on behalf of the imprisoned Englishmen, imploring the governor to release them. "These men come from the West where the sun sets," he said, "we know nothing of their country except that beyond it lies nothing but water." "Why should we punish them?" mused the governor, seemingly quickly convinced that the English monks were harmless. "Allow them to depart and go on their way." Willibald's Syrian companions, though, paid a fine (or had it paid for them), before being "let off scot-free."[6]

Willibald and his comrades wandered throughout Syria and Palestine for four years. The fellowship fluctuated—some pilgrims peeled off, and new travelers joined; only Tidbercht remained loyal to the end. Willibald visited Damascus (twice), Tiberias on the Sea of Galilee ("on which our Lord walked dry-shod and where Peter sank"), Caesarea, Gaza, Hebron, Bethlehem, Tripoli, Tyre (twice), Sidon, and dozens of other small villages and towns. He remembered seeing "wonderful herds of cattle, long in the back and short in the leg, bearing enormous horns," with deep dark ruddy coats, "plunging themselves up to their necks" in the river Jordan to escape the searing heat of summer. A lion, "growling and roaring," once scared Willibald half to death as he traveled through a vast grove of smoke-colored olive trees in the caravan of a friendly "Ethiopian," two camels, and a woman on a mule.

More than anything, the old Englishman told Huneberc about his four visits to Jerusalem. He especially recalled how in and around the city were a multitude of crosses, massive and small, wooden and stone, singular or in groups of three, out in the open (exposed or under canopies), in houses, or in churches. A mighty column in front of the city gate was crowned with a cross "as a sign and memorial of the place where the Jews attempted to take away the body of our Lady." Just outside the city in the valley of Josaphat were another two columns inside a roofless church, and if you squeezed between them, all your sins disappeared. Underneath the city fifteen golden lamps burned day and night in the tomb where Christ's body was placed after the Crucifixion.

In late November 727, Willibald and Tidbercht stopped rambling in the footsteps of the Lord and sailed from Tyre to Constantinople (with some contraband balsam hidden from Umayyad customs officials in a calabash); then, after two years (mostly hanging around the tomb of John Chrysostom in the Church of the Holy Apostles), they tagged along with papal and imperial envoys to Reggio Calabria.[7]

Southern Italian bishops did not quite know what to make of Willibald and Tidbercht, alarmed by the strange, glamorous, and now distinctly undisciplined holiness of the Englishmen after years of living amongst "pagan Saracens." They were wild and exotic gyrovagues, the worst kind of monk in Benedict's *Rule*. Eventually the bishop of Teano dispatched the two Englishmen to the monastery at Monte Cassino, hoping they might learn what it meant to be monks again. "So for ten years the venerable man Willibald tried to observe, as far as possible, every detail of the monastic observance as laid down by the *Rule* of Saint Benedict." In that decade the fame of the two young English monks who had traveled to the "ends of the earth" for seven years and survived the "wickedness of pagans" spread all the way to the Elbe River, where another English monk and archbishop, formerly named Wynfrith and now known as Boniface, was so impressed that he requested from the pope that his compatriots join him in converting "pagan Saxons." Willibald willingly agreed (once the pope released him from Benedict's *Rule*) even though he was now forty; Tidbercht declined, staying at Monte Cassino.[8]

After seven months of traveling, including a visit to his father's grave in Lucca, Willibald reached Eichstätt on the river Ailtmühl in late November 740. Boniface ordained him a priest. Astonishingly, earlier that year Boniface had also ordained Wynnebald as a priest in Thuringia; after the older brother departed for Jerusalem, the younger one, after convalescing in Rome, had returned to Britain and become a monk. Now, like Willibald, he too was part of the English exodus of monks and nuns colonizing and Christianizing the German lands on the ever expanding frontier of the Frankish realm.

The brothers finally greeted each other for the first time in eighteen years when the beech leaves turned red and gold in 741. "And they were glad to see each other," Huneberc understatedly observed, "and congratulated each other on their meeting." Soon after, Boniface consecrated Willibald as bishop of Eichstätt. "And so like a busy bee that flits through the meadows, purple with violets, aromatic with scented herbs and through tree branches yellow with blossom, drinking the sweet nectar but avoiding bitter poison, and returns to the hive bearing honey on its thighs and body," Huneberc wrote (discarding all understatement) of Willibald as bishop, "so the blessed man chose out the best from all that he had seen abroad with his own eyes," miraculously transforming Bavaria into a land "worthy of the Lord."[9]

Huneberc stressed that her *Life* of Willibald was based upon what she heard from "his own lips." "I say this so that no one may afterward say that it was an idle tale."[10] It was the story of a journey as wondrous as that undertaken by Barontus into heaven, and much less common. Apart from imperial ships and galleys sailing between southern Italy and Constantinople, regular shipping routes connecting the western Mediterranean to the east, while already erratic in the late sixth century, had disappeared by 700.[11] This dangerous uncertainty about even reaching Syria and Palestine was part of the appeal to Willibald, a danger enhanced by the conquest Muhammad's nomads had made four generations earlier. Yet he never discussed Muslims or Islam with Huneberc. Even when imprisoned by Umayyad officials he never mentioned their religion or beliefs. Huneberc inserted "pagan Saracens" as vague descriptors of persons who were not Christians or Jews in Willibald's memories of the Levant. Admittedly, there would have been comparatively few Muslims in Syria and Palestine in the early eighth century, apart from the *ashraf*, Arab elite soldiers and administrators. Nevertheless, it is striking that Willibald, for example, did not recall the Dome of the Rock, which, even if he did not understand what it signified, he clearly must have seen in Jerusalem.

Willibald's holy rambling in Syria and Palestine was guided (if that is the right word, as he never seemed to follow a straight path to anywhere) by what he had read about Christ, Mary, and the Apostles in the Gospels. He prayed at Bethlehem; he bathed in the Jordan where Jesus was baptized (holding a rope stretched across the river); he climbed Golgotha; "he trod with his own feet" wherever the Lord had once walked.[12] Huneberc's *Life* of Willibald often reads like a biography written four or five centuries later in the West, where imitating Christ was the very definition of what it meant to be human and Christian. Except that was not what Willibald or his biographer thought he was doing when he occasionally reenacted what Christ had done in the same places where He did them. The Englishman was undeniably special in going where he went and doing what he did, but he himself was not transformed into Christ by imitation. He never even thought he was copying an apostolic life. Willibald's journey, though, was a rare prefiguration of a much later and widespread medieval phenomenon.

Willibald was surprisingly pliant and adaptable as a pilgrim (and a person), more than willing to live like a transient Syrian monk or follow the rites of local East Roman churches or stay in Palestinian monasteries or be given alms by Muslims. According to Huneberc's portrait, he had a touch of the holy fool about him, a perpetual hopefulness transcending the mundane reality of how to get from one place to another or find something to eat. "Blessed is the man who lives in trust," as the English poem known as "The Seafarer" describes another Englishman wandering far from Britain, "grace shall come to him from the heavens."[13] (Willibald, unlike other Englishmen, never seemed to sing. Or he never did for Huneberc.)

The participation of Willibald's father and brother in his pilgrimage to Rome, when neither of them were monks, was an early example of the penitential expeditions soon embraced by lay men and women throughout the West. It was an enthusiasm that ultimately reached its fullest and most volatile expression in the martial pilgrimage of the First Crusade. Huneberc in her own way exemplified this democratization of pilgrimage and exilic holiness, for although she was already a nun, her journey from southern Britain all the way to Bavaria in the middle of the eighth century was the kind of *peregrinatio* that two centuries earlier the Liffey River nun had lamented to Columbanus was forbidden to women. Of course, Huneberc moved from one monastery to another, as the open-ended years-long holy wanderlust of a Willibald was still prohibited for her. And in all the hearsay stories of Englishwomen who risked traveling alone as pilgrims, they ended up as prostitutes.

Nevertheless, Huneberc overcame her limitations as a woman by suggesting that in writing Willibald's *Life*, she too experienced in a very real sense what he had done in Syria and Palestine. She was momentarily a pilgrim in Jerusalem along with him and Tidbercht. She too briefly trod where Christ walked. And when she reread what she had written, she again reexperienced what it was like to be a handsome (if frequently sunburned) young man reliving what he had read in the Gospels. This fleeting but powerful mimesis meant that Huneberc's *Life* of Willibald was in itself a transporting act of penance when heard or read by any woman or man.

Huneberc never really explains how Willibald's sojourn in Syria and Palestine related to his work as a bishop in Bavaria, except that the renown of his travels eventually led him to Eichstätt. Whatever honey the middle-aged Englishman carried on his thighs (as Huneberc's apian analogy would have it) seemed to be more from his years at Monte Cassino, a decade where he remorselessly erased who he was as a younger man. Either way, Huneberc ended Willibald's *Life* by listing the monasteries following Benedict's *Rule* (which included Heidenheim), the churches, the priestly houses, the saintly relics, and the crosses now dotting Bavaria thanks to him. "From these places antiphons now resound, sacred lessons are chanted, a noble throng of believers shout aloud the miracles of Christ," echoing from mouth to mouth, so that even the Frankish king heard them, that is to say, Charles, the grandson of Charles Martel, more commonly known as Charles *le magne* (from Latin *magnus*, "great") or Charlemagne.[14]

2 A Hard Man

In 723—the same year that Willibald left Rome for Syria—Daniel, bishop of Winchester, sent a letter to his old friend Boniface in Germany, giving advice about debating with pagans. He listed questions about gods and goddesses—mostly involving their sexual habits, which, being all too human, were proof they lacked divinity—that should be put to the heathens, "not in an offensive and irritating way but calmly and with great moderation." Ultimately, though, if the old Saxon gods were so powerful, why were they "banished from the rest of the world" to the frozen north, abandoning the lands "rich in oil and wine and other goods" to Christians? This sunny Mediterranean vision of the good life as irrefutable proof of God's omnipotence, while an odd verdict from a prelate in a frigid island distinctly lacking olive groves, vineyards, and sunshine but not, as Daniel well knew, monks or nuns, was less compelling as a climatic argument than as a mildly amusing play upon Boniface's "Roman" persona as a missionary bishop commissioned a year earlier by Pope Gregory II with bringing warmth and light to Germans east of the Rhine "still lost in the darkness of ignorance."[15]

Five years earlier, Boniface, who was still known as Wynfrith, had carried a letter of introduction from Daniel when he left Exeter as a pilgrim.[16] This was no youthful wide-eyed decision, as he was close to forty and had been a studious but unexceptional monk since childhood (and a priest for a decade).

Around 716, though, a monk from Wenlock (in Shropshire) had told Wynfrith about an out-of-body journey very much like that experienced by Barontus three decades earlier. One night, while the monk was suffering extreme pain, his soul suddenly jumped from his body. Angels swooped in and carried his soul "high in the air" to a place between hell and paradise, where a multitude of other night-flying souls were gathered. Terrifyingly, all his sins since he was a boy crowded around him like an angry mob, each one crying out an accusation. "I am vainglory," yelled one. "I am falsehood," screamed another. "I am stubbornness and disobedience." "I am sluggishness and neglect in sacred studies." "I am the idle errand." And so on. His virtues, while a smaller group, forcefully defended him. "I am obedience, which he has shown to his spiritual superiors." "I am fasting." "I am the service of the weak." "I am the psalm, which he chanted before God to atone for an idle word." And so on. Demons and angels cheered and helped one side against the other. This scrum of self-aware sins and virtues was what constituted a life. The monk's virtues won this time. But what about when his soul flew away again? Or when he finally died? Sins were the offspring of complacency and idleness; they must not be allowed to breed.[17]

Wynfrith, soon after hearing this story of otherworldly flight, abruptly fled to Frisia, where another Englishman, Willibrord, was battling paganism on the edge of the North Sea as bishop of Utrecht, but he swiftly returned to Britain flustered and disheartened.

Two years later, Wynfrith, his virtues finally shouting down his sins (and doubts), departed forever (with Daniel's letter of introduction) as an exile, reaching Rome in 719.

Wynfrith, as was common with English monks after visiting Rome, adopted a "Roman" name, which for him was Boniface. But unlike other English pilgrims, he (or anyone else) rarely used his old name again. Wynfrith had been a troubled and diffident man, but Boniface, shedding his old sins and some virtues (such as humor) with his old name, was now an austere, zealous, and uncompromising individual. He kept his ties with southern Britain, but he was not the same man that his friends once knew. He now imagined himself as a "Roman" like Gregory the Great, scanning the far horizons for opportunities to convert pagans into Christians. Such a man stood out amongst the hundreds, if not thousands, of other Englishmen remaking themselves in Rome (and he was over six feet, too). He did not leap into the unknown like Willibald; instead, he lobbied Gregory II for recognition as a missionary.

As the pope was worried about supposed North African Manichaean refugees masquerading as monks and priests on the German frontier of Francia, he readily ordained Boniface a bishop in 722 with the mission of purifying Thuringia of heresy and paganism.[18] He also recommended his new evangelical bishop to Charles Martel, *maior* of the puppet Merovingian king of Austrasia and overlord of the former Neustrian kingdom in the Paris basin.[19] The Frankish strongman had already attacked Saxon territory in 718, 720, and 722, campaigning over an area more than 120 miles east of the Rhine. Boniface was soon placed under the protection of Charles—two hard men whose fortunes were now intertwined.

Boniface found neither Manichaeans nor pagans living near the Rhine; instead, what he discovered were complacent Christians, carelessly risking their souls with practices that, even if they thought them harmless, reeked of paganism and heresy. Before he reached Thuringia he showed his severity, strength, and showmanship by chopping down "a certain oak of extraordinary size called in the old tongue of the pagans the Oak of Thunor" at Geismar beside the river Fulda. Hessian Christians prayed at this great tree, offering it sacrifices. According to the *Life* of Boniface written by Willibald (a different English monk from the Syrian wanderer), all it took was one nick of an axe and "suddenly the oak's vast bulk, shaken by a mighty blast of wind from above, crashed to the ground shivering its topmost branches into fragments in its fall."[20]

Daniel would have been disappointed, as this was hardly an argument offered "calmly and with great moderation" (but then he had been writing with his old friend Wynfrith in mind). Gregory the Great would have been disappointed, as this was against his advice to Augustine about preserving pagan places of worship. Boniface knew better than his friend or the pope he emulated, for his miraculous axemanship showed the futility of any lingering beliefs about holy trees other than the Rood. It also showed that he could get away with it, as he was protected by the *maior* Charles. By destroying the great oak Boniface eliminated all the past and future sins it had and would have caused; yet he still acknowledged its ancient divinity, or rather that he could remodel such holiness as he saw fit, by building an oratory to Saint Peter out of its timber.

Again, as has often been the case over the last few centuries, Boniface's German mission raises the question of the genuine reality of a paganism distinct from Christianity, rather than just accusations from a censorious bishop. If there once had been a separate religion of the old Saxon gods, where, say, Wodan or Thor lived in a universe without Christ, that was long gone by the eighth century. If the old gods still existed, along with some of the old ways, then they survived as Christianized versions of themselves, completely compatible with the rough and ready "unchurched"

Christianity that had been developing for more than two centuries east of the Rhine.

A mid-eighth-century penitential list of "superstitions" that may have been drawn up by Boniface catalogued behaviors such as yelling "Triumph, Moon!" at lunar eclipses; saying this or that place is holy; setting aside days for Wodan and Thor; believing women commanded the moon; worshipping at trees and springs; adoring idols of dough and rags; and carrying idols through fields.[21] These were all superstitions held by men and women who thought of themselves as Christian. Not surprisingly, Boniface was a great reader of the sermons of Caesarius of Arles, so some of the *rusticitas* of fifth-century Provence was superimposed on eighth-century Bavaria. What was different in time and place, though, were the wandering Irish, English, and Frankish holy men who, at least since the late sixth century, had exiled themselves along the river Weser spreading their own version of a personal charismatic Christianity, so that, as the penitential list lamented, it was widely believed that living and "dead persons of whatever sort are saints."[22] These entrepreneurial holy men (dead and alive) with their laissez-faire religiosity annoyed Boniface for more than thirty years.

In 745, for example, Boniface demanded that a Roman synod condemn two such men and their heretical ways. The first was an Irishman named Clement. His crimes were encouraging Judaism by marrying his brother's widow, fathering two children, calling himself a bishop, and preaching that Christ had freed all believers and unbelievers from hell. The second, whom Boniface really loathed, was a Frank named Adelbert. This charlatan said "he could obtain from God whatever he might wish" because an angel had bestowed upon him marvelous relics, such as a letter written by Christ that, after falling from heaven in Jerusalem and passing through many Mediterranean hands, had ended up at Saint Peter's tomb in Rome. Adelbert even distributed his own hair and fingernails as relics. Boniface fumed that stupid bishops, dazzled by this flimflam, had ordained the swindler a bishop. "I know all your hidden sins," Adelbert would tell anyone begging him for penitential forgiveness, so there was no need to confess; indeed, there was no need for penances either, as he had already absolved all past and future sins. Such an obvious con, grumbled Boniface, yet many fell for it. And like an English nobleman, Adelbert erected crosses at springs or on fields or in copses.[23]

Such freelance Christianity infuriated Boniface with its complete disregard for institutions like monasteries and churches—and, of course, him. When Willibald traveled to Eichstätt in 740, his years slumming it in Syria and Palestine were much less important than his ten years at Monte Cassino, where his wild and careless holiness was steadfastly brought under control, if not erased. For Boniface, Willibald was a living rebuke to men like Clement and Adelbert.

Boniface was an institutionalist; he founded monasteries following Benedict's *Rule*, built churches, and established dioceses. He wanted to transform Germany as Gregory the Great had transformed Britain. In 738, as a step in this direction, he called upon all English bishops, priests, abbots, abbesses, monks, and nuns to pray for all pagan Saxons. "Take pity upon them," pleaded Boniface (even mentioning his old name, Wynfrith, as a way of soliciting as many English prayers as possible), "for they themselves are saying: 'We are of one blood and one bone with you.'" This supposedly widespread Saxon sentiment was less about ethnic affinity (if at all) than a declaration that some of them already were, just like the English, "children of Mother Church."[24]

Apart from English prayers, Germany also needed English books. Like Bede, Boniface knew the importance of books not only as reservoirs of knowledge but also as magnificent things in themselves symbolizing power. He badgered his English friends for volumes from their libraries. In 735, for instance, he requested from Eadburga, abbess of Minster-in-Thanet, a copy of the epistles of Saint Peter in gold, so that he might "impress honor and reverence for the sacred scriptures visually upon the carnally minded to whom I preach." He also promised to send her the gold leaf.[25] The golden sheen of an open folio would convert any pagan or excise any heresy.

A decade later he wrote to Daniel in Winchester asking him to hunt out a book of the Prophets from the Old Testament that had belonged to his teacher more than half a century earlier in the monastery of Nursling (in Hampshire). He remembered the letters in this book as large, well-spaced, and clearly written out; as his eyesight was fading, "I cannot read well writing which is small and filled with abbreviations." Boniface accompanied his request with a prayer for Daniel's health (which had not been good for two decades) and "a bath towel, not of purest silk, but mixed with rough goat's hair, to dry your feet."[26]

On Wednesday, June 5, 754, as "the morning light was breaking through the clouds after sunrise," Boniface was murdered beside the river Boorne near where it flows into the North Sea. Four decades earlier, after hearing the story of the Wenlock monk, he had briefly (and ineptly) dashed off to Frisia. Now, in his late seventies, he returned to the Frisian marshlands in a great summer evangelical procession, "destroying pagan worship and turning away the people from their pagan errors by his preaching of the Gospel." This cavalcade was almost over—just one more group baptism of scattered homesteaders remained—when estuary pirates (most likely Christians themselves) chanced upon Boniface's poorly defended encampment overflowing with hefty iron-bound chests. After killing everyone in the camp, they greedily broke open the chests. Instead of treasure, all they found were books, lots of books, "manuscripts instead of gold vessels, pages of sacred texts instead of silver plate." Enraged, "they littered the fields with the books they found, throwing some of them into the reedy marshes." Even though Boniface died as the consequence of a bloody smash-and-grab, he was remembered as a martyr, which, for his biographer Willibald writing a decade later, was a "glorious end."[27]

3 The Battle of Poitiers

In late August 733, according to an anonymous Christian chronicler writing in Córdoba twenty years later, the Umayyad governor of al-Andalus, 'Abd ar-Rahman al-Gafiqi, "cut through the rocky mountains of the Basques so that, crossing the plains, he might invade the lands of the Franks." Such "invasions" across the western Pyrenees into the lands of Eudes, duke of Aquitaine, had been occurring since 721. They were end-of-summer sorties in which Berber and Syrian Muslim soldiers, along with Christian Visigoths serving the new regime, swooped in and pillaged the farms, monasteries, and towns between the Garonne, Dordogne, and Aude Rivers. (It was one of these summer raids, along with two comets, that Bede noted in 729.) Eudes, while troubled by these Iberian raiders, was much more worried about the seemingly unstoppable northern aggression of Charles Martel. He even handed over the last Merovingian king of Neustria to the Austrasian *maior* as a sop in 721. 'Abd ar-Rahman's foray exploited the turmoil of these Frankish civil wars.

In early October 733, more by accident than design, Eudes ran across the Iberians near Bordeaux as he himself was traveling north to parley with Charles and his Austrasians gathering around Tours. The Aquitanians were caught off guard and routed. "God only knows the number of those who died or fled," wrote the anonymous Andalusian. 'Abd ar-Rahman, elated by his victory, "decided to despoil Tours by destroying its palaces and burning its churches." Instead, "he confronted the consul of Austrasia by the name of Charles." As Tours was no more than a ten-day march away, such an encounter was likely. "In the blink of an eye," the northern Franks, "holding together like a glacier in the cold regions," crushed the smaller raiding party, killing 'Abd ar-Rahman.[28]

Charles was so indifferent to his easy triumph that he allowed the surviving "Ishmaelites" to escape in the night "in tight formation, returning to their home country." The next day the northern Franks "joyfully" ransacked the plunder looted from the southern Franks left behind in the Iberian camp. Although the anonymous Andalusian chronicler rebuked the "Europeans" for their nonchalance in not pursuing the Saracens, he did not view what had happened as the opening gambit of an enduring holy war between Christians and Muslims.[29]

This unequal contest in early autumn 733 between a few hundred skirmishers far from home and a few thousand well-rested infantrymen has been rather grandly known since at least the early ninth century as the Battle of Poitiers or Tours. The courtier and lay abbot Einhard in his *Life* of Charles the Great (Charlemagne), written after 820, commented that, if it were not for Charles Martel, the Saracens would have occupied all of Gaul.[30] More insidiously, there is still a lingering modern myth that the battle was a turning point in world history, stopping the spread of Islam in the West. Edward Gibbon in *The History of the Decline and Fall of the Roman Empire* (1788) at once famously expressed and mocked this view when, tongue firmly in his cheek, he observed that if not for the Battle of Poitiers stopping the furious Muslim onslaught into Europe, "perhaps the interpretation of the Koran would now be taught in the schools of Oxford, and her pulpits might demonstrate to a circumcised people the sanctity and truth of the revelation of Mahomet."[31]

4   Iconoclasm

In January 730 the East Roman emperor Leo III, according to an anonymous (and contemporaneously written) *Life* of Pope Gregory II, decreed that in the churches and monasteries of Rome, Constantinople, Alexandria, Antioch, and Jerusalem, "no image of any saint, martyr or angel, should be kept, as he declared them all accursed." All paintings in Constantinopolitan churches were whitewashed and, "what is painful to mention," all icons "of the Savior, His Holy Mother and all the saints" were consumed in a great bonfire in front of Hagia Sophia.[32]

Gregory was horrified. What Leo actually mandated is lost, and he was much less destructive than what was reported in Rome, but his iconoclasm is without question, as was the pope's complete opposition to destroying images. The polymath astrologer Theophilus of Edessa, writing in Syriac a few decades later in newly founded Baghdad, even recorded Gregory's anger in his chronicle, noting that the pope dispatched letters to Leo, objecting that "a king ought not to make pronouncements concerning the faith nor to alter the ancient doctrines of the Church."[33] Both papal biographer and Syrian chronicler said there were rebellions in East Roman Italian enclaves, such as Ravenna or the Veneto. The pope, while opposing these uprisings, encouraged the withholding of taxes from the emperor.[34] Theophilus also commented that Leo's condemnation of images was similar to an edict by Caliph Yazid II seven or so years earlier prohibiting Christian symbols and the representation of living things.[35]

Since the fourth century, the walls, ceilings, and floors of churches, houses, and palaces throughout the Mediterranean had been decorated with paintings, sculptures, and mosaics of Christ, Mary as the Mother of God, angels, saints, martyrs, bishops, and other assorted holy individuals. This was just an artistic changing of the heavenly guard, for although ancient paintings and statues of the old gods never really disappeared from the public square in most cities and towns—recall that even Constantine the Great adorned his new eponymous capital with godly antiques requisitioned from throughout the empire—these portrayals were no longer seen as representations of the holy or deserving of worship. Christ and a panoply of Christian luminaries stepped into this sacred aesthetic space. Perhaps even from the beginning of such distinctively Christian art, customary behaviors once lavished upon pagan statues, such as praying to them or offering them gifts, were given to a painting of Saint Peter or a figurine of Mary without a second thought. By the fifth century some images of Christ, His Mother, and the saints had acquired a holy aura that made them more exceptional than any artistic ornamentation around them. These portraits were literally entry points to heaven, and far from being two-dimensional images, they really were what they represented. A painting on a wooden board of Christ was actually Him, ready to listen, ready to help any petitioner, ready to bless anyone looking upon His face. Emperors, senators, soldiers, mothers, sickly merchants, childless wives, monks, and peasants all worshipped these icons (from the Greek *eikôn*, "image"), bowing before them, kissing them, talking to them, nailing little votive objects to them, perfuming them with incense, and illuminating them with candles.

Such worshipfulness toward images always ran the risk of accusations of idolatry. In the late sixth century Serenus, bishop of Marseille, went on a rampage destroying the images of saints in churches he was convinced were being worshipped as idols. Gregory the Great rebuked him for his arrogant "blind fury." Did Serenus think himself wiser and holier than other bishops? Did Serenus know of other bishops throwing sacred portraits into the sea? "To adore images is one thing; to teach with their help what should be adored is another. What scripture is to the educated, images are to the ignorant, who see through them what they must accept; they read in them what they cannot read in books."[36] This famous formulation was frequently repeated (and as frequently misunderstood) by Latin Christian intellectuals for the next nine centuries in the medieval West.

For Gregory, images were especially important in the conversion of pagans accustomed to adoring likenesses of the old gods. When Augustine was dispatched on his mission to Britain, the pope made sure there were teaching images for the ignorant English. Indeed, in the very first meeting between the missionaries and King Æthelbert on the island of Thanet, the Roman monks brandished, according to Bede, "a silver cross as their standard and the likeness of our Lord and Savior painted on a board."[37]

By 700, similar paintings on boards, either affixed in churches or carried in religious and civic processions, and their private and public worship as icons was more common amongst Christians in the eastern Mediterranean than in Francia or Britain. Willibald even remembered for Huneberc that when he visited the Church of the Holy Fathers in Nicaea around 729, lining the walls were 318 portraits of the bishops who attended the ecumenical council in the lakeside town four centuries earlier. He was not interested in the paintings. Instead, Willibald was curious to see if the church was really built like the one he had seen in Jerusalem at the Mount of Olives, marking the spot where Christ ascended into heaven.[38]

Two years before Willibald's architectural tourism, Nicaea was besieged by an Umayyad army. The East Roman monk Theophanes, writing in Greek in his sickbed beside the Sea of Marmara in the early ninth century, not only said that the "venerable images" still existed in the Church of the Holy Fathers but that on account of these portraits being "exact likenesses," the saintly bishops themselves had intervened and defeated the Arab forces in 727. During the siege, though, one young iconoclastic officer named Constantine, after seeing that someone had set up a Mother of God icon for protection, "picked up a stone and threw it at her." He then trampled on her image. Later that night she appeared to him in a vision, saying: "See, what a brave thing you have done to me! Verily, upon your head have you done it!" The next morning Constantine's head was crushed by a stone hurled from a catapult—"a just reward for his impiety."[39] Theophanes was an iconophile (lover of images), and the victory over the Saracens at Nicaea (and the story of sacrilegious Constantine) four generations earlier was a confirmation of the power of holy images. Ironically, for Leo III it was his success in stemming the seemingly unstoppable Umayyad onslaught that convinced him of the sinfulness of images painted on boards.

Soon after Leo ascended the throne in March 717, he skillfully defended Constantinople from a mighty Umayyad fleet (more than a thousand galleys and ships) by setting the Bosporus aflame with "Greek fire" (an incendiary concoction that ignited in water).[40] He knew he was living through apocalyptic times, one in which a diminished East Roman Empire was fighting for its survival. Already in the late seventh century the imperial rump left over from the conquests of Muhammad's nomads had been reorganized into four massive territorial *themata*, standing armies of fifteen thousand men under regional commanders. Cities and towns were deserted for a more rural and hopefully safer existence, where fortified castles were surrounded by the small farmsteads of yeoman soldiers and the vast ranches of their generals. Even Constantinople was an empty husk, with orchards and market gardens in derelict neighborhoods, and no more than sixty thousand inhabitants.

Emperors forcibly moved populations around like chess pieces, settling
them in whatever *thema* was most strategically appropriate. Leo in the aftermath of the siege of Constantinople refashioned the *themata* and the remaining imperial fragments in western Asia Minor, the Peloponnese, the
Balkans, Calabria, and Sicily (where he swiftly executed a pretender to
the purple) into a close-knit Greek-speaking holy and "orthodox" commonwealth. As the Latin of the *Justinianic Code* was largely useless in such
a Byzantine Empire—the caveats remain, but the name is now more
apposite—he published a practical legal handbook in Greek, the *Ekloga*
(*Selections*). In a state of constant emergency, both worshipping spurious
images and exalting unreadable laws were immoral. In summer 726 the
impending apocalypse was confirmed when an underwater volcano
vomited forth a new island in the Aegean. As ash clouds darkened the skies
over Constantinople, Leo atoned by removing a large icon of Christ at the
Chalkê entrance to the imperial palace—the same Chalkê entrance where
a mosaic still showed, now somewhat incongruously, Justinian receiving
"honors equal to those of God."[41]

Yazid II also knew he was living during the Last Day. Remarkably, much
of the apocalyptic zeal that had so motivated the Believers two or three generations earlier still inspired the great Umayyad assault on Constantinople
in 717. Yet the failure of the siege, far from dissipating this eschatological
fervor, only intensified it amongst Muslim elites, especially in Syria. Indeed,
this sense that the Last Day was at hand even affected Syrian Jews and
Christians. When Yazid became caliph in 720, according to Theophilus, a
Christian named Severus decided he was Jewish and traveled throughout
Syria telling Jews "that he had come to deliver them." "I am the Messiah,"
he would say in one place, "I am the Messenger of the Messiah" in another.
Although a grifter, swindling dinars here and there, he was widely believed
(even by himself, it seems) and worshipped. Yazid arrested and executed
him as a fraud.[42]

Three years later, in 723, Yazid ordered all images, "whether of bronze,
wood or stone, or of paint, be completely destroyed."[43] As many Muslims
still prayed in churches, he wanted all Christian images erased from these
buildings. He also apparently ordered the killing of all "blue-eyed people"
and pigs. He wanted to purify Syria of messianic hucksters, evil eyes, unclean beasts, and idolatry before the Day of Judgment. He even commissioned his half-brother Maslama ibn 'Abd al-Malik, who had led the failed

attack on Constantinople, to undertake this cleansing. (Willibald was imprisoned in Hims around the time of the edict. Did the authorities view
him as a holy con artist? Did he have blue eyes?) Yazid died less than a year
after his edict, which, in turn, was immediately repealed by his successor. A
few mosaics in Transjordanian churches were smashed, although it seems no
blue-eyed people or pigs were harmed.[44]

Despite the later prohibition on images, especially human representation,
becoming such a fundamental tenet of Islam, it was not yet fully articulated
or widely accepted by Muslims at the beginning of the eighth century.
Unquestionably, the early Believers, if they gave any thought to images,
would have dismissed them as unnecessary artifices with the approach of
the Hour. There is no injunction on images in the Qur'an. Nevertheless,
how one viewed and represented the world was a sharp way of saying who
was and was not a follower of Muhammad. It was the apocalypticism before
and after 723 that finally set in place an aesthetic principle that eventually
developed into dogma. Yazid's edict may have been fleeting zealotry—and
more bark than bite—but it was the start of something rather than its confirmation. Did the developing Muslim view of images affect Leo? Perhaps.
He was certainly accused of it by later iconophiles like Theophanes.

More likely, as great apocalyptic swaths entwined Constantinople and
Damascus around 700, with each side constantly experimenting with ways
of winning God's approval, the distrust of images was, momentarily for
some Christians and more enduringly for many Muslims, one tactic for
surviving the Day of Judgment.

5 The Last Merovingian King

After the last Merovingian king of Austrasia died in 737, Charles Martel
ruled as *maior* without a monarch until his death four years later. He saw
no reason for a king, even as a hollowed-out symbol. He was the suzerain
of the kingless "kingdoms" (*regna*) of Austrasia and Neustria and other
lands all the way from the North Sea to the Mediterranean and from the
Pyrenees to the Harz. There was still enough residual meaning in what defined kingship, at least for other Frankish aristocrats, that he would never
have usurped the crown. In death, though, Charles affirmed he was equal if
not superior to any Merovingian king by having himself buried in the royal

abbey of Saint-Denis in Paris alongside two (admittedly mediocre) heirs of Merovech.[45]

The sons of Charles Martel, Carloman and Pippin (known as "the Short"), shared the kingdoms. The former became mayor and duke of Austrasia and Swabia; the latter was mayor and duke of Neustria, Burgundy, and Provence. Both affirmed their father's patronage of Boniface. Indeed, Carloman went further, asking him to reform the clergy and laity in his kingdom. Boniface immediately complained to the new pope, Zacharias, that in Francia, "for the most part, the episcopal sees in cities are in the hands of greedy laymen or are exploited by adulterous and vicious clergymen." Everywhere he looked was corruption, paganism, or heresy.

Of course, much of the problem lay at the pope's doorstep. Many Franks wondered why they should stop doing this or that pagan practice or be better Christians when it was widely known that Romans were even worse. Boniface, channeling Caesarius of Arles, therefore thought it about time that the pope banned the street parties on the Kalends of January when men and women dressed and danced like pagans, "shouting and chanting sacrilegious songs." How could he make the Franks properly "Roman"— as only an Englishman knew how—if Rome did not set the example?[46] Carloman agreed with Boniface about Francia. Like his father, he thought too much land had been given away in the previous century as ecclesiastical gifts and that greedy fools mismanaged it. He confiscated the corrupt properties, while extracting yearly grants from all endowments for his armies. It was still the monasticized realm of the last three generations, but it had become too lax and needed a tougher rule. His brother Pippin agreed. Many nobles, abbots, and bishops did not; so, in 743, the brothers plonked a Merovingian on the throne, Childeric III. This king, while perhaps not quite the long-haired inbred imbecile described by Einhard, provided royal gloss to the ascendency of Carloman and Pippin.[47]

In 747 Carloman, after a savage campaign against the Alamanni (not the same barbarians attacked by Julian and Clovis four centuries earlier, but a confederation of farmers and lordlings living in the same upper Danube region and so given the old name by eighth-century Franks), "walked away from the oppressive chore of governing an earthly kingdom."[48] He was thirty-eight years old and, after handing over his lands to Pippin, emulated Boniface at a similar age by traveling to Rome in search of a new life. There, shedding his old self, he became a monk, first in a small monastery he built for himself on a lonely limestone ridge within the city, then, when that proved too convenient for visiting Frankish well-wishers, he locked himself away at Monte Cassino. Three years later, Pippin, after first gaining the approval of Pope Zacharias, deposed the straw man Childeric (cutting his hair, dumping him in a monastery) and, with Boniface officiating, had himself anointed like an Old Testament king with oil at the abbey of Saint-Médard in Soissons.[49]

In summer 754 another pope, Stephen II, again anointed Pippin as king in a more elaborate ceremony at Saint-Denis, even blessing his sons Carloman and Charles (the future Charlemagne) and his wife, Bertrada. This affirmed the new Carolingian dynasty—named after Charles Martel by modern historians—as at once deeply Christian, Frankish, and "Roman." (Boniface would have been there, no doubt still grumbling that neither pope nor king were "Roman" enough, had he not been murdered in Frisia just before the ceremony.) Pippin, now with the pope as his "spiritual father," agreed to defend Rome from the renewed aggression of the Lombards. He did so in two ruthlessly successful campaigns in 755 and 756, looting the Lombard capital, Pavia, and recapturing East Roman enclaves, like Ravenna, that the Lombards had snapped up while Constantinople was focused on destroying icons. In a revolutionary move, Pippin "donated" these territories to the papacy.[50]

Rome, while even more decrepit than the crumbling city described by Gregory the Great over a century earlier, and with perhaps no more than twenty-five thousand residents, was, largely thanks to the thousands of English, Irish, and Frankish pilgrims, who often stayed for years on end, now "Roman" and Christian in a way defined by these hard but idealistic northerners. The popes, since the late seventh century but certainly after the iconoclasm of Leo III, had been trying to disentangle themselves from Constantinople, and it finally seemed such an unraveling might actually succeed with the heirs of Charles Martel. Pope Stephen and Pippin, while acknowledging the northern drift of Latin Christianity since the late sixth century, also initiated a new political, cultural, and martial orientation for the West.

6 The Last Umayyad Caliph

On Saturday, January 22, 750, the Umayyad caliph, Marwan II, assembled his Syrian foot soldiers and cavalry on the western side of the Greater Zab, a tributary of the Tigris. On the other side of the river was an insurgent army from the eastern Iranian province of Khurasan. There had been scattered rebellions and uprisings against Marwan's rule almost from the moment he became caliph in 744. The most serious was the apocalyptic Shi'ite Hashimiyya movement, which believed that caliphs should only come from the family of Muhammad. Although it began in the Euphratean city of Kufa, its most zealous revolutionaries came from Khurasan. In 748 the Khurasani Hashimi, dressed in black and carrying black banners, launched their holy war against the Umayyads. In less than a year they had taken over much of western Iran and eastern Iraq. They still had no specified leader, trusting that God would reveal *al-rida min al-Muhammad*, "the one selected from the family of Muhammad." The Abbasids, claiming descent from an uncle of the Prophet named Abbas, stepped into this sacred void, harnessing the Hashimi revolution by naming Abu al-Abbas as caliph in Kufa in November 749. A few months later, Marwan arrived on the Greater Zab to kill this insurgency and its pretender.[51]

"When the two sides encountered each other," eulogized Theophilus of Edessa, "Marwan found the Khurasanis to be heroes, not wavering in battle, like a wall of stone, unaffected by iron or fire, possessing courage and fortitude." The battle surged back and forth over a wide expanse of river shallows and, more ferociously, a narrow pontoon bridge thrown across a swirling deep channel. After one last Khurasani assault, the Syrians crumbled, trampling comrades as they fled, stampeding the bridge; "some piled on others and many fell into the Euphrates, where they drowned." Marwan escaped (apparently with three thousand servants, three thousand camels, and wagons of gold). "On this day the rule passed from the sons of Umayya to the sons of Hashim and Abu al-Abbas," intoned Theophilus. The "wearers of black" pursued the fugitive Marwan for ten months until one night on a hill near the whitewater rapids of the upper Nile they trapped him, but the former caliph "kept on fighting until he fell and was killed."[52]

The so-called Abbasid Revolution erupted because what it meant to be Muslim was no longer synonymous with being Arab (or, as it had been only a few generations before, a Believer). The Umayyads never successfully embraced the coherent Islamic universalism necessary for a changing caliphate. The Hashimiyya movement, despite obsessing over the ancestry of one holy Arab, envisioned an Islam unmoored from any ethnic exclusivity—which was also what Muhammad preached a century and a half earlier. The Abbasids adroitly usurped this militant religious utopianism.

"I was myself a constant witness of these wars," recalled Theophilus about the "Abbasid Revolution" in the decade before he died aged ninety in 785. "I would write things down so that nothing of them should escape me."[53] During his last years, he lived and wrote his partially autobiographical chronicle (which only survives as extracts copied into four other chronicles) in the Round City of Baghdad, founded by the caliph Abu Ja'far al-Mansur as his capital in 762, just fifteen miles north of the former Sasanian capital of Ctesiphon. Theophilus, though, was more than just a memoirist and historian; he was also court astrologer to al-Mansur's son, al-Madhi, publicly forecasting the future as he privately pieced together what he remembered of the past.

7 The Donation of Constantine

A few years after Pippin's death in 768, an unknown group of clerics (most likely English and Frankish monks) concocted a blatantly obvious forgery in Rome. This *Constitutum Constantini*, or "Donation of Constantine" as it was known in later centuries, was an extravagant rewriting of history in which the emperor Constantine, following his conversion to Christianity after Pope Sylvester cures him of leprosy, rewards the pope and all his successors with the inalienable gift of "the city of Rome and all the provinces, districts and cities of Italy or of the western regions." It pretended to be a fourth-century Latin (from a Greek original) imperial edict written in the form of an eighth-century penitential confession. Some of its fabrication, like Constantine's leprosy, was lifted from the fifth-century *Actus Sylvestri* (which, as discussed earlier, shaped Gregory of Tours' disease metaphors for the baptism of Clovis).

Overall, though, the "Donation" was a polemical justification for why the new Frankish kings, Charles and Carloman, should esteem and aid the popes against the Lombards, the emperors in Constantinople, and any bishop or abbot in the "western regions" unwilling to submit themselves to the papacy. The fictional Constantine repeatedly exalts the pope and the Roman Church over himself and his earthly realm. The fictional Sylvester even reaffirms him as emperor in a ceremony replicating the real Stephen anointing Pippin. The "Donation" asserted what its fabricators believed to be the historical "truth" about emperors and popes; given that documentation was lacking from the past, they faked what they knew should exist. Like the heavenly letter from Christ that Adelbert said an angel had given him, so the late eighth-century popes had their own documentary relic affirming what they now claimed about themselves—and like Adelbert's letter, it was dismissed as much as it was believed. The odd thing is that over the centuries the specific circumstances and doubts behind the "Donation" were forgotten and, whether from convenience or conviction, quite a few popes believed it to be authentic.[54]

8 Emperor and Augustus

On Christmas Day, 800, Charles was praying at the shrine of Saint Peter in Rome. Einhard was watching him. In his *Life* of Charles, which he modeled on Suetonius' early second-century *Life* of Augustus, he described the fifty-eight-year-old royal pilgrim as having a "cheerful and attractive face" with two large eyes either side of a nose "a little longer than average" beneath a short crop of handsome gray hair. Charles had "a large and powerful body" just over six feet tall, "although his neck seemed short and thick and his stomach seemed to stick out."[55] (His little pot belly resulted from a fondness for eating only roast meat and a conviction that fasting was bad for his health.) It was twenty-nine years since his younger brother Carloman had died—a petty and jealous man, in Einhard's opinion—leaving him sole king of the Franks.

In these years Charles had waged almost continuous, frequently overlapping, and increasingly brutal wars in Aquitaine, Brittany, northern Spain (in which Roland, lord of the Breton March, was killed by Basques), the Italian peninsula (destroying the Lombard kings and annexing their lands in 774), Bavaria, the northwestern Hungarian plain (decimating the Avar khaganate), and, most especially, Saxony. He was always on horseback or sailing a river, camping in fields, staying in royal villas, or lodging in monasteries, an itinerant ruler visiting his vast realm. Around 794, though, he began building a rural palace as a permanent retreat near hot sulfur springs at Aachen (Aix-la-Chapelle) in the Ardennes. In assemblies and capitularies (short sharp decisions "from the mouth of the king") he admonished every individual and group within and even outside his kingdom so that they were more properly Christian, "Roman," and loyal to him.

All this and much more was in Einhard's mind as he watched his king pray, not the least of which was that he knew what was about to happen even if he and his king pretended otherwise. As Charles was getting up from kneeling, Pope Leo III "unexpectedly" placed a golden diadem upon his gray head and proclaimed him "Emperor and Augustus."[56]

Einhard kept up the Christmas Day charade by writing that if Charles "had known in advance of the pope's plan, he would not have entered the church that day." Despite the new emperor's false modesty and feigned surprise—which he undoubtedly performed in the moment—his adoption of such a glorious title, more than three hundred years after it was last used in the West, was at once hardheaded, deeply holy, a touch idealistic, and inevitable for a ruler already profoundly "Roman." Of course, "Roman" for Charles and his advisors did not mean the pagan empire of Augustus or Marcus Aurelius; it meant the Christian empire of Constantine the Great and Theodosius II and, most crucially, of Latin Christian intellectuals like Jerome, Augustine of Hippo, and Caesarius of Arles. They were not "renewing" an imperial past or lost Latinate culture, which is why the modern scholarly notion of a "Carolingian Renaissance" is a misnomer; they were asserting a "Romanness" that never really went away for them, and while it was sometimes forgotten, smothered by paganism, or knocked asunder by barbarian invasions, it was now, at long last, reaching its divine apogee. It was "Romanness" epitomized in someone like Boniface and his vision of Christianity and the Church. In this sense, Einhard "baptized" Suetonius, "correcting" him with his portrait of a Christian Augustus in the manner of an up-to-date "Roman." Such *correctio*, whether in books, law, war, or religion, defined kingdom and empire. It was a penitential realm, requiring ever watchful emendation and correction. After that fateful Christmas Day, Einhard in an epic poem (in the style of Virgil) gushed, "For twelve hours the sun is without its light, but Charles continues to shine like an everlasting star," always enlightening, forever rectifying the holiness of his Roman Empire.[57]

Eleven years before becoming Augustus and an "everlasting star," Charles proclaimed in the sweeping capitulary *Admonitio generalis* ("A General Warning") that King Josiah in the Old Testament "strove to recall the kingdom which God had given him to the worship of the true God" by relentless "visitation, correction, and admonition." Of course, "I say this not to compare myself with his holiness," but because all persons and not just kings were duty-bound "to follow the examples of holy men." Charles dispatched his *missi* (envoys, emissaries, investigators) to all his bishops with copies of the capitulary, "so that, with the authority of our name, they may correct, together with you, those things that must be corrected." What needed correcting was listed like a penitential, with the same eclectic mix of the generally Christian ("honor thy father and mother") and the specifically pagan ("prohibiting sorcerers, enchanters or enchantresses"). Despite being rather verbose and rambling, a powerful apocalyptic urgency ran through the capitulary—"ye not know day or hour" of the Last Judgment, so every man, woman, and child must heed what bishops preached and what "I, Charles," admonished.[58]

This End of Days sensibility was more widespread than just amongst the intellectuals and soldiers in the royal entourage, which was why it frequently needed correction too. Quite wonderfully, Adelbert's heavenly letter from Christ, which had so infuriated Boniface half a century earlier, was still making the rounds along the Rhine as a sign of the End of Days. Charles in his *Admonitio* declared, once and for all, that this "most evil and most false letter" had not fallen from the sky, should not be believed or read, and needed "to be burned lest the people be cast into error by such writings."[59]

The *Admonitio*, despite the frequency of *ego Carolus*, was mostly written by an English deacon from York named Alcuin. Charles had first met him in Parma in 781; he was going to Rome, the other was leaving it. Whatever passed between the two of them, they impressed each other, with Alcuin becoming an advisor and teacher to the king, at first briefly in 782 and then more permanently in 786. (It was around this time that Willibald, after a long life, died at Heidenheim.) Einhard called him "the most learned man in the entire world."[60] Alcuin, like Bede, was a man defined by words and books, by his reading and writing. (He was also probably born soon after Bede died in 735.) In a relentless flow of words, he wrote poetry, dialogues, biblical exegesis, textbooks, biographies, and hundreds of letters that were affectionate, playful, correctional, and censorious, often within the same missive. Curiously, he never wrote a history like Bede; then again, no Carolingian writer did. Alcuin, like Boniface, knew the importance of being "Roman." Like Boniface, he was contemptuous of the talents of most bishops, abbots, monks, and priests in the Frankish kingdom. And in a nod to Boniface in the *Admonitio*, he hated the letter from heaven too. His outsider's disdain, though, was softened by his scholarly earnestness in wanting to teach what he thought was right and correct. Nevertheless, after the *Admonitio*, Alcuin returned to York in 790.[61]

Charles tempted him back to Francia three years later. "God led you, and brought you back, O revered master Albinus," says Karlus (Charles) to Albinus (one of Alcuin's nicknames) in *De Rhetorica*, a little Ciceronian dialogue Alcuin composed for the king on the art of public speaking in 794. Of course, there was vanity at work here, but there was also truth. Charles was genuinely happy at Alcuin's return and enjoyed talking with him. "Who could dare to say that we have talked in vain?" concludes Karlus.[62] Certainly not Einhard, who admired how Charles and Alcuin studied together for hours, going over rhetoric, dialectic, "the art of calculation," and astronomy "with deep purpose and great curiosity." They talked to each other in Latin, which the king spoke as well as his "native language," which would have been a mix of "rustic Roman" or early Romance (French) and Old High German. "Indeed," joked Einhard about the king's Latin, "he was such a fluent speaker, that he actually seemed verbose." Charles even tried learning to write Latin, placing wax tablets and notebooks under his bed pillows "so that, if he had any free time, he might accustom his hand to forming letters." Einhard regretted that such efforts were "too late in life and achieved little success."[63]

Charles may not have known how to write Latin, but he and advisors like Alcuin were deeply concerned about "correcting" its grammar, spelling, and how even it looked on parchment. According to the *Admonitio*, too many priests and monks, while desiring "to pray to God properly, pray badly because of incorrect books."[64] Charles often complained that letters sent to him, especially from monasteries, while sound in sentiment, were barely legible and appeared to have been written by uncouth clods. Dialects of Latin were still spoken as the vernacular in large parts of his realm, such as west of the Rhine, the Pyrenees, and northern Italy. In Britain, Ireland, Frisia, and now the German lands east of the Rhine, Latin was the language of precious books in iron-bound chests, missionaries, and colonizers. There is still a tendency to refer to Latin as a "dead language" for individuals like Alcuin, Boniface, or Huneberc, as their knowledge of it was only from what they read and discussed. This is misguided. No language was more alive for them than Latin, as it was the language of learning, friendship, and

Christianity. It evoked a Christian past that went back through Bede to Gregory the Great to Augustine of Hippo. If for Alcuin, like Bede, autobiography was bibliography, then without Latin he would have no sense of self, as he would have no books. For Huneberc, Latin briefly transformed her (or anyone reading or hearing what she had written about Willibald) into a handsome young man in the Holy Land. Ultimately, Latin was the language of heaven and God.

Which was why it was so important to write clear and "correct" Latin. What this meant for Alcuin was the language he knew and cherished from the schoolrooms and libraries of Northumbria. When Patricius wrote his *Confession* in fifth-century Britain, his words would have run together with no punctuation, no space between them, no lower-case letters, and no demarcation between sentences and paragraphs. This was and had been the convention for Latin writers and their manuscripts for generations, even for a man barely clinging to *Romanitas*. Patricius, though, still lived in a world that spoke and read Latin as its vernacular, and so he and his readers knew how to make sense of a seemingly messy alphabet soup on the page.

By the sixth century, Irish and then English monks found it more and more difficult, if not impossible, to read ancient books in their libraries or recently copied volumes from the continent. Gradually they added spaces between words and punctuation based upon the rhythms (breathing, pausing, emphasis, quickening, slowing) of reading aloud. Older books were then recopied in clearer, more distinct, and more uniform scripts. This "English Latin" was precise, pedantic, enunciated clearly, easy to read by sight, and unquestionably "Roman." This was why Boniface asked his friend Daniel to send him a book from an English library copied half a century earlier, as its script and punctuation were superior to the contemporary Frankish scrawl he was struggling to read. Alcuin flamboyantly talked about "flowers from Britain," that is, books from his old "walled garden in York," wafting their corrective fragrance on the wind throughout Francia.[65] It was this "English Latin" that Charles ordered should be taught and used by his "Christian people."

In 799, three years after Alcuin became abbot of the monastery of Saint Martin in Tours, he sent a letter to "King David" (Charles' nickname) from "Flaccus" (Alcuin's other nickname, aside from Albinus) about Latin, haste, headaches, and punctuation mistakes. He was replying to a letter accompanying a returned book, which the king, after listening to it read out loud, said had too many errors and needed correction. "Speed of thought often results in spelling and punctuation being less accurate than the rules of grammar demand," Alcuin offered by way of apology. "Nor, when I am weary with headaches, can I weigh the words which pour out in dictation." The book, which was not his own work, he had quickly dictated to a monk without proofreading the final product. Like most copyists, Alcuin tepidly added, the monk was ignorant and knew nothing of punctuation. It was a stinging embarrassment for the new abbot. Especially as the scriptorium at Saint Martin was perfecting and promoting what we now call Caroline minuscule, a neat, regular, punctuated script that still makes Carolingian manuscripts a pleasure to read. "I ... battle daily against ignorance in Tours," Flaccus sighed at the end of his letter to King David.[66]

One way Alcuin fought the stupidity of copyists was with a Latin poem on the scriptorium wall in Tours:

> May those who copy the pronouncements of the holy law
> and the hallowed sayings of the saintly fathers sit here.
> Here let them take care not to insert their silly remarks;
> may their hands not make mistakes through foolishness.
> Let them zealously strive to produce emended texts
> and may their pens fly along and follow the correct path.
> May they distinguish the proper meaning by colons and commas.[67]

For Alcuin, all knowledge that ever was and would be—indeed, the ineffable goodness of God Himself—was visible in a well-placed comma.

As Latin was corrected and "Englished," fewer and fewer monks, priests, and laypersons grasped what was being written or said in laws or sermons, let alone the infinite virtues of a comma. Charles and Alcuin were acutely aware of this reality, and so it was always assumed that a capitulary like the *Admonitio* would be translated (usually extemporaneously) into the vernacular. If no one understood why they were being admonished, then *correctio* was just a quaint and donnish notion. One of the more remarkable consequences of reforming Latin amongst intellectual elites was the encouragement and advocacy of vernacular languages developing west and east of the Rhine. In 813 a council of bishops in Tours formally decreed what had long been informally practiced: after preaching sermons in Latin, clerics should then translate them *in rusticam Romanam linguam aut theotiscam*, "into the language of rustic Romans or into German."[68] Truth was not lost in translation.

Theodulf, another intellectual in the entourage of Charles, in a remarkable treatise on images now known as the *Opus Caroli* (*Work of Charles*) or *Libri Carolini* (*Books for Charles*), forcefully argued that paintings and paint always lacked truth, unlike books and words (and commas). What provoked this aesthetic *correctio* was the reaffirmation of the adoration of icons at the East Roman Council of Nicaea in 787 (which, sadly, was not held in the Church of the Holy Fathers with its 318 portraits). Or rather, it was a lousy Latin translation—pens flying incorrectly, indeed!—made in Rome of the Greek canons. Three or so years later, it was sent to Charles and his advisors. Even if the translation had been good and the impression of superstitious idolatry not so pronounced, they probably would still have objected to "the errors of the Greeks." Charles was no iconoclast, but he saw nothing holy or truthful in paintings. Theodulf's treatise elaborated why this opinion was correct. (Amazingly, the surviving draft of the treatise even has marginal editorial comments from Charles as he listened to it.) In holy scripture, "nothing impure, and nothing false can be found," declared Theodulf. "But in painting, much that is false, wicked, foolish, and unsuitable can be found." God, "like a lord to his servants," was so distant in heaven as to be almost unimaginable. ("Excellent," agreed Charles.) This was why a painter cannot truthfully portray the "celestial fatherland which the eye has not seen nor has the ear heard," and which was promised in the New Testament. ("Reasonable," commented Charles.) This chasm between the Creator and humanity could be overcome only by the words of scripture and divine law, not by images. "Moses took the Book," not the painting, when he corrected Israel. Leaving aside Theodulf's sincere doubts about holiness, truth, and imagery, his treatise was a powerful and politic assertion that Charles, like God, was only truly known to his people by his words and his laws.[69]

Yet for all the godlike grandiosity of laws issued from on high, and intellectuals constantly writing about the importance of words and commas, what was just as important throughout kingdom and empire, if not more so, were the intimate face-to-face bonds of love, oaths of loyalty, and vassalage between Charles and his Christian people. By 789, the king required yearly oaths of loyalty from all fighting men in the fatherland, especially before the summer campaign season. According to the *Admonitio*, these oaths were given in "everyday speech" and in Latin, with individuals placing their hands upon the Gospels, or on altars, or on the relics of saints.[70] If the king could not personally be present when an oath was taken, then his *missi* fulfilled that function as if he were present. Nevertheless, part of Charles' relentless journeying throughout his realm was the need to constantly hold the hands of his secular and ecclesiastical lords as oaths were sworn to him.

In 802 a new and more radical oath was required. Charles commanded that every man in every part of his kingdom older than twelve, "whether ecclesiastical or layman, and each one according to his vow and occupation, should now promise to him as emperor the fidelity which he had previously promised him as king." It was to be sworn in public, "so that each might know, how great and how many things are comprehended in that oath," because what was being sworn was much more profound than just the old fidelity. Each man was to willingly "strive, in accordance with his knowledge and ability, to live completely in the holy service of God in accordance with the precept of God and in accordance with his own promise, because the lord emperor is unable to give to all individually the necessary care and discipline."[71] In promising faithfulness to Charles, all men (and some women, like abbesses) promised faithfulness to God. The more they struggled in correcting themselves as individual Christians, the more they proved their individual loyalty as vassals and "Romans." The new oath to Charles was a "gift" of free will from him, which was why he no longer personally corrected anyone, for if an individual justified the love of God, then they justified the love of their lord and emperor too.

Most men and boys, clerical or lay, west or east of the Rhine, neither comprehended nor cared about the gift of free will, seeing their new oath as just one more sign that their lord and emperor was now a distant, impersonal figure living in majesty at his palace in Aachen, the "second Rome." Ironically, while the sacred ideology undergirding the empire was monumental, the imperial capital was, especially when compared to Constantinople or Baghdad, quite modest. Charles (along with his courtiers, concubines, sons, daughters, bodyguards, monks, priests, servants, craftsmen, and horses) lived in a sprawling arc of colonnaded wooden buildings. On the edges of this half-moon were the workshops of thousands of masons, carpenters, sculptors, painters, mosaicists, and metalworkers. Inside this timbered constellation (of which no trace remains) was a royal church and an audience hall constructed of local rough-hewn stone and mortar. The church (whose design changed as builders experimented with different techniques during construction) was sixteen-sided, just over a hundred feet high, covered in a thin coat of red plaster, with a dome nestled on top, and in the middle of that was a golden apple. The interior was an airy octagonal space of two levels supported by surprisingly complicated vaulting. The church and the audience hall were connected by a long narrow portico. Hundreds of columns, sheets of marble, shiny mosaic shards, and other materials were shipped from Rome and Ravenna. (The masons for the audience hall were from Rome too.) Charles even transported a sixth-century bronze equestrian statue of King Theodoric from Ravenna to Aachen. Italian *spolia* and trophies were intentionally symbolic and not just evidence of a lack of skills and resources in the Ardennes. The "second Rome" was literally built from the ruins of the first.[72]

On the gallery of the church at Aachen was the royal and imperial throne, solid and simple in slabs of marble, like a chair made from oversized children's blocks. It was placed opposite a mosaic or fresco on the domed ceiling of Christ enthroned. The emperor on his throne looked down upon the congregation and, with only a slight tilt of his head, upward to a shimmering portrayal of the heavenly Judge. Charles hovered between humanity and divinity.[73]

Einhard, as if responding to criticism that Charles was cocooning himself in ceremony and pomposity at Aachen, stressed in his *Life* of Charles that the emperor was like any other Frank when it came to the little (well, Frankish) things in life. "He normally wore the customary attire of the Franks," which was a linen shirt and underwear, silk fringed tunic and stockings, belt, and gold-pommeled sword. Charles rode and hunted almost every day, something in which "hardly a people on earth can rival the Franks." Although he liked to listen to Augustine's *City of God* read aloud in Latin while he dined, he was also fond of "the very old Germanic poems, in which the deeds and wars of ancient kings were sung." He even wished for these songs to be "written down and preserved for posterity." Unfortunately, nothing has survived of these old Frankish poems. Charles was apparently an excellent swimmer—"no one was considered better"—and when he was not hunting or riding he swam in the hot springs near his palace. Nevertheless, Einhard admitted, even something as quotidian as a quick dip was a great ceremonial occasional at Aachen, with the emperor usually paddling and floating amidst "such a crowd of courtiers and bodyguards, that there might be more than a hundred people bathing together."[74]

And then there was the elephant at Aachen. This fabulous beast arrived as a gift from the Abbasid caliph Harun al-Rashid in 802. His name was Abul Abaz. Charles had asked the caliph for such an animal when he sent his own envoys to Jerusalem and Baghdad, equally loaded with presents and expressions of goodwill. More gifts from Harun al-Rashid arrived in 807, such as a brass water clock with twelve little copper horsemen, two massive brass candelabra, "robes, spices, and other riches of the East."[75] Charles mainly "struck up friendships with kings overseas," wrote Einhard, "so that the poor Christians living under their rule might receive some relief and assistance." He lavishly and often spontaneously distributed charity, "which the Greeks call 'alms,'" amongst impoverished Christians in "Jerusalem, Alexandria, and Carthage." Which was why perhaps the greatest gift from Harun al-Rashid was that the Holy Sepulcher in Jerusalem, this "sacred and salvific place . . . might be considered as under the control of Charles."[76]

Even if Charles' authority over the Holy Sepulcher was just diplomatic show, it was still a pantomime with enough purpose for him to commission "An Inventory Memorandum of God's Houses or Monasteries in and around the Holy City of Jerusalem." Sometime before 808, a party of imperial investigators from Aachen, accompanied by Arabic and Greek interpreters, questioned, counted, and classified all Christian monks, nuns, hermits, and clergy living within and near Jerusalem. All told, 405 religious persons were tallied, as well as fifteen lepers. For example: "A monastery of 26 women[, of whom] 17 nuns who serve at the Holy Sepulcher are from the empire of Lord Charles." Or in a list of thirty-five hermits "who reside scattered amongst their cells," the languages in which they prayed were noted, from eleven "who sing the psalms in Greek" to five singing in Latin to "one who sings the psalms in Arabic."

In Bethlehem, "where Our Lord Jesus Christ deigned to be born from the Holy Virgin Mary," there were, quite marvelously, two hermits "who sit on top of columns on the example of St. Symeon." At Nablus there was another hermit on a column. The investigators even counted steps. "When you go down from Jerusalem into the Valley of Jehoshaphat, where the tomb of St. Mary is, there are 195 steps; to go up on the Mount of Olives, 537." The inventory was terse, quirky, and surprisingly vivid in the way that seemingly banal lists often can be. One thing that obviously did not interest the imperial investigators, but does reveal itself in their religious accounting, was that English wanderers like Willibald seem to have disappeared from the Holy Land. [77]

In 813 earthquakes shook Aachen. The portico between the church and the audience hall collapsed. There was an eclipse of the sun. A fiery meteor fell from the sky. The golden apple atop the church dome was struck by lightning. Inside the church the red letters that spelled out "Princeps" in "Karolus Princeps" suddenly faded so that they were almost invisible. "Yet Charles either rejected all these things," said Einhard, "or acted as if none of them had anything to do with him."

Nevertheless, the emperor knew he was dying. He slept barely three hours a night, one foot was lame, and fevers racked his body with shivers and sweats. In September, as all his other sons were dead, and on the recommendation of his lords and advisors, especially Einhard, he crowned his surviving son Louis (known as "the Pious") at Aachen "as the co-ruler of the entire kingdom and the heir to the imperial title." Then the limping, feverish insomniac went off hunting, enjoying himself to the last as a Frank. By November, though, as the snow was starting to fall in the Ardennes, he took to his bed, hot and damp, breathing with difficulty. He died at nine o'clock in the morning of Saturday, January 28, 814, aged seventy-two, having reigned for forty-seven years. Charles the Great, "who gloriously increased the kingdom of the Franks," was buried in his church at Aachen. [78]

9 A Beautiful Mountain

Thirteen to fourteen years later, Charles was in agony as animals mauled his genitals halfway up an infinitely high and stunningly beautiful white mountain. The base of the mountain rose out of hell, while its chilly, windswept peak brushed against heaven. It was encircled by a surging river of fire. An elderly monk named Wetti from Reichenau (a monastery on an island in Lake Constance) was flying around the mountain with his angel companion in early November when he recognized the suffering soul, "who formerly ruled the kingdoms of the people of Rome and Italy."

Lower down the mountain Wetti had already discovered that priests and monks and the women they "defiled" were beaten on their genitals "every third day without fail." (These fornicators were also clothed in clinging flames—all over for the men, only as far as the pudenda for the women.)

Wetti asked the angel why a prince, "who seemed to be very special amongst others in defending the Catholic faith and the rule of the Holy Church in the present day, could be afflicted by a punishment so degrading." The angel replied that while the prince certainly had done many splendid things admired by God, his good deeds were squandered in the "charms of sexual defilement." An individual, even an emperor, could never bury "a little obscenity" under a mound of virtuous acts. God saw and remembered everything. "Nevertheless," said the angel about Charles, "he is destined to the fate of the elect in eternal life."[79]

Wetti's vision of Charles suffering on the beautiful mountain was part of an out-of-body journey he breathlessly described a day before he died and which was hastily copied on a wax tablet by Heito, the former abbot of Reichenau, around 824. Unlike the flight of Barontus and the archangel Raphael a century and a half earlier, this monk and his anonymous angel never visited hell and paradise, mostly only floating around the great white mountain, which was a place for the purgation of sins rather than eternal damnation. Boniface's Wenlock monk traveled to a similar betwixt-and-between place. Confusingly, Wetti and the angel visited a cavernous palace where God sat enthroned, except this vast building constructed out of cosmic *spolia* (celestial sculptures, starlight, infinite arches of precious metal) was not explicitly heaven. Moreover, unlike what Barontus experienced, where God was so distant as to be almost unimaginable, He now talked to and even touched the soul in His presence. The reason the angel brought Wetti to God's throne was that the old monk was going to die tomorrow—shockingly, the angel only told him just as they stood before the throne—and they must plead for mercy. What sins had Wetti not excised through penance? What little obscenities had he forgotten? "He should have given edifying examples," scolded a voice from the throne, "but he did not." Eventually God relented—after a mass of holy virgins rushed the throne and begged on Wetti's behalf—saying, "If he teaches good and leads with good example and corrects to whom he had previously provided bad example, your request will be granted."[80]

Wetti's vision now took a quite explicit confessional turn, and this was why the torment of Charles was so important. For the angel turned to him when they floated away from His throne and said in a seeming non sequitur, "God is offended by nothing more than when a person sins contrary to nature." Wetti knew what he meant. "Sodomy," said the angel, just to be sure. "Sodomy," the angel went on, warming to his subject, not only infected "the polluted souls of males who lie together, but is even found in the ruin of many couples." Wetti acted nonplussed. "So you are ordered by divine authority to proclaim this publicly," instructed the angel. "In the end, those polluted in this obscenity will never deserve entry to the kingdom of heaven." Wetti demurred, saying that he was the wrong person for such admonishments. "What God wishes and commands you to do, through me," yelled the angel, "do not dare put off!" After calming down, he listed other vices—gluttony, fancy dress, overweening pride—that barred monks "from the entrance of eternal life." Again and again, though, as Wetti noted bemusedly, "the angel introduced a discussion of the sin of sodomy," at least five times, maybe more.[81]

Wetti got the less-than-subtle hint—the angel had once failed with that long-haired sexual athlete Samson and he was not about to fail now—as did those to whom he told his vision. He had either defiled himself with "sodomy" or tolerated it in others. (This need not mean anal sex, for as Theodore's penitential pointed out, "the worst of evils" was semen ejaculated into the mouth of a man or a woman. Both were acts of sodomy. But then so was any sexual activity not explicitly reproductive.) Either way, this was the bad example Wetti must now correct before he died. Or even after death.

Charles on the beautiful mountain vividly showed that the penitential culture on earth now carried over into the afterlife. It was still better to undergo penance while alive, but if one overlooked "a little obscenity," then it was possible, if painful for eons, to ultimately be redeemed and enter heaven. Even fornicating emperors. Even Wetti.[82]

10 Cloud-Ships and Storm-Makers

Cloud-ships sailed through the summer skies over the Saone and Rhône valleys in the early ninth century. They floated in the upper air waiting for a "raised wind" conjured by the incantations of "storm-makers" on the ground. When the incanted wind shot up into the sky, emerald-black storm clouds appeared, exploding with thunder, flashing with lightning, lacerating fields and vineyards with hail. The cloud-ships quickly descended in

the aftermath, scooping up all the crushed grain and grapes, before stealing far away over the horizon. These magical storms and sky raids were so
common in the summer around Lyon that whenever a light breeze rustled
the leaves, everyone knowingly said, "The wind has been raised," followed
by the oath, "Curse that tongue, let it wither and be torn out!"[83]

In 817, Agobard, the new archbishop of Lyon, gave an angry sermon
denouncing this "great and foolish belief" in storm-makers and cloud-
ships. What shocked him was how "almost everyone, nobles and non-
nobles, from the city and from the countryside, old and young, think that
hail and thunder can be made at the will of men." Yet everyone he questioned about the storm-makers and cloud-ships, while adamant that such
persons and things existed, had never seen one or the other. "Once it was
reported to me that someone said that he himself had seen such things.
With great interest I myself set out to see him, and I did." A dead end. This
fellow, despite naming a storm-maker, a storm, and a ruined field, "nevertheless confessed that he himself had not been present," only hearing what
had happened secondhand.

Once, though, a mob showed Agobard three men and a woman who had
supposedly fallen out of the sky from their ship. These cloud-sailors were in
chains, waiting to be stoned to death. He convinced the crowd they were
mistaken, but only in this instance, not generally about the reality of flying
ships. "This stupidity is not the least part of this unfaithfulness," he sighed,
as it was widely believed that some men, while not knowing how to raise
the wind, "nevertheless know how to defend the inhabitants of a place from
storms." What added to this madness was that anyone wishing to be defended from hailstorms gave these "storm-defenders" a regular gift of grain
and grapes known as *canonicum*. And yet no matter how many times he
preached about giving tithes to priests, or alms to widows, orphans, or other
poor people, he was ignored, while everyone gladly handed over their canonical gifts to the storm-defenders. Amazingly, the cloud-sailors were from
a land named Magonia—and so, at least in Agobard's rendering of what he
heard, they were *mangones*, the airborne descendants of the Galatian slavers
condemned by Augustine of Hippo four hundred years earlier.[84]

Agobard never doubted that it was possible for men to raise winds and
dash a vineyard with hail, except that, if it did happen, only a saint could
do it, and even then only if God allowed it, which, as He never shared the

treasures of His household, like hail, He would not.[85] Anyone who believed in storm-makers and storm-defenders simply did not understand
that it was impossible for humans to do what God would never let them do.
Intriguingly, Agobard never accused his listeners of being pagans or tricked
by the devil, he just thought them foolish, half-formed Christians.

Overall, Agobard was more exasperated than anything, especially as he
knew exactly what was going on around (and above) him. He wanted
the men and women of the Lyonnais to come to him with their worries about the unpredictability of summer weather, their fears of starving,
their suspicion of strangers, and their acquiescence to individuals more
powerful and threatening than themselves. Of course, he would have
been no help, as everyone, including himself, knew. The storm-makers
and storm-defenders, with the potential for *complete* harm and protection,
were amongst the local Frankish elites. (In many past societies, the talent
for calamity was often imagined as dwelling in the dark social fringes;
not so in early ninth-century Lyon.) They entrenched their power over
weaker men and women through their supposed ability to unleash or stop
hail. The system of thought accounting for environmental disaster, and in
which it was sensible that winds were raised or banished by humans, was
also the system of society. In other words, coercive and subservient relationships already existed in Lyon before they were realized in the erratic
savagery of a hailstorm.

Agobard, as a Visigothic refugee from northern Spain, was an outsider to
Lyon and the empire. (Theodulf had a similar background but was much
smarter and cannier.) He was not a powerful man in his own right and was
not related to anyone with power. The previous archbishop, Leidrad, was
from an influential Bavarian noble family and had been a *missus* of Charles.
Agobard did not even control all of the possessions of his church; rather,
some properties were held in beneficiary and usufructuary right by local
nobles, such as the count of Lyon, who possessed heritable *precaria* (ecclesiastical property granted to a powerful layman by a secular ruler, who was
then able to support and reward his followers at no real cost to himself).[86]
He bitterly opposed laymen, even emperors, having authority over clergy
and rights over the lands of churches and monasteries. This was why tithes
mattered so much to him and why he hated the *canonicum* given to storm-
defenders. It was not just that he needed the funds, which he did, but
tithing was the duty of all good Christians.

Yet the tithe—that is, a yearly tax of a tenth of the income of a household given to the local church (and so the Church in the broadest sense)—was still a relatively new innovation. It was neither consistently observed nor even demanded throughout much of Latin Christendom. In Francia, despite repeated capitularies enforcing the tithe, it was an easily ignored duty going back no more than three generations. "Even we who have been born and brought up in the Catholic faith find it hard to agree to a full tithing of property," Alcuin observed to Charles twenty years earlier when suggesting that Saxons, as "beginners in the faith," perhaps should not be burdened with the tithe. "It is better to lose the tithe than destroy the faith."[87] Agobard was not so charitable.

Agobard's sermon was a less-than-sympathetic lesson about the precariousness of the agrarian rhythms upon which all medieval existence depended. The destruction of vines and crops by hail and tempests just before or during the twenty or so days of the summer harvest was (as it still is) a catastrophe. The need to cross this dangerous threshold was especially pronounced in the untidy patchwork of localized subsistence economies, more inclined to gift-giving than moneylending and colored with only the most minor of regional specializations, that stitched together the early ninth-century West. (Charles may have "renewed" the coinage in 793 with new, heavier silver pennies, but Francia was far from being a monetarized economy.)[88] Three to five million people (depending upon whether one assumes that roughly fifty persons or vaguely seventy-five lived within each square mile) lived in the empire west of the Rhine, farming the stony, dry soils of the Brittany coast to the rich, heavy clays and loams of the Ardennes to the porous limestone hills of the Saône and Rhône valleys. Agricultural techniques were competent, but there was little to no surplus.

Although more land was under cultivation than a century earlier, there were still vast areas either untouched by the plow or abandoned after previously being farmed and settled. For instance, when Leidrad surveyed the properties of the church of Lyon between 809 and 812, he counted 1,091 individual farms, of which 131 were vacant and unpopulated.[89] Around 800, as the climate was becoming ever so slightly warmer, albeit stormier, and so the husbandry of crops and animals somewhat easier, even with good harvests, starvation was always a threat—such as the terrible famines that ripped through Francia in 792–793 and 805–806.[90]

In 810 a devastating cattle plague swept through the empire, which Agobard recalled in his sermon, less because of bovine suffering and human deprivation than the conspiratorial reasoning and murderous reaction of many rural communities:

> A few years ago, when the cattle were dying, a certain foolishness was being disseminated, so that people said that Grimoald, the Duke of Benevento, because he was an enemy of the most Christian Emperor Charles, had dispatched men with dust, which they spread through fields, mountains, meadows, and springs—and from that dispersed dust, the cattle died. For this reason we heard and saw that many people were captured and some were killed.[91]

Many of the men killed were tied to planks and thrown in the Rhône. They came from outside the Lyonnais. They were strangers, easily accused of spreading dust and killing cattle. They were the loose and rootless humanity of beggars, thieves, refugees from hunger, and roving holy men and women whose miracles had failed one too many times. A few of them had even flown in from Magonia. The power behind hailstorms was specific and identifiably elite, whereas dust spread surreptitiously was obviously harm from the margins. An accusation of killing cattle widely and covertly was irrefutable when the accused lacked local protectors like storm-defenders. Agobard noted how "the captured men gave false testimony against themselves," admitting to having and spreading "dust of such a nature." These men, despite flogging, torture, and imminent death, never stopped saying "they really did do it."[92]

Agobard's learned allusion to the cloud-sailors engaging in slave raiding was more than just misunderstanding what he was told (and then tried saying) in "rustic Roman." While there were household slaves, which were remarkably more often possessed by families of low social standing than by wealthy aristocrats, there was no widespread economy of humans captured and sold in the Roman Empire of Charles and Louis.[93] Agobard himself, while once ranting about his fear of Christian slaves converting to Judaism in Jewish households, assumed these slaves were either inherited or were freemen who had sold themselves into slavery.[94] In 793, when Charles employed roughly six thousand men for three months digging a canal between the rivers Rednitz and Altmühl, and so connecting the Rhine and the Danube, none of them were slaves.[95] (This pharaonic project failed, as the ground was too waterlogged.) Certainly, with the end of the great summer campaigns of the Frankish host around 810, so that no new lands were taken and the yearly flow of loot and plunder stopped, nobles and their retainers looked closer to home for spoils, becoming the bullying oppressors of lesser free men.[96]

This harsh reality was implicit in Agobard's sermon. Even in Wetti's vision there was a place on the beautiful mountain for counts and nobles, "blinded by the expectation of gifts," viciously persecuting the powerless.[97] But this oppression was not about seizing and selling weaker men, women, and children as slaves. It was much easier and more profitable to get canonical gifts every summer. A slave trade did exist, but it was on the edges of the Frankish empire, undertaken by Iberian Saracen pirates and the shadowy, swift-sailing Northmen or Vikings—and it was to the latter that Agobard linked Augustine's fifth-century African slavers and his contemporary cloud-sailors from Magonia.

11 Correction

The history of the eighth and early ninth centuries is overwhelmed by the seeming inevitability of Charles and his new Roman Empire. This is inescapable, as the consequences reverberated throughout the West. Nevertheless, it should never be forgotten that for all the conquests and capitularies, what was achieved by the Carolingians was surprisingly fragile, easily shattered if more than one son survived the father.

What endured, more than even the idea and reality of a Western Roman Empire, was the notion of a "corrected" Latin Christianity that was recognizable from the North Sea to the Mediterranean, from the Garonne to the Rhine. This was a Christendom that, because every man, woman, and child was always in need of *correctio*, saw paganism or heresy in every forest clearing, misplaced comma, and storm cloud. It took centuries for this to be attained, and even then, it fractured the moment it was, but it began with men like Boniface, Alcuin, and Charles. It also began with a holy fool like Willibald, who, by living his twenties following in the footsteps of Christ, radically prefigured by four centuries what would eventually define, for good or ill, what was a "correct" Christian.

THE SCANDINAVIAN LANDS OF
THE NORTHMEN (OR VIKINGS)

N
W E
S

White Sea

Borg

Lake Onega

Lake Ladoga Staraya Ladoga

Frösö

Lade

FINLAND

Gorodishe *Lake Ilmen*

Volkhov R.

NORWAY

SWEDEN Uppsala

ESTONIA

Bergen

Birka

Lake Mälaren Helgö

VIKEN

Styrstad

Dvina R.

Skiringssheath

Gotland

SEMIGALLIA

Paviken

Slöinge

Öland

North Sea

Samsø SKANIA

Baltic Sea

JUTLAND

Lund

Barnholm

DENMARK

Jelling Leire Uppakra

Zealand

Truso

Ribe

Hedeby

Rügen

Danevirke

Wollin

Vistula R.

Hamburg

FRISIA

Bremen

Weser R. *Elbe R.*

Oder R.

0 km 100   200

0 miles   100   200

VI

The Harrying of the Heathen

825–972

1 Findan's Cave

Around 825, Findan, a noble young warrior from Leinster, was sent by his father to a long sandy beach on the Irish Sea to buy back his sister, kidnapped by "those pagans called Northmen." He feared these pirates from the Norwegian fjords, Denmark, and southern Sweden, having once cowered behind a door when they chased him through a house during one of their sudden attacks. This time, though, accompanied by spearmen, an interpreter, and the market value of his sister, he felt safe enough. "But, early on the journey, he was captured by the pagans, thrown into chains, and carried without delay to their ships," lying in low water by the beach. He lay shackled all night, starving and thirsty. Fortunately, the next morning he was released, as some of the Northmen decided it was bad policy to snatch an individual delivering a ransom. Findan, while elated, failed at securing his sister, as she was long gone across the sea, sold by one Northman to another.[1]

A decade or so later, Findan's father and brother were brutally murdered (arson while sleeping, speared while escaping) by one of the two petty kings of Leinster in a blood feud. "Not surprisingly, this event caused fierce and inexorable hostility." The surviving son wanted revenge, as everyone knew and expected. Peace was penitentially restored when some "faithful men" compelled a hefty compensation from the king. "In the same year, however, Findan's enemies, fearing his vengeance might descend upon them, and that resentment at his father's death might revive in his heart, and equally from a desire of being rid of him, secretly devised a trap." They planned a grand beach party and invited their unsuspecting prey. Findan naively accepted, lulled by his reparation. In the middle of the feasting, he was grabbed by Northmen allied with his enemies, and swiftly carried out to sea. The leader of his captors, "unwilling to return home just yet, as was customary, sold him on to another, who sold him to a third, and the third to a fourth." This last Northman, "wishing to see his homeland again," and whose ship already had a brace of Irish slaves apart from Findan, sailed away toward the long summer twilight of the North Atlantic.[2]

As Findan's Northmen neared Orkney (an archipelago of roughly seventy islands huddled around the top of Britain) they encountered other ships from their homeland sailing toward the Irish coast. One of the new ships glided alongside. A spritely fellow jumped aboard and asked what the spoils were like in Ireland. On Findan's ship, "however, was a man whose brother had been killed by the questioner, who was no sooner recognized than killed." Immediately, a bitter sea skirmish erupted between the two ships, with warriors leaping between the vessels. "Findan, wishing to support his master and companions, got to his feet despite his chains." Whatever he imagined himself doing was never tested, as the crews from the other ships, while initially letting the vendetta play out, intervened to stop the fighting. Findan's ship, bloodied but unbowed, sailed away.[3]

But not very far, as the Northmen rowed into the Bay of Ireland and moored in the Loch of Stenness, a natural harbor on Orkney Mainland (the largest island in the archipelago). They wanted a respite and "a fair wind" after their fight. Findan was unchained as a reward for his loyalty in battle, although not freed from slavery. His brief fidelity was not a ruse, as he believed in the inviolability of blood feuds—his whole life up to this point had been shaped by them—but now, left alone to wander unguarded, "he began to explore the island, wondering anxiously about how to get away safely." On a lonely pebble beach he hid inside a sea cave. As the wind and tide were rising, his captors wanted to leave, so they started searching for him, calling out his name. "On one side the sea threatened, and on the other fear of his enemies tormented him." Massive waves started crashing and flooding Findan's cave. He even heard some Northmen walking on the rock above him, but he stayed silent, drowning in the suffocating sea. He gulped for air when he could, his body stinging with pain. After a day and a night, the sea receded, apart from the odd wind-whipped wave slugging him in the face as it barreled in and out of the cave. "Robbed of his physical strength," Findan crawled on all fours over the slippery pebbles and onto the dry scrubby land behind him.[4]

Findan was terrified of the Northmen finding him, but they had left. He was worried about other humans, as there were ancient cairns and henges near the shore, but he saw no one. He discovered nothing but the vast sea all around. He stumbled about this island for three days, eating heather and bog myrtle. When all hope seemed lost, "he saw the monsters of the sea and huge dolphins playing and diving close to the shore." (Pods of whales, dolphins, and porpoises are still spotted every summer in Orkney.) He fell to his knees, tearfully praying, "God, Creator of both these brute breasts and of me, a human, You gave them the sea as their element and to me You gave the earth on which to set my feet. As is Your merciful custom, help me in my present troubles. . . . I dedicate my service to You. . . . I shall journey into exile and never return to my homeland." Findan then dived fully clothed into the sea. "Instantly, divine mercy made his clothing rigid so that its support kept him from sinking." It even seemed as if his clothes swam dolphin-like independent of him, surfing through the boisterous waves to another island, probably Hoy to the south. Once ashore, this strange man from the sea lived with a kindly English bishop who had once studied in Ireland. Findan thanked God for escaping the Northmen.[5]

Findan died forty years later, around 880, as a seventysomething Benedictine monk at the monastery of Rheinau on an island in the Rhine (in what is now modern Switzerland). He had lived his last twenty-two years as a recluse entombed in his own private "cave" beside the monastery church, nibbling tiny fish, praying to Saint Patrick, sleeping on a bed of pebbles, and nightly battling demons trying to enslave him.[6] Another Rheinau monk wrote a *Life* of Findan soon after his death; apart from his long and largely anecdote-less existence as a walled-in holy man, it was entirely about his early troubles with the Northmen. In a coincidence too obvious not to be deliberate, Findan's seclusion from the world in his Rhenish cave occurred during some of the most tumultuous decades of the so-called Viking Age—as he had once escaped from the Northmen, so he did again.

2 The Northmen Were Beyond Counting

In 793 the Northmen attacked Lindisfarne, a small tidal island off the northeast coast of Northumbria long settled by Irish and English monks as a sister monastery to Iona in the Inner Hebrides. This was one of their earliest recorded raids outside Scandinavia. News of this "harrying of the heathen"—in the words of an English chronicler—reverberated all the way to Aachen, where Alcuin quickly dashed off a letter to the surviving monks.[7] He consoled ("God chastises every son whom He accepts, so perhaps He has chastised you more because He loves you more") and censured (such a punishment must be the result of some sin) before ending with a promise that he would talk to King Charles to see what could be done "about the boys who have been carried off by the pagans as prisoners."[8]

It is not known what or if Charles did anything about the boys from Lindisfarne, but his last campaign before becoming too infirm to fight was against a Danish king and his "two hundred ships" ravaging the islands and coastal settlements of Frisia in early summer 810. Or it almost was. After the emperor hastily gathered an army at the river Aller, he was told that the Northmen had sailed home and that their king had been assassinated by a rival. The only casualty in the Frankish ranks was the elephant Abul Abaz, collapsing in mortal exhaustion beside the Rhine.[9]

After Charles died in 814, Northmen raids into Francia increased in frequency and magnitude every year for a century. All along the Frisian coast, farmhouses, fishing villages, monasteries, and especially the trading entrepôt of Dorestad were relentlessly assaulted, pillaged, and burned. Even in the aftermath of high Christmas tides flooding Frisia and drowning thousands in 840, Danish pirates floated over the lingering floodwaters at Easter and kidnapped survivors. The emporium of Quentovic on the English Channel was razed in 842. "They left nothing in it except for those buildings they were paid to spare."

In 820 thirteen ships attempted to sail into the Seine but were beaten back by a coastal guard; in 845 "one hundred and twenty ships" rushed the river estuary and ransacked Paris two months later; in 856 another fleet wintered on an island in the river before burning Paris in the summer; five years later, what was left of the city was set on fire again by a different host. In 845 "six hundred ships" journeyed down the Elbe, picking off monasteries and abducting boys and girls. In 843 a flotilla sailed along the northeast Atlantic coast and, after entering the Loire, destroyed Nantes. A year later ships sailed up the Garonne and looted Toulouse. In 858 some Northmen, after hugging the eastern Atlantic from Brittany to Gibraltar, sailed into the Mediterranean and up the Rhône, plundering Arles before wintering in the Camargue wetlands. (In 842 "Moorish pirates" did the same thing, "ravaging everything on their route.") In 882 a band of Danes even burned the palace at Aachen. Monarchs, abbots, soldiers, and villagers sometimes abated the ferocity of the Northmen with "canonical" payments of silver coins, horses, cattle, crops, and, despite capitularies repeatedly banning such gifts, swords and shirts of mail.[10]

In 863 a monk named Ermentarius lamented how his Benedictine community and the bones of their patron saint, Philibert, were refugees for thirty years in the wake of the Northmen. Initially, bones and monks lived on the long flat tidal island of Noirmoutier in the Bay of Biscay near the mouth of the Loire. Except "the sudden and unforeseen attacks of the Northmen" were so horrific that the monks feared these "faithless men would dig up the grave of the blessed Philibert and scatter whatever they found in it hither and yon, or rather throw it into the sea." In 836, bones and monks departed Noirmoutier, fleeing inland along the Loire valley to Samur, then a place called Cunauld, and after that a series of nameless hideouts farther and farther away from the sea. "Everywhere there were massacres of Christians, raids, devastations, and burnings." Untold ships stormed ocean beaches and choked flowing rivers, "and the Northmen were beyond counting." Everyone everywhere was in flight; "rare was the man who said: 'Stay, stay, resist, fight for the fatherland, for children and relatives.'" Only in 862 were the bones of Philibert finally "smuggled away from the grasp of the Northmen" when the surviving monks crossed over the Massif Central to safety in Tournus on the banks of the Saône, three hundred miles from Noirmoutier.[11]

A young monk from the monastery of Saint-Germain-des-Prés in Paris named Abbo witnessed a great assault by the Northmen on the city in November 885. Soon afterward he composed an epic Latin poem (as an exercise modeled after Virgil's *Eclogues*) about the siege, whose opening description of the ships on the Seine—not the seven hundred he wrote about, but more likely a still-astonishing two to three hundred—vividly captured the shock and marvel of seeing a river overgrown with a merciless forest:

> Ships—seven hundred, not to mention smaller ones,
> Tall ships, beyond a number that could reckon them—
> In vulgar tongue the custom is to call them "barques."
> The Seine's deep surge was packed so full with ships like
>   these—

Extending two miles' distance and a little more—
That you would wonder where the river'd gone, unseen,
Into a cave: the pine had thrown a veil to cover it,
And oaks and elms and alders that grow by the streams.[12]

3 Ships, Bloodshed, and Death

The oldest and most wonderful Northman ship so far excavated was built around 820 and buried in a mound at Oseberg (near Tønsberg) in Norway in 834. This well-preserved oak ship is seventy feet long and sixteen feet across. It is low (just over five feet from the keel to the upper sides) with a modest draft (thirty-two inches under water). Stern and bow rise lissomely into elegant curlicues. There are fifteen oar ports for thirty rowers. The ship-wright awkwardly positioned the thirty-eight-foot mast three feet forward of midships, either as compensation for the slight distortion in the hull or just as a product of inexperience, as sails were a relatively new nautical tech-nology for Scandinavians. It was rigged with a square sail (twenty-eight feet in length either side) made of tightly woven wool and dyed, waterproofed, and stiffened with red ochre and horse mane fat (or beef suet). The rigging was made from horsehair rope, hemp rope, or walrus-skin rope. Modern reconstructions of the Oseberg ship have achieved remarkable speeds of ten or more knots under sail and three to four knots when rowed. In a squall or blow it would have been dangerously difficult to handle no matter the rate. Its shallow waterline would have required constant bailing out by the crew in even slightly choppy seas. Yet it was in ships like this that the Northmen attacked Lindisfarne and stole away with Findan.[13]

It is not known where the Oseberg ship sailed before it became a mag-nificent tomb for two women, one in her eighties and the other around fifty. Neither is it known who these women were or what relationship, if any, they had with the ship. A wooden bucket amongst the grave goods bears the runic inscription "Sigrid owns [me]," so perhaps that was the name of one of the deceased. The women were buried in a ritual lasting over four months from early spring until late summer. After the ship was dragged in-land along a specially excavated trench, a wooden burial chamber or cabin was erected just behind the mast. Cooking pots and a freshly butchered ox were placed in the cabin and then it and the stern were covered with rocks and soil. The women, in beautifully embroidered clothes, were laid inside the now underground chamber with cushions, sleds, beds, tapestries, ten chests, and Sigrid's bucket. This half a mound with half a ship sticking out were the proscenium arch and stage for the last acts honoring the two voyagers. The bow was tied to a large stone as if the ship were moored in a bay. Three sets of pine oars were put in place ready for rowing out to sea. In the very late summer, just as apples and bilberries were added to the provisions aft, ten horses and three dogs were decapitated in the fore part of the ship, soaking the prow in blood. Finally, what was visible was buried under seventy tons of rock and turf.[14]

The Oseberg ship was a subterranean barge for royalty, although whether one or both of the women were princesses or queens is unknown. Or was the younger woman (whose DNA suggests her family was of partially Iranian descent) a servant to the older? Or vice versa? And was one of these women sacrificed for the other? Despite the grandeur of this ship mound, hundreds if not thousands of boat burials, lavish and modest, involving men and women of high and low standing, occurred throughout Denmark, Sweden, Norway, and other lands, including Orkney, settled by Northmen from the late eighth century onward. And if an individual was not buried in a ship, then ships were carved on gravestones. What is so striking about the ubiquity of ships in the sacred, social, and martial universe of Scandinavians was that it was a recent phenomenon, beginning perhaps less than a century before Sigrid and her companion set sail for the afterlife.[15]

In the middle of the eighth century most people in Denmark, Sweden, and Norway were farmers living in hamlets. In northern Scandinavia such communities were usually two or three farmsteads of small turf and wood-paneled stone buildings beside fjords and bays, growing barley, oats, and rye wherever they could. In the late ninth century a Northman lord named Óttarr (or Ohthere in English) from "the North Way"—the Norwegian coast—described his homeland to King Alfred of Wessex as "very long and very narrow," so whatever livestock or fields his people "grazed or plowed lies close to the sea, and even that is in some places very rocky."[16] Danish and southern Swedish hamlets were slightly larger, at six or seven farmsteads with bigger wooden buildings (half a dozen sheds around a longhouse) and fields sowed with a greater variety of cereal crops. Flax, hemp, and woad were raised everywhere for weaving and dyeing. Horses, cattle, sheep, and goats were widespread, cosseted, and closely guarded.

Overall, though, it was a hard existence, and most individuals suffered periodically from malnutrition. Hunting reindeer and moose helped, but more than anything, fishing, trading, and raiding were necessary for survival. Almost all farmers had some type of boat or ship, often no more than a hollowed-out tree-trunk canoe or a rowed skiff. As hardwoods and bog iron were plentiful and the skills of some shipwright-farmers developed exponentially—clearly techniques were shared, stolen, or traded between hamlets—ships of astonishing sophistication were being built soon after 750. Around this time masts and sails were added to ships, allowing for longer and swifter journeys. (Of course, Scandinavians had long known about sails; they just saw no use for them until, mysteriously, they did.) Large and small vessels started traversing these little communities from the Arctic Circle to the Baltic Sea, so seasonal trading towns emerged. Companies or coalitions of farmers began following "captains" and "kings" in raids against other hamlets. The word *víkingr* in Old Norse meant "pirate" or "adventurer," deriving from *vík*, "a sea bay"—the target and sanctuary of a "Viking." By the beginning of the ninth century the lands of the Northmen were overwhelmingly maritime societies.[17]

There is no definitive explanation for why suddenly, and without any apparent forewarning, the Vikings broke away from their coastal waterways and started raiding across the North Sea and the Atlantic. This suddenness was undoubtedly less abrupt than what was chronicled by stupefied English, Irish, and Frankish writers. Nevertheless, the raids really did represent a momentous shift in Scandinavian society. What seems crucial was that these ocean-roving ships and their crews were escaping from the consequences of petty wars and local hit-and-runs, which, apart from diminishing material and honorific returns, entrapped more and more men (and women) in never-ending blood feuds. A broadening of sailing and looting horizons was a moral and financial necessity. Ransacking a monastery off the Northumbrian coast or pillaging a Frisian fishing village possessed none of the ethical repercussions that inevitably ended with a young stranger quickly and piously slicing the throat of an old man he recognized as the killer of his father's uncle two decades earlier. Of course, as Findan witnessed, blood feuds from back home still traveled with Northmen on their ships. Yet such invisible and sacred burdens, which every man carried with him, as did his children after him, were miraculously lifted or at least lightened when men sailed away from their oppressive little worlds. A holy metamorphosis, inseparable from commercial and pecuniary rewards, occurred when a Viking went on a raid—a kind of pagan warrior *peregrinatio*.

Most Scandinavians in the eighth and ninth centuries were "pagan." That is to say, they imagined life and death within a religious and mythical framework that, while aware of and even partially influenced by Christianity, was uniquely their own. Unfortunately, much of what we know, or think we know, about

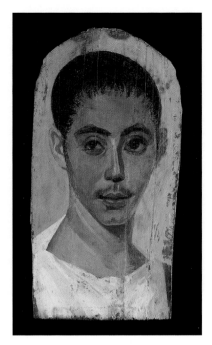

1. This funerary portrait of a young man from the same region as Antony of Egypt was placed over his mummified body or atop his coffin, c. 190–200. Courtesy of The Metropolitan Museum of Art of New York City.

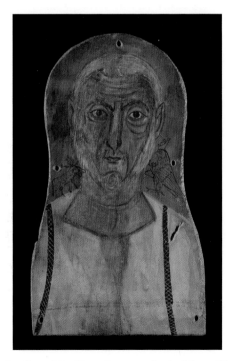

2. Funerary portrait of an older Egyptian man flanked by a falcon representing the sky god Horus and a ram symbolizing either the sun god Re in the underworld, the god Khnum (who was an incarnation of Re after nightfall), or his own daemon guiding him into the afterlife, c. 250. Courtesy of The Metropolitan Museum of Art of New York City.

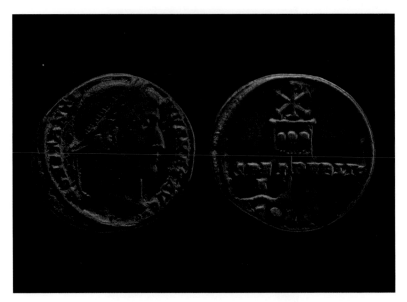

3. Roman copper coin, c. 327. Obverse is the head of Emperor Constantine I and reverse is the *labarum* (imperial standard displaying the Greek letters *chi* and *rho* from Constantine's vision before the Battle of the Milvian Bridge) impaling a serpent (representing Constantine's enemies). Courtesy of The British Museum, © The Trustees of the British Museum.

4. Portraits of a twelve-year-old bride, Projecta, and her slightly older husband, Secundus, on the lid of a massive glided silver casket (weighing eighteen pounds) given to her as a wedding gift, c. 380. He wears the great heavy cloak and barbarian-style brooch of an imperial official. Around the casket rim is the inscription *Secunde et Proiecta vivatis in Christo* (Secundus and Projecta, may you live in Christ). Sadly, Projecta died in late December 385, just before her seventeenth birthday. Her wedding gift was discovered at the foot of the Esquiline Hill in Rome in 1793. The British Museum, © The Trustees of the British Museum. Courtesy of Art Resource, New York.

5. Hagia Sophia (Holy Wisdom), Istanbul (until 1930 known as Constantinople). The East Roman emperor Justinian I began rebuilding the church as a monument to his piety after the *Nika* revolt in 532, and it was finished five years later. The minarets were added when the church became a mosque after the conquest of Constantinople by the Ottoman sultan Mehmed II in 1453. Courtesy of Art Resource, New York.

6. Portraits of Emperor Justinian I, his general Belisarius, Archbishop Maximian of Ravenna, priests, and East Roman soldiers in a mosaic panel on the north wall of the presbytery of the Church of San Vitale, Ravenna. On the south wall opposite was another mosaic panel with Empress Theodora, her ladies-in-waiting (including Belisarius' wife), and imperial eunuchs. These mosaics were planned between 540 and 544 to commemorate the imperial recovery of Ravenna from the "Arian" Goths and finished in 547. Courtesy of Art Resource, New York.

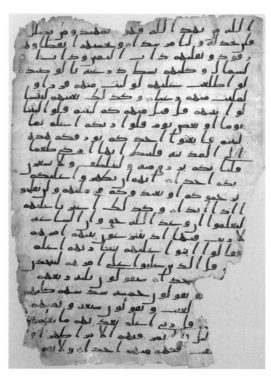

7. A fragment of Surat al-Kahf (The Cave) from the Qur'an, written in Arabic Hijazi script on parchment that came from a goat or sheep that died between 568 and 645. The verses, though, were not written when the parchment was made. The idiosyncratic spellings and distinctive orthography suggest the scribe was writing after 650 and before 700. This fragment was a draft copy intended to help Believers (*mu'minun*) in reciting from memory what the Prophet Muhammad had once heard from the One God. Mingana Arabic Islamic MS. 1572a, folio 1r. Courtesy of © Cadbury Research Library: Special Collections, University of Birmingham.

8. The Dome of the Rock, Jerusalem, completed in 691 or 692 and built by the Umayyad caliph 'Abd al-Malik atop the platform on which the Jewish Temple had stood before its destruction by the Roman general (and future emperor) Titus in 70. Encircling the roof are 787 feet of inscriptions from the Qur'an. Although the building was clearly conceived to be in dialogue with other monuments to monotheism in Jerusalem, especially the Church of the Holy Sepulcher, its precise function is still unclear. Courtesy of Art Resource, New York.

9. Portrait of the prophet Ezra at the beginning of a colossal Bible (1,030 folios, 77 pounds, 515 skins of young calves) copied by nine monks at the monastery of Wearmouth and Jarrow in Northumbria between 688 and 716. It is the earliest surviving full copy of the Bible in the West and so the most reliable transcription of Jerome's Latin (Vulgate) translation from the fourth century. The inscription above the portrait reads: *Codicibus sacris hostile clade perustis / Esra D[e]o fervens hoc reparavit opus* (When the sacred books were destroyed by fire, Ezra, inspired by God, restored this work). Codex Amiatinus, folio 5r, Biblioteca Medicea Laurenziana, Florence. Courtesy of Art Resource, New York.

10. Portrait of Saint Matthew, Ebbo (or Ebo) Gospels, c. 816–835 or possibly c. 840, copied and illuminated at the monastery of Saint-Pierre in Hautvillers in the Marne. MS. 1 folio 18v. Courtesy of Bibliothèque municipale, Epernay.

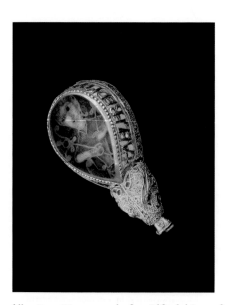

11. The "Alfred jewel," c. 871–889, named after Alfred, king of Wessex, because around the tear-shaped rock crystal is inscribed in English: *Aelfred mec heht gewyrcan* (Alfred ordered me to be made). It is probably the head of a reading aid known as an aestel (a pointer for following words would have been inserted in the base). It was plowed up in a field at North Petherton, Somerset, in 1693, close to the marshes in which Alfred had been hiding from the Viking Great Army (*micel here*) during the winter of 878. © Ashmolean Museum, University of Oxford. Courtesy of Art Resource, New York.

12. This ship was built around 820 and buried in a mound at Oseberg (near Tønsberg) in Norway in 834. It was a tomb for two women, one in her eighties and the other around fifty. The "Oseberg ship" is the oldest Northman or Viking vessel so far discovered. Courtesy of Museum of Cultural History, University of Oslo.

13. The Jelling Stone, erected by King Harald (later nicknamed "Bluetooth") at Jelling in southwest Jutland around 965. The stone has an image of the crucified Christ on one side—visible in the photograph—while on the other side in lines curving around the stone are runes proclaiming: "King Harald ordered this monument to be carved in memory of Gorm, his father, and Thyrve, his mother. [This was] the Harald who conquered Denmark and all Norway and made the Danes Christian." Courtesy of Art Resource, New York.

luxta foluf hyftorię textū teneni · ne li hęc
ad indaganda myfteria trahim̄ ꝰuertitatem
fortaffe opif uacuare uideamur ;

EXPL LIB · XX ·

INCIPIT · XXI ;

NTELLECTVS
facri eloquii inter textū & myfte
rium tanta eft libratione penfand̄ ·
ut utriufꝗ partif lance moderata ·
hunc neꝗ nimię difcuffioni ponduf
deprimat̄ · neꝗ rurfuf torpor incu
rię uacuū relinquat ; Multę quip
pe eiuf fententię tanta allegoriaꝛ
conceptione funt grauidę · ut qfqf
eaf ad folam tenere hyftoriā nitit̄ ·
earū notitia p̄ fuā incuriam p̄uet ;
Nonnullę uero ita exterioribꝰ p̄cep
tif inferuiunt · ut fi quif eaf fubti
luif penetrare defiderat̄ · nttꝰ quidē
nil inueniat · fed hoc fibi etiā quod
forif locuntur abfcondat ; Unde be
ne quoꝗ narratione hiftorica per
fignificatione dicitur ; Tollenf iacob
uirgaf populeaf uiridef · & amigda
linaf · & ex platanif · ex parte deco
ticauit eaf · detractifꝗ corticibuf · in
hif quę expoliata fuerant candor
apparuit · Illa ū quę integra erat̄ ·
uiridia p̄manferunt · atꝗ inhunc
modū · color effectuf · e uariuf ; Vbi
& fubditur ; Pofuitꝗ eaf incanalibꝰ :

14. The Cistercian monk and his companion hacking at the tree (which is also
the letter "I") is an allegory of exegesis—debating and interpretating texts is as
vigorous and physically demanding as assarting forests. Pope Gregory I, *Moralia
in Job*, copied and illuminated at the monastery of Cîteaux in 1111, MS. 170, folio
41r. Courtesy of Bibliothèque municipale, Dijon.

15. The Church and Basilica of Saint-Sernin, Toulouse, begun around 1080 and mostly completed by 1120. The architectural theorist Eugène-Emmanuel Viollet-le-Duc began restoring the building in 1845 to a condition more medieval than anything to which the Middle Ages could ever have aspired. Saint-Sernin has since undergone *dérestauration* and remains one of the largest surviving Romanesque structures. Courtesy of Eva Garb.

16. The Church of Notre Dame de Paris, begun in 1163 and mostly completed by 1260, is an example of Gothic architecture. Eugène-Emmanuel Viollet-le-Duc started restoration work on the church in 1844 with his usual romantic medievalism. On Monday, April 15, 2019, a fire erupted in the roof during renovation work (some of which included removing Viollet-le-Duc's handiwork) and burned for fifteen hours. This photo shows the ongoing reconstruction as of June 2022. Courtesy of Eva Garb.

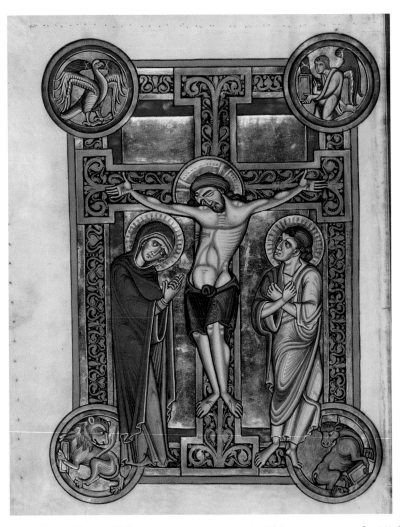

17. Crucifixion, Berthold Sacramentary, c. 1215–1217. This sacramentary for High Mass was commissioned by Berthold, abbot of the Benedictine monastery at Weingarten (in modern Württenburg in the Schussen River valley) from 1200 to 1232. The illumination of Christ on the cross exemplifies the Romanesque style in representation. MS M.710, folio 10v, © The Morgan Library and Museum. Courtesy of Art Resource, New York.

זה עוף שקורין איתו בר יוכני

חכם בני

זה שלמה המלך העושה משפט משתי נשים

18. Judgment of Solomon and Bar-Yokhani, a mythical bird symbolizing Jewish hopes for the Messiah, in a North French Hebrew Miscellany complied and illuminated over twenty years between 1278 and 1324. The manuscript contains texts such as the Pentateuch (the Torah) and a Christian calendar listing saints' days in Hebrew (folio 542v). The calendar's scribe punned on the names of the saints with crude and mordant wit, such as *hariah* for Mariah (Mary), which sounds like the Hebrew word for "excrement." The illuminations were mostly painted by Christian artists in Parisian workshops. Add MS 11639, folios 517v–518r. Courtesy of the British Library, © The British Library Board and Granger Collection Ltd.

19. The Hereford Cathedral *mappa mundi* (map of the world) is the largest surviving medieval map. Created on the hide of one large calf (whose veins can still be seen), it measures 5 feet 2 inches by 4 feet 4 inches. It is circular, with Jerusalem and the Crucifixion at the center of the world. It was designed by Richard of Haldingham and Lafford at Lincoln Cathedral (where he was treasurer) before his death in 1278 and transferred to Hereford Cathedral after 1283. It was originally brightly colored and displayed in the central panel of an altar triptych. The map was an explicit statement that Latin Christendom encompassed all time and space. Courtesy of the © Dean and Chapter of Hereford Cathedral and the Hereford Mappa Mundi Trust.

20. Francis of Assisi receiving the stigmata from Christ as a six-winged angelic seraph, Giotto di Bondone, 1300–1325. Originally in the Church of San Francesco, Pisa, and likely commissioned by a "White Guelf" family exiled from Florence. Emperor Napoleon I requisitioned the painting for the Louvre Museum (then known as the Musée Napoléon) in 1813. Courtesy of Musée du Louvre.

21. Beatrice showing Dante the nine heavenly spheres leading to the Empyrean in Dante Alighieri, *Commedia,* with a commentary in Latin, copied in the first half of the fourteenth century in Padua or Emilia. The illumination is attributed to the Master of the Antiphonar. Egerton MS 943, folio 176r. Courtesy of the British Library, © The British Library Board and Granger Collection Ltd.

22. Dante with Bernard of Clairvaux sees Beatrice's last smile in Egerton MS 943, folio 182r. Courtesy of the British Library, © The British Library Board and Granger Collection Ltd.

23. Dante Alighieri, *Commedia*, copied and illustrated by Giovanni Boccaccio between 1357 and 1373. This drawing shows Dante the Pilgrim and Virgil at the very beginning of the poem when a leopard, a lion, and a she-wolf block their way. Boccaccio copied the whole *Commedia* three times, and each one has slight variations, as he researched and read other manuscripts in the hope of capturing exactly what Dante had written. Ri MS 1035, fol. 4v. Courtesy of Biblioteca Riccardiana, Florence.

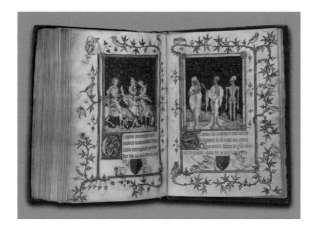

24. The Three Living and the Three Dead, The Psalter (Prayer Book) of Bonne of Luxemburg, duchess of Normandy, attributed to the illuminator Jean Le Noir, Paris, before 1349. This psalter was a gift for Bonne from her husband, Jean, duke of Normandy, soon after they married in 1332. Unfortunately, she died of the plague aged thirty-four in 1349. Jean would become the king of France a year after her death and, despite losing the Battle of Poitiers in 1356 and being captured by the English, was known somewhat incongruously as "the Good." The Cloisters Collection (69.86), folios 321v–322r. Courtesy of The Metropolitan Museum of Art of New York City.

25. Pen and ink drawing of Jeanne la Pucelle holding a sword and a banner emblazoned with JHS (for Jesus), Tuesday, May 10, 1429, by Clément de Fauquembergue, greffier of the Parlement de Paris. Paris, Archives Nationales, Registre du Conseil du Parlement de Paris, AE/II/447 (X1a 1481), fol. 12r. Clément wrote next to his sketch that all Parisians were talking about "a virgin girl [*pucelle*] alone with a banner" who had accompanied the victorious soldiers of the dauphin six days earlier against the English army at Orléans. This drawing of Jeanne was a fanciful doodle as she is wearing a dress and has long hair. It is the only surviving image of her (however imaginary) by a contemporary. Courtesy of Art Resource, New York.

Viking paganism comes from what was written in the early thirteenth century by the Icelandic historian, antiquarian, and poet Snorri Sturluson. In what was ostensibly a handbook on Old Norse poetry, now known as the *Prose Edda*, he copied old poetry from other books, listed synonyms and odd turns of phrase, fabricated or reimagined ancient myths, composed his own version of lost songs, and offered commentary on everything he collected and dreamed up—in short, he invented a coherent pre-Christian "religion" for Scandinavia.

In Snorri's new-old religion there were probably fragments of incompletely remembered stories from half a millennium earlier, but while it is tempting to extrapolate backward from such a wonderful text, and many scholars do, it is extremely naive. If nothing else, for all of the frost giants, elves, and dwarves in the *Prose Edda*, the great All-Father god Odin was repeatedly envisaged as a Christ-like figure: in the marvelous *Gylfaginning*, a Platonic dialogue between Odin and a Swedish king named Gylfi, the former is a three-person deity in one, Hárr (High One), Jafnhárr (Just as High), and Thridi (Third), whose greatest achievement "was to create man and give him a soul that will live and never perish, even though his body molders to dust or is burned to ashes."[18] For Snorri's thirteenth-century readers, it showed that Scandinavian paganism was really just a prefiguration of Christianity.[19]

In the late eighth, ninth, and early tenth centuries, the Viking cosmos was shaped less by a panoply of gods than by ships, water, sailing, prestige treasure (unburied and buried), opportunism, bloodshed, and death. The Oseberg ship burial was an awesome testament to these sacred assumptions. A century later and more than thirteen hundred miles to the southeast, another elaborately macabre ship funeral, this time of a Rus lord, was vividly described by Ahmad ibn Fadlan, an Abbasid diplomat traveling up the Volga in 921.

Who were the Rus? It is difficult to say, although some of them were descended from early Swedish adventurers who, as soon as they equipped their ships with sails, journeyed eastward and established a trading post at Staraja Ladoga on the Volkhov River near Lake Ladoga around 750. These Northmen raided amongst the various Finnish, Saami, and Slavic peoples in the region, stealing and bartering slaves, furs, amber, and whalebone. They quickly dominated the indigenous populations and, just as quickly, married them. They soon sailed south down the Volga into the Caspian Sea and the Dnieper into the Black Sea. They even unwisely assaulted Constantinople in 860. These Northmen were known by the river communities living along the Volkhov, Dnieper, and the Volga as the Rus (from whom modern Russia derives its name). The Rus encountered by Ahmad, eight or nine generations removed from the pirate-settlers of Staraja Ladoga and now quite ethnically and culturally eclectic, nevertheless still enacted death rites similar to many of their Scandinavian contemporaries in the North Sea and Atlantic.[20]

"Which of you will die with him?" the family of the dead Rus lord asked his slave girls and young slave boys. "I will," said a girl. "Usually," observed Ahmad, "it is the slave girls who offer to die." Two other slave girls now followed her everywhere, while she "spends each day drinking and singing, happily and joyfully." Ten days later, the dead man's ship was dragged from the river, placed upon a wooden platform, and fitted with a cabin or pavilion before the mast. A woman—"gloomy, corpulent, neither young nor old"—known as the "Angel of Death" arranged silk cushions on a bed inside the pavilion. The dead man's corpse, which had been buried in a temporary grave with mead (*nabidh*), fruit, and a drum, was now unearthed—"he had turned black because of the coldness of the country"—and dressed in beautiful silks, furs, and gold buttons. He was then placed on the bed amongst the silk cushions. Near him were bread, fruit, fragrant herbs, meat, onions, mead, and a lute. "After that, they brought in a dog, which they cut in two and threw on the boat." Two horses were then galloped until lathered, hacked to pieces by swords, and thrown onboard. Two cows, a cock, and a hen were similarly butchered and scattered over the bow. An axe, a knife, and a sword "broad-bladed and grooved like Frankish ones"—the weapons carried by all Rus men—were laid beside the bed.[21]

"Meanwhile, the slave girl who wanted to be killed" was led to a wooden structure near the ship that was like a door frame, where, balancing on the flattened palms of six men like a tiny acrobat, she was lifted up three times to look over it. "There I see my father and my mother," she said the first time. "There I see my dead relatives seated," was her second vision. "There I see my master seated in paradise," was her third revelation. "There are men with him, and boy slaves, and he is calling me. Take me to him." After cutting off a chicken's head and throwing the remains on the ship, she was gently hoisted on deck. Outside the pavilion, she was given a cup of mead by men armed with shields and staves. She bade farewell to her girlfriends in song and emptied the cup. She was given more to drink, so she sang more songs.

When it was time to enter the pavilion, the girl swayed and fell over. The Angel of Death grabbed her head and pushed her inside. The men with the shields and the staves began beating them, rat-a-tat, rat-a-tat, which Ahmad assumed was to drown out the girl's cries, "so that other slave girls would not be frightened and try to avoid dying with their masters." The six men who had previously lifted the girl up to see paradise entered the pavilion and raped her, saying, "Tell your master that I only did this for your love of him." Then they placed her on the bed next to the dead lord. Finally, two of the six men strangled the girl with a rope, while the Angel of Death repeatedly stabbed her in the ribs with a dagger.[22]

After the Angel of Death and her accomplices climbed down from the blood-drenched ship, a naked male relative of the dead lord with his back to the ship threw a blazing torch over his shoulder onto the deck. Then all the Rus men and women, including slave girls, who had been watching and listening to the ritual so far hurled burning pieces of wood at the ship. "A violent and frightening wind began to blow, the flames grew in strength and the heat of the fire intensified," so that within an hour, "ship, wood, girl and master were no more than ashes and dust." A mound, "like a round hill," was then built over the gray and white powdery residue.

"You Arabs are fools!" one of the Rus men said to Ahmad at the end of the funeral. "Why is that?" "Because," the man laughed, "you put the men you love most into the earth, and the earth and the worms and insects eat them. But we burn them in an instant and without delay they enter paradise."[23]

Ahmad, who was usually dismissive of the habits and beliefs of the idolatrous Rus in the expected manner of a cosmopolitan Muslim, was surprisingly dispassionate about the remarkable funeral he witnessed—with the exception of the sacrificial slave girl, whose willingness to die was deeply shocking and moving for him. Although he wanted to doubt that she knew what she was doing, he kept convincing himself that she did know. By the end, Ahmad genuinely believed the girl thought she saw her parents, relatives, and master in paradise, and so, transported by that vision, intoxication, and song, she was, he hoped, already with them before her last brutal moments on the ship.

4 Lines of Blood

In 839, shortly after Easter, King Æthelwulf of Wessex sent a letter to Emperor Louis the Pious—Charlemagne's son and heir—describing an ominous and terrifying out-of-body journey that an English priest had experienced at Christmas. "One night when the pious priest was asleep, a certain man came to him and told him to follow him. So he got up and did so."

The man led him to a mysterious land and into a magnificent church where thousands of boys were reading and writing. The priest saw that for every line written by the boys in black ink, the next line was written in blood. "The lines of blood," said the man, "are all the various sins of Christian people." The boys were actually the souls of saints grieving for the sins they copied out. "If Christian people don't quickly do penance for their various vices and crimes," the man told the priest, the world will be smothered in a very dense fog for three days and nights, "and then all of a sudden pagan men will lay waste with fire and sword most of the people and the land of the Christians."

The priest's vision had convinced Æthelwulf that the Northmen were an apocalyptic punishment from God and that unless rulers like himself and Louis devoted more attention to the souls of their people, the saints in their celestial scriptorium would be compelled by their bloody lists into allowing the destruction of Christians by pagan fires and swords.[24]

Louis died a year later, and while his reply to Æthelwulf is lost, he needed no convincing that the Last Judgment was at hand. In June 837, Einhard had already instructed him on the meaning of a comet that had blazed over Francia two months earlier. "I suspect that this supplies us with fitting signs of an approaching disaster that we deserve and of our just punishments. For what does it matter whether humans are forewarned of God's impending anger by a human, an angel, or a star?" Why were Louis and his realm deserving of catastrophe? Because only seven years earlier his sons by his first wife had rebelled and deposed him, plunging the empire into chaos, and while he reclaimed the throne again in 834, it was obvious such faithless anarchy would return.

Einhard viewed the raids of the Northmen as "penitential remedies" for the sins of sons and fathers. "I wish," he said, "that the destruction which the Northmen's fleet is said to have recently brought upon parts of this kingdom could have made full payment for the appearance of that horrible star." Regrettably, while the infidel onslaught from the sea was a pentitential penalty for many but not all Christians, "I fear that the punishment that awaits us will be even heavier."[25] Einhard died four months before the emperor; they were both around sixty-four. Louis, moments before death, yelled at a demon lurking near his bed, "Hutz! Hutz!" ("Go away! Go away!")—and then he died, apparently looking as if he were laughing in joy at what was revealed to him.[26]

The Northmen were at once a horror of almost unfathomable depravity and an instrument of God punishing, cleansing, and redeeming Christian lands—a fortuitous interpretation by emperors, kings, bishops, and monks of the seemingly endless heathen violence that Christian swords and prayers were unable to stop, but not an insincere one. The savagery of the Vikings was understood as divinely efficacious within a universe shaped by penitential salvation. What was said and written about them was more often than not an exaggeration of their ferocity because, in what might seem a perverse paradox, the more viciously outrageous they were assumed to be, the easier it was to comprehend the shock of what they did and what they achieved. There had to be something otherworldly about the Northmen; otherwise, how could they be instruments of God's anger?

In reality, they were just as brutish and mercenary as the Franks. What was unquestionably different about them was their own sense of the sacred, embodied and enhanced in the very acts of sailing and raiding, and which they and their victims recognized as different (or different enough) from Christianity. Nevertheless, despite their differing perspectives on what defined divinity, the Northmen and the Franks saw their hostilities with each other as holy wars. Wetti's angelic companion was already saying as much around 827. Just after telling the old monk that the end of the world was rapidly approaching, he praised a certain Frankish soldier named Geroldus, who "met the horde of the infidel and suffered with the loss of his temporal life, so that he is made a participant in eternal life." By fighting and dying against the Northmen, this Christian warrior "was sharing in heaven in the glory of the martyrs."[27]

After the death of Louis, the greater punishment foretold by the "horrible star" was fulfilled when the empire was ripped apart by his sons (and a grandson) in civil wars. The Northmen exploited and abetted this fratricidal bloodshed. In late June 841 at Fontenoy (near Auxerre in Burgundy) the eldest son, Lothar, was defeated in battle by his younger brother, Louis (known as "the German"), and his younger half brother, Charles (known as "the Bald"). "No slaughter was ever worse on any field of war," sang the warrior and poet Engelbert, who fought on Lothar's side. "The law of the Christians was shattered by this shedding of blood."[28] Famously, two years later the three brothers came together at Verdun in the summer and divided the Roman Empire of their father and grandfather into three kingdoms (regna) between themselves. "Louis received the eastern part, Charles the western, and Lothar . . . chose the middle portion," recorded the monk Rudolf in the annals of Fulda monastery.[29] Nevertheless, the civil wars continued, with the brothers, their sons, and grandsons fighting amongst themselves for the next four decades, with the result that after 870 there were only two Frankish kingdoms, one west of the Rhine and one east of it. "For this reason God led the Northmen into Gaul and they devastated it both from the land and sea," judged Audradus Modicus, the former suffragan bishop of Sens, in 849. "It was as if the very anger of God raged throughout the lands of these kings in the savagery of these evil men."[30]

In 846 a wandering holy woman named Thiota preached in Mainz—now in the eastern kingdom ("across the Rhine," *transrhenania*) of Louis the German—that the world was about to end and she knew the exact date. "As a result many of the common people of both sexes were struck by fear; they came to her with gifts and commended themselves to her prayers," noted Rudolf in his Fulda annals. Even worse, "men in holy orders, ignoring the teaching of the Church, followed her as a teacher sent from heaven." This was too much for some bishops, and they questioned Thiota about her prophecy. Unexpectedly, she quickly confessed that it was all a scam and that a priest had coached her on what to say. She was "ignominiously stripped of the ministry of preaching" and publicly flogged. Rudolf and the bishops, while doubting Thiota's divine insight, never doubted that the end of the world was imminent, as the signs of God's anger were all around them.[31]

A year later the same bishops in Mainz condemned the roaming visionary priest (and former monk) Gottschalk as a heretic for his preaching on dual predestination. "I, Gottschalk, believe and confess," he succinctly stated, "that predestination is twin, whether of the elect to peace or of the reprobate to death."[32] That is to say, God by His freely given grace had already decided before the cosmos even existed which men or women were elected to paradise or damned to hell on the Day of Judgment. Although Gottschalk's theology was partially inspired by his reading of Augustine of Hippo, he was still a man of the ninth century, so, in what at first seems contradictory, or at least superfluous, his predestined souls lived and died within a penitential universe. One of the wrongheaded or deliberately misleading accusations against him was that he rejected penance; quite the contrary, it was vitally important for him, not because it wiped away sin but because it was a sign of the elect. An elected person (while obviously never knowing this about themselves while on earth) was a person always engaged in penitential confession and piety. When such an individual fasted on this day of that week in such-and-such a year they were erasing a sin that God had already erased from them before the existence of days, weeks, and years. The mark of the reprobate was skipping, dismissing, or mocking penances for their sins, which, of course, was also predetermined about them.

But not all was lost for the wicked. Paradoxically, it was possible for an unrepentant sinner to become one of the elect by finally doing penance, because, as time was irrelevant to immutable God, with past, present, and future all the same to Him, the gift of His grace—say, to a woman in 840— was already and always freely given by Him. Gottschalk had preached his doctrine around the Adriatic before journeying down the Rhine, confusing and angering as many people as he inspired.

After Gottschalk's condemnation at Mainz, he was dispatched to the monastery of Orbais—near Reims, now in the western kingdom of Charles the Bald—for confinement. There he wrote his *Longer Confession* (*Confessio prolixior*), modeled on Augustine's *Confessions*, which was the first time a Latin Christian author had explicitly imitated the earlier work. Although Gottschalk's *Confession* was a long prayer to God, mostly defending himself from the charge of heresy, it was not an autobiography interweaving personal memories, theology, and philosophy like the *Confessions*. Augustine's thrilling sense of the self was meaningless to him, as it would have been to any ninth-century person. (At least sixteen manuscripts of the *Confessions* have survived from the ninth century, so it was widely read, just not as an autobiographical text.)

Augustine's sense of humor was also irrelevant—except, perhaps, where Gottschalk proposed in his *Confession* being tested for his faith in an elaborate theatrical ordeal. Before an audience of kings, popes, priests, and monks, four barrels would be placed in a row, "and filled one by one with boiling water, oil, lard, and pitch," and then finally a fire. As Gottschalk dipped into each barrel and walked through the flames, God would hold his hand "until I come out unharmed so that at last the clarity of the Catholic faith should shine out."[33] As one of the elect, he would have survived such a penitential obstacle course, but only in risking his life was such predestination divinely affirmed. Obviously, he was not serious about being poached, fried, and scorched, but what his imagined scenario revealed about how he viewed himself was serious indeed. Gottschalk saw himself as a martyr and his suffering as affirming his election to paradise, which, in a world ablaze with the chaos of civil war and the Northmen, was the consoling (if rather smug) joy of the elect.

5 As If

On Friday, February 2, 843, "in the course of the worsening turmoil of this wretched world, in the midst of much agitation and discord in the realm," a Frankish noblewoman in her early thirties named Dhuoda finished writing a learned and poignant book known as the *Liber Manualis* for her sixteen-year-old son William (whose name in the vernacular was probably Guilhem). The youth was newly a vassal— really, a hostage—of the twenty-year-old Charles the Bald. His father, Bernard of Septimania, had surrendered him as a pledge of loyalty in the aftermath of Fontenoy.

Dhuoda's "little book" to her "beautiful and lovable son" is a rare text by a ninth-century laywoman, revealing her impressive education and Latin literary skill, which, while clearly exceptional, she never assumed were all that unusual for an aristocratic woman like herself or men like her son and husband. She wrote chapters that mixed homilies, family reminiscences, mystical numerology, acrostic poems, biblical quotations, paraphrases of Augustine and Gregory the Great, advice on setting up a household, maternal affection, paternal obedience, jokes, penitential piety, political discretion, the limitless horror of hell, and the grandeur of God. Quite profoundly, though, her "little book of moral counsels" was a living "memento" of herself for William. When he read (and reread) her words, he would "gaze upon me as in an image in a mirror." This was why Dhuoda's book was greater than any book by any male author, even a "learned doctor," as "they are not of equal status with me, nor do they have a heart more ardent than I, your mother, have for you, my firstborn son!" The *Liber Manualis* was a book only a mother could write.[34]

Dhuoda was acutely aware that Charles would read or at least hear about her "little book," so she stressed over and over that William must be faithful to his overlord. "Never once let yourself fall into the folly, the outrageous affront of breaking faith. Never let such an idea of disloyalty against your lord grow or arise in your heart." More subtly, she even warned against dreaming of vengeance and rebellion. William must never mistake the "as if" of what he dreamed—"as if" he were a strong and victorious warrior, "as if" he were riding a wild mare in the Spanish March—for the truth. Too many foolish men were seduced and doomed by "as ifs" into the glassy-eyed sleep of vanity. "Oh, the deep, heavy sleep from which there is no awakening for those who live badly and who race toward the abyss without the fruit of penance! What do they own? Nothing but the 'as if'!"

Unfortunately, seven years after reading his mother's admonition, William was executed by Charles as a traitor and rebel. He had led a valiant but delusional "as if" insurgency, even attacking Barcelona and allying himself with the Andalusian Umayyad emirate, after the king murdered his father in 844. Dhuoda was not alive to mourn her son and husband, dying soon after finishing the *Liber Manualis*. She had worried that what eventually did happen to William would occur, as more lives than not were cut short like cloth snipped by a merchant, but she could not keep herself from dreaming that her "beautiful boy" would survive the turbulent world in which they lived. And so Dhuoda succumbed to her own "as if," imagining that her death was far enough in the future so that her son, secure as a great lord in his estates, would carve on her tomb for all to see the verses with which she ended the *Liber Manualis*.

> Dhuoda's body, formed of earth,
>   here lies buried in the tomb.
>   Great King, receive her . . .
> No wayfarer shall pass this way
>   without reading this! I beg all to pray:
>   "Grant her rest. Kindly One."[35]

6 Murderers of Their Own Souls

On Wednesday, June 3, 851, a young monk named Isaac was "decapitated, elevated, and suspended upside down on a post" placed on the other side of the Guadalquivir River in full view of the city of Córdoba. A few days earlier, having discarded his monastic attire for nondescript Andalusian dress, he walked into the audience hall of an Umayyad judge and politely asked in Arabic: "Judge, I would like to become a more resolute worshipper of the faith, if only you do not delay explaining to me its logic and reason."

The judge, thinking the youth was a sincere and inquiring Muslim, lectured on the Prophet's life, the Qur'an, and how "the kingdom of heaven was filled with feasts and streams of women." "He lied to you!" Isaac suddenly yelled about Muhammad. "Why do you not renounce the sore of this pestilential dogma and opt for the eternal and evangelical protection of the Christian faith?" The judge slapped his face. "Perhaps you are drunk on wine or you have been seized with madness!" Isaac was quite sober when he uttered his blasphemies. "If," he goaded the judge, "a savage death should follow, I will welcome it gladly and submit to it calmly." A brutal execution was what he had planned all along for the final scene of his little performance—and on cue it happened, allowing him to bow out like a glorious martyr under the pagan Roman emperors. Isaac "seized the kingdom of heaven with a kind of violence through the shedding of [his] own blood."[36] Between 850 and 859, forty-eight other Christians were beheaded in Córdoba for disrespecting Muhammad and Islam.

Yet most of these executed Christians were not chasing after death and martyrdom like Isaac. What transformed all of them into the very special dead, the "martyrs of Córdoba," were the writings of a local priest named Eulogius. He sketched a brief *vita vel passio* (life or passion) soon after each execution as part of a larger narrative, most clearly articulated in his *Memorial of the Saints* (*Memoriale sanctorum*), in which every decapitated man or woman was predestined since childhood to be a martyr on earth and a saint in heaven. Unquestionably, some of the dead were copycat self-sacrificers hoping for martyrdom. For example, Sanctius—kidnapped as a youth from Albi during a Saracen raid and, while growing up to be a palace guard for the amir, neither a slave nor a secret Christian—was beheaded two days after Isaac for reenacting the young monk's provocation.

Most of the "martyrs of Córdoba" did not want to die—especially the first one on the list, Perfectus, a priest who was executed a year before Isaac at the end of Ramadan. He, too, was condemned for blasphemy, but it was inadvertent, the consequence of a genuinely curious group of Muslim men asking him on the street in "good faith" for his opinion on the virtues and errors of Christ and Muhammad. Unfortunately, as he was less than gracious in what he said about the Prophet, two or three of his street audience denounced him later in the week. Eulogius acknowledged that Perfectus was not seeking a "savage death" like Isaac, but his decapitation nevertheless demonstrated the "pagan" persecution under which all Christians lived in Córdoba, and so in retrospect his injudicious criticism of Muhammad furnished the "fuel for a more ardent desire to die for the sake of justice."[37]

The trouble for Eulogius was that most Christians in Córdoba, including the bishop, did not think they suffered persecution like their ancestors under pagan Rome and so any contemporary "martyrdom" was foolish, fraudulent, and sinful. "There are many amongst the faithful," he bristled, "asserting that a martyrdom of this kind is unusual and profane, for no violence on the part of authorities compelled them to renounce their faith, or separated them from the worship of the holy and pious religion." Instead, he lamented, the faithful accused the "martyrs" of dying by "their own free will . . . murderers of their own souls." And in any event, the faithful said to him, how could a modern Christian be like an ancient martyr when it was blatantly obvious that Muslims were not Roman pagans worshipping the old gods but, just like us, worshipped the "one true God"? An exasperated Eulogius, while acknowledging there was some truth in these criticisms, brushed them aside as irrelevant technicalities.[38]

There was something Eulogius had a harder time dismissing: if the "martyrs" were the very special dead, why were there no miracles associated with their bodies, like with other saints? Fortunately, Gregory the Great in his *Moralia in Job* helpfully pointed out that during the End of Days, which was what everyone in Córdoba was clearly living through even if they did not know it, all "miracles" and "signs of power" will be absent to most people. "Heavenly dispensation does not entirely withdraw them," Eulogius quoted the pope on these miracles in absentia, "but it does not exhibit them openly and in such different ways as in former times." The "martyrs" would have bestowed miracles upon the world if God had allowed them, but regrettably everyone in Córdoba, Christian and Muslim alike, was not "worthy of contemplating such heavenly powers." Eulogius, worried that he was perhaps being too harsh, admitted that he was "not rejecting outright the honor of miracles as a celestial gift" from God to the people of Córdoba—just not now, and only when the time was right. "We are simply trying to stop the barking of the dogs who seek to weaken the intention of our martyrs and hope to refute them on the grounds of miracles."[39]

Eulogius saw signs of the apocalypse everywhere in Córdoba, which was why he so tirelessly (and tiresomely to his detractors) promoted his "martyrs." The greatest portent for him was not just the passivity of most Christians toward "pagan" Muslims, but that for many of them this docility easily transitioned into apostasy. Christians and Jews, as "people of the book," were classed as *dhimmis* under Islamic law, that is, they and their religious traditions were protected as long as a poll tax, *jizya*, was paid either each year or, as in the case of Córdoban Christians, according to Eulogius, each month.

It was a status whose burdens and inconveniences varied from one locale to another. During the ninth century Abbasid caliphs and their jurists steadily proclaimed more severe laws erasing these communal variations. The Umayyad regime in al-Andalus was less rigorous. Church bells, for example, were now required to ring softly in Jerusalem and Alexandria, whereas in Córdoba their "reverberating metal" clanged throughout the day announcing the hours for prayer, often overlapping with the muezzin's call to prayer five times each day, which Eulogius spitefully said sounded like "asses, with unhinged jaws."[40] Or the clothes of *dhimmis* throughout the Abbasid caliphate were now ordered to be different from those of Muslims, while Córdobans (except priests and monks) all dressed alike—and which, of course, helped Isaac in his initial charade before the judge. Although Eulogius halfheartedly complained that Muslim children threw rocks at priests like him or that the monthly tax was crushing, it was the effortless slippage of individuals moving from Christianity to Islam, and which was inevitable no matter how lightly the *dhimma* was enforced, that signaled the End of Days and the necessity of "martyrs."

A few of the "martyrs" exemplified this religiously fluid environment. For instance, the sisters Nunilo and Alodia, who, despite having a Muslim father, were raised by their Christian mother in her faith. When their indulgent father died, their mother married another Muslim, who demanded his new wife and stepdaughters adopt his religion. The sisters escaped to live in hiding with a maternal Christian aunt. Umayyad officials soon discovered them, and from their perspective, the girls were apostates from Islam. Nunilo and Alodia, after refusing husbands and religious instruction by learned Muslim women, were beheaded and buried in a ditch in late October 851.

Or Flora, who also had a Christian mother and an easygoing Muslim father. Her brother, though, was an ardent Muslim, who, disgusted with what he thought was his sister's apostasy after their father died in 845, dragged her before an Umayyad judge for punishment. Flora argued that she had always been a Christian. "I have known Christ since my childhood," she told the judge. "I promised Him the integrity of my body to be enjoyed in His bed-room." She was so viciously whipped about the head for these outrageous words that her hair and skin were flayed away, revealing skull and glistening white neck bone. (Eulogius viewed Flora's "martyrdom" as beginning with her flogging.) When her wounds healed, she ran away from her brother's house, living as a fugitive. During this time, Eulogius met her and "touched with both of my hands the scars of her most reverent and delicate neck, where her virginal hair had been removed by the blows of the whips."

After six years Flora walked into the audience hall of the same judge who had scourged her. "I am the woman," she announced, "who you previously injured with a cruel lashing hoping I would deny Him." She embraced blasphemy and death; her years of hiding were over. She confessed that "Christ is truly God" and that Muhammad "is a false prophet, an adulterer, a magician, and a sorcerer." A month after Nunilo and Alodia, Flora was decapitated beside the Guadalquivir and her body devoured by dogs and carrion birds.[41]

If the lives and deaths of Nunilo, Alodia, and Flora were not enough evidence for why Córdoban Christians should resist becoming Muslims, in 857 Eulogius inserted in his *Apologetic Book of the Martyrs* (*Liber apologeticus martyrum*) a short anonymous Latin *Life* of Muhammad he un-expectedly discovered inside another book in the monastery of Leyre in Pamplona a decade earlier. This "little history about that nefarious prophet"—the first Latin history of Muhammad in the West and known in later manuscripts as the *Istoria de Mahometh*—was a caustic, scathing, and often silly diatribe, but its unknown Christian author was also knowledgeable and well-read in what by the ninth century was now the received version of the Qur'an and biography of His Messenger for Muslims, whether in Córdoba or Baghdad. Moreover, the unknown author presupposed a similar knowledge in his Christian readers of the Qur'an (which he repeatedly and insightfully referred to as a "song") and Muhammad's revelations, wars, marriages, and worship of the "one true God." The anonymous *Life* of Muhammad was written to browbeat, bully, or just sow doubt within complacent Andalusian Christians who viewed Islam as more similar than not to Christianity—which was why Eulogius copied it out.[42]

The End of Days that Eulogius so feared and desired almost happened during the summer of 853 when the amir Muhammad I, furious at what seemed like a never-ending parade of Córdoban suicidal blasphemers, decreed the mass murder of all Christian men and the conversion of all Christian women or their enslavement and sale if they refused Islam. The amir changed his mind when his advisors argued that most Christians in Córdoba, especially the nobles, thought the so-called martyrs were reckless, arrogant fools. "I believe he would have utterly extinguished our Christianity, partly by the sword and partly by apostasy," wrote Eulogius, at once relieved and giddy that this was not, and yet almost was, the Last Judgment.[43]

The apocalypticism of Eulogius should be seen within the broader Christian phenomenon from the North Sea to the Mediterranean of believing that God's anger was punishing the sinful and the unrepentant by pagan fires and swords. (Although he never mentioned the Northmen or the devastation in Francia, Eulogius was well aware of it from letters, refugees, and travelers, such as two Parisian monks from Saint-Germain-des-Prés hunting for relics in northern Spain whom he met in 858.)[44] The Córdoban variation on this apocalyptic theme was that Eulogius himself and a zealous cadre of his "martyrs" actually created the very pagan persecution that they so sincerely believed was compelling them in their violent seizure of heaven.

Eight years after Isaac's execution, Eulogius hid a girl named Leocritia in his house. Her parents were both Muslim, but she had recently and secretly converted to Christianity, promising Christ her virginal body in His bedroom. She was soon found by Umayyad officials. Eulogius, who never entirely envisioned himself as being like the "martyrs" he so assiduously groomed and catalogued, was beheaded at three o'clock in the afternoon on Saturday, March 11, 859. Leocritia was decapitated three days later.[45]

7 Alfred's Wisdom

Philosophy floated back down from heaven at the end of the ninth century. Except now the old nurse of Boethius was a man (although sometimes he was a she again) named Wisdom, singing and chatting away in a West Saxon dialect of English. Alfred, king of Wessex, possibly translated the *Consolation of Philosophy* before he died in 899, though it was more likely he did not. He certainly encouraged the translation of Latin texts into English, such as

Orosius' *History Against the Pagans* (which is where we find Óttar describing Norway and the Northmen to Alfred), Bede's *Ecclesiastical History*, Gregory the Great's *Regula Pastoralis*, and Augustine's *Soliloquies*. (Alfred is often assumed to be the translator of the *Regula Pastoralis* and the *Soliloquies* as well. Again, it is unlikely.)

Whoever Englished the *Consolation* cut out most of what Boethius wrote about himself, reshaping much of the book as a dialogue between Wisdom and the inquiring Mind of an unnamed king. Overall, the original Latin functioned more as a springboard for vernacular reflections on a variety of new and more pressing subjects, most especially what it meant to be a Christian and a monarch in a violent world. "The material for any skill is that without which one cannot exercise that skill," observes Mind to Wisdom. "Then the material for a king and his tools for ruling are that he has his land fully manned. He must have praying men, fighting men, and working men. You know that without these tools no king can show his skill." Further, a king must have the resources to support "the three classes of men" that are his tools. Accordingly, says Mind in his most majestic voice, "I desired resources in order to exercise power, so that my skills and authority should not be forgotten and hidden." Even if the *Consolation* was not translated and rewritten by Alfred, it very much encapsulated what he thought of himself, his kingdom, and his God after decades of debilitating if ultimately triumphant warfare with the Northmen.[46]

In 851, when Alfred was three years old, a Viking fleet, after wintering on the island of Thanet, sailed up the Thames and sacked London (which was something of a ghost town in any case) and Canterbury. For the next fourteen years, naval "brotherhoods" (as a Frankish annalist called them) from Denmark, Sweden, and Norway joined together for summer raiding throughout Britain before dispersing for the winter, either returning to Scandinavia or bivouacking on islands in the Thames, Seine, and Rhine estuaries. In 865 and 866, though, instead of scattering during the colder months, the fraternities and their ships not only moored permanently on British rivers but were joined by other Northmen from Ireland, Francia, and perhaps as far away as the Danube (in which case they might even have been Rus). English chroniclers called this new occupying and constantly warring confederation the *micel here*, the "Great Army."

In less than twelve months, York was captured and Northumbria reduced to a client kingdom. Two years later the last king of East Anglia,

Edmund, was killed. The kingdoms of Mercia and Wessex clashed with the *micel here* separately and as allies, often with success. In 871 they won no fewer than eight land battles against the Northmen, killing two of their "kings." But such victories were still not decisive, merely causing the surviving four leaders to momentarily sue for peace as they retreated to Northumbria or East Anglia. Soon enough, the fighting started again, except now the Northmen were the victors. In 874 the Mercian king and queen fled as exiles to Rome after their kingdom was overrun. Four years later at Christmas, thirty-year-old Alfred was skulking and starving in the icy marshes of Somerset, fearful of being captured by the Northmen or betrayed by English collaborators.[47]

Asser, Welsh monk and later bishop of Sherborne, in his *Life* of Alfred written around 893, swiftly pivoted from the lonely despair of wintry swamps to the glorious exhilaration of the king destroying the Great Army three months later at Edington. The English forces consisted of all the men (and quite a few women) of Somerset, Wiltshire, and Hampshire—basically, everyone "who had not sailed overseas for fear of the pagans." Asser was not a very artful or necessarily reliable biographer, but as with Einhard's *Life* of Charles, which was his model, amidst all the dull formulaic prose there are often sparks of surprising authenticity, if rarely insight. He never explained how Alfred's ragtag militia defeated the Northmen's forces so conclusively in 878—a fierce "shield-wall" was the most he said—but he deftly conveyed the shock of their victory for both sides. What was left of the *micel here* swiftly disbanded; some stayed in Britain, returning, for example, to their homesteads in Yorkshire, while others sailed off to join "brotherhoods" assaulting Francia and Ireland. "And, Guthrum, their king, promised to accept Christianity and to receive baptism at King Alfred's hand." This conversion of the leader of the Northmen in East Anglia, along with thirty of his lords, was crucial in confirming the superiority of the Christian God and of the Wessex king as His champion.

Of course, Scandinavian soldiers of fortune continued raiding Britain for another century, either on horses from their Northumbrian farms or in ships dashing across the English Channel or the Irish Sea. They were just never as coordinated, threatening, or successful as the Great Army. Alfred adroitly used all his "tools" as a king in these wars, especially in the construction of a fleet of longships, which were like Danish or Swedish vessels but apparently longer (at least sixty oars) and with higher sides.

Slowly but surely, he ruled less as a king of Wessex and more as king of all the Angelcynn, the "English folk." By 886, "all the Angles and the Saxons," according to Asser, "turned willingly to King Alfred and submitted themselves to his lordship."[48]

At one point in the *Consolation* Wisdom describes God in an analogy that was obviously intended for an audience of recently converted Northmen, or at least how divine authority was imagined after a lifetime of sea and river fighting by a Christian king like Alfred. "Through goodness, God created all things. . . . And He alone is the stable ruler, steersman, rudder, and helm, since He guides and governs all creation as a good steersman guides a ship." Wisdom repeatedly refers to God in this way. Indeed, there is a slight brininess to the Englished *Consolation*, with numerous marine and riverine metaphors and analogies. For example, according to Wisdom, humans as creatures of motion are similar to motionless shellfish, in that both have some measure of reason, but that is where the sameness ends, as the latter cannot "flee from what they hate and seek what they love." Yet even animals that can run away from their fears or chase after their desires are no different from mollusks, as they all lack the "gift of intelligence" given to humanity by God. Alfred until the end of his life was concerned with the ragged Christianity of his realm after years of violence and mayhem, because, like shellfish, so many Christians, old and new, were spiritually inert. But then, as Mind says to Wisdom about a door that God the steersman has partially opened for him, "I was able to see with difficulty a tiny ray of light in this darkness."[49]

8 Three Irishmen in a Boat

A wonderful and surreal moment of brightness shone through the gloom in 891. Three Irishmen named Dubslaine, Macbethath, and Maelinmuin washed up on the Cornish coast in a curragh made of animal skins. They had gone to sea without a paddle, "to go on pilgrimage for the love of God, they cared not where," according to an English chronicler. Somehow or other, despite aimlessly drifting about for seven days, they escaped capture by the Northmen. Alfred was delighted with these heirs of Columbanus, whose holy naivety he rewarded by sending them off to Rome.[50]

9 The Ships Are Far Away

Anskar, a monk from Corbie (in the Somme River valley), accompanied a Danish émigré king and recent Christian convert named Harald Klak back to his homeland in 826. Louis the Pious had commissioned him to be a new Boniface amongst the Northmen, a missionary traveling throughout Denmark and southern Sweden smashing idols and converting pagans. Despite becoming bishop of Hamberg-Bremen and living until 865, Anskar mostly failed. He was hobbled from the beginning, when Harald, whom Louis had personally baptized, was stopped by other Danish kings from even crossing into Jutland. The returning exile's Christianity, imperial connections, and shipless entourage were dismissed as signs of weakness. His evangelizing companion, though, persevered in his perilous mission, traipsing across (and boating between) hundreds of Danish islands, and even sailing as far as the Swedish trading port of Birka on an island in Lake Mälaren. Shortly after Anskar's death, Rimbert, a Danish disciple, wrote his *Life*, which turned four decades of lackluster achievement into visionary triumph.[51]

Anskar discovered that the Christian God and His Son were well known wherever he preached, and while accepted by most Danes and Swedes as impressive deities, they were still just two more gods milling about in a universe full of immortal beings. He never converted anyone by the force of his character (again, he was no Boniface); instead, like a wandering prompt, he reminded kings and warriors of the sacred options available to them when their usual gods let them down. Rimbert illustrated this point in a story about fear and confusion during a Swedish assault on a Baltic people known as the Cori in 854. A fleet of longships sailed from Birka across the Baltic Sea to the Couronian port town of Seeburg (Grobina in modern Latvia), swiftly capturing and burning it. "They left it with strengthened hopes and, having sent away their ships, set out on a journey of five days," and thirty-nine miles, to the Couronian hill fort of Aputra (Apuole in modern Lithuania). After nine days of bloody but inconsequential slaughter, the exhausted Swedes were overwhelmed with doubt and dread. "Here," they said, "we effect nothing and we are far from our ships."

In search of holy guidance, they cast lots as to whether their gods would aid them in victory. "No," answered the gods. "Our ships are far away," lamented the Swedes, justifying their godly abandonment. "What hope have we?" Then some older men remembered Anskar's preaching in Birka a few weeks earlier. "The God of the Christians," they said, "frequently helps those who cry to Him." Lots were cast and it was divined that Christ wanted to help. As His favor would not last forever, the fidgety younger warriors wished to attack Aputra immediately, but before they could, the pagan Cori surrendered. Despite the Swedes reimbursing the Christian God by penitentially fasting like His followers for seven days back in Birka, very few of them converted. Anskar, though, encountered less outright opposition from now on, as Christ had proven Himself a God of war, willing to fight even when, unlike other gods, "the ships are far away."[52]

Over the next century and a half as scattered Swedish, Norwegian, and Danish communities were forcefully gathered under the rule of overbearing kings, and former Scandinavian pirates permanently colonized areas of Britain, Ireland, and Francia, the deep intimacy between ships, sailing, and paganism steadily fractured. The enthusiasm for a warrior Christ after the old gods rebuked the Birka Swedes for being too distant from their ships was a phenomenon inevitably experienced in one form or another by most Scandinavians. As the old gods became less useful and their scolding more easily dismissed in a North Atlantic with fewer sea-roving "brotherhoods" and more consolidated kingdoms, the only deity regularly sanctioned by fate when the lots were cast was the Christian God.

Of course, Scandinavians still sailed with flair and virtuosity, especially as innovations in ship design during the later ninth century allowed for longer and safer voyages of discovery, but the old indivisible bond with their ships in life and death, and by which they defined themselves in relationship to each other, their victims, and the divine, frayed and unraveled within four or five generations. The Christianization of the Northmen between the late ninth and early eleventh centuries was very much a refrain that played upon "the ships are far away" in reality and in the imagination.

A century after Anskar's death, a Danish king named Harald (later nicknamed "Bluetooth") erected at Jelling, in southwest Jutland, a large and magnificent runestone around 965. On one side was an image of the crucified Christ dressed like a Dane, and beginning on the other side in sinuous lines curving around the stone were runes proclaiming: "King Harald ordered this monument to be carved in memory of Gorm, his father, and Thyrve, his mother. [This was] the Harald who conquered Denmark and all Norway and made the Danes Christian."[53] A strong king was a Christian king. This may seem paradoxical, as the English and Frankish Christian kingdoms were disrupted and weakened by more than a century of raiding and warfare by the Northmen. But the lesson that Scandinavian kings like Harald learned from all this turmoil—which often was caused by them in their younger days—was that they could rule as unchallenged monarchs only when their own indigenous and inherently fractious sea- and freshwater "brotherhoods" and "kings" were crushed, overthrown, and "made Christian."

Harald's Jelling runestone was initially placed in the "stern" of a great and much older "ship setting" of large rocks outlining a vessel 1,115 feet long. In the middle of the ship setting was a Bronze Age mound that had a new wooden burial chamber built in 958–959. Five years after Harald put up his runestone, he destroyed the ship setting, burying the rest of the stern under a second, bigger mound (thirty-three feet high, twenty-three feet in diameter). The stone now stood equidistant between the two mounds. There are no surviving human remains in the burial chamber of the ancient mound, although there was an abundance of grave goods, including a horse. Harald placed nothing inside the new mound. A wooden church (over which a stone church was constructed in the eleventh century) was also built between the runestone and the ancient mound. A broken-up skeleton that might have been King Gorm, and which was likely taken out of the ancient mound's new burial chamber, was interred with grave goods beneath the wooden church.

Christ on the runestone in the ship setting was initially God as a steersman, an amalgam of the old ways with the new deity. Harald soon regretted this religious and political concession, so he not only razed the holy ship setting but smothered its lingering impression beneath the ancient symbol of a burial mound now rendered as a Christian monument by being deliberately empty inside—the ship was not just far away, it was as if it had never existed.[54]

10 Fever Dreams

The appearance of the Northmen in the late eighth century and their continued raiding, conquest, and colonization into the tenth (and even into the eleventh) provided another transformative moment in the West. Even taking into account the exaggeration of Latin Christian writers elevating the ferocity of the Scandinavian naval "brotherhoods" into the violently supernatural, the pagan holy warfare embodied in the longships was shocking and destabilizing from the North Atlantic to the Mediterranean. While the splintering of Charlemagne's empire was inevitable sooner or later, the inherent fractiousness of the Franks on either side of the Rhine was exacerbated and hastened by the Northmen.

Yet, without downplaying the violence of the Danish, Swedish, and Norwegian pirate fleets, they helped reinforce and in some regions actually create a more universal sense of Christianity transcending the many smaller parochial Christendoms. A shared siege mentality, certainly, but crucial in the formation of Western identity. Finally, the apocalypticism that was never far from the surface in the West, and which affected men, women, and children of all ranks, was sent into overdrive by the Northmen—a great engulfing fever dream that only intensified in the eleventh century.

THE MEDIEVAL WEST, 1000

–·–·– Approximate borders of kingdoms and larger domains

N
W E
S

ALBA

IRELAND

WALES
ENGLAND
London
Winchester
Bruges
FLANDERS
Ghent
VERMAINROIS
Rouen
NORMANDY
Reims
Paris
WEST
FRANCIA
ANJOU
Poitiers
FRANCIA
Clermont
AQUITAINE
Lyon
Aurillac

North
Sea

DENMARK

Hamburg
SAXONY
Arneburg
Hildesheim
Gandersheim
Tiel
Goslar
Cologne
Mainz
Gorze
Metz
EAST
FRANCIA
BURGUNDY
Cluny
Mâcon
Charvines
Cremona
BURGUNDY
Milan
Canossa

NORTHERN
MARCH
LIUTIZI
Magdeburg
Quedlinburg
Meissen
BOHEMIA
Elbe R.

Baltic
Sea

Vistula R.
POLES

Kiev

Dnieper R.

Augsburg
BAVARIA
CARINTHIA
HUNGARY

Danube R.
Venice
Adriatic Sea

Black Sea

Constantinople

ATLANTIC
OCEAN

ASTURIAS
Léon
LÉON
CASTLE
Duero R.
NAVARRE
Ebro R.
CATALONIA
Barcelona

ITALY
Rome
Gaeta
Naples
Amalfi
Salerno
Benevento

EAST ROMAN
(BYZANTINE) EMPIRE

Toledo

AL-ANDALUS
Córdoba

SARDINIA

Palermo

SICILY

Tunis

FATIMID
CALIPHATE

Mediterranean Sea

Sijilmasa

0 km 200 400
0 miles 200 400

VII

Hermits in Mail

972–1099

1 Leutard and the Bees

A poor farmer named Leutard was napping in a field in Champagne at the end of the year 1000. He dreamed that a great swarm of honeybees flew into his body through "nature's secret orifices" and then out of his mouth, loudly buzzing and viciously stinging him, until, after what seemed like an eternity, the last of the hive spoke to him as they departed his swollen lips, "ordering him to do things impossible for a human."

Leutard awoke, groggy and exhausted, convinced his dream was a revelation from God. What the bees commanded were edicts of the Lord, which included leaving his wife and smashing the "cross and the image of the Savior" in the village church. Leutard, emboldened by his newfound celibacy and iconoclasm, started preaching that paying tithes was foolish and that while the Old Testament prophets "said many good things, they were not to be believed in everything." Many "common rustic people" soon viewed him as a holy man radiating faith and wisdom. The local bishop did not. He diagnosed the lowborn dreamer as poisoned with the vile "madness" of heresy. The rural Champenois, fearful of being judged as heretics too, renounced their modern prophet as swiftly as they had once worshipped him. Leutard, feeling abandoned by God (and His insects), killed himself by leaping into a well.[1]

2 Events Around the Millennium

Leutard's sorrowful tale of millennial prophecy, heresy, and suicide was recorded by a fiftysomething Burgundian monk named Rodulfus Glaber in his *Five Books of the Histories* (*Historiarum libri quinque*) around 1030. It was one of many such stories interwoven into a self-consciously literary and historical endeavor unlike anything written for almost three centuries in the West: the first Latin "history" since Bede's *Ecclesiastical History*, which was itself only preceded by Gregory of Tours' *Histories*.

Of course, there were other writings before the eleventh century concerned with narrating past events, especially biographies of saintly individuals and the laconic annals of monastic communities. But histories concerned with the linear movement of events through time, and the inescapable interconnectedness of these events within a grand narrative, were the very antithesis of the penitential culture that had developed since the seventh century. The whole point of penance was the repeated erasure of actions and events in an individual life—the excision of the very stuff that constituted history, whether in a person or in a society. Most men and women understood themselves as living within a universe that haltingly moved forward in time (the widespread obsession with the approaching apocalypse guaranteed that), but their own individual salvation depended upon a kind of relentless historical bowdlerization. Bede was unusual in trying to reconcile his historical thinking with a penitential worldview. Rodulfus not only achieved such reconciliation but moved beyond it in his *Histories*, offering a new vision of the relationship of humanity and history as he narrated "the many events which occurred with unusual frequency about the millennium of the Incarnation of Christ our Savior."[2]

Rodulfus was at once frightened and thrilled that he lived around the year 1000. He was unusual. Most men, women, and children did not know they were living through the millennium, or if they did, they were either indifferent or confused about why it was important that a thousand years had passed since the birth and death of Christ. Anxiety about the End of Days certainly shadowed them—as it had done for the previous seven or eight generations—but the consequences of this always-approaching but never-arriving apocalypse, when it finally happened, would be the cessation of all time and earthly existence.

Rodulfus' millennialism, while infused with some of this apocalypticism, was very different. The many events, mostly calamitous, that he diligently collected and described in stylish prose were all signs of the second coming of Christ, and while these portents heralded evils worthy of the Day of Judgment, the world would be reborn rather than annihilated. Such millennialism, or more precisely chiliasm, required not only that time flowed uninterrupted into the future but also that it could be studied as a constant in the past. Christ had once experienced days, weeks, and years as a human, and yet as His life was not interrupted by penance—"without any contagion of sin," nothing needed erasing from His life—His earthly existence was an unbroken progression to His Crucifixion. The writing of history was therefore a sacred act in which the historian replicated Christ's own experience of terrestrial time.

At the very beginning of his *Histories* Rodulfus acknowledged Bede's *Ecclesiastical History* as a rare antecedent—he was shocked that no one for hundreds of years was "anxious to leave any written record for posterity"—and while he admired the Englishman, he faulted him for being too parochial, whereas he was grandly "going to tell what happened in the four parts of the globe." History and so the past and present clues revealing Christ's triumphant return happened in more places than just Britain.

3 At the End of a Bed

Sometimes these clues even appeared at the end of a bed. Rodulfus recalled in his *Histories* how as a sleepy adolescent in the monastery of Saint-Léger-de-Champceaux he saw the devil just after midnight. "As far as I could judge he was of middling stature with a thick neck, skinny face, jet-black eyes," pointy head, wrinkled brow, pinched nostrils, puffy moist lips, dog-like fangs in an elongated mouth, wispy goatee, furry pointy ears, pigeon chest, and a hunchback protruding through raggedy, filthy clothes.

This charming vision leaned over the half-awake lad and, quivering with excitement, violently shook the top of the bed, barking: "You will not remain longer in this place! You will not remain longer in this place! You will not remain longer in this place!" Rodulfus leaped out of bed, ran into the monastery church, and prostrated himself before the altar, "trying desperately to recall all the grave sins of which I had wantonly or carelessly been guilty since childhood."

Rodulfus confessed to his readers that he had been a sinful youth, as "my character was more intractable and my behavior more intolerable than words can tell." Indeed, he was only at Saint-Léger-de-Champceaux because his previous community of monks had expelled him as a delinquent bully, "knowing full well that I should find somewhere to take me in because of my literary ability—this was proved many times." He moved between at least seven different monasteries as an adult, always an obstreperous loner, usually leaving before he was forced out. And it amused the devil to follow him, once even racing out of the lavatories in a new monastery crying, "Where is my young man? Where is my young man?"

Despite the devil's rude awakenings (and creepy toilet humor), Rodulfus admitted that he almost never did enough penance for his sins. Or, rather, what he did do was not necessarily the spotless penitential cleansing of the last four centuries. He still performed penances, but he never assumed such acts completely wiped away whatever sins he had done in his life. Sins and the memory of them remained a vital part of him. Ultimately, Christ's love superseded all penance for Rodulfus, which was why, prostrated before the altar at Saint-Léger-de-Champceaux, "I could say nothing but: 'Lord Jesus, Who came to save sinners, through Your great mercy have pity upon me.'"

Everything Rodulfus wrote about in the *Histories* revealed how Jesus saved the world and individuals through His great mercy. The devil at the end of his bed was as revelatory of the redemptive importance of the millennium as Leutard's bees or any other event in the four corners of the globe. This was not just self-obsession—well, not completely; it was a belief that the history of the world, the history of any one person, and the history of Christ were all intimately connected.[3]

4 Too Many Pilgrims

An explicit example of these connections was the extraordinary surge in pilgrimages to the Sepulcher of the Savior in Jerusalem noted by Rodulfus. "First to go were the petty people, then those of middling estate, and next the powerful, kings, counts, marquesses, and bishops; and finally, something which had never happened before, numerous women, noble and poor, undertook the journey." In the eleventh century more and more ordinary Christians rather than just monks or nuns were traveling as pilgrims to the Holy Land.

Yet even the shortest journey was risky. While the harrying of the Northmen and Saracens was receding for most communities between the Mediterranean and the North Sea by the early eleventh century, the threat of violence by local Christian lords and their mounted thugs was actually intensifying. If these pilgrims were, as estimated, only 1 percent of the roughly 35 million persons living in the West, 350,000 individuals were clogging roads and rivers and expecting to be fed and housed along the way at monasteries. Most of these pilgrims walked through Hungary (whose first Christian monarch, the usurper Stephen, was crowned either on Christmas Day 1000 or a year later), rather than sailing steerage in merchant ships from southern Italy. Most of these pilgrims, according to Rodulfus, never intended to return to their homes, as they hoped to die upon reaching Jerusalem.

Rodulfus reported that the cautious consensus amongst monastic intellectuals was that these pilgrim hordes, far from being good news, were proof of the imminent arrival of the Antichrist and so the end of the world. He politely (rare for him) dismissed this interpretation. And while all those ordinary Christians, especially the poor and women, may have undertaken their journeys partially prompted by a fear of the End of Days, they certainly did not think they were setting in motion the world's destruction. After more than four centuries of the universe being steadily monasticized and the culture of penance shaping almost every thought and action, it was inevitable not only that lay individuals would seek to copy what it was like to be a monk or a nun exiling themselves in a great *peregrinatio*, but also that such a pilgrimage was the ultimate penitential expression of the cleansing of sins—which was why a sinless death in Jerusalem was the hope of so many. Yet, as Rodulfus observed, most churchmen were shocked by this fervor, seeing in it only ominous terror. For him such pilgrimages were an affirmation of the advent of Christ, obviously with some attendant disasters but not the end of everything.[4]

One very relevant disaster for Rodulfus was the destruction of the Church of the Holy Sepulcher in Jerusalem by the Shi'ite Fatimid caliph al-Hakim in 1009. Two years earlier the caliph had issued edicts against Christians and Jews, ignoring their rights as *dhimmis*, confiscating or destroying churches and synagogues in Egypt and Syria; he also persecuted Sunni Muslims. He was widely viewed as dangerously unstable and erratic, eventually disappearing in an "accident" outside Cairo in 1021—though most likely his sister had him murdered. Rodulfus, though, perversely judged him a tool of the Jews, specifically the Jews of Orléans, and that he was their unwitting pawn in an elaborate conspiracy against Christians. This "dastardly plot" involved bribing a fugitive "serf" named Robert (originally belonging to one of the monasteries where Rodulfus had briefly lived) to journey to Cairo disguised as a pilgrim with parchment strips hidden in an iron staff warning in Hebrew that if al-Hakim did not immediately raze the Holy Sepulcher, then he would be overthrown. Somehow or other, the caliph read these secret notes and did as he was told.

News of this Jewish plot apparently spread throughout Latin Christendom, and Jews "became the objects of universal hatred," driven from cities, put to the sword, or drowned in rivers; "some even took their own lives in diverse ways." Like the conspiracy itself, these massacres only occurred in Rodulfus' imagination—the cruel wishfulness of what he knew should have happened in a world properly gripped by his millennial obsessions. Most Latin Christians were either unaware of or indifferent to the destruction of the Holy Sepulcher—let alone the collapse of the Dome of the Rock from an earthquake in 1015—and the few who knew or cared never blamed the Jews.[5]

Rodulfus was unusual in his hatred of the Jews in the early eleventh century, but for him such loathing was inescapably entwined with his fixation on the birth and death of Christ a thousand years earlier. He was more ambiguous about Muslims, as his justification for al-Hakim's actions suggests. Or when he told the well-known story of the kidnapping of the abbot of Cluny, Maiolus, in the Alps by Saracen marauders from La Garde-Freinet (near modern Saint-Tropez) in July 972. "I will not eat this," said the abbot after his captors offered him meat and hard dry bread, "for it is not what I am used to." One of the Muslims, "recognizing the sanctity of this man of God," washed his shield and cooked the prisoner some fresh flatbread. Then another bandit carelessly stepped on the abbot's Bible; shocked at this sacrilege, his companions immediately cut off his foot. "For the Saracens read the Hebrew prophets (or, rather, those of the Christians), claiming that what they foretold concerning Jesus Christ, Lord of all, is now fulfilled in the person of Muhammad [*Mahomed*]," and so the swift amputation, explained Rodulfus, was necessary after the words of the older prophets were trampled upon. (This reference to Muhammad in the *Histories* was the first mention of the Prophet in Latin outside the Iberian peninsula.) Rodulfus thought most of what the Saracens believed was "erroneous fiction," but he emphasized more than once how the marauders recognized and revered the holiness of Maiolus. Of course, these "hordes of Belial" still expected their ransom for the abbot, but then so would any Christian gang of mercenary raiders. Although Rodulfus viewed the followers of Muhammad as members of a distinct religion, he also saw them as essentially misguided Christians and so similar to heretics.[6]

5 There Must Be Heresies

"There must be heresies," Rodulfus agreed with (and quoted) Saint Paul in the *Histories*, so "that they who are of the Faith may be proved." Heresies also confirmed the prophecies of Saint John, "who said the devil would be freed after a thousand years." Leutard's tragic example demonstrated such apostolic wisdom. As did all the other heretics Rodulfus heard about and described with his usual millennial zeal—most notoriously, a sect of thirteen discovered in Orléans in 1022.

The beliefs of these heretics supposedly had been "dispersed like poison" years earlier by a wandering Italian woman, but for more than a decade they had been secretly nurtured by two learned and influential clerics named Lisois and Herbert. The thirteen were exposed when a priest from Rouen, whom they foolishly hoped would be a fellow traveler, denounced them. "We have long believed in this sect which you have only now uncovered," Lisois and Herbert defiantly confessed as they were questioned by a shocked Robert II, king of western Francia or what can now be called France. Rodulfus considered their heresy to be "more stupid and miserable than any of the ancient heresies." Apparently they believed that the unity of the Trinity is an illusion; that heaven and earth had always existed and were not created by God; that there were no carnal sins ("very like the Epicureans," Rodulfus tsk-tsked); and that piety and justice as the price of salvation were "so much useless labor." Rodulfus then refuted these ideas in a long and convoluted diatribe that revealed just how seriously he took such stupidity. What the thirteen failed to understand was that the universe was made by God and that humans by their labors could genuinely resemble their "good Creator." Where once God had sent Christ as a man to renew humanity by taking "upon Himself in this world the image which He had formerly created," now in this new millennium the salvation of all men and women lay in imitating Him as the Son had once imitated them. Dismissing or misunderstanding such redemption, "undoubtedly, is the origin of all the heresies and perverse sects which exist all over the globe."

King Robert and his bishops most likely never thought about (or would not have agreed with if they did) what was so self-evident to Rodulfus about the salvation of humanity. They did, though, know what should be done with the proud and recalcitrant Lisois, Herbert, and the eleven other sect members (a mix of men and women, clerical and lay). In late December 1022 the king "ordered a huge fire should be lit not far from the city, hoping that the sight of this would frighten them into giving up their malign belief." It had the opposite effect, with the heretics laughing and saying "that this was just what they wanted!" Once in the flames, however, "they cried as loudly as they could from the middle of the fire that they had been terribly deceived by the trickery of the devil," and that what they suffered now for their blasphemies was nothing compared to what was to come after their deaths. "Many of those standing nearby heard this, and, moved by pity and humanity, approached seeking to pluck them from the furnace even when half-roasted." But nothing could be done, and the burning bodies were soon piles of ash. "Later," Rodulfus wrote approvingly, "wherever adherents of this perverse sect were discovered, they were everywhere destroyed by the same avenging punishment."

The thirteen individuals incinerated at Orléans were the first men and women executed as heretics since the fourth century in the West. They would not be the last.

Heresy exemplified a broader phenomenon that at once pleased and disturbed Rodulfus. He liked that lay men and women of all social classes were actively embracing what it meant to be a Christian, such as going on pilgrimages to the Holy Land. As far as he was concerned, they were all struggling in their own ways to resemble Christ. Or at least he hoped they realized that this was what they were doing. He was not opposed in principle to peasants like Leutard or clerical and lay elites like the Orléans sect thinking for themselves about the relationship of heaven and earth or divinity and humanity. The trouble was that without proper spiritual guidance such persons could easily think and do what was heretical. It was a slippery slope. The old penitential model was not enough of a bulwark against the spread of heresy for Rodulfus, which was why a renewed Christendom guided by a reformed Church was necessary for a new millennium.

Even if very few of Rodulfus' contemporaries shivered with his excitement and anxiety about the year 1000, much of what this quirky, stroppy, and moody loner envisioned for ordinary Christians (and Jews) would within a century become, if not completely commonsensical, then less exceptional in Latin Christendom.

6 Peace! Peace! Peace!

Around 1033, according to Rodulfus, after three years of never-ending rain that flooded fields and putrefied crops, and an accompanying famine in which many succumbed to cannibalism, suddenly "the happy face of the sky began to shine and to blow with gentle breezes and by gentle serenity to proclaim the magnanimity of the Creator." Starvation (and the bestial evil of eating human flesh) swiftly disappeared as the "whole surface of the earth was benignly verdant."

At the same time, beginning in Aquitaine and then spreading across France, councils were summoned by abbots and bishops in villages, towns, and fields. In these councils, surrounded by the bones of saints in gilded and jeweled caskets, local lords, secular and ecclesiastical, promised to reestablish and maintain peace after years of famine, banditry, and turmoil. The "great, middling, and the poor" all rejoiced at the promise of peace, "ready to obey the commands of the clergy no less than if they had been given by a voice from heaven speaking to men on earth."[7] By the middle of the eleventh century these assemblies were collectively known as the "Peace of God."

These peace councils were great festivals of penitential revivalism. Thousands of people gathered to hear abbots and bishops read from long lists on parchment rolls, "divided into headings," of what they wanted prohibited throughout the land and "what men had, by sworn undertaking, decided to offer to Almighty God." The lists varied from council to council, but some prohibitions were common. Robbers and those who seized other men's farms and fields "were to suffer the whole rigor of the law, either by a heavy fine or corporal punishment." If criminals sheltered inside a church, they were to be unharmed, unless they were guilty of breaking their own peace oath, in which case they could be grabbed (even before the altar) and punished without hesitation. Clerics, monks, nuns, and any persons traveling with them were never to be threatened or harmed. And the most important interdiction, the one from which every other injunction derived, was that all men and women, lay and religious, "whatever threats hung over them before, could now go about their business without fear and unarmed."

A raucous back-and-forth between the bishops and the crowd frequently added items to the lists that, while normally rather mundane penances for specific sins, were rendered into extraordinary self-sacrifices by "perpetual edict." For example, in some councils everyone agreed they would abstain for the rest of their lives from wine on the sixth day of the week and meat on the seventh. Amongst the chanting and cheering throngs were the sick, maimed, and deformed, who, Rodulfus stressed, were miraculously healed not by the bejeweled relics of dead saints but by the prayers of abbots and bishops as living holy men. Finally, after all the lists were read and the oaths were sworn, the bishops raised their croziers to heaven, the people went silent as thousands of hands were lifted in imitation, and then, as a sign of their eternal covenant with God, everyone cried in unison: "Peace! Peace! Peace!" *Pax! Pax! Pax!*[8]

Despite Rodulfus linking these peace councils with happy skies, abundant food (apart from meat and rare spices), "and the millennium of the Lord's Passion," at least twenty-six similar assemblies had occurred since a great public spectacle orchestrated by the archbishop of Bordeaux at Charroux in 989. They were mostly clustered in Poitou, Limousin, Berry, and Auvergne, that is, modern central-western and southern France. They all attempted in their lists, oaths, and acclamations to create local enclaves of peace, safety, and holiness. There was an odd modesty in the grandeur of these councils. Each individual peace covenant with God only went so far spatially—and even temporally, as Rodulfus noted that all oaths needed renewing every five years (even for perpetual edicts). But this localism should not diminish the lasting and unexpected consequences such peace councils had for all of Latin Christendom. The repeated emphasis on the inviolability of ecclesiastical lands and persons from the violence and greed of the laity, while playing an old tune recited and ignored since at least the ninth century, was now declared and heard with singular gravity. Likewise, if monks, priests, and even grandees like abbots and bishops deserved such sacrosanctity, then they must live up to what was expected of them—no weapons, no wives, no sex, no simony (that is, the buying or selling of ecclesiastical offices).

Such principles consciously echoed what famously had been agreed upon when Dhuoda's grandson William I, duke of Aquitaine, founded the monastery of Cluny in 910. Rodulfus, who was at Cluny for four years in his forties, lauded the holiness, independence, and influence of its abbots (like Maiolus) and monks as "an example for imitation by future generations." What most impressed him was the strict enforcement of Benedict's *Rule*.[9] He was not alone. As much as the peace councils were festivals of penitential revivalism, they were also public displays of obedience modeled upon the great *Rule*.

By the middle of the eleventh century, these Peace of God councils ended with another oath, which was called, "in the vulgar tongue, the Truce of God." This covenant, though cried out by everyone in the crowd, was specifically directed toward local nobles and their armed followers. What was agreed, "through both love and fear of the Lord," was that from the setting of the sun on Wednesday until dawn the following Monday, no man would seek out vengeance upon his enemies, kill under any circumstances, commit violent thefts, or even receive an oath of fealty from another man. Individuals breaking these public decrees were punished with steep fines, exile, and even the possibility of death. There were variations on these penalties. In 1041 a council held in a great meadow at Toulouges (near Perpignan on the Mediterranean coast) ordered that if a man deliberately killed another, then the murderer was perpetually exiled, but if a victim was accidentally killed, then the slayer was banished for as long as the bishop judged just. This council also banned all construction work on castles during the usual four days of the Truce as well as during Advent and Lent.

What was so remarkable about the Truce of God was that everyone swearing this oath readily accepted that certain forms of intensely parochial violence (*violentia*) between lords and their gangs of warrior hangers-on was inevitable, even necessary, within the broader Peace of God, but that these blunt and bloody demonstrations of lay power needed their own *Rule* as well. The bishops could not stop such small-scale sadism, but they could try to miraculously suspend it in time and space by public oaths to the Lord. In so doing, they conceded that such violent behavior was special and even holy when controlled by the Church. By regulating vengeance, killing, thievery, raiding, fighting, kidnapping, extortion, and oath-taking—basically, what defined eleventh-century nobles and their mounted retainers—bishops and abbots were not only confirming that such behavior was customary but sanctifying it.[10]

This is a new development in the relationship of churchmen and warriors. Under Charlemagne or Louis the Pious, the run-of-the-mill cruelty of nobles and their martial lackeys throughout the empire was repeatedly condemned in capitularies. The emperors "corrected" with the purpose of eliminating such sinful activity, not metamorphosing it into something virtuous by issuing restraining orders. An abbot like Alcuin and most emphatically a bishop like Agobard never thought a lordly ruffian was or ever could be like them.

The familiar apocalypticism of the last few centuries enveloped the Peace of God and the Truce of God. Now, though, it was transformed into the giddy possibility that the oaths sworn might delay, perhaps permanently, the End of Days. This was not quite the millennialism of a Rodulfus, but it was very close, and represented the beginning of a religious shift that reached an apotheosis by the end of the century.

7 Loyal Oaths

Yet was the world, or rather the small worlds, in which the Peace of God and the Truce of God oaths were sworn significantly more violent and lawless than in previous centuries? The bishops and the crowds thought so when they cried, "Peace! Peace! Peace!" There was certainly a marked intensification of parochial murderousness and larceny by petty lords and their bully boys on horseback. The violence was short-lived, limited, and granular—which, far from lessening its horror, only added to its hellishness.

This was vividly illustrated by the proliferation of castles constructed (mostly out of wood) by big and small lords after the millennium. Such encastellation overwhelmingly began in the same regions as the early peace councils—for example, in Auvergne there were only nine castles in the tenth century, whereas by the middle of the eleventh there were forty-one—but within three or four decades, whether in northern England, Catalonia, or the German lands across the Rhine, castles dominated the landscape.

Often the building of a castle merely confirmed an earlier, more freelance domination. Around 1000, for instance, a tiny tyranny was established by a noble boss and his gang encamped on a hill overlooking some free peasants raising sheep and pigs within the ruins of a Roman villa six hundred feet beneath them in Olargues (in Hérault in southern France). Archeological excavations have revealed that the hilltop racketeers gorged themselves on suckling pigs and lambs either stolen from or offered up as protection payments by the peasants, who themselves rarely consumed meat, apart from the occasional haunch of chewy old mutton. This small-time despotism, like so many others, was soon fixed in place by a castle.[11] The well-fed thugs on the hill in Olargues, though, were still just that. It was only when such men and their martial ways were sanctified by steadily more and more complex oaths and rituals between themselves, their lords, and the Church throughout the eleventh century that they changed into something more than just local toughs in mail; they were transformed into "knights."

This encastellation was part of the great transformation in how the rural world was exploited and experienced from the eleventh century onward. Lords in their castles and abbots in their monasteries, through rough coercion or gentle persuasion, gathered formerly free peasants into villages as their unfree "serfs." These new and permanent communities of a few hundred inhabitants gradually replaced the transitory and widely dispersed single-family farmsteads and hamlets of twenty or so people that had settled the plains, valleys, and forests from the North Sea to the Mediterranean since the sixth century. When these villages were not formed higgledy-piggledy around small castles, they were usually established on hills and enclosed within walls. Of course, there were always peasants in some regions holding their lands freely as allods even if they lived in villages dominated by one or more lords. Nevertheless, inseparable from this village formation was the imposition of unfreedom upon hundreds of thousands of individuals, who, while often poor and powerless, were not and had never been slaves.

What this unfreedom meant as a day-to-day reality varied from the barely noticeable to the brutally oppressive, yet such variety does not lessen that something, arguably intangible for many, was lost. Even as such unfreedom remorselessly spread throughout the West, slavery itself never quite disappeared as a category for some unfree persons, even if, like sharing the name *servus*, there was often no real difference between slave and serf.[12]

Around these villages the formidable early medieval forests, so beloved by Columbanus for their wildness and lack of humanity, were slowly but steadily cleared or (as it is technically known) assarted. Eighty-five percent of England's tree cover was already hacked away by the end of the eleventh century, and it shrank a further 9 percent by 1300. And while 74 million acres of woodland carpeted imperial western Francia in the ninth century, there were only 32 million acres in the French kingdom by the end of the thirteenth century. The lands around the Fulda and Weser Rivers, which had been almost entirely forested when Boniface chopped down the Oak of Thunor in the eighth century, were largely treeless and arable by 1290. There were exceptions. Despite peasant farmers and gardeners around Rome moving from the remnants of ancient villas or isolated farmsteads into villages after 1000, they mostly left the old groves and thickets alone, so the wooded landscape of Lazio in the fourteenth century was almost the same as that into which Benedict escaped as a youth in 503.[13]

All this assarting involved the backbreaking labor of ripping out the stumps and roots of felled trees so that the ground could be plowed. Across the European plain this allowed for what is known as the heavy moldboard plow (iron blades cutting into the ground, picking up and turning over the earth) to be used on heavier and formerly intractable soils. Around the Mediterranean the light scratch or ard plow traced shallow furrows in the flaky soils as it had for thousands of years. Unlike the scratch plow, which was dragged by men, the heavy plow was pulled by horses (mares and geldings) and oxen. An improved plowing collar that did not strangle draft horses appeared in the eleventh and twelfth centuries.

And what covered these new fields were cereal grasses. Wheat and rye for the white bread that lords and knights hungrily devoured with meat. Barley, oats, millet, and spelt for the porridge and beer that nourished peasants (and as fodder for horses).[14]

Crucially, a lord needed villages, serfs, and farmable terrain so that when a fighter in mail swore an oath of fealty (*fidelitas*) to him, he was able to give in return a piece of land variously known as a benefice (*beneficium*) or fief (*feudum*). Yet for a lord to have enough land to bestow, he needed to defend what he possessed with a company of already enfeoffed (in possession of fiefs) knights from the predations of other lords as well as grab further property or serfs from weaker lords so as to receive the homage of more and more fighting men. As for the peasants living and farming on fiefs, while they often pledged loyalty to the new noble who now owned them, their servitude and that of their children was constant.

At least this was the theory if not always the practice after the millennium. "He who takes the oath of fealty to his lord should always keep these six things in mind," Fulbert, bishop of Chartres, theorized in a letter to Guilhem V, duke of Aquitaine, in 1021. First, be "harmless" by never injuring your lord's body. Second, be "safe" by never betraying your lord's secrets or the defenses of his castles. Third, be "honorable" by never harming your lord's honor or his rights of justice. Fourth, be "useful" by never damaging your lord's property. Fifth, be "easy" by never making anything too difficult for your lord. Sixth, be "practicable" by never making impossible what was possible for your lord. Along with these six ways of abstaining from evil, the vassal must actively do good to be worthy of his benefice. And his lord must reciprocate the same six things as well as goodness to him. Fulbert, worried that his analysis of fealty was less rigorous and insightful than the duke wanted, excused himself by saying that his mind was elsewhere, busy with rebuilding Chartres after a fire. He was acutely aware that there was much more to be said than what he had quickly dashed off.[15]

The deep and profound loyalty mandated by such oaths of fealty was new, often rapidly changing in meaning and practice from one region to another, so that even those willing to be bound by them were uncertain of everything that was entailed. It was the obligations of lords to their vassals that most needed clarification. Earlier oaths of loyalty, such as what Charlemagne required throughout his empire in 802, explicitly excluded the emperor from any reciprocity. He was not bound by any oath to him. Four decades later, in a remarkable passage in her *Liber Manualis*, Dhuoda not only referred to herself as the vassal of her husband because she protected his lands like a faithful servant when he was away but also bluntly stated he would abandon her and their son without a second thought, "as is the custom with many men," if she even vaguely faltered in her "servitude." (She lamented that her unwavering servitude required having to take out loans from Jews to pay for soldiers.)[16]

This imbalance in what constituted loyal servility was already shifting into less lopsided relationships by the end of the ninth century. The fracturing of the Frankish realm, especially west of the Rhine, because of civil wars and the invasions of the Northmen, made it more difficult and then simply impractical for kings and lords to solicit loyalty and peace from warriors and strongmen without forfeiting lands in perpetuity and so some of their lofty superiority. Famously, in 911, the king of west Francia, Charles the Simple, received an oath of fealty from the Viking leader Rollo as the new lord of a massive swath of the lower Seine already colonized by two generations of Northmen (or "Normans") and soon known as Normandy. In this relationship the king was very much the weaker party and he knew it. Rollo, while letting the king clasp his hands, refused to bend the knee to him.[17] (The Carolingian west Frankish kings slipped even further into irrelevancy throughout the tenth century, especially when compared with an east Frankish king like Otto I, "the Great," who assumed the old imperial title in 962, or even the dukes of Normandy after Rollo. In 987 a duke named Hugh Capet usurped the west Frankish throne, establishing the Capetian dynasty, which ruled France for the next three hundred years.)

A century later, as Fulbert observed, oaths of fealty were ideally more mutual in their obligations.

8 The Three Orders

An ideal of mutuality tied society into an unbreakable triple knot for other bishops in the early eleventh century. Around 1020, Adalbero, bishop of Laon, in a poem to King Robert II observed that within the world some people "pray, others fight, and others work." These three groups were "together and suffer no split; the workings of two thus stand on the office of one," and yet despite the burdens suffered by serfs supporting churchmen and warriors, everyone was inescapably bound together, so this "three-way connection is therefore single." In his perfect schema, Adalbero admitted, "there is no end to the groans and tears of serfs." Regrettably, "no free man could live without serfs" and the fields they plowed and harvested. But this divine threefold order needed protecting, as evil and rapacious men currently threatened it. The king must control these sinners by forcing them back into the social trinity.

Although Adalbero saw a landscape of violence in northern France similar to what other bishops decried further south, he denounced the Peace of God and reformers like the abbots of Cluny.[18] Another northern

French bishop during the same decade, Gerard of Cambrai, also condemned and countered the Truce of God with a vision in which God had from the beginning of the world divided humanity into "prayers, farmers, and fighters." (He even mocked one bishop for saying he had a letter from heaven mandating what oaths should be sworn.)[19] These two men angrily opposed bishops and abbots controlling violence through peace assemblies. That was the role of kings, even a largely powerless one like Robert. Yet both Adalbero and Gerard, just like the bishops they loathed, saw fighting men (*bellatores*) as needing to be held in check, and equally, they elevated them into an order (*ordo*) on a par with monks, except it was within an imaginary eternal triad and not by public oaths of peace.

Adalbero and Gerard's model of the three orders as a response to social tumult was, for all its head-in-the-clouds impracticality and prickly traditionalism, intellectually significant, though not so much at the time. Although it seems no one had ever carved up society in this way before—apart from the notable exception of the English translator of the *Consolation of Philosophy* more than a century earlier, where the three tools of a king were praying men, fighting men, and working men—and while later medieval intellectuals imagined humanity classified in any number of orders, it was this tripartite system that found most favor in the twelfth century and beyond.[20]

In late June 1027, Fulbert in a hastily written letter—he was always so busy—to Robert II explained a recent freakish summer storm that apparently rained blood by arguing that it not only prophesied (or, as it were, precipitated) a forthcoming catastrophe but also indicated who amongst the "three kinds of men" would survive. After copying out a long extract from Gregory of Tours' *Histories* on how plague in the sixth century was always preceded by showers of blood from the sky, he judged that the new red rain "portends the coming of a public disaster." (Such "blood rain" may be a case of the meteorological phenomenon in which fine reddish Saharan sand is carried by powerful winds over Europe, where it mixes with storm clouds and colors precipitation. For example, in July 1968 blood rain fell on southern England.)[21] As to the king having heard that the recent deluge of blood was unable to be washed off stone or flesh, unlike wood, this clearly signified the well-known tripartition of humanity. Stone symbolized the impious; flesh, the fornicators; and wood, "which is neither hard like stone nor soft like flesh," neither the impious nor the fornicators. "When the sword or plague foretold by the blood comes upon the people for whom it was portended," then if the "hard" or the "soft" remain uncleansed, they will perish in their own blood, while men and women standing in the spotless middle will be saved. Fulbert's forecast that a wooden but virtuous third would be God's chosen survivors in a looming great war or pestilence was more moral triage than mutual triad.[22]

The three orders, untrammeled violence, the Peace of God and the Truce of God, encastellation, oaths of fealty, serfs, knights, assarting, vassalage, white loaves, gruel, and the fief are all frequently wrapped up and described by the controversial (at least amongst medieval historians) adjective "feudal." It is an anachronistic descriptor, derived from *feudum* by French and English legal scholars in the seventeenth and eighteenth centuries as a way of characterizing ancien régimes, medieval and modern. However, no "feudal society" in any schematic way ever existed in the Middle Ages, and certainly not in the eleventh century, when it was supposedly formed. Yet most of the components of this theoretical model did exist, just never all of a piece and rarely in more than one or two regions in the same decade or even century. Hence, if used sparingly, "feudal" aptly delineates some aspects of the later medieval West.

9 The Patarenes

"There are three orders in the holy Church," the young priest Arialdo preached to a crowd in Milan in 1057; "the first, those who preach, the second, those who are continent, and the third those who are married." Whoever belonged to these three orders, he exhorted, "and has not fought ardently against the heresy of simony" will suffer eternal damnation. This was one of many sermons raging against simony—the selling of Church offices—Arialdo had given in the streets and piazzas of Milan since arriving in the city twelve months earlier. He had been shocked at the corruption he saw amongst the clergy: "Some served the pleasures of the hunt, wandering about with hounds and hawks, others were tavern-keepers and wicked overseers, while others were impious usurers." All of them had wives or concubines.

But what most disgusted Arialdo was that "all were so deeply implicated in the heresy of simony that from the least to the greatest there was no order or clerical rank that could not be had unless it was bought just as a pig is bought." His passionate exhortations against heretical priests, including Guido da Velate, the archbishop and de facto lord of Milan, so stirred everyone up, whether noble or commoner, that now "those whom they had formerly venerated as ministers of Christ, they condemned and declared enemies of God and deceivers of souls."[23] Arialdo's followers, especially amongst the holy "married" third, were known as Patarenes, a pun on the lowly street-corner rag-sellers known as *pattari*. Even if their enemies used it as an insult, the Patarenes themselves embraced it as marking them out as humble, like Christ.[24]

The spring after Arialdo had given his first anti-simoniac tirade—"For just as those deceived long ago believed rocks and wood to be gods, so you suppose your priests to be true priests!"—a young cleric of aristocratic family named Landulfo stepped out of the crowd and, in a joyful voice, said, "Before you all I thank omnipotent God that He allowed me to hear now things that have long burned in my heart." Then one of the wealthy "married" named Nazarius came forward and loudly agreed with Arialdo about the priests of Milan, especially "as the life of those men should be superior and different from mine whom I summon to my home to bless it, whom I feed according to my ability, to whom I offer a gift after kissing their hands, and from whom I receive the sacraments for which I expect eternal life!" He offered the angry but eloquent young man his family chapel as a place of sanctuary from the simoniacs and whatever monies might be needed (he had the hereditary right to mint coin in Milan). Landulfo became Arialdo's constant companion in the fight against heresy.[25]

"In those days," recalled the monk Andrea da Strumi about simony in Milan twenty years later in his *Life* of Arialdo, "if you were to walk through the city, you would hear scarcely anything but debate on this matter." Everywhere there was confusion and contention. "Some excused the simoniacal heresy, others condemned it constantly, and no wonder since one house was faithful, another completely unfaithful, in a third the mother and son were believers, while the father and son were unbelieving." Frequently these quarrels spilled into the streets, with the Patarenes and their supporters fighting the lay and clerical partisans of the archbishop. According to Andrea, one impious priest tried and failed to assassinate Landulfo with a poisoned sword ("a sword I saw later many times").[26]

Arialdo embraced the threat of violence as signifying his righteousness. When he was excommunicated by Guido da Velate as a heretic himself, he mocked and dismissed the sanction. In the chapel of Nazarius he established a community of men and women, lay and clerical, rich and poor, living less like monks under a *Rule* than as pious and chaste individuals replicating the lives of the Apostles and Christ. These most precious of the Patarenes were an example to the faithful and a rebuke to the faithless. Every morning Arialdo departed the chapel on long processions throughout the city, visiting shrines and churches, constantly praying, preaching, and singing—he saw himself as a living holy man who by undertaking these daily pilgrimages throughout Milan was purifying every sacred urban space, even the tombs of saints, of the pollution of heresy.

After 1061 the new pope, Alexander II, enthusiastically encouraged Arialdo in his efforts at reforming the clergy of Milan. It helped that he too came from the city and that only five years earlier, when he had been a priest named Anselmo da Baggio, he had been one of the first Patarenes like his close friend Landulfo. He may have even hoped to root out simoniacal priests as the next archbishop, but before that could happen, a vengeful Guido da Velate shunted him off to what should have been obscurity at the papal court in Rome. In a demonstration of the kind of poor judgment that was a hallmark of the archbishop, the annoying priest he had dismissed from his thoughts rapidly became bishop of Lucca and then pope. Unsurprisingly, Alexander detested Guido, and vice versa.

Landulfo, while preparing to visit his old friend in Rome, suddenly died (natural causes, no foul play). At his bedside was his brother Erlembaldo, who, after more than a year away, had just returned from a pilgrimage to Jerusalem. Arialdo looked at him closely and was impressed with what he saw, all the more so as the brother was a *capitaneus*, a martial aristocrat of Milan, and he needed a charismatic fighting man in the battle against heresy. Erlembaldo, while sympathetic to the Patarenes, had decided that after having walked where Christ had once walked, he "wanted to leave the world and give himself over to the monastic life." Arialdo would have none of it, forcefully telling him that he would be more esteemed in the eyes of God if he stayed exactly as he was and joined him as a soldier "defending the Catholic faith and resisting heretics and the enemies of Christ." Erlembaldo was tempted, but he was still unsure about whether remaining a fighter was really better than being a prayer. The new pope, who was a friend of his too, would know.

Alexander could not have been more enthusiastic about Erlembaldo staying in the world as a warrior on behalf of God, giving him a banner emblazoned with the image of Saint Peter to hold aloft in the streets of Milan, "when the madness of the heretics raged beyond measure," and commanding him "to fight Christ's enemies bravely with Arialdo in defense of justice even to the point of shedding his own blood." As the French bishops had done and were still doing in the Peace of God and the Truce of God, the pope not only affirmed the holiness of fighting men who submitted themselves to the Church but went further and suggested that such laymen were exactly the same as monks, perhaps even holier in some respects, if they fought the enemies of Christ and died battling them. Erlembaldo epitomized such an ideal—"like a duke arrayed in fine clothes and surrounded by knights and arms, but in secret before God he was like a hermit in the wilderness, dressed in woollens."[27]

This ideal also started going the other way, so that hermits in the wilderness were dressing like men-at-arms. In 1045, Dominic Loricatus, known as "the Mailed," wore mail as a hermit at Fonte Avellana (in the Marche) until his death fifteen years later, according to his *Life* written by the ascetic (and cardinal in 1057) Peter Damiani. He was at once a prayer and a fighter, a monk and a knight, "always prepared for the fight" against the enemies of Christ. He never removed his mail, so his skin was scraped raw, and he ceaselessly whipped himself, with the never-healing scars forming "the banner of the cross" on his forehead and "the stigmata of Jesus on his body." (This seems to be the first reference to a living person replicating Christ's stigmata, that is, His five wounds.)

And why did Dominic punish himself so severely? He was expiating his own sin of simony—or, rather, the sin of his parents when they purchased his ordination as a priest while he was still a small child.[28] Peter, who knew and deeply admired Dominic, was equally obsessed with simony, even intervening at one point in the Milan struggle, arguing that if the clergy did penance for their simoniacal ways and never returned to their heresy, they could stay in their offices. This satisfied no one: for Arialdo it pardoned heretics, while for Guido it was irrelevant as there were no sins to cleanse.

Peter, while despising simony, believed it might be forgiven, whereas he thought clerical marriage could never be absolved. Priests "ready for themselves a thousand years in hell for every fleeting enjoyment of intercourse."[29]

Arialdo was oddly indifferent about whether "heretics have wives or not."[30] Nevertheless, both he and Peter shared a passion for suffering like Christ and wishing to be martyrs—and while it never happened to the latter, no matter how hard he tried, for the former it happened all too soon.

In 1066, Guido da Velate, hoping to end the Patarenes once and for all, had five assassins kidnap Arialdo as he was traveling in northern Lombardy. The killers bundled their victim onto a boat and rowed out to an island in Lake Maggiore. "Arialdo," they asked, pulling on their oars, "why don't you deny what you have said until now and proclaim that our lord is the true bishop?" The bundle in the bow replied, "God forbid that the crown which I have acquired during my life by speaking the truth, I lose at the end of my life by lying." Once ashore, the assassins tied Arialdo to a rock but, losing heart, decided they could not kill him. "What are we going to do?" Suddenly, two Milanese clerics raced up the rocky shore from another boat, yelling, "Where's Arialdo?" "He's dead," lied the five (not especially bright) penitents. As Arialdo was clearly visible tethered on the rock, the clerics barreled forward and, viciously pulling his ears, growled, "Tell us, you gallows rogue, if our lord is the true archbishop." "He is not and never was," was the cool reply. The clerics cut off both ears with swords. Arialdo smiled, raised his eyes to heaven, and said, "I thank You, Christ, that today You deigned to number me amongst Your martyrs." The clerics then slowly butchered him—as he murmured "He is not and never was"—cutting off his nose, upper lip, right hand, and genitals ("Until now you have been a preacher of chastity, now you shall be chaste!") before finally tearing out his tongue. Arialdo's body was dumped in the lake, where it bobbed and floated undiscovered for ten months.[31]

The Patarene movement did not end with the murder of Arialdo. Erlembaldo still marched through the streets of Milan with his banner flying, encouraged and financed by Alexander II and his zealous re-forming archdeacon Hildebrand. The pope and his archdeacon even fo-mented Patarene outbursts in other Lombard cities. After Guido da Velate died in 1073, Erlembaldo effectively ruled as the sanctimonious dictator of Milan, "like a pope to judge the priests and like a king to bruise the populace."[32] At first he demanded oaths of fidelity from all Patarenes and then more broadly from all Milanese nobles. He and his "fighters of Christ" scoured churches and chapels for heretical priests, banishing (after thrashing) them, their wives, and their children. In 1074 he even stopped

Easter baptisms, as he decided that every drop of chrism (baptismal oil and balsam) in Milan was impure with heresy.

A year later, after a fire (the second in four years) ripped through Milan, destroying the cathedral, a band of *capitanei*, having had enough of their hermit duke and seeing their charred streets as a sign of God's anger, ambushed and killed Erlembaldo. The Patarenes almost immediately dispersed, and while a few elderly survivors were still willing to call themselves such after 1100, their purifying fury disappeared from Milan.[33]

The Patarenes were inspired by the same social and moral renovation as seen in the Peace of God and the Truce of God, except in an urban environment. Milan even underwent its own version of encastellation, with its first noble tower-house erected in 1043.[34] As the city was steadily pockmarked with tiny overlapping circles of aristocratic violence radiating outward from these tower-houses, there were calls for controlling this escalating danger on the streets. Erlembaldo's brutality was what was expected from men like him, even if the puritanical fanaticism was all his own. This is why it should not be underestimated that Guido da Velate and his supporters, which were always a majority of the Milanese, were equally in favor of spiritual and communal reform, just in a more incremental traditionalist manner and without any papal intervention.

Fundamentally, it was the aggressive involvement of the papacy with the Patarenes that had lasting consequences far removed from Milan, especially when Hildebrand became Pope Gregory VII in 1073.

10 A War Penitential

In 1070, Alexander II, while encouraging Erlemblado as his unfettered holy warrior, affirmed through his legate, Ermenfrid, bishop of Sion, a "war penitential" for all Norman lords, soldiers, and clerics who had fought at the Battle of Hastings four years earlier and subsequently conquered England with their duke (and now king), William.

Like the lists of penances read out by bishops at Peace of God assemblies, this ordinance, while recalling the older penitential understanding of what constituted a person, was shaped by the shifting eleventh-century formula that now the sins of an individual were never completely erased whatever penances they did. For instance, the penitential opened with this sweeping statement: "Whoever knows that he has killed in the great battle is to do one year's penance for each man slain." This was followed by "Whoever struck another but does not know if that man was thereby slain, is to do forty days penance for each case, if he can remember the number, either continuously or at intervals." Both of these rules were potentially lifelong and continuous, with the same penances perpetually overlapping with one another. Even just the desire to hit someone in the war was three days of penance. Archers, who obviously had no notion of how many were killed by their arrows, were to do penance for three Lents.

The penitential acknowledged that clerics and monks had fought at Hastings, but like the condemnation of simony and marriage amongst the clergy, such fighting was forbidden if all too common. The penitential made a sharp distinction between killing before and after William's consecration as king of England on Christmas Day 1066: beforehand, all the various war penances applied; afterward, just the penance for quotidian homicide. And warfare neither excused nor afforded a special category of penances for "adulteries or rapes or fornications" committed by warriors.

As to whether the Norman lords and their knights were constrained by this penitential—especially as William's army "utterly ravaged and laid waste" northern England in 1070—it was still a trenchant statement of papal greatness, declaring that the power of penance ultimately derived only from the pope.[35]

11 That He May Depose Emperors

In early March 1075, Gregory VII drafted an extraordinary memorandum listing twenty-seven powers and prerogatives of himself as pope. It was a radical assertion of papal grandeur: "That only the Roman Pontiff may by right be called universal." That his title of "pope" is unique. That only he may establish new laws. That no one may judge him. That he may depose, reinstate, or transfer bishops as decided by him alone. "That his name alone may be read out in churches." That all serious problems in churches everywhere be referred to him. And so on, in a series of statements affirming that no ecclesiastical individual, whether exalted like a bishop or admirably holy like a hermit, was more magnificent or sacred than the pope.

Most crucial, though, were the papal claims of absolute authority over secular rulers, especially emperors: "That all princes should kiss the feet of the pope alone." That only he may use imperial insignia. That he may release vassals from fealty to unjust men. "That he may depose emperors."[36] Gregory's privately sketched-out vision of himself as pope and of all future pontiffs was no ineffectual daydream; quite the contrary, his twenty-seven points shaped and underpinned the final decade of his papacy, most particularly what is known as the Investiture Controversy (or Conflict) with Henry IV, German king and eventual emperor.

Gregory, as Hildebrand, had already sparred with Henry a couple of years earlier over his tacit support of Guido da Velate against the Patarenes. In late 1075 they tussled over the king appointing two new archbishops in Milan and bishops in Fermo and Spoleto. The pope, while not ready just yet to bluntly deny that Henry had such prerogatives, angrily objected that he had never heard of these men and that he should have been consulted. The king, who was only twenty-five, replied in kind, dismissing Gregory, who was fifty, as corrupted by simony and violence—the pope did, after all, bless Erlambaldo's reign of terror—and whereas he was called to kingship by Jesus Christ, only emptiness and vanity called Hildebrand (as he snidely referred to Gregory) to the priesthood.

The pope retaliated by excommunicating Henry and releasing his vassals from their oaths of fealty. In January 1077, the king, genuinely upset about his soul but also worried about rebellious lords along the Rhine, penitentially walked through the snow to a mountain castle at Canossa (in Reggio Emilia) where Gregory was staying, begging for forgiveness. The pope forgave him. A year later he did not. "We decree that no one of the clergy shall receive the investiture with a bishopric or abbey or church from the hand of an emperor or king or of any lay person, male or female." Henry was excommunicated again for "investing" (choosing and installing, dressing and equipping) bishops in the German lands and northern Italy. Gregory issued an even stronger condemnation against lay investiture in 1080. Henry, enraged and exasperated with the presumptuous pontiff, attacked and besieged Rome over the next five years. He vowed that Hildebrand and all his clerical "thickheads" would soon kiss his feet. In 1084, after capturing Rome, Henry installed his own pope,

Clement III, who then obediently crowned him emperor. Gregory, broken and unwell, retreated to Salerno, where he died on Sunday, May 25, 1085, saying at the end, "I loved justice and I hated iniquity, therefore I die in exile."[37]

What Gregory envisioned for the papacy specifically and the Church more generally did not end with these last words. Far from it. The Gregorian Reform associated with his name continued well into the thirteenth century, as did the conflict between popes and emperors, and a king or two, over who truly ruled Christendom. More remarkably, though, was how so many ordinary men, women, and children throughout the West passionately embraced this reform, often willing to risk their lives for what they thought it demanded and for what they thought it promised—as was exemplified in what happened a decade after Gregory's death.

12 The First Crusade

"Most beloved brethren," announced Pope Urban II in a field outside the city of Clermont (in Auvergne, by the shallow Tretaine River) on Tuesday, November 27, 1095, "by God's permission placed over the whole world with the papal crown." Most of his shivering audience, more than a hundred bishops and thousands of ordinary Christians, assumed they were participating in a raucously redemptive Peace and Truce of God council, if one that was more marvelous than usual, as the festival impresario was the pope himself.

Everyone in the field knew Urban was exiled from Rome, and yet they all agreed he was the rightful pontiff as the successor of Gregory VII (once removed, as there was the brief three-year papacy of the abbot of Monte Cassino as Pope Victor III). The pope began by praising the bishops around him as the "salt of the earth," as men whose salinity, if it was "kind, provident, temperate, learned, peace-making, truth-seeking, pious, just, equitable, pure," would preserve humanity from becoming rancid with maggoty sins. But this holy saltiness would save the world only if the bishops were themselves unsullied, so they must never submit to secular lords or turn a blind eye to the heresy of simony.

Urban then recited the customary Peace of God exhortations against anyone seizing or kidnapping bishops, monks, nuns, clerics, pilgrims, and merchants, before calling for a renewal of the Truce of God—except he did not mean just around Clermont; quite radically, he meant in every diocese of every bishop who was present. A patchwork of over a hundred local Peaces and Truces, almost all of them in France, were now stitched together into a great whole cloth by the pope. When the crowd swore their oaths promising to uphold the Peace and Truce of God, it was this grandiose papal vision they were affirming. Most in the audience assumed the council was over, especially as what had happened was already exciting enough. But Urban was not finished just yet.[38]

Urban told those assembled that, having sworn their oaths of fealty to God, there was now even greater work to be done for Him. "O sons of God, you must help your brothers living in the Orient, who need your aid for which they have already cried out many times." Eight months earlier the East Roman emperor, Alexios Komnenos, had asked Urban for help against the Turcoman Saljuqs of Rum, who were threatening Constantinople from their capital in Nicaea. (The Saljuqs of Rum were formerly a confederacy of warrior nomads from the Asian steppes who, after two decades of fighting Byzantine armies, had overwhelmed Anatolia, a territory they knew as Bilad al-Rum, "land of the Romans," or simply Rum.)[39] Urban described these "Turks" as occupying and laying waste to God's kingdom. "I, with suppliant prayer—no, not I, but the Lord" was calling upon all bishops to coax knights and foot soldiers, rich and poor, "to help expel that wicked people from our Christian lands before it is too late."

Urban then offered his great gift. Everyone journeying to Romania (as he called Anatolia) as pilgrims, even if they died on land in chains or in crossing the sea or in fighting the heathen, "will be granted remission of sins." All warriors, he commanded, instead of fighting fellow believers, must fight faraway infidels; instead of being thieves on horses, they must be "soldiers of Christ"; and instead of earning a few grubby shillings as hirelings, they must win eternal reward in heaven. Urban looked out at the mass of men, women, and children in the field of Clermont and saw their wonder at what they had heard. He ended with the hope that the *peregrinatio* or *expeditio* would be under way by the next summer.

Whether Urban had planned all along to say what he did or if he was carried away in the apocalyptic and millennial moment, what he unleashed over the next four years, and which he could never have imagined, was an extraordinary fighting pilgrimage now known as the First Crusade.[40]

Despite the thousands present at Clermont, very few of them wrote down what Urban said. Fortunately, a fastidious thirty-six-year-old priest from Chartres named Fulcher was in the audience taking notes. He also went on the great pilgrimage himself, jotting down his impressions and recording what he witnessed, eventually compiling and editing everything into what he called *The Jerusalem History* (*Historia Hierosolymitana*) around 1102. In Fulcher's vivid description of Clermont, though, Urban never mentions Jerusalem or the Holy Sepulcher as the goal of his warrior pilgrims. This reveals just how impromptu and even experimental the last part of the pope's sermon was. He clearly thought his admonition to help the emperor in Constantinople was the obvious extension of what he had just achieved with his wide-ranging Peace and Truce of God. He was unmistakably saying that this continuation of papally sanctioned fighting—basically, Peace and Truce oaths on the move—was the equivalent of going on a pilgrimage, but not necessarily one to Jerusalem. He was explicitly proclaiming that he was the final arbiter of imperial legitimacy in Christendom—which for him was Alexios Komnenos as emperor and not Henry IV.

All this was amazing and revolutionary enough. Yet even before the crowd at Clermont dispersed, Urban soon realized that many of them, although not all, just assumed that once they liberated Romania, they would inevitably set free the Holy Sepulcher. And this assumption only escalated once more and more ordinary Christians heard what the pope said. Urban adapted his message and penitential gift accordingly; he was forced into it by the very enthusiasm he had unleashed.

Lambert, bishop of Arras, who was at Clermont, tersely outlined this papal modification in a decree a few months later: "Whoever shall set forth to liberate the church of God at Jerusalem for the sake of devotion alone and not to attain honor or money will be able to substitute that journey for all penance."[41] More than anything, Lambert's decree reasserted that the journeying in and of itself was all that mattered for the remission of sins, although now freeing the Holy Sepulcher was explicitly the purpose of the pilgrimage.

Urban himself was soon reiterating this revised version of his Clermont sermon before crowds in France and northern Italy over the next six months. He also commanded that after taking their vows as pilgrims, all individuals should sew crosses on their cloaks or cassocks in silk, woven gold, or whatever cloth they could afford. "They imprinted the ideal," wrote

Fulcher about these embroidered crosses, "so that they might attain the reality of the ideal."[42]

Other charismatic preachers, most famously a priest from Amiens known as Peter the Hermit, traveled the German lands whipping up excitement and gathering followers in what quickly became great meandering mobs of pilgrims, wearing crosses often stitched on rags. These preachers extrapolated wildly from what Urban was saying (and had said). Albert, a canon of Aachen cathedral, writing only twenty years after Clermont in his *History of the Journey to Jerusalem*, even concocted a fanciful tale that it was the eremetical Peter and not the pope who came up with the idea of capturing and cleansing the Holy Sepulcher—or, rather, Christ came up with the idea and relayed it to Peter in a dream.[43] What Urban had said at Clermont was still being debated (and distorted) a generation later.

These messianic preachers and their amorphous wandering catchalls of men and women, rich and poor, fighters and farmers—"the leftover shit," as Guibert, abbot of Nogent, described them—attacked Jews throughout the Rhineland as soon as the warmth of spring arrived. In Speyer, Worms, Cologne, Trier, Metz, Regensburg, and Mainz, Jewish families were dragged into the streets and threatened with death if they did not convert to Christianity. Bishops, horrified by this savagery, tried and mostly failed to protect Jews in their dioceses; of course, these same bishops also warned newly converted Jews against apostasy. Peter, while equally appalled by this perversion of the great pilgrimage, had no qualms about extorting funds from the Jews of Trier.

Many Jews fought back, winning victories here and there, but they were outnumbered. "Mother, do not slaughter me!" screamed sons and daughters in Mainz as they were sacrificed before the pilgrims could murder them. Jewish parents surrounded by the bodies of their children committed suicide as martyrs.[44] The apocalypticism of the mob was embraced by their victims. Everything Rodulfus imagined in his vicious millennial dreams seventy years earlier had come to pass.

After this Easter bloodshed, these various pilgrim hordes started walking toward Constantinople, usually starting out from Cologne. Most of them disappeared in the grassy plains of Hungary as the first poppies were blooming, cut down by locals infuriated at the untrammeled brigandry and violence of supposedly fellow Christians. Peter's followers, roughly ten thousand or so, while similarly inclined to sanctimonious pillaging, fought off the Hungarians and managed to reach the Bosphorus by October.[45]

Fulcher, while briefly mentioning Peter and his shitty mob, recorded nothing about the attacks on the Jews. He was more interested in "the heroes crossing the sea," the noble pilgrims in mail. They were Hugh of Vermandois, brother of the French king; Raimon of Saint-Gilles, count of Toulouse; Godfrey, duke of Lower Lorraine; Bohemond, "an Apulian of Norman descent," son of Robert Guiscard; Robert, duke of Normandy and brother of the English king; and Étienne, count of Blois and Duke Robert's uxorious brother-in-law. Fulcher himself ("a beautiful cross" sewn on his cloak) traveled in the entourage of Robert and Étienne. Each of these expeditions departed in summer 1096 and, apart from Godfrey traveling unscathed through Hungary, they sailed on ships and galleys from southern Italy.

When these pilgrims finally gathered before the walls of Constantinople a year later in May, they pitched tents for seven thousand horsemen, thirty thousand foot soldiers, and somewhere between twenty thousand and sixty thousand other individuals. Not surprisingly, the emperor Alexios Komnenos, while grateful that his call for help was answered more extravagantly than he had ever expected, was extremely wary of these holy warriors on his doorstep.[46]

"Let it be known to you, my sweet," Étienne began a letter to his wife, Adèle, on Wednesday, June 24, 1097, "that I am honored and well rested." He described how Alexios had received him "as if I were his son." The emperor had charmed Étienne. "I tell you truthfully that there is no man under the heavens like him today. He has generously enriched all our leaders, he has given gifts to every knight, and he has refreshed all the poor with great meals." The emperor reminded him a lot of Adèle's father, William. Anyhow, what Étienne really wanted to tell his wife about was the siege of Nicaea. After crossing the Bosphorus, which he assured her was no more dangerous than sailing the Seine or Marne, he hurried to the pilgrim camp encircling the city. He did not mention to Adèle that the plains around Nicaea were littered with thousands of rotting severed heads and bloated carcasses of the dead followers of Peter. A few months earlier they had attacked the city as a frenzied rabble and the Saljuqs had slaughtered them mercilessly. (Anna Komnene, the daughter of Alexios, in her *Alexiad*, a history dedicated to her father, remembered how Peter arrogantly called the massacre of his acolytes their own fault. "He called them brigands and robbers," disobedient and foolish.)[47] Étienne swiftly narrated how the "army of God" had constructed tall and hefty wooden towers from which arrows and spears could be launched over the walls of Nicaea. In less than a month, the Saljuqs surrendered to Alexios. Étienne was in the city even as he dictated this letter to his "sweetest friend." It was the city, he reminded her, of the great council that had affirmed the Trinity and demolished the Arian heresy. "I tell you, my sweet," Étienne concluded, "that from this oft-mentioned Nicaea we should arrive in Jerusalem in just five weeks, unless Antioch should slow us down."[48]

"You may surely believe, dearest," Étienne wrote to Adèle in March 1098, "that this messenger whom I have sent to your sweetness left me safe and healthy and enriched by good fortune at Antioch." He had been there for four indecisive months and, to his surprise, had been elected leader of the expedition of the Lord. "Antioch is a city great beyond belief, one we have found most powerful and invincible." The Saljuq amir Yaghi-Siyan (formerly a Mamluk) had adroitly repulsed all assaults by the "army of Christ." The pilgrims were starving, their horses were emaciated, and their tents were little more than ribbons flapping in the wind. The winter was brutal and the rain cut into their flesh like thousands of icy knives. "It is false what some say about the unbearable heat of the Syrian sun, for their winter is similar to ours in the West." Étienne ended his letter by telling Adèle, "You will surely see me as soon as I am able."[49]

Indeed, sooner than she expected. Three months later, pleading illness and feeling that he had done enough for his sins to be erased, Étienne departed "invincible" Antioch and sailed home. He had incredibly poor timing, as the next day, Thursday, June 3, the city was captured after Bohemond bribed a Saljuq guard named Firuz into dropping ropes over the walls. Étienne would probably still have fled, as a coalition of northern Syrian Saljuq amirs under Karbuqa (or Kerbogah) of Mosel was rapidly marching to Antioch. The army of God was frightened. Miraculously, the lance that pierced Christ's side on the cross was discovered by a pilgrim peasant in a church in Antioch. Everyone was elated. Unfortunately, it turned out to be false.[50] After four more weeks of such frantic mood swings, and just when all seemed lost, Karbuqa's coalition fractured and disappeared.[51]

Étienne was mocked and humiliated throughout Christendom for fleeing Antioch.

Even by Adèle. She frequently urged him to return to Holy Land, as he was held in such scorn. Étienne did in 1101—and died there within a year.

On Saturday, September 11, 1098, as the army of Christ moved south toward Jerusalem, Raimon of Saint-Gilles and the other noble leaders (those who had not died or fled) dispatched an audacious letter to Urban. "You started this expedition!" they bluntly told him. "Your sermons made us all leave our lands and what was in them, follow Christ by taking up the cross and exalt the Christian name." They wanted him to come east and lead them. "So what on earth could appear more appropriate than that you, the father and leader of the Christian religion," they said flatteringly, "should personally complete the war which is your own." Why they needed Urban so desperately was that while they were triumphing over "Turks and pagans," they were failing with eastern Christians (Greeks, Armenians, Syrians, and Jacobites), all of whom were "heretics." (Even in the late eleventh century, there were more Christians than Muslims in the Levant.) They pleaded for him to command them in the eradication and destruction of all types of heresy. "In this way you will complete the expedition of Jesus Christ which we began and you preached." Finally, "if you do come to us to complete the expedition you began, the whole world will obey you." (They added an addendum, clearly with individuals like Étienne in mind, that it was wrong for Urban to let anyone signed with the cross have their sins forgiven if they either ran away from or put off joining the holy expedition.)

This manifesto, composed before the pilgrimage had even reached Jerusalem, revealed that, at least amongst the leaders, what they were now waging was a holy war against Muslims (as pagans), heretics, and by association Jews—an apocalyptic and millennial campaign that would transform all the world into Latin Christendom.[52]

Nine grueling months later, on Tuesday, June 7, 1099, the holy warriors, numbering around fifteen thousand, finally reached the walls of Jerusalem. Urban had not come out to lead them. The Shi'ite Fatimids, reveling in the turmoil of the Sunni Saljuqs, had besieged and retaken the city only the previous September. Now, the twenty thousand inhabitants—many of whom were Jews, Muslims, and Christians (Western and Eastern) on their own private pilgrimages—huddled down and waited for another onslaught. It came soon enough. On Friday, July 15, after towering wooden war machines dressed in leather had hurled missiles into the streets and long-nosed battering rams thumped and smashed holes in the stone walls, the soldiers of Christ rushed into the city under the blistering midday sun, blowing trumpets and yelling "Help! God!" and "God wills it!" Anyone not obviously signed with the cross was slaughtered. "Nowhere was there a place where the Saracens could escape the swordsmen," gushed Fulcher, adding:

> On the top of Solomon's Temple, to which they had climbed in fleeing, many were shot to death with arrows and cast down headlong from the roof. Within this Temple about ten thousand [more like a still awful three hundred] were beheaded. If you had been there, your feet would have been stained up to the ankles with the blood of the slain. What more shall I tell? Not one of them was allowed to live. They did not spare the women and children.[53]

In late 1099, Manasses, bishop of Reims, sent a letter to Lambert, the bishop of Arras, who had been present at Clermont. "Let it be known to you," he wrote, barely able to contain his excitement, "that a true and joyful rumor has recently come to our ears, and we believe it to have happened not through human power but by divine majesty: Jerusalem is fixed joyfully and happily in heaven." The sons of God had freed the city from paganism and heresy. "We rejoice!"[54] At least Lambert did. Urban did not—he had died two weeks after the walls of Jerusalem were breached, never knowing that what he had started four years earlier had reached its bloody ending.

13 Behind His Head

Rodulfus Glaber had a theory about why there were religious differences between East and West. "When He was hung from the cross the immature peoples of the East were hidden behind His head, but the West was before His eyes, ready to be filled with the light of the faith. So too His almighty right arm, extended for the work of mercy, pointed to the North," while His left sagged toward the South, "which swarmed with barbaric peoples."

It was on account of Christ's blind spots on Golgotha that so much of humanity was still trapped in the "wildness of their errors" in the decades after 1000.[55] Rodulfus would have been astonished—and probably pleased, although with his character, it is hard to tell—that by the end of the century not only had a great fighting pilgrimage in His name journeyed from the West to those eastern lands hidden behind His head, but miraculously these pilgrims had captured Jerusalem for the faith.

The First Crusade, of course, was not called that at the time, as there was no word yet for such holy wars—one would not be coined until the early thirteenth century—or even a name for a fighting pilgrim signed with the cross, although soon enough such a *crucesignatus* was known as a "crusader." What is certain is that this great expedition epitomized the radical blending of early medieval apocalypticism with an ardent reforming millennialism that was first articulated by Rodulfus and other Latin Christian intellectuals seventy or so years earlier. It also embraced and transformed the long tradition of pilgrimage and penitential redemption going back to Columbanus at the end of the sixth century. The First Crusade conveniently marks out how powerfully transitional was the eleventh century, decades in which we move, surprisingly quickly, from the Early to the High Middle Ages.

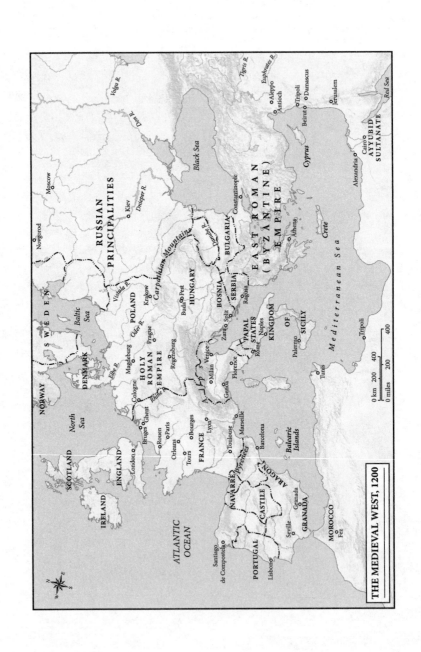

THE MEDIEVAL WEST, 1200

VIII

Uncle, What Troubles You?

1099–1220

1 A Love Story

"The true story!" promised Peter Abelard in his *History of My Calamities* (*Historia calamitatum*), written around 1132. "I now want you to know from the facts, in their proper order, instead of from hearsay."[1]

Fifteen or so years earlier, when Abelard was in his late thirties, "there was in Paris at the time a young girl named Heloise." She was in her mid-twenties, prettier than usual, and the niece (or more probably the daughter) of Fulbert, a canon of Notre Dame cathedral in Paris. "A gift for letters is rare in women," but she was brilliant and "renowned throughout the realm." But then so was he—almost from the moment he had arrived in Paris from Le Pallet (east of Nantes on the Brittany border) "like a true peripatetic philosopher" in 1100. Unlike a knight, such as his father, he preferred the "weapons of dialectic," choosing "conflicts of disputation instead of trophies of war." He battled and defeated various intellectual foes in the cathedral schools of Paris and Laon for more than a decade, all of whom he dismissed as stunning mediocrities. "As my reputation grew, so other men's jealousy was aroused." Nevertheless, "through persecution my fame increased," and just before he first saw Heloise he was appointed to a chair at the Notre Dame school.[2]

"But success always puffs up fools with pride," Abelard bitterly recalled. "I began to think myself the only philosopher in the world, with nothing to fear from anyone, and so I yielded to the lusts of the flesh." Heloise seemed the perfect prize. "I considered all the usual attractions for a lover and decided she was the one to bring to my bed, confident that I should have easy access." Of course, he flattered himself: "I had youth and exceptional good looks as well as my great reputation to recommend me." How could any woman refuse such a man? "All on fire with desire," Abelard insinuated himself as a lodger in Fulbert's house; even more amazingly, the uncle, who was thrilled at having such a renowned scholar living under his roof, begged him to tutor Heloise night and day. "Need I say more?"

Abelard did, quite effusively. "And so with our lessons as a pretext we abandoned ourselves entirely to love." There was more kissing than teaching. "My hands strayed oftener to her bosom than to the pages; love drew our eyes to look on each other more than reading kept them on our texts." He sometimes hit her so as to avoid suspicion, "but these blows were prompted by love" and not the common irritation of a teacher. "In short, our desires left no stage of lovemaking untried, and if love could devise something new, we welcomed it." Abelard was soon bored with school; his days were listless and his lecturing uninspired, "when my nights were sleepless with lovemaking." He composed love songs instead of writing philosophy. Everyone knew what he and Heloise were doing—except, that is, Fulbert. "But what is last to be learned is somehow learned eventually, and common knowledge cannot easily be hidden from one individual."[3]

One day the uncle walked in unawares upon his niece and her teacher. "And so we were caught in the act as the poet [Ovid] says happened to Mars and Venus." Fulbert separated them—"separation drew our hearts still closer while frustration inflamed our passion even more"—but by now Heloise was pregnant. Abelard helped her escape (at night, through a window) to Brittany, where, staying with his sister, she gave birth to a boy named Astralabe.[4]

Fulbert was out of his mind with grief and worry about Heloise. "In the end I took pity on his boundless misery," Abelard wrote, promising that "I would marry the girl that I had wronged." Nevertheless, he wished for the marriage to be a secret, "so as not to damage my reputation." Fulbert agreed; the two men reconciled with a kiss. "But his intention was to make it easier to betray me."[5]

"I set off at once for Brittany and brought back my friend to make her my wife." But Heloise was appalled at Abelard's proposal. "Nature had created me for all humanity," she furiously praised him (and which he assiduously remembered), and "it would be a sorry scandal if I should bind myself to a single woman!" "What honor could she win, she protested, from a marriage which would dishonor me and humiliate us both?" She angrily listed arguments why intellectuals should never marry, ranging from the Apostles, pagan philosophers such as Socrates, ancient Jews, and Augustine of Hippo to the crushing banalities of daily married life. "Who can concentrate on thoughts of scripture or philosophy and be able to endure babies crying, nurses soothing them with lullabies, and all the noisy coming and going of men and women about the house?" Who can really put up with the squalor and nuisance of children anyhow? (Astralabe, not surprisingly, was raised by Abelard's sister.) Perhaps, she mused, only the rich with their mansions and servants should have children. "The great philosophers of the past have despised the world, not so much renouncing it as escaping from it." She said that the name of "lover [amica]" was dearer to her than "wife." She only wanted Abelard's love if it was freely given and not yoked by marriage vows. He stood firm that his proposal was the right thing to do. Heloise, crying and sighing deeply, finally relented, bitterly saying, "We shall both be destroyed. All that is left us is suffering as great as our love has been."[6]

Abelard and Heloise were married in a dawn ceremony in a Paris church in the presence of Fulbert and some friends in 1118. Afterward, they separated so as to hide what they had done, only seeing each other late at night in out-of-the-way places. Fulbert, though, "seeking satisfaction for the dishonor done to him, began to spread the news of the marriage," breaking his promise of secrecy. Heloise cursed her uncle; he replied in kind. Abelard, thinking he was protecting her from such abuse, moved her into the convent where she had been educated as a girl, disguising her as a novice nun. Fulbert, convinced this easily discovered subterfuge was just a callous husband tossing aside a wife, and already seething with barely concealed hatred for "nature's gift to humanity," surprised Abelard as he slept and, with some accomplices, "cut off the parts of my body whereby I had committed the wrong of which they complained." Next morning, "the whole city gathered before my house," horrified, shocked, and amazed. "What road could I take now? How could I show my face in public, to be pointed at by every finger, derided by every tongue, a monstrous spectacle to all I met?"[7]

Abelard's castration was not the last of his calamities, far from it, but—and while this seems like stating the obvious—he viewed it as the singular event shaping the narration of his life. He had written the *History of My Calamities* as if were a letter for an imaginary friend in need of consolation: "In comparison with my misfortunes you will see that your own are nothing, or only slight, and will find them easier to bear."[8] Before Abelard's savage mutilation, everything he wanted as a scholar and as a lover played out with pleasing inevitability; afterward, while achieving much if not more intellectually, there was nothing delightful about the flow of time, only the inevitable and seemingly effortless gathering of one humiliating misfortune after another.

Abelard's new tribulations began when he entered the abbey of Saint-Denis as a monk so as to hide from all the fingers he imagined pointing at him. He hated it there, soon retreating to a small stone shed (or cell) away from all the other monks, who he thought were depraved idiots. He started teaching again, lecturing on "faith by analogy with human reason," even writing a theological treatise, *Theologia scholarium*, on divine unity and trinity for his students, "who were asking for human and logical reasons on the subject . . . something intelligible rather than mere words." It was absurd for anyone to preach what they first did not understand, his students argued; "nothing could be believed unless it was first understood."[9]

As always, Abelard said everyone admired his ideas; as always, he was attacked by his "jealous enemies"—except, unlike before, he was accused of heresy and dragged before a council at Soissons in 1121. The council judged him guilty of teaching that the Trinity was constituted of three Gods (or at least that only God the Father was omnipotent). Abelard's three punishments were burning a copy of his treatise by his own hand, reciting the Athanasian creed as if he were an ignorant child (this upset him more than anything), and imprisonment in the monastery of Saint Médard in Soissons (whose unsympathetic abbot, Goswin, mocked him as "delirious" with self-pity).[10]

Soon, though, Abelard was transferred back to Saint-Denis, and then, after appealing to the abbot, he became a hermit in a lonely grove on the marshy banks of the river Ardusson, four miles southeast of Nogent-sur-Seine. "I built a sort of oratory of reeds and thatch and dedicated it in the name of the Holy Trinity." The other name he gave his holy shack was "Paraclete, that is, Comforter." Into this raw wilderness students still followed him, at first slapping together their own huts and living rough, but very quickly they constructed stone buildings, gardens, and a library for their teacher. Yet his enemies would not leave him alone, especially a "new apostle" (as Abelard sarcastically named him) like Bernard, abbot of Clairvaux, who, despite involving himself in almost every major event during the middle decades of the twelfth century, always found more than enough time to denounce the "world's philosopher."[11]

Abelard was frightened. "I waited like one in terror of being struck by lightning to be brought before a council or synod and charged with heresy." God knows, "I fell into such a state of despair that I thought of quitting the realm of Christendom and going over to the heathen, there to live a quiet Christian life amongst the enemies of Christ."[12]

Instead, Abelard ran away from the Paraclete to be the abbot of a monastery on the Breton coast that was shrouded in sea fog, fatuousness, and monks who soon tried to kill him. He ran away again, this time to Heloise, whom he had largely ignored since his castration, apart from ordering her to become a nun when he became a monk, but now he offered her the Paraclete as a refuge for herself and some other nuns in 1129.[13]

"Not so long ago, my beloved," wrote Heloise in a long and impassioned letter to Abelard four or so years later from the Paraclete, "by chance someone brought me the letter of consolation you had sent to a friend." She had his *History of My Calamities* before her, and while she had hoped it "would picture for me the reality I have lost," instead all it did was remind her, "with gall and wormwood," of why she was now a nun and he a monk, "and the cross of unending suffering which you, my only love, continue to bear." But she carried her own cross too: "You know, beloved, as everyone knows, how much I have lost in you," how her uncle's treachery "robbed me of my very self in robbing me of you!"

So where were her letters of consolation? Abelard destroyed her when he commanded she become a nun. "I changed my clothing along with my mind, in order to prove you the sole possessor of my body and my will alike." God knows, she had never wanted anything except him. She certainly never wanted to be called his wife, just lover, "or, if you will permit me, whore or concubine." They had done nothing wrong. "It is not the doing of the thing but the intention of the doer which makes the crime," she reminded him of what they both believed. So why was he so silent? When he had wanted her young body, she sarcastically recalled, your letters were "thick and fast." And he had sung love songs of his beautiful Heloise, charming everyone who heard them, "so that every street and house resounded with my name." She softened at the memory. "Farewell, my only love."[14]

Abelard's *History of My Calamities* exemplifies the shift from the penitential culture that had so shaped the world between the seventh and eleventh centuries to the confessional one that defined the next three hundred years in the West. Autobiographies as narrative histories of the self, as reflections upon an individual life moving through time in a linear progression, multiplied from the twelfth century onward. They were spiritual and literary innovations. Although autobiographical writing had existed previously, such as Bede's few words about himself at the end of his *Ecclesiastical History*, there had been nothing like Abelard's memoir since Augustine's *Confessions* seven hundred years earlier. Of course, the latter deeply influenced the former, as it did every other autobiography written after 1100. Augustine, though, never assumed that in writing so intimately about himself he was in any sense imitating Christ, whereas Abelard absolutely thought that in writing about himself he was ultimately emulating Him—his life was as consoling as His.

The *History of My Calamities* was written as if it were part of an epistolary dialogue, even if the imaginary interlocutor never replied. Really, though, Abelard was in dialogue with himself. A few years earlier he had begun but never finished the *Soliloquium*, which was a chat between "Peter" and "Abelard"—"the same self spoke to the same."[15] Around this time he also scripted the *Collationes*, a playlet between a philosopher, a Jew, and a Christian. He viewed all knowledge, whether of the self or not, as only truly grasped through the Platonic dialogue.

Plato was important for many intellectuals in the twelfth century, especially his *Timaeus* with its Demiurge who, as a Creator God and Divine Craftsman, imposed order upon the universe and endowed the world with a soul. Bernard of Clairvaux, despising all pagan philosophers, accused Abelard of turning the Holy Spirit into Plato's world soul. He also slandered him with the sarcastic compliment of being a "new Aristotle." Abelard was as influenced by Aristotle as by Plato, particularly on logic and dialectic. Ironically, what he knew of Aristotle was derived from the third- and sixth-century Latin translations by the Neoplatonists Porphyry and Boethius. After reading them, he compiled *Sic et Non* ("Yes and No") with hundreds of seemingly contradictory quotations, ranging from the Bible to anyone he had ever read, as "by inquiry we perceive the truth."[16] As a dialectician, however, what mattered was asking the right questions (*questiones*), as this was the only way "to establish the truth or falsehood of something."[17] Or of yourself. An autobiography or a confession was fundamentally about asking or being asked the right questions.

Abelard in his mid-fifties tried and failed more than once to ask Heloise the right question about love. Soon after she had finished reading the *History of My Calamities*, he sent her a letter wondering why she still loved him, when she should only love Christ. "In Him, I beseech you, not in me, should be all your devotion, all your compassion, all your remorse."[18] It is often difficult to know what role Abelard (or "Abelard") was playing in his epistolary dialogues with Heloise. In this instance, he knew before he even put pen to parchment that she saw no incompatibility between loving him and loving Him. Indeed, neither did he, if what he wrote in his autobiography was true about the passion of his former love for her. To have experienced temporal love with the ardor that they both claimed to have felt, and which she said she still did, was to have lived so intensely as humans that they recreated the eternal love that Christ had for humanity on account of His having once lived as a man. (Bernard of Clairvaux actually believed the same thing about love and Christ.)

Individuals had loved before them, but this notion that loving was in and of itself an imitation of Him was new. Does this mean that the flamboyant amorousness of Abelard and Heloise was just extravagant mimesis, two souls playacting in the hope of grasping the holy? Yes, of course it was—and, yes, that made it no less authentic. This is especially so in Heloise's letters to Abelard from the Paraclete, where she defined herself only by the enduring love she had for him and how she suffered at his lack of reciprocation. In humbling herself before her lover so unflinchingly she was explicitly copying Christ. Love was a perpetual form of penance, at once wonderful, humiliating, sacrificial, and redemptive. Even when it was lost or never given, His love was always there as compensation and salvation. In the end, all love stories were now the story of Christ.

2 Fin'Amor

"Love descends from a wicked line," sang the troubadour Marcabru after 1130. "It has slain many without a sword." None so famously as Abelard, whom he mocked:

> God made no grammarian so smart
> > *Listen!*
> That love can't make him a dolt
> If it catches him in its trap.

More generally:

> Love spreads like a spark
> That mixes with soot,
> Burning the wood and the straw.
> > *Listen!*
> Whoever gets caught by the fire
> Doesn't know where to flee.
> He who strikes a deal with love . . .
> Ties his tail to the devil;
> If another rod beats him, what does he care?
> > *Listen!*
> Nothing to do but scratch your hide
> Until you've skinned yourself alive!

More confessionally:

> Marcabru, son of Marcabruna,
> Was engendered under a moon
> That showed love falling, a seed from the husk.
> > *Listen!*
> He never truly loved a woman.
> Nor has a woman loved him.[19]

Marcabru was one of the most sublime, satiric, sharp-witted, and suavely ribald of the *trobadors* singing in Old Provençal or Occitan, the vernacular of a vast region between the Garonne and Rhône Rivers known as Provincia (Province or Provence) in the twelfth and early thirteenth centuries and which, give or take a mile here and there, is now modern southern France. He was also one of the first troubadours, with only Guilhem IX, duke of Aquitaine and count of Poitou, singing a decade or two before him. Many more would follow, including a few women troubadours sometimes known as *trobairitz*.

Apart from the gorgeously austere melancholy of English poetry before the eleventh century, next to nothing has survived of songs that were sung in languages other than Latin in the early medieval West. One of the reasons, despite Charlemagne's supposed intention of preserving old poems celebrating Frankish deeds, was that, outside of Britain (and the

Arabian peninsula), vernacular songs were not considered artistic or spiritual achievements. A poem as glorious as "Dream of the Rood," while more than likely known to Boniface or Alcuin, was never promoted as a model for the literati of the Carolingian Renaissance. This all changed with the troubadours.

Significantly, the songs (*cansos*) of Marcabru, like all troubadours with one or two exceptions in the late twelfth and early thirteenth centuries, were extremely short when compared with, say, *Beowulf*, easily sung in less than five minutes, and more often less than three. Unlike earlier songs, they were not extemporized by a singer from twenty or more similar poems. They were to be sung exactly the same way each and every time. There was meant to be no difference between what was sung and what was originally composed on wax tablet and parchment (or possibly paper). These songs were also to be sung from beginning to end, which, in part, was why they were so much shorter. And they were deeply self-referential, even if the poet's persona was more often an overtly stylized version of him- or herself. Troubadours understood themselves and their songs as moving narratively forward through time in a continuous uninterrupted melody.

"The other day I found a shepherdess," sang Marcabru in another song. "Beside a hedge. Witty and full of happiness." A knowing and humorous dialogue ensues as "Marcabru" tries to seduce the pretty *toza* (young girl) with his verse. "Sir," she says, dismissing him,

> a man who's up to foolish play
> Takes oaths and says that he will pay;
> It's that kind of homage you throw my way . . .
> But not for the paltry entrance fee
> Will I trade my virginity
> For the name of whore! . . .
> Sir, yes—but according to their nature:
> A fool cuts a foolish caper,
> A courtly man has a courtly venture,
> And a peasant, a toss with a *toza*:
> All around there's lack of order
> For man has lost all measure,
> So say the ancient people.

"Marcabru" suddenly realizes the shepherdess is Jewish, teasingly calling her *trefana*, "deceptive," an Occitan word derived from Hebrew. "That one man gapes at an image," the girl ends the song, lampooning a Christian looking at the crucified Christ in comparison to a stoical Jew, who just "hopes for manna."[20]

In this song Marcabru invented the genre of the medieval *pastorela* or *pastourelle*. Such songs involved conceited and swaggering nobles attempting and failing in the seduction of shrewd and virtuous peasant girls in bucolic surroundings. They were at once entertainingly risqué and deeply moralizing. They were lessons in decorum and sexual probity for a nobility willing to be amused and admonished. Marcabru, who more likely than not was a petty Gascon noble not much higher than a peasant, cleverly played upon the self-admiring delusion of men even grander than himself, easily tripped up in their wantonness by supposedly simple shepherdesses and, quite brilliantly in his first *pastorela*, a *toza* who turns out to be Jewish and so was even more of a rebuke to Christian lords who merely gaped at pictures or sculptures of Christ without modeling themselves on Him.

Of course, there were no shepherdesses (tending sheep was the job of a *tos*, a boy), let alone Jewish ones, but such recognizable artifice did not take the sting out of the song for any listener, especially as Marcabru's *toza* was so vividly imagined as a distinct and nuanced individual. Equally, the barely submerged reality of rampant noble violence, sexual or otherwise, captured an obsessive theme in all troubadour songs. This was why being a "courtly man" constrained by "courtliness" or *cortezia* was so vital.

"A man who knows well how to observe moderation can pride himself on possessing *cortezia*," Marcabru sang of courtliness in 1148. Any man "who wants to hear everything that is said or aims to possess all that he sees must need moderate this 'all'—or he will never be very courtly." He advised:

> Moderation lies in noble speaking
> and *cortezia* comes from loving;
> and a man who does not want to be misjudged
> should guard against all base, deceitful, and villainous acts,
> although it might not make him any happier, he'll be wise.[21]

Courtliness was not a stylish pastime, a mannerism without meaning. It was the very thing moderating the violence so inherent to what it meant to be a noble and knight since the middle of the eleventh century, especially between the Garonne and the Rhône. If a man was not courtly, then basically he had no identity. His individuality was achieved only through prudent speech, righteous behavior, and perfect love.

Cortezia entrapped women too. They were meant to be loved, even seduced, but never so far that they might be called sluts. Most famously, the troubadours sang of the *fin'amor*, the ideal love between men and women undergirding all courtliness, which they simultaneously satirized and exalted—for instance, it was equally the "cunt game," as Marcabru so charmingly put it, and spiritually transcendent.[22] When a man loved a woman he experienced ecstasy and horror, delighting in the feminine as much as degrading it, joyously celebrating what he must aggressively demean because, if he was not careful, then every lady was just like a Jewish shepherdess, ready to deceive and humiliate him. Such notions of love and courtliness as sung by the troubadours were soon imitated by other poets throughout Latin Christendom.

3 A True Vassal

Those notions were not imitated by the anonymous copyist who wrote down what is now known as *The Song of Roland* in either England or Normandy after 1130. This poem is a *chanson de geste*, a song of heroic deeds sung in Old French (specifically Anglo-Norman) and, unlike any of Marcabru's *cansos*, around four thousand lines long.

There were a number of such epic *chansons* either copied from older songs or newly composed in the twelfth century, but *Roland* is the oldest. Unlike the songs of the troubadours, these northern French songs were creations of a more overtly oral poetic culture, and so closer in performance and reception to a poem like *Beowulf*. Perhaps *Roland* was already being sung in some form in the late eleventh century, fifty or more years before it was written down. Either way, the twelfth-century version was clearly shaped by the aftermath of the capture of Jerusalem in 1099, even if the First Crusade is never mentioned. Then again, the actual event that seemingly inspired the song—Basque raiders ambushing Charlemagne's rear guard at Roncesvalles in 778—was transfigured into a momentous last stand by a vainglorious Count Roland during a great war between an elderly, slightly out-of-it Emperor Charles and the sly but sympathetic pagan (which is to say Muslim) king of Saragossa, Marsile.

Overall, though, *Roland* was a song for the new knightly order who wanted to hear about themselves as loyal vassals, valiant fighters, and men whose characters, even when proud and downright foolhardy, were nevertheless inherently glorious by the very fact that they were Christian fighters.

> Count Roland is bleeding from the mouth;
> In his skull the temple is burst.
> He blows his oliphant with pain and anguish;
> Charles heard it and so did the Franks.
> The king said: "The sound of the horn is long drawn."
> Duke Naimes replies: "A true vassal makes the effort . . .
> You can hear clearly the distress cry which Roland sends."[23]

The irony here is that when Roland finally blows his horn alerting Charles that he needs help against Marsile's host, his companion Oliver, after repeatedly begging for him to blow the oliphant, has just angrily denounced him for sounding the alarm when it was too late. "For a true vassal's act, in its wisdom, avoids folly . . . Franks are dead because of your recklessness."[24] But Charles knows nothing of this and assumes Roland has been a true vassal all along, which, the song suggests, is all that really matters in the end. And yet Oliver's idea of what defines a true vassal is never fully undermined either. "Today our loyal comradeship is at its end," he poignantly tells his unwise companion before dying.[25] Of course, Roland never doubts himself at any point, a galloping celebration that pride and heedless daring (and a sword named Durendal) make a true vassal too.

Roland lacks the humor, condensed complexity, and sharp awareness of human character of a troubadour *canso*. It rarely sings of love, except of that between comrades like Roland and Oliver or of that between a lord and a vassal. It was a rollicking, boozy song about days gone by that was at once archaic in style and anachronistic in content, never pretending to be formally innovative or too clever for its audience. It was sung in snatches with the assumption that some if not all of the story (although not necessarily the *chanson* itself) was known. It was translated into Old Norse, German, Spanish, and English, as well as Latin in the so-called *Pseudo-Turpin Chronicle* (which was itself translated into Old French). *Roland* in its own bluff way evoked a tangled, often contradictory, and even occasionally nuanced (or, rather, more nuance was heard and appreciated by later generations of listeners) understanding of what constituted vassalage, loyalty, and noble male identity as a Christian warrior.

4 I Am Neither Perfectly a Jew nor a Christian

A curious twentysomething named Judah ben David ha-Levi wandered into Münster cathedral around December 1127. "I saw, among the artful varieties of carvings and paintings, a particularly monstrous idol." More precisely, "I discerned one and the same man abased and exalted, despised and lifted up, ignominious and glorious. Below, he hung wretchedly on a cross. Above, by means of the deception of a painting, he was enthroned, handsome enough to seem to have been deified. I admit, I was stupefied." Twenty or so years later, Judah, having converted to Christianity and now known as Herman, recalled having seen this sculpture of the crucified Christ beneath a painting of Him as God in the autobiographical *Short Work on His Conversion (Opusculum de conversione sua)*.[26]

When thirteen-year-old Judah was living in Cologne he had a vision that middle-aged Herman looked back upon as a premonition of his future. He dreamed that Emperor Henry V—who would finally end the Investiture Controversy with the Concordat of Worms two years later in 1122—presented him with a strapping white horse, an exquisite golden belt, a silk purse with seven coins, and the confiscated lands of a dead prince. "Know," says the emperor, "that my dukes and princes take serious umbrage at the benefice that I have conferred on you." Judah should ignore them, for "I shall add to these many more benefices by far." Judah graciously thanks him and, after buckling on his splendid belt and riding his white horse to a lustrous palace, he and the emperor share a salad of herbs and roots as "the dearest of friends."

Judah woke up, "still in the joy of this vision." The boy knew his dream was a prophecy, but of what? A wise old relative named Isaac told him it signified success in life with a pretty wife (she was the white horse). Judah was less than satisfied with this interpretation.[27]

Seven years later, and a few months before Judah saw the monstrous idol of Christ, he was in Mainz on business, specifically loaning money to an insolvent Egbert, bishop of Münster. "By the custom of the Jews, as I knew very well, I ought to have exacted a pawn twice the amount of the loan," but he did not, thinking the bishop's good reputation was pledge enough. This angered and worried his family and friends, who thought it uncommonly foolish and incipiently weak, so he was required to remain in Egbert's household until the debt was repaid. "Assuredly, all Jews are serfs to commerce," Judah wrote, reflecting upon this fact more as a social constraint imposed on him and his ancestors by Christians, especially princes, than as a symptom of any inherent nature. An old family friend stayed and watched over him, as his recent behavior suggested to his parents a sympathy for Christianity that might, if not checked, easily slip into apostasy. (Herman later acknowledged how insightful were his parents.) Judah had to wait five months for his money, and by the end, while seemingly the same on the surface, he had almost but not quite renounced his old faith within "the treasure chest of my heart."[28]

Judah in these months attended the cathedral school in Münster, studying Latin, borrowing books from other students, and reading (as best he could) the Gospels. He openly argued the merits of Judaism over Christianity. Indeed, when Rupert, the learned abbot of Deutz, once visited the school-room, "I invited him to lock horns in debate." The abbot generously agreed.

"You Christians bear a great prejudice toward the Jews," began Judah. "You spit on them with curses and loathing as though they were dead dogs, although you read that of old, God chose them for Himself, as His own people." God even wrote with His own hand the law for them on stone. "But you"—and here he looked around at his audience—"blinded by envy of the divine benefits toward us, consider loathsome above all mortals the very ones whom, as you have read, you know to be more honorable and beloved to God than all other humans." The Jews have never abandoned His law, even when mocked and derided for their faithfulness. "You are not doers of the law, as you say, but plainly judges of it. Laughable as it is to say, you correct it just as you want," adding whatever "stupid, asinine, and depraved fictions anyone pleases." Above all else, Christians worship a man who hangs on wood! "I have seen it with my own eyes!"

Rupert answered that Judah's arguments, while clever, were not daunting. Obviously, Christians were not idolators. "Images"—and here he repeated Gregory the Great's famous justification—"were devised to benefit the simple and uneducated so that those who could not learn the Passion of their Redeemer by reading in books could see the very price of their redemption through the visible appearance of the cross." He offered no comment on the persecution of Jews. As recollected by Herman, Rupert's response was somewhat pat compared to what young Judah argued; nevertheless, it was impressive enough in hindsight.[29]

When Judah returned to Cologne in late spring 1128 (or 1129), the old family friend watching over him for the last twenty weeks reported that the youth "could now be thought, not a Jew, but a Christian." (This informer conveniently died fifteen days later of a fever and went on to suffer the "eternal torments of hell.") His parents were deeply anguished by what they heard. Judah denied such slander, but he looked back as Herman and admitted his continued piety was a sham, just him going through the motions, "practicing my ancestral religion out of habit." He trusted God would soon show him the truth. (After all, He swifly punished his informer.) As a way of enticing a conclusive response from Him, he decided to fast in the manner of both Jews and Christians, which, after some dietary mathematics and menu compromises, was bread and water eaten sparingly in the evening. After three days he was a sleepless, red-eyed wreck groaning and weeping in his room. God ignored him, but his parents did not, convinced that their son's malnourished eccentricity was proof that he was slipping into Christianity. It distressed Judah that his parents were upset, so he ended his (barely begun) fasting regime without any word from heaven.[30]

Judah, still unsure about whether to stay a Jew or become a Christian, then hemmed and hawed about marrying a girl to whom he was betrothed. The girl's father was furious, convinced that his prospective son-in-law was procrastinating because "I had been so depraved by the pestilential tales of the Christians." Judah was dragged before a "council of Jews" to explain himself. He stupidly replied that he wanted to go to France to study, not with Christians but with Jews, and, fumbling for something else to say, added that he lacked the funds to get married just yet. "They all opposed me with one accord, shouting with raucous voices that this was a sign of apostasy." He was given an ultimatum: marry the girl or leave the synagogue. "In case anyone perhaps considers this a light matter amongst them, he should know that, amongst Jews, to be outside the synagogue is the same as, amongst Christians, to be cast out of the Church by excommunication."

Judah, "smitten rigid with immense fear," married the girl. "How," some Christian friends asked him at the wedding feast, "did you fall so quickly and easily from your good intention to such a depth of perdition?" Judah regretted inviting them.

As a husband, Judah discovered to his surprise that he enjoyed sex and that he liked his wife . . . for all of three months, until his doubts returned. "What hope of salvation can there be for me," he said to himself, "since I am neither perfectly a Jew nor a Christian?" He remembered that in Cologne there were two holy sisters, Bertha and Glismut, living enclosed in a cell next to a monastery and "whose odor of good repute" perfumed the whole city. "I humbly begged them to see fit to direct their prayers to God for my enlightenment." They did, and Christ finally answered him. "It was indeed an appropriate about-face for women to raise up by their prayers a man who had fallen because of a woman." What converted him was not reading books or debating with great scholars "but the devout prayer of simple women." Judah, overjoyed, readied himself for abandoning his now pregnant wife (whom he never names in his memoir).[31]

First, though, Judah wished to kidnap his seven-year-old half brother (same father, different mother) living in Mainz, so that they could be baptized together. He was not very discreet about either his conversion, going and sitting in a church every day, or his planned abduction, as everyone seemed to know what he intended to do. Indeed, a group of Cologne Jews dispatched some letters written in Hebrew to their brethren in Mainz viciously denouncing him. Judah intercepted the courier (an oddly compliant and incurious imperial chaplain) on a road outside Worms, easily purloined the letters, read their contents in horror, then burned them.

Euphoric, Judah galloped all the way to the nearby city and, convinced he could do anything, calmly walked into a synagogue and started lecturing on prophecy and the superiority of Christianity. "Can you imagine how great a stupor of amazement then seized all the Jews who were present?" As his exhilaration receded and the insulting calls of "half-Christian" grew louder, he feared he himself might be abducted and harmed. And so he said it was all a ruse: "Since I frequently dispute with Christians, I have learned, for the greatest part, their subtle arguments against the Jews." He was only playacting, offering a lesson in what a Christian might say. "They gratefully accepted this."

Judah soon reached Mainz and easily kidnapped his half brother. Yet, as he tried to get away, he just kept running around in circles, lost in streets that all looked the same, unable to find the city gate—"an astonishing thing!" Some Christians laughed at him when he hoisted his weary brother on his shoulders. Judah ignored them, as even His followers could be fools; still, they reminded him to make the sign of the cross, which instantly revealed the gate and his waiting horse.[32]

Three weeks later, Judah was again seemingly ridiculed by Christians during his baptism in Cologne cathedral. (The unnamed half brother was dropped off in a monastery and, despite what was involved in grabbing him, largely forgotten.) "I stepped into the waves of the life-giving font." He stood up, "water running down the hairs of my head," shivering from the bitter cold of the font, blinking furiously in the candlelight, everything silent as his ears were waterlogged. Around him he vaguely saw but could not hear clerics yelling something, which, after wiping the water from his face and hair, he understood as "More times!" Apparently, the one thing that his Christian patrons had forgotten to tell him was that "baptism involved threefold immersion in the name of the Holy Trinity."

Judah reluctantly agreed to be dipped again. "I did what had to be done for my salvation." He had had enough and wanted to get out of the font. "I was almost frozen rigid by its extreme cold." But the clergy kept shouting for one more time, so under the icy water he went. "I suspected they were making a laughingstock of me." He convinced himself they were not (or, at least, not all of them). Either way, he was "invisibly cured of the leprosy of his soul." Crucially, "I, who was Judah, now took the name Herman."[33]

Herman after his baptism became a Premonstratensian canon at Cappenberg (formerly a castle overlooking the Ruhr valley) and, after perfecting his Latin within five years, a priest. In the final paragraphs of his *Short Work on His Conversion* he returned to the dream he had had at thirteen and, as far as he was concerned, finally discerned its meaning. The emperor was God, the white horse was baptism, the golden belt checked the "torrential desires of the flesh," the seven coins were the seven gifts of the Holy Spirit (all easily lost, hence the purse), the jealous princes were his former Jewish friends and family, and the salad of herbs and roots was the Gospels.

Yet whatever comfort Herman derived from this interpretation, it was all a bit too obvious, even rather trite, which he basically acknowledged. It flattened a conversion he was at pains to stress was not a "swift or unanticipated change," as was often the case with other "infidels, Jews, and pagans" (by which he meant not only contemporary heretics, Jews, and Muslims but also ancient pagans). Rather, "my conversion was gained in the face of powerful waves of temptations, which ever mounted at the beginning . . . of long suffering amid continual ebb and flow, and finally, with the greatest toil." Dreams might foretell how a life will be lived, but a person actually needed to live and remember that life as it continually unfolded in the waking world to truly understand it—without memories of being Judah, there was no Herman moving forward.[34]

The memory of the savage violence of crusaders against Jewish men, women, and children in Mainz, Cologne, and Worms half a century earlier pervaded Herman's autobiography without him ever needing to explicitly say it. Christians rather than their religion frequently come off as mean-spirited, suspicious, and potentially lethal. He evoked the overwhelming inescapability of Christianity for Jews and so the inevitable possibility of apostasy. For example, Jewish mothers were repeatedly warned not to engage Christian wet nurses, as their babies "may be lured to *minut* [Christianity]."[35] A poignancy, if not sadness, was mingled with the joy Herman felt about his conversion.

Some modern scholars argue that Herman's *Short Work on His Conversion* was a twelfth-century fiction composed by the Premonstratensian canons at Cappenberg for their own edification, an allegorical autobiography of an imaginary Jewish convert whose imagined confession was a text that, if they studied it closely enough, revealed how the canons should understand themselves before and after entering into a religious life.[36] A shrewd if slightly convoluted argument, it is ultimately unconvincing, as it presupposes from the outset that a Christian who had formerly been Jewish could and would not have written such a book. Unquestionably, Herman's memoir was written for other Christians and not for Jews. Equally, while it was certainly written for the Cappenberg canons, it assumed an audience much wider than them, especially women like the holy recluses Bertha and Glismut.

Even if Herman embellished his life with more adventure and excitement than it actually had, such as debating with Rupert of Deutz or superciliously confronting a crowded synagogue in Worms, this hardly demonstrates that the whole autobiography was fictional, as such enhancement was expected in the recollection of a life (as witnessed in Abelard's recollection of his calamitous life). In the end, the young Jewish Judah was not some figment of a Christian imagination—that is, apart from his older self.

5 Just Like Cancer

"For I do not recall having heard anything new or extraordinary in all their assertions," Bernard of Clairvaux preached about heretics, portraying them as foxes and their doctrines as spreading throughout the "Lord's vineyard" in 1144, "but only trite commonplaces long vented amongst the heretics of old."

This was Bernard's sixty-fifth sermon inspired by the Song of Songs and his third on the verse "Seize for us the little foxes that are destroying the vineyards." He was replying to an anxious letter from Eberwin, prior of the Premonstratensian abbey in Steinfield, about two new unnamed groups of heretics living and preaching in Cologne. "Recent damage to the vine, in truth, shows that the fox has been at work," and although the cunning animal hid its tracks, so that it was almost impossible to find it, "the Church from the beginning has always had her foxes," and all of them were eventually discovered and taken. He told Eberwin not to worry; the Cologne heretics would, as had all skulks before them, soon be trapped and forgotten.

A year later Bernard was less nonchalant about a wolf named Henri. "I have learned and realize fully how great are the evils which the heretic Henri has committed and is still committing daily against the churches of God," Bernard informed Anfoz-Jordas, count of Toulouse, in the summer of 1145. This "ravening wolf in sheep's clothing" was traveling and preaching throughout the Toulousain. "That man is not from God who thus acts and speaks in contradiction of God! O woe! He is nonetheless listened to by many and has a following who believe him!" Bernard admitted that Henri had the "appearance of piety," for he was once a monk and a scholar, but now he was just wandering the earth, selling at retail what he had once studied of the Gospel, "preaching in order to eat."

Most shamefully, the wolf denied that baptism was necessary for children. Then why, Bernard asked, "did the mighty Lord become a little child, not to mention that He was scourged, was spat upon, was crucified, and finally died"? Although sickly, "I am undertaking a hurried journey to those places where that singular wild beast is ravaging, since there is no one to resist him or offer protection from him." Heretical preachers always mixed their poisonous words with honey, Bernard warned, so that what sounded sweet and mellifluous actually putrefied their listeners from within, "imperceptibly just like cancer."[37]

Bernard was a Cistercian—that is, he was a member of a monastic order whose first foundation was at Cîteaux in Burgundy around 1098. Like the monks at Cluny almost two hundred years earlier, these monks were reformers. Except the Cistercians thought that the Cluniacs had lost their way, becoming corrupt and misguided, and that it was up to them to finally enact Benedict's great *Rule* in its true historical purity and simplicity. They built monasteries away from towns and cities, clearing the land with their own hands. (Bernard, whose stomach was always upset and whose body was slight, helped out as a young monk by praying more than usual rather than by chopping wood.) They shunned (although not as much as they some-times claimed) all decoration in their churches. Their habits or monastic dress were white or undyed wool, as opposed to Cluniac black, so they came to be known as the "white monks." Remarkably, by the middle of the twelfth century, more than three hundred monasteries were affiliated with Cîteaux, one of which was Clairvaux, where Bernard was abbot.

Most importantly, though, the Cistercians believed that the *Rule* was quite literally the Gospel of Christ. By following it they imitated Him. "In My life you may know your way," Bernard once imagined himself as Him in a Pentecostal sermon, "so that just as I held the unswerving paths of pov-erty and obedience, humility and patience, love and mercy, so you too will follow these footsteps."[38] The *Rule* was now a *Life* of Christ. (Cistercians opportunely forgot that Gregory the Great said it was a partial memoir of Benedict.) But then almost every text, artwork, sermon, song, act of fealty, memory of love, and moment of love was possibly a model for living like Christ, if you thought deeply enough about what you were reading, writing, hearing, seeing, or just doing. "This is why He was born an infant and advanced to manhood through all the stages of life, so that He might be lacking in no age," Bernard preached in his sixty-sixth sermon inspired by the Song of Songs, against vulpine heretics denying not only the hu-manness of Christ but also that He had lived in a seamless forward temporal flow of unique thoughts and actions.[39]

The trouble is that most if not all individuals accused of heresy largely agreed with this view of Him too. Abelard certainly did, and most likely so did the bestial Henri. But that was not good enough for Bernard, who, as a Cistercian following His footsteps in the *Rule*, knew better than anyone else who truly was like Christ and who was a misguided heretic. As he said of Abelard, "He looks like a monk on the outside, but inside he is a heretic."[40]

After 1140 accusations of heresy were more widespread and increasingly more virulent throughout Latin Christendom—and leading the way with a vengeance were the Cistercians.

6 The Curious Case of Catharism

Catharism is the most famous heresy of the Middle Ages—or so we have been told in one history of the medieval West after another since the nineteenth century. The Cathars, so says conventional wisdom, thought the universe was torn asunder with an active wicked devil manipulating the earth and a passive good God serenely dwelling in heaven. Consequently, they looked upon matter and spirit, including their own bodies and souls, as implacably divided.

The Cathars acquired this theology either wholly or in part from shadowy Bogomil heretics journeying from the Balkans to southern France and northern Italy, perhaps during the eleventh century, definitely by 1170. Or if these beliefs were not derived from these clandestine Byzantine missionaries, then they and their dualism were the last gasp of a Manichaeism that had survived underground since the fourth century in the West (or perhaps since the early eighth century when Pope Gregory II worried about Manichaean refugees from North Africa swarming along the Rhine).

Either way, a far-reaching "Cathar Church" existed from the North Sea to the Mediterranean with an elaborate episcopate and a priestly elite of ascetic "perfects" by the end of the twelfth century. The heartland of Catharism lay between the Garonne and Rhône, particularly in the Toulousain, Carcassès, Biterrois, and Albigeois, although many Cathars lived in the northern Italian towns and villages of the Trevisan March. This traditional narrative reaches its tragic crescendo in the bloody violence of the Albigensian crusade in the early thirteenth century and, thereafter, the relentless persecutions by inquisitors until the heresy all but disappeared in the early fourteenth century. It is a saga of spiritual resistance and religious intolerance, a warning and a lesson from the past, always worth telling.

Except none of it is true, as Catharism never existed. Or rather, Catharism exists only as a revolutionary historical and religious paradigm invented in the late nineteenth century by scholars (at first mostly German, then French, Italian, American, and British) as they restyled history and religion as modern sciences. Catharism is a fin-de-siècle artifact with no likeness to medieval reality, designed (even down to its name) as much as the historical and religious patterns delineating it were discovered, ingeniously fabricated as a discrete world religion with Eurasian roots. It functioned as an Oriental agent provocateur in Western history, instigating almost all heresy in the Middle Ages, inciting the Church to reform and repression, and ultimately suggesting (especially to Protestant scholars) a more progressive, comparative, and scientific vision of what constituted a religion, past and present.

Catharism exemplified historical and religious modernism. As striking in its own way as a lithograph by Henri de Toulouse-Lautrec or a novella by Joseph Conrad, it was fiction then and it is fiction now.

Some have argued that even if nineteenth-century scholars invented Catharism, what they thought they discerned really did exist, no matter what it was called. This is not the case. Catharism does not exist outside of its own historiography. Its history is only the history of what historians have written about it since the nineteenth century. No "living Cathars" underpin the historiography of Catharism. By contrast, underpinning the historiography of medieval Judaism, no matter what historians argue, is the fact that there were "living Jews" in the Middle Ages. Just as there were no "living Cathars," there were no "living heretics" either, at least not before around 1220.

What nineteenth-century historians were trying to explain when they constructed Catharism was why, especially after 1140, so many Latin Christian intellectuals (monks, priests, nuns, bishops, popes, university teachers, and students) started accusing each other of heresy—and, with growing apocalyptic fury, accusing so many ordinary Christians throughout the West of the same. These thousands of accusations were so overwhelming for modern scholars before the First World War (especially when collected together in the "scientific" laundry lists of which they were inordinately fond) that they thought there had to be some connection between all of them—and that was where Catharism came in, fortuitously explaining the very phenomenon by which it was itself supposedly explained.

Ironically, what connected all these accusations was not some fictional heretical "counter-Church" but the tumultuous reality of the ongoing "reformation" (*reformatio*) of the actual twelfth-century Church itself. So many of the ideas and practices that Latin Christian intellectuals were articulating and codifying, especially the imitation of Christ or a sense of the self as linear and confessional, while widely and enthusiastically adopted by every order of society (including many Jews), were understood and enacted in surprisingly varied ways depending on local circumstances. Much of the twelfth-century reformation was about eliminating this regional variation, whether in monasteries, schoolrooms, cities, or villages. As Bernard of Clairvaux never tired of pointing out, it was all too easy to unthinkingly step over the line from being a Catholic to being a heretic.

Therefore, accusations of heresy functioned as reprimands, criticisms, admonitions, acts of spiritual guidance, rhetorical threats, and, for the first half of the twelfth century, an affirmation of the historical continuity of the Church. The heresies of the past (as revealed in the condemnations by ancient ecclesiastical councils and, especially, in the voluminous writings of Augustine of Hippo against the Manichaeans) provided templates into which the heretical ideas of the present could be fitted and, as a consequence, explained. It was a historical and analytical method that necessitated finding coherence in the beliefs of heretics, so that not only were all heresies continuous over the centuries but, as all heretical thoughts were perceived as similar from Toulouse to Cologne, from London to Milan, deep and secretive connections must exist between all individuals or groups accused of heresy.

Heretics were the enduring and persistent witnesses to the immortal and infinite Church. Accusations of heresy were crucial to the making of medieval Latin Christianity.

7 Some Strange Region of the Universe

"The recollection of the past is the promise of the future," wrote Suger, abbot of Saint-Denis, in his *On What Was Done Under His Administration* (*De rebus in administratione sua gestis*) around 1150.[41] He was celebrating and justifying what he had accomplished a decade earlier when he remodeled his abbey church and in the process established a new architectural style now known as Gothic. (This designation was initially an early eighteenth-century insult against late medieval art before becoming within a generation a term of romantic longing for an imaginary Middle Ages as exemplified by Horace Walpole in his Gothic Revival house at Strawberry Hill and his *The Castle of Otranto: A Gothic Story* from 1765.) Suger was aware that what he had achieved was artistically novel, but, as with his reform of the Saint-Denis monks, he viewed his aesthetic reformation as remembering and enhancing a spiritual and material past that had been forgotten.

Suger's description of radiating arches that seemingly allowed the masonry to float, colored glass that bathed him in a heavenly glow, and a sensation of infinite lightness as he walked through his revamped church (especially the choir) were all early manifestations of what would be recognizable characteristics of Gothic from the thirteenth century onward. He covered chalices, plates, massive candlesticks, relics of saints, altar panels, and the back of a great golden crucifix—on whose front was the "adorable image of our Lord the Savior, suffering, as it were, even now in remembrance of His Passion"—with a "wealth of precious gems, hyacinths, rubies, sapphires, emeralds and topazes, and also an array of different large pearls." The loveliness of many-colored gems, he observed, "has called me away from external cares, and worthy meditation has induced me to reflect, transferring which is material to that which is immaterial, on the diversity of the sacred virtues." As Suger stared at his dazzling gems, "I see myself dwelling, as it were, in some strange region of the universe which neither exists entirely in the slime of the earth nor entirely in the purity of heaven."[42]

Suger's feeling of a delightful holy strangeness when looking at his treasures was achieved with even more breathtaking effect by later patrons and architects of Gothic form throughout Latin Christendom. Such radiant transcendence is often seen now as starkly contrasting with the supposedly less numinous experience associated with churches constructed from the late eleventh century until the late twelfth in a style classified as Romanesque (an early nineteenth-century term initially used as way of differentiating architectural forms that were viewed as being more similar to those of ancient Rome than those of the medieval Gothic style). Unquestionably, such churches possess a gloomy dolefulness, like walking through fog, as their use of rounded arches (similar to those seen in a Roman aqueduct or the Colosseum) necessitated great heavy walls with only a handful of small windows. The pointed arches characteristic of the Gothic style are stronger and allow for soaring, less hefty walls. Romanesque churches often look like mighty fortresses towering over the landscape, such as those built by the Normans in northern England. They were usually constructed on pilgrimage routes and often, but not always, outside of towns.

Indeed, as sanctuaries housing relics themselves, they were frequently the end of a journey for many pilgrims. What this meant was that they were buildings into which as soon as one entered them the eye rushed and darted through the twilight to the end of the nave where a saint (or bit of a saint) was buried or on display. Once inside, men, women, and children felt a tingling kinetic quality compelling their movement along the colonnaded interiors in a procession around the saintly relics. Despite the buildings' lack of windows, they were lit with candles and often quite gaudy with wall paintings; yet as one moved through the regions of light and dark until reaching the blazing candelabra around a tomb or relic, there was a feeling no less sublime than Suger's many-hued transport. Romanesque churches were recollections in stone of the older penitential culture, but as all of them displayed images of the crucified Christ, they very much looked to the future as well.[43]

"O vanity of vanities, but above all insanity!" Bernard of Clairvaux said, dismissing all church decoration as wasteful when the poor needed feeding.[44] Suger, aware of such criticism (and having once suffered from Bernard specifically attacking him), explicitly stated that the whole point of his gems, painted windows, gilded surfaces, and strange sensations was, "first and foremost, for the administration of the holy Eucharist." Surely, the blood of Christ deserved no less! "The detractors also object that a saintly mind, a pure heart, a faithful intention ought to suffice for this sacred function." He countered that his beautiful things were signs of his loyal homage to Christ, "with all inner purity and with all outward splendor."

Fundamentally, argued Suger, his magnificent treasures demonstrated that what Christ and humanity shared was, like a glittering alloy, inseparably fused "into one admirable individuality."[45]

8 Pray Like *This*

"Whenever I went to the holy sites in Jerusalem," reminisced the noble Syrian mercenary, diplomat, and *littérateur* Usama ibn Munqidh in 1183, "I would go in and make my way to the al-Aqsa mosque," or rather, as it had been for six decades, the headquarters of the Knights of the Temple of Solomon, or Templars. There was a chapel attached to this building (heavily renovated, as the old al-Aqsa mosque had been in disrepair), and this was where he had liked to pray. The Templars, "who are my friends," would shoo everyone out of the chapel so that, momentarily, it became a little mosque.

Once, while Usama prayed toward Mecca in the chapel, a "Frank" ("Ifranj" were what Latin Christians were collectively called by Muslims in the eastern Mediterranean since the ninth century) rushed inside and forcefully turned Usama's face to the east, saying, "Pray like *this!*" A group of Templars seized the intruder and bustled him out. "I then returned to my prayers." But before he even drew a breath, the same wild-eyed Frank grabbed him again, crying, "Pray like *this!*" The Templars quickly dragged the zealot outside, this time for good. "This man is a stranger," they apologized, "just arrived from Frankish lands sometime in the past few days. He had never seen anyone who did not pray towards the east." Usama smiled, replying sardonically, "I think I've prayed enough."[46]

This memory was one of the many stories about the crusades and Latin Christian settlers in the Levant that Usama scattered throughout *The Book of Contemplation* (*Kitab al-I'tibar*), written at the age of eighty-eight, while he was a courtier of the sultan Salah al-Din Yusuf, or Saladin, in Damascus. Although it was an anthology of mostly autobiographical anecdotes, it was not a memoir; rather, it was a collection of marvelous and mundane tales that revealed upon reflection the omnipotence of God. All too often Usama's descriptions of Franks and his interactions with them, while seemingly vivid and detailed, were knowing caricatures offered with a wink. "Indeed, when a person relates matters concerning the Franks, he *should* give glory to God and sanctify Him! For he will see them to be mere beasts possessing no other virtues but courage and fighting."[47]

There is a shaggy-dog quality to *The Book of Contemplation* in which an urbane, charming companion rambles slightly in the telling of his tales. This is emphasized by Usama's unusually informal Arabic, which, while it shocked some readers expecting the contorted mannerism of similar books, involved experimentation and skill in achieving such an easygoing style. (For example, he has someone dismissively say "Pfft!," which, onomatopoeically, evokes the verb *darata*, meaning both "to scoff" and "to fart.") What was also unusual were the autobiographical stories, which, even if highly stylized, Muslim authors rarely if ever composed. It would be too much to suggest that Usama was influenced by the confessional autobiographies being written by Latin Christian intellectuals; nevertheless, his exception to a general rule does highlight how different was the sense of the self developing in the West.[48]

Although the profusion of autobiographical and confessional writing was a distinctive feature of Latin Christendom, especially from the twelfth century onward, other, more mundane documents, such as court records and marriage contracts, were not—and yet there is still a widespread notion that the medieval Islamicate Middle East either never produced such documents or indifferently preserved what little was supposedly written. This is usually held as demonstrating a lack of archival skill or bureaucratic sensibility in comparison to the West. What gives the lie to such assumptions are the thousands of documents surviving from the attic of the medieval Ben Ezra synagogue in Fustat, Egypt, and known as the Cairo Geniza. The Jewish custom of *geniza* was to deposit worn-out texts in Hebrew script into "dignified limbo." The Ben Ezra chamber was emptied between 1888 and 1897 and its contents (Hebrew and Arabic texts) dispersed into mostly European and American libraries. Of course, why very few archives from the medieval Islamicate Middle East have survived is still an unanswered question. Nevertheless, there were more than enough differences developing between Latin Christendom and its neighbors without adding quotidian documentation and archives into the equation.[49]

The events described in Usama's anecdote about his interrupted prayers happened between 1140 and 1150, so roughly twenty to thirty years after the founding of the Templars and half a century since Latin Christian colonists (mostly martial pilgrims who stayed after 1099) established the kingdom of Jerusalem, the county of Tripoli, the principality of Antioch, and, to the northeast of this principality, the county of Edessa.

The origins of the Templars are hazy. William, archbishop of Tyre, in his *Chronicle* of the kingdom of Jerusalem, written around the same time as Usama was compiling his stories, recorded that in 1118 a few "noble men of the equestrian order"—in other words, knights—"wished to live perpetually in chastity and obedience and without their own property, following the custom of the regular canons." The most prominent of these warriors were Hugh de Payns and Godfrey de Saint-Omer, who, along with perhaps only nine other knights, were instructed by the patriarch of Jerusalem that, for the remission of their sins, "they should protect the roads and routes, especially for the safety of the pilgrims against the ambushes of brigands and raiders." William, for all his virtues as a historian—the last chapters of his *Chronicle* possess a gripping and affecting poignancy, as he saw only darkness gathering around the kingdom—was often wrong in his chronology. It seems that the Templars were officially founded between January and September 1120, even if, as was likely, Hugh and Godfrey were already protecting pilgrims in an improvised way. In 1129 the pope commissioned some French bishops and abbots, most especially Bernard of Clairvaux, with devising a monastic *Rule* for the Templars at a council at Troyes.[50]

Bernard, soon after the council, famously wrote a sermon of encouragement for the Templars entitled *In Praise of the New Knighthood* (*De laude novae militiae*). "A new sort of knighthood, I say, unknown to the world, is fighting indefatigably a double fight against flesh and blood as well as against the immaterial forces of evil." As for the old secular sort of knight, they fight for reasons that are quite frivolous. For those knights, "the only things that cause conflicts and start wars are feelings of irrational anger, the pursuit of vainglory, or the desire for some piece of land. It is certainly not safe to kill or be killed in such causes!" However, "the knights of Christ fight the battles of their Lord in all peace of mind, in no way fearing to sin in killing the enemy or die at his hands." Christ willingly accepts the death of His enemies and willingly consoles His vassals. "The knight of Christ, I say, kills in safety and dies in greater safety." Indeed, all secular knights should look upon him as "a model to imitate." Unlike them, he would never flounce about in flamboyant clothes that trip him up, sheathe his horse in silks, grow his hair long like a girl, or titivate his sword and spurs in silver, gold, and jewels. He knew the difference between military insignia and a woman's baubles!

Instead, a knight of Christ was never well-groomed, and rarely clean; his skin was burned by sun and sizzling breastplates; his only clothes were white vestments over mail; his tonsured hair was always short, scruffy, and neglected. His only thoughts were of battle and victory, not pomp and show. He instilled fear, not adulation. "In short, in some wonderful, unique way," enthused Bernard about the new knighthood, "I am almost in doubt as to whether they ought to be called knights or monks. Unless, of course, I were to call them by both names, which would be more exact, as they are known to have the gentleness of a monk and the bravery of a knight."[51]

The Templars were the first of numerous military orders that would be established throughout Latin Christendom from the Iberian peninsula to the Baltic. The most famous and longest-lasting were the Knights of the Hospital of Saint John, or the Hospitallers, who, while initially only providing shelter and medical care for pilgrims at a small house in Jerusalem as early as 1080, and for which the papacy recognized them as a religious order in 1113, were inspired by the Templars to be both healers and warriors after 1130. The Templars, unlike other monastic orders such as the Cluniacs and Cistercians, initially accepted men who were not nobles as knights of Christ. Nevertheless, as Bernard hoped, they quickly became a model and inspiration for aristocratic warriors.

In 1131 Alfonso I "the Battler," king of Navarre and Aragon, dictated a will in which he conceded his whole kingdom upon his death to the Holy Sepulcher in Jerusalem, the Hospitallers, and the Templars. He was childless and had greatly expanded his realm by capturing Zaragoza, Tudela, Tarazona, Daroca, and Calatayud between 1118 and 1120. He wanted the martial holiness of the new knighthood fighting Saracens in the Holy Land extended to Spain. He died four years later, and while his will was ignored by rival family factions, the military orders were already firmly established in his lands. By the early fourteenth century the Templars possessed thousands of properties (from serfs to villages to town houses to the ovens of Paris) throughout the West.[52]

Templars were perpetually martial pilgrims, forever signed with the cross—an eight-pointed red cross was sewn on their white robes by 1140. They epitomized the ideal of the knight as a warrior pilgrim fighting for Christ.

9 Pseudo-Prophets

Such an ideal was sorely tested in what is now known as the Second Crusade, in 1147 and 1148. Imad al-Din Zangi, a Turcoman amir and atabeg of Mosul, captured Edessa in December 1144. (Usama ibn Munqidh loyally campaigned with Zangi in Iraq, Armenia, and Syria between 1131 and 1138—then abandoned him.) Almost exactly a year later Pope Eugenius III issued the papal bull *Quantum praedecessores*, which, after recalling the words (as he understood them) of Urban II at Clermont, the victory of 1099, and his sorrow at the loss of Edessa, promised the protection of property, suspension of debts, and the remission of sins for all who signed themselves with the cross. As a former Cistercian, he asked—who else!—Bernard of Clairvaux to preach the crusade during Easter at Vézelay. It was here that Louis VII, king of France, received his pilgrim cross. (Suger advised the king against going on crusade.)

Bernard continued preaching throughout northern France, the Rhineland, and Saxony. He vehemently denounced any threats of violence against Jews; sadly, there were a few attacks spurred on by another Cistercian. He welcomed the German king Conrad III as a crusader. Somewhat surprisingly, he judged that Saxon nobles fighting and converting the pagan Wends across the Elbe River had fulfilled their pilgrim vow to go to the Holy Land. Similarly, in October 1147 when Flemish, Norman, and English crusaders successfully besieged Almoravid Lisbon at the request of the Portuguese king, Afonso Henriques, they assumed this Iberian fight was part of (although not equivalent to) their greater pilgrimage to Jerusalem. This notion that different crusading arenas were nevertheless all still part of a single phenomenon is an element of what was so extraordinary and revolutionary about the Second Crusade.

The other extraordinary thing is how Louis and Conrad bungled and failed so completely in Syria, to the point that many Latin Christians wondered if God had forsaken them.[53] An anonymous Würzburg chronicler scathingly observed that the failure of the crusade in the Holy Land was God punishing the "Western Church . . . since its sins required this punishment." He implicitly blamed the pope and Bernard: "Pseudo-prophets were in power, sons of Belial, heads of the Anti-Christ, who by stupid words misled the Christians and by empty preaching induced all sorts of men to go against the Saracens for the freeing of Jerusalem." No wonder, the chronicler concluded, the pilgrimage was such a fiasco.[54]

The anonymous Würzburg chronicler was explicitly linking his Western "pseudo-prophets" with the great Eastern "pseudo-prophet" Muhammad. In 1143 the English Cluniac, Robert of Ketton, had translated the Qur'an into Latin as Lex Mahumet pseudoprophete (The Religion of Muhammad the Pseudo-Prophet). A year earlier the powerful abbot of Cluny, Peter the Venerable, had commissioned him and other monks in northern Spain with translating Arabic works; he hoped that with a better understanding of "Arabic civilization" it would be easier to defeat and convert the followers of Muhammad. "All Latin civilization [*Latinitas*]," said Robert, needed his translation so as to overcome its ignorance and resulting failure "in driving away the cause of its enemies." Robert viewed *Latinitas* as the equivalent of *Christianitas*, as Latin was the language of learning, scripture, and God.

As the Qur'an epitomized Arabic and so Muslim civilization for him, Robert wished his translation to get across just how important and holy was the book for Saracens—even if he thought Islam was a "death-dealing religion" (*lex letifera*) and the enemy of Christianity. His translation was therefore grandiose, solemn, and elegant; but, in rendering it in his high Latin style, he heavily paraphrased the text. Paradoxically, the elegance of the *Lex Mahumet pseudoprophete* was at once greatly admired (and widely read for centuries) and damning proof as to why the Qur'an was such a seductive false scripture by a pseudo-prophet.[55]

Such seductiveness and falseness were why the Würzburg chronicler (who was obviously a Cluniac) thought a Cistercian like the abbot of Clairvaux was a pseudo-prophet, harming the cause of *Latinitas* by preaching so eloquently in favor of a crusade that was lost before it even began. Bernard was widely criticized (just less apocalyptically) by other clerics who had always resented his self-righteousness. (Abelard would have enjoyed such opprobrium, but he had died in 1142.) Although somewhat chastened, he brushed aside such sniping; nevertheless, he agreed with the view that the fiasco of the Second Crusade was a sign of sinfulness within Christendom. Clearly the little foxes were more widespread in the Lord's vineyard than he had realized, so he (and other Cistercians, especially after his death in 1153) preached even more passionately against heresy. As to whether Bernard grasped how similar the attacks on his crusade preaching were to what he had accused and continued accusing heretics of doing, he never mentioned it.

Usama ibn Munqidh referred to the Second Crusade only once, in a brief but telling anecdote in *The Book of Contemplation*: "Amongst men there are those that go to battle just as the Companions of the Prophet (may God be pleased with them) used to go to battle: to obtain entrance to Paradise, and not to pursue some selfish desire or to gain a reputation." He offered two examples from when Conrad III (*malik al-Alman*, "king of the Germans") marched on Damascus in July 1148: the jurist al-Findalawi and the ascetic sheikh Abd al-Rahman al-Halhuli. "Aren't these the Romans?" the former said to the latter as they lined up in formation outside the city gate. "Yes, indeed." "Then how long are we going to stand here?" "Go, in the name of God!" exhorted Abd al-Rahman; "may He be exalted!" The two of them raced out to meet the crusaders and died together as martyrs.

Al-Findalawi and Abd al-Rahman al-Halhuli were engaging in *jihad* by imitating the "striving" of Muhammad and his Companions. They offered themselves up as gifts to their fellow Muslims—most gloriously, as neither was a trained soldier, which was a virtue and not a flaw. They even offered themselves up to the infidel Romans as holy exemplars of what it truly meant to be embraced by God's mercy. The invasion of Syria and Palestine in the late eleventh century by the first crusaders may have necessitated *jihad* for some Muslim warriors, but for many if not most it did not. Usama, despite his many years fighting the Franks, never engaged in *jihad*.[56]

Saladin, on the other hand, did. In 1186 he ruled a sultanate from Damascus which, while fractious—with one too many seditious sons and uncles—majestically stretched from the Euphrates to the Nile and from northern Mesopotamia to southern Yemen. Achieving such glory from his beginnings as a Kurdish lackey in the retinue of Zangi's son, Nur al-Din Mahmud, had involved talent, ruthlessness, and almost continuous warfare against other Muslims for more than two decades. He had returned Egypt to the Sunni and Abbasid fold when the last Shi'ite Fatimid caliph died in 1171, but he had also treacherously overthrown the Zangids in becoming master of Muslim Syria. He may have been granted rights to all past and future conquests by the Abbasid caliph and married Nur al-Din's widow as a show of dynastic continuity, but the restlessness of his soldiers and insubordination of his kinsmen (which his own example demonstrated was worth risking) necessitated finally waging his much-talked-about but long-neglected *jihad* against the Franks.[57]

In summer 1187, after adroitly maneuvering the Latin Christian army (Templars, Hospitallers, and the troops of the kingdom of Jerusalem) into an indefensible position near Lake Tiberias (modern Sea of Galilee), Saladin crushed the crusaders at the Horns of Hattin. Three months later he captured Jerusalem.[58]

Just over a year later, on Thursday, November 17, 1188, Usama died in Damascus aged ninety-three; yet he viewed his last years as more like prison than anything prodigious. "Enfeebled by years, I have been rendered incapable of performing service for sultans . . . the goods of such a very old man cannot be sold . . . I have now confined myself to my own house, therefore, taking obscurity as my by-word."[59]

10 Puddles in the Street

One spring Sunday in 1173 an urban *mediocris* (neither noble nor peasant) and merchant named Valdes, "who had amassed a great fortune through the iniquity of usury," was walking through the streets of Lyon when he came across a crowd listening to a *joglar*. The minstrel was singing a song about Alexis of Rome, who, after renouncing his wealth, wandered and begged in Syria during the reign of Constantine the Great, until finally dying the "happy death" of a nameless pauper in his father's Italian mansion.

Valdes, deeply moved by what he heard, invited the minstrel to his house so that he could hear the song from start to finish. The next morning, overwhelmed with doubt about his soul's welfare, he rushed to the cathedral school in search of answers, "and when he had been instructed in the many ways of coming to God, he asked the master which was the most sure and perfect way of all." The master replied with the words of Christ: "If you would be perfect, go and sell what you have, give all to the poor, and come follow me and you will have treasure in heaven"—the very same words that had inspired Antony of Egypt almost a millennium earlier to sell all his goods and become the first monk. In the late twelfth century such words prompted Valdes to model his life upon that of the Apostles—the *vita apostolica*—and so, at one remove, the life of Christ.

Valdes offered his wife "the choice of keeping for herself all his possessions in either movable goods or in property, that is, lands and water, woods, meadows, houses, rents, vineyards, mills, and ovens." Sad and confused, she chose the property. From the remaining movable goods, he returned what he had gained unjustly, bestowed a large sum upon his two little daughters, "whom he placed in the order of Fontevrault without his wife's knowledge," and distributed what was left amongst the poor. "No man can serve two masters, God and Mammon," Valdes cried out on the Feast of the Assumption of the Blessed Virgin as he cheerfully "scattered money to the poor in the streets."[60] A crowd gathered around him, thinking he was mad. "My friends and fellow townsmen," Valdes addressed them. "Indeed, I am not, as you think, insane, but I have taken vengeance on my enemies who held me in bondage to them, so that I was always more anxious about money than about God and served the creature more than the Creator." He told them that he gave away his wealth for their salvation, "so that you may learn to fix your hope in God and to trust in riches."

Three years later, Valdes had acquired a following of individuals who gave all they possessed "to the poor and willingly devoted themselves to poverty." Little by little, his followers began preaching, publicly and privately, "against their own sins and the sins of others." Valdes himself, after learning parts of the Gospel by heart, sang songs and preached sermons in the streets and broadways of Lyon and other towns in the Lyonnais.

In March 1179, during the Third Lateran Council, summoned by Pope Alexander III, the English cleric Walter Map "saw simple and illiterate men called Waldenses, after their leader, Valdes, who was a citizen of Lyon on the Rhône." These grubby men, these puddles in the street, presented the pope "with a book written in French which contained a text and a gloss of the Psalms and many of the books of both Testaments." They sincerely requested that the pope give them formal permission to preach, "although they were nothing more than dabblers." These Waldenses "go about two by two, barefoot, clad in woollen garments, owning nothing, holding all things common like the Apostles, naked, following a naked Christ." Walter, who fancied himself as a wit, mostly mocked the Waldensians, except for one serious observation amidst his laughter: "If we admit them, we shall be driven out."[61]

An anonymous and sympathetic chronicler from Lyon, however, had Alexander embracing Valdes at the council, "approving his vow of poverty but forbidding preaching by either himself or his followers unless welcomed by the local priests."[62] In 1184 this partial approval was removed when Pope Lucius III decreed at the Council of Verona that any persons, especially "the Poor Men of Lyon," who preached without the permission of popes or bishops were condemned to perpetual anathema.[63] Valdes and his followers ignored such decrees and condemnations. Thirty years later the Waldenses were being persecuted and killed as heretics.

Valdes and his followers highlight the growth and importance of towns and cities and the individuals who lived in them during the twelfth century. Around 1050, 90 percent of all men, women, and children lived in the countryside in the West. It had been that way for the previous six hundred years and remained roughly the same (with the proportion of rural dwellers never dropping lower than 80 percent) for the next five hundred. Nevertheless, for the first time since the sixth century cities and towns were growing in population and infrastructure. At the beginning of the thirteenth century the largest cities were Paris and Milan, with over 150,000 inhabitants each (adding another 50,000 by 1300); Genoa, Venice, and Florence, with perhaps 70,000 each (adding another 30,000 by 1300); London, with less than 60,000 (adding another 20,000 by 1300); and Lyon, with 25,000 (adding another 10,000 by 1300). Rome, which in the tenth century was easily the biggest city in the West with a population of 20,000–30,000, was only just over 40,000 by 1200 (and would add perhaps another 10,000 a century later).[64]

These towns and cities were not cut off from the countryside around them, far from it. Often, as in the Italian peninsula or in what is now southern France, rural nobles frequently lived in town houses or towers. A distinct urban culture, though, began forming most clearly after 1130, when the middling order, the *mediocres*, merchants and tradesmen (often living in the *burgum* part of a town, hence "bourgeois" or "burgher"), started demanding and winning new economic and political rights from their nominal secular and ecclesiastical overlords—economic and political rights inseparable from the new kind of urban holiness asserted by Valdes.

11 Below God but Above Man

It was an exhilarating sunrise for a young German cleric as he stood excitedly in a great crowd before the church of Saint John Lateran (the ancient basilica of Constantine and church of the Savior) in Rome on Wednesday, November 11, 1215. The surrounding houses and towers were draped in purple cloth, and lanterns were "suspended on ropes throughout the streets and alleys." He watched as Pope Innocent III, 71 cardinals, 412 archbishops and bishops, and 802 abbots ("who, unlike the bishops, wore no miters") paraded into the church for a dawn mass. "When the mass had been said" and these ecclesiastical grandees were seated, "many thousands, even ten times a hundred thousand clerics and people," surged with hurrahs and hosannas into the church.

The German, whooshed along with the crush, eventually gained a foothold toward the front, even if the constant swell of the crowd pushed him this way and that. The pope, standing on a raised stage surrounded by his cardinals, began singing the hymn "Veni Creator Spiritus." He was soon accompanied by everyone in the church. In the lull after the song, he preached, "Our actions, we beg you, Lord . . ."—and that was all the German clearly heard; "because no one was able to calm the tumult of the people, I could unfortunately only understand very little of his sermon." As far as he could tell, it was about the sacrifice of Christ and the recovery of the Holy Land. "Then the patriarch of Jerusalem gave a sermon to the same effect," although he too was barely audible. The pope and patriarch preached until around the ninth hour of the day (so around three in the afternoon), undeterred by the constant hoots, cries, and chatter in the raucous church. The German, despite hearing next to nothing, having sore feet, and nursing bruises from a sea of sharp elbows, was immensely proud of himself for having attended (and survived) the first day of the great Fourth Lateran Council.[65]

Nine days later, the final session of the council in the Lateran church was even rowdier. Innocent submitted sixty-eight canons (or constitutions) and two dogmatic decrees for approval. They were read aloud, one after the other, until well past the ninth hour of the day. These elaborate canons—often small legal, historical, social, and moral essays in themselves—were the rules and principles by which the Church was to govern itself and, in turn, oversee all persons, whether Christian or not, living within Christendom. They were the monumental statutory outcome of almost a century of ecclesiastical intellectuals codifying, centralizing, and unifying the laws and institutions of the Church. Whereas the early medieval world was a hodgepodge of "Christendoms" with often very different and varying laws and customs, what had been happening since at least Gregory VII, but which advanced exponentially in the twelfth century, was the notion that there was only one Christendom under the pope, similar everywhere in every way, and that Christian men, women, and children should be recognizably similar in what they thought and did.

Around 1140 the monk Gratian famously had compiled his *Concordance of Discordant Canons*, or *Decretum*, which, while partially inspired by the magisterial uniformity and ambition of Justinian's sixth-century *Code* and *Digest*, was equally motivated by collecting and then erasing all the contradictions of ecclesiastical law that had accumulated over half a millennium in the West. The legal and historical constancy relentlessly articulated in the canons of the Fourth Lateran Council depended upon the achievement of the *Decretum*.[66]

As the laws of the Church were now written down and applied in exactly the same way in each and every place, rather than memorized and extemporized depending on local circumstances, they could be systematically taught and studied with the same rigor as the Bible, Plato, or Augustine. Abelard may not have studied the law, but the skills of logic and dialectic that he championed were applied to it. Indeed, all of the general study, *studia generalia*, that schools across Latin Christendom started teaching was useful in training the lawyers and bureaucrats that the Church now required. These were the seven liberal arts: the *trivium* (grammar, rhetoric, and dialectic) and the more advanced *quadrivium* (music, arithmetic, geometry, and astronomy). These schools would soon become the great medieval universities (from *universitas*, meaning a corporation or guild of masters and students).

The first was the school of law at Bologna, chartered by Emperor Frederick I "Barbarossa" in 1158. By the end of the twelfth century the masters and students at Notre Dame in Paris, where Abelard had taught, had moved to the Left Bank of the Seine, separating themselves from the cathedral as a university, which the French king, Philip II Augustus, formally recognized in 1200. Such recognition by secular rulers corresponded to their own developing chanceries and bureaucracies staffed by university men, especially lawyers. The growth and clarification of canon law for popes, bishops, and abbots was replicated in secular law by kings, princes, and emperors.

Innocent III studied as a young man (named Lotario dei Conti di Segni) in both Paris and Bologna and saw theology and law as intertwined. The canons of the Fourth Lateran Council were unprecedented and revolutionary in their legal and spiritual scope. Yet so much of what was legislated took more than a century to eventually affect the lives of ordinary Christians. For some individuals, such as those accused of heresy in the lands of the count of Toulouse, the effects were all too immediate. What is certain, though, was that unlike earlier councils, the consequences of this council were immense and long-lasting for the West. An example is the first canon, which stated that by ingesting the Eucharist—"His body and blood are truly contained in the sacrament of the altar under the forms of bread and wine"—"we receive from God what He received from us." The divinity of Christ was literally absorbed by the individual as a consequence of His humanity. Or the eighteenth canon, prohibiting clerics from carrying out any punishment involving blood or death and, by extension, participating in ordeals of water (boiling or cold) and hot irons. Or the sixty-eighth, requiring that Jews and Saracens dress differently from Christians. Or the twenty-first, which mandated that every Christian man over fourteen and every Christian woman over twelve confess all their sins at least once a year to a priest and then try to do whatever penance was imposed upon them. Confession was what mattered, more so than whatever atonement followed. Also, as one clearly went with the other, the same canon required that the Eucharist was to be received by all Christians at least once a year, preferably at Easter.[67]

Innocent died in Perugia on Wednesday, July 16, 1216, less than a year after the Fourth Lateran Council. He was only fifty-five and had been pope for eighteen years. "This bride of mine, the Roman Church," he preached on the first anniversary of his consecration, "did not come empty handed. She brought me a dowry precious beyond price: a plenitude of spiritual goods and a broad sweep of temporal power."[68] His vision of the infinite authority of the Apostolic See was unparalleled. Innocent imagined himself as existing somewhere between God and humanity, "below God but above man, less than God but greater than man, who judges all things but who no one judges."[69]

Jacques de Vitry, traveling as the new bishop of Acre, arrived in Perugia soon after Innocent died. When he saw the naked papal corpse, he reflected, as its stench choked him, "Brief and empty is the deceptive glory of this world."[70]

12 The Question

On a snowy Good Friday, sitting next to a fire in the cave of the hermit Trevrizent, the youthful knight Parzival nervously confesses that he is searching for the Grail. "So much may I say of the Grail," sighs the hermit. "I know it and have seen it in truth." He tells what he knows.

The Grail is a most pure stone that fell from heaven in the company of angels neither loyal to Lucifer nor God. It presently resides in the marvelous castle of Munsalvæsche, where rough and pugnacious Templars guard it. The Grail summons girls and boys from many lands as companions by fleetingly inscribing their names on its surface. As these children grow up sinless, happiness awaits them in heaven. All who look upon the stone retain or return to their moment of most perfect beauty. Nor can they die in the week that follows, so it is possible to live for centuries without a hair turning gray. Every Good Friday (coincidentally today, muses Trevrizent), the power of the stone is renewed by a translucent white dove flying down from heaven and depositing a small white wafer on it. "Sir, this is the nature of the Grail."[71]

Trevrizent's eyes start welling as he recounts the great sadness that now surrounds the Grail. First, though, he realizes that Parzival is his nephew. What a coincidence! This adds even more pathos to the tragic story of his brother, Anfortas, who is the king and steward of the Grail. "Amor" was once the battle cry of the king, and while such a call is "not entirely compatible with humility," he was a glamorous knight of Love.

Unfortunately, the stone demands by its inscriptions whom the Grail's steward can love, and Anfortas loved whomever he wanted. One day, as the king was romping about outside Munsalvæsche, "seeking joy with Love's guidance," a poisoned spear pierced his genitals during a joust with a heathen, "so that he never regained his health, your gentle uncle." Anfortas writhed in constant agony, his wound forever oozing, his body reeking of decay. No doctor, herb, or monicirus (unicorn) could cure him. "We fell in genuflection before the Grail." Words appeared on the stone describing a young knight destined to visit Munsalvæsche who would heal Anfortas when he asked the appropriate question. "Have you understood this?" continued the Grail. "If he does not ask on the first night, then his question's power will disappear. If his question is put at the right time, then he shall possess the kingdom, and the duress will be at an end."

Trevrizent had become a hermit after reading these messages. Parzival sat silently listening to his host, holding back a secret. "Afterwards a knight came riding to the Grail," just as the stone foretold. "He might as well have left it alone!" spat Trevrizent. The young fool simply could not ask this question: "Lord, what is the nature of your distress?"[72]

"That man who rode up to Munsalvæsche and who saw the true anguish, and who spoke no question," Parzival shamefully admits, "I am he, child of misfortune that I am!" Four or so years earlier, he had come across Anfortas on a boat in a lake enjoying the sweet breeze over the water (it dispersed the sour stink of his wound), and "that sad fisherman, far from merry," had invited him to stay the night in the Grail castle. "Nephew, what are you saying now!" exclaims Trevrizent. Parzival had had his chance to ask the question but did not. Fortunately, after a few more adventures, in which he meets King Arthur and even sits at the Round Table, he again comes upon the magical Munsalvæsche and, in the presence of the Grail, says to Anfortas, "Uncle, what troubles you?"[73]

This question is the climactic moment in the long (twenty-five thousand lines) poem *Parzival* by Wolfram von Eschenbach, composed in Middle High German around 1215. Before and after this moment swirls a luxuriously convoluted and often deliberately misleading story of chivalric quests and exploits by Parzival within a Christendom that encompasses the whole world. The poem simultaneously celebrates and denigrates love and women, Christianity and knighthood, Sir Gawain and King Arthur, beauty and grace, youthfulness and the gaining of wisdom, and the loutishness and divine purpose of its hero. Nothing is clearly this rather than that. Even the Grail, that most perfect of all things, has a nasty edge to it. "Wolfram," in the poem, never gives a straight answer about himself or his song. At one point he says, "I don't know a single letter of the alphabet." And if anyone wants to think he does, "I would rather sit naked without a towel, as if sitting in the bath—provided I didn't forget the bundle of twigs"—a bawdy boast underscoring that Wolfram outside the poem (as well as the "Wolfram" within) was not a clerical *literatus* only writing in Latin but rather a knight of the vernacular, which, as far as he was concerned, was equal to if not more transcendent than *Latinitas*.

Soon afterward, though, "Wolfram" goes off on the first of two tangents about how he knows the story of Parzival only from Kyot the Provençal, who by chance discovered it in an Arabic (or possibly Hebrew) manuscript in Toledo written by a heathen (on his father's side) named Flegetanis. "What he told of it *en franzoys* [in French], if I am not slow of wit, I shall pass on in German." So "Wolfram" is only translating a troubadour's translation (into French, not Occitan) of an obscure Arabic song about Parzival and the Grail.[74]

Wolfram admitted more truthfully at the very end of *Parzival*, albeit with dismissive wit, that his song was indebted to another great poet, Chrétien de Troyes, whose *Perceval or The Story of the Grail* was written in Old French around 1180. This earlier poem was the first time that anyone had heard of the Grail, the sickly "Fisher King," and the question (or, in this case, two linked questions). Chrétien, singing in the court of the countess of Champagne, created the stories of King Arthur and his knights in the poems *Yvain*, *Lancelot*, and *Perceval*. He also restyled the *fin'amor* of the troubadours into a northern French version called now (but not then) "courtly love."

Chrétien's and Wolfram's poems also stressed primogeniture, the rights of inheritance of the firstborn son, and the importance of familial lineage and ancestry. This was radically different from the southern world of the troubadours, where, with the notable exception of the counts of Toulouse, partible inheritance between all brothers and sisters was the convention. And yet in northern France, Germany, and England, this practice was still the most common as well. These poets of Arthurian chivalry were promoting in their poems new forms of inheritance and family structures that their grander patrons desperately wanted as the social norm.

What is so extraordinary is that Wolfram took the story of the Grail (which for Chrétien was a shallow dish or vessel) from a poem he back-handedly acknowledged was superb and transformed it into an even more dazzling artistic and spiritual achievement.[75]

Wolfram's *Parzival* was a poem that mocked and exalted the importance of autobiographical self-awareness and confession. He may have only been a poor wandering knight from Franconia or Bavaria, singing himself into the patronage of various Bavarian and Thuringian barons and margraves, but the sophistication of his understanding of what defined human existence was the equivalent of any philosopher's, theologian's, monk's, or pope's. "Wolfram" constantly steps out in front of his poem, confessing what he thinks of his characters and their adventures, addressing what he knows his audience is thinking, admiring the cleverness of his own metaphors (almost always mixed).

Parzival is therefore as much a narrative about its own composition as it is about the adventures of a knight named Parzival. There is a constant dialogue between the poet and his poem. The creator and what he has created are constantly questioning each other—just like the Creator and His creations. This is why the question that has to be asked of Anfortas is so vital. When Parzival finally poses the question, it is, in and of itself, all that is necessary for the cleansing of his uncle and himself. After the question he becomes the Grail's steward, that is, he becomes like Christ. Abelard would have applauded the elevation of asking the right question at the right moment as a holy and heroic quest. (He might also have been sympathetic to Anfortas' wound.) Parzival's question was the very definition of the confessional culture that had been developing for more than a century.

13 Renaissance, Revolution, Reformation

Modern scholars have labeled the twelfth century as a "renaissance," a "revolution," and a "reformation" in the West. It was all of these things and more. Certainly, the early penitential culture, at least for most intellectuals, shifted into an overwhelmingly confessional and autobiographical one. This was inspired by the broader phenomenon of the imitation of Christ affecting how many ordinary Christians now understood themselves, holiness, and their existence in the world.

There is an irony that the individuality and sense of self that marked the last centuries of the Middle Ages were premised upon copying the life of an individual man—admittedly, the godhead as a human in the past. Further, this confessional distinctiveness in the lives of men, women, and children throughout Latin Christendom was equally determined by the efforts of popes and kings, preachers and poets, at achieving doctrinal, behavioral, and even physical similarity between all Christians from the North Sea to the Mediterranean. But in so sharply and aggressively defining what it was to be a Christian, there was now an awful clarity in defining the opposite, such as Jews and Muslims, and most especially heresy and heretics.

As much as a confessional society was forming in the twelfth century, so too was (as it has been famously called) "a persecuting society." The two were inextricably linked, reaching their grand and grotesque fruition in the next century.

IX

Love Moves the Sun and All
the Other Stars

1209–1321

1 Divine Vengeance Raged Marvelously

Five thousand horsemen, ten thousand foot soldiers, and around twelve thousand other ragtag men, women, and children surrounded the city of Béziers (between Toulouse and Marseille) on Wednesday, July 22, 1209. All of them, from great lords to beggar boys, from noble ladies to washerwomen, wore a cross of cloth on their clothing as "the sign of the living God." They were crusaders in a holy war against the "Provençal heretics" in the lands of the count of Toulouse proclaimed sixteen months earlier by Innocent III. Arnau Amalric, abbot of Cîteaux and papal legate leading this crusade, threatened the people of Béziers with wholesale carnage unless they handed over the heretics he accused them of protecting. The towns-people denied the accusation. Around the middle of the next day, a foolhardy French crusader was killed and mutilated on the bridge leading into the city. This enraged the thousands of boys (runaways, servants, thieves, young monks) in the crusader camp. These ribauds, as these children and adoles-cents were known, started chanting, "Let's attack! Let's attack!" Suddenly, jumping defensive ditches, clambering over one another, they swarmed the walls of Béziers. Scratching and clawing the ramparts, loosening stones and rocks, hundreds of boys irrupted inside the city through cracks and crevices.

Terrified by such fury, the people of Béziers abandoned their defenses. Mobs of delirious boys surged through the streets, clubbing to death everyone they met. As they slaughtered, they searched for treasure. After an hour or so, the crusader knights and soldiers entered the city and, whipping the wild boys like dogs, seized all their prizes. Outraged, the boys howled, "Burn it! Burn it!" Piles of corpses and kindling were set alight. The city was soon an inferno. Knights and soldiers, unable to breathe, unable to see, fled the city. Any survivors from the earlier bloodshed were consumed by fire. Many of the arsonists themselves, blinded by smoke, scalded by ashes, suffocated. Less than three hours elapsed from the first ribaud shout to the last fleeing knight. Béziers and all the people who lived there were annihi-lated in an afternoon.[1]

"To our wonderment," Arnau wrote to Innocent a month later, "these ribauds of ours spared no order of persons (whatever their rank, sex, or age), putting to the sword almost twenty thousand people. After this great slaughter the whole city was despoiled and burnt, as divine vengeance raged marvelously."[2] In his joy, the papal legate exaggerated the number of men, women, and children killed by about seven thousand.

A decade after the massacre, with the crusade still another decade from ending in 1229, the Cistercian Caesarius of Heisterbach summar-ized the exemplum of the destruction of Béziers in an all too famous an-ecdote applauding Arnau's wisdom. In this story there were no furious boys or fiery infernos, only confused crusaders worrying about how to sort out the faithful from the heretics inside the captured city. "Lord," the crusaders ask Arnau, "what shall we do?" "Kill them [all]!" he re-plies. "Truly, God will know his own!"[3] This much-quoted (and much-misunderstood) exchange was imagined by Caesarius. Nevertheless, he encapsulated two profound truths for Latin Christian intellectuals in the early thirteenth century: first, heretics and ordinary Christians were indistinguishable from each other; and second, a moral imperative for mass murder was an essential principle of the holy war on the "Provençal heretics" (*Provincales heretici*), or, as it was commonly known to northern French knights, poets, bureaucrats, and preachers after 1211, the crusade against the Albigensians.

A decade before Innocent called for a crusade against the "Provençal heretics," and only seven months after he ascended the papal throne, he had declared another crusade, except this one was to the Holy Land. "Following the pitiable collapse of the territory of Jerusalem, following the shameful massacre of the Christian people, following the deplorable invasion of that land upon which the feet of Christ once stood," he grieved as he recounted Saladin's victory at the Horns of Hattin and conquest of Jerusalem in 1187. Yet even now, in late summer 1198, the Holy Sepulcher was still "imprisoned by the impious," despite a crusade (known as the Third) led by the lustrous English king Richard the Lionheart and the much less starry French king Philip II Augustus in 1191.

"Where is your God? He can neither deliver Himself nor you from our hands," Innocent imagined Saracens taunting all of Latin Christendom. "How, brothers and sons, are we to rebut the insults of insulters?" He answered his question by ordering that cities and nobles should equip soldiers for a two-year pilgrimage beginning Easter 1199. He granted a full pardon of sins for any man who endured the rigors and cost of this journey in person. A pilgrim's debts and interest payments were suspended, and interest already charged by Jews was to be reimbursed. Significantly, Innocent granted a full pardon of sins to men and women who merely sent other pilgrims at their own expense.

Innocent's crusade, known as the Fourth, took longer to get under way than he had hoped, but when it did four years later, consisting mostly of French and Venetian pilgrims, the flotilla, instead of sailing straight to Acre, seized and occupied the Catholic city of Zara, belonging to the king of Hungary, Imre, on the Dalmatian coast. The pope was appalled. When Christians attacked Christians without apostolic approval they "injured" Christ. The French begged forgiveness. The Venetians argued that Zara belonged to them and denied any culpability. Innocent absolved the former and excommunicated the latter.

The French and Venetian crusaders, undeterred by potential consequences or excommunication, then intervened in the politics of the East
Roman Empire. Alexios Angelos, whose aunt was married to the brother
of the leading crusader, Boniface, marquis of Montferrat, promised the return of the Greek Church to Rome, two hundred thousand silver marks,
and his support invading Ayyubid Egypt if the pilgrims overthrew his
uncle, Emperor Alexios III Angelos. The crusader nobility agreed and, with
a shockingly poor plan, assailed Constantinople by land and sea in June
1203. It seemed to be a quixotic enterprise, considering the city's magnificent urban walls and fortifications, yet a small fire set by the Venetians soon
blasted through the city, devouring more than twelve acres. The citizens of
Constantinople renounced the uncle and acclaimed the nephew as emperor or *basileus*.

Innocent was saddened by the further corruption of the crusade when
he heard the news. Alexios IV Angelos was strangled in a palace coup eight
months later as a pretender in thrall to the crusaders. On Monday, April
12, 1204, the crusaders responded by savagely looting Constantinople.
A month later they elected their own *imperator* and proclaimed a Latin
Empire of Constantinople. Innocent was initially elated that the Greek and
Latin Churches were seemingly reunited, seeing it as a sign of the Second
Coming. As more details reached Rome, his mood changed, and the sack
of Constantinople was "nothing other than an example of pestilence and
the works of hell"—it was a sign that Christendom itself was more diseased
with the cancer of heresy than even he had thought.

This apocalyptic sensibility was similar to what had gripped many individuals, ecclesiastical and secular, in the aftermath of the Second Crusade,
except now, three generations and so many more Levantine catastrophes
later, it was inescapable that Jerusalem would never be recovered unless the
heresy poisoning Christendom was eliminated. "Indeed, such pestilential
Provençals not only strive to devastate all we possess, but they strive to an-
nihilate us!" declared Innocent in his crusading exhortation of 1208. "Truly,
they have become perverters of souls and putrefiers of bodies!"[4]

These metaphors simultaneously evoked the spatial specificity of heresy
growing within the lands of the count of Toulouse, the temporal continuity
of heresy within the Church, and the insidious way in which heresy secretly
poisoned careless Christians, so that they and their neighbors were unaware
of their own pestilence. What made this threat so apocalyptic was that all

Christians, including popes, would eventually be corrupted by heresy unless it was exterminated. The crusade against the "Provençal heretics" was the first holy war in which Christians were guaranteed salvation through the killing of other Christians. "Attack the followers of heresy more fearlessly than even the Saracens," thundered Innocent, "since heretics are more evil!"[5]

The massacre at Béziers in its haphazard beginning, escalating feral fury, and whirlwind ferocity was at once the result and justification of this millennial exhilaration of imitating Christ by killing His supposed enemies. Although Innocent's crusading exhortations exalted the necessity of expunging and exterminating "Provençal heretics" from Christendom, it was not until Béziers that this homicidal ethic was fully adopted by those doing the killing. This moral imperative to mass murder was starkly different from all crusades (past and future) to the eastern Mediterranean, the Iberian peninsula, or the Baltic. The Cistercian Pierre des Vaux-de-Cernay, who witnessed much of the crusade and wrote a history of it, compared purged Béziers to purified Jerusalem—except he was thinking not of the first crusaders in 1099 but of when the emperor Vespasian and his son Titus had destroyed the Temple and expelled the Jews a thousand years earlier.[6] Innocent warned, over and over, that most persons who lived in and around the county of Toulouse were wholly or partially diseased with heresy and did not know it. Unless men and women ostentatiously announced themselves opposed to heresy, by default they were either heretics or supporters of heretics. The crusaders never thought they were fighting a "counter-Church" of heretics, as the nineteenth-century invention of Catharism would have it. What added to their ardor, and so their murderousness, was the conviction that if heresy was not erased, then sooner or later they too would be corrupted by this plague. It was only through the precautionary killing of all and sundry in a city like Béziers that the crusaders avenged and imitated Christ and so saved themselves.

A "genocidal moment" erupted at Béziers. It was a maelstrom within the framework of crusading, appearing as if out of nowhere and engulfing everyone within it before subsiding. Violence as a redemptive act, the escalating terror of heresy, and the holiness of being signed with the cross all converged at Béziers. It is the underlying sacrality of genocides, rarely discussed by modern historians and theorists, that differentiates them from other mass murders. The Albigensian crusade itself was not a sustained genocidal enterprise over twenty years. Nevertheless, after the nominal leader of the crusade, Simon de Monfort, died in 1218 (his skull was crushed by a rock flung from a mangonel worked by noble ladies, merchant wives, and little girls), an anonymous troubadour sang with bitter irony of the epitaph above the count's tomb, all but labeling him a mass murderer.

> The epitaph says, for those who can read it,
> that he is a saint and a martyr and that he shall breathe again
> and inherit and flourish in marvelous joy
> and wear a crown and be seated in the Kingdom.
> And me, I have heard it said that this must be so
> if, by killing men and by spilling blood
> and by squandering souls and by sanctioning deaths
> and by trusting evil counsel and by setting fires
> and by destroying barons and by dishonoring *paratge*
> and by seizing lands and by nourishing pride
> and by lauding evil and mocking the good
> and by massacring ladies and by slaughtering children,
> a man can win over Jesus Christ in this world,
> then the count of Montfort wears a crown and shines in heaven.[7]

2 A Ghost Story

In July 1211 a dead adolescent boy named Guilhem suddenly appeared in rags one night in the room of an eleven-year-old girl. "Cousin, do not be afraid," he said, stepping out of the shadows into the dim lamplight. "For I come to you by divine permission, drawn by my old abundant affection for you, and you must not suppose that you can be harmed in any way by me."

Three or five days earlier he had been murdered on the road from Apt to Beaucaire (near the mouth of the Rhône) traveling to see his cousin. "How can you come back to this world, since you are dead?" asked the girl. The word "dead" made him wail and sob. "My dearest, may this word never cross your lips! For the bitterness of death is so great and so beyond compare that someone who has once tasted death cannot endure even the mention of the word!" The dead preferred saying "departing this life."

The girl's mother and father had been asleep in the same room but were awakened by what, so it seemed to them, was their daughter chatting away to herself. They asked her what she was doing. "Don't you see my cousin Guilhem, who died recently, but is now standing here and speaking to me?" They crossed themselves in stunned amazement, as they did not see or hear their nephew. The boy withdrew back into the shadows, returning to wherever it was he dwelled. Guilhem's supernatural visit and conversation with his cousin was one of the first times that a revenant or ghost was seen or heard in the West.[8]

Guilhem and a hideous companion reappeared next to the girl a few days later at nine in the morning as she was standing alone in her father's room. She greeted her cousin fondly, but immediately asked where he had returned from and whom he had brought with him. He said he currently lived in the air amongst the spirits, was suffering the "torments of the fire of purgatory," and his ugly companion, conspicuously spitting flames and breathing fire, was a horned devil scourging him. "The girl, following the custom of the Provençals, flung out her hand to the holy water which was kept in the room, and sprinkled the devil." The creature vanished and the pain of purgatorial fire lessened for Guilhem. The two cousins then arranged to meet and chat at specific times every day. These visitations were soon well known on both sides of the Rhône.[9]

"Where is he standing, what is he doing, where has he come from, and what companion has he brought?" a skeptical and pushy prior from Tarascon asked the little girl as he barged into her house. She told him to be careful, as he had almost trodden on Guilhem's foot. This startled the prior into politeness. He wondered if she might ask the dead boy some questions on his behalf. She agreed, but first she herself wanted to know: who was her cousin's new just out-of-sight companion, apparently telling him what to say? Guilhem told her that while he was still "undergoing purgatory in the air," he suffered less than usual, as a guardian angel named Michael now accompanied him. The angel stepped forward, his wings enfolded about him, "his face shining with infinite splendor." The girl was dazzled, but then wanted to know why her cousin was no longer dressed in rags. Guilhem replied that he was actually dressed in his very own clothes from when he was alive, because the girl's mother, his aunt, had finally given them to the poor. He then answered the prior's questions with the help of Michael. Could he see God? At present, no, but after completing his spell in purgatory, "he would see God with a certain degree of clarity," although after the Day of Judgment he would see Him clearly and endlessly. "How does he know what is being done on earth?" Guilhem answered that all spirits can see everything at a glance, that what every human says and does is being watched and remembered, which was why shameful deeds should be avoided at all costs.[10]

A learned priest, distrusting what he had heard about the revenant, visited the girl and asked if he could see, hear, and so question Guilhem directly without her intervention: "Why draw things out?" The priest's request was reluctantly granted. Guilhem again repeated that at the moment of "departing this life" he had been terrified, and that both good and bad angels had come for him, with the former prevailing and taking him to purgatory. Where exactly was purgatory? Nearer to Jerusalem than the Rhône. Do the damned go to purgatory? No, they suffer infernal punishment in the air, only entering hell after the Day of Judgment. And saints? No, they enter their own heaven immediately, far from purgatory. Can you see all the souls in purgatory? Yes, "he could hear the groans of some, and the rejoicing of others who had completed their purification." Indeed, he could even see heaven and hell, standing within reach of both, "so that as a result of his proximity he can contemplate the joy of the just and the bitterness of the lost." Do souls in purgatory ever rest? Yes, every week from Saturday evening until Sunday evening, and whenever a mass is specifically sung for one of them. Does purgatory have a nighttime or is it always daytime? No, night follows day, but it is not as dark as on earth. What was the highest good after mass and giving alms? Never lying.

"When asked if the death and extermination of the Albigensians were pleasing to God, he replied that nothing that had ever been done in that region had pleased God so much." Guilhem, with Béziers in mind, stressed that when heretics were burned here in the body, they "are burned more severely after death in the spirit," and he warned that tolerating heresy was as bad as being a heretic.[11]

Michael was pleased with Guilhem's answers to the priest. By the way, said the dead boy, every Christian had a guardian angel. They were all called Michael, as it was an official title for a legion of angels. Crucially, the holiness of one angelic clone, no matter how loving, could be violent and unbearable. One day Guilhem's particular Michael stretched out his hand to bless the little cousin, and "such a blinding light struck the girl that she could not look at it or endure it without losing her senses." After this incident, the dead boy, apart from engaging in a few more wondrous things, stopped visiting his cousin, staying in purgatory with his guardian angel.[12]

Guilhem's ghost story was one of hundreds of tales, vignettes, sketches, curios, theological rants, puzzles, jokes, puns, travelogues, word games, geography lessons, map quizzes, and reportage that Gervase of Tilbury packed into a door-stopper known as the *Recreation for an Emperor* (*Otia Imperialia*). The Englishman (for Tilbury is in Essex) had dedicated his extravagant book to the emperor Otto IV around 1215: "I have decided to present something for your hearing to refresh you in the midst of your worldly cares." Gervase exemplified the university *literatus* as a worldly and learned bureaucrat. He had studied law at Bologna and had traveled widely as an administrator, working for the kings of England and Sicily, various archbishops, and a few abbots before being appointed marshal of Arles by the emperor in 1209. He had been collecting interesting things for his book for more than thirty years. It had long refreshed him before he presented it to Otto (who probably never read it). What Gervase knew of the ghostly Guilhem was largely copied from the notes taken by the learned priest and from his own firsthand investigations.[13]

"Let hearts be awed, minds amazed, and limbs tremble at the wonder of it!" intoned Gervase in his best carnival barker voice about the dead boy who returned.[14] Yet like so many of his tales, there was, as he intended, profundity in the story of the revenant. The whole point of ghosts was that they were not visions; rather, they really were the dead interacting with the living in the here and now. More than this, though, they were proof of the linear continuity of individual selves, which were unbroken in life and carried over unbroken in death. Revenants were the logical outcome of the confessional culture developing in the twelfth century. Who you were when alive, warts and all, was the same you in death.

Guilhem may have been the first recorded ghost, but we should assume there were other visitations beginning around 1200. Revenants like him would have made no sense in the earlier penitential culture, where the hope was a "happy death" basically bleached of any earthly identity. Which was why purgatory became so essential from the twelfth century onward. There were clearly purgatorial spaces between hell and heaven in the visions of Barontus (handsome Abraham on a throne ruling an empty middle kingdom) and Wetti (the beautiful white mountain), but none of them were as elaborate or so obviously a continuation of the human experience of the mundane world, especially time, into the afterlife. Only eternity existed in hell and heaven, but in purgatory there was, like night becoming day, a temporal limit to a soul's suffering, perhaps ten thousand years, but still an endpoint, which gloriously led to paradise.

Guilhem stressed over and over the interconnectedness of terrestrial existence with the celestial, most obviously in purgatory, but even in hell and heaven. The reality of purgatory was difficult to grasp for most Christians in the early thirteenth century, which was why ghost stories like that of the dead boy who returned one night in Beaucaire were so important.

3 So Small

In 1205, Marie d'Oignes, a married woman from a wealthy merchant family in Liège, had a vision of the coming crusade that Innocent III would launch against the "Provençal heretics." "When this happened there had been no

mention of these heretics in our lands," observed Jacques de Vitry disingenuously in his *Life* of Marie written a decade later, "but then that was the time
when God spoke to her in the spirit and it was as if He were complaining that
He had lost almost all His realm and had been banished like an exile from His
lands."

In 1211, "although she lived far away," Marie had another vision of the crusaders fighting and dying in battle near Toulouse. Amidst the carnage she saw
angels rejoicing as they carried the souls of the "holy martyrs of Christ" directly to paradise without needing the purification of purgatory. She immediately wanted to travel south and join the war against the heretics. "She could
barely be restrained from doing so." Jacques was Marie's confessor and, sympathetic toward her desire to fight and be a martyr, asked what she would do
if she were a crusader. "I would honor my Lord," she replied, "by witnessing
His name where so many impious men have denied Him by blasphemy."

"When her tiny body was washed after death," recalled Jacques when
Marie died aged thirty-six in 1213, "it was found to be so small and shriveled
by her illness and fasting that her spine touched her belly." It was also discovered that she had secretly scarred her body with the wounds of Christ.
Marie, crippled by starvation and chronic weeping, gripped with an un-
quenchable thirst for the "vivifying blood of Christ," and marked like Him,
was to be admired rather than imitated, said her biographer, for only He
should be copied. Yet, such imitation, while now widespread and encouraged, nevertheless required supervision by the Church. For example, in
1229 in the diocese of Liège, according to Jacques in a sermon, a demon
masquerading as an angel tricked a well-meaning but foolish man into nailing himself to a cross on Good Friday. Fortunately, some shepherds took
him down, and "after a few days he recovered sufficiently that any signs of
the wounds scarcely appeared on him."[15]

Marie, though, for all her untrammeled ecstasy and loving ferocity toward
her own body, was, at least according to Jacques, deferential to the Church.
Similar freelance holy urban lay women, almost always from mercantile
families, were common (although perhaps not as common as is sometimes
assumed by historians) from the thirteenth century onward. These women,
obsequious before priests, obsessed with the Eucharist, and starving themselves in glorifying Him, were "soldiers of God" in the eradication of heresy
within Christendom. Whatever violence they inflicted upon their own
bodies they intended to be inflicted with infinitely more violence against

heretics and unbelievers. The wounds of Christ were at once marks of His persecution and, if imitated with genuine holiness from genuine angels, weapons for persecuting sinners.

4 The Ends of Nails

On Tuesday, September 13, 1224, a radiant vision of a six-winged angelic seraph with hands and feet nailed to a cross was seen by Francis of Assisi inside his hut on La Verna (a lonely mountain overlooking the valley of Casentino in central Italy). Two wings stretched out above the seraph's head and another two were extended ready for flight, while the final two wrapped themselves around his body.

Francis was confused by what he was seeing. "Still, he was filled with happiness and he rejoiced very greatly because of the kind and gracious look with which he saw himself regarded by the seraph, whose beauty was beyond estimation." And yet he was frightened by how much the seraph was suffering on the cross. What did this vision mean? Why did it elicit both joy and sorrow in him? "And while he was thus unable to come to any understanding of it and the strangeness of the vision perplexed his heart, the marks of the nails began to appear in his hands and feet, just as he had seen them a little before in the crucified man above him." Blood dripped from these marks. "Some small pieces of flesh took on the appearance of the ends of nails, bent and driven back and rising above the rest of the flesh." Simultaneously, on his right side a bleeding wound appeared, as if he had been stabbed with a lance. As Francis intellectually struggled to comprehend what he was seeing and experiencing, the answer to his question famously appeared on his body as the stigmata of Christ.[16]

This was the culmination of more than twenty years of Francis being obsessed with Christ. "Jesus he bore in his heart, Jesus in his mouth, Jesus in his ears, Jesus in his eyes, Jesus in his hands, Jesus in the rest of his members," as his first biographer and early follower, Tommaso da Celano, encapsulated the all-consuming and eventually transformative nature of this obsession. Until Francis was twenty-five, though, he barely thought about Jesus; or, rather, he thought about Him no more than any other wealthy urban knight of Assisi. His youthful wantonness, foolishness, fondness for "soft and flowing garments," and squandering of the family mercantile fortune, while overdone by him in hindsight, were nevertheless abruptly and flamboyantly cast aside in his conversion to poverty, perpetual penance, and imitating Christ.

What caused this change in him is unclear. Shortly before he died in 1226, he said that it had been triggered by the sight of lepers; despite initially feeling physically nauseous, he soon felt nothing but spiritual consolation. "After that I did not wait long before leaving the world." It is important to note that individuals either called or calling themselves "lepers" were rarely infected with leprosy (Hansen's disease); rather, it was a synonym for the poor, often the urban homeless, but just as likely impoverished families living together in "leper houses" in towns and villages like religious communities. It was this extreme poverty, associated with abuse, persecution, "purgatory on earth," and even heresy, that provoked Francis into embracing the perfect holy poverty of the abused and persecuted Christ.[17]

In 1207 Francis discarded everything he owned, including all his clothes apart from a frayed tunic, and began praying in abandoned buildings, empty churches at night, huts on hills, and forlorn groves in the hilly crevasses around Assisi. As he wandered shoeless from one deserted spot to another, he preached, sometimes to just one shepherd, often to thousands of townspeople. His sermons were impromptu, seemingly given without any thought beforehand, and were in bad French. He even composed and sang songs in rough and ready French. There were too many Italian dialects, even within the same region or town, and makeshift French—a mix of Occitan picked up from troubadour songs and aristocratic northern French—was more easily understood by merchants and nobles in Umbria, Tuscany, Marche, and Lazio.[18] These sermons and songs were about redemption through replicating the poverty of Christ—His humanity was most powerfully revealed in His impoverishment.

Francis soon attracted followers, imitating him imitating Him. A seventeen-year-old noble girl named Clare was one of them. Unlike Valdes of Lyon, though, he was always deferential to episcopal authority, never preaching without the permission of the bishop. Innocent III rewarded such submissiveness by allowing Francis to draft a *Rule* for an Order of Friars Minors in 1210, and which, after a few revisions, was finally formulated in 1223. The pope refused to let this new *Rule* include Clare or women like her. "Surely," Innocent supposedly exclaimed about Francis, "this is the man who, by his works and by the teaching of Christ will give support to the Church."[19]

The *Rule* of Francis was, unlike that of Benedict, deliberately short and succinct. It was for itinerant mendicants and not immured monks. It stressed that the friars—literally "brothers," as they were "members of the same family"—owned nothing, just one tunic with a hood (which they could patch with sackcloth), shoes only when necessary, no money at all, and no permanent buildings. It was indifferent to learning; "those who are illiterate should not be anxious to study." Rather, what mattered was being humble, "and patient in persecution or illness, loving those who persecute us." Francis thought of himself as persecuted by the enemies of Christ, such as heretics and Saracens. Indeed, in 1219, during a crusade (numbered as the Fifth) he even walked into the camp of the Ayyubid sultan al-Kamil outside Damietta (at the eastern mouth of the Nile) hoping to convert him; fortunately, the Egyptians assumed he was a holy fool and politely sent him back.[20] Nevertheless, this expectation of persecution in the *Rule*, which easily transitioned into a desire to be persecuted, powerfully shaped the zealous pursuit of martyrdom by some brothers.[21]

Although Francis expected persecution like Him, for his contemporary Dominic de Guzmán (or de Caleruega), Christ Himself was the model of the perfect holy persecutor. Dominic was formerly the subprior of the cathedral at Osma (east of the river Ucero in northwestern Spain) and had initially accompanied the bishop of Osma on a preaching campaign against heresy in the lands of the count of Toulouse in 1206. He continued preaching in villages throughout the Toulousain, Carcassès, and Albigeois during the Albigensian crusade with a small coterie of other monks, canons, priests, and laymen. He was not charismatic like Francis, but he was fervent and relentless in the war on heresy, and it was this fervor that his followers admired and copied. Pope Honorius III officially recognized Dominic and his "brothers" as the Order of Friars Preachers in 1216.

Dominic wrote no *Rule*; indeed, he wrote very little at all. Dominicans replicated Christ's love and existence on earth not through His poverty like the Franciscans, although His impoverishment was important to them, but rather through His salvation of souls, which for them was the conversion or, if necessary, elimination of heretics. They even dug up the corpses of supposed heretics and burned them. The Dominicans and the Franciscans, known as mendicants from their itinerant ways and beggarly appearance,

took over from the Cistercians as the great preachers, promoters, and enfor-
cers of Christianity in the West. Also, despite what Francis put in his *Rule*
and Dominic's lack of concern for learning, both the Friars Preachers and
the Friars Minors soon dominated the universities within a generation. The
turning point was when Alexander of Hales, the regent master of theology
at Paris, became a Franciscan in 1236.

Pope Gregory IX canonized Dominic thirteen years after he died in 1234,
largely because of his own enthusiasm for a man he viewed as holy, rather
than any clamoring from the Dominicans, who, curiously, were ambivalent about their founder's sacrality. In 1228 he had already made a saint of
Francis, whose holiness almost no one doubted. A year before Gregory elevated Dominic to sainthood (and really what provoked him to do it), he had
asked the Dominicans to hunt out and extinguish the newly revived serpent
of heresy in France and Provincia by undertaking "inquisitions into heretical
depravity" (*inquisitiones heretice pravitatis*). Christ now came as an inquisitor.[22]

5 A Demon in Her Belly

One morning in 1222, Aimerzens Viguier, adolescent and pregnant, was
taken by her aunt, Geralda de Cabuer, to the house of Esquiva Aldric in
a village near Toulouse. Inside the house were Esquiva's husband and son,
both named Guilhem, and two unknown noble women. Aimerzens soon
realized these anonymous women were fugitive heretics when everyone,
including herself as instructed by Esquiva, genuflected thrice before them,
saying, "Bless us, good ladies, pray God for these sinners."

Later that day, other noble men and women joined Aimerzens and her
aunt in the Aldric house. The good ladies preached to this gathering, and
then everyone, including Aimerzens, offered them the same bows and words
as in the morning. The heretics, relaxing in the admiration of those present,
then teased the obviously awkward and unsure girl, saying, as she later recalled, that "since I was a pregnant adolescent, I was carrying a demon in
my belly." This jest provoked raucous laughter in everyone, including her
aunt Geralda. Aimerzens was so deeply embarrassed, so humiliated by everyone's lack of *cortezia*, but most especially by that of the good ladies, that
she was never courteous again to another person she knew was a heretic.
In the following weeks her husband, Guilhem Viguier, repeatedly beat her,

yelling insults, warning "me that I had to love the heretics" like him and everyone else they knew. "But I didn't wish to love them," Aimerzens told the Dominican inquisitor Bernart de Caux twenty-three years later, "after they told me I was pregnant with a demon."[23]

Aimerzens, now close to forty when she remembered her adolescent humiliation and spousal abuse, was just one witness amongst almost six thousand men, women, and children interrogated by the Dominican inquisitors Bernart de Caux and Johan de Sant Peire in the abbey cloisters of the basilica of Saint Sernin in Toulouse between May 1245 and August 1246. This "great inquisition" was not only the largest *inquisitio* in the Middle Ages but also one of the first, happening only a decade after the pope's request for the Friars Preachers to search out heretics in the very same villages and hamlets that had only recently suffered two decades of a holy war against heresy.

"Now they've made themselves into inquisitors and they judge just as it suits them," sarcastically sang the troubadour Guilhem de Montanhagol about the Dominicans in 1233. "But," he added, tongue in cheek, "I've nothing against the inquisition, far from it, I like those who pursue errors and who, with their lovely delightful words, devoid of anger, restore to the faith who have strayed and turned away."[24] In 1235 one inquisitor caused a riot in Narbonne when he accused most of the town of being heretics. That same year Raimon VII, the count of Toulouse, expelled the Dominicans from his city for four months because their inquisitions were causing too much turmoil, especially as they demolished the houses of accused heretics (and kept digging up and burning corpses).

Much of the trouble was that neither the inquisitors nor those they questioned actually understood what constituted an inquisition into heretical depravity in these early years. Moreover, these inquisitions were ad hoc and not permanent institutional courts. The Dominicans were dependent upon the support of local secular lords, like the count of Toulouse, for the functioning of their tribunals. Otherwise, it was risky. In May 1242, two inquisitors, one of whom was a Franciscan, were brutally murdered (tongues cut out, heads caved in) along with nine companions in Avignonet, a tiny village near Toulouse. Seven months later Raimon finally supported the inquisition, partially because it was rumored he had encouraged the Avignonet massacre in the spring, but mostly because he was too exhausted to resist after failing miserably in an autumn war against the French king, Louis IX.

In 1245, Aimerzens began her testimony by first abjuring all heresy and then taking an oath that she would "tell the full and exact truth about oneself and about others, living and dead, in the matter of the fact or crime of heresy or Waldensianism." She then answered a series of questions, which a scribe simultaneously translated from her oral first-person vernacular into written third-person Latin on parchment. When she had finished testifying, what was recorded of her confession was then read back to her, now translated by the scribe from his Latin into her vernacular, so she could confirm that what she was hearing was what she had testified. Aimerzens verifying the truth of what she had just confessed before the inquisition, or rather confirming the truth of what a scribe had transcribed of her confession, was the final legal step that turned her testimony into a notarized public document. For many witnesses interrogated by the inqusitors it was this writing down of a confession that was confusing and frightening, as yearly confession to a priest was explicitly never to be copied out. Even the inquisitors themselves were at first unsure, taking no notes or records of what they were told. Importantly, though, no one would have thought it unusual that one language could truthfully resemble another or that Latin words on parchment truthfully captured a life remembered in the vernacular.

Latin was a language that all medieval men and women, no matter how high or humble, regularly heard and saw and had translated for them. Charters, wills, oaths of loyalty, bequests, deeds, debts, accounts, contracts, and letters were all mundane acts that needed notarized authentication and were almost always written in Latin, even if the individuals involved could not read the language. In this sense, Latin was vigorously alive, not just in the schoolroom but in the marketplace and courtroom, as so much of ordinary existence depended on its ability to faithfully record the wishes of a dying man, the size of a house being sold, the length of a vineyard, or the freedom of a manumitted serf. Most people knew a smattering of Latin, or at least enough to recognize a few words. In England, for example, three languages flowed back and forth at an assize: the nobility spoke French, the peasantry and many merchants spoke English, and notaries who spoke both French and English transcribed everything into Latin. In Catalonia, documents were frequently a mélange of Catalan, Arabic, Hebrew, and Latin. Of course, a Latin testimony transcribed by the inquisition was an explosive collection of words, abbreviations, and pen strokes that could potentially destroy a person or a village.

Most of the individuals questioned by the inquisition in these early decades genuinely assumed that things they had said or done years or even decades earlier, especially when they were children, were in no way evidence of heresy or sympathy for heretics. Much of the confusion was because the men and women now labeled as heretics by the inquisitors had not been seen as such around 1200. The good ladies who had mocked Aimerzens were the fugitive descendants of a much wider phenomenon in the twelfth century between the Garonne and Rhône, the "good women"—literally thousands of noble prepubescent girls and widowed older women living together secluded in village houses. Similarly, there were the "good men"—prepubescent boys, although not as many as the girls, and older, mostly widowed men—who lived more openly and publicly.

These good men and good women were in their own way understood to be copying Christ as holy individuals. They did not think of themselves as heretics and, apart from some Cistercian preachers, neither did everyone else. Their holiness and the complex social and moral universe swirling around them were certainly distinctive to this region, particularly as they involved elaborate performances of sacred *cortezia*, but there can be no doubt that other, equally parochial versions of what it meant to be a Christian in the aftermath of the First Crusade existed everywhere in Latin Christendom. None of these individuals, or the communities that needed and admired them, thought that what they were doing was antithetical to the Church. It is these good men and good women that modern scholars erroneously call "Cathars."

Only after 1220, and so during the last decade of the Albigensian crusade, did some, but not all, of these good men and good women become wandering refugees, barely clinging to memories of who they once had been in a world that no longer existed. The inquisitors then transformed these clandestine figures into a "heresy" by transforming them into a "religion," or, more correctly, transfiguring them into a sect or an *ecclesia*, a "church." As for the Waldensians, while there were very few of them in comparison to the good men and good women, they too were now explicitly viewed by the inquisition as a heretical sect. Fundamentally, the inquisitors changed how the past was remembered and so experienced by thousands of men, women, and children, so that what were once inescapably innocent interactions with local holy persons were now consciously guilty relationships with heretics.

What is just as astounding is how these fugitive good men and good women actually came to think of themselves as heretics, that is, as individuals self-consciously saying and doing things they knew were "heretical" and potentially dangerous, if not life-threatening. They welcomed their persecution as a confirmation of their holiness, just as Francis had understood himself in his *Rule*. It is perhaps one of the terrible ironies of history that it was only on account of the inquisitions into heretical depravity that the medieval heretic—self-aware, authentic, full of agency—can be said to have come into existence, to have become *real*.

In May 1245, Aimerzens was stuffed inside a wine barrel by Guilhem Sais, the lord of her village. "Boy," Guilhem screamed at her son (perhaps the demon originally in her belly) when the lad interceded, "do you want to help this old bag destroy us all?" And he squeezed the youth inside the barrel as well. He hoped this rough treatment would persuade Aimerzens to keep her mouth shut when she testified to the inquisition a few weeks later. Mother and son were released after a night in the barrel, although Guilhem still extorted three shillings and seven pence from them for the privilege. Aimerzens, not surprisingly, confessed everything she knew of heresy in the recent and distant past to the inquisitors, fulfilling exactly what so many in her village feared.[25]

6 The Mongols

"We Mo'als [Mongols]," said the great khan Möngke, grandson of Chinggis Khan, to the Franciscan Guillaume de Rubruck in the imperial palace of Qaraqorum in the Orkhon valley (in modern central Mongolia) in late May 1254, "believe that there is only one God, through whom we have life and through whom we die, and towards whom we direct our hearts."[26]

Möngke was speaking of Tengri, the everlasting God of the sky or heavens as well as everything awe-inspiring in the world (like a high mountain or a mighty tree). Tengri radiated *sülde*, the force that endowed Mongol warriors with majesty, masculine strength, and good fortune. It was from Tengri that Chinggis Khan and his successors were granted the right and the duty of ruling the world. Guillaume knew Möngke was referring to Tengri but, as always, he restated his conviction that the God of the Mongols was really the Christian God. Möngke asked Guillaume's interpreter, the adopted son of a

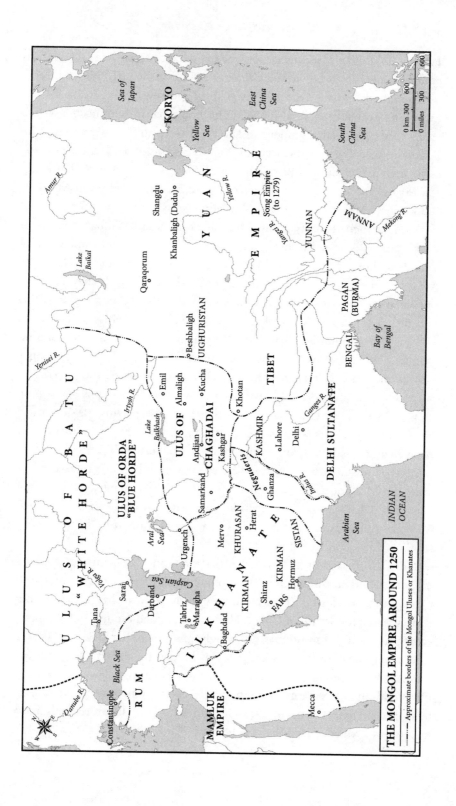

THE MONGOL EMPIRE AROUND 1250

- - - - - Approximate borders of the Mongol Uluses or Khanates

Parisian goldsmith working at Qaraqorum, what the friar had said. He was amused, especially as he viewed Christ as a gift from Tengri. "Nevertheless," he continued, "just as God has given the hand several fingers, so he has given human beings several paths." (The noble pagan Symmachus, as we recall, made a similar argument in late fourth-century Rome.) Tengri, he pointed out, had given the scriptures to Christians, "and you do not observe them." Guillaume opined that he did, even if it was true that many Christians did not. Whereas Tengri, observed Möngke, had given Mongols "soothsayers, and we do as they tell us and live in peace."[27]

Möngke then abruptly pointed his staff at the friar. "You have been here a long time. It is my wish that you go back." He wanted Guillaume to carry a letter to Louis IX, who was last known to be on crusade in Damietta. Möngke concluded the audience, saying, "You have a long journey ahead."[28]

Guillaume described his final meeting with Möngke in a report of his expedition across the Mongol Empire written for Louis IX in late 1255. He was not a diplomat, as he was at pains to point out to everyone he met, and while he took seriously keeping an account of "everything I saw amongst the Tartars" for the French king, it was not the overriding purpose of his journey. ("Tartars" as a name for the Mongols was a pun, supposedly made by the usually humorless Louis IX, playing off "Tartarus," the name for hell in the *Aeneid*.) Guillaume's journey was primarily an evangelizing mission, at once intending to convert the Mongols and to comfort Latin Christians enslaved by them. Or, rather, he endeavored to make the Mongols understand that they, like all of humanity, were already essentially Christians as His creations living in His universe, even if they were not fully aware of it just yet. He assumed something similar about Muslims, Jews, and Buddhists.

This Christian essentialism meant that everyone Guillaume met on his trek of more than three and a half thousand miles from Constantinople to Qaraqorum he viewed as only one step away from realizing that within them was the revelation of Christ. This even included Nestorian Christians, whom he mostly dismissed as shockingly misguided, heretical, and drunk. There were no longer lands and peoples hidden behind His head on the cross, as had been the case for Rodulfus Glaber two centuries earlier. Christendom now encompassed the world, even if much of the world pretended to be ignorant of this fact. Guillaume's report therefore reads like a memoir of a journey into the strangely familiar.[29]

According to Guillaume in his report, Möngke's grandfather had been declared "chief and commander of the Tartars and Mo'als" half a century earlier after telling a large and secret assembly of warriors: "It is because we have no leader that we are oppressed by our neighbors."[30] Indeed, in spring 1206, the Mongol warrior Temüjin was acclaimed as Chinggis Khan at a great assembly of nomadic steppe tribes, known as a *quriltai*, or gathering of the Felt-Walled Tents, near the head of the Onon River in the Khentii Mountains (in modern northeastern Mongolia). His novel title meant "mighty" or "universal." He embodied Tengri. In submitting themselves to him the Felt-Walled Tents acknowledged that they were now members of a new *ulus*, an all-encompassing sacred and sovereign community with new rules and a new hierarchy in which biological kinship and older loyalties were now subsumed. They were a new Mongol "people." They further accepted that they would only ever be ruled by the "golden kin" (*altan orugh*) descending from Chinggis Khan. At the same time they were also members of a new great "horde."

A horde (*orda*) for Mongols implied many things, such as an army, a place of power, subjects under a ruler, and a vast camp; overall, though, and so encompassing all these meanings, it defined and celebrated the kinetic existence of nomads in constant movement. Hordes migrated, dispersed, came together again, and were composed of differing ethnic and religious groups. And, while not tied to specific lands like sedentary regimes, they were political and martial entities like kingdoms, khanates, or empires. Many hordes could and soon did exist within the new Mongol *ulus*. Nevertheless, under Chinggis Khan, *ulus* and horde, while not synonymous, were inseparable, so that by his death in 1227, the imperial Mongol state, the *yeke Mongghol ulus*, was known as the "great horde."[31]

The great horde as a realm in motion was constantly swallowing other, less agile nomadic peoples and clashing with more sedentary states. As the notion of borders was fundamentally meaningless, it was always simultaneously beginning, fighting, and ending wars on various fronts. Chinggis Khan reorganized the Mongol military structure, or *tümen*, with this reality in mind. He introduced a system that grouped his horse soldiers in ever larger decimal units: ten within one hundred within one thousand within ten thousand. His army was probably 150,000 men. He exploited the traditional wild fluidity of Mongol fighting by focusing it through mass regimentation. Around himself he gathered an elite imperial guard of ten thousand known as the *keshig*, who, apart from their superior fighting skills, were administrators, stewards, official cooks, doorkeepers, quiver guards, and diplomats. He created the first Mongolian script, based on the Uighur, for these guardian bureaucrats. Chinggis Khan fashioned a new nobility dedicated to himself and his golden kin out of the *keshig*.

Chinggis Khan quickly tested his martial and governmental innovations with wars against the Tibetan-Burmese Tangut (or Xi Xia) Empire, the formidable Jin (or Chin) Empire in northern China, and the Khwarezmian Empire (which covered Transoxiana, that is, parts of modern Afghanistan, Iran, Uzbekistan, and Turkmenistan). Chinggis Khan, while dying before these wars were brutally and victoriously concluded, had established the sweeping movement of the great horde across Eurasia, an imperial momentum that ended only in 1279.[32]

In March 1241, as many as 130,000 Mongol warriors crossed the Dnieper River into the kingdom of Hungary. This army within the greater horde was known as the "white horde" (*ak orda*) and its leader or khan was Batu, another grandson of Chinggis Khan. (Confusingly, Batu was also head of the *ulus* founded by his father, Jochi.) This was a war of conquest and punishment against the Hungarian king, Béla IV, for the sanctuary he had given thousands of Qipchak (or Cuman) nomadic refugees fleeing as the white horde overran their steppe lands stretching from the northern shores of the Black Sea to the northern shores of the Caspian Sea. The old *keshig* general Sübötei meticulously planned the invasion, with the main host charging through the Verecke Pass, while other contingents galloped through the Carpathian Mountains and Poland.

Béla had already written to Pope Gregory IX begging for help— specifically, a crusade against the pagans, plus Venetian catapults that he could position along the Danube. The catapults never arrived. However, a crusade was preached in the German lands, though very few knights signed themselves with the cross. Béla waged a hapless and incoherent campaign against the Mongols. In April at the Sajó River on the Plain of Muhi, the Hungarians were crushed. The king miraculously survived and fled to the Dalmatian coast. In February 1242, the white horde cantered over the frozen Danube, advancing toward Austria and Dalmatia, intending to hunt down the fugitive monarch. Suddenly, in March, the Mongols wheeled around and bolted back over the Danube and the Dnieper.[33]

What caused this stunning turn of events? Apparently the main reason was that the great khan Ögödei, son and successor of Chinggis, had died three months earlier, and so Batu, as a member of the golden kin, and Sübötei, as a member of the *keshig*, were required to hurry back to Qaraqorum for an assembly of the Felt-Walled Tents. Equally, though, their invasion was stumbling into disaster. The winter of 1241–1242 was the coldest in living memory, and the Mongols and their horses, usually great fighters and for-agers in icy conditions, were shivering and starving. Then the torrential spring rains turned the plains into a quagmire, devouring men, carts, siege engines, animals, and new grass shoots. Apart from these logistical problems, there were unexpected military setbacks, with at least twelve cities and cas-tles in western Hungary deftly resisting the Mongols.

On top of all this, Batu and Sübötei loathed each other. The latter thought the former was an inept warrior, lacking the *sülde* of his grandfather and other golden kin; the former thought the latter was deliberately making him look weak in comparison to his cousins Möngke and Qubilai. The death of Ögödei, while a sacred call for choosing a new Great Khan by the Felt-Walled Tents, was a fortuitous excuse for both men to abandon their western war. Indeed, in the end, Batu did not even go to Qaraqorum, dis-trusting his golden kin and their *keshig* supporters, camping with his white horde in the recently conquered Qipchaq steppe along the lower Volga. The Mongols never again threatened Latin Christendom.[34]

Béla, of course, assumed the Mongols were soon coming back. A decade later he was still worrying about their return. Around 1250 he complained to Pope Innocent IV that when the Tartars had attacked his kingdom, nei-ther pope nor emperor nor French king, "the three principal courts of Christendom," had offered any real help—words, yes, but no soldiers—against the "pestilence." Hungary, "if it is possessed by the Tartars, will be for them an open gate to other regions of the Catholic faith." So why, he wondered, was Louis IX allowed to go crusading in the Levant, when the Mongols were so obviously the greater threat to Christendom? As far as Béla was concerned, Christendom had frontiers, or least fragile gateways, and the most vulnerable was the kingdom of Hungary.[35]

Batu, in sullen majesty, remained with his white horde, moving up and down the eastern bank of the Volga, until he died aged around fifty in 1255. Two years earlier, Guillaume and his Franciscan companion Bartolomeo da Cremona had visited him during the late summer near Ukek on their way to Qaraqorum. "On sighting Batu's camp, I was struck with awe." Thousands of gleaming white felt tents and pavilions (tinted even whiter with chalk, clay, and crushed bone) were organized like a great circular city as the khan's palatial compound. (A few of Batu's white tents were different from the others, as they had once belonged to Béla.) Around this cantonment, extending for two or three miles, were tens of thousands of other white and gray felt tents belonging to individual warriors and their families. These dwellings could be as large as thirty feet across or as small as fifteen, and all of them were topped with bright embroidery and doorways sewn from colorful felt and silk strips to look like vines, trees, birds, and animals. Guillaume described how the Mongols carried their tents, large and small, on flatbed wagons, some of which were so massive that they were pulled by as many as twenty-two oxen. An elite Mongol man or woman easily owned between one hundred and two hundred wagons and tents. Batu's twenty-six wives, for example, each possessed two hundred. Guillaume noted that the khan's residence was called "in their language *orda*, meaning 'the middle,' since it is always situated in the midst of his men." He may have confused what he heard with the Turkish *orta*, "middle," but more likely it was just another of the multiple meanings of "horde." Batu's camp somehow moved every two or three days, as "slow as a lamb or an ox might walk." Guillaume worried in his report that his words poorly conveyed the grandeur and beauty of the Mongol felt-walled tents, but, sadly, his skill at drawing was even worse.[36]

Guillaume had his audience with Batu in a special ceremonial pavilion made of felt and silk that shimmered with chalk dust and kaleidoscopic needlework. "We took up our stand there, with bare feet, wearing our habits, but with our heads uncovered, and we presented quite a spectacle for them." The Mongols thought it very strange that Guillaume and Bartolomeo never wore footwear; even when the Franciscans reluctantly wore shoes because of weather or etiquette, they took them off again as soon as possible. ("People gathered around us," Guillaume amusingly remembered when he first arrived at Qaraqorum, "gazing at us as if we were freaks, especially in view of our bare feet, and asked whether we had no use for our feet, since they imagined that in no time we should lose them.")[37]

Batu in his pavilion was seated on a golden throne that looked like a broad couch with one of his wives next to him. "He regarded us with a keen gaze, as we did him." His face had reddish blotches, and his build was the same as a French knight that Guillaume knew in Acre. Batu asked about Louis IX. Why had he left his kingdom and who was he fighting? "'With the Saracens,' I replied, 'who are profaning Jerusalem, the house of God.'" The khan already knew a great deal about the French king and his crusade. A scribe copied down everything that was said. Batu permitted Guillaume and Bartolomeo to continue on their way to Qaraqorum, even making sure that their new noble Mongol guide (the son of a commander of a thousand white horde warriors) properly outfitted them for the coming winter—"so intense that rocks and trees split apart with the frost"—paying particular attention to putting their bare feet into felt boots.[38]

In early July 1254, Guillaume, after five months in Qaraqorum and having failed to convert Möngke, or anyone else for that matter, was readying himself for the long slog back to Acre. Bartolomeo broke down, refusing to go. "Brother, look what you are about. I will not leave you," said Guillaume. "You are not leaving me," whimpered Bartolomeo. "I am leaving you, since if I accompany you, I see danger to my body and my soul, for I cannot face the unbearable hardship." He had complained throughout their expedition, always hungry, exhausted, freezing, and frightened; in Qaraqorum he stayed in the household of the Parisian gold-smith. Guillaume returned alone, only accompanied by an interpreter, a Mongol guide, and a servant, "who was in possession of a warrant enti-tling him to receive every four days a sheep for the four of us." The return journey took just over a year.[39]

Louis IX had already left Acre for Paris in April 1254. Guillaume in his report lamented that had he known of the king's departure from Syria before leaving Qaraqorum, he would have traveled straight to France via Hungary, instead of the more dangerous route he took.[40] He stayed in Acre for a year or so, writing and teaching, before finally reaching Paris around 1257. It seems Louis never read the report. The English Franciscan Roger Bacon, who did attentively read it after meeting its author in Paris, thought that the king was perhaps told about it.[41]

Louis most likely never received Möngke's letter either. Guillaume trans-lated it for him, as best he could, in his report. It was short and blunt. "This is the order of the everlasting God," Möngke began. "In heaven there is only one eternal God. On earth there is only one lord, Chinggis Khan. This is the word of the son of God." After hearing and understanding this order, "King Louis, ruler of the French ... if you are willing to obey us, you should send envoys to us: in that way we shall be sure whether you wish to be at peace with us or at war." The entire world, "from the sun's rising to its setting, has become one in joy and in peace" by obeying the order of everlasting God. "But, if on hearing and understanding the order of the everlasting God, you are unwilling to observe it or to place any trust in it," with Louis saying to himself, "Our country is far away, our mountains are strong, our sea is broad," then he had chosen war and not peace. "How can we know what will happen?" The everlasting God, Möngke menacingly ended his letter, "He knows."[42]

Another Franciscan, Giovanni del Pian di Carpini, carried a similar letter back to Pope Innocent IV from the great khan Güyük (son and successor of Ögödei) after visiting Qaraqorum in summer 1246 (and he also wrote another, less confessional travelogue of his journey).[43] Möngke and before him Güyük conceived of themselves as sons or embodiments of Tengri by virtue of being the heirs of Chinggis Khan, and what constituted the limits of the *yeke Mongghol ulus* were whatever constituted the limits of the world. All wars by the great horde and other lesser hordes were holy wars merely affirming this fact. All rulers and peoples unwilling to obey the Mongols were therefore rebels against the order of the everlasting God.

In 1258, Möngke ordered his brother Hülegü to conquer the lands of the Abbasids as their grandfather had intended four decades earlier. An army of three hundred thousand, of which over half were Mongol horsemen, marched against Baghdad. A letter was delivered to the Abbasid caliph al-Musta'sim requiring his submission to the "army of God on His earth." He refused. Baghdad was swiftly seized in February and the caliph, wrapped in a carpet, was trampled to death by thousands of horsemen. (It would have offended Tengri to spill the blood of a ruler upon His earth.) Hülegü even boasted in a letter to Louis IX that more than two hundred thousand people were massacred in Baghdad. After five centuries the Abbasid caliphate was over.[44]

"I tell you with confidence that if our peasants, to say nothing of kings and knights, were willing to travel in the way the Tartar princes move," Guillaume concluded his report, "they could conquer the whole world."[45]

7 The Existence of God

"The attempt to prove that God exists would perhaps seem superfluous to some," wryly suggested the Dominican Thomas Aquinas in his *Summa contra Gentiles* (*Summary Against Unbelievers*) in 1259, "namely those who assert that it is self-evident that God exists." Specifically, he meant anyone still persuaded by what the monk Anselm had famously argued in his *Proslogion* from 1078 (when he was abbot of Bec and fifteen years before he was unexpectedly chosen as archbishop of Canterbury) and what modern philosophers since Emmanuel Kant call an "ontological argument."[46]

But what about Him existing was supposedly self-evident? Thomas listed five considerations. First, God exists by the very meaning of the term "God." Second, as something that cannot be thought to exist cannot be thought, and as nothing can be thought greater than God, therefore He exists by virtue of being thinkable and by the inability of thinking of anything greater than Him. Third, His existence is His essence, and therefore God exists because "the predicate is the same as the subject or it is included in the definition of the subject." Fourth, God exists as He is naturally known and cannot be known by any inquiry of reason. Fifth, because "that by which all other things are known must be known of itself," therefore God exists, as nothing can be known without knowing Him and so to know anything is to know Him.[47]

This was all lazy thinking to Thomas. Regrettably, "the foregoing opinion prospers." His explanation for such misguided notions was similar to how his fellow Dominicans as inquisitors explained heretical ideas. "Custom, especially that which dates from childhood, takes on the force of nature and as a result the things with which the mind has been imbued from childhood take such firm root that it is as if they were naturally known of themselves." Consequently, these individuals as adults were unable to distinguish what was self-evident as such and what was self-evident for them. "Simply speaking, God exists is self-evident since what God is, is His existence."[48]

Thomas systematically dismisses the five considerations he viewed as affirming this common opinion about the self-evident existence of God. First, it was trivial and unnecessary that God be known to exist upon knowing that the name "God" required that nothing greater can be thought. "Even if everyone granted that the name 'God' means that than which nothing greater can be thought, it is not necessary that that than which nothing greater can be thought should exist in reality." Second, it was therefore not foolish to deny the existence of God, for such denial had nothing to do with His perfection and everything to do with the imperfection of human intellect, "which cannot intuit Him in Himself but can know Him only through His effects." Third, even if we cannot see His essence, we know of His existence by His effects in the world. Fourth, humans naturally knew God in the way they naturally desired Him in the way they naturally desired happiness, "which is a kind of likeness of the divine goodness." Fundamentally, it was not necessary that God Himself be naturally known, just "a likeness of Him." And it was from His likeness, discovered in His effects, such as men and women imitating Him, "that we come to knowledge of God through reasoning." Fifth, knowledge existed outside of knowing Him, "because all knowledge is caused in us by Him." Ultimately, by dismissing such popular and slipshod arguments, Thomas wanted to show "that it is not idle to try to prove that God exists."[49]

Thomas proved the existence of God by relying upon the "Philosopher," that is, Aristotle. The proof involved motion. "Whatever is moved is moved by another. It is evident to sense that something is moved, for example, the sun. Therefore it is moved by some other mover. And either that mover is moved or not." If the mover is not moving in this distinctly Ptolemaic universe, then there is something moving that is immobile. *Et hoc dicimus Deum*—"and this we call God." Of course, if the mover is moving, then there is another mover that in turn is being moved by another mover, which in turn ... but Aristotle had shown that there cannot be an infinite regress in causes and effects. "Therefore we must hold that there is some immobile mover." *Et hoc dicimus Deum*. After proving God's existence in quick and elegant fashion, Thomas then proceeded to lay out why he and the Philosopher might be wrong in smart if excruciating detail before reasserting in equally sophisticated and hairsplitting thoroughness why he and the Philosopher had been right all along. "Therefore it must be said that the separate prime mover is completely immobile." *Et hoc dicimus Deum*.[50]

Thomas epitomizes what was so brilliant and absurd about medieval Scholasticism: a cleverness and extravagance in thought that were derived from a deep and profound reading of Aristotle. He was not alone in being inspired by the Philosopher in the thirteenth century. Abelard had been a century earlier, though his knowledge was based upon poor translations, summaries by earlier scholars, and his own astute talent for imagining what he thought Aristotle might have argued. By the early decades of the thirteenth century the translation of the Philosopher had quickened immensely, mostly with translations from Arabic, although by the middle decades all translations were from the Greek, such as the *Politics* and the *Poetics*, which had never previously been translated.

There were also Latin translations of what Muslim and Jewish scholars had written on Aristotle. The most influential were the eleventh-century Persian polymath Ibn Sina, or Avicenna as he was known in Latin Christendom, who had actually outlined an ontological argument that was similar to Anselm's and which Thomas thought much smarter and so more mischievous by being so much more persuasive; Solomon Ibn Gabirol, or Avicebron, an eleventh-century Andalusian Jewish Aristotelian who wrote in Arabic; and the twelfth-century Andalusian Ibn Rushd, or Averroës, who praised Aristotle as approaching "very near to the highest dignity humanity can attain." A telling example of this translating fever was Robert Grosseteste, the first chancellor of the university of Oxford, who after becoming bishop of Lincoln in 1235 learned Greek in his sixties and translated many Aristotelian works, most importantly the *Nicomachean Ethics* around 1246.[51]

Scholasticism was the intellectual equivalent of what Gothic art and architecture managed to do in stone, colored glass, paint, and precious metal. In the way that Gothic art seems to push further and further into the unforeseen intricacies of space and light, in the way that a cathedral is both universally massive and delicately precise, encompassing the world but always reaching out to heaven, so the exquisite manner in which the infinite is always suggested in the finite, like the unimaginability and untouchability of God being seen and felt in the stained light of a Gothic window.

Thomas had entered Benedict's monastery at Monte Cassino when he was five and, rather than pursuing a grand ecclesiastical career culminating in an abbacy or bishopric, as his noble family from Aquino had hoped, he became a poor Dominican in 1244, when he was twenty. (His family was so angered by this decision that they kidnapped him and locked him up in a castle for a year as dissuasion.) He went on to study in Paris and in Cologne with the gifted Dominican Aristotelian Albertus Magnus. In 1256 he was appointed the first Dominican regent master or chaired professor in the university of Paris. The equally talented Bonaventure (miraculously healed when gravely ill at ten by the prayers of Francis of Assisi) held the complementary Franciscan professorship. These two professorial chairs were instituted by Louis IX, or rather he pressured the pope and university masters into establishing them, after more than a decade of strife (often involving bloody Left Bank street fights) between mendicant and secular scholars about whether the former should be allowed to teach. As more than 10 percent of all university students throughout Latin Christendom were mendicants by now, such antipathy by the Parisian dons to Dominican and Franciscan professors was just petty insecurity masquerading as academic integrity.

Thomas resigned as regent master and returned to Italy to teach in various Dominican houses in 1259. Nine years later he was called back to the professorship in Paris. He once again left for Italy in 1272. He was unwell. A chubby man all his life, he dramatically lost weight. What had once been a charming tendency to absentmindedness was now an alarming stillness for hours each day. He collapsed in spiritual ecstasy during a mass in Rome in late September 1273. "I cannot do any more," he supposedly said afterward. "Everything I have written seems to me straw in comparison with what I have seen." He stopped writing his *Summa theologica* (*Summary of Theology*), his other great work apart from the *Summa contra Gentiles*. Thomas died six months later, soon after hitting his head on a tree branch while traveling to the Second Council of Lyon.[52]

What Aristotle provided for Thomas and so many other Latin Christian intellectuals were methods for grasping the divine truth of God by the logical processes of human thought. The Aristotelian emphasis on dialectical inquiry, empirical observation, and the systematic collection and classification of evidence, while hardly unknown before the thirteenth century, was now adopted and adapted as the "scientific" scaffolding by which an individual might think out the contours of the universe. It helped that Aristotle had written so much and on so many topics, from metaphysics to politics to poetry to biology, consistently demonstrating the astonishing applicability of his methodology. The mystical vagueness and beauty of Neoplatonism never completely lost its appeal for intellectuals, even for Thomas, but the Aristotelian insistence upon methodically contemplating the temporal world in all its sensate complexity as the way to truth was now more persuasive.

The methods of the Philosopher were surprisingly compatible with the confessional culture of the late medieval West. The intricacies of cause and effect in an individual life were potentially limitless in their temporal permutations. Paradoxically, this afforded men and women free will in how they lived their lives, while at the same time stressing that God as the immobile mover set in motion everything they did or thought and would do and think. Aristotle's methods also confirmed for intellectuals like Thomas that thinking itself was a form of *imitatio Christi*. Of course, he stressed that even the most talented thinker with a copy of the *Metaphysics* under his arm could never answer some sacred questions, and so revelation, or knowledge of Him through His grace, was still important. Such statements often read like lip service to what he wished he believed rather than what he actually did believe—until he collapsed in that mystical stupor in Rome. Except when Thomas said that everything he had written was like straw in comparison to what was revealed to him—and it should be noted we only have a thirdhand report of him saying this—he never stopped reading Aristotle or even writing before he died, although he never added another word to his *Summa theologica*.

In March 1277, Étienne Templier, the bishop of Paris, issued a condemnation of 219 theological and philosophical propositions supposedly argued by university faculty from their reading of Aristotle (and, for a few scholars, what they had read in Averroës). Some of what Thomas had taught and written was condemned. Étienne stressed that despite what some professors had been saying for the last two decades, "God's absolute power" meant He could do whatever He pleased and not what the Philosopher allowed Him to do. The condemnation was chilling in its censoriousness, even if the propositions were incoherent, slanderous, contradictory, and mostly misunderstood what they attacked—basically, the very opposite of Aristotelian logic.[53]

8 God Opposes the Crusades

In October 1273, Humbert de Romans, the former master general of the Dominicans, finished an Aristotelian treatise, *Short Work in Three Parts* (*Opusculum tripartitum*), in which he defended the crusades against Saracens, attacked heresy, suggested options for the reunification of Latin and Greek

Christians, fretted that there were too many men and women pretending to be mendicants, and generally offered remedies for what he diagnosed as the aliments of Christendom. He had written it in response to an appeal from Pope Gregory X for advice on what should be discussed at the Second Council of Lyon in May 1274. Thomas Aquinas was bringing to the council a short work he had written a decade earlier, *Against the Errors of the Greeks* (*Contra errores Graecorum*), which, despite its title, was about what he thought Latin intellectuals had misunderstood about the theology of the Greeks.[54]

Humbert's defense of crusading is the first and longest part of his *Short Work*. It was important to him. He listed seven kinds of men and their arguments opposing martial pilgrimages against the Saracens.

The first kind say that Christians should not shed blood, "even of wicked infidels." Nonsense. "For who is so stupid as to dare to say that, were the infidels or evil men to desire to kill every Christian and to wipe out the worship of Christ in the world, one ought not to resist them?"

The second kind of men say that "while one ought not to spare Saracen blood, one must, however, be sparing of Christian blood and deaths." More nonsense. "The purpose of Christianity is not to populate the earth but to populate heaven! Why should one worry if the number of Christians is lessened in the world by deaths endured for God? By this kind of death people make their way to heaven who perhaps would never reach it by another road."[55]

The third kind of men say that Saracens always have the advantage of fighting on lands they know. Fair enough; but the advantages of their "human wisdom" will inevitably succumb to the "divine wisdom" of God.

The fourth kind of men say that while Christians should defend themselves if attacked by Saracens, why invade their lands if they leave us in peace? "I would reply that the Saracens are so hostile to Christians that they do not spare them whenever they have a chance of defeating them." In any event, all Saracen realms had once belonged to Christians before Muhammad, so what was once owned should be regained.[56]

The fifth kind of men say that "if we ought to rid the world of the Saracens, why do we not do the same to the Jews?" Or idolators? Or Tartars? Or other infidels? "I would reply that, as far as the Jews are concerned, it has been prophesied that in the end the remnant of them will be converted," and so Jews should be tolerated and not harmed. Indeed, Saracens living within Christendom should be shown leniency too, as they might convert.

"Since it had been prophesied that every tongue shall serve the Lord Jesus Christ," idolators, Tartars, and infidels will eventually convert, and so Christians do not seek their extermination when fighting them. Saracens outside Christendom will never be Christian and so must be eradicated.

The sixth kind of men say, why attack them if they will not convert? Because it sows fear in enemies like the Tartars—and one never knows whether the faith of some Saracens in Muhammad might be shaken.[57]

Finally, the seventh and loudest kind of men say that it appears that God disagrees with crusading against Saracens, as He has allowed and continues to allow so many misfortunes to happen to Christians signed with His cross. Why did God allow Saladin to seize in just one stroke nearly all of the Promised Land, won with so much Christian blood in 1099? Why did God allow Louis IX to fail in two mighty crusades (now known as the Seventh and Eighth)? Indeed, these men say, God did not just let the French king fail miserably twice; He let him be captured by the Egyptians during his first pilgrimage in 1250 and then die of dysentery in Tunis during his second in 1270. Why does God allow these and other catastrophes if the crusades against the Saracens were pleasing to Him? "I would reply that it should be said that people who speak like this do not understand at all well how God acts." When misfortunes fall upon some people, rather than it being a sign of His displeasure with them, it is the reverse, "since in this world calamities befall more often those who do good than those who do evil." And some misfortunes suffered by the good while on crusade were because of their sins. King Louis knew this was why God let him be captured by the Egyptians, for afterward he boasted that on the Day of Judgment he would proudly tell Him that he was maltreated for the sake of all Christians and, as his maltreatment was like what Christ had suffered, for His sake too. Adversity does not destroy good men; it makes them stronger and more holy.[58]

Humbert blamed the widespread criticism of crusading, and the resulting lack of enthusiasm for holy war, on the incompetence of clerical preachers and, much more disturbing for him, the outright hostility of many bishops to the whole enterprise. He also blamed knights for forgetting their sacred purpose as fighters for the Church. Although Humbert somewhat overstated the low regard in which the crusades were held by most Latin Christians in the late thirteenth century—exaggeration was and is a rhetorical feature of the Aristotelian method—the cachet of being signed with the cross was unquestionably diminished by everything his seven kinds of men opined.[59]

Except, of course, in the Iberian peninsula, where the ongoing holy wars of Christians against Muslims had been successful, often spectacularly so, since the beginning of the thirteenth century. On Monday, July 16, 1212, the grand army of the Almohad caliph Muhammad al-Nasir was crushed by a Christian coalition led by Alfonso VIII, king of Castile, on the Andalusian plain of al-'Iqab or Las Navas de Tolosa. Although the Muslim cities of Córdoba, Granada, and Jaen were not captured by Alfonso after the battle, the Almohad caliphate in al-Andalus was broken. Muhammad was soon assassinated in Marrakesh by one of his own men, and his young son, Yusuf al-Mustansir, died within a few years of becoming caliph. The following Almohad civil war, in which Castilian and Portuguese knights zealously involved themselves, merely confirmed that the time of Muslim al-Andalus was coming to an end. What is now known as the Reconquista, the Christian reconquest of the Iberian peninsula, was all but over after Las Navas de Tolosa, even if the last campaign would not be for another two and a half centuries.[60] (The term *reconquista* was actually first used by Spanish loyalists in their war against the French usurper Joseph Bonaparte when his brother, Emperor Napoleon I, made him king of Spain in 1808. The expulsion of the French was a second *reconquista*, like the medieval holy war.)

Arnau Amalric, the abbot of Cîteaux and the papal legate leading the Albigensian crusade at Béziers, was present at Las Navas de Tolosa, writing afterward that the victory was a triumph against "the three plagues of humanity and enemies of His Holy Church; namely, schismatics from the East, heretics from the West, and Saracens from the South." As far as he was concerned, the slaughter of Muslims in Spain, heretics in the Biterrois, and Greek Christian schismatics in Constantinople were all part of the same great crusade. Sixty years later, Humbert still viewed Saracens and heretics as enemies of the Church, whereas he was not so sure about Greek schismatics.[61]

Humbert's distinction between heretics and schismatics was crucial for him. Arnau was not known for his fine distinctions, even apocryphally; nevertheless, most Latin Christian intellectuals used "heretic" and "schismatic" interchangeably in the twelfth and early thirteenth centuries. Gratian, for all his legal precision, mostly blurred the difference, except at one point in his *Decretum* he did repeat Jerome's contrast between "heresy" as the perversion of dogma and "schism" as episcopal dissent from the Church. This was Humbert's opinion about the Greeks as schismatics—they were only institutionally and liturgically separated and so reconcilable to the Church. He blamed both Latins and Greeks for the split in Christianity. His remedies for reunion included more schools and universities teaching Greek, a scholarly exchange program, and the pope allowing the patriarch of Constantinople the courtesy of assuming equality with him (even if it was not true). Humbert's other suggestion for reunification was that there should be a Latin emperor again in the East.[62]

Twelve years earlier, Michael VIII Palaiologos had entered Constantinople as the restored Greek emperor in August 1261. A small contingent of his armed followers had previously snuck into the city while the Frankish garrison was absent. The Latin Empire founded in the aftermath of the Fourth Crusade ended that easily. Michael had been the emperor of Nicaea, an East Roman rump state established by Greek aristocrats fleeing the crusaders in 1204. There were two other Greek remnant states, known as the Empire of Trebizond and the Despotate of Epirus. Oddly enough, Michael was sympathetic to reconciling with the Roman Church. Most Greek Christians were adamantly opposed to such an accord. During the interregnum of the Latin Empire the importance of the emperor and Constantinople had waned for many East Romans in exile. Of course, the recovery of the city was always the dream, but after five decades it was no longer fundamental in defining Byzantine identity. Greek Christianity and Hellenic tradition were now the primary components in shaping a common culture rather than the imperial Roman past. Michael's attempts at asserting his authority like that of past emperors were rebuffed and his talk of compromise with Rome was denounced as betrayal. By the end of the thirteenth century, the largely ruined and empty Constantinople was more meaningful for Latin Christians in the West than for Byzantines in the East.[63]

Humbert ended his *Short Work* with recommendations for reforming Christendom. He argued that there were too many feast days, interfering with the ability of ordinary Christians to make a living. Only prostitutes, so he heard, profited from this surfeit of holidays. What really bothered him were the "dishonest and infamous persons" working as the hirelings of bishops who went around selling indulgences and relics by the cartload to naive buyers. How could the pope allow such scams? With all this corruption in Christendom, Humbert concluded, it was little wonder that so many Latin Christians thought God opposed the crusades against Saracens.[64]

Two decades later, such opinions were dramatically confirmed when the last crusader city, Acre, was captured by the Mamluk sultan al-Ashraf

Khalil in May 1291. "The nation of the cross has fallen," sang an anonymous Egyptian poet, "the religion of the chosen Arab has triumphed!"[65]

9 They Deserve to Be Killed, Just as They Killed Him!

"Listen, all you peoples, to the shame and the disgrace which these Jews committed on our Savior Jesus, in that, for no crime of His, they afflicted Him and killed Him and hanged Him and tortured Him," declaimed the Dominican and Jewish convert Paul Chrétien (formerly Saul of Montpellier) to a large audience of Jews, clergy, and ordinary Christians while debating with the rabbis of Paris in 1273. "They deserve to be killed, just as they killed Him!"

Paul supported his savage opinion in good Aristotelian fashion with five proofs against Judaism. First, the Messiah "has already come and departed." Second, He was born of a virgin. Third, He was "divine and assumed human flesh." Fourth, He suffered death for the redemption of all humanity. Fifth, "He annulled all of the law of Moses and despised anyone who observed it." Paul quoted from the Mishnah, the Talmud, *halakhot* (rabbinic law), and *haggadot* (rabbinic lore) to show that the Jews had always known that Christ was the Messiah and had deliberately turned away from Him as heretics. "I wish to prove to you," he said to the Parisian Jews with sadistic reasonableness, "that you are without a faith, a people called Bougres, heretics, worthy of being burned." (Bougres was another northern French name for the Albigensians.) A decade earlier he had made similar arguments in a disputation with Rabbi Moses ben Nahman (Nachmanides) in Barcelona. In Paris it was Rabbi Abraham ben Samuel arguing with Paul, at first bravely and wittily, but once the Dominican invoked the Crucifixion the rabbi was, according to an anonymous Hebrew chronicler, "very much afraid to speak of the slaying of Jesus because this revealed his [Paul's] intention to exterminate all of the Jews."[66]

In 1236 another French Jewish convert to Christianity, Nicholas Donin, had presented a short treatise to Pope Gregory IX listing thirty-five accusations against the Talmud. He alleged that Jews believed the Talmud was given to them by God; that it was preserved for a long time without being written; that it was longer than the Bible when written out; that it was more important than the Bible, even forbidding Jewish children from reading the latter; that it reviled Jesus and Mary; and that it promoted hatred of Christianity. Three years later the pope sent letters to archbishops and princes throughout Latin Christendom repeating these allegations and ordering that all copies of the Talmud were to be confiscated. In March 1240 the books were seized throughout France. Soon afterward a trial regarding the contents and meaning of the Talmud was conducted in Paris. Jewish intellectuals, especially Rabbi Yehiel ben Joseph and Rabbi Judah ben David, were interrogated in two inquiries modeled on the new inquisitions into heretical depravity.

The more official investigation involved Dominicans, Franciscans, and scholars from the university of Paris. The other examination was pursued by Nicholas Donin himself. Rabbi Yehiel ben Joseph was particularly clever at answering his accusers, but it was all to no avail. The Talmud was judged "full of errors." It misled the Jews spiritually and literally, blocking them from understanding their own religion and ultimately from converting to Christianity. It was a work of heresy. Twenty-four cartloads of the Talmud were incinerated in a great bonfire in Paris in 1242. Rabbi Meir ben Baruch of Rothenburg, who witnessed the book burning as a student, later lamented in a poem:

> How were you given over to a consuming fire?
> How were you devoured by man-made flames
> and the oppressors not scathed by your coals?
> How long, O lovely one, will you lie quietly,
> While my young ones bear your shame.[67]

Four decades later, Paul Chrétien, while still enthusiastic about incinerating the Talmud, wanted to burn people too. Humbert de Romans, even as he championed the extermination of heretics and Saracens, opposed such savagery toward the Jews. His attitude regarding the Jews was more widely held than is often realized. Nevertheless, by the end of the thirteenth century most Latin Christians either stridently agreed with or were easily persuaded by the demagoguery of men like Paul. Jews were denounced—by mendicants and kings alike—as heretics deliberately turning away from the revelation of Christ. They had seen and were still seeing His wonders, accused Paul, "but they still do not confess their sins." They had known He was the Messiah even before His Crucifixion. They had even recorded knowing it in the Talmud. They refused in their willful blindness to admit what they had always known about Him.[68]

These accusations swiftly mutated into stories where Jews, in a mix of self-loathing, archaic use of the ordeal, Aristotelian empiricism, and Crucifixion reenactment, secretly "tested" the Host during Easter. Knife, hammer, nails, spear, fire, and boiling water were the testing tools. The Host as the body of Christ, while indestructible, sometimes bled and occasionally screamed in pain. The first such desecration supposedly happened in Paris in 1290—"I shall know whether the insane things that Christians prattle about are true," says the dastardly Jew to himself in one version of the story—but soon these anti-Jewish fictions were more common in German-speaking lands such as Franconia, Austria, and Bohemia. The Jews now apparently acted out their own clandestine versions of the Passion during Holy Week.[69]

In 1290, Edward I, king of England, expelled all the Jews from his realm. Thirteen years later the French king, Philip IV, known as "the Fair" or "the Pretty," had all the Jews in his kingdom, roughly one hundred thousand, arrested in a single day during the summer. After a brief imprisonment, during which royal officials ransacked synagogues and town houses, he banished every Jewish man, woman, and child from France. Both kings were convinced that the Jews were a pestilence within their kingdoms and Christendom. Philip personally believed the stories of Host desecration. Both kings justified what they were doing as holy acts of purification and argued that by expelling the Jews they were at once casting out the enemies of Christ and imitating Him. One French Jew sang of his banishment and exile in a poem:

> My enemy said to me yesterday:
> I will destroy the country of your dwelling,
> I will take away all that your ancestors have amassed.
> I will pursue
> I will overtake
> I will divide
> I will scatter the promise of God.[70]

10 The Romance of the Rose

Genius, flapping his wings more swiftly than the wind, swoops down into the army of the God of Love and Venus, encamped outside a beautiful high-walled rose garden. Lady Nature, God's high servant and the smith of humanity, sent him as her confessor to read a sermon to the troops.

The God of Love invests the winged envoy as a bishop in clothes more limpid than glass.

"By the authority of Nature, custodian of the whole world, vicar and constable of the Eternal Emperor," announces Genius as he unrolls the parchment upon which his text is written. Venus giggles with excitement. The barons and knights nudge and wink at each other.

"Let all disloyal renegades, great or humble, who scorn those works by which Nature is maintained, be excommunicated and ruthlessly condemned." Of course, says Genius, any man making a "good confession" that he uses the tools given him by Nature as best he can as a true lover will wear a floral crown in paradise.

Unfortunately, Genius sighs, too many treasonous men have stopped using their styli on wax tablets, their hammers on anvils, or their sharp-edged plows on fields. "If no one drives the plowshares into the fallow fields, they will remain fallow." Humanity will come to an end if these tools are neglected for sixty years.

So why, wonders Genius, does God want chastity for some men and women? "If anyone wishes to reply, let him do so, I know no more about it." And what of two hammers hammering without an anvil? Such men are reading Nature's rules back to front. May they be excommunicated and condemned to hell! "May the hammers inside them be torn out!" What is to be done when too many men let their tools go rusty for the sake of chastity or refuse to use them as Nature intended? "Plow barons!" Genius exhorts his audience. "Plow for God's sake!"[71]

Genius implores the barons and knights to learn his sermon by heart. "Fair sirs, my Lady needs preachers for her law, to denounce those sinners who transgress her rules." He promises that all who preach and practice the laws of Nature will eventually enter the "fair and verdant park where the Virgin's Son, the white-fleeced lamb, brings the sheep with Him, leaping ahead over the grass."

In this verdant and eternal park the sweet-smelling flowers are indestructible. There is no night there either, nor twilight, nor dawn, "for evening is one with morning and the morning resembles the evening." The day exists as an eternal moment. "There is neither future nor past for, if I understand the truth correctly, all three tenses are present and the day is ordered by the present."

Genius abruptly denounces anyone in his audience who thinks that the rose garden that they will soon assail as knights of the God of Love is like the eternal park of the white-fleeced lamb. "For God's sake, my lords, take care! The truth is that the things in the garden are trumpery toys." You have been told that there is a spring in the rose garden with water brighter than pure silver. Lies! "In fact, it is so ugly and muddy that anyone who hangs his head over in order to look at himself will be unable to see a thing. Everyone goes wild with anguish because he cannot recognize himself." Narcissus died beside this spring.

In the white-fleeced lamb's park, though, there is an everlasting spring coursing through three channels before becoming one, whose water, clear and delicious, faithfully reflects your face and lets you understand yourself. "In God's name, my lords, what do you think of the park and garden together?" You must judge according to Reason. You must judge which is fiction and which is truth.

"But what business have I chattering on?" And Genius vanishes, leaving innuendo and ambiguity in his wake.

The God of Love and Venus, hearing only what they wanted to hear, spread news of the sermon throughout the world, "so that no lady could protect herself from it."[72]

"Amen, Amen, fiat, fiat," cheer the barons and knights in the afterglow of what they think Genius has told them to do. "To arms! No more delay! If we understand the verdict correctly, our enemies are quite discomfited!" Venus leads them in assaulting the rose garden. She loosens invisible fiery arrows on the outer fortifications constructed by Jealousy, setting them ablaze.

Rebuff, Fear, and Shame cry out, "Treason, treason! Alas, alas! We are all dead! Let us flee the country!" Courtesy races into the flames to free her son, Fair Welcome, long imprisoned in a tower by Jealousy. She tells him to help a young man standing amidst the battle, whose desire for the rose in the garden, against the advice of Reason, is the cause of this great war. "Love conquers all," she quotes Virgil.

"I will give it up to him most willingly," says a smiling Fair Welcome.

"I thanked him a hundred thousand times," says the young man. He is as happy as a pilgrim about to fulfill his pilgrimage, "whose staff was so stiff and strong that it needed no ferrule." Nature forges his weapons, even giving him a bag with two hammers just in case one fails.

The young man soon finds a small opening in the inner garden wall, forcing his way in, eager to pluck the rosebud. Fair Welcome begs him in God's name to do nothing violent. "And so I won my bright red rose. Then it was day and I awoke." It was all a dream.[73]

This dream of innuendo, double entendres, less-than-subtle dirty jokes, surprisingly nuanced allegory, rape fantasy, misogyny, and chronic ambivalence about what it all really symbolized was *The Romance of the Rose* (*Le roman de la rose*), an immensely long poem in Old French by two authors writing almost half a century apart: Guillaume de Lorris composed the first four thousand lines around 1230, while Jean de Meun added another seventeen thousand before 1278. Nothing is known of Guillaume. Jean, although almost as enigmatic, wrote other surviving vernacular poems and prose, even translating Boethius' *Consolation of Philosophy* and the letters of Abelard and Heloise. (Genius, clearly with Abelard in mind, goes off on a bizarre tangent about castration in his sermon.)

Guillaume framed *The Romance of the Rose* as a confession in verse of a dream the young man had had one night five years earlier, when he was aged twenty. Indeed, within the dream the young man even names the song of his dream as *The Romance of the Rose*. Jean further accentuated this self-awareness within the poem by having the dreamer sing about the changing of the poets singing of him singing of his dream. He acknowledged the decades between himself and Guillaume as authors, but skipped over the jump in time as all part of the young man's dream. What he could not hide was that his attitude toward love was more ambiguous, satiric, and bitter than Guillaume's. Even his allusive salaciousness often sounds more like a parody of bawdy humor, a conscious mockery of those who would enjoy such *wink wink nudge nudge* amusement.

Did these attitudes lead him to a more scathing view of women? Did the quest for rosebuds turn men away from the park of the white-fleeced lamb? Or was he suggesting the opposite? Is it better to follow Nature or go against her? Is plowing, so to speak, a way of imitating Christ or not? And was he ridiculing knights, holy wars, and courtly love? Or the opposite? Jean de Meun's verses were knowingly like an Aristotelian *summa* in which he sang out the contours of the universe one double entendre at a time. Such crude, cruel, and complex humor was why *The Romance of the Rose* quickly became the most popular and controversial song throughout Latin Christendom.

11 The End of the Templars

On Tuesday, October 24, 1307, Jacques de Molay, grand master of the Templars, was interrogated in Paris by the Dominican inquisitor Guillaume de Paris. "He swore on the holy Gospels of Christ which were placed before him and physically touched by him to tell the full, whole, and complete truth about himself and others."

Guillaume questioned Jacques about his reception into the Order of the Temple forty-two years earlier in Beaune. The Templar recalled that in the presence of several brother knights he was ordered to deny Christ while a bronze cross with an image of His Crucifixion was held in front of him. "Against my will I did this." He was ordered to spit on this image of Him. "I spat on the ground." "How many times?" quizzed Guillaume. "Only once," replied Jacques, "I remember this clearly."

Guillaume then asked if, after Jacques had vowed chastity, anything was said about sexual practices with his brother knights. "He said on oath that this was not the case and that he had never done this." Guillaume wanted to know if all brother knights of the order were received this way. Jacques believed that there was no difference between his experience as a young man in his twenties and that of other youthful Templars in 1265. He confessed that over the years he had commanded other brother knights to receive new members into the order in the same way. "My intention was that they should do to them what had been done to me."

Guillaume ended his interrogation for now. Jacques was asked if had told any lies or omitted any facts in his deposition because of threat, fear of torture, imprisonment, or any other reason. "I have not; indeed, I told the whole truth for the salvation of my soul."[74]

Two days later, Jean de Tour, Templar and treasurer of the order in Paris, was questioned by Guillaume. He said that thirty-two years earlier, when he was about twenty-seven, his receptor into the order, coincidentally also named Jean de Tour, showed him a cross with an image of the crucified Christ and asked whether he believed in Him. "I replied that I did." He was then ordered to deny Christ, which he did once, and spit on the cross, which also did once. He was then kissed three times by his receptor: "firstly on the base of the spine of the back, secondly on the navel, and thirdly on the mouth." Guillaume asked Jean about his vow of chastity. "I was prohibited from knowing women, but if any natural heat should move me, I could unite myself with my brothers, and similarly I should suffer this from them." Nevertheless, he swore that he had never done such things or seen anyone else do them. Guillaume again wanted to know if all Templars were received this way into the Order. "Yes," replied Jean.

The inquisitor's final question was about whether the witness had ever seen "a certain head depicted on a board." "Yes," said Jean, but only once, and only in one particular Templar preceptory, where, with several other brother knights, he had "adored" it. The witness, fearing neither torture nor prison, swore that he had told no lies in his deposition; "on the contrary, he had presented the pure and full truth."[75]

Two weeks earlier, on Friday, October 13, all members of the order in France had been suddenly arrested as heretics by officials of Philip the Fair. Only the previous day, Jacques de Molay, having traveled from Cyprus, had participated in the funeral of the king's sister-in-law in Notre Dame cathedral. Apart from his and Jean de Tour's confession to Guillaume de Paris, another 132 Templars confessed almost word for word the same heretical depravities to the inquisitor between October and November. Only four brother knights denied the accusations. Pope Clement V, while initially opposing what he viewed as blatantly illegal actions by the French crown, soon accepted that perhaps there was some truth in the allegations. On Wednesday, November 22, he ordered the general arrest and investigation of all Templars throughout Latin Christendom. The kings of England and Aragon thought the accusations against the Templars were dubious, to say the least; nevertheless, they instituted haphazard inquiries. Clement was himself French, mostly in thrall to Philip the Fair, and the first pope of seven in a row residing in the "Babylonian captivity" of Avignon rather than Rome. Yet, for all his cravenness, he paused the investigations into the order in early 1308. Then in July of that year he established two inquisitorial proceedings, one in which bishops examined individuals within their dioceses, with the second a papal commission in Paris investigating the whole order.

The commission ended after three years, whereas the diocesan examinations (and occasional executions by fire) were still continuing. On Wednesday, March 22, 1312, Clement abolished the order after judging that too many Templars had turned against Christ by succumbing to apostasy, idolatry, sodomy, and various other heresies. Two months later he transferred all property of the Temple to the Hospitallers. On Monday, March 18,

1314, Jacques de Molay, after bravely but belatedly renouncing the accusations against himself and the Order, was burned as a relapsed heretic on the Île-des-Javiaux in the middle of Paris.[76]

The debate about the truthfulness of the accusations against the order of the Temple has been ongoing since the first lightning arrests in 1307. There has always been the question of whether Philip the Fair even believed his own allegations justifying his actions. If he did not, then the argument usually goes that he wanted to destroy the Temple simply to get their wealth and that accusing them of heresy was a convenient and largely irrefutable indictment once made. He certainly had financial problems, especially as he had debased the silver content of the *gros tournois* (the main French currency) for years, and inflation was rampant. Moreover, he owed the Templars large sums of money, and so, like his expulsion of the Jews a year earlier, destroying them was a way of avoiding paying his debts. Yet, as with his casting out of the Jews, pecuniary reward and genuinely believing that the Templars were a pestilence within France and Christendom were more than compatible.

As to why and when Philip came to think that the brother knights were secretly heretics, that is harder to pinpoint. It seems to have been a decision, or really a revelation, that came upon him quite suddenly, perhaps no more than a month before the October arrests. The Templars had lost much of their rationale for existence after the fall of Acre in 1291, and, unlike the Hospitallers, they had never fully articulated a new vision for themselves and their *Rule*. Despite this quandary, they were still widely respected. Philip's accusations against them were a return to an older understanding of heresy in which those accused of it were unaware that they were so diseased. What was different in the early fourteenth century, though, was that sodomy, or any supposed sexual perversion, was in and of itself a form of heresy, rather than just being one more vice attributed to heretics. More than anything, it was the covert and unnatural sexuality of the Templars, as imagined by Philip, that was the heretical depravity corrupting Christendom.[77]

What is significant was how so many Templars themselves confessed to what they were accused of doing behind closed doors—unless, of course, they really did what they confessed to the inquisition and other tribunals. This is unlikely. The accusations themselves were resolutely unimaginative; prurient and blasphemous, certainly, but very much textbook *exempla* from inquisitorial manuals. An allegation of heresy was almost impossible to dismiss once an individual was accused of such depravity, so the only way of escaping serious punishment, let alone death, was by acknowledging the truth of the accusation and hoping for absolution. Many Templars therefore just acquiesced in shock and confusion.

For others it was the pain and threat of torture that persuaded them to confess their guilt. Moreover, the actual experience of being interrogated, especially more than once, and being asked to recall actions from decades earlier, as well as being told what they had done in the past even if they had no recollection of such acts, was effective in eliciting penitent confessions. It would be foolish to deny that some Templars sincerely came to believe that they and some of their brother knights were guilty of what they were accused of. Equally, just as the sincerity of Philip must be taken seriously, so must the conviction of Clement V in finally believing that the Templars as individuals, rather than the Temple as an institution, were poisoned with heresy.

12 Beatritiz Confesses

"What will I do if I become pregnant by you?" Beatritiz de Plannisoles asked Peire Clergue after she began a sexual relationship with him in 1299. "I shall be dishonored and lost!" He told her not to worry, as he had a special herb that stopped a woman from conceiving. "What is this herb?" she inquired doubtfully. "It isn't the one that cowherds put over a pot of milk in which they put rennet and it doesn't allow the milk to curdle as long as it's in the pot?" Peire said never you mind what kind of herb it was; all she had to know was that he had some and it was potent.

Peire's herb was wrapped inside a tiny linen bag, not much larger, thought Beatritiz, than "the joint of the little finger on my left hand." A long cord was attached to the bag, which, just before intercourse, he looped over her head and threaded between her breasts so that the herb dangled just above her vagina. "He always placed it so when he wanted to know me and the cord stayed around my neck until he was done." Sometimes, "if he wanted to know me two or more times during the same night, he asked me before he joined himself to me, where is the herb?" Beatritiz once asked if she could keep the herb. Peire angrily refused, saying that she "could then give herself to another man without becoming pregnant."[78]

Beatritiz was initially very reluctant to begin her liaison with Peire. She was young, noble, and recently widowed, whereas he was older, a peasant, and, moreover, her priest in the village of Montaillou, high in the Pyrenees. She was also the abused and unwilling mistress of his cousin, Raimon Pathau, who had raped her even before her husband died. Peire began his seduction—if sacrilegious groping can be called that—when Beatritiz was kneeling before him for confession during Lent and he suddenly kissed her, "saying that there was no woman in the world that he loved as much as me." She was so surprised, "I left without having confessed." He harassed her over Easter, dogging her doorstep. "I would rather give myself to four men than a single priest," she rebuked him, if for no other reason than she had heard that a woman who slept with a priest would never see the face of God. "You're an ignorant fool," he retorted. The sin was the same whether the man was a priest or not. In fact, it was worse if the man was her husband, because a wife mistakenly assumed sex within marriage was not a sin. "I asked him how he, who was a priest, could speak like that." Peire shrugged.[79]

Indeed, "speaking of marriage," Peire argued that a couple were married as soon as they promised themselves to each other, and that a church ceremony was just pomp and worldly glory. "A man and a woman could freely commit any sort of sin," he said, as long as in death they were received into the faith of the "good Christians," whom some people wrongfully called "heretics." (And whom some modern historians wrongfully call "Cathars.") This was when Beatritiz admitted to herself what she had suspected all along about Peire—that while he was not a "good Christian" himself, he was a believer in them and in the heresy they preached. Yet this realization, far from scaring her away, was what finally convinced her to wear his special herb five nights a week. By promising herself to him like a wife, it gave her the confidence to escape from Raimon Pathau, even if Peire, like an absolute bastard, at first suggested he and his cousin share her. Beatritiz stayed in this relationship for a year and a half until, wanting children and more property, she married another nobleman in another village lower down the mountain.[80]

Two decades later, Beatritiz talked about herself, Peire, his special herb, love, regret, aging, motherhood, angels falling to earth, heresy, and so much more over nine interrogations with the inquisitor Jacques Fournier,

Cistercian bishop of Pamiers, during August 1320. She had actually been summoned to appear before the inquisition in late July but, frightened of being burned as a heretic, had fled as far as the village of Mas-Saintes-Puelles in the Lauragais before being caught and dragged back to Pamiers by the bishop's serjeants.

Astonishingly, even before Beatritiz was questioned about the heresy of the "good Christians," she was suspected of being a sorceress on account of the jumble of extraordinary things discovered on her when she was apprehended: "two umbilical cords of infants found in her purse; linens stained with blood which seemed to be menstrual blood in a leather sack with rocket seed and slightly burned grains of incense"; a mirror and a small knife bundled in linen; a plant seed wrapped in muslin; a piece of dry bread; some formulas written on parchment; and a few pieces of linen. "Why do you possess these items?" asked Jacques.[81]

Beatritiz explained all of her things. "I have the cords of the male children of my daughters and I keep them because a Jewish woman, since baptized, had told me that if I carried them with me and I had a lawsuit, I would not lose." Now, the blood on the linens was from her daughter Philipa's first period because that same baptized Jew had once said that if her daughter's husband (or any man, really) drank this blood he would never look at another woman. "This is why a long time ago, when my daughter Philipa, who was young, had her first period, I looked her in the face and seeing that she was flushed, asked her what was wrong. She told me that she was losing blood through her vulva." Beatritiz, remembering the words of the baptized Jew, cut off a small piece of her daughter's underclothes stained with blood. Just to be sure, she gave Philipa another scrap of cloth to soak up more blood. She dried the linens with the intention of one day extracting the blood (by steeping in warm water) for her future son-in-law to drink. "Philipa was to marry this year and I had intended to give it to her fiancé to drink, but I thought that it would be better to wait until the marriage was consummated and that it should be Philipa herself who should give it to her husband to drink." Unfortunately, said Beatritiz, she was arrested before her daughter's wedding, "so I did not give it to him to drink."

Everything else had nothing to do with magic or evil spells. The grains of incense were left over from trying to help Philipa when she had a headache. The seeds were to cure Beatritiz's grandson (one of the umbilical cords was his) of epilepsy, but God had already healed him when his mother, her other daughter, Condors, took him to a church.[82]

"Have you cast any other evil spells, taught them, or learned them from anyone?" asked Jacques. "No," replied Beatritiz. Except possibly in the last few months a priest named Bartomieu Amilhac "had cast some sort of evil spell on me because I loved him so much and I wanted to be with him so much, even though when I met him my periods had stopped." Beatritiz was no older than forty, once again a widow, and surprised that sexual desire and love for this priest was overwhelming her, when, as a woman whose fertile years had ended, she should have moved beyond such longing. It just had to be sorcery.[83]

Beatritiz's confessions to Jacques Fournier are some of the most compelling autobiographical narratives ever spoken by a woman or man that have survived from the Middle Ages. Of course, her testimony was elicited under duress, and while she confessed in the vernacular, the translation and transcription of her words into Latin unavoidably modified (and still modifies) much of the immediacy of her stories about herself. Nevertheless, it would be wrong to assume that Beatritiz was not consciously trying to tell the history of her life in such a way that was at once truthful in the context of what she thought other people had already testified about her and what she hoped was redemptive in the eyes of Jacques and of God. She may have been illiterate, but her skill in crafting the memories of what she said and did as an individual existing within linear time was just as sophisticated as Abelard's two centuries earlier. After a century of confession to priests and most especially inquisitors, women like her had been taught how to think and talk about themselves as women.

More so than would be true of a man, Beatritiz's sexuality was tied to her identity as a woman, and so she spoke of it often, correctly assuming that this emphasized for Jacques just how "natural" and so inherently orthodox she was. She may not have narrated her life in exactly the same way outside the courtroom, but she most definitely did think of her life as an unbroken narrative moving forward through the years. She clearly thought confession was a form of penance in and of itself and that talking about herself was a way of imitating Christ. The confessional culture that had first developed amongst elite intellectuals at the beginning of the twelfth century had finally permeated into how ordinary people now understood themselves. This was a momentous shift in the history of the West.

As this confessional culture was now more or less ubiquitous throughout Latin Christendom, some individuals began loudly denouncing such an understanding of the self as oppressive and unnecessary. Peire, not surprisingly, was such a person. He once told Beatritiz that confession to priests was useless, as they only knew what you had done and thought once you told them, whereas God had known for eternity what you would one day do and think, so only He could absolve you. The "good Christians" had taught him about the futility of confession. They had a vision that was remarkably like the penitential culture between the seventh and eleventh centuries, especially in their assertion that Christ had never been a man who had once lived on earth from childhood to crucifixion, and so human existence was obviously not temporally linear either. "Why then do you hear confessions?" Beatritiz asked Peire. Why, if it was all pointless? "It was necessary for him and for other priests to do this, even though it meant nothing," she reported. "Otherwise," laughed Peire, "we'd lose our revenues and no one would give us anything."[84]

On Sunday, March 8, 1321, Beatritiz, unwell, stood in the cemetery of Sant-Johan-Martyr in Pamiers as Jacques Fournier sentenced her to death for the crimes of heresy and sorcery. Four months later the sentence was commuted to wearing two yellow crosses for life.

13 Beatrice Smiles

> Midway along the journey of our life
> I awoke to find myself in a dark wood,
> for I had wandered off from the straight path.

Dante Alighieri the Pilgrim famously begins his journey through hell, purgatory, and heaven in the first of three canticles (or books)—*Inferno, Purgatorio, Paradiso*—of the *Comedy* (*Commedia*) composed by Dante Alighieri the poet. It is Good Friday, 1300, and the Pilgrim is at the bottom of a mountain whose high shoulders are shawled in soft morning light. As he climbs to the summit his fear and confusion dissipate until, suddenly, a leopard, a lion, and a she-wolf block his way. This last animal, "slowly, step by step, forced me back to where the sun is mute."

As the Pilgrim stumbles backward into the murky wilderness, what looks like a man is coming toward him. "Is it a shade or a man I see?" "No, not a man," replies the figure. "No, not now"—though once, under the emperor Augustus, "I was a poet."

"Are you Virgil?" cries the Pilgrim.

"I was in Limbo," replies the pagan poet, when Beatrice, beatific and beautiful, stepped out of the nothingness, her scintillating green eyes shining bright. "I begged her to command me." She told him that the Virgin in heaven, pitying the Pilgrim, had asked Lucia, "the spirit of Grace," to tell her to order him to rescue that frightened man from the deep river of bad dreams. "To disobey? Impossible."

Virgil comforts the Pilgrim by saying that while the three beasts are stopping their ascent up the mountain, "three women loved in heaven do their best to make you loved there too." He will guide him to that eternal place of love by another way. "Let us start, for both our wills, joined now, are one," says the Pilgrim to Virgil, calling the poet his guide, master, and teacher. "On the high, hard road, I followed, and he led."

The Pilgrim and Virgil approach the antechamber of hell, upon whose gate is written:

> I am the way into the doleful city,
> I am the way into eternal grief,
> I am the way to a forsaken people.
> My Creator, moved by justice, lies above;
> Through Him, the holy power, I was made—
> Made by the Highest Wisdom and First Love . . .
> Abandon every hope, all who enter.

The living soul hesitates, but his spectral guide rebukes him: "Here you must renounce your slightest doubt. And kill your every weakness."

Inside the stifling antechamber a cacophony of shrieks and lamentations engulfs them as naked shades who did nothing good nor bad in life are stung again and again by wasps. Outside beneath a starless sky the river Acheron morosely encircles hell. "And you, living soul, you over there, get away from all these people who are dead," angrily shouts Charon the white-haired boatman to the Pilgrim. "Another way, by other ports, not here!"

"Charon, never fear," replies Virgil calmly, telling him that this living soul has permission to cross the river. The boatman, his furious eyes glowing like hot coals, ferries them over the dark water, grumbling all the way. Dante the poet in an aside says this memory still makes him sweat. Dante the Pilgrim swoons as a gust of blood-hued and tear-drenched wind knocks him unconscious.

The Pilgrim awakens at the edge of Limbo, the first circle of hell. "Now, let us go down into the sightless well," says Virgil, his cheeks pale with pity. These souls do not suffer, as they have not sinned, but they were born before His Son and so were never baptized or knew Him sufficiently. For this defect and no other, "we're doomed to live without hope for all time." A few (Adam, Abel, Noah, Moses, David) were plucked out for heaven when Christ descended into hell. There are so many souls in Limbo that it is like walking through a thick forest.

The Pilgrim soon sees a great domed castle blazing with the flames of divine wisdom. The inhabitants are great philosophers, poets, and warriors, such as Plato, Aristotle, Euclid, Ptolemy, Avicenna, Averroës, Homer, Ovid, the Amazon queen Penthesila, "falcon-eyed" Julius Caesar, and Saladin—all of them "were like the first sunrays that build the dawn." After Limbo, the air trembles and all light disappears.

"This way I went, descending from the first into the second circle, that holds less space, but much more pain." Minos stands at the circle's lip as a monstrous magistrate listening to the confessions of the damned before, with a sharp whip of his tail, hurling them into the abyss to whatever punishment he judges most fits their crimes. "Be careful how you enter and whom you trust!" he snarls at the Pilgrim.

In this second circle the lustful swirl in a tempest of impenetrable darkness like an infernal murmuration of starlings. Two inseparable shades catch the Pilgrim's eye; they alight, and although the man stays silent, the woman, Francesca, tells him of their sublime if adulterous (and incestuous) love. "There is no greater pain than to remember, in our present grief, past happiness," she laments.

Once more, the Pilgrim swoons. He awakens in the third circle, where the gluttonous, watched over by the three salivating canine heads of Cerberus, lay stretched out in filthy slush as icy rain lashes them. He and his guide quickly journey through the fourth circle, where the prodigal and the miserly are punished, reaching the rotting banks of the river Styx, more dismal swamp than rushing torrent, whose turgid gray water is the fifth circle. Wrathful souls caked in mud fight tooth and nail in the boggy shallows. Bubbles pop the viscous river surface with the submerged sighs of the slothful. "I thought at first that my eyes were playing tricks," says the Pilgrim.

A high signal tower summons the boatman Phlegyas. "Aha, I've got you now, you wretched soul!" he yells, dashing over the filthy waves. Not this time, laughs Virgil. As the seething boatman punts his passengers across the Styx, a man-shaped lump of stagnant muck rises out of the water and almost sinks them.

"Get out! Here is the entrance!" bellows Phlegyas as he moors before the gates of the city of Dis, where a thousand fallen angels lean over the iron walls and furiously cry, "Who, without death, dares walk into the kingdom of the dead?"

Suddenly, a booming crash like summer lightning rips a doorway in the putrid air, and out strides a majestic angel sent from heaven. After opening the iron gates of Dis with the touch of a scepter, he returns the way he came, closing up the cosmic gash.

The Pilgrim and Virgil quickly traverse the vile city, upon whose avenues crouch the screaming sarcophagi of arch-heretics entombed in fire. Once they are outside, a choking stench wells up around them like a "wound's pus." The fetor only worsens as they scramble down the rocks and gravel of a landslide (not unlike what you see in the Alps, thinks the Pilgrim) between the sixth and seventh circles. (This avalanche happened when Christ harrowed hell.) They evade the bull-headed fury of the Minotaur guarding this level and reach the river Phlegethon, where souls who inflicted violence on others are poached in boiling blood. Three centaurs gallop along the river shooting arrows at the damned, making sure they boil at just the right depth.

Across the Phlegethon is a leafless forest in which the Pilgrim, while hearing immeasurable weeping, sees no souls. Virgil tells him to snap off a twig. "Why are you wounding me?" howls a trunk as blood drips from the break. These barren trees are the souls of suicides.

At the edge of the wood a small stream from the Phlegethon flows through a vast burning desert swept by flurries of fire-flakes. Blasphemers, usurers, and sodomites suffer upon these sands. This scalding wasteland ends (cruelly) in a great waterfall, whose deafening roar "is like the hum of bee-hives," cascading into the eighth circle. Virgil takes a cord wrapped around the Pilgrim's waist and throws it over the edge of the cataract. Instantly, Geryon, a monster with the face of an honest man spliced upon a serpentine physique, swims upward through the thick stale air and, with the two souls on his broad shoulders (sagging a little under the weight of the living one), he gently undulates back down again like an eel.

The Pilgrim, wriggling through the sodden air, sees laid out below ten concentric valleys cut from iron-colored stone, like welts beaten into the earth, with bridges of scabby rock between them. These "evil pockets" are the eighth circle, called Maleborge. "New torments, new tormentors."

In the first valley (or bolgia) are two lines of mewling souls, pimps and seducers, marching in opposite directions as demons scourge them. In the second are flatterers, swimming in slimy shit, steaming and stinking as if fresh from human privies. In the third are the fire-licked soles and legs of simoniacs poking out of holes. (The Pilgrim predicts that Pope Clement V, "that lawless shepherd from the West," will be here soon.) In the fourth ravine is a lake of tears in which slosh the soothsayers, their heads twisted right around, so they blubber down their backs.

"Watch out! Watch out!" shouts Virgil as an inky devil flits over the fifth bridge and tosses a grafter's soul into the trench of bubbling pitch beneath. He boldly confronts a band of devils on the bridge (busily stabbing the simmering souls with pitchforks, like cooks prodding chunks of meat in soup) with his heavenly passport. Their suspiciously affable leader, Malacoda (Evil-Tail), says the sixth bridge collapsed during the earthquake when Christ was crucified but, luckily, he knows of a secret span, which his mates will gladly reveal. He salutes the departing fellowship "with the trumpet of his arse."

Of course, there is no other bridge, and so the two souls must escape their escorts by clambering in and out of the sixth dike, dodging the hypocrites dressed like glamorous Cluniacs (gold cloth lined with lead).

In the seventh gorge are thieves shattering into ashes from snakebites, only to reform to be bitten again. In the eighth are individual flames dancing like fireflies as a deceiving soul (such as Ulysses) burns within. In the ninth are sowers of schism and dissent: Muhammad, as a heretic, is split from groin to chin, and the troubadour Bertran de Born, whose songs inspired rebellion, swings his severed head like a lantern. The miasma of a summer hospital suffocates the tenth valley as the falsifiers are smitten with leprous sores and pestilence.

As the Pilgrim crosses Maleborge's last bridge he hears a sound more arrogant than Roland's horn ringing out from some looming ghostly towers. "Master," he asks his guide, "what city lies ahead?" Virgil lovingly takes his hand and says, "They're giants."

These titans are sunk up to their belly buttons in rock around the crater of this last circle of hell—except for one, Antaeus, who picks up the two souls and carefully places them below on the massive ice lake known as Cocytus. All the weight of hell converges on this grim glacial hole. In this ice are the souls of traitors, "like straws in glass," although a few faces and heads break through the surface with eyes shut tight with frozen tears.

In the middle of Cocytus is the once beautiful angel Lucifer, who, after rebelling against God, tumbled into hell as the foul and ugly Satan. The ice imprisons him around his hairy torso. He has six mighty wings, whose constant flailing, like a ghastly windmill, maintains the frigid temperature entrapping him. His head has three faces, six weeping eyes, and three mouths, each chewing an unholy rebel (Judas Iscariot, Brutus, Cassius) with threshing teeth.

Virgil, with the Pilgrim hanging on to his neck, skates toward the hirsute stomach and, with perfect timing between the oscillating wings, grabs a tuft of hair. He crawls downward through the ice along the furry thighs until, suddenly, he leaps—and instead of falling backward, he and his ward land upright next to Satan's colossal legs, which now soar vertically like shaggy obelisks. The Pilgrim and Virgil are in the Southern Hemisphere, "where I saw the lovely things the heavens hold, and we came out to see once more the stars."[85]

"To run through better waters now the little ship of my talent here must lift her sails and put behind her that so cruel sea," sings Dante the poet as Dante the Pilgrim and Virgil, like survivors of a shipwreck, end up on the beach of the mountainous island of purgatory.

It is dawn on Easter Sunday, and the sky, suffused with sapphire, is "flawlessly pure, from zenith to horizon."

As all humanity lives in the Northern Hemisphere, no living souls, apart from Adam and Eve, have ever seen the stars now contemplated by the Pilgrim.

"And who are you two?" inquires Cato, silver-maned watchman of the shore, who thinks the two souls are fugitives from hell. Usually, repentant souls arrive on flying ships steered by angels. Virgil explains everything. The just old man nods, letting them approach the high mountain, but first the Pilgrim must be girded with a humble reed and his face bathed with morning dew to wash away the filth of hell.

As the sun rises only one soul casts a shadow. The Pilgrim wonders why it is him. Virgil replies that light passes through his kind of body, "even if Divine Power permits it to suffer both torments of heat and cold."

The companions begin climbing to the gate of purgatory by clawing their way slowly up the foothills past the late-repenting souls (such as the indolent). The Pilgrim, breathing heavily under the hot afternoon sun, frequently needs to rest, and Virgil, unsure of what path to take, asks different souls for directions. One shade, the poet Sordello, offers to guide them as far as he can, except as it is almost nightfall, they must rest until the morning. "How is that?" snaps Virgil. "Look! After sunset you could not go a step beyond this line," retorts Sordello as he traces his finger on the ground.

Lucia, "the spirit of Grace," is sent from heaven to carry the sleeping Pilgrim to the gate of purgatory. When he awakens, the angel guarding the portal traces seven Ps (for *peccata*, "sins") upon his brow with an incandescent sword. "You're in," says the ashen-clothed gatekeeper. "Try not to think the worst. These wounds wash off."

As the Pilgrim and Virgil enter purgatory, the gate abruptly slams behind them. They zigzag along a tiny track, then squeeze through a "needle's eye" of split rock, before finally coming to a ledge where once proud souls carry crushing slabs of stone on their backs. "You must not think about the punishment, think but what will come of it," Dante the poet joyfully reminds his reader. "At worst it cannot go beyond the Last Judgement."

As Dante the Pilgrim ascends to the next terrace one of the letters on his forehead is erased by the touch of an angel's wings. "When the Ps that still remain (though they have almost faded) on your brow shall be excised like the first," observes Virgil, "then your feet will be light with good desire."

It is dusk when the companions reach the fourth terrace, where the slothful sing of zeal, and as all movement will soon cease, the weary Pilgrim prepares to sleep. Virgil, though, lectures him until midnight on how all the sins purged in purgatory are perversions of love. "Neither the Creator nor His creatures ever, my son, lacked love." And as the Pilgrim well knows, there are two kinds of love, the natural and the rational. "The natural is always without error, but the heart can err by choosing the wrong object or by excessive or too little ardor." Even sodomy or bestiality is natural love, while being errors of the heart. "Love is the seed of every virtue and of every act that calls for condemnation."

As the mountaineers leave the seventh and final terrace, where the lustful furiously rush about yelling out *exempla* of their lust, an angel stops them, saying they can go no further without passing through a wall of fire. The Pilgrim is gripped with fear.

"Now, my son, look, only this partition keeps you from Beatrice," says Virgil tersely before lovingly ushering him through the flames, whose searing pain is like stepping into a curtain of molten glass.

"You've now seen, my son, both temporal and eternal fire, but you've reached where I can now discern no further." What? "I crown and miter you lord of yourself!" But? "You'll never hear from me again."

"I left the steep incline without delay, and slowly, slowly, took the level ground that breathed out fragrances from every side."

At the summit of purgatory is a "lovely, dense, divine, and living forest." Playful zephyrs tickle the Pilgrim's forehead (now scrubbed of all the Ps). His former guide stands mutely behind him. A stream blocks his way, no wider than three feet, and pure, so pure, unlike any earthly water.

On the other bank the Pilgrim sees a beguiling woman. What is this place? he asks her. This is the Garden of Eden, she replies, and the stream separating them is really two rivers: on her side flows the Lethe, which erases the memory of sin, while the current near him is the Eunoë, which restores the memory of good deeds.

"My brother, look," says the woman. The Pilgrim sees behind her a luminous parade (living candelabra as heralds, twenty-four elders wreathed with lilies, a quartet of six-winged animals plumed with feathers and eyes, a chariot pulled by a griffin, six dancing nymphs, seven dawdling ancient men garlanded with red roses) and a squadron of angels scattering flowers upon a woman in a white veil.

It is Beatrice. Virgil! Look! But he is gone. "Dante, though Virgil leaves you, do not weep . . . not yet," the veiled woman commands both Pilgrim and poet.

"Yes, look at me! Yes, I am Beatrice! So, you at last have deigned to climb the mount? You have learned at last that here lies human bliss?"

The angels wonder why Beatrice so shames Dante. When he was young and gifted, "I let him look into my young eyes," but in death, despite becoming more beautiful after shedding flesh for spirit, "he loved me less." He forgot her, chasing after any pretty skirt—and so forgot his inspiration. She tried reaching him in dreams, but to no avail, so his journey through hell was the only way to save his soul.

"Speak!" Beatrice abruptly orders Dante. "If the accusation I make is true, you must seal it with your confession!"

Dante confesses his guilt and faints. He awakes as the beguiling woman dips him in the Lethe, but so as not to forget his good memories, he sips some water from the Eunoë.

Beatrice lifts her veil, revealing her mouth. Dante "is now ready for the stars."[86]

Beatrice stares intently into the sun. Dante imitates her and metamorphoses beyond mere humanity. "Transhumanize [*trasumanar*]," he says, trying to encapsulate what has happened to him, "but it cannot be explained *per verba*."

Dante starts flying beyond the earth. "Tell me how," he excitedly asks Beatrice. She sighs like a mother with a delirious child, fondly guiding him through all nine heavenly spheres to the Empyrean. "God's greatest gift," she says as they soar beyond the moon, "and the one most like Himself—free will."

As they reach the sun (having chatted to the emperor Justinian in Mercury) a circle of intellectuals sing and dance around them like twinkling stars, such as Isidore of Seville, Bede, Bonaventure, and most genially Thomas Aquinas.

Dante thinks Beatrice is looking lovelier as they approach Saturn, and yet she no longer smiles. "If I were to smile," she answers, knowing his thoughts, "you would be burned to a heap of ashes." She is becoming more beautiful as they approach the eternal place of love, and so her smile is more devastatingly divine, even for one transhumanized.

"Open your eyes, look straight into my face," Beatrice soon consoles Dante as they arrive amongst the fixed stars. "You have the power to endure my smile!"

Dante is now in the presence of Christ, "the Rose in which the Word of God took on flesh," and the Virgin Mary, which gives him the strength to survive Beatrice's smile.

Indeed, "I seemed to see all of the universe turn to a smile."

Finally, "appearing before me in the form of a white rose was heaven's Sacred Host, those whom Christ with His own blood made His bride." This vision of the Elect is like what the barbarians must have felt when they first saw Rome.

"Where is she?" cries Dante, suddenly alone.

"Look up there," says Bernard of Clairvaux—as ubiquitous as ever— pointing to the third row of the white rose.

> And she, who seemed so far off, smiled
> and though she looked at me awhile,
> she turned once more to the Eternal Fountain.

"Love," Dante realizes in a flash of understanding after Beatrice's last smile, "moves the sun and all the other stars."[87]

Dante began his *Comedy* around 1307 and finished it shortly before his death at fifty-six in 1321. It is a poem so magnificent—which the preceding summary hopefully captures in some small way—that one inevitably stumbles into sophomoric clichés. It was considered a masterpiece even while Dante was alive, despite the *Paradiso* being published posthumously, and such esteem only increased throughout the fourteenth and fifteenth centuries. ("Divine," *divina*, was added to the title by these later readers.) It is at once a visionary eschatological epic about the destiny of humanity, an urgent autobiography of what had happened and was happening to Dante, often on the very day when he was writing a verse, and a love story melding such cosmic grandiosity with the insistently human. It is a relentless linear narrative moving through time, hour by hour, day by day. It constantly interweaves the past tense of Dante as the Pilgrim remembering and the present tense of Dante as the poet in the act of writing. The *Comedy* is the poetic epitomization of the confessional culture that had been developing for more than two centuries in the medieval West.

Dante's poem was a *commedia* (from *comus* and *oda* and meaning a "rustic song") because, unlike a tragedy, which begins blithely and ends with sadness, a comedy starts out inauspiciously and yet always concludes with happiness. It was in Italian rather than Latin, as a comedy should be in the language of ordinary people. Except, of course, Dante in two earlier books, the *Convivio* (*Banquet*) and especially the *De vulgari eloquentia* (*On Eloquence in the Vernacular*), had argued that as the vernacular varied throughout the Italian peninsula, indeed even varying within one city, it needed to be unified and perfected like Latin, so that in this ideal synthesis it could guide and inspire all the local variations of itself. As we have already seen, Francis of Assisi got around all this linguistic diversity by preaching and singing in make-do French.

Dante was one of the first Western intellectuals to grasp that languages possessed a history and changed over time, "so that if the ancient citizens of Pavia were to rise from the grave today, they would speak in a language that was separate and distinct from that of modern Pavians." Further, he observed that as most Italian nobles only spoke the vernacular rather than Latin, which had become the language of professors and professionals, then ordinary speech needed to be viewed as able to carry any message, no matter how sophisticated or esoteric. The troubadours, he asserted, had shown that this was possible. (He was aware of the irony of making this argument in Latin in the *De vulgari eloquentia*, but he was addressing other intellectuals unconvinced that the vernacular could ever convey anything of worth.) Dante invented his own perfect version of Italian, which, while similar to what was spoken in his native Florence, was nevertheless his own linguistic distillation.[88]

In March 1302, Dante was exiled from Florence as a "White Guelf," and if he ever returned, he would be "burnt with fire until he dies." A coalition of "Black Guelfs" had seized power in the city and were purging leading Whites. Four generations earlier the Guelfs were individuals within Italian cities supporting the authority of the pope over that of the emperor, whose supporters were known as Ghibellines. It was a continuation of the Investiture Controversy from the eleventh and twelfth centuries. In Florence the Guelfs had been dominant since 1278, only fracturing into Blacks and Whites around 1300, with the former adamantly defending the pope, while the latter were now opposed to (or at least ambivalent about) the papacy. Dante would, perhaps not surprisingly, become an advocate of the emperor over the pope, stating in his *De Monarchia* (*On Monarchy*), written after a decade as an émigré wandering from city to city, that government by a single ruler "is necessary for the good of the world" and that the power of a prince came directly from God rather than the Church. As Dante never returned to Florence, the *Comedy*, while imagined in some form before 1302, was born in and shaped by exile.[89]

Dante was almost ten when he saw a girl who had just turned nine named Bice, but whom he and others called Beatrice. "I can truly say that at that very moment my vital spirit, which dwells in the heart's most secret space, began to tremble so violently, even my smallest veins were throbbing," he vividly recalled his first sight of her in his *Vita nuova*, a vernacular memoir combining prose and poetry written in his late twenties (and very much a portrait of the artist as a young man). "From then on, I swear, Love was lord of my soul."[90]

Beatrice's father, Folco Portinari, was the leading member of a prominent family in trade and finance, and while Dante's father was no more than a petty moneylender and usurer, they lived in the same neighborhood of Florence. At fourteen she married the knight Simon dei Bardi, whose family was even more illustrious than her own, and died ten years later, in 1290.

Dante married Gemma Donati, whose family was wealthier and more powerful than the Alighieris, when he was around twenty and she was probably sixteen. (Her dowry of only two hundred small florins was quite pathetic, but dowries were calculated based on the future wealth of the husband.) He genuinely seems to have liked his wife, but the fictional image he crafted of himself in his poetry, and which to some extent became more and more his reality as he wrote the *Comedy*, was that he had only ever loved Beatrice. "Remember," Love speaks to his youthful heart in the *Vita nuova*, "to bless the day I took you captive."[91] Ultimately, it really is impossible to know if Dante ever spoke, let alone spoke of his love, to Beatrice outside of his imagination.[92]

But what an imagination. Dante's love for Beatrice, like the separate prime mover for Thomas Aquinas, had to be enduringly immobile within his heart from the very first moment he experienced it, because such eternal love was what moved everything in the universe. *Et hoc dicimus Deum.* Loving was more than just knowing God; it was truly imitating Him. As love was the seed of every virtuous and sinful act, then every action, no matter how mundane or ordinary, like speaking in vernacular, was an imitation of Christ. And the only way of discovering such love within oneself was through finally confessing it to one's beloved—which is God.

Love eventually transhumanized every man and woman into Christ, but you had to go through hell to get there, and even then, if you were not careful, a loving smile might turn you into ashes.

14 And Love, Just Love

The autobiographical sense of self that was first clearly articulated by intellectuals (male and female) in the early decades of the twelfth century had, more or less, become commonplace amongst ordinary men, women, and children throughout Latin Christendom by the beginning of the fourteenth. (Abelard is not in Dante's heaven with Bernard of Clairvaux, which, while perhaps wise, is a little unfair. Then again, somewhat surprisingly, he and Heloise are never mentioned in the *Comedy*.) The mendicant orders and their role in undertaking inquisitions into heretical depravity, especially the Dominicans, reinforced this linear understanding of what defined individual existence. But then so too did the emphasis upon the continuity of human identity after death.

Indeed, the movement and experience of earthly time quite literally carried over into purgatory. Furthermore, this sense of time and space covered all individuals who had ever lived and would live, so that Latin Christendom now encompassed the entire world—past, present, and future. Individual redemption therefore depended upon the coherent existence of a man or a woman from crawling child to elderly adult, and upon everyone understanding this about themselves and, crucially, being able to confess it. The ability to talk about oneself, whether peasant or prince, was vital. This led to cogent and consistent sexual identities being impressed upon and adopted by most men and women.

The violent and cruel persecution of heretics and Jews (as heretics) was fundamental in creating this distinctly Western sense of self, as was the powerful notion that even the most mundane behavior was by its everyday humanity an imitation of Christ. No other culture in world history, for good or ill, has assumed that ordinary persons, through their sheer ordinariness, were copying the godhead. And love, just love, was where the divine and the human most met, causing everything that was wonderful in the universe, like a last smile, as well as the most malevolent, like an apocalyptic plague.

X

Only Death Wakes Us from Dreaming

1321–1431

1 The Black Death

I say, then," so Giovanni Boccaccio began his interweaving of tales within tales, stories within stories, known as the *Decameron*, "that the sum of thirteen hundred and forty-eight years had elapsed since the fruitful Incarnation of the Son of God, when the noble city of Florence, which for its great beauty excels all others in Italy, was visited by the deadly pestilence." Some said this great plague descended upon humanity through the influence of the stars and planets, others that it was a punishment from God. "But whatever its cause, it had originated some years earlier in the East, where it had claimed countless lives before it unhappily spread westward, growing in strength as it swept relentlessly on from one place to the next."

The early symptoms of the plague, continued Giovanni, "in men and women alike, were the appearance of certain swellings in the groin or the armpit, some of which were egg-shaped whilst others were roughly the size of the common apple." These swellings were popularly known as *gavòccioli*. "Later on, the symptoms of the disease changed, and many people began to find dark blotches and bruises on their arms, thighs, and other parts of the body, sometimes large and few in number, at other times tiny and closely spaced." Most men, women, and children died within three days after the appearance of these swellings and blotches. What made the pestilence so frightening was the speed with which it consumed the healthy whenever they mixed with the sick, like fire racing through kindling. All physicians were useless, all medicines were ineffective, and all the medical quacks promoting whatever healing nonsense entered their heads only made things worse, but a dying man will try anything. "In any event," sighed Giovanni, "few of those who caught the plague ever recovered."[1]

Giovanni's deadly pestilence was, sadly, no fiction; rather, he was describing the bubonic plague or (as it has been called since the nineteenth century, despite no one naming it so in the Middle Ages) the "Black Death." Between 1347 and 1351, when this plague first swept through Latin Christendom, almost forty million people died—that is, roughly 50 to 60 percent of the population of the West. This was the most devastating pandemic—so far—in world history.[2]

Giovanni himself witnessed (or if he did not, then his father certainly did) the pestilence in Florence, where "many dropped dead in open streets," while others collapsed indoors, forgotten until the stench of rotting corpses was too much for their neighbors. Around sixty thousand out of the hundred thousand citizens of the commune perished. "Bodies were here, there, and everywhere."[3]

Giovanni wrote most of the *Decameron* during the height of the plague, vividly using the horrific reality of the pestilence as a way of opening and so framing his fictional "comedy" of a "happy band" (*lieta brigata*) of bright young things—seven women, three men—escaping into a secluded garden in the countryside where they entertained one another with a hundred tales over ten days. (*Decameron* means "ten days.") Despite his stories often being wildly comical and so closer to *The Romance of the Rose*, he was inspired by Dante's *Comedy*. Indeed, he copied the entire poem three times in his own hand, along with long learned commentaries, especially on the *Inferno*. If nothing else, Giovanni's description of the plague in the streets of Florence deliberately evoked the Pilgrim in the circles of hell.

2 It Began in the Land of Darkness

"It began in the land of darkness," speculated the Syrian scholar Abu Hafs 'Umar ibn al-Wardi in his *Epistle on Reports of the Pestilence* (*Risalah al-naba' 'an al-waba'*) about the origins of the plague shortly before it killed him in Aleppo in March 1349.[4] The region he had in mind was central Asia—modern Kazakhstan, Kurdistan, Kyrgyzstan, and western China—and perhaps even specifically around Lake Issyk Kul, in eastern Kyrgyzstan. Modern research has confirmed that Abu Hafs' hunch was correct.[5]

The fourteenth-century plague bacterium was unquestionably *Yersinia pestis*, but it was not the same organism that had caused the sixth-century Justinianic plague, having suddenly mutated into four new strains in central Asia around 1268. (The Justinianic strain might have even gone extinct.) What allowed these mutations to spread, and probably helped cause them in the first place, were earthquakes, wildfires, climate change, and, most significantly, the Mongols. The habitat of *Yersinia pestis* was repeatedly disturbed by the conquests, mass migrations, long sieges, and massive mobile armies of the great horde. Moreover, the imperial Mongol state interlaced many different ecological zones, allowing all sorts of usually isolated pathogens to travel. As more than three hundred species of mammals (two-thirds of them rodents) host fleas that can carry *Yersinia pestis*, the ever-rolling felt-walled tents inadvertently herded such animals over thousands of miles. And as the Mongols were particularly fond of the fur and meat of marmots—which, like rats or voles, can carry enormous numbers of plague bacteria when septicemic, anywhere from a hundred million to one billion per milliliter (0.03 of an ounce) of blood—they repeatedly exposed themselves to infection.

In the early fourteenth century three waves of the plague (1307–1313, 1331, 1344–1345) swept through the Yuan Mongol-Chinese Empire, the *yeke Yuwan ulus*, founded by Qubilai Khan in 1271. Across the Eurasian steppes the so-called Silk Road through the various Mongol successor states functioned as a series of irregular staging posts for *Yersinia pestis*, ravaging an oasis here before skipping two towns and infecting a caravan encampment there, as it haphazardly but inexorably moved westward.[6]

The notary Gabriele de Mussis wrote a *History of the Disease or Mortality That Occurred in the Year of Our Lord 1348* (*Historia de morbo sive mortalitate quae fuit anno Domini 1348*) before he died in Piacenza in 1356. Famously, he judged

the moment when the plague first infected Latin Christians as occurring during the siege of the Genoese in Caffa (modern Feodosiya) by Janibek Khan
and the Mongol "golden horde" in summer 1346. The khan was reminding
the arrogant Italians that this Black Sea entrepôt belonged to him and they
were merely his mercantile guests. "And lo! The whole army of the Tartars was
struck down, thrown into disarray by a rampaging disease, and every day, it
seemed, many thousands were laid low, as if arrows rained down from heaven."

The Mongols abandoned the siege, but not before catapulting the fetid
corpses of their fallen comrades into the city, hoping to kill the inhabitants.
"Yes, yes, what seemed like a mountain of the dead was hurled inside! . . .
And soon the whole air was infected, and the water poisoned, by a corrupt
putridity, and the stench increased to such an extent that hardly one out
of a thousand was left alive." When the surviving remnant finally escaped,
they supposedly first infected Constantinople, then Genoa, until finally one
sickly Genoese man unleashed the plague in Piacenza.[7]

Gabriele's theory for how the plague spread to Italy, while horribly convincing, was nevertheless mostly his imagination trying to make sense of what
he had heard from Genoese and Venetian merchants about the pestilence in
Crimea. He also needed a hypothesis based upon the widespread assumption that the plague was spread by miasmas, that is, the foul smells of blotchy
and swollen corpses. The dead as "biological weapons" was a clever touch, if
completely out of character for actual Mongols. Janibek's army was certainly
decimated by disease outside Caffa, but then most of Mongol Crimea had
already been infected for almost a year. Undoubtedly, some Italian refugees
from the Black Sea must have been sick and so spread the disease across the
Mediterranean. Ultimately, the plague most likely reached Genoa and Venice
when grain ships from Caffa and Tana (a Venetian trading post on the river
Don) sailed in spring 1347, and apart from the recent harvest in their holds,
they carried rats, mice, ticks, lice, and fleas infected with *Yersinia pestis*.[8]

Yersinia pestis stepped ashore at Genoa in November 1347 and Venice in
February 1348. Between these months the plague seeped into Marseille,
then hopped between the Mediterranean islands of Sardinia, Corsica, Elba,
and Mallorca before reaching western Italy and eastern Spain. By March,
it was in the streets of papal Avignon, Narbonne, Montpellier, Carcassonne,
and Toulouse. By late spring, it was in Rome, Florence, and most of northern
Italy, soon crossing the Alps into Switzerland. Between June and August,
it passed through Bordeaux, Lyon, and Paris, then spread into Burgundy
and Normandy, where it jumped the Channel into southern England in
November.

By the end of 1349, the plague had cast a death-dealing shadow over the Iberian and Italian peninsulas, France, England, Ireland, Norway, parts of Denmark, Flanders, the Low Countries, most of the Balkans, all of the German lands, Hungary, and much of Poland. In 1350 and 1351 the sickness reached Scotland, the rest of Denmark, Sweden, the lands around the Baltic, and the last untouched Polish regions. A year later the plague entered the Grand Duchy of Moscow. Iceland and Finland were seemingly unaffected in this first great pestilential wave.[9]

The previous paragraph is a little too neat. The plague actually spread throughout Latin Christendom much more randomly and erratically, so that while mapping its movement gives insights, such cartography can make it seem that *Yersinia pestis* was consciously on a march of conquest (rather like an old newsreel with its sweeping arrows of battalions on the move).[10] The bacterium traveled with incredible speed, making great metastatic leaps across distances, usually on account of ships swiftly traversing seas and rivers, but often with baffling quickness in the company of wagons and pedestrians over roads. For example, the plague moved roughly 0.6 miles a day in England, taking just over a year to spread throughout the kingdom. This swiftness suggests *Yersinia pestis* entered the island simultaneously through a number of seaports. (By comparison, it took more than a century for the bubonic plague to spread from Yunnan Province in southwest China in the late eighteenth century to Hong Kong in the late nineteenth.)

Also, two different but contemporaneous mid-fourteenth-century strains of *Yersinia pestis* have been discovered, one strain in Saint-Laurent-de-la-Cabrerisse (southeastern France) and Hereford (southwestern England) and the other strain in Bergen op Zoom (southern Netherlands), suggesting overlapping varieties of the disease, with one perhaps more virulent than the other. Possibly pneumonic plague (rapidly infecting the lungs and killing with almost 100 percent efficiency) might explain some of the briskness of *Yersinia pestis*; however, while pneumonic plague was a distinct manifestation of the bacterium, bubonic plague overwhelmingly accounted for most infections and deaths in the fourteenth century.

Finally, despite the vaulting momentum of the disease, it also moved very slowly sometimes, more so in cities than the countryside, and it almost always stalled with the onset of winter.[11]

This erratic randomness was observed by contemporaries. "The said mortality, from what I can gather," noted the priest Konrad of Megenberg at the papal court in Avignon around 1350, "now moves towards the east and now in the opposite direction and then changing direction leaps from the south to the north and retraces its steps in places already visited, in such a way as if it moves with an accidental or involuntary motion like some bodily form propelled by winds in the airy regions."[12] Or according to Matteo Villani in his continuation of his brother Giovanni's *New Chronicle* (a sweeping world history that the latter stopped writing when he died of the plague in Florence in 1348), the pestilence was "like a hailstorm leaving one area intact while destroying another." Matteo himself later died of the plague in Florence during an outbreak in 1361.[13]

3 Waiting Amongst the Dead for Death to Come

"Since the beginning of the world it has been unheard of for so many people to die of pestilence, famine or other infirmity in such a short time," wrote John Clynn, an English Franciscan in Kilkenny, southeastern Ireland, in 1349. "Plague stripped villages, cities, castles and towns of their inhabitants so thoroughly that there was scarcely anyone left alive. The pestilence was so contagious that those that touched the dead or the sick were immediately infected themselves and died." He counted twenty-five Franciscans succumbing at Drogheda before Christmas, as did another twenty-three in Dublin, while eight Dominicans perished at Kilkenny during Lent when the plague was rampant. "It is very rare for just one person to die in a house, usually husband, wife, children and servants went the same way, the way of death." John saw the whole world encompassed by evil, and yet there he was alone, "waiting amongst the dead for death to come."

But if the worst was to happen to John, his chronicle of the present horrors should be carried on as a confirmation of the survival of humanity, "so I leave parchment for continuing the work, in case anyone should still be alive in the future and any son of Adam can escape this pestilence." He died from the plague soon after writing these words.[14]

How quickly and indiscriminately did the plague kill? In England, for which we have the most extensive records (especially rural) for tabulating statistics, there were vast discrepancies in mortality between the nobility and everyone else. The death rates of higher nobles were perhaps 4.5 percent in 1348 and 13 percent in 1349, while wealthy landowners averaged 27 percent over both years. Bishops succumbed at a rate of 18 percent, whereas secular and monastic clergy were cut down at rates of 45 to 51 percent. Male peasants were shattered by a mortality rate of roughly 50 percent. It was even higher amongst poor landless males, being somewhere between 56 and 57 percent. The evidence for the frequency of death for English peasant women is limited, but it seems they died at a rate a few percentage points higher than servile men. This is supported by an analysis of thousands of death duties (known as mortmains, literally "dead hands") in the Hainaut (now in modern Belgium), where significantly more peasant women than men died in 1348 and 1349.

Overall, the mortality for both peasant men and women in the English countryside was somewhere between 54 and 61 percent. As for English towns, such as Canterbury, two-thirds of the taxpaying population was dead by 1352. In London, at least going by wills, the mortality was 51 percent in 1349, but it was probably much higher. The English elderly, anyone between fifty and ninety (it is difficult to tell the difference in skeletons), had a greater susceptibility to the plague than younger individuals in 1349. Interestingly, anyone with skin lesions was particularly vulnerable to *Yersinia pestis*. If England had a population of 4.8 million (a low estimate) before 1348, then around two million people died within two to five years.[15]

At a mass grave in East Smithfield, London, twenty-four hundred individuals were buried in the early months of 1349. Rather movingly, even though the bodies were stacked in layers, they were still interred respectfully, with their heads oriented to the west and their feet to the east. (Six hundred and thirty-six skeletons from East Smithfield have been excavated and studied.)[16] John Clynn noted that Pope Clement VI had approved similar mass graves in Avignon, although he had heard the corpses were just dumped without ceremony in a trench.[17] Likewise, Giovanni Boccaccio in the *Decameron* wrote that at first, when the dead were not so overwhelming, they were buried in traditional Florentine fashion (a procession of family, neighbors, priests) in single graves, but soon "no more respect was accorded to dead people than would nowadays be shown towards dead goats." As the multitude of corpses increased, especially amongst the poor, "huge trenches were excavated in churchyards, into which new arrivals were placed in their hundreds, stowed tier upon tier like ships' cargo, each layer of corpses being covered over with a thin layer of soil till the trench was filled to the top."[18] A later Florentine chronicler described this method of burying the dead to be "just as one makes lasagna with layers of pasta and cheese."[19] In Piacenza, according to Gabriele de Mussis, when there was no more room in the cemeteries, even for trenches, "pits had to be dug in colonnades and piazzas, where nobody had ever been buried before."[20]

Between 1348 and 1350 the plague killed with shocking vehemence, wiping out great swaths of the population of Latin Christendom, especially in the countryside. But it was not, as we have seen, completely indiscriminate; nobles survived more often than peasants, the wealthy more than the poor, the young more than the old, and, despite the loneliness of John Clynn in Kilkenny as he waited for death, the clergy more than the laity.

4 Corruption of the Air

"We say that the distant and first cause of this pestilence is the configuration of the heavens," reckoned the medical faculty of the university of Paris on Monday, October 6, 1348. "In the year of our Lord 1345, at precisely one hour after noon on the twentieth day of the month of March, there was a major conjunction of three planets in Aquarius. This conjunction, along with earlier conjunctions and eclipses, by causing deadly corruption of the air around us, signifies mortality and famine." Most particularly, during a conjunction of Jupiter and Mars, as happened when the planets lined up in 1345, the former, "being hot and wet, drew up evil vapors from the earth," but the latter, "since it is immoderately hot and dry, then ignited the risen vapors, and therefore there were many lightning flashes, sparks, and pestiferous vapors and fires throughout the air."

The earthly cause, "the particular and near," was corruption of the air. "Thus, the corrupted air, when it is breathed in, necessarily penetrates to the heart and corrupts the substance of the spirit that is in it and putrefies the surrounding moisture, so that the heat that is created goes forth and by its nature corrupts the principle of life, and this is the immediate cause of the current epidemic." Also, winds, which had been so prevalent lately, undoubtedly dispersed poisonous vapors from faraway swamps, lakes, and deep valleys. And all of this particular and near putrefying air and water obviously only happened on account of the configuration of the planets, "the aforesaid universal and distant cause."[21]

Seven months earlier, Jacme d'Agramont, a physician and professor of medicine at the university of Lérida, composed in Catalan what seems to have been the earliest treatise on the plague, *Regime of Protection Against Epidemics or Pestilence and Mortality* (*Regiment de preservacio a epidimia o pestilencia e mortaldats*). He too argued that the plague was caused by putrefaction of the air, which also may have been the result of earthly infection or the conjunction of opposing planets, but it may have been equally, if not more so, "chastisement for our sins." If the corrupt air was because of the sins of humanity, "the remedies of the medical art are of little value." Nevertheless, Jacme offered some cures: do not exercise, eat well, sleep after eating, give up sex, undergo gentle enemas and light bleedings, and stop bathing, as this opens the pores, letting in corrupt air.

Jacme also warned that perhaps the plague was being spread by evil men, "children of the devil," secretly poisoning food and water. "I wished to mention it because we are now in a time when many deaths have occurred in nearby regions, such as in Collioure, in Carcassonne, in Narbonne, and in the barony of Montpellier and in Avignon and in all Provence."[22]

Another Spanish physician, Alfonso de Córdoba, teaching at the university of Montpellier—the most important medical school in Latin Christendom—issued a similar warning against poisoners, albeit in Latin, at the end of the year. "Before all else, one must be on one's guard against all food and drink which can be infected and poisoned, especially against non-flowing water, because this can easily be infected." He dismissed the thesis of the Parisian faculty as nonsense. Ignore all this talk about the conjunction of planets or the elemental infection of the earth, he stressed, as it was obvious from experience that the plague was the result of "deep-seated malice through the most subtle artifice that can be invented by a profoundly wicked mind." Alfonso suggested some antidotes against poisoned food and drink, but really there were no prophylactics against the conspiracy of wicked men spreading the pestilence by poison.[23]

5 Poison

In early April 1348, when Jacme d'Agramont was writing his *Regime of Protection*, some of the poisoners that he tentatively and later Alfonso de Córdoba definitively blamed for the plague were arrested in Narbonne during Lent. They were "poor men and beggars of diverse nations" supposedly spreading powdered poisons in "water, houses, churches and foodstuffs in order to kill people." Remarkably, at least according to the *viguier* (official) of the viscount of Narbonne, "some freely confessed, while some only on pain of torture." These men confessed that they had been given the poison from certain individuals, "whose names they say they do not know," and that they had been paid money for their venomous acts.

"Nevertheless, it is true that those who confessed were torn apart by red-hot iron pincers, then quartered, their hands cut off, and then they were burned." The *viguier* counted four men discovered and executed in Narbonne, five in Carcassonne, two in another town, but he knew there were many others elsewhere. "Justice was done!" These anonymous wandering beggars were the first individuals accused of infecting people with the plague by poison.[24]

Soon after these eleven men were executed, there were more accusations of poisoning throughout Languedoc and Provence, except now the accused were Jews. Between April and May 1348, at least eleven Jewish communities were attacked as purveyors of pestilential poison. For example, in Toulon (a port city on the Mediterranean) forty Jews were murdered and thrown naked on the streets during the early morning hours of Palm Sunday, April 13. As one local official phrased it, "All the Jews in Provence were killed, as they were suspected of poisoning and contaminating the wells and springs, so that a true report and rumor spread it about that the universal mortality . . . arose from poison."[25]

These allegations quickly crossed the Pyrenees into towns throughout Catalonia. "Kill the traitors!" yelled a mob in Tàrrega as they murdered with vicious savagery three hundred Jews, many of them children and babies, on Sunday, July 6, 1348. In 1321, not coincidentally, lepers throughout these very same regions were accused of sprinkling poisonous powders in wells and springs, so as to kill or make the healthy just like them. As already noted, most if not all "lepers" were actually communities of poor families living together like confraternities. Almost every village in southern France had such "leper houses." The only reason the leprous on either side of the Pyrenees were not now blamed for the plague was that most of them (men, women, and children) had been tortured and incinerated a generation earlier.[26]

Toward the end of 1348, five Jewish men and one Jewish woman from the county of Savoy were interrogated in the castle of Chillon (on the eastern shore of Lake Geneva) about poisoning streams, lakes, and wells. One of these men was a surgeon named Balavigny from Thonon-les-Bains (on the southern shore of Lake Geneva). Under torture he confessed that a certain Rabbi Jacob from Toledo had sent him during Easter "through a certain Jewish servant boy a heap of poison about the size of an egg, which was in the form of a powder in a sack of fine, sewn leather," along with a letter ordering him, under pain of excommunication from his religion, "to put the said poison into the greatest and most public well of the town." He also testified that similar mandates had been sent by other rabbis to other Jews in various other places. "In the presence of very many trust-worthy witnesses, he confessed by the faith in his religion and in all that is contained in the five books of Moses that the aforementioned things were absolutely true."

Later, Balavigny, "without being tortured," confessed about talking to other Jews about how he and they were poisoning streams and wells around Lake Geneva. Indeed, at one point his interrogators even rowed him across the lake in search of a poisonous linen rag he had secreted near a public water source. "Here is the spring where I put the poison," he said, con-veniently showing them. "The linen rag or cloth was taken away and is in safe keeping," noted a scribe recording the confession. Also, "speaking as a surgeon," Balavigny professionally observed that when someone was sick from his poison, their sweat and breath would infect anyone near them with the plague. By the way, "he believes the poison to come from the basilisk." Balavigny was executed as a Jew as a saboteur deliberately spreading the pestilence, and not, as he would have been only forty years earlier, a Jew as a heretic poisoning Christendom by his mere existence.[27]

More than anywhere else, though, it was in the German lands where Jews were massacred in more than four hundred towns for poisoning wells. Interestingly, the first accusations and killings occurred when the plague was subsiding as the weather turned colder in November 1348. Indeed, even as deaths from the plague abated, the persecutions rapidly escalated during winter 1349. For example, on the Rhine near Basel in January, 600 Jews were burned in a specially constructed wooden house, while 130 of their children were forcibly baptized.[28]

Or Strasbourg in February, where in another "specially-prepared house" two thousand Jews were set ablaze and, once again, children were snatched from their mothers for baptism, but most "refused this invitation." (The number of Jews killed during this one horrific month in Strasbourg equaled all the Jews massacred in the Rhineland by the "leftover shit" signed with the cross in 1096.) Or Erfurt in March, where three thousand Jews were killed, many of them supposedly taking their lives before their persecutors could. The slaughter slowed during the spring as the plague returned, but quickened during the summer.[29]

However, in Mainz and Cologne in July and August, according to Gilles li Muisis, abbot of Saint Martin in Tournai, "the Jews armed themselves and sought out arms, along with those arms that they had in their possession as pledges from Christians, and they manfully resisted many times, nor were the citizens and others from the city able to vanquish them." The Christian butchers of Mainz and Cologne sent messages to the Jews saying that they would join them in their fight, but it was a trick, and so the Jews were unexpectedly attacked on all sides. "More than 25,000 Jews were slain," and every Jewish house and building was burned to the ground.[30]

Almost exactly a year earlier Clement VI had issued the encyclical *Sicut Judeis* demanding that no "hot-headed" Christian, "under the pain of excommunication," should capture, strike, wound, or kill Jews. "Our Savior chose to be born of Jewish stock when he put on mortal flesh for the salvation of the humanity," and so the Jews were to be protected. In any event, "it cannot be true that the Jews, by such a heinous crime, are the cause of the plague, because throughout many parts of the world the same plague, by the hidden judgement of God, has afflicted and afflicts the Jews themselves and many other peoples who have never lived alongside them."[31]

Around 1350, Konrad of Megenberg reaffirmed the pope's opinion about Jews and poison, a year or so after the massacres in the German lands had petered out. "My reasoning is as follows: It is well known that in most places where the Hebrew people had remained, they themselves had died in droves from the exact same cause of this common mortality." If the wells were really poisoned, "then without a doubt horses, cows, and sheep and livestock that drink the water ought to have been infected and died in great numbers like humans." Just as conclusively, "the whole population of Bavaria in the cities bordering on the Danube and other navigable rivers only use the water of these same rivers and most scrupulously avoid well water, nevertheless they have died." Finally, "even after all the Jews in many places have been killed and completely driven out for nearly two years prior, Death strikes these same places with a strong hand." And so "it does not seem to me that the pitiful Jewish people is the cause of this general mortality which has spread throughout almost the whole world."

Much of the violent maelstrom that engulfed Jews between 1348 and 1349, even as they themselves were dying from the plague, while clearly deriving from a brutal animosity that had been intensifying amongst some but not all Christians for more than two centuries, was nevertheless different. Most clearly, poisoning wells was not seen as a quality inherent to them as Jews and, most especially, as heretics who had had the revelation of Christ but deliberately turned away. Instead, Jewish men, women, and children had supposedly chosen to inflict the pestilence on the world, often in alliance with vagabond Christians, in a deliberate endgame that would bring about the Last Judgment.

For many of their attackers, the Jews were the instruments of an angry and punishing God. And so some if not all the fury against them should also be understood as raging against Him. The poison accusations must be seen in this context. This was why Balavigny, even after torture, sheer resignation at his fate, and prompting from his interrogators, still had no idea why he was supposedly ordered to poison springs around Lake Geneva. He had merely been acting out something he was told to do. Paul Chrétien may have wanted to eliminate Jews as heretics eighty years earlier, but for many Christians the poison accusations and subsequent killings had transformed Jews into hollow men, more like puppets than humans, easily manipulated by divine, demonic, or even earthly forces, and therefore so much easier to murder—then and in the future.

Still, as Clement and Konrad perhaps vainly tried to point out, the Jews were human, dying like everyone else. Or as said in a Hebrew epitaph from Toledo commemorating the death from plague of Sitbona, daughter of Judah ben Sahwan, wife of Meir haLevi:

> At the end of days, He will raise you up and compensate your actions
> There is hope for your future with the resurrection of His pious few.
> He will say to you, "Do not grieve!
> Shake off the dust! Arise and return!"[32]

6 The Flagellants

Toward the end of 1348, there suddenly appeared in Austria and the southern German lands penitential companies of men, women, and even children who, upon entering a town, would remove their outer garments and then recite and perform a liturgy while whipping themselves until the blood pooled around their feet. They were known as the "flail-brothers," "brethren of the cross," "crossbearers," the "red knights of Christ," and, most commonly, the "flagellants."

These companies soon multiplied and, with anywhere from forty to three hundred flagellants, were scourging themselves in northern town squares between the Seine and the Rhine throughout 1349, with a small Dutch-speaking group even crossing the Channel for a whirlwind performance in London. Every company was a mix not only of men and women, of young and old, but also of nobles, peasants, bishops, priests, mendicants, knights, and merchants. Individuals joined a company for only thirty-three and a half days, replicating the number of years that Christ was human. Large wooden crosses with the crucified Christ, banners of silk or velvet painted with a cross or whip, and large twisted candles were carried before the flagellants as they traipsed from one town to another. They dressed in a habit of a shoulder- or knee-length black hooded cloak embroidered with a red cross on the front and the back. They wore a black mushroom-shaped hat on top of the hood. A flagellant's whip was typically a stick with three leather cords into which one needle-like iron splinter was knotted at the ends.[33]

When the flagellants gathered in a town square or in an open field, their performance was precisely choreographed. The men stripped down to white smocks that covered them from their waists to their ankles, exposing their upper bodies. Women undressed similarly, but with a covering over their breasts. Then they would sing as they whipped themselves:

> Jesus Christ was taken prisoner,
> To a cross He was hung.
> This cross turned red from blood.
> We lament God's martyr and His death . . .
> Because of God we spill our blood . . .
> Now flail yourself heavily for Christ's honor!
> Through God now leave your sins behind . . .
> Jesus, through all Your wounds red
> Shelter us from the [sudden] death! . . .
> So help us, Mary, queen,
> That we will win your Child's praise![34]

And so on, for more than twenty minutes, interspersed with falling face-down upon the ground, making the shape of a cross with outstretched arms, and "confessing themselves clean." Sometimes they fell to their knees, sobbing and beseeching God. The flagellants were imitating Christ, mimicking

His bleeding on the cross. But in doing so they were hoping to pacify Him and His wrath as manifested in the plague. They were saving themselves and all of humanity by lacerating their flesh and offering up their blood to an angry and not at all loving Christ.

Clement VI suppressed the flagellant movement in October 1349. Although he did not accuse them of heresy, he came close, saying they were deluding the "simple and ignorant" with lies and superstitions. He had also heard that some flagellants had participated in killing German Jews. Many princes and town councilors were reluctant to follow the papal lead, but eventually, within two or three years, they complied. The flagellants disappeared, even as the plague remained.[35]

7 Leave My Earth!

"From imagination alone, can come any malady," wrote Jacme d'Agramont in his *Regime of Protection*. "Thus, it is evidently very dangerous and perilous in times of pestilence to imagine death and to have fear. No one, therefore, should give up hope or despair, because such fear only does great damage and no good whatsoever." Jacme died from the plague within a few months of writing these words.

Unfortunately, many people succumbed to their imaginations and gave up all hope during the plague. There were all sorts of reasons for the unusual swiftness of the pestilence in killing so many so quickly, most obviously fleas (and, perhaps even more so, lice) swarming with virulent strains of *Yersinia pestis*, but certainly the crushing sense that God had forsaken His creations made surrendering to death, however dreadful, so much easier than fighting for life. Gabriele de Mussis in his *History of the Disease* imagined a furious God saying to the humanity polluting His earth:

> When you compelled Me, Who upheld the spheres, to descend into the womb of a virgin I endured hunger, thirst, toil, crucifixion and death—and your deeds, you ingrate, condemn Me still to the cross. I ought to have punished you with eternal death, but pity conquered Me. . . . You are unworthy of eternal bliss, showing yourself instead to be worthy of the torments of hell. Leave My earth, I abandon you to be torn into pieces by dragons! . . . Behold the image of Death! . . . Let the planets poison the air and corrupt the whole earth. . . . Let the sharp arrows of Death have dominion throughout

the world! Let no one be spared, either for their sex or their age! Let the innocent perish with the guilty and no one escape![36]

He imagined God as passionately resentful that a sinful humanity had once
forced Him into taking human form. The very thing that individuals shared
with Christ, their humanness as revealed in their bodies, was now a liability
used by Him to sow death and destruction.

Giovanni Boccaccio in his *Decameron* even wondered how was it possible
to imagine a loving God when all familial love was destroyed. "It was not
merely a question of one citizen avoiding another, and of people almost
invariably neglecting their neighbors and rarely or never visiting their relatives, addressing them only at a distance." No, it was much worse, he lamented: "This scourge had implanted so great a terror in the hearts of men
and women that brothers abandoned brothers, uncles their nephews, sisters
their brothers, and in many cases, wives deserted husbands." Much, much
worse: "Fathers and mothers refused to nurse and assist their children, as
though they did not belong to them."[37]

And the plague seemingly never went away. There were at least fifteen
further general outbreaks within Latin Christendom before 1500, with
England in particular specifically suffering seventeen. Perhaps the most devastating was the "second pestilence" between 1361 and 1362, which, unlike
the great pestilence a decade earlier, mostly killed children and adolescents.
In England, again the most studied statistically, while the mortality was
significantly lower than between 1347 and 1351—for example, 20 percent
for London instead of 51 percent, and just 10–30 percent for secular clergy
rather than 45 percent—the burials of children were 6–10 percent higher.
Perhaps more boys died than girls, but this might just be a question of
bioarcheological sampling. Perhaps older individuals, having survived the
earlier plague, acquired an immunity, while anyone born after 1348 had
not, but this is only speculation. All that is certain was that a cruel God
slaughtered more innocents this time around. What is also certain is that
the relentless presence of the plague in the West for more than 150 years is
unparalleled in world history.

Around 1350, Francesco Petrarch—formerly Francesco Petracchi before his self-transformation into the more euphonious and classically res-
onant Franciscus Petrarca, a White Guelf exile from Florence, if forty years
younger than Dante, a brilliant scholar and sensual poet, and whose Beatrice
was named Laura—told a friend how comforting it would be to surrender

to death instead of living in the nightmare of the plague: "The life we lead is a sleep; whatever we do, dreams. Only death breaks the sleep and wakes us from dreaming. O, I wish I could have woken before this!"[38]

8 The Beginning of the End

The Black Death was the beginning of the end of the Middle Ages. No civilization could have remained unchanged by it. The various Mongol *uluses*, hordes, khanates, and empires disappeared within a few generations as a consequence. There had been a Great Famine from 1315 to 1322 across a swath of lands bordering the North Atlantic and the North Sea, in which for those seven years it rained almost every day in summer and the winters were unbearably cold, and yet, despite thousands dying from starvation, the West remained culturally coherent.[39] It is almost unimaginable—almost, but sadly not quite—what it must have been like to live during a pandemic where the dying and the dead were all around you.

The plague started the fragmentation and metamorphosis of Latin Christendom into "Europe." Obviously, Europe has always existed as a geographical entity, but as a historically meaningful religious and cultural configuration it came into existence only in the aftermath of the plague. To call, say, Willibald, Findan, Rodulfus Glaber, Heloise, Herman, Beatritz, or Dante Alighieri, a "European," while understandable and convenient, would be anachronistic and wrong. All the more so as each of them was struggling much more profoundly with what it meant to be Christian or Jewish, or even at a more basic level what it meant to be human in relationship to the divine. When individuals wrote and spoke of "Europe," they used it only as a geographically handy designation borrowed from classical authors for the variously defined landmass (it differed from author to author) that some but not all of them lived and traveled upon. People might have referred to themselves as, say, Frank and eventually French, or as living within specific regions, empires, kingdoms, principalities, villages, towns, and farmhouses, but these epithets, localities, or institutions were never understood as existing apart from or outside of *Christianitas*. Christendom was—or, more precisely, the many micro-Christendoms of the early Middle Ages were— much more important in defining the world in which individuals lived for more than a millennium.

More specifically, it was the Christendom of Innocent III, which, encompassing all time and space and any human who had ever lived and would ever live, that began splintering during and after the plague. This vision of Christendom was powerfully and intimately tied to the confessional culture that had developed since the twelfth century, so it is not surprising that what confession meant for individuals shifted and changed.

Ralph of Shrewsbury, bishop of Bath and Wells, acknowledged the necessity of this shift when he informed the clergy of his diocese on Saturday, January 10, 1349, "that because priests cannot be found for love or money" to visit the sick and hear confessions during the pestilence, then, especially in an emergency when someone was on the point of death, people "should make confession of their sins . . . to any lay person, even to a woman if a man is not available." Moreover, "lest anyone should hesitate or refuse to make confession to a lay person in an emergency, imagining that lay confessors are likely to reveal what was said to them," he promised that what was said would be secret, "unless the person making the confession wishes it to be revealed." Of course, he ended with the caveat that if the dying individual miraculously recovered from the plague after confessing to their friend, son, or wife, "they should confess the same sins again to their own parish priest." [40]

Since the late thirteenth century, many individuals, especially in regions where inquisitors were a constant presence, such as southern France or northern Italy, were encouraged to question and confess to themselves privately as a form of imitating Christ. Nevertheless, constantly talking about oneself to oneself, while a penance in and of itself, did not absolve persons from confessing to priests in life or on the point of death. All men, women, and children understood that confession sooner or later involved the Church. Now, though, the bishop of Bath and Wells stressed that confession was so important that in an emergency—and for the next century, living was nothing but a pestilential emergency—there was no need for the Church.

9 A Roman! A Roman!

If the Church was unnecessary for individuals in a crisis, why not for kingdoms and communes? This question was answered by the so-called Great Schism, which began in 1378. The seventh Avignon pope, Gregory XI, despite being French, decided that the papacy should return to Rome. He entered the city in January 1377; unfortunately, he died a year later. In April 1378, as the mostly French cardinals met in the Vatican palace to elect a new pope, whom they intended would be French too, outside the citizens of Rome began chanting, "A Roman! A Roman! A Roman or at least an Italian! Or else we'll kill them all!" The cardinals, frightened and flustered, picked the archbishop of Bari, Bartolomeo Prignano, who, while not from Rome, was at least from Naples. Their fear descended into farce when, still hearing the chant "Roman! Roman! Roman!," they wheeled out the elderly and barely conscious Cardinal Pietro Tebaldeschi, who was Roman, and pretended he was the new pope, diverting the mob and so escaping the city.

Bartolomeo was soon crowned Urban VI on Easter Sunday and immediately surprised the cardinals when, instead of being the amiable mediocrity they had assumed they could push around, he denounced their corruption and affirmed that the Avignon papacy was at an end. This was too much for the French cardinals, who decided that Urban was unstable (he actually might have been) and that his election was illegal because it had been made under duress. In late September, they elected a Frenchman, Robert of Geneva, as Clement VII. The two popes then anathematized each other. Christendom took sides: England, the German lands and emperor, Poland, Scandinavia, Hungary, Sicily, and most of Italy were for Urban; France, Burgundy, Savoy, Scotland, Castile, Aragon, and Navarre were for Clement; and a few realms fluctuated back and forth, such as Portugal, which changed sides four times. There had been papal schisms before, such as when Urban II proclaimed the First Crusade, but never for too long, whereas this emergency lasted thirty-nine years until the election of Martin V in 1417. At the beginning of the fifteenth century, while there may have been a Christian Europe, there was no Christendom, except perhaps in name only.[41]

10 The Jacquerie

Other violent and fractious events after the plague only accelerated the disintegration of Christendom. For example, at the end of May 1358, as the weather was warming and everyone was preparing for the Feast of Corpus Christi, thousands of French peasants in the Île-de-France, Normandy,

Picardy, and Champagne suddenly assaulted the castles and houses of the aristocracy, brutally killing noble men, women, and children. This rampage, which included Paris, lasted for two months until, with vengeful ferocity, the nobility regained their martial advantage and indiscriminately slaughtered peasants and burned villages. This insurrection was soon known as the Jacquerie, from the nickname "Jacques Bonhomme" adopted by some rebels.

The causes of this summer rebellion were varied, including anger at the obvious unfairness of the plague in sparing so many nobles, the aristocratic unwillingness to keep paying higher wages for farm work after the death of so many laborers, a related revanchism by the nobility in asserting a harsher model of serfdom that they imagined had existed before the pestilence, and the widespread instability from the warfare between England (always victorious) and France (never) now known as the Hundred Years War. What was distinctive about the Jacquerie, though, was that most of the peasants embraced their violence as a way of purifying the kingdom of France from the corruption of the nobility, and so while there was a sense of holy war about their uprising, there was no assumption that what they did was redemptive for Christendom.[42]

11 Sorcery and Demons

In 1376 the Dominican Nicolau Eymeric—an exile at the papal court in Avignon after being expelled from the kingdom of Aragon for being too zealous an inquisitor—posited two important questions in his encyclopedic *Directorium inquisitorum*: "The first is, whether sorcerers and diviners are subject to the judgement of the inquisitor of heretics. The second, posed thusly, is whether they are to be considered as heretics or as those suspected of heresy."

Nicolau answered both questions affirmatively. However, because he was an academic trained in Paris and a dedicated reader of Thomas Aquinas, this conclusion was painstakingly reached through Aristotelian convolutions. He stressed that astrologers or palm readers were not his concern; undoubtedly, they were sinful, but they were mostly harmless, having nothing to do with demons or heresy. What mattered to him were perversions of *latria* and *dulia* by humans and demons. *Latria* was the adoration that should be shown only to God. *Dulia* was the veneration that should be given only to saints, holy individuals (who had been judged as such by the Church), and popes and kings.

When a man, woman, or child offered demons the honor of *latria*—prayers, sacrifices, songs, promises of obedience, vows of chastity, genuflections, candles, incense, specially chosen clothes—they were judged by the Church as heretics. If they recanted and abjured heresy, they should be perpetually imprisoned. But if they relapsed afterward, "they are to be relinquished to the secular arm, and punished by the ultimate torture." ("Whoever invokes the aid of Mohammad," added Nicolau almost as an afterthought, "even if he does nothing else, falls into manifest heresy," as this was an act of *latria* too.)

"Certain other invokers of demons show to the demons they invoke not the honor of *latria*, but that of *dulia*, in that they insert in their wicked prayers the names of demons along with those of the blessed or the saints, making them mediators in their prayers heard by God." These individuals were also judged by the Church as heretics.

Nicolau added a Neoplatonic twist to *dulia* by noting that when such reverence was offered properly by Christians to popes, kings, "or any person who wields power," then God Himself received *latria* as a divine echo reverberating from one of His vicars on earth.

Sometimes the invocation of demons seemingly involved neither *latria* or *dulia*. Nicolau offered a very specific case study that he apparently heard in many confessions as an inquisitor in Aragon. A circle was traced on the ground and a boy placed inside it. A mirror, a sword, an amphora, "or something else" was placed in front of the child. A necromancer then read from a magic book and invoked the demon. This summoning of a demon was still a form of worship, argued Nicolau, and so *latria* and so manifest heresy.[43]

Nicolau's *Directorium inquisitorum*, while overtly technical, frequently arcane, and exhausting in its endless logical digressions, was nevertheless more than just a vast inquisitorial *summa* written by a man with too much time on his hands. In particular, what he wrote on magic, divination, demonology, adoration, and heresy was adapted as the theoretical and practical framework for the trials of men and women accused of witchcraft from the middle of the fifteenth century onward. The *Directorium inquisitorum* was the most influential and widely read inquisitorial manual for the next three hundred years.[44]

For example, the *Malleus maleficarum* (commonly if incorrectly translated as *The Hammer of Witches*) published by the Dominican inquisitors Jacob Sprenger and Heinrich Kramer in 1487—and oddly famous amongst modern readers of the occult on account of Montague Summers' translation from 1928—cribbed generously from Nicolau's work.[45]

A crucial implication of Nicolau's argument was that a man, woman, or child may genuinely believe that they were praying to God or hearing the voices of saints without realizing that they were actually adoring, venerating, and obeying demons. Such individuals were as guilty of heresy as any person explicitly invoking them. Being tricked or fooled by a demon into offering him *latria* or *dulia* was, even after his subterfuge was revealed, still a demonstration of complicity. Demons were everywhere, insinuating themselves into everything.

Although demons had been around since at least the third century—Antony of Egypt had constantly wrestled with them—the world after the plague swarmed with these malevolent entities. *Maleficium* (sorcery or witchcraft) was, at least from the perspective of inquisitors, a pragmatic response to such an infestation. Why suffer the deprecations of demons when they could so easily be manipulated through ordinary human behavior like praying, giving tokens of love, lighting candles, wearing different clothes, or solitary confession in a darkened room or a forest grove? Such *superstitio*—and superstition had a more profound and diabolical meaning then than it does now—possessed an understandable if wicked logic for persecutory intellectuals like Nicolau.[46] What is so striking about most accusations of sorcery and witchcraft against men, women, and children from the fifteenth century onward is the sheer ordinariness and banality of their supposed evil.

Ordinary human behavior had been celebrated for almost two hundred years by preachers and poets as the very thing that humanity shared with Christ. This closeness had already been breaking apart for half a century, and now the growing obsession by the Church with finding and punishing sorcerers and witches only strained this bond further.

12 Clean Blood

"Wail, holy and glorious Torah, and put on black raiment," lamented Reuven, son of the Barcelona rabbi Nissim Gerundi, in the margins of his father's Torah scroll, "for the expounders of your lucid words perished in the flames. For three months the conflagration spread through the holy congregations of the exile of Israel in Sepharad."

Reuven was remembering when thousands if not tens of thousands of Jews were massacred or forced to convert by Christian mobs (usually orchestrated by nobles and churchmen) in the kingdoms of Aragon and Castile in 1391. "The sword, slaughter, destruction, forced conversions, captivity, and spoilation were the order of the day," he wrote. The fate of Sodom and Gomorrah "overtook the holy communities of Castile, Toledo, Seville, Mallorca, Córdoba, Valencia, Barcelona, Tàrrega, and Girona, and sixty neighboring cities and villages." Reuven had survived the massacres, but so many did not.[47]

The Jewish men, women, and children who had converted were known as "New Christians" or *conversos*, as opposed to those who had forced them to convert, who now called themselves "natural Christians" or "Old Christians." This sudden and violent influx of new Christians radically changed Christianity in the Iberian peninsula. The older notion that Jews were heretics on account of deliberately turning away from the revelation of Christ—and which the earlier Jewish massacres during the Black Death had already hollowed out—now evaporated when so many had converted in so short a time. Accusations of heresy were meaningless against the surviving Jewish remnant. Instead, if there were heretics in Spain, they existed amongst the *conversos*. Many Old Christians were convinced that New Christians secretly maintained Jewish practices and beliefs. Perhaps some did, but many were, despite the violence of their conversion, eventually (or resignedly) sincere in their Christianity. Either way, as many *conversos* still had Jewish neighbors—having not moved from houses where they had formerly lived as Jews—harsher laws segregating Jews from Old and New Christians were enforced throughout the kingdoms of Aragon and Castile. Despite (or because of) the remarkable success of some *conversos*—Fernando de la Cavalleria became royal treasurer of Aragon in 1414, while Pablo de Santa Maria, who had converted in 1390, became bishop of Burgos and chancellor of Castile and León—New Christians were under constant surveillance by Old Christians.[48]

The trouble for Old Christians was that within a generation it had become almost impossible to identify New Christians. Old and New looked and acted alike. Seemingly, we are back in the Christendom of Bernard of Clairvaux or Innocent III, where Christians and heretics looked alike, which was why monks and popes were so obsessed with discovering who was secretly diseased with heretical pestilence. But there was a profound and lasting difference in the fifteenth century. Biological metaphors were still being used, except now instead of leprosy, cancer, or plague (although they never quite disappeared), there was an obsession amongst Old Christians with having "clean blood" (*sangre limpia*), which New Christians were accused of innately never having possessed or never being able to possess, however many generations after 1391.

There is a tendency amongst some modern scholars to read any biological metaphor in the Middle Ages as being a racial one. All such metaphors before the fifteenth century were not, or at least not in any sense analogous to modern racism. This changed with ideas about clean blood. Even Innocent III thought pestilential heretics were not inherently unable to cleanse themselves of their disease. As Christians, they still shared their humanity with Christ, and so His love might redeem them. Indeed, for the previous twelve hundred years, as we have seen, some form of divinity was assumed to ebb and flow within all persons. But from the fifteenth century onward some humans were, by their very biology, by their very blood, by their very skin color, supposedly so polluted that they could and never would experience the holy.

It was only after this late medieval excision of the sacred from particular individuals and groups that a fixation with race and so racism arose in the West.

13 Chauntecleer's Dream

As the sun rises on an English cottage one spring morning the cock Chauntecleer wakes up screaming. His favorite wife, Lady Pertelote, is aghast, almost falling off her perch. "Madam," he says, "I pray, don't take offence. By God, I dreamed I was in such danger!" His little heart thumps with fear. His gallant cockscomb, usually fiercely upright like the crenellations of a castle, droops in terror. In his dream a red and yellow beast similar to a hound had tried to grab and kill him in the cottage yard. This vision is so real to Chauntecleer.

"For shame," snaps Pertelote, "fie on you, faintheart." Dreams are delusions and it is vanity to think otherwise. They are nothing more than the choler (yellow bile) of blocked bowels. Is his heart not as manly as his beard? All wives desire strong and brave husbands, not constipated milksops frightened by dreams. "I cannot love a coward, by my faith."

"Madam," says Chauntecleer pretending not to be hurt, "thank you for your lore." But her lore is wrong. Dreams are not delusions, no, not at all; they are significations of the triumphs and tribulations that have happened and that will happen to every creature living in this world. The proof is all around them. Now, if experience is not good enough for her, then she should read of dreams in Macrobius, the Old Testament, Homer, or the *Life* of Saint Kenelm, an old king of Mercia. "And therefore, fair Pertelote, no man should be too reckless with dreams."

"Now," says Chauntecleer with a smile, "let's speak of mirth and stop all this!" He looks into Pertelote's beautiful face, admiring the scarlet loveliness around her eyes, and the anguish of his dream disappears. Yet, for all his love, he cannot forgive her for mocking him. So he makes fun of her, even if he only gets the joke.

"*In principio,*" lectures Chauntecleer like a cocksure scholar, in the beginning was the Word ... but enough of that. "*Mulier est hominus confusio* is what I know for sure. Madam, this Latin is 'Woman is man's joy and all his bliss.'" Really, he chuckles to himself, it says "Woman is man's ruin." Of course, he never tells this to Pertelote's beautiful face. In a fog of love, fear, and recrimination, he forgets all about the portent of his dream.

Soon after nine o'clock that same spring morning, Chauntecleer sees out of the corner of his eye a brindle fox lurking in the cabbages of the cottage yard.

"Cok cok!" Chauntecleer barely crows, horror in his heart.

"Gentle sir," the fox salutes him, leaping from his hiding place. "Don't be afraid of me as I'm your friend." Indeed, he is a connoisseur of singing, and he is only in the cabbages hoping to hear the crowing of Chauntecleer. It is widely known, he purrs, that the cock sings as skillfully as Boethius. His voice is that of an angel. Even the sun will not rise unless it hears a song from him.

Such flattery ravishes Chauntecleer's heart. He stands high upon his toes, stretches out his neck, shuts his eyes, opens his beak, and crows with all his might. Silly cock! The fox seizes him by the throat and races off toward the woods.

Pertelote shrieks along with her six sisters (who are also her husband's wives). The old widow and her daughters living in the cottage hurry outside at their alarm. "Ha! Ha! The Fox!" they cry, and after him they run like Achilles after Hector. Men with staves and their furious dogs soon join the chase. Everyone is yelling like fiends in hell—or peasants on a murderous rampage. So hideous is the noise that even the bees swarm out of their hives in fright.

"Lo, how Fortune suddenly turns!"

"Sir," rasps Chauntecleer to his captor in one last desperate bid for survival, "if I were you, God help me, I'd turn upon these churls and shout, 'Go back! . . . A very pestilence upon you fall! . . . The cock is mine no matter what you do!'" "In faith, it shall be done," laughs the fox, but when he opens his mouth, his prisoner escapes and flies into a tree.

Chauntecleer, his throat sore, but not as sore as his pride, curses both himself and the fox for vanity—and pretty Pertelote for dismissing dreams.[49]

A fictional Priest recounts this fable of a cock, a hen, and a fox within a collection of twenty-three other stories and their equally fictional narrators largely written between 1387 and 1389 by a middling English bureaucrat in his late forties named Geoffrey Chaucer in a work now known as *The Canterbury Tales*.

All of Chaucer's storytellers are on a pilgrimage to the shrine of Saint Thomas Becket in Canterbury Cathedral. (Becket, archbishop of Canterbury, was murdered by four knights inside the cathedral in 1170; three years later Pope Alexander III canonized him.) These pilgrims are an eclectic crowd, neither too high nor too low in English society, including a Miller (sixteen stone, rude, and rambunctious), a Merchant (forked beard, money troubles, but decent), a Reeve (old, choleric, and thin), a Pardoner (deceitful with ratty waxen hair), a Friar (boozy seducer of young girls), a Monk (always out hunting on a horse), a Clerk (Oxford student and, spending what little he has on the works of Aristotle, penniless), a Man of Law (wary and wise), and a Doctor (knows his humors and profits from the plague). There is a kind and chivalrous Knight, who, while socially superior to his companions, is a little worse for wear in his rust-stained tunic. There are only three women pilgrims: the Wife of Bath (gap-toothed, fun, and married five times), a Nun (devoutly loathes idleness), and another nun, the Prioress (perhaps too preciously a gentlewoman, whose little dogs drink milk and who, despite adorning herself with the inscription *Amor vincit omnia* on a brooch, gladly tells tales of Jews killing Christian children). The Priest (muscular, ruddy complexion) is the less-than-enthusiastic confessor to the Prioress (and so is known as the Nun's Priest).

According to the prologue of The Canterbury Tales, the pilgrims initially gather in the Tabard Inn in Southwark (on the south bank of the Thames) just as the sweet April showers are beginning. There, the host of the Tabard, Harry Bailly, while admiring the individual sprightliness of each pilgrim, jovially warns that riding to Canterbury will be a very dull journey if everyone keeps to themselves. Instead, he proposes, why not tell each other stories in a competition for the most entertaining and edifying tale. "I myself will kindly ride with you—at my own expense—and be your guide." Harry organizes the pilgrims into a new "fellowship" in which they are equally storytellers and listeners, so that the peregrination to Canterbury, far from being a tedious, silent slog to be gotten through quickly, will now be a noisy, communal literary pleasure to be enjoyed for as long as possible—which is why no one ultimately reaches Becket's shrine.[50]

When Chaucer died in 1400—in a retirement house on the grounds of Westminster Abbey—he left behind ten different fragments of his text. To the very end he was not quite sure in which order his characters and their stories should be told. Fortunately, his Prologue was one of the surviving bundled quires, giving a framework to seemingly disparate tales with its Canterbury conceit and Harry's wager. (Chaucer at first intended that every pilgrim tell two tales going to Becket's shrine and two tales on the way back to the Tabard Inn. Harry still announces this astonishingly ambitious plan in the Prologue.) The Canterbury Tales is a posthumous compilation of Chaucer's poetic remains by later scribes and editors—fittingly, perhaps, as Chaucer had always called himself a "compiler" (compilator) rather than "poet."[51]

Chaucer was partially inspired by Giovanni Boccaccio's Decameron with its ten secluded storytellers entertaining one another with a hundred tales over ten days. Indeed, his Knight's Tale—a courtly romance with a mix of influences from Homer to the troubadours to Thomas Aquinas—was a translation of a story by the Italian. Even more than this artful pilfering, his earlier epic poem Troilus and Criseyde from around 1386—the story of a Trojan warrior punished by the gods with loving a woman who cruelly betrays him—was an English adaptation of Boccaccio's Filostrato. Yet Chaucer never mentioned the Italian in any of his writing. He acknowledged other

Italian poets, such as Francesco Petrarch and Dante Alighieri, even jovially ridiculing the *Comedy* and its Pilgrim in the witty *House of Fame* (where a naïve Geffrey bumbles along searching for the truth without a Virgil), written in his early thirties. He most likely gathered manuscripts for translation (and inspiration) in the 1370s when he traveled to northern Italy in the train of at least two English diplomatic missions. In any event, while Chaucer's vernacular aesthetic was deeply affected by the previous two generations of Italian poets, especially Boccaccio, the unfinished tales of the Canterbury pilgrims exemplify much more than just the anxiety of influence.[52]

The Canterbury pilgrims, their stories, and how they tell them are sublime exemplars of the late-medieval confessional culture. Chaucer imagined each of them as distinct individuals with long personal histories inescapably shaping who they once were, currently are, and will be in the future. Even when some of his pilgrims seemingly veer toward caricature, they do so because he understood that people often go through life living as clichés of themselves, having either chosen, stumbled into, or been forced by society or gender (especially for women) into this path. This was an awareness of the individuality of other humans that could only have happened after two centuries of emphasizing what it meant to talk about oneself as an individual with an inescapably intertwined past, present, and future. Chaucer shared in the humanity of others by being able to fully imagine them as different from himself.

Such humanness shone through in humor. We have come across jokes and jokers over the centuries—Augustine stands out as quite the wit, except when he corresponded with pagans, and then there are the vicious wags ("More times!") watching Judah's baptism—but here humorousness seems a defining quality of being human. Christ was not known as especially funny when He was a man. Chaucer unquestionably believed that he and other people imitated Him in the world, especially in their experience of love, but the intimacy between Creator and His creations had been fracturing since the plague and humor was now a sign of this growing rupture. *The Canterbury Tales* makes this point explicit by ending with the (unfinished) Parson's Tale, a prose sermon rather than a poetic tale and a relentlessly dull display of Christian platitudes that, far from elevating the tone of what has come before—the bawdy fun of it all—only underscores its joyfulness.

The cock Chauntecleer is one of the most fully human individuals in *The Canterbury Tales*, and the Nun's Priest's Tale is an artistic and intellectual triumph. It is at once a parody of the *Iliad*, *chansons* like the *Song of Roland*, troubadours singing (or crowing) of *fin'amor*, and Arthurian romances like *Parzival*. It is a satire of Scholasticism. It is a reflection on the meaning and purpose of dreams, which, going all the way back to Vibia Perpetua, was a distinctly medieval way of connecting and communicating with the holy. It comically alludes to what is now known as the Peasant Revolt (similar to the Jacquerie), which swept through southern England in 1381. And it is an affectionate spoof of Boethius' *Consolation of Philosophy* and the problem of free will. Chaucer had read Jean de Meun's French translation of the *Consolation* and was deeply moved by it. (He also admired and translated *The Romance of the Rose*.) "Blessed be your breeches and your balls!" says an equally moved Harry Bailly to the Nun's Priest. "That was a merry tale of Chauntecleer!"[53]

Chauntecleer's dream and his sense of impending doom in the cottage yard remind us of Boethius awaiting death in Pavia nine hundred years earlier—except without Philosophy, a lot more poultry, and a last-minute and quick-witted escape from his executioner.

14 I, Christine

Christine de Pizan loathed *The Romance of the Rose*. She thought it vile, humorless, and immoral, an ugly book that encouraged the degradation and mistreatment of women.

"Go ahead," Christine dared a Parisian champion of Jean de Meun's work named Pierre Col in a letter (more of a treatise, really) from October 1402, "turn the bad into good, then I will believe that *The Romance of the Rose* is good!" She knew such alchemy was beyond him. "Come on now! Ha!" Did Pierre even know how to read? Books were not for dipping into, skimming here and there, liking just one or two parts and ignoring everything else. In the Qur'an, wrote Christine, will be found many good and pious points, even beauty, but taken as whole—and that was the only way to read a book, she stressed—it was worthy of scorn, although less so than *The Romance of the Rose*. Further, she argued, authors and their characters were one and the same, so in reality Jean de Meun was as mean-spirited, foul-mouthed, and hateful toward women as his fictional Genius. She never wanted *The Romance of the Rose* banned, just understood for what it was. Debating and arguing over books were vital to her as a scholar and a woman—especially when she was right. What more could Christine say to Pierre than she already had—having previously corresponded with him and his brother Gontier on the same topic—except that, once again in her opinion as a humble woman who loved to read, *The Romance of the Rose* was poisonous rubbish.

Christine had been debating the merits of *The Romance of the Rose* with a cadre of influential French male ecclesiastical scholars for over a year. But enough was enough. "Let each person believe what he wants to the best of his ability," she told Pierre Col. "What I have written is written."[54]

For more than a decade, writing had been Christine's intellectual, spiritual, and financial salvation. Her husband, Estienne de Castel, had died during an epidemic in 1389—probably one of the plague's many late brushfires—and she was widowed at twenty-five with three small children, a niece, and a mother to support. (Her father had died a year earlier.) She had loved her husband deeply, but remorse was a vanity she could not afford.

"Fortune," Christine recalled in her *Book of Fortune's Transformation* (*Le livre de la mutacion de Fortune*) from 1403, "remembered me when it pleased her to help me quickly in my great need." Fortune's charity was cruel. "She transformed me, my body and my face, completely into those of a natural man. And I who was formerly a woman, am now in fact a man." She hated this transformation, revealing, as it did, the spitefulness of Fortune and of the society in which she lived. She was forced into being like a man ("my current self-description is the truth") in order to earn her living as a writer. But Christine was a natural woman with free will, and she would overcome the cruelty of Fortune—just as Boethius had done in his *Consolation of Philosophy*—by embracing books and writing.[55]

Christine had come to Paris from Venice aged four when her father, Tommaso di Benvenuto da Pizzano, was appointed royal astrologer and physician to the French king, Charles V. Tommaso had encouraged his daughter to read and study (even if she was a disappointment as a girl when he had wanted a son). He was a bookish man, and his daughter could not prevent herself "from stealing scraps and flakes, small coins and change" from his wealth of knowledge.[56] Nevertheless, however learned Christine was at home—and Estienne had also supported her self-education—becoming a journeyman writer in French was a radical decision. And having decided that was her new life, she worked incredibly hard at it. She wrote love poetry, devotional tracts, ballads, rondels, and poems on various subjects (including widowhood). Whatever her patrons (mostly in the French court) wanted, she swiftly supplied a text. She even oversaw the copying and illumination of her manuscripts. But she was no hack; or, rather, whatever she wrote was always very good and she knew it. Christine has been called—with not too much exaggeration—the first professional female writer in the West.

"Between the years 1399," Christine calculated, "and the present year, 1405, during which I am still writing, I have compiled fifteen major works, without counting some smaller works, which together are contained in seventy large-size quires."[57] (Amongst her smaller works was a *Dit de la Rose* in which knights form an "Order of the Rose" to defend the honor of women.) She still accepted commissions—such as from the duke of Burgundy, Philip the Bold, to write a biography of his brother, Charles V—but, buoyed by her growing reputation as a writer and an intellectual, she began writing whatever she passionately believed needed to be written by a woman. And so she wrote *The Book of the City of Ladies* (*Le livre de la cité des dames*) in 1405.

"I, Christine," she imagined herself at the beginning of *The Book of the City of Ladies*, "was sitting in my study, surrounded by books on many different subjects." She has been immersed in too many weighty tomes, so she searches for something frivolous to read. By chance she comes across a small book, which, while purportedly a satire, viciously mocks women as naturally "inclined to and full of every vice." Why, why, she laments, do so many male poets and philosophers think this? (Or, if she had known, cocks like Chauntecleer.)

"Thinking deeply about these matters, I began to examine my character and conduct as a natural woman." Perhaps the male poets and philosophers are right. God, Christine concludes, formed a vile creature when He made woman. "Alas, God," she cries, "why did You not let me be born as a male?" Why is she trapped in a female body? She leans back in her chair and weeps, her head bowed in shame.

Suddenly a ray of light falls upon Christine's lap. She lifts her head and sees three crowned ladies glowing in splendor. They are Lady Reason, Lady Rectitude, and Lady Justice. "Dear daughter," says Lady Reason, "do not be afraid." The three ladies have come to lead her out of her ignorance and shame at being a woman. "Fair daughter," continues Lady Reason, "the pre-rogative amongst women has been bestowed on you to establish and build the City of Ladies."

This City of Ladies will be established on the Field of Letters, "where all fruits and fresh rivers are found and the earth abounds in good things." Christine will dig up all the books by men slandering women—which she admits are most books—littering this field. "I assure you," Lady Reason tells her, "that any man who slanders does so out of a great wickedness of heart, for he is acting contrary to reason and contrary to nature." Against reason because he fails to recognize all the good deeds that women have done for him. Against nature because there is "no naked beast anywhere, nor bird, which does not naturally love its female counterpart." No greater love exists than that between a man and a woman.

Lady Reason carries away upon her shoulders all the male literary de-tritus that Christine excavates from the Field of Letters. And then Christine constructs upon this gouged and trenched field—following the architec-tural plans of Lady Reason—a magnificent and eternal city of soaring pal-aces, grand boulevards, and towering walls. The mortar, bricks, and stones of the City of Ladies will be the stories of great and virtuous women, pagan and Christian, from the past and the present. Lady Reason, Lady Rectitude, and Lady Justice supply these building materials by answering the many questions that Christine asks them about the nature and history of women—it is Platonic dialogue as lumberyard. Finally, when the City of Ladies is finished (or nearly, as there is still a bit of work to be done on the roofs), the Virgin Mary rules as queen.

Christine hopes that all women, especially women of the future, will see themselves reflected in the mirrored surfaces of the City of Ladies—that is, in a history of women not shaped by the books and slanders of men. She hopes that the city will be a refuge for women and a defense against their enemies and assailants. She hopes it will remind women that God loves them and that they always have been and always will be the equal of men. "In brief, all women, whether noble, bourgeois, or lower-class," will find consolation and sanctuary in the City of Ladies.[58]

Christine's *The Book of the City of Ladies* was heavily indebted to Giovanni Boccaccio's *De mulieribus claris* (*Concerning Famous Women*). Most of her sto-ries about pagan women were copied from him. She probably read his book in French translation, although some of the scraps and flakes she stole from her father included Latin. Boccaccio included no Christians amongst his famous women, preferring notorious and entertaining pagans over virtuous martyrs. Christine appropriated only his stories of "good" pagan women (such as Gaia Cirilla, wife of King Tarquin, who governed wisely). And like everyone else with a quill and inky fingers—or so it seems—she borrowed a few tales from the *Decameron*.

Christine in *The Book of the City of Ladies* never suggested that any of her famous women, however chaste, ethical, learned, martial, or holy, were engaged in imitating Christ. She was deeply Christian, but the humanity or naturalness of women was no longer a quality she believed they shared with Him. *The Book of the City of Ladies* was still written within a confessional culture—it was itself a form of confession, especially as Christine believed an author and her characters were one and the same—but writing was no longer an act of *imitatio Christi*. Neither was human love, which now existed in a separate ideal realm divorced from His experience as a man. And this human love reached perfection in the love of married men and women.

Not surprisingly, after reading Heloise's letters to Abelard (probably in Jean de Meun's translation), Christine thought that the twelfth-century woman's belief that the love between lovers, no matter how unrequited or degrading, overlapped and replicated Christ's love for humanity was nonsense. She dismissed Heloise's preference for the label *meretrix* (whore) over "wife" as morally absurd and obviously a male fantasy (especially as it was repeated in *The Romance of the Rose*).[59] Heloise's story is not one of the building blocks of the City of Ladies.

In 1418 Christine retired to the abbey of Poissy, outside Paris, where her daughter was a nun. She was seeking safety in a ravaged and broken France, suffering from never-ending war with England. Paris had been captured by the Burgundian allies of the English.

Eleven years later Christine heard of a peasant girl named Jeanne who dressed like a man and had led the French army to victory over the English at Orléans. This girl had then escorted the dauphin to Reims, where he was crowned Charles VII, king of France. (Soon afterward the ten-year-old English king, Henry VI, was taken to Notre Dame in Paris and anointed king of France by an English bishop. His father, Henry V, had been affirmed as heir to the French throne by the Treaty of Troyes in 1420.)[60]

Jeanne was a living exemplar of the glorious women inhabiting the City of Ladies. Christine was inspired to write "a most beautiful poem"—her last work—in praise of the Maid or Virgin, in praise of la Pucelle.

> I, Christine, who have wept for eleven years in a closed abbey . . .
> I begin now for the first time to laugh . . .
> In 1429 the sun began to shine again . . .
> You, Jeanne, were born at a propitious hour,
> blessed be He who created you . . .
> Oh! What an honor for the female sex!
> That God loves women is clear with all these wretched people
> and traitors who laid waste the whole kingdom . . .
> now recovered and made safe by a woman . . .
> something a hundred thousand men could not have done!
> Before, one would not have believed it possible.
> A young girl of sixteen years (isn't this something beyond nature?)
> to whom arms seem weightless . . .
> She will restore harmony in Christendom and the Church.
> She will destroy the unbelievers one talks about
> and the heretics with their vile ways . . .
> She will destroy the Saracens, by conquering the Holy Land . . .
> I understand that some people will be displeased
> by the contents [of this poem], for if one's head is lowered
> and one's eyes are heavy one cannot look at the light.[61]

Christine de Pizan died a few months later, never knowing the tragic fate of Jeanne la Pucelle.

15 The Voices Go Silent

"The voice first came at noon, on a summer's day, in my father's garden," recalled Jeanne la Pucelle six years later on Thursday, February 22, 1431, for Pierre Cauchon, bishop of Beauvais, and the Dominican Jean Lemaître, deputy inquisitor of Rouen. "What teaching did this voice give you about the salvation of your soul?" questioned Jean Lemaître. "It taught me how to behave," quipped Jeanne. "Since when have you heard your voice?" the theologian Jean Beaupère asked her two days later in the chapel royal of Rouen's castle. "I heard it both yesterday and today," she answered. Jeanne had been asleep in her prison room when the divine voice woke her, she said. "Did the voice wake you with its sound or by touching you on the arms or elsewhere?" Jean Beaupère was curious to know. "I was woken by the voice without being touched," Jeanne replied, and although it said some things before she was fully awake, she did remember being told to "answer boldly" when questioned. The voice came from God and was always accompanied by light. "Do you see anything with the voice?" "I'm not going to tell you everything," Jeanne retorted, "for I don't have permission," but she did add that the voice was beautiful, righteous, and worthy. "There's also a saying amongst little children that people are often hanged for telling the truth," she wryly added.[62]

Three days later, Jeanne was back before the inquisition in heavy iron fetters and once more was asked about whether the voice was an angel, a saint, or directly from God. "The voices are those of Saint Catherine and of Saint Margaret," she now specified. "How do you know it was these two saints?" "I well know one from the other." It was, however, Saint Michael's voice she had first heard at thirteen. The voice, no matter who was speaking, was always lovely, low, sweet, and in French. "Did the voice, that is to say Saint Margaret, speak English?" Pierre Cauchon urbanely quizzed her two days later. "Why should she speak English?" Jeanne replied, laughing. After all, "she's not on the side of the English!"[63]

Two weeks later, Pierre Cauchon and six other clerics privately questioned Jeanne in her prison cell. "Asked if she spoke to God when she promised Him to keep her virginity, she replied that it should be quite enough to promise it to those who were sent by Him, namely Saints Catherine and Margaret." Jeanne was not a bride of Christ. Did Saints Catherine and Margaret sometimes not come when she summoned them? "I never needed them without having them." Did she see her voices? "They came often amongst Christians and were not seen," she replied, "but I often saw them." What did her voices call her? Every day, she said, they called her "Jeanne la Pucelle, daughter of God."[64]

Three years earlier, the holy French voices of Jeanne ordered the sixteen-year-old to leave the hamlet of Domrémy and expel the armies of the English king Henry VI from France. Remarkably, this stocky and illiterate peasant girl persuaded the dauphin Charles, the heir to the French throne, to let her not only join his army but also help lead it. Immediately, Jeanne adopted a great white standard with the names of Jesus and Mary on it (designed by her voices) and a sword discovered behind the altar of Saint Catherine at Fierbois (which the saint had told her about). Even before discovering the sword, she was already wearing the tunic, armor, and rounded bowl haircut of a knight.

"Did the voice make you wear men's clothes?" Jean Beaupère sneered at Jeanne during her trial. "Dress is of little matter," was her equally dismissive answer. "I didn't take these clothes or do anything except by the command of Our Lord and the angels."[65]

On Monday, May 4, 1429, inspired by her voices, Jeanne led the French army to success over the English at Orléans. A day, as Christine de Pizan laughed, when "the sun began to shine again."

Unfortunately, almost exactly a year later, Jeanne fell off her horse in an attack on Compiègne and, captured by the Burgundian allies of the English, she was given to the bishop of Beauvais to be judged for sorcery and heresy. The trial began at Rouen's castle on Saturday, January 13, 1431, and lasted four months. Pierre Cauchon along with the faculty of the university of Paris believed that Henry VI was the rightful king of France and, though taking their interrogation very seriously, were convinced that either Jeanne's holy voices were demonic and invoked by her or that she sincerely believed her voices were those of Saints Catherine and Margaret when, in fact, they were demons tricking her. (Pierre Cauchon would certainly have read Nicolau Eymeric's *Directorium inquisitorum*.) Four months later, the inquisition and the university judged her to be a heretic.[66]

Jeanne's voices went silent. Confused and frightened, wearing a woman's dress and with her head shaven, she signed (a notary held her hand to help her make "a sort of signature") an abjuration denying them on Thursday, May 24, 1431. "I, Jeanne, commonly called la Pucelle," began the abjuration, "confess that I have sinned very grievously in falsely pretending to have had revelations and apparitions from God, His angels, Saint Catherine and Saint Margaret . . . and in leading others astray . . . and in making superstitious divinations . . . and in wearing a dissolute, shameful and immodest outfit, against natural decency, with hair cut round like a man, against all decency of womanhood . . . and practicing idolatry by invoking and adoring demons . . . I will never through any exhortation or other means return to these errors from which it has pleased Our Lord to deliver and remove me." [67]

Five days later, Pierre Cauchon and Jean Lemaître visited Jeanne in her prison cell (where she was to stay for the rest of her life) and were shocked to discover her dressed once more as a man. "I would rather die than be kept in irons," she told them. "But you admitted that you falsely boasted that the voices you heard were those of Saint Catherine and Saint Margaret!"

Pierre and Jean yelled at her. "I never intended to deny them," she told the two men; it was the fear of fire that had made her do it. Jeanne was instantly condemned as a relapsed heretic. [68]

The next morning Jeanne, after receiving the Host (a rare privilege for a heretic), was led into the town square of Rouen. She was wearing women's clothes and a long pointed hat shaped like a bishop's miter, upon which was written: "Heretic, relapse, apostate, idolator." An executioner fastened her to a wooden stake atop a small platform made of plaster. A placard in front of the platform read: "Jeanne who had herself named 'la Pucelle,' liar, pernicious woman, abuser of people, soothsayer, superstitious woman, blasphemer of God, presumptuous unbeliever in the faith of Jesus Christ, boaster, idolator, cruel, dissolute, invoker of demons, apostate, schismatic and heretic." Pierre Cauchon proclaimed to the crowd of thousands who had come to watch the execution what the condemned had done and why she was to be burnt.

Jeanne, barely nineteen years old, was crying. An Englishman (hiding his tears) stepped out of the crowd and gave her a small cross as a comfort. The executioner lit a fire under the plaster platform. Jeanne soon suffocated. As the flames subsided it was revealed that her body was unharmed, apart from some scorched hair and clothing. She was stripped by the executioner and her naked body displayed to the crowd as proof that she was a woman. Her corpse was then placed upon what was left of the plaster platform and incinerated in another fire. Finally, Jeanne's ashes were gathered by the executioner and scattered in the Seine. [69]

A startling observation about Jeanne is that, despite her incredibly active life, she was decidedly passive in relation to her divine voices. She never assumed she was imitating Christ, and she never tried to grasp the sacred by being like Him; instead, she took it for granted that it would come to her. She simply could not imagine being a young girl and not hearing sacred voices. And these voices never attempted to be human either.

Similarly, Jeanne never actually thought she had achieved a sensation of divinity through her actions, despite the inquisition trying to imply this about her. On the contrary, she simply did whatever her voices, and so God, told her. She did not believe, and no one else did, that any residue of the sacred adhered to her, got mixed into her flesh, after she heard her voices or won her victories. This is in stark contrast to all the preceding centuries, whether Christianity was involved or not. It was the sheer ordinary humanity of Jeanne that God liked and so used to reveal His divinity. She remembered Him telling her this was why He chose her. "It pleased God," she told Pierre Cauchon two months before her execution, "to act through a simple virgin girl."[70]

Unquestionably, Jeanne passionately believed that humans and the divine had a holy intimacy, where one needed the other, but a new distance had developed between the two. In fifteenth-century art, for instance, we still see this yearning for the sacred, the idea that some sort of divinity dwells in a person, but it was becoming harder and harder to imagine Christ and humanity as having any real compatibility. It was not for nothing that in 1512 Michelangelo's God and Adam in the Sistine Chapel reach out to each other but fail to touch.

Jeanne exemplifies the shift after the Black Death in which Latin Christendom was transforming into Europe and in which the individual sense of self, which had been forged during the twelfth and thirteenth centuries, while maintaining a linear identity that moved forward through time, was no longer intimately tied to Christ. She certainly still lived within a confessional culture knowing how to talk about herself inside the courtroom and out. (Again, like Beatritz confessing to Jacques Fournier a century earlier, everything Jeanne confessed was mediated by coercion and being translated into Latin, and yet an incredibly charismatic, witty, and vivid personality still comes through in the record of her trial.) Nevertheless, her understanding of herself was first and foremost as a Christian French woman and as a Christian European. Jeanne's God spoke to her in French, as did His saints and angels, and He had a clear idea what constituted the kingdom of France and that only a Frenchman could be king.

In this sense, something called "medieval Europe" really only existed for less than a century at the very end of the Middle Ages. Obviously, a lot happened after 1431, not the least of which was the Ottoman sultan Mehmed II capturing Constantinople in 1453, the final campaign of the Reconquista and the expulsion of Iberian Jews in 1492, and the Spanish conquest and colonization of the Americas. But this book is not about medieval Europe, and so we shall end with the death of Jeanne la Pucelle, daughter of God

16 A Vision Without End

It has been a long and hopefully not too perilous journey from Vibia Perpetua to Jeanne la Pucelle.

We began with the Roman Empire and ended with Europe. We have seen societies and cultures collapse, coalesce into new formations, then fracture once again. We have moved from a universe of many gods to a cosmos with only one God. We have watched as small and fragile western Christendoms metamorphosed into an all-embracing Latin Christendom. We have followed the shift from a penitential culture to a confessional one. We have viewed heaven and hell become extravagant places of punishment and redemption even as some of the here and now overflowed into the hereafter as purgatory. We have traced the change from a world in which no one either could or wanted to copy Christ to one in which the most inescapably ordinary thoughts and deeds, especially as realized in love, were imitations of Him. We have surveyed invasions, crusades, inquisitions, and plagues. We have experienced men, women, and children struggling with their identities as pagans, Jews, Muslims, and especially as Christians.

What has given continuity to these twelve centuries has been the splendor and sorrow of existence as shaped by the ebb and flow of the divine and the human in the living of millions of lives.

The formation of Europe from a fractured Latin Christendom was by no means the final summation of the West; rather, it was merely one more configuration of a phenomenon that first began in the third-century Roman Empire. The West in the centuries after the Middle Ages has shifted and changed in many more regions than just Europe.

Like Isidore of Seville in the seventh century, I have tried to cast a wide net over what can never be fully captured. As he knew all too well, such scholarly endeavors are visions without end. Too many things are always left out, and even more are yet to be discovered. My history of the Middle Ages is therefore a narrative of how I presently envision these centuries and a stepping-stone for my readers and myself for further reflection on the medieval West. Unlike Isidore and his *Etymologies*, I have not written this book as a bulwark against the imminent disappearance of truth.

If, for no other reason than that Beatrice's last smile promises that even when everything we hold dear turns away from us, never to look back, the truth of what we had endures forever.

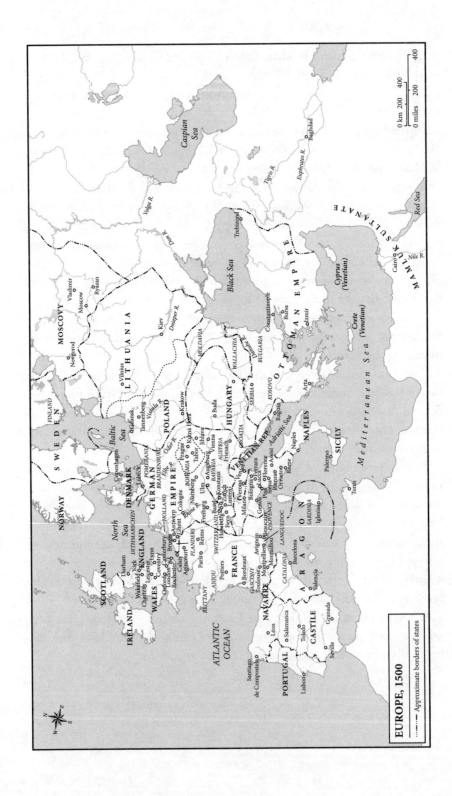

EUROPE, 1500

----- Approximate borders of states

Acknowledgments

Tim Bent is a superb editor and friend. This book would never have been finished without his encouragement and certainly would not read as it does without his skill.

Zara Cannon-Mohammed, project editor, Sue Warga, copy editor, and Amy Whitmer, senior production editor, were expert guides on the final stages of publication.

I thank my undergraduates over the years who have listened to much of this book as lectures (or rambling asides) and who prompted me to clarify what I thought. Their brilliance more than compensated for my institutional loneliness (quite common for medieval historians) outside the classroom.

The second chapter was written while I was a fellow at the Collegium de Lyon: Institut d'Études Avancées. I am grateful to Julien Théry for the invitation and to Hervé Joly for his directorship.

The fourth chapter (and the book more generally) is indebted to the Andrew W. Mellon Foundation for awarding me a New Directions Fellowship to study Arabic and medieval Islamic history.

Final revisions were undertaken while I was a visiting professor at the Université Paul Valéry–Montpellier 3. I am grateful to Alessia Trivellone for the invitation (and her advice on images).

My gratitude goes to Elizabeth Redgate, Jeff Gerecke (G Agency), Ussama Makdisi, Julie Berry, Sunjoo Moon, Camille Peck, Leticia Connell, Cassie Adcock, Madeline Linder, Sabrina Hu, Mia Bloss, Chloe West, Peter Kastor, Jonathan Cohen, Jessica Rosenfeld, Emily Rose, Maribel Dietz, Isaac Amon, Sean McWilliams, Daniel Bornstein, Michael Schaefer, Sean Field, Lauren Staub, Kevin Ohlinger, Amanda Scott, John Arnold, Anna Matevosyan, Will Winter, Laura Winter, Andrew Collings, Amanda Power, Jay Rubenstein, Thomas Granier, Tim Parsons, Ivona Percec, Jean-Paul Rehr, Nicole Jacobs,

Rich Cohen, Chris Kasamis, Sonia da Silva, Betsy Farrell, Babs Davy, Anne Lester, Laurent Guitton, and Christine Caldwell.

My sister, Trescha Knowles, brother-in-law, Grahame, nephew, Andrew, niece, Victoria, and sister-in-law, Emily Garb, are invaluable.

Three individuals read the book as I was writing it. Anthony Peck, my oldest friend, offered superlative advice and criticism. Randall Pippenger—a former student who ended up studying with my own graduate advisor—is a brilliant historian and writer, and his judgments and opinions (especially on the ending) were indispensable. Bob Moore, a great scholar and friend, has shaped this book (and me) in so many ways.

This book is dedicated to my late wife, Margaret Garb, and my late mother, Veronica Lacy, who died within a few months of each other after long and cruel illnesses. It is also dedicated to my daughter, Eva, whose love moves the sun and all the other stars for me.

Notes

PREFACE

1. Jorge Luis Borges, "La última sonrisa de Beatriz," in his *Nueve ensayos dantescos* (Madrid: Espasa-Calpe, 1982), pp. 155–161, esp. p. 155, and translated by Esther Allen as "Beatrice's Last Smile," in *Jorge Luis Borges: Selected Non-Fictions*, ed. Eliot Weinberger (New York: Penguin, 1999), pp. 302–305, esp. p. 302.
2. Marc Bloch, "Pour une histoire comparée des sociétés européenes" [orig. 1928], in *Mélanges Historiques* 1, ed. Charles-Edmond Perrin (Paris: SEVPEN, 1963), pp. 16–40, esp. p. 38.

I

WHAT GOD?

203–337

1. *Passio Sanctarum Perpetuae et Felicitatis*, ed. and trans. Joseph Farrell and Craig Williams, in *Perpetua's Passions: Multidisciplinary Approaches to the* Passio Perpetuae et Felicitatis, ed. Jan N. Bremmer and Marco Formisano (Oxford: Oxford University Press, 2012), pp. 14–23 (translation), pp. 24–32 (Latin text); Brent Shaw, "The Passion of Perpetua," *Past and Present* 139 (1993): 3–45. On the amphitheater in Carthage, see David L. Bomgardner, "The Carthage Amphitheatre: A Reappraisal," *American Journal of Archaeology* 93 (1989): 85–103, esp. 88–91.
2. Marcus Aurelius, *Meditations*, ed. and trans. C. R. Haines (Cambridge, MA: Harvard University Press, 1994), pp. 28–29 [and trans. Maxwell Staniforth (New York: Penguin, 2005), p. 17; references to page numbers in this translation are in square brackets].
3. On population, see Bruce Frier, "Demography," in *The Cambridge Ancient History. Vol. 11: The High Empire, A.D. 70–192*, ed. A. K. Bowman, Peter Garnesey, and Dominic Rathbone (Cambridge: Cambridge University Press, 2000), pp. 787–816, esp. pp. 813–816, and Walter Scheidel, "Demography," in *The Cambridge Economic History of the Greco-Roman World*, ed. Walter Scheidel, Ian Morris, and Richard P. Saller (Cambridge: Cambridge University Press, 2007), pp. 38–86, esp. pp. 47–49.
4. Kyle Harper, *Slavery in the Late Roman World, AD 275–425* (Cambridge: Cambridge University Press, 2011), pp. 25, 66–99.

5. Chris Wickham, *Framing the Early Middle Ages: Europe and the Mediterranean, 400–800* (Oxford: Oxford University Press, 2005), p. 17.

6. Marcus Aurelius, *Meditations*, pp. 164–167 [Staniforth, p. 75].

7. Marcus Aurelius, *Meditations*, pp. 30–31 [Staniforth, p. 18].

8. Marcus Aurelius, *Meditations*, pp. 294–295 [Staniforth, p. 139]. The phrase "as is the case with the Christians" may have been added by a later copyist. See also Peter Brown, *The Ransom of the Soul: Afterlife and Wealth in Early Western Christianity* (Cambridge, MA: Harvard University Press, 2015), p. 7.

9. On *paideia*, see Peter Brown, *Power and Persuasion in Late Antiquity: Towards a Christian Empire* (Madison: University of Wisconsin Press, 1992), pp. 35–70.

10. Aeschylus, *Agamemnon* in *Oresteia: Agamemnon. Libation-Bearers. Eumenides*, ed. and trans. Alan H. Sommerstein (Cambridge, MA: Harvard University Press, 2008), pp. 22–23.

11. Now, see Kim Bowles, *Private Worship, Public Values, and Religious Change in Late Antiquity* (Cambridge: Cambridge University Press, 2008).

12. Ovid, *Ex Ponto*, in *Tristia. Ex Ponto*, trans. A. L. Wheeler, rev. G. P. Goold (Cambridge, MA: Harvard University Press, 1924), pp. 266–267.

13. *Passio Sanctorum Scilitanorum*, trans. Herbert Musurillo, in *The Acts of the Christian Martyrs* (Oxford: Oxford University Press, 1972), p. 87.

14. *The Book of the Laws of Countries: Dialogue on Fate of Bardaisan of Edessa*, ed. and trans. H. J. W. Drijvers (Piscataway, NJ: Gorgias Press, 2006), p. 61.

15. *Book of the Laws of Countries*, p. 53.

16. Beate Dignas and Engelbert Winter, *Rome and Persia in Late Antiquity: Neighbours and Rivals* (Cambridge: Cambridge University Press, 2007), pp. 9–18.

17. Dio Cassius, *Roman History*, ed. and trans. Earnest Cary and Herbert B. Foster (Cambridge, MA: Harvard University Press, 1927), 9, pp. 482–483.

18. Dio Cassius, *Roman History*, vol. 9, pp. 482–483.

19. *Kephalaia*, ed. Alexander Böhlig and Hans Jacob Polotsky (Stuttgart: Kohlhammer, 1940), 14–16, pp. 46–54; *Der Kölner Mani-Kodex (Über das Werden seines Leibes)*, ed. and trans. Ludwig Koenen and Cornelia Römer (Opladen: Westdeutscher Verlag, 1988), p. 12; Iain Gardner and Samuel N. C. Lieu, *Manichaean Texts from the Roman Empire* (Cambridge: Cambridge University Press, 2004), pp. 49–51, 73–75.

20. Michel Tardieu, "La diffusion du Bouddhisme dans l'empire kouchan, l'Iran et la Chine d'après un Kepahalaion manichéen inédit," *Studia Iranica* 17 (1988): 153–182.

21. On Manicheanism and "blessed poverty," see Peter Brown, *Treasure in Heaven: The Holy Poor in Early Christianity* (Charlottesville: University of Virginia Press, 2016), esp. pp. 36–50, 72.

22. *A New Eusebius: Documents Illustrating the History of the Church to AD 337*, rev. W. H. Frend (London: SPCK, 1987), p. 155.

23. On Caracalla's general grant of citizenship, see Myles Lavan, "The Spread of Roman Citizenship, 14–212 CE: Quantification in the Face of High Uncertainty," *Past and Present* 230 (2016): 3–46.

24. Mary Beard, *SPQR: A History of Ancient Rome* (New York: Liveright, 2015), pp. 527–529, ends her history of "classical" Rome with Caracalla's grant of citizenship.

25. Wickham, *Framing the Early Middle Ages*, pp. 609–635. On urban density and transportation in the eastern Mediterranean, see Colin Adams, *Land Transport in Roman Egypt* (Oxford: Oxford University Press, 2007), esp. pp. 44–47.

26. Peter Brown, *Through the Eye of a Needle: Wealth, the Fall of Rome, and the Making of Christianity in the West, 350–550 AD* (Princeton, NJ: Princeton University Press, 2012), pp. 6–7.

27. On the number of *curiales*, see W. C. Scheidel and S. J. Friesen, "The Size of the Economy and the Distribution of Income in the Roman Empire," *Journal of Roman Studies* 99 (2009): 61–99, esp. 77. On taxation, see Keith Hopkins, "Rome, Taxes, Rent and Trade," *Kodai: Journal of Ancient History* 6–7 (1995–1996): 41–75, for an overall tax rate of 5–7 percent.

28. Michael McCormick et al., "Climate Change During and After the Roman Empire: Reconstructing the Past from Scientific and Historical Evidence," *Journal of Interdisciplinary History* 43 (2012): 169–220, esp. 183, 188–189.

29. Raffaella Cribiore, "A Hymn to the Nile," *Zeitschrift für Papyrologie und Epigraphik* 106 (1995): 97–116, esp. 98–100.

30. On the edict of Decius, see J. B. Rives, "The Decree of Decius and the Religion of Empire," *Journal of Roman Studies* 89 (1999): 135–154.

31. Eric Rebillard, "Popular Hatred Against Christians: The Case of North Africa in the Second and Third Centuries," *Archiv für Religionsgeschichte* 16 (2015): 283–310, esp. 288.

32. Dignas and Winter, *Rome and Persia in Late Antiquity*, pp. 56, 80.

33. Matthew P. Canepa, *The Two Eyes of the Earth: Art and Ritual of Kingship Between Rome and Sasanian Iran* (Berkeley: University of California Press, 2009), pp. 54–56.

34. Lactantius, *De mortibus persecutorum*, ed. and trans. J. L. Creed (Oxford: Clarendon Press, 1984), pp. 10–11.

35. Athanasius of Alexandria, *Vie d'Antoine: Introduction, texte critique, traduction, notes et index*, ed. and trans. G. J. M Bartelink (Paris: Cerf, 2011), pp. 125–377. Carolinne White translated Evagrius of Antioch's Latin translation as "Life of Antony" in *Early Christian Lives* (Harmondsworth, UK: Penguin, 1998), pp. 7–70.

36. Bartelink, *Vie d'Antoine*, pp. 27–76, and White, *Early Christian Lives*, pp. 3–6.

37. Porphyry, *On the Life of Plotinus and the Order of His Books. Ennead I*, trans. A. H. Armstrong (Cambridge, MA: Harvard University Press, 1969), pp. 68–69.

38. Porphyry, *On the Life of Plotinus*, pp. 4–5, 28–35.

39. Porphyry, *On the Life of Plotinus*, pp. 70–71.

40. Porphyry, *On the Life of Plotinus*, pp. 56–57.

41. *Le traité de Porphyre contre les chrétiens. Un siècle de recherches, nouvelles questions. Actes de colloque international organisé les 8 et 9 septembre 2009 à l'Université de Paris IV–Sorbonne*, ed. S. Morlet (Paris: Institut d'Études Augustiniennes, 2011).

42. Lactantius, *De mortibus persecutorum*, pp. 20–21. Now, see David Potter, *Constantine the Emperor* (Oxford: Oxford University Press, 2013), p. 92.

43. "Diocletian's Edict Against the Manichaeans, 297 (or 302)," trans. in Dignas and Winter, *Rome and Persia in Late Antiquity*, pp. 216–217.

44. Gardner and Lieu, *Manichaean Texts from the Roman Empire*, pp. 84–88.

45. Brown, *Through the Eye of a Needle*, p. 36.

46. Potter, *Constantine the Emperor*, p. 94.

47. "Panegyric of Constantine Augustus," trans. C. E. V. Nixon and Barbara Saylor Rodgers in their *In Praise of Later Roman Emperors: The Panegyrici Latini* (Berkeley: University of California Press, 1994), pp. 294–333, esp. pp. 295–296, 332–333.

48. Eusebius, *Life of Constantine*, trans. Averil Cameron and Stuart G. Hall (Oxford: Oxford University Press, 1999), book I, chap. 28, p. 81.

49. Lactantius, *De mortibus persecutorum*, pp. 62–63.

50. Potter, *Constantine the Emperor*, p. 143.

51. Lactantius, *De mortibus persecutorum*, pp. 62–63.

52. Eusebius, *Historia ecclesiastica*, trans. G. A. Williamson as *The History of the Church from Christ to Constantine* (New York: New York University Press, 1966), book 10, sec. 7.1, pp. 407–408.

53. Peter Brown, *The Rise of Western Christendom: Triumph and Diversity, AD 200–1000* (Oxford: Wiley-Blackwell, 2013), p. 70.

54. Council of Elvira, canon 5, in *Acta et symbola conciliorum quae quarto saecula habita sunt*, ed. E. J. Jonkers (Leiden: Brill, 1954), p. 6.

55. Diarmaid MacCulloch, *Christianity: The First Three Thousand Years* (Harmondsworth, UK: Penguin, 2011), p. 137.

56. Judith Herrin, *The Formation of Christendom* (Princeton, NJ: Princeton University Press, 2021 [orig. 1987]), pp. 58–59, 62–63.

57. Herrin, *The Formation of Christendom*, pp. 63–64; Brown, *Through the Eye of a Needle*, pp. 120–148.

58. Potter, *Constantine the Emperor*, pp. 164–169.

59. Brown, *Through the Eye of the Needle*, pp. 14–18.

60. Brown, *Through the Eye of the Needle*, pp. 21–22.

61. On "pagans" and "paganism," see Alan Cameron, *The Last Pagans of Rome* (Oxford: Oxford University Press, 2011), esp. pp. 14–32.

62. Athanasius of Alexandria, *Vie d'Antoine*, 78, pp. 334–335.

63. Cameron, *The Last Pagans of Rome*, pp. 18–24.

64. *Athanasius Werke Band III/Teil 1: Urkunden zur Geschichte des arianischen Streites 318–328*, Lieferung 1–2, ed. Hans-Georg Opitz (Berlin: W. de Gruyter, 1934), no. 1.3, pp. 2–3.

65. Peter Green, *Alexander to Actium: The Historical Evolution of the Hellenistic Age* (Berkeley: University of California Press, 1990), esp. p. 322.

66. MacCulloch, *Christianity: The First Three Thousand Years*, pp. 127–137.

67. *Athanasius Werke*, no. 20, pp. 41–42.

68. "Nicaea 1 325," in *Decrees of the Ecumenical Councils*, vol. 1, ed. and trans. Norman P. Tanner (London: Sheed and Ward, 1990), p. 5.

69. Kevin W. Wilkinson, "Palladas and the Age of Constantine," *Journal of Roman Studies* 99 (2009): 54.

70. Eusebius, *Life of Constantine*, book IV, chap. 10, p. 157.

71. Eusebius, *Life of Constantine*, book IV, chap. 9, p. 157.

72. Eusebius, *Life of Constantine*, book III, chap. 30, p. 134.

73. Eusebius, *Life of Constantine*, book III, chap. 53, p. 142.

II

SWAN SONGS

337–476

1. Augustine, *Confessions*, trans. Henry Chadwick (Oxford: Oxford University Press, 1992), VIII, vi–vii, pp. 142–145.

2. Augustine, *Confessions*, VIII, vii–xii, pp. 145–153.

3. Augustine, *Confessions*, VIII, xii, p. 154.

4. Peter Brown, *Augustine of Hippo: A Biography* (Berkeley: University of California Press, 2013 [orig. 1967]), pp. 154–156.

5. Augustine, *Confessions*, X, viii, p. 187.

6. Augustine, *Confessions*, IX, ix–xii, pp. 170–173.

7. Augustine, *Confessions*, IX, xii, p. 174.

8. Possidius, *Vita S. Augustini*, ed. Jacques-Paul Migne, *Patrologiae cursus completus: Series Latina 32* (Paris: Garnier, 1841), c. 18, col. 49.

9. Julian, *Oration 1: Panegyric in Honour of Constantius* in *Orations 1–5*, ed. and trans. Wilmer C. Wright (Cambridge, MA: Harvard University Press, 1913), pp. 33–34, 86–87.

10. Ammianus Marcellinus, *History I Books 14–19*, ed. and trans. J. C. Rolfe (Cambridge, MA: Harvard University Press, 1950), XVI, pp. 6–11, 244–247 [and Walter Hamilton's translation, *The Later Roman Empire (A.D. 354–378)* (Harmondsworth, UK: Penguin, 1986), pp. 100–101; references to page numbers in this translation are in square brackets].

11. Athanasius of Alexandria, *Apology to Constantius*, trans. Miles Atkinson, in *Historical Tracts of S. Athanasius*, Library of Fathers of the Holy Catholic Church 13 (Oxford: John Henry Parker, 1848), p. 180.

12. Ammianus Marcellinus, *History*, XVI, 2, pp. 204–205 [Hamilton, pp. 89–90].

13. Ammianus Marcellinus, *History*, XVI, 2, pp. 206–207 [Hamilton, pp. 89–90].

14. Ammianus Marcellinus, *History*, XVI, 2, pp. 208–209 [Hamilton, pp. 89–90].

15. Ramsay MacMullen, *Changes in the Roman Empire: Essays in the Ordinary* (Princeton, NJ: Princeton University Press, 1990), pp. 78–106; Susanne Hakenbeck, "Roman or Barbarian? Shifting Identities in Early Medieval Cemeteries in Bavaria," *Post-Classical Archeologies* 1 (2011): 37–66; Peter Brown, *Through the Eye of a Needle: Wealth, the Fall of Rome, and the Making of Christianity in the West, 350–550 AD* (Princeton, NJ: Princeton University Press, 2012), p. 27.

16. Guy Halsall, *Barbarian Migrations and the Roman West, 376–568* (Cambridge: Cambridge University Press, 2007), pp. 144–149.

17. Halsall, *Barbarian Migrations and the Roman West*, pp. 118–137.

18. Philipp von Rummel, *Habitus barbarus: Kleidung und Repräsentation spätantiker Eliten im 4. und 5. Jarhundert* (Berlin: de Gruyter, 2007), p. 400.

19. Ammianus Marcellinus, *History*, XXII, 5, pp. 202–213 [Hamilton, pp. 238–239].

20. Ammianus Marcellinus, *History*, XXII, 14, pp. 274–275 [Hamilton, pp. 250–251].

21. *Artemii Passio*, in *Die Schriften des Johannes von Damaskos*. vol. 5, *Opera homiletica et hagiographica*, ed. Bonifatius Kotter (Berlin: de Gruyter, 1988), 70.5, p. 244, and trans. in *The Roman Frontier and the Persian Wars (AD 226–363)*, ed. Michael H. Dodgeon and Samuel N. C. Lieu (London: Routledge, 1991), p. 239.

22. Ammianus Marcellinus, *History*, XXXI, 2–4, pp. 381–403 [Hamilton, pp. 410–418].

23. Kyle Harper, *The Fate of Rome: Climate, Disease, and the End of an Empire* (Princeton, NJ: Princeton University Press, 2017), pp. 191–195.

24. Jordanes, *Romana et Getica*, ed. Theodor Mommsen, Monumenta Germaniae historica, Auctores antiquissimi 5 (Berlin: Weidmann, 1882), xxiv, pp. 89–91 [and translated by Peter Van Nuffelen and Lieve Van Hoof as *Romana and Getica* (Liverpool: Liverpool University Press, 2020), pp. 279–280; references to page numbers in this translation are in square brackets]. On Jordanes, see Michael Kulikowski, *Rome's Gothic Wars from the Third Century to Alaric* (Cambridge: Cambridge University Press, 2007), pp. 54–56.

25. Ammianus Marcellinus, *History*, XXXI, 4, pp. 402–403 [Hamilton, pp. 416–417].

26. Ammianus Marcellinus, *History*, XXXI, 4, pp. 406–407 [Hamilton, p. 418].

27. Kulikowski, *Rome's Gothic Wars*, pp. 132–137.

28. Ammianus Marcellinus, *History*, XXXI, 13, pp. 402–483 [Hamilton, pp. 435–437]. See also Kulikowski, *Rome's Gothic Wars*, 137–143.

29. Ammianus Marcellinus, *History*, XXXI, 14, pp. 416–417 [Hamilton, p. 420].

30. Ambrose, *De officiis*, ed. and trans. Ivor J. Davidson (Oxford: Oxford University Press, 2001), 2, 15.70, 28.136–143, pp. 306, 342–348.

31. Kulikowski, *Rome's Gothic Wars*, pp. 144–153.

32. Maximus, "Letter 16," trans. James Houston Baxter, in *Augustine: Selected Letters* (Cambridge, MA: Harvard University Press, 1953), no. 5, pp. 16–21.

33. Roger S. O. Tomlin, "The Curse Tablets," in *The Temple of Sulis Minerva at Bath: Volume 2, The Finds from the Sacred Spring*, ed. Barry Cunliffe (Oxford: Oxford University Press, 1988), no. 98, pp. 232–234.

34. Augustine, "Letter 17," trans. James Houston Baxter, in *Augustine: Selected Letters* (Cambridge, MA: Harvard University Press, 1953), no. 6, pp 21–31.

35. *The Theodosian Code and Novels and the Sirmondian Constitutions*, trans. Clyde Pharr (Princeton, NJ: Princeton University Press, 1952), 16.1.2, p. 440.

36. Peter Brown, "Christianization and Religious Conflict," in *The Cambridge Ancient History. Vol. 13: The Late Empire, A.D. 337–425*, ed. Averil Cameron and Peter Garnsey (Cambridge: Cambridge University Press, 1997), pp. 646–647.

37. Symmachus, *Relatio* 3.8–9, ed. and trans. R. H. Barrow in *Prefect and Emperor: The* Relationes *of Symmachus, A.D. 384* (Oxford: Clarendon Press, 1973), pp. 39–41.

38. Brown, *Through the Eye of a Needle*, pp. 107–108.

39. Jerome, "Letter 128," trans. F. A. Wright, in *Jerome: Selected Letters* (Cambridge, MA: Harvard University Press, 1933), pp. 466–481.

40. Jerome, "Letter 14," trans. F.A. Wright, in *Jerome: Selected Letters* (Cambridge, MA: Harvard University Press, 1933), pp. 28–29.

41. Jerome, "Letter 128," pp. 480–481.

42. Megan Hale Williams, *The Monk and the Book: Jerome and the Making of Christian Scholarship* (Chicago: University of Chicago Press, 2006), pp. 50–52.

43. Brown, *Through the Eye of a Needle*, pp. 264–265.

44. Jerome, "Letter 128," pp. 474–475.

45. Jerome, "Letter 128," pp. 479–481.

46. Halsall, *Barbarian Migrations*, 200–217; Kulikowski, *Rome's Gothic Wars*, pp. 154–184.

47. Paulus Orosius, *Seven Books of History Against the Pagans* [*Historiarum adversus paganos libri VII*]: *The Apology of Paulus Orosius* [417], trans. Irving Woodworth Raymond (New York: Columbia University Press, 1936), 7, pp. 386–391.

48. Brown, *Augustine of Hippo*, pp. 298–301.

49. Augustine, *Concerning the City of God Against the Pagans*, trans Henry Bettenson (London: Penguin, 1972), I, Preface, p. 5, XXII, 30, p. 1091, and Brown, *Augustine of Hippo*, pp. 300–302.

50. Brown, *Augustine of Hippo*, pp. 302–311.

51. Peter Brown, *The Rise of Western Christendom: Triumph and Diversity, AD 200–1000* (Oxford: Wiley-Blackwell, 2013), pp. 88–91.

52. Brown, *Through the Eye of a Needle*, p. 362.

53. Santo Mazzarino, *Aspetti sociali del quarto secolo* (Rome: Bretschneider, 1951), p. 239.

54. Kyle Harper, *Slavery in the Late Roman World, AD 275–425* (Cambridge: Cambridge University Press, 2011), p. 15.

55. Chris Wickham, *Framing the Early Middle Ages: Europe and the Mediterranean, 400–800* (Oxford: Oxford University Press, 2005), pp. 161–163.

56. Steffen Diefenbach, *Römische Erinnerungsräume: Heiligenmemoria und kollektive Identitäten im Rom des 3. bis 5. Jahrhunderts n. Chr* Millennium-Studien 11 (Berlin: de Gruyter, 2007), pp. 404–413.

57. Jerome, "Letter 128," pp. 479–481.

58. On this point, see Brown's superb *Through the Eye of a Needle*, vii, x, xix–xx, 15, 54, 72, 83–88, 207, 216, 231–234, 246, 282, 437–438, 470, 524, and passim, and his *Treasure in Heaven: The Holy Poor in Early Christianity* (Charlottesville: University of Virginia Press, 2016).

59. John Chrysostom, *In epistulam I ad Corinthios*, ed. Jacques-Paul Migne, *Patrologiae cursus completus: Series Graeca 62* (Paris: Garnier, 1862), 40:5, cols. 353–354.

60. John Chrysostom, *In epistulam ad Ephesios*, ed. Jacques-Paul Migne, *Patrologiae cursus completus: Series Graeca 62* (Paris: Garnier, 1862), 15:3–4, cols. 109–110. An excellent discussion is in Harper, *Slavery*, pp. 206–207, 211.

61. Augustine, "[New] Letter 10*," *Epistolae ex duobus codicibus nuper in lucem prolatae*, ed. Johannes Divjak, *Sancti Aurelii Augustini opera* 2:6, Corpus scriptorum ecclesiasticorum Latinorum 88 (Vienna: Tempskey, 1981), pp. 166–182. See esp. Brown, *Augustine of Hippo*, pp. 470–471, and Harper, *Slavery*, pp. 92–95.

62. David L. Thurmond, "Some Roman Slave Collars in *CIL*," *Athenaeum* 82 (1994): 460–492, esp. 471–472; Harper, *Slavery*, p. 258.

63. Halsall, *Barbarian Migrations*, pp. 206–224; Walter Goffart, *Barbarian Tides: The Migration Age and the Later Roman Empire* (Philadelphia: University of Pennsylvania Press, 2006), pp. 73–118.

64. Halsall, *Barbarian Migrations*, pp. 224–234.

65. *Proclus of Constantinople and the Cult of the Virgin in Late Antiquity: Homilies 1–5, Texts and Translations*, ed. and trans. Nicholas Constas (Leiden: Brill, 2003), pp. 52–69. Now, see Diarmaid MacCulloch, *Christianity: The First Three Thousand Years* (Harmondsworth, UK: Penguin, 2011), pp. 224–225, and Brown, *Rise of Western Christendom*, pp. 118–120.

66. MacCulloch, *Christianity*, pp. 220–221.

67. MacCulloch, *Christianity*, pp. 225–226; Brown, *Rise of Western Christendom*, pp. 120–121.

68. Christopher Kelly, "Rethinking Theodosius," in *Theodosius II: Rethinking the Roman Empire in Late Antiquity*, ed. Christopher Kelly (Cambridge: Cambridge University Press, 2013), p. 10.

69. *The Theodosian Code*, 14.10.4, p. 415.

70. *The Theodosian Code*, 14.10.1, p. 415.

71. *The Theodosian Code*, 15.5.5, p. 433. Now, see Richard Flower, "'The Insanity of Heretics Must Be Restrained': Heresiology in the Theodosian Code," in *Theodosius II: Rethinking the Roman Empire in Late Antiquity*, ed. Christopher Kelly (Cambridge: Cambridge University Press, 2013), pp. 172–194.

72. Brown, *Rise of Western Christendom*, pp. 121–122.

73. MacCulloch, *Christianity*, p. 227.

74. Halsall, *Barbarian Migrations*, pp. 240–242; Wickham, *Framing the Early Middle Ages*, p. 711.

75. *Chronicle of 452*, ed. Theodor Mommsen, in *Chronica Minora*, saec. IV.V.VI.VII, Monumenta Germaniae historica, Auctores antiquissimi 9 (Berlin: Weidmann, 1892), p. 660.

76. Halsall, *Barbarian Migrations*, pp. 244–250.

77. Jordanes, *Romana et Getica*, xl, p. 112 [Van Nuffelen and Van Hoof, p. 318].

78. Halsall, *Barbarian Migrations*, pp. 250–254; Peter Heather, *The Fall of the Roman Empire: A New History of Rome and the Barbarians* (Oxford: Oxford University Press, 2007), pp. 310–369.

79. Sidonius Apollinaris, *Poems and Letters*, trans. W. B. Anderson (Cambridge, MA: Harvard University Press, 1965 [repr. 1984]), 1.II, pp. 340–341.

80. Sidonius Apollinaris, *Poems and Letters*, 1.II, pp. 336–337.

81. Halsall, *Barbarian Migrations*, pp. 278–283; Heather, *The Fall of the Roman Empire*, pp. 425–437.

82. Ralph Mathisen, "Dating the Letters of Sidonius," in *New Approaches to Sidonius Apollinaris*, ed. Johannes A. van Waarden and Gavin Kelly (Leuven: Peeters, 2013), pp. 221–247, esp. pp. 226, 230, 232; Brown, *Through the Eye of a Needle*, pp. 405–407.

83. Sidonius Apollinaris, *Poems and Letters*, 8.IX, pp. 441–451. Now, see Jill Harries, *Sidonius Apollinaris and the Fall of Rome* (Oxford: Clarendon Press, 1995), pp. 241ff.

84. *Receuil des inscriptions chrétiennes de la Gaule*, vol. 8, ed. Françoise Prévot (Paris: Éditions du Centre National de la Recherche Scientifique, 1991), no. 21, p. 126; Brown, *Through the Eye of a Needle*, p. 406.

III

THE FLUTTER OF BLACKBIRDS

440–613

1. Patricius, *Confessio*, in *St. Patrick: His Writings and Muirchu's Life*, ed. and trans. A. B. E Hood (London: Phillimore, 1978), pp. 41–45.

2. Patricius, *Confessio*, pp. 45–54.

3. Robin Fleming, *Britain After Rome: The Fall and Rise, 400–1070* (London: Penguin, 2011), pp. 23–38.

4. Fleming, *Britain After Rome*, pp. 28–29.

5. Sidonius Apollinaris, *Poems and Letters*, trans. W. B. Anderson (Cambridge, MA: Harvard University Press, 1965 [repr. 1984]), 8.IX, p. 447.

6. Patricius, *Epistola*, in *St. Patrick: His Writings and Muirchu's Life*, pp. 55–59.

7. Patricius, *Confessio*, p. 54.

8. Patricius, *Confessio*, pp. 46–47.

9. Guy Halsall, *Barbarian Migrations and the Roman West, 376–568* (Cambridge: Cambridge University Press, 2007), pp. 303–310.

10. Gregory of Tours, *The History of the Franks*, trans. Lewis Thorpe (London: Penguin, 1974), II.25, pp. 139–140.

11. Gregory of Tours, *The History of the Franks*, II.30, p. 143.

12. Helmut Reimitz, *History, Frankish Identity and the Framing of Western Ethnicity* (Cambridge: Cambridge University Press, 2015), p. 47.

13. *Lex Salica*, ed. Karl August Eckhardt, Monumenta Germaniae historica, Leges nationum Germanicarum 4.1 (Hanover: Hahn, 1962). Cf. Reimitz, *History, Frankish Identity and the Framing of Western Ethnicity*, pp. 103–108.

14. Gregory of Tours, *The History of the Franks*, III, p. 161.

15. Gregory of Tours, *The History of the Franks*, II.42, p. 158.

16. Boethius, *The Consolation of Philosophy*, trans. P. G. Walsh (Oxford: Oxford University Press, 2008), pp. 3–8.

17. Boethius, *The Consolation of Philosophy*, pp. 17, 35, 59, 65.

18. *Anonymi Valesiani pars posterior*, ed. Theodor Mommsen, Monumenta Germaniae historica, Auctores antiquissimi 9 (Berlin: Weidmann, 1892), pp. 85ff. [and trans. J. C. Rolfe in his *Ammianus Marcellinus: Res gestae* (Cambridge, MA: Harvard University Press, 1939), p. 563; references to page numbers in this translation are in square brackets].

19. Halsall, *Barbarian Migrations*, pp. 286–293.

20. *Anonymi Valesiani pars posterior*, p. 61 [Rolfe, p. 547].

21. Bryan Ward-Perkins and Carlos Machado, "410 and the End of the New Statuary in Italy," in *The Sack of Rome in 410 AD: The Event, Its Context and Its Impact*, ed. Johannes Lipps, Carlos Machado, and Philipp von Rummel (Wiesbaden: Dr. Ludwig Reichert Verlag, 2013), pp. 353–364.

22. Procopius, *The Secret History*, ed. and trans. Anthony Kaldellis (Indianapolis, IN: Hackett, 2010), 26.29, p. 117.

23. Cristina La Rocca, "An Arena of Abuses and Competing Powers: Rome in Cassiodorus's *Variae*," in *Italy and Early Medieval Europe: Papers for Chris Wickham*, ed. Ross Balzaretti, Julia Barrow, and Patricia Skinner (Oxford: Oxford University Press, 2018), pp. 203–204.

24. La Rocca, "An Arena of Abuses and Competing Powers," p. 202; M. Shane Bjornlie, *Politics and Tradition Between Rome, Ravenna, and Constantinople: A Study of Cassiodorus and the Variae, 527–554* (Cambridge: Cambridge University Press, 2013), pp. 244–245.

25. *Selected Variae of Magnus Aurelius Cassiodorus Senator*, trans. S. J. B. Barnish (Liverpool: Liverpool University Press, 1992), XI.39, pp. 161–162.

26. La Rocca, "An Arena of Abuses and Competing Powers," p. 201.

27. Procopius, *The Wars of Justinian,* trans. H. B. Dewing, rev. Anthony Kaldellis (Indianapolis, IN: Hackett, 2014), 5.14.14–15, p. 287.

28. Procopius, *The Secret History*, 7.8–14, pp. 32–33.

29. Procopius, *The Secret History*, 7.15–21, p. 33.

30. Procopius, *The Wars of Justinian,* 1.24.3–6, pp. 60–61.

31. Procopius, *The Wars of Justinian,* 1.24.7–10, p. 61.

32. Peter Brown, *The Rise of Western Christendom: Triumph and Diversity, AD 200–1000* (Oxford: Wiley-Blackwell, 2013), p. 178.

33. Procopius, *The Wars of Justinian,* 1.24.33–37, p. 64.

34. Procopius, *The Wars of Justinian,* 1.24.38–58, pp. 65–67.

35. Michael Maas, "Roman Questions, Byzantine Answers: Contours of the Age of Justinian," in *The Cambridge Companion to the Age of Justinian*, ed. Michael Maas (Cambridge: Cambridge University Press, 2005), pp. 5–6.

36. "Law of Justinian I on Conversion of Pagans to Christianity, (?)529," *Codex Justinianus*, 1.11.10, trans. P. R. Coleman-Norton, in *Roman State and Christian*

Church: A Collection of Legal Documents to A.D. 535, vol. 3, ed. P. R. Coleman-Norton (London: SPCK, 1966), pp. 1048–1050.

37. Christian Wilberg, "Philosophy in the Age of Justinian," in *The Cambridge Companion to the Age of Justinian*, ed. Michael Maas (Cambridge: Cambridge University Press, 2005), p. 320.

38. Procopius, *Buildings*, trans. H. B. Dewing (Cambridge, MA: Harvard University Press, 1940 [repr. 1996]), 1.1.15–78, pp. 9–33, esp. p. 27.

39. Fabio Barry, "Walking on Water: Cosmic Floors in Antiquity and the Middle Ages," *Art Bulletin* 89 (2007): 627–656.

40. According to the eleventh- or twelfth-century *Narratio de aedificatione templi Sanctae Sophiae*, in *Scriptores originum Constantinopolitanarum*, ed. Theodor Preger (Leipzig: B. G. Teubner, 1901), p. 105.

41. Justinian, *Novellae*, in *Corpus iuris civilis*, vol. 3, ed. Rudolf Schoell and Wilhelm Kroll (Berlin: Weidmann, 1904), 30.11.2, p. 234.

42. Procopius, *Buildings*, 1.10.15–19, pp. 85–87.

43. Procopius, *The Wars of Justinian*, 2.22–23, pp. 120–124.

44. Procopius, *The Secret History*, 2.11.14–17, p. 58.

45. Kyle Harper, *The Fate of Rome: Climate, Disease, and the End of an Empire* (Princeton, NJ: Princeton University Press, 2017), p. 244.

46. Lee Mordechai and Merle Eisenberg, "Rejecting Catastrophe: The Case of the Justinianic Plague," *Past and Present* 244 (2019): 3–50.

47. Harper, *The Fate of Rome*, p. 218, refers to Procopius as his "star witness" for the plague.

48. Mordechai and Eisenberg, "Rejecting Catastrophe: The Case of the Justinianic Plague," 26–32.

49. Sharon N. Dewitte and Maryanne Kowaleski, "Black Death Bodies," *Fragments* 6 (2017): 1–37, esp. 5; Mordechai and Eisenberg, "Rejecting Catastrophe," 32–33.

50. Mordechai and Eisenberg, "Rejecting Catastrophe," 36–39.

51. Now, see Michael McCormick, "Gregory of Tours on Sixth-Century Plague and Other Epidemics," *Speculum* 96 (2021): 38–96.

52. *Vita S. ius ii Arelatensis a discipulis scripta*, trans. in J. N. Hillgarth, *Christianity and Paganism, 350–750: The Conversion of Western Europe* (Philadelphia: University of Pennsylvania Press, 1986), p. 32.

53. Peter Brown, *Through the Eye of a Needle: Wealth, the Fall of Rome, and the Making of Christianity in the West, 350–550 AD* (Princeton, NJ: Princeton University Press, 2012), pp. 414–415.

54. John Cassian, *Jean Cassian: Institutions cénobitiques*, ed. and trans. Jean-Claude Guy, Sources chrétiennes 109 (Paris: Cerf, 1965), 4.14, p. 138.

55. Cassian, *Institutions Cénobitiques*, 12.32, p. 498.

56. Brown, *Through the Eye of a Needle*, p. 419.

57. *Vita S. Caesarii Arelatensis a discipulis scripta*, pp. 33–34.

58. *Vita S. Caesarii Arelatensis a discipulis scripta*, pp. 36–40.

59. Caesarius of Arles, *Sermons (1–80)*, trans. Peggy Meuller (Washington, DC: Catholic University of America Press, 1956), "Sermon 44," pp. 221–222, "Sermon 52," pp. 259–262, and *Sermons (187–238)*, trans. Mary Meuller (Washington, DC: Catholic University of America Press, 2004), "Sermon 192," pp. 27–30.

60. Caesarius of Arles, *Sermons (1–80)*, "Sermon 33," p. 165.

61. William E. Klingshirn, *Caesarius of Arles: The Making of a Christian Community in Late Antique Gaul* (Cambridge: Cambridge University Press, 2004), p. 46.

62. *Vita S. Caesarii Arelatensis a discipulis scripta*, p. 37.

63. Gregory I, *Life of Benedict*, trans. Carolinne White, in her *Early Christian Lives* (London: Penguin, 1998), pp. 166–170.

64. Gregory I, *Life of Benedict*, pp. 172–204; *The Rule of Saint Benedict*, ed. and trans. Bruce Venarde (Cambridge, MA: Harvard University Press, 2011).

65. *The Rule of Saint Benedict*, Prologue, pp. 2–9.

66. Brown, *The Rise of Western Christendom*, pp. 221–226.

67. *The Rule of Saint Benedict*, LIV–LV, pp. 176–181.

68. *The Rule of Saint Benedict*, VI, pp. 42–43.

69. *The Rule of Saint Benedict*, II, pp. 20–27.

70. *The Rule of Saint Benedict*, I, pp. 16–19.

71. Gregory of Tours, *The History of the Franks*, trans. Lewis Thorpe (London: Penguin Books, 1974), IV.5, pp. 199–200.

72. Gregory of Tours, *The Lives of the Fathers*, in *Lives and Miracles*, ed. and trans. Giselle de Nie (Cambridge, MA: Harvard University Press, 2015), 6, pp. 67–89, esp. pp. 83–89.

73. Gregory of Tours, *The Miracles of Bishop Martin*, in *Lives and Miracles*, ed. and trans. Giselle de Nie (Cambridge, MA: Harvard University Press, 2015), pp. 423–427.

74. Gregory of Tours, *History of the Franks*, V.18, pp. 277–278.

75. Wickham, *Medieval Europe*, pp. 30–36; Chris Wickham, *Framing the Early Middle Ages: Europe and the Mediterranean, 400–800* (Oxford: Oxford University Press, 2005), pp. 102–124.

76. Gregory of Tours, *History of the Franks*, V.34, pp. 296–297.

77. Wickham, *Framing the Early Middle Ages*, pp. 186–187.

78. Peter Brown, *The Ransom of the Soul: Afterlife and Wealth in Early Western Christianity* (Cambridge, MA: Harvard University Press, 2015), pp. 149–180.

79. Venantius Fortunatus, *Poems*, ed. and trans. Michael Roberts (Cambridge, MA: Harvard University Press, 2017), I.6, 4.4, pp. 22–23, 220–221.

80. Gregory of Tours, *The Miracles of Bishop Martin*, 2.36, pp. 608–609.

81. Gregory of Tours, *The Lives of the Fathers*, 9, pp. 148–149.

82. Gregory of Tours, *History of the Franks*, VIII.15, pp. 445–447; Judith Herrin, *The Formation of Christendom* (Princeton, NJ: Princeton University Press, 2021 [orig. 1987]), pp. 109–110.

83. Gregory of Tours, *The Lives of the Fathers*, 9, pp. 149–151.

84. Peter Brown, *The Cult of the Saints: Its Rise and Function in Latin Christianity*, 2nd ed. (Chicago: University of Chicago Press, 2014).

85. Procopius, *The Wars of Justinian*, 8.29–35, pp. 528–544.

86. Procopius, *The Wars of Justinian*, 2.10, p. 93.

87. Beate Dignas and Engelbert Winter, *Rome and Persia in Late Antiquity: Neighbours and Rivals* (Cambridge: Cambridge University Press, 2007), p. 109.

88. Diarmaid MacCulloch, *Christianity: The First Three Thousand Years* (Harmondsworth, UK: Penguin, 2011), p. 327; Brown, *The Rise of Western Christendom*, p. 184.

89. Anthony Kaldellis, *Romanland: Ethnicity and Empire in Byzantium* (Cambridge, MA: Belknap Press of Harvard University Press, 2019), pp. 81–120, esp. pp. 84–85.

90. Halsall, *Barbarian Migrations*, p. 507.

91. "The Third Council of Toledo, Sixty-Two Bishops Attending in Which the Arian Heresy Was Condemned in Spain," trans. David Nirenberg, in *Medieval Iberia: Readings from Christian, Muslim, and Jewish Sources*, ed. Olivia R. Constable, 2nd ed. (Philadelphia: University of Pennsylvania Press, 2012), pp. 12–20.

92. Halsall, *Barbarian Migrations*, pp. 505–506.

93. Jonas of Bobbio, *Life of Columbanus, Life of John of Réomé*, and *Life of Vedast*, trans. Alexander O'Hara and Ian Wood (Liverpool: Liverpool University Press, 2017), I.1–5, pp. 96–107.

94. Jonas of Bobbio, *Life of Columbanus*, pp. 107–132.

95. Jane Barbara Stevenson, "The Monastic Rules of Columbanus," in *Columbanus: Studies on the Latin Writings*, ed. Michael Lapidge (Woodbridge, UK: Boydell, 1997), pp. 203–216; Brown, *The Ransom of the Soul*, pp. 188–193.

96. Jonas of Bobbio, *Life of Columbanus*, pp. 133–176.

97. In general, see Donald Bullough, "The Career of Columbanus," in *Columbanus: Studies on the Latin Writings*, ed. Michael Lapidge (Woodbridge, UK: Boydell, 1997), pp. 1–28.

IV

MAD POETS

597–735

1. Bede, *The Ecclesiastical History of the English People*, ed. and trans. Bertram Colgrave and R. A. B Mynors (Oxford: Clarendon Press, 1969), i.25–26, pp. 72–79.

2. Bede, *The Ecclesiastical History*, i.26, pp, 76–77.

3. Gregory I, *Life of Benedict*, trans. Carolinne White, in her *Early Christian Lives* (London: Penguin, 1998), p. 183.

4. Peter Brown, *The Rise of Western Christendom: Triumph and Diversity, AD 200–1000* (Oxford: Wiley-Blackwell, 2013), pp. 198–202.

5. Gregory I, "Letter 7.5," in *Registrum epistularum*, ed. Dag Norberg, Corpus Christianorum 140 (Turnhout: Brepols, 1982), p. 449.

6. Brown, *The Rise of Western Christendom*, pp. 205–207.

7. Gregory I, *Moralia in Job*, ed. Marc Adriaen, Corpus Christianorum 143, 143A, 143B (Turnhout: Brepols, 1979–1985), 5.29.52, 8.30.49, 9.33.50, 10.9.15, 10.10.17, 34.3.7, 35.1.1, pp. 254, 421, 491, 548, 550, 1727–1728, 1774.

8. Gregory I, *Pastoral Care* [*Regula pastoralis*], trans. Henry Davis (London: Longmans, 1950), esp. pp. 90–226.

9. Robin Fleming, *Britain After Rome: The Fall and Rise, 400–1070* (London: Penguin, 2011), pp. 102–119.

10. Fleming, *Britain After Rome*, pp. 90–102; Heinrich Härke, "'Warrior Graves'? The Background of the Anglo-Saxon Weapon Burial Rite," *Past and Present* 126 (1990): 22–43.

11. *Beowulf: A New Verse Translation*, trans. Seamus Heaney (New York: Farrar, Straus and Giroux, 1999), ll. 3137–3168, pp. 210–213.

12. Nancy Edwards, "Early Medieval Inscribed Stones and Stone Sculpture in Wales: Context and Function," *Medieval Archeology* 45 (2001): 15–39, esp. 25–28.

13. Gildas, *The Ruin of Britain* [*De excidio et conquestu Britanniae*], trans. Michael Winterbottom (London: Phillimore, 1978), c. 8, p. 18.

14. Fleming, *Britain After Rome*, pp. 80–88.

15. Adomnán, *Life of Columba*, ed. and trans. Alan Orr Anderson and Marjorie Ogilvie Anderson (Oxford: Clarendon Press, 1991), i.7, pp. 30–31.

16. Adomnán, *Life of Columba*, ii.25, pp. 130–131.

17. Fleming, *Britain After Rome*, p. 105.

18. Bede, *The Ecclesiastical History*, ii.1, pp. 122–135.

19. Bede, *The Ecclesiastical History*, ii.12, pp. 174–183.

20. Bede, *The Ecclesiastical History*, ii.12, pp. 180–181.

21. Bede, *The Ecclesiastical History*, ii.13, pp. 182–187.

22. Fleming, *Britain After Rome*, pp. 101–102.

23. Gregory I, "Letter 11," trans. J. Barmby, in J. N. Hillgarth, *Christianity and Paganism, 350–750: The Conversion of Western Europe* (Philadelphia: University of Pennsylvania Press, 1986), pp. 152–153.

24. Bede, *The Ecclesiastical History*, ii.13, pp. 182–185.

25. Bede, *The Ecclesiastical History*, ii.5, pp. 150–151.

26. *Beowulf*, ll. 866–874, pp. 58–59.

27. *The Laws of the Earliest English Kings*, ed. and trans. Frederick Levi Attenborough (Cambridge: Cambridge University Press, 1922), pp. 4–17.

28. "Deor," trans. Michael Alexander, in *The First Poems in English* (London: Penguin Books, 2008), pp. 71–72.

29. The following paragraphs rely upon these texts and translations of the Qur'an: *The Meaning of the Holy Qur'an*, trans. 'Abdullah Yusuf 'Ali (Beltsville, MD: Amana, 1997); *Der Koran*, trans. Rudi Paret (Stuttgart: Kohlhammer, 1996); *Qur'an: A Contemporary Translation*, trans. Ahmed Ali (Princeton, NJ: Princeton University Press, 1993); and *The Koran Interpreted*, trans. A. J. Arberry, 2 vols. (New York: Macmillan, 1955).

30. Fred M. Donner, *Muhammad and the Believers: At the Origins of Islam* (Cambridge, MA: Belknap Press of Harvard University Press, 2010), pp. 39–49.

31. Michael Philip Penn, *When Christians First Met Muslims: A Sourcebook of the Earliest Syriac Writings on Islam* (Berkeley: University of California Press, 2015), pp. 21–24.

32. Penn, *When Christians First Met Muslims*, pp. 25–28.

33. Chase F. Robinson, "Reconstructing Early Islam: Truth and Consequences," in *Method and Theory in the Study of Islamic Origins*, ed. Herbert Berg (Leiden: Brill, 2003), pp. 101–123.

34. Much of what follows is informed by Donner, *Muhammad and the Believers*, pp. 57–61.

35. Patricia Crone, "The Religion of the Qur'anic Pagans: God and the Lesser Deities," *Arabica* 57 (2010): 151–200.

36. Donner, *Muhammad and the Believers*, pp. 82–89.

37. Matthew P. Canepa, *The Two Eyes of the Earth: Art and Ritual of Kingship Between Rome and Sasanian Iran* (Berkeley: University of California Press, 2009), p. 204.

38. Theophylakt Simokatta, *The History of Theophylakt Simokatta*, trans. Michael Whitby and Mary Whitby (Oxford: Clarendon Press, 1986), 4.11.2–3, p. 117.

39. Cf. Crone, "The Religion of the Qur'anic Pagans," 200.

40. "Lamiyyat," trans. Warren Treadgold, in *Night and Horses and the Desert: An Anthology of Classical Arabic Literature*, ed. Robert Irwin (New York: Anchor Books, 2002), pp. 19–23, esp. p. 23.

41. Donner, *Muhammad and the Believers*, pp. 145–226.

42. Finbarr B. Flood, "Faith, Religion, and the Material Culture of Early Islam" and "The Qur'an," in *Byzantium and Islam: Age of Transition 7th–9th Century*, ed. Helen C. Evans with Brandie Ratliff (New Haven, CT: Yale University Press, 2012), pp. 244–258, 266.

43. *The* Etymologies *of Isidore of Seville*, trans. Stephen A. Barney et al. (Cambridge: Cambridge University Press, 2007), pp. 166–168.

44. *The* Etymologies *of Isidore of Seville*, pp. 39, 139, 150, 174–178, 186, 174, 195, 233, 298, 311.

45. *The* Etymologies *of Isidore of Seville*, p. 413.

46. Hugh Kennedy, "The Muslims in Europe," in *The New Cambridge Medieval History. Vol 2: c. 700–c. 900*, ed. Rosamond McKitterick (Cambridge: Cambridge University Press, 1995), pp. 249–271.

47. Bede, *On Genesis*, trans. Calvin B. Kendall (Liverpool: Liverpool University Press, 2008), pp. 53, 279.

48. *Visio Baronti monachi Longoretensis*, in *Passiones vitaeque sanctorum aevi Merovingici*, ed. Wilhelm Levison, Monumenta Germaniae historica, Scriptores rerum Merovingicarum 5 (Hanover: Hahn, 1910), pp. 377–378 [and trans. J. N. Hillgarth, in J. N. Hillgarth, *Christianity and Paganism, 350–750: The Conversion of Western Europe* (Philadelphia: University of Pennsylvania Press, 1986), pp. 195–196; references to page numbers in this translation are in square brackets].

49. *Visio Baronti*, pp. 379–380 [Hillgarth, pp. 196–197].

50. *Visio Baronti*, pp. 381–386 [Hillgarth, pp. 198–199].

51. *Visio Baronti*, pp. 387–390 [Hillgarth, pp. 199–200].

52. *Visio Baronti*, p. 391 [Hillgarth, p. 200].

53. *Visio Baronti*, pp. 390–392 [Hillgarth, pp. 201–203].

54. *Visio Baronti*, p. 393 [Hillgarth, p. 203].

55. *Visio Baronti*, p. 394 [Hillgarth, p. 204].

56. Bede, *The Ecclesiastical History*, ii.19, pp. 198–203.

57. Jonas of Bobbio, *Life of Columbanus, Life of John of Réomé*, and *Life of Vedast*, trans. Alexander O'Hara and Ian Wood (Liverpool: Liverpool University Press, 2017), pp. 206–208.

58. Peter Brown, *The Ransom of the Soul: Afterlife and Wealth in Early Western Christianity* (Cambridge, MA: Harvard University Press, 2015), pp. 193–197; Jamie Kreiner, *The Social Life of Historiography in the Merovingian Kingdom* (Cambridge: Cambridge University Press, 2014).

59. Ian Wood, "Entrusting Western Europe to the Church, 400–750," *Transactions of the Royal Historical Society* 23 (2013): 37–73, esp. 41; Ian Wood, *The Transformation of the Roman West* (Leeds: Arc Humanities Press, 2018), pp. 91–124; Ian Wood, *The Christian Economy in the Early Medieval West: Towards a Temple Economy* (Binghamton, NY: Punctum, 2022).

60. Wickham, *Medieval Europe*, pp. 35–37.

61. Brown, *The Rise of Western Christendom*, pp. 15, 355–380.

62. Brown, *The Rise of Western Christendom*, pp. 368–371; John Haldon, *The Empire That Would Not Die: The Paradox of Eastern Roman Survival, 640–740* (Cambridge, MA: Harvard University Press, 2016), pp. 26–78.

63. Bede, *The Ecclesiastical History*, iii.25, pp. 294–309, iv.1–2, pp. 328–337.

64. "The Ruin," trans. Michael Alexander, in *The First Poems in English* (London: Penguin Books, 2008), p. 3.

65. Bede, *The Ecclesiastical History*, v.23, pp. 556–561.

66. Theodore, *Penitential*, trans. John T. McNeill and Helena Gamer, in their *Medieval Handbooks of Penance: A Translation of the Principal Libri Poenitentiales* (New York: Columbia University Press, 1938 [repr. 1990]), pp. 182–184, 215.

67. Theodore, *Penitential*, pp. 184–213.

68. Theodore, *Penitential*, pp. 184–213.

69. Muirchú, *Vita*, trans. A. B. E. Hood, in *St. Patrick*, pp. 81–98.

70. Bede, *The Ecclesiastical History*, IV.24, pp. 414–421; "Caedmon's Hymn," trans. Michael Alexander, in *The First Poems in English* (London: Penguin Books, 2008), p. 44.

71. Bede, *The Ecclesiastical History*, iv.24, pp. 416–417.

72. "The Dream of the Rood," trans. Michael Alexander, in *The First Poems in English* (London: Penguin Books, 2008), pp. 30–42.

73. George Molyneaux, "Did the English Really Think They Were God's Elect in the Anglo-Saxon Period?," *Journal of Ecclesiastical History* 65 (2014): 721–737.

74. Bede, *The Ecclesiastical History*, iv.24, pp. 418–421.

75. Bede, *The Ecclesiastical History*, v.24, pp. 566–571.

76. Wood, "Entrusting Western Europe to the Church," 67; R. S. L. Bruce-Mitford, "The Art of the Codex Amiatinus: Jarrow Lecture, 1967," *Journal of the British Archaeological Association* 32 (1969): 2.

77. Brown, *The Rise of Western Christendom*, p. 358.

78. Adomnán, *Life of Columba*, i.23, pp. 50–51.

79. "Cuthbert's Letter on the Death of Bede," trans. Bertram Colgrave and R. A. B. Mynors in Bede, *The Ecclesiastical History*, pp. 580–587; "Bede's Death Song," trans. Michael Alexander, in *The First Poems in English* (London: Penguin Books, 2008), p. 45.

V

AN EVERLASTING STAR

722–824

1. Huneberc, *Vita Willibaldi episcopi Eichstetensis et vita Wynnebaldi abbatis Heidenheimensis auctore sanctimonale Heidenheimensis,* ed. Oswald Holder-Egger, Monumenta Germaniae historica, Scriptores 15.1 (Hanover: Hahn, 1887), pp. 86–88 [and trans. Thomas Head as "The *Hodoeporicon* of Saint Willibald," in *Soldiers of Christ: Saints and Saints' Lives from Late Antiquity and the Early Middle Ages*, ed. Thomas F. X. Noble and Thomas Head (University Park: Pennsylvania State University Press, 1995), p. 145; references to page numbers in this translation are in square brackets].

2. Huneberc, *Vita*, pp. 88–89 [Head, pp. 145–147].

3. Huneberc, *Vita*, pp. 90–92 [Head, pp. 148–150].

4. Huneberc, *Vita*, pp. 92–94 [Head, pp. 150–153].

5. Mattia Guidetti, "The Contiguity Between Churches and Mosques in Early Islamic Bilad al-Sham," *Bulletin of SOAS* 76 (2013): 229–258, esp. 237–239.

6. Huneberc, *Vita*, p. 95 [Head, p. 153].

7. Huneberc, *Vita*, pp. 96–102 [Head, pp. 153–160].

8. Huneberc, *Vita*, pp. 102–105 [Head, pp. 160–162].

9. Huneberc, *Vita*, pp. 104–106 [Head, pp. 162–164].

10. Huneberc, *Vita*, p. 105 [Head, p. 163].

11. Michael McCormick, *Origins of the European Economy: Communications and Commerce AD 300–900* (Cambridge: Cambridge University Press, 2001), pp. 129–134, 502–508; Chris Wickham, *The Inheritance of Rome: A History of Europe from 400 to 1000* (New York: Viking, 2009), p. 225.

12. Huneberc, *Vita*, p. 98 [Head, p. 144].

13. "The Seafarer," trans. Michael Alexander, in *The First Poems in English* (London: Penguin Books, 2008), p. 58.

14. Huneberc, *Vita*, p. 106 [Head, p. 164].

15. Boniface, *The Letters of Saint Boniface*, trans. Ephraim Emerton (New York: W. W. Norton, 1976), XV, pp. 48–50.

16. Boniface, *Letters*, III, p. 32.

17. Boniface, *Letters*, II, pp. 25–31.

18. Boniface, *Letters*, X, pp. 43–44.

19. Boniface, *Letters*, XII, p. 45.

20. Willibald, "The Life of Saint Boniface," trans. C. H. Talbot, in *Soldiers of Christ: Saints and Saints' Lives from Late Antiquity and the Early Middle Ages*, ed. Thomas F. X. Noble and Thomas Head (University Park: Pennsylvania State University Press, 1995), pp. 126–127.

21. "An Eighth-Century List of Superstitions," trans. John T. McNeill and Helena Gamer, in their *Medieval Handbooks of Penance: A Translation of the Principal Libri Poenitentiales* (New York: Columbia University Press, 1938 [repr. 1990]), pp. 419–421.

22. "An Eighth-Century List of Superstitions," p. 420.

23. Boniface, *Letters*, XLVII, pp. 98–107.

24. Boniface, *Letters*, XXXVI, pp. 74–75.

25. Boniface, *Letters*, XXVI, pp. 64–65.

26. Boniface, *Letters*, LI, p. 116.

27. Willibald, "The Life of Saint Boniface," pp. 134–136.

28. *The Chronicle of 754*, trans. Kenneth Baxter Wolf, in his *Conquerors and Chroniclers of Early Medieval Spain*, 2nd ed. (Liverpool: Liverpool University Press, 2011), pp. 116–117.

29. *The Chronicle of 754*, pp. 24–37, 117.

30. Einhard, *Life of Charlemagne*, in *Charlemagne's Courtier: The Complete Einhard*, ed. and trans. Paul Edward Dutton (Peterborough: Broadview Press, 1998), p. 17.

31. Edward Gibbon, *The History of the Decline and Fall of the Roman Empire*, ed. J. B. Bury, vol. 9 (New York: Fred De Fau, 1907), p. 254.

32. *The Book of the Pontiffs (Liber pontificalis)*, trans. Raymond Davis in *The Lives of the Eighth-Century Popes AD 715–817*, 2nd ed. (Liverpool: Liverpool University Press, 2007), 91.23, p. 15.

33. *Theophilus of Edessa's Chronicle, and the Circulation of Historical Knowledge in Late Antiquity and Early Islam*, trans. Robert G. Hoyland (Liverpool: Liverpool University Press, 2011), pp. 224–225.

34. *The Book of the Pontiffs (Liber pontificalis)*, 91.17, p. 11; *Theophilus of Edessa's Chronicle*, p. 225.

35. *Theophilus of Edessa's Chronicle*, p. 225.

36. Gregory I, "Letter 11.10," in *Registrum epistularum*, ed. Dag Norberg, Corpus Christianorum 140A (Turnhout: Brepols, 1982), pp. 873–876, esp. pp. 873–875. Now, see Celia M. Chazelle, "Pictures, Books, and the Illiterate: Pope Gregory I's Letters to Serenus of Marseilles," *Word and Image* 2 (1990): 138–153, esp. 139–140; Brown, *The Rise of Western Christendom*, p. 10; Judith Herrin, *The Formation of Christendom* (Princeton, NJ: Princeton University Press, 2021 [orig. 1987]), pp. 177–179.

37. Bede, *The Ecclesiastical History*, i.25, pp. 74–75.

38. Huneberc, *Vita*, p. 101 [Head, p. 159].

39. Theophanes the Confessor, *The Chronicle of Theophanes the Confessor: Byzantine and Near Eastern History AD 284–813*, trans. Cyril Mango and Roger Scott (Oxford: Clarendon Press, 1997), A.M. 6218, pp. 560–561.

40. John Haldon, "'Greek Fire' Revisted: Recent and Current Research," in *Byzantine Style, Religion and Civilization: In Honour of Sir Steven Runciman*, ed. Elizabeth Jeffreys (Cambridge: Cambridge Unversity Press, 2006), pp. 290–325.

41. Herrin, *The Formation of Christendom*, pp. 325–343; Judith Herrin, *Ravenna: Capital of Empire, Crucible of Europe* (Princeton, NJ: Princeton University Press, 2020), pp. 326–334; Peter Brown, *The Rise of Western Christendom: Triumph and Diversity, AD 200–1000* (Oxford: Wiley-Blackwell, 2013), pp. 387–393; John Haldon, *The Empire That Would Not Die: The Paradox of Eastern Roman Survival, 640–740* (Cambridge, MA: Harvard University Press, 2016), pp. 79–119.

42. *Theophilus of Edessa's Chronicle,* p. 220.

43. *Theophilus of Edessa's Chronicle,* p. 222.

44. Christian C. Sahner, "The First Iconoclasm in Islam: A New History of the Edict of Yazid II (AH 104/AD 723)," *Der Islam* 94 (2017): 5–56.

45. Janet L. Nelson, *King and Emperor: A New Life of Charlemagne* (Berkeley: University of California Press, 2019), pp. 50–55.

46. Boniface, *Letters*, XL, pp. 78–83.

47. Einhard, *Life of Charlemagne*, pp. 16–17.

48. Einhard, *Life of Charlemagne*, p. 17.

49. Nelson, *King and Emperor*, pp. 69–72.

50. Herrin, *Ravenna*, pp. 343–346.

51. Paul M. Cobb, "The Empire in Syria, 705–763," in *The New Cambridge History of Islam. Vol. 1: The Formation of the Islamic World, Sixth to Eleventh Centuries*, ed. Chase F. Robinson (Cambridge: Cambridge University Press, 2010), pp. 226–268.

52. *Theophilus of Edessa's Chronicle*, pp. 275–278.

53. *Theophilus of Edessa's Chronicle*, p. 278.

54. *Das Constitutum Constantini (Konstantinische Schenkung)*, ed. Horst Fuhrman, Monumenta Germaniae historica, Fontes iuris Germanici antiqui (Hanover: Hahn, 1968), and trans. E. F. Henderson in Paul Edward Dutton, *Carolingian Civilization: A Reader*, 2nd ed. (Toronto: University of Toronto Press, 2009), pp. 14–22. Also see Herrin, *The Formation of Christendom*, pp. 385–387.

55. Einhard, *Life of Charlemagne*, p. 30.

56. Nelson, *King and Emperor*, pp. 380–385, and Rosamond McKitterick, *Charlemagne: The Formation of a European Identity* (Cambridge: Cambridge University Press, 2008), pp. 34, 115.

57. Einhard (?), *Karolus Magnus et Leo Papa*, ed. and trans. Peter Godman, in his *Poetry of the Carolingian Renaissance* (Norman: University of Oklahoma Press, 1985), pp. 198–199. On *correctio*, see McKitterick, *Charlemagne*, pp. 292–380.

58. *Die Admonitio generalis Karls des Grossen*, ed. Hubert Mordek, Klaus Zechiel-Eckes, and Michael Glatthaar, Monumenta Germaniae historica, Fontes iuris

Germanici antiqui 16 (Hanover: Hahn, 2012), prologue, pp. 180–185, c. 17, pp. 192–193, c. 67, pp. 218–221, c. 80, pp. 234–238; Nelson, *King and Emperor*, pp. 258–264.

59. *Admonitio generalis,* c. 78, pp. 230–231.

60. Einhard, *Life of Charlemagne*, p. 32.

61. Nelson, *King and Emperor*, pp. 14, 259, 261–262, 315.

62. Alcuin, *Disputatio de Rhetorica et de virtutibus*, ed. and trans. Wilbur Samuel Howell as *The Rhetoric of Alcuin and Charlemagne* (Princeton, NJ: Princeton University, 1941), pp. 66, 154; Nelson, *King and Emperor*, pp. 316–318.

63. Einhard, *Life of Charlemagne*, p. 32.

64. *Admonitio generalis*, c. 71, pp. 224–225.

65. Alcuin, "To the King on Books, Learning, and Old Age (796)," trans. Paul Edward Dutton in his *Carolingian Civilization: A Reader*, 2nd ed. (Toronto: University of Toronto Press, 2009), p. 121.

66. Alcuin, "To the King on the State of Learning in His Day (799)," trans. Paul Edward Dutton in his *Carolingian Civilization: A Reader*, 2nd ed. (Toronto: University of Toronto Press, 2009), pp. 122–123.

67. Alcuin, *On Scribes*, ed. and trans. Peter Godman, in his *Poetry of the Carolingian Renaissance* (Norman: University of Oklahoma Press, 1985), pp. 138–139.

68. Council of Tours (813), Monumenta Germaniae historica, Concilia 2 (Hanover: Hahn, 1906), c. 17, p. 288; Brown, *The Rise of Western Christendom*, p. 451; McKitterick, *Charlemagne*, p. 317.

69. Theodulf, *Opus Karoli regis contra synodum*, ed. Ann Freeman with Paul Meyvaert, Monumenta Germaniae historica, Concilia 2, Supplementum I (Hanover: Hahn, 1998), 1.1, pp. 105–115, 1.15, pp. 169–175, 2.30, p. 305, 4.21, p. 540, 5, pp. 598–600; partially trans. in Paul Edward Dutton in his *Carolingian Civilization: A Reader*, 2nd ed. (Toronto: University of Toronto Press, 2009), pp. 95–98. Now, see Herrin, *The Formation of Christendom*, pp. 437–439; Brown, *The Rise of Western Christendom*, pp. 456–462; McKitterick, *Charlemagne*, p. 313; Nelson, *King and Emperor*, pp. 289–292.

70. *Admonitio generalis*, c. 63, pp. 214–217.

71. Nelson, *King and Emperor*, pp. 395–398.

72. Charles B. McClendon, *The Origins of Medieval Architecture: Building in Europe, A.D. 600–900* (New Haven, CT: Yale University Press, 2005), pp. 108–113.

73. McClendon, *The Origins of Medieval Architecture*, pp. 119–121.

74. Einhard, *Life of Charlemagne*, pp. 30–31, 36.

75. Einhard, *Life of Charlemagne*, p. 26; *Annales regni Francorum*, ed. Georg Heinrich Pertz and Friedrich Kurz, Monumenta Germaniae historica, Scriptores rerum Germanicarum in usum scholarum separatim editi 6 (Hanover: Hahn, 1895), pp. 123–124.

76. Einhard, *Life of Charlemagne*, pp. 26, 33.

77. Michael McCormick, *Charlemagne's Survey of the Holy Land: Wealth, Personnel, and Buildings of a Mediteranean Church Between Antiquity and the Middle Ages* (Washington, DC: Dumbarton Oaks, 2011), pp. 200–217.

78. Einhard, *Life of Charlemagne*, pp. 35–37.

79. Heito, *Visio Wettini*, in *Poetae Latini aevi Carolini*, ed. Ernst Dümmler, Monumenta Germaniae historica, Poetae Latini medii aevi 2 (Berlin, 1884), pp. 267–271 [and Eileen Gardiner's translation in her *Visions of Heaven and Hell Before Dante* (New York: Italica Press, 2019), pp. 62–65; references to page numbers in this translation are in square brackets].

80. Heito, *Visio Wettini,* pp. 271–272 [Gardiner, pp. 65–67].

81. Heito, *Visio Wettini,* pp. 272–275 [Gardiner, pp. 67–71].

82. Heito, *Visio Wettini,* pp. 272–275 [Gardiner, pp. 67–71].

83. Agobard of Lyon, *De Grandine et Tonitruis*, in *Agobardi Lugdunensis: Opera Omnia*, ed. Lieven van Acker, Corpus Christianorum: Continuatio Mediaevalis 52 (Turnhout: Brepols, 1981), pp. 3–11.

84. Agobard of Lyon, *De Grandine et Tonitruis*, pp. 3, 11–14.

85. Agobard of Lyon, *De Grandine et Tonitruis*, p. 9.

86. According to two diplomas of Lothar I issued between 841 and 853 dealing with the restoration of ecclesiastical property in Lyon. For the diplomas, see *Die Urkunden Lothars I und Lothars II,* ed. T. Schieffer, Monumenta Germaniae historica, Diplomata Karolinorum 3 (Berlin: Weidmann, 1966), nos. 117, 124, pp. 270, 284.

87. Alcuin, "Advice to the King on Converting Saxons," trans. Paul Edward Dutton in his *Carolingian Civilization: A Reader*, 2nd ed. (Toronto: University of Toronto Press, 2009), p. 126.

88. Rory Naismith, "The Social Significance of Monetization in the Early Middle Ages," *Past and Present* 223 (2014): 14–17; Nelson, *King and Emperor*, pp. 288–289.

89. Alfred Colville, *Recherches sur l'histoire de Lyon du Ve siècle au IXe siècle (450–800)* (Paris: Picard, 1928), pp. 287–288.

90. Adriaan E. Verhulst, "Karolingische Agrarpolitik. Das *Capitulare de villis* und die Hungersnöte von 792/93 und 805/6," *Zeitschrift für Agrargeschichte une Agrarsoziologie* 13 (1965): 175–189, and Jean-Pierre Devroey, *La nature et le roi: Environnement, pouvoir et société à l'âge de Charlemagne (740–820)* (Paris: Albin Michel, 2019), pp. 12–13, 61–75, 255–258, 308–313, 409–412, and passim.

91. Agobard of Lyon, *De Grandine et Tonitruis*, p. 14.

92. Agobard of Lyon, *De Grandine et Tonitruis*, p. 15. On the cattle plague, see Devroey, *La nature et le roi*, pp. 130, 173, 350, 355.

93. Alice Rio, *Slavery After Rome, 500–1100* (Oxford: Oxford University Press, 2017), pp. 19–41, 160–161. Cf. Michael McCormick, "New Light on the 'Dark Ages': How the Slave Trade Fuelled the Carolingian Economy," *Past and Present* 177 (2002): 17–54.

94. Agobard of Lyon, *De Insolentia Iudeorum (ad Ludovicum)*, in *Agobardi Lugdunensis: Opera Omnia*, ed. Lieven van Acker, Corpus Christianorum: Continuatio Mediaevalis 52 (Turnhout: Brepols, 1981), p. 192.

95. Nelson, *King and Emperor*, pp. 292–298.

96. Timothy Reuter, "The End of Carolingian Military Expansion," in *Charlemagne's Heir: New Perspectives on the Reign of Louis the Pious (814–840)*, ed. Peter Godman and Roger Collins (Oxford: Oxford University Press, 1990), pp. 391–405.

97. Heito, *Visio Wettini*, pp. 271–272 [Gardiner, pp. 65–66].

VI

THE HARRYING OF THE HEATHEN

825–972

1. *Vita Sancti Findani*, ed. Oswald Holder-Egger, Monumenta Germaniae historica, Scriptores 15.1 (Hanover: Hahn, 1887), p. 503.

2. *Vita Sancti Findani*, p. 504.

3. *Vita Sancti Findani*, p. 504.

4. *Vita Sancti Findani*, p. 504.

5. *Vita Sancti Findani*, pp. 504–505.

6. *Vita Sancti Findani*, pp. 505–506.

7. *The Anglo-Saxon Chronicle*, trans. G. N. Garmonsway (London: J. M. Dent, 1960), pp. 56–57.

8. Alcuin, "On the Sack of Lindisfarne by the Northmen in 793," trans. Paul Edward Dutton in his *Carolingian Civilization: A Reader*, 2nd ed. (Toronto: University of Toronto Press, 2009), pp. 123–125.

9. Einhard, *Life of Charlemagne*, trans. Paul Edward Dutton in his *Charlemagne's Courtier: The Complete Einhard* (Peterborough, ON: Broadview Press, 1998), pp. 24–25, and *Annales regni Francorum*, ed. Georg Heinrich Pertz and Friedrich Kurz, Monumenta Germaniae historica, Scriptores rerum Germanicarum in usum scholarum separatim editi VI (Hanover: Hahn, 1895), pp. 91–92.

10. *Annales regni Francorum*, pp. 78–125; *The Annals of St-Bertin: Ninth-Century Histories I*, trans. Janet L. Nelson (Manchester: Manchester University Press, 1991), pp. 21–138; *The Annals of Fulda: Ninth-Century Histories II*, trans. Timothy Reuter (Manchester: Manchester University Press, 1992), pp. 15–76.

11. *Ex Ermentarii miraculis sancti Filiberti*, ed. Oswald Holder-Egger, Monumenta Germaniae historica, Scriptores 15.1 (Hanover: Hahn, 1887), pp. 298–303; trans. David Herlihy as "The Wandering Relics of St. Philibert Described by the Monk Ermentarius," in his *The History of Feudalism* (Atlantic Highlands, NJ: Humanities Press, 1979), pp. 8–13.

12. Anthony Adams and A. G. Rigg, "A Verse Translation of Abbo of St. Germain's 'Bella Parisiacae urbis,'" *Journal of Medieval Latin* 14 (2004): 22–23.

13. Anders Winroth, *The Age of the Vikings* (Princeton, NJ: Princeton University Press, 2014), pp. 71–79, 92; Vibeke Bischoff, "Viking-Age Sails: Form and

Porportion," *Journal of Maritime Archaeology* 12 (2017): 1–24, esp. 3–7; Neil Price, *Children of Ash and Elm: A History of the Vikings* (New York: Basic Books, 2020), pp. 198–203.

14. Winroth, *The Age of the Vikings*, pp. 92–94.

15. Winroth, *The Age of the Vikings*, pp. 88–91; Price, *Children of Ash and Elm*, p. 199.

16. *The Old English History of the World: An Anglo-Saxon Rewriting of Orosius*, ed. and trans. Malcolm R. Godden (Cambridge, MA: Harvard University Press, 2016), p. 37.

17. Robin Fleming, *Britain After Rome: The Fall and Rise, 400–1070* (London: Penguin Books, 2011), pp. 213–219; Winroth, *The Age of the Vikings*, pp. 157–180; Price, *Children of Ash and Elm*, pp. 7–8, 64–106.

18. Snorri Sturluson, *The Prose Edda*, trans. Jesse Byock (London: Penguin Books, 2005), p. 12.

19. Winroth, *The Age of the Vikings*, pp. 187–191.

20. Winroth, *The Age of the Vikings*, pp. 94–103; James E. Montgomery, "Ibn Fadlan and the Rusiyyah," *Journal of Arabic and Islamic Studies* 3 (2000): 1–25.

21. Ahmad Ibn Fadlan, *Ibn Fadlan and the Land of Darkness: Arab Travellers in the Far North*, trans. Paul Lunde and Caroline Stone (London: Penguin, 2012), pp. 49–51; Montgomery, "Ibn Fadlan and the Rusiyyah," pp. 12–14.

22. Ahmad Ibn Fadlan, *The Land of Darkness*, pp. 51–53; Montgomery, "Ibn Fadlan and the Rusiyyah," pp. 14–20.

23. Ahmad Ibn Fadlan, *The Land of Darkness*, pp. 53–54; Montgomery, "Ibn Fadlan and the Rusiyyah," pp. 20–21; Winroth, *The Age of the Vikings*, pp. 94–97.

24. *Annals of St-Bertin*, pp. 42–43.

25. Einhard, "To the Emperor Louis the Pious. After June 837," trans. Paul Edward Dutton in his *Charlemagne's Courtier: The Complete Einhard* (Peterborough, ON: Broadview Press, 1998), pp. 160–161.

26. Allen Cabaniss, *Son of Charlemagne: A Contemporary Life of Louis the Pious* (Syracuse, NY: Syracuse University Press, 1961), p. 125.

27. Heito, *Visio Wettini,* in *Poetae Latini aevi Carolini*, ed. Ernst Dümmler, Monumenta Germaniae historica, Poetae Latini medii aevi 2 (Berlin, 1884), p. 274; trans. Eileen Gardiner in her *Visions of Heaven and Hell Before Dante* (New York: Italica Press, 2019), p. 70.

28. Engelbert, "The Battle of Fontenoy" in *Poetae Latini Aevi Carolini*, Monumenta Germaniae historica, Poetae Latini medii aevi 2, pp. 138–140; trans. Paul Edward Dutton in his *Carolingian Civilization: A Reader*, 2nd ed. (Toronto: University of Toronto Press, 2009), pp. 332–33.

29. *Annals of Fulda*, p. 22.

30. Audradus Modicus, *Liber Revelationum*, ed. Ludwig Traube, "O Roma nobilis. Philologische Untersuchungen aus dem Mittelalter," in *Abhandlungen der philosophisch-philologischen Classe der königlich Bayerischen Akademie der Wissenschaften* 19 (1982): 378–387, esp. 382; trans. Paul Edward Dutton in his *Carolingian Civilization: A Reader*, 2nd ed. (Toronto: University of Toronto Press, 2009), p. 357.

31. *Annals of Fulda*, pp. 26–27.

32. Gottschalk, *Fragmentum* 15, in *Oeuvres théologiques et grammaticales de Godescalc d'Orbais*, ed. Cyrille Lambot (Louvain: Spicilegium Sacrum Lovaniense, 1945), p. 38; Mathew Bryan Gillis, *Heresy and Dissent in the Carolingian Empire: The Case of Gottschalk of Orbais* (Oxford: Oxford University Press, 2017), pp. 77–117.

33. Gottschalk, *Confessio prolixior*, in *Oeuvres théologiques et grammaticales de Godescalc d'Orbais*, ed. Cyrille Lambot (Louvain: Spicilegium Sacrum Lovaniense, 1945), pp. 74–75; Gillis, *Heresy and Dissent*, pp. 118–146.

34. Dhuoda, *Liber Manualis: Handbook for Her Warrior Son*, ed. and trans. Marcelle Thiébaux (Cambridge: Cambridge University Press, 1998), pp. 68–71, 94–97.

35. Dhuoda, *Liber Manualis*, pp. 165–169, 228–231.

36. Eulogius, *Memoriale sanctorum*, trans. Kenneth Baxter Wolf in his *The Eulogius Corpus* (Liverpool: Liverpool University Press, 2019), Preface.2–4, pp. 153–157.

37. Eulogius, *Memoriale sanctorum*, Preface.5–6, 2.3, pp. 157–158, 211.

38. Eulogius, *Memoriale sanctorum*, 1.18, pp. 178–179.

39. Eulogius, *Memoriale sanctorum*, 1.12–16, pp. 172–177.

40. Eulogius, *Liber apologeticus martyrum*, trans. Kenneth Baxter Wolf in his *The Eulogius Corpus* (Liverpool: Liverpool University Press, 2019), 19, p. 340.

41. Eulogius, *Memoriale sanctorum*, 2.7.1–2.8.16, pp. 215–230.

42. Eulogius, *Liber apologeticus martyrum*, 15–17, pp. 334–338.

43. Eulogius, *Memoriale sanctorum*, 3.7.4, pp. 275–276.

44. Kenneth Baxter Wolf, "Introduction," in his *The Eulogius Corpus* (Liverpool: Liverpool University Press, 2019), p. 49.

45. Paul Alvarus, *Vita Eulogii*, trans. Kenneth Baxter Wolf in his *The Eulogius Corpus* (Liverpool: Liverpool University Press, 2019), pp. 124–146, esp. p. 141.

46. *The Old English Boethius: With Verse Prologues and Epilogues Associated with King Alfred*, ed. and trans. Susan Irvine and Malcolm R. Godden (Cambridge, MA: Harvard University Press, 2012), pp. 99–101.

47. Fleming, *Britain After Rome*, pp. 219–220, 226–228.

48. Asser, *Asser's Life of King Alfred*, ed. William Henry Stevenson (Oxford: Clarendon Press, 1959), pp. 30–35, 44–47, 68–69; and translated by Simon Keynes and Michael Lapidge in their *Alfred the Great: Asser's Life of King Alfred and Other Contemporary Sources* (London: Penguin Books, 1983), pp. 80–85, 96–98.

49. *The Old English Boethius*, pp. 260–261, 390–391.

50. "The Ango-Saxon Chronicle 880–900," trans. Simon Keynes and Michael Lapidge in their *Alfred the Great: Asser's Life of King Alfred and Other Contemporary Sources* (London: Penguin Books, 1983), pp. 113–114.

51. Peter Brown, *The Rise of Western Christendom: Triumph and Diversity, AD 200–1000* (Oxford: Wiley-Blackwell, 2013), pp. 470–472.

52. Rimbert, *Vita Anskarii*, ed. Georg Waitz, Monumenta Germaniae historica, Scriptores rerum Germanicarum in usum scholarum (Hanover: Hahn, 1884), esp. pp. 59-63; trans. Paul Edward Dutton in his *Carolingian Civilization: A Reader*, 2nd ed. (Toronto: University of Toronto Press, 2009), pp. 400–451, esp. pp. 435-437.

53. "Denmark: The Jelling Stone," in *The Viking Age: A Reader*, ed. Angus A. Somerville and R. Andrew McDonald (Toronto: University of Toronto Press, 2020), p. 426.

54. Winroth, *The Age of the Vikings*, pp. 147–151.

VII

HERMITS IN MAIL

972–1099

1. Rodulfus Glaber, *Historiarum libri quinque*, in *Opera*, ed. Neithard Bulst, trans. John France and Paul Reynolds (Oxford: Clarendon Press, 1989), 2.xi.22, pp. 88–91.

2. Rodulfus Glaber, *Historiarum libri quinque*, 1.1, pp. 2–3.

3. Rodulfus Glaber, *Historiarum libri quinque*, 1.i, 5.i.1–5, pp. 4–5, 217–223.

4. Rodulfus Glaber, *Historiarum libri quinque*, 4.vi.18, pp. 198–205.

5. Rodulfus Glaber, *Historiarum libri quinque*, 3.vii.24, pp. 133–137.

6. Rodulfus Glaber, *Historiarum libri quinque*, 1.iv.9, pp. 18–23.

7. Rodulfus Glaber, *Historiarum libri quinque*, 4.v.14, pp. 194–195.

8. Rodulfus Glaber, *Historiarum libri quinque*, 4.v.14, pp. 194–199.

9. Rodulfus Glaber, *Historiarum libri quinque*, 3.v.17–18, pp. 122–125.

10. Rodulfus Glaber, *Historiarum libri quinque*, 5.i.15, pp. 236–239; "The Peace and Truce of God at the Council of Toulouges," trans. David Herlihy in his *The History of Feudalism* (Atlantic Highlands, NJ: Humanities Press, 1979), pp. 286–288.

11. Richard C. Hoffmann, *An Environmental History of Medieval Europe* (Cambridge: Cambridge University Press, 2014), pp. 117–118.

12. Alice Rio, *Slavery After Rome, 500–1100* (Oxford: Oxford University Press, 2017), pp. 215–249.

13. Hoffman, *An Environmental History*, pp. 119–122; R. I. Moore, *The First European Revolution, c. 970–1215* (Oxford: Blackwell, 2000), pp. 46–47.

14. Hoffman, *An Environmental History*, pp. 122–125; William Chester Jordan, *The Great Famine: Northern Europe in the Early Fourteenth Century* (Princeton, NJ: Princeton University Press, 1996), pp. 35–36.

15. Fulbert of Chartres, "Letter 52," ed. and trans. Frederick Behrends, in *The Letters and Poems of Fulbert of Chartres* (Oxford: Clarendon Press, 1976), pp. 90–93.

16. Dhuoda, *Liber Manualis: Handbook for Her Warrior Son*, ed. and trans. Marcelle Thiébaux (Cambridge: Cambridge University Press, 1998), 10.4, pp. 226–227.

17. Alice Taylor, "Homage in the Latin Chronicles of Eleventh- and Twelfth-Century Normandy," in *People, Texts and Artefacts: Cultural Transmission in the Medieval Norman Worlds,* ed. David Bates, Edoardo D'Angelo, and Elisabeth van Houts (London: Institute of Historical Research, 2018), pp. 231–252.

18. Adalbero, *Carmen ad Rotbertum regem*, ed. Claude Carozzi (Paris: Les Belles Lettres, 1979), pp. 20–22.

19. *Gesta episcoporum Cameracensium*, trans. Richard Landes, in *The Peace of God: Social Violence and Religious Response in France Around the Year 1000*, ed. Thomas Head and Richard Landes (Ithaca, NY: Cornell University Press, 1992), pp. 335–337.

20. Giles Constable, *Three Studies in Medieval Religious and Social Thought: The Interpretation of Mary and Martha, The Ideal of the Imitation of Christ, and The Orders of Society* (Cambridge: Cambridge University Press, 1995), pp. 249–360.

21. Paul Edward Dutton, "Observations on Early Medieval Weather in General, Bloody Rain in Particular," in *The Long Morning of Medieval Europe: New Directions in Medieval Studies*, ed. Jennifer R. Davis and Michael McCormick (Aldershot, UK: Ashgate, 2008), pp. 167–180, esp. pp. 172, 178–179; Michael McCormick, "Gregory of Tours on Sixth-Century Plague and Other Epidemics," *Speculum* 96 (2021): 69.

22. Fulbert of Chartres, "Letter 125," ed. and trans. Frederick Behrends, in *The Letters and Poems of Fulbert of Chartres* (Oxford: Clarendon Press, 1976), pp. 224–227.

23. Andrea da Strumi, "Passion of Arialdo," trans. William North, in *Medieval Italy: Texts in Translation*, ed. Katherine L. Jansen, Joanna Dell, and Frances Andrews (Philadelphia: University of Pennsylvania Press, 2009), pp. 339–345.

24. On the Patarenes, see R. I. Moore, *The War on Heresy* (Cambridge, MA: Belknap Press of Harvard University Press, 2014), pp. 71–86.

25. Andrea da Strumi, "Passion of Arialdo," pp. 341–342.

26. Andrea da Strumi, "Passion of Arialdo," p. 343.

27. Andrea da Strumi, "Passion of Arialdo," p. 374.

28. Peter Damiani, *Vita Dominici Loricati*, ed. Jacques-Paul Migne, *Patrologiae cursus completus: Series Latina* 144 (Paris: Garnier, 1867), cols. 1007–1024; Katherine Allen Smith, "Saints in Shining Armor: Martial Asceticism and Masculine Models of Sanctity, ca. 1050–1250," *Speculum* 83 (2008): 585–586; Constable, *Three Studies*, pp. 202–203.

29. Peter Damiani, "Letter to Bishop Cunibert of Turin, 1064," trans. Maureen C. Miller in her *Power and the Holy in the Age of the Investiture Controversy: A Brief History with Documents* (Boston: Bedford-St. Martin's, 2005), p. 47.

30. Andrea da Strumi, "Passion of Arialdo," p. 344.

31. Andrea da Strumi, "Passion of Arialdo," pp. 349–350.

32. Landulf Senior, *Historia Mediolanensis*, ed. Ludwig Conrad Bethman and Wilhelm Wattenbach, in Monumenta Germanie historica, Scriptores 8, ed. Georg Heinrich Pertz (Hanover, Hahn, 1848) iii.30, p. 95, and H. E. J. Cowdrey, "The Papacy, the Patarenes and the Church of Milan," *Transactions of the Royal Historical Society* 18 (1968): 35.

33. Chris Wickham, *Sleepwalking into a New World: The Emergence of Italian City Communes in the Twelfth Century* (Princeton, NJ: Princeton University Press, 2015), pp. 24–25.

34. Chris Wickham, *Medieval Rome: Stability and Crisis of a City, 900–1150* (Oxford: Oxford University Press, 2015), p. 160.

35. "Penitential Ordinance (*poenitentiae institutio*)," trans. R. Allen Brown in his *The Norman Conquest: Sources and Documents* (Woodbridge, UK: Boydell, 1984), pp. 156–157; E. J. Cowdrey, "Bishop Ermenfrid of Sion and the Penitential Ordinance Following the Battle of Hastings," *Journal of Ecclesiastical History* 20 (1969): 241–242; David Carpenter, *The Struggle for Mastery. The Penguin History of Britain, 1066–1284* (London: Penguin Books, 2003), pp. 72–78.

36. Gregory VII, "*The* Dicatus papae," trans. Maureen C. Miller in her *Power and the Holy in the Age of the Investiture Controversy: A Brief History with Documents* (Boston: Bedford-St. Martin's, 2005), pp. 81–81.

37. See the documents translated by Maureen C. Miller in her *Power and the Holy in the Age of the Investiture Controversy: A Brief History with Documents* (Boston: Bedford-St. Martin's, 2005), pp. 83–115, and William Chester Jordan, *Europe in the High Middle Ages* (London: Viking-Penguin Books, 2001), pp. 90–99.

38. Fulcher of Chartres, *Historia Hierosolymitana*, ed. Heinrich Hagenmeyer (Heidelberg: Carl Winters, 1913), I.3.7, p. 136 [and Martha McGinty's translation in *The First Crusade: The Chronicle of Fulcher of Chartres and Other Source Materials*, ed. Edward Peters, 2nd ed. (Philadelphia: University of Pennsylvania Press, 1998), pp. 50–51; references to page numbers in this translation are in square brackets].

39. Paul M. Cobb, *The Race for Paradise: An Islamic History of the Crsuades* (Oxford: Oxford University Press, 2014), pp. 78–88.

40. Fulcher of Chartres, *Historia Hierosolymitana*, I.3.7, p. 136 [McGinty, pp. 52–53]. Out of the many books on the First Crusade, see especially Jay Rubenstein, *Armies of Heaven: The First Crusade and the Quest for Apocalypse* (New York: Basic Books, 2011), and his *Nebuchadnezzar's Dream: The Crusades, Apocalyptic Prophecy, and the End of History* (Oxford: Oxford University Press, 2019).

41. Lambert of Arras, "Urban II's Crusading Indulgence 1095," trans. Robert Somerville, in *The First Crusade: A Brief History with Documents*, ed. Jay Rubenstein (Boston: Bedford-St. Martin's, 2015), p. 62.

42. Fulcher of Chartres, *Historia Hierosolymitana*, I.4.4, pp. 140–142 [McGinty, p. 54].

43. Albert of Aachen, *Historia Ierosolimitana* [*History of the Journey to Jerusalem*], ed. and trans. Susan B. Edgington (Oxford: Clarendon Press, 2007), i.2, pp. 2–5.

44. Solomon Ben Simson, *Chronicle*, trans. Robert Chazan in his *European Jewry and the First Crusade* (Berkeley: University of California Press, 1987), pp. 250–254, 258–259, 266–267.

45. Rubenstein, *Armies of Heaven*, pp. 55–67.

46. Fulcher of Chartres, *Historia Hierosolymitana*, I.6.1–14, pp. 153–163 [McGinty, pp. 57–59].

47. Anna Komnene, *The Alexiad*, trans. E. R. A. Sewter, rev. Peter Frankopan (London: Penguin Books, 2009), p. 279.

48. Étienne de Blois, "Letter, June 24, 1097," trans. Jay Rubenstein in his *The First Crusade: A Brief History with Documents* (Boston: Bedford-St. Martin's, 2015), pp. 94–96.

49. Étienne de Blois, "Letter, March, 1098," trans. Jay Rubenstein in his *The First Crusade: A Brief History with Documents* (Boston: Bedford-St. Martin's, 2015), pp. 103–106.

50. Fulcher of Chartres, *Historia Hierosolymitana*, I.18.1–5, pp. 235–245 [McGinty, pp. 76–77].

51. Cobb, *The Race for Paradise*, pp. 88–94.

52. "Letter to Pope Urban II, 11 September, 1098," trans. Malcolm Barber and Keith Bate in their *Letters from the East: Crusaders, Pilgrims, and Settlers in the 12th–13th Centuries* (Farnham, UK: Ashgate, 2013), pp. 30–33.

53. Fulcher of Chartres, *Historia Hierosolymitana*, I.27.1–13, pp. 292–301 [McGinty, pp. 89–91].

54. Manasses of Reims, "Latin Christian Reaction to the Crusade," trans. Jay Rubenstein in his *The First Crusade: A Brief History with Documents* (Boston: Bedford-St. Martin's, 2015), pp. 154–155.

55. Rodulfus Glaber, *Historiarum libri quinque*, I.v.24, pp. 40–43.

VIII
UNCLE, WHAT TROUBLES YOU?
1099–1220

1. Peter Abelard, *Historia calamitatum*, ed. J. Monfrin (Paris: J. Vrin, 1959), p. 71 [and trans. Betty Radice, rev. M. T. Clanchy, as *The Story of His Misfortunes* in *The Letters of Abelard and Heloise* (London: Penguin Books, 2003), p. 9; references to page numbers in this translation are in square brackets].

2. Peter Abelard, *Historia calamitatum*, pp. 63–71 [Radice and Clanchy, pp. 3–9].

3. Peter Abelard, *Historia calamitatum*, pp. 73–74 [Radice and Clanchy, pp. 11–12].

4. Peter Abelard, *Historia calamitatum*, p. 74 [Radice and Clanchy, p. 12].

5. Peter Abelard, *Historia calamitatum*, p. 74 [Radice and Clanchy, p. 12].

6. Peter Abelard, *Historia calamitatum*, pp. 75–78 [Radice and Clanchy, pp. 14–16].

7. Peter Abelard, *Historia calamitatum*, p. 79 [Radice and Clanchy, p. 17].

8. Peter Abelard, *Historia calamitatum*, p. 63 [Radice and Clanchy, p. 3].

9. Peter Abelard, *Historia calamitatum*, pp. 79–83 [Radice and Clanchy, pp. 17–20].

10. Peter Abelard, *Historia calamitatum*, pp. 83–90 [Radice and Clanchy, pp. 20–25].

11. Peter Abelard, *Historia calamitatum*, pp. 90–98 [Radice and Clanchy, pp. 25–32].

12. Peter Abelard, *Historia calamitatum*, p. 98 [Radice and Clanchy, p. 33].

13. Peter Abelard, *Historia calamitatum*, pp. 99–109 [Radice and Clanchy, pp. 33–43].

14. Heloise, "Lettre I," ed. J. Monfrin, in Peter Abelard, *Historia calamitatum* (Paris: J. Vrin, 1959), Appendix, pp. 111–114, and trans. Betty Radice, rev. M. T. Clanchy, as "Letter 2" in *The Letters of Abelard and Heloise* (London: Penguin Books, 2003), pp. 47–50.

15. M. T. Clanchy, *Abelard: A Medieval Life* (Oxford: Blackwell, 1999), p. 271.

16. Clanchy, *Abelard*, p. 274.

17. Clanchy, *Abelard*, p. 108.

18. Clanchy, *Abelard*, pp. 286–287.

19. Marcabru, *Dire vos vuelh ses duptansa*, trans. William D. Paden and Frances Freeman Paden in their *Troubadour Poems from the South of France* (Cambridge: D. S. Brewer, 2007), pp. 38–39.

20. Marcabru, *L'autrier jost'una sebissa*, trans. William D. Paden and Frances Freeman Paden in their *Troubadour Poems from the South of France* (Cambridge: D. S. Brewer, 2007), pp. 40–42.

21. Marcabru, *Cortesamen vuoill comensar*, ed. and trans. Simon Gaunt, Ruth Harvey, and Linda Paterson in their *Marcabru: A Critical Edition* (Cambridge: D. S. Brewer, 2000), pp. 202–203.

22. Marcabru, *Dirai vos e mon latin*, ed. and trans. Simon Gaunt, Ruth Harvey, and Linda Paterson in their *Marcabru: A Critical Edition* (Cambridge: D. S. Brewer, 2000), pp. 230–231.

23. *The Song of Roland*, trans. Glyn Burgess (London: Penguin Books, 1990), p. 86.

24. *The Song of Roland*, p. 84.

25. *The Song of Roland*, p. 84.

26. Herman the Former Jew, *Short Work on His Conversion* [or *Short Account of His Own Conversion*], trans. Karl F. Morrison in his *Conversion and Text: The Cases of Augustine of Hippo, Herman-Judah, and Constantine Tsatsos* (Charlottesville: University Press of Virginia, 1992), pp. 76–113, esp. p. 80.

27. Herman the Former Jew, *Short Work on His Conversion*, pp. 77–78.

28. Herman the Former Jew, *Short Work on His Conversion*, pp. 78–80.

29. Herman the Former Jew, *Short Work on His Conversion*, pp. 81–88.

30. Herman the Former Jew, *Short Work on His Conversion*, pp. 91–93.

31. Herman the Former Jew, *Short Work on His Conversion*, pp. 94–102.

32. Herman the Former Jew, *Short Work on His Conversion*, pp. 102–107.

33. Herman the Former Jew, *Short Work on His Conversion*, pp. 107–109.

34. Herman the Former Jew, *Short Work on His Conversion*, pp. 76, 110–113.

35. Elisheva Baumgarten, *Mothers and Children: Jewish Family Life in Medieval Europe* (Princeton, NJ: Princeton University Press, 2007), p. 140.

36. Jean-Claude Schmidt, *The Conversion of Herman the Jew: Autobiography, History, and Fiction in the Twelfth Century*, trans. Alex J. Novikoff (Philadelphia: University of Pennsylvania Press, 2010), and a translation of *Opusculum de conversione sua*, pp. 202–239.

37. Bernard of Clairvaux, "Letter 242," in *Sancti Bernardi Opera VIII: Epistolae*, ed. Jean Leclercq and Henri Rochais (Rome: Éditions cisterciennes, 1977), pp. 128–129.

38. Bernard of Clairvaux, "Sermon 2 on Pentecost," in *Sancti Bernardi Opera V: Sermones II,* ed. Jean Leclercq and Henri Rochais (Rome: Éditions cisterciennes, 1972), p. 168.

39. Bernard of Clairvaux, "Sermon 66," in *Sancti Bernardi Opera II: Sermones super Cantica Canticorum 36–38*, ed. Jean Leclercq, Charles Talbot, and Henri Rochais (Rome: Éditions cisterciennes, 1958), p. 185.

40. Bernard of Clairvaux, "Letter 331," in *Sancti Bernardi Opera VIII: Epistolae*, ed. Jean Leclercq and Henri Rochais (Rome: Éditions cistercienses, 1977), p. 269.

41. Suger, *De rebus in administratione sua gestis*, ed. and trans. Erwin Panofsky as *Abbot Suger on the Abbey Church of St.-Denis and Its Art Treasures*, 2nd ed. by Gerda Panofsky-Soergel (Princeton, NJ: Princeton University Press, 1979), pp. 52–53.

42. Suger, *De rebus*, pp. 56–65, 72–77.

43. Eric Fernie, *Romanesque Architecture* (New Haven, CT: Yale University Press, 2014).

44. Bernard of Clairvaux, *Apologia ad Guillelmum abbatem* [*An Apologia for Abbot William*], trans. Pauline Matarasso in her *The Cistercian World: Monastic Writings of the Twelfth Century* (Harmondsworth, UK: Penguin Books, 1993), p. 56.

45. Suger, *De rebus*, pp. 66–67.

46. Usama ibn Munqidh, *The Book of Contemplation: Islam and the Crusades*, trans. Paul Cobb (London: Penguin Books, 2008), p. 147.

47. Usama ibn Munqidh, *The Book of Contemplation*, p. 144.

48. Usama ibn Munqidh, *The Book of Contemplation*, pp. xv–xli, 84, and 296n113 for Cobb's brilliant word choice of "Pfft!"

49. Marian Rustow, *The Lost Archive: Traces of a Caliphate in a Cairo Synagogue* (Princeton, NJ: Princeton University Press, 2020).

50. William of Tyre, *Chronicon*, ed. R. B. C. Huygens, Corpus Christianorum, Continuatio Mediaevalis 63 (Turnhout: Brepols, 1986), pp. 553–555; Malcolm Barber, *The New Knighthood: A History of the Order of the Temple* (Cambridge: Cambridge University Press, 1994), pp. 1–64; Helen J. Nicholson, *The Knights Templar* (Leeds, UK: Arc Humanities Press, 2021), pp. 11–20, esp. pp. 11–12.

51. Bernard of Clairvaux, *In Praise of the New Knighthood*, trans. Malcolm Barber and Keith Bate in their *The Templars: Selected Sources Translated and Annotated* (Manchester: Manchester University Press, 2002), pp. 215–227.

52. Barber, *The New Knighthood*, pp. 26–37.

53. Giles Constable, "The Second Crusade as Seen by Contemporaries," *Traditio* 9 (1953): 213–279, remains superlative and seminal.

54. *Annales herbipolenses*, ed. Georg Heinrich Pertz, Monumenta Germaniae historica, Scriptores 16.3 (Hanover: Hahn, 1859), pp. 3–8, esp. pp. 3–4; Constable, "The Second Crusade," 268.

55. Thomas E. Burman, *Reading the Qur'an in Latin Christendom, 1140–1560* (Philadelphia: University of Pennsylvania Press, 2007), pp. 16–17, 14–35.

56. Usama ibn Munquid, *The Book of Contemplation*, p. 108; Paul M. Cobb, *The Race for Paradise: An Islamic History of the Crusades* (Oxford: Oxford University Press, 2014), pp. 28–33.

57. Anne-Marie Eddé, *Saladin*, trans. Jane Marie Todd (Cambridge, MA: Belknap Press of Harvard University Press, 2011), pp. 67–332.

58. Cobb, *The Race for Paradise*, pp. 160–193.

59. Paul Cobb, *Usama ibn Munqidh: Warrior Poet of the Age of the Crusades* (Oxford: Oneworld, 2005), p. 65.

60. *Chronicon universale anonymi Laudunensis*, ed. Georg Waitz, Monumenta Germaniae historica, Scriptores 26 (Hanover: Hahn, 1882), pp. 447–449 [trans. Walter Leggett Wakefield and Austin P. Evans in their *Heresies of the High Middle Ages: Selected Sources Translated and Annotated* (New York: Columbia University Press, 1991 [orig. 1969]), pp. 200–202; references to page numbers in this translation are in square brackets].

61. Walter Map, *De nugis curialium*, ed. Montague R. James (Oxford, 1914), pp. 60–62, trans. Walter Leggett Wakefield and Austin P. Evans in their *Heresies of the High Middle Ages: Selected Sources Translated and Annotated* (New York: Columbia University Press, 1991 [orig. 1969]), pp. 203–204.

62. *Chronicon universale anonymi Laudunensis*, p. 449 [Wakefield and Evans, p. 203].

63. *Corpus iuris canonici*, ed. Aemilius Friedberg (Leipzig: B. Tauchnitz, 1879; reprint, Graz: Akademische Druck-u. Verlagsanstalt, 1959), 2, cols. 780–782.

64. Chris Wickham, *Medieval Europe* (New Haven, CT: Yale University Press, 2017), pp. 130–133; and his *Medieval Rome: Stability and Crisis of a City, 900–1150* (Oxford: Oxford University Press, 2015), p. 112.

65. "Fourth Lateran Council," ed. and trans. Norman P. Tanner in his *Decrees of the Ecumenical Councils*, vol. 1 (London: Sheed and Ward, 1990), pp. 230–271. The text of the anonymous German cleric is edited in Stephan Kuttner and Antonio García y García, "A New Eyewitness Account of the Fourth Lateran Council," *Traditio* 20 (1964): 115–178, and translated by Constantin Fasolt in *Medieval Europe: Readings in Western Civilization*, ed. Julius Kirshner and Karl F. Morrison (Chicago: University of Chicago Press, 1986), pp. 369–376. Now, see Brenda Bolton, "A Show with Meaning: Innocent III's Approach to the Fourth Lateran Council, 1215," in her *Innocent III: Studies on Papal Authority and Pastoral Care* (Aldershot, UK: Ashgate, 1995), XI, pp. 53–67.

66. Anders Winroth, *The Making of Gratian's Decretum* (Cambridge: Cambridge University Press, 2000).

67. "Fourth Lateran Council," pp. 230–271.

68. Innocent III, "Sermon 3," ed. Jacques-Paul Migne, *Patrologiae cursus completus: Series Latina* 217 (Paris: Garnier, 1890), col. 665.

69. Innocent III, "Sermon 2," ed. Jacques-Paul Migne, *Patrologiae cursus completus: Series Latina* 217 (Paris: Garnier, 1890), col. 658.

70. Jacques de Vitry, "Letter I," ed. R. B. C. Huygens, in *Lettres de Jacques de Vitry (1160/70), évêque de Saint-Jean d'Acre* (Leiden: Brill, 1960), pp. 71–78, esp. 73–74.

71. Wolfram von Eschenbach, *Parzival (with Titurel and the Love-lyrics)*, trans. Cyril Edwards (Woodbridge, UK: D. S. Brewer, 2004), IX, pp. 139–152.

72. Wolfram von Eschenbach, *Parzival*, IX, pp. 153–156.

73. Wolfram von Eschenbach, *Parzival*, V, IX, XVI, pp. 71–89, 157–161, 254.

74. Wolfram von Eschenbach, *Parzival*, "Wolfram's Self-Defense," VIII, IX, pp. 36–37, 134, 145–147.

75. Wolfram von Eschenbach, *Parzival*, XVI, p. 264.

IX

LOVE MOVES THE SUN AND ALL THE OTHER STARS

1209–1321

1. Guilhem de Tudela, *La Chanson de la Croisade Albigeoise* [*La Canso de la Crozada*], ed. and trans. E. Martin-Chabot, 2nd ed. (Paris: Les Belles Lettres, 1960), 1, laisses 15–23, pp. 44–65; Pierre des Vaux-de-Cernay, *Historia Albigensis*, ed. P. Guébin and E. Lyon, Société de l'Histoire de France (Paris: Librairie Ancienne Honoré Champion, 1926), 1, §§ 84–90, pp. 84–91 [trans. W. A. Sibly and M. D. Sibly in their *The History of the Albigensian Crusade* (Woodbridge, UK: Boydell Press, 1998), pp. 48–50; references to page numbers in this translation are in square brackets]. Now, see Mark Gregory Pegg, *A Most Holy War: The Albigensian Crusade and the Battle for Christendom* (New York: Oxford University Press, 2008), pp. 71–78, and his "The Albigensian Crusade and the Early Inquisitions into Heretical Depravity," in *The Cambridge World History of Genocide. Vol 1: Genocide in the Ancient, Medieval, and Premodern Worlds* ed. Ben Kiernan, T. M. Lemon, and Tristan Taylor (Cambridge: Cambridge University Press, 2022), pp. 470–497.

2. Arnau Amalric, "De victoria habita contra hereticos," ed. Jacques-Paul Migne, *Patrologiae cursus completus: Series Latina* 216 (Paris: Garnier, 1891), cviii, cols. 138–141, esp. cols. 138–139.

3. Caesarius of Heisterbach, *Dialogus Miraculorum*, ed. J. Strange (Cologne: H. Lempertz, 1851), 1, V, xxi, p. 302; and trans. H. von E. Scott and C. C. Swinton Bland as *The Dialogue on Miracles* (London: George Routledge & Sons, 1929) 1, V, xxi, pp. 345–346.

4. *Historia Albigensis*, 1, § 61, p. 60 [Sibly and Sibly, p. 35].

5. *Historia Albigensis*, 1, § 64, pp. 63–65 [Sibly and Sibly, pp. 37–38]. Peire de Castelnau's murder was also described by Guilhem de Puylaurens, *Chronica Magistri Guillelmi de Podio Laurentii*, ed. and trans. J. Duvernoy, Sources d'Histoire Médiévale (Paris: Éditions du Centre National de la Recherche Scientifique, 1976), ix, p. 52, and trans. W. A. Sibly and M. D. Sibly as *The Chronicle of William of Puylaurens: The Albigensian Crusade and Its Aftermath* (Woodbridge, UK: Boydell Press, 2003), p. 27.

6. *Historia Albigensis*, 1, § 91, p. 93 [Sibly and Sibly, p. 51].

7. Anonymous Continuator (after Guilhem de Tudela), *Crozada,* 3, laisse 208, p. 228. Now, see Daniel Power, "The Albigensian Crusade After Simon of Montfort (1218–1224)," in *Simon de Montfort (c. 1170–1218): Le croisé, son lignage et son temps*, ed. M. Aurell, G. Lippiatt, and L. Macé (Turnhout: Brepols, 2020), pp. 161–178.

8. Gervase of Tilbury, *Otia Imperialia* [*Recreation for an Emperor*], ed. and trans. S. E. Banks and J. W. Binns (Oxford: Clarendon Press, 2002), III, 103, pp. 761–763.

9. Gervase of Tilbury, *Otia Imperialia*, III, 103, pp. 763–764.

10. Gervase of Tilbury, *Otia Imperialia*, III, 103, pp. 765–769.

11. Gervase of Tilbury, *Otia Imperialia*, III, 103, pp. 771–779.

12. Gervase of Tilbury, *Otia Imperialia*, III, 103, pp. 779–780.

13. Gervase of Tilbury, *Otia Imperialia*, Introduction, pp. xxvi–lxiii, Preface, pp. 12–15.

14. Gervase of Tilbury, *Otia Imperialia*, III, 103, p. 761.

15. Jacques de Vitry, *Vita Mariae Oigniacensis*, ed. Daniel von Papenbroeck, Acta Sanctorum . . . editio novissima 23 June 5 (Paris: Palmé, 1867), pp. 542–572, esp. pp. 547–550, 586; and trans. Margot H. King as *The Life of Marie d'Oignes by Jacques de Vitry* (Saskatoon, SK: Peregrina, 1986), esp. pp. 2–4, 79–80, 103; Giles Constable, *Three Studies in Medieval Religious and Social Thought: The Interpretation of Mary and Martha, The Ideal of the Imitation of Christ, and The Orders of Society* (Cambridge: Cambridge University Press, 1995), pp. 216–217.

16. Thomas of Celano, *Life of Saint Francis*, trans. Marion A. Habig, in *Medieval Europe: Readings in Western Civilization*, ed. Julius Kirschner and Karl F. Morrison (Chicago: University of Chicago Press, 1986), pp. 294–295.

17. Francis of Assisi, *Testament* (1226), trans. Marion A. Habig, in *Medieval Europe: Readings in Western Civilization*, ed. Julius Kirschner and Karl F. Morrison (Chicago: University of Chicago Press, 1986), pp. 286–289.

18. Augustine Thompson, *Francis of Assisi: The Life* (Ithaca, NY: Cornell University Press, 2013), pp. 23, 47, 51.

19. Thomas of Celano, *Life of Saint Francis*, p. 304.

20. John Tolan, *Saint Francis and the Sultan: The Curious History of a Christian-Muslim Encounter* (Oxford: Oxford University Press, 2009).

21. Francis of Assisi, *Rule*, trans. Marion A. Habig, in *Medieval Europe: Readings in Western Civilization*, ed. Julius Kirschner and Karl F. Morrison (Chicago: University of Chicago Press, 1986), pp. 281–286.

22. Christine Caldwell Ames, *Righteous Persecution: Inquisition, Dominicans, and Christianity in the Middle Ages* (Philadelphia: University of Pennsylvania Press, 2009).

23. Toulouse, Bibliothèque municipal, MS 609, fol. 239v; Mark Gregory Pegg, *The Corruption of Angels: The Great Inquisition of 1245–1246* (Princeton, NJ: Princeton University Press, 2001), pp. 20–27.

24. "Del tot vey remaner valor," in *Les Poésies de Guilhem de Montanhagol: Troubadour Provençal du XIIIᵉ Siècle*, ed. and trans. Peter T. Ricketts (Toronto: Pontifical Institute of Medieval Studies, 1964), I, 19–20, p. 44.

25. Toulouse, Bibliothèque municipal, MS 609, fols. 239v–240r.

26. Guillaume de Rubruck, *Itinerarium*, ed. Anastasius van den Wyngaert, *Sinica Franciscana, I. Itinera et relationes Fratrum Minorum saeculi XIII et XIV* (Florence-Quaracchi: Apud Collegium S. Bonaventurae, 1929), XXXIV, p. 298 [and trans. Peter Jackson and David Morgan in their *The Mission of Friar William of Rubruck: His Journey to the Court of the Great Khan Möngke, 1253–1255* (Indianapolis, IN: Hackett, 2000), p. 236; references to page numbers in this translation are in square brackets].

27. Guillaume de Rubruck, *Itinerarium*, XXXIV, pp. 298–299 [Jackson and Morgan, pp. 236–238]; Marie Favereau, *The Horde: How the Mongols Changed*

the World (Cambridge, MA: Belknap Press of Harvard University Press, 2021), pp. 22, 31–33, 144, 162, 166, 222.

28. Guillaume de Rubruck, *Itinerarium*, XXXIV, p. 300 [Jackson and Morgan, p. 239]; Favereau, *The Horde*, pp. 22, 31–33, 144, 162, 166, 222.

29. Peter Jackson and David Morgan, "Introduction," in their *The Mission of Friar William of Rubruck: His Journey to the Court of the Great Khan Möngke, 1253–1255* (Indianapolis, IN: Hackett, 2000), pp. 1–55.

30. Guillaume de Rubruck, *Itinerarium*, XVIII, pp. 209–211 [Jackson and Morgan, pp. 124–125].

31. Favereau, *The Horde*, pp. 10–13, 36–42.

32. Favereau, *The Horde*, pp. 42–62; David Morgan, *The Mongols* (Oxford: Blackwell, 1990), pp. 32–96.

33. Favereau, *The Horde*, pp. 86–89; Morgan, *The Mongols*, pp. 138–141.

34. Favereau, *The Horde*, pp. 89–92.

35. Nora Berend, *At the Gate of Christendom: Jews, Muslims, and "Pagans" in Medieval Hungary, c. 1000–c. 1300* (Cambridge: Cambridge University Press, 2001), pp. 163–171.

36. Guillaume de Rubruck, *Itinerarium*, II, XIX, pp. 172–176, 211–216 [Jackson and Morgan, pp. 72–78, 130–132].

37. Guillaume de Rubruck, *Itinerarium*, XXVII, p. 240 [Jackson and Morgan, p. 173].

38. Guillaume de Rubruck, *Itinerarium*, XIX, XX, pp. 211–218 [Jackson and Morgan, pp. 132–134, 136–137].

39. Guillaume de Rubruck, *Itinerarium*, XXXVI, pp. 311–312 [Jackson and Morgan, pp. 252–253].

40. Guillaume de Rubruck, *Itinerarium*, XXXVII, p. 315 [Jackson and Morgan, p. 257].

41. Amanda Power, *Roger Bacon and the Defence of Christendom* (Cambridge: Cambridge University Press, 2013), p. 256.

42. Guillaume de Rubruck, *Itinerarium*, XXXVI, pp. 306–309 [Jackson and Morgan, pp. 248–250].

43. David Morgan, *The Mongols* (Oxford: Blackwell, 1990), pp. 180–181.

44. Favereau, *The Horde*, pp. 142–143; Morgan, *The Mongols*, pp. 147–152; Peter Jackson, *The Mongols and the Islamic World: From Conquest to Conversion* (New Haven, CT: Yale University Press, 2017), pp. 128–129.

45. Guillaume de Rubruck, *Itinerarium*, "Epilogue," p. 331 [Jackson and Morgan, p. 278].

46. Thomas Aquinas, *Summa contra Gentiles*, trans. Ralph McInerny, in *Thomas Aquinas: Selected Writings* (London: Penguin Books, 1998), p. 244.

47. Thomas Aquinas, *Summa contra Gentiles*, pp. 244–246.

48. Thomas Aquinas, *Summa contra Gentiles*, p. 246.

49. Thomas Aquinas, *Summa contra Gentiles*, pp. 247–248.

50. Thomas Aquinas, *Summa contra Gentiles*, pp. 249–255.

51. Bernard G. Dod, "Aristoteles latinus," in *The Cambridge History of Later Medieval Philosophy*, ed. Norman Kretzmann, Anthony Kenny, and Jan Pinborg (Cambridge: Cambridge University Press, 1982), pp. 45–79.

52. Jean-Pierre Torell, "Life and Works," in *The Oxford Handbook of Aquinas*, ed. Brian Davies (Oxford: Oxford University Press, 2012), pp. 15–28, and his *Saint Thomas Aquinas, vol. 1, The Person and His Work*, trans. Robert Royal (Washington, DC: Catholic University Press, 1996), esp. pp. 289–295.

53. Edward Grant, "The Effect of the Condemnation of 1277," in *The Cambridge History of Later Medieval Philosophy*, ed. Norman Kretzmann, Anthony Kenny, and Jan Pinborg (Cambridge: Cambridge University Press, 1982), pp. 537–539; Ian P. Wei, *Intellectual Culture in Medieval Paris: Theologians and the University, c. 1100–1330* (Cambridge: Cambridge University Press, 2012), pp. 167–169.

54. Humbert de Romans, *Opusculum tripartitum*, in Ortuin Gratius, *Fasciculus rerum expetendarum et fugiendarum*, ed. Edward Brown (London: Richard Chiswell, 1690), and partially trans. Louise and Jonathan Riley-Smith in their *The Crusades: Idea and Reality 1095–1274* (London: Edward Arnold, 1981), pp. 103–117.

55. Humbert de Romans, *Opusculum tripartitum*, pp. 186–193.

56. Humbert de Romans, *Opusculum tripartitum*, pp. 193–194.

57. Humbert de Romans, *Opusculum tripartitum*, pp. 195–196.

58. Humbert de Romans, *Opusculum tripartitum*, pp. 197–201. On the 1270 crusade, see Michael Lower, *The Tunis Crusade of 1270: A Mediterranean History* (Oxford: Oxford University Press, 2018).

59. Humbert de Romans, *Opusculum tripartitum*, pp. 202–204.

60. Paul M. Cobb, *The Race for Paradise: An Islamic History of the Crusades* (Oxford: Oxford University Press, 2014), pp. 182–184.

61. Arnau Amalric, *Letter* [*Ex Epistola Arnaldi Narbonensis archiepiscopi ad abbatem Cisterciensem*], ed. Martin Bouquet, *Recueil des historiens des Gaules et de la France*, vol. 19 (Poitiers: Oudin, 1880), pp. 250–254, esp. p. 253.

62. Humbert de Romans, *Opusculum tripartitum*, pp. 205–223.

63. Michael Angold, "After the Fourth Crusade: The Greek Rump States and the Recovery of Byzantium," in *The Cambridge History of the Byzantine Empire c. 500–1492*, ed. Jonathan Shepard (Cambridge: Cambridge University Press, 2008), pp. 731–778.

64. Humbert de Romans, *Opusculum tripartitum*, pp. 223–229. Now, see Edward Tracy Brett, *Humbert of Romans: His Life and Views of Thirteenth-Century Society* (Toronto: Pontifical Institute of Mediaeval Studies, 1984), esp. pp. 176–194; Brett Edward Whalen, *Dominion of God: Christendom and Apocalypse in the Middle Ages* (Cambridge, MA: Harvard University Press, 2009), pp. 196–198.

65. Cobb, *The Race for Paradise*, p. 239.

66. *La Deuxième Controverse de Paris: Un chapitre dans la polémique entre chrétiens et juifs au Moyen Âge*, ed. Joseph Shatzmiller (Paris: E. Peeters, 1994), pp. 44–57.

67. *The Trial of the Talmud, Paris, 1240*, ed. and trans. John Friedman, Jean Connell Hoff, and Robert Chazan (Toronto: Pontifical Institute of Mediaeval Studies,

2012); William Chester Jordan, *The French Monarchy and the Jews: From Philip Augustus to the Last Capetians* (Philadelphia: University of Pennsylvania Press, 1989), pp. 138–141.

68. *La Deuxième Controverse de Paris*, p. 56; Jeremy Cohen, *Living Letters of the Law: Ideas of the Jew in Medieval Christianity* (Berkeley: University of California Press, 1999), pp. 317–363, esp. pp. 335–352.

69. Miri Rubin, *Gentile Tales: The Narrative Assault on Late Medieval Jews* (Philadelphia: University of Pennsylvania Press, 1999), pp. 40–69.

70. Jordan, *The French Monarchy and the Jews*, pp. 214–216.

71. Guillaume de Lorris and Jean de Meun, *The Romance of the Rose*, trans. Frances Horgan (Oxford: Oxford University Press, 1994), pp. 301–304.

72. Guillaume de Lorris and Jean de Meun, *The Romance of the Rose*, pp. 304–318.

73. Guillaume de Lorris and Jean de Meun, *The Romance of the Rose*, pp. 319–335.

74. "Depositions of the Templars at Paris (October–November 1307)," trans. Malcolm Barber and Keith Bate in their *The Templars: Selected Sources Translated and Annotated* (Manchester: Manchester University Press, 2002), pp. 252–253.

75. Malcolm Barber, *The New Knighthood: A History of the Order of the Temple* (Cambridge: Cambridge University Press, 1994), p. 302.

76. Malcolm Barber, *The New Knighthood*, pp. 280–313.

77. Now, see *The Debate on the Trial of the Templars*, ed. Helen Nicholson, Paul F. Crawford, and Jochen Burgtorf (Farnham, UK: Routledge, 2010).

78. "Beatrix de Ecclesia [Beatritiz de Plannisoles]," in *Le Registre d'Inquisition de Jacques Fournier, Évêque de Pamiers (1318–1325)*, ed. Jean Duvernoy (Toulouse: Édouard Privat, 1965), I, pp. 243–245.

79. "Beatrix de Ecclesia [Beatritiz de Plannisoles]," pp. 224–225, 238.

80. "Beatrix de Ecclesia [Beatritiz de Plannisoles]," pp. 225–226.

81. "Beatrix de Ecclesia [Beatritiz de Plannisoles]," pp. 247–248.

82. "Beatrix de Ecclesia [Beatritiz de Plannisoles]," pp. 248–249.

83. "Beatrix de Ecclesia [Beatritiz de Plannisoles]," p. 249.

84. "Beatrix de Ecclesia [Beatritiz de Plannisoles]," pp. 226–227.

85. For the preceding paragraphs on the *Inferno*, see Dante Alighieri's *Commedia: A Digital Edition*, ed. Prue Shaw, 2nd ed., 2021, www.dantecommedia.it, and translations in *The Portable Dante*, trans. Mark Musa (New York: Penguin Books, 2003), pp. 1–191, and *The Divine Comedy*, trans. Clive James (New York: Liveright, 2013), pp. 1–171.

86. For the preceding paragraphs on the *Purgatorio*, see the *Commedia: A Digital Edition*, and translations in *The Portable Dante*, pp. 195–387; *The Divine Comedy*, pp. 173–345; and *Purgatorio*, trans. D. M. Black (New York: New York Review of Books, 2021), pp. 26–411.

87. For the preceding paragraphs on the *Paradiso*, see *Commedia: A Digital Edition*, and translations in *The Portable Dante*, pp. 391–585 and *The Divine Comedy*, pp. 349–526.

88. Marco Santagata, *Dante: The Story of His Life*, trans. Richard Dixon (Cambridge, MA: Belknap Press of Harvard University Press, 2018), pp. 178–184.

89. Santagata, *Dante*, pp. 142–145, 217–218, 266–269.

90. Dante Alighieri, *Vita Nuova: A Dual Language Edition*, trans. Virginia Jewiss (New York: Penguin Books, 2022), pp. 2–3.

91. Dante, *Vita Nuova*, pp. 82–83.

92. Santagata, *Dante*, pp. 37–42.

X

ONLY DEATH WAKES US FROM DREAMING
1321–1431

1. Giovanni Boccaccio, *Decameron*, ed. Vittore Branca (Milan: Mondadori, 1989), pp. 11–19 [and trans. G. H. McWilliam as *The Decameron*, 2nd ed. (London: Penguin Books, 1995), p. 412; references to page numbers in this translation are in square brackets].

2. In general, see Monica H. Green, ed., *Pandemic Disease in the Medieval World: Rethinking the Black Death*, Medieval Globe 1 (Kalamazoo, MI: Arc Medieval Press, 2015).

3. Giovanni Boccaccio, *Decameron*, p. 18 [McWilliam, p. 11]; John Aberth, *The Black Death: A New History of the Great Mortality in Europe, 1347–1500* (New York: Oxford University Press, 2021), p. 1.

4. Michael W. Dols, "Ibn al-Wardi's Risalah al-naba' 'an al-waba', a Translation of a Major Source for the History of the Black Death in the Middle East," in *Near Eastern Numismatics, Iconography, Epigraphy and History: Studies in Honor of George C. Miles*, ed. Dickran K. Kouymjian (Beirut: American University of Beirut, 1974), pp. 447–448.

5. Monica Green, "The Four Black Deaths," *American Historical Review* 125 (2020): 1601–1631; Aberth, *The Black Death*, pp. 18–19.

6. Aberth, *The Black Death*, pp. 14–20; Marie Favereau, *The Horde: How the Mongols Changed the World* (Cambridge, MA: Belknap Press of Harvard University Press, 2021), pp. 250–257.

7. Gabriele de Mussis, *Historia de morbo sive mortalitate quae fuit anno Domini 1348*, trans. Rosemary Horrox in her *The Black Death: Selected Sources Translated and Annotated* (Manchester: Manchester University Press, 1994), pp. 14–21.

8. Favereau, *The Horde*, pp. 248–250.

9. Aberth, *The Black Death*, pp. 20–27.

10. Cf. Ole J. Benedictow, *The Complete History of the Black Death* (Woodbridge, UK: Boydell Press, 2021).

11. Aberth, *The Black Death*, pp. 27–31; Sharon N. Dewitte and Maryanne Kowaleski, "Black Death Bodies," *Fragments* 6 (2017): 4–5.

12. Konrad of Megenberg, *De mortalitate in Alamannia*, trans. John Aberth in his *The Black Death: The Great Mortality of 1348–1350: A Brief History with Documents*, 2nd ed. (Boston: Bedford-St. Martin's, 2017), p. 137.

13. Aberth, *The Black Death*, p. 25.

14. John Clynn, *Annalium Hibernae Chronicon*, trans. Rosemary Horrox in her *The Black Death: Selected Sources Translated and Annotated* (Manchester: Manchester University Press, 1994), pp. 83–84.

15. Dewitte and Kowaleski, "Black Death Bodies," 3–12.

16. Abeth, *The Black Death*, p. 179; Jacme d'Agramont, *Regime of Protection Against Epidemics or Pestilence and Mortality* [*Regiment de preservacio a epidimia o pestilencia e mortaldats*], trans. John Abeth in his *The Black Death: The Great Mortality of 1348–1350: A Brief History with Documents*, 2nd ed. (Boston: Bedford-St. Martin's, 2017), pp. 52–56; David Nirenberg, *Communities of Violence: Persecution of Minorities in the Middle Ages*, 2nd ed. (Princeton, NJ: Princeton University Press, 2015), p. 235.

17. John Clynn, *Annalium Hibernae Chronicon*, p. 82.

18. Giovanni Boccaccio, *Decameron*, pp. 18–19 [McWilliam, pp. 11–12].

19. Abeth, *The Black Death*, p. 32.

20. Gabriele de Mussis, *Historia*, p. 21.

21. "Medical Faculty of the University of Paris. Consultation, October 6, 1348," trans. John Abeth in his *The Black Death: The Great Mortality of 1348–1350: A Brief History with Documents*, 2nd ed. (Boston: Bedford-St. Martin's, 2017), pp. 41–45.

22. Jacme d'Agramont, *Regime of Protection Against Epidemics or Pestilence and Mortality* [*Regiment de preservacio a epidimia o pestilencia e mortaldats*], pp. 52–56.

23. Alfonso de Córdoba, *Letter and Regime Concerning the Pestilence* [*Epistola et regime de pestilentia*], trans John Abeth in his *The Black Death: The Great Mortality of 1348–1350: A Brief History with Documents*, 2nd ed. (Boston: Bedford-St. Martin's, 2017), pp. 46–47.

24. André Benedict, "Letter to the Jurors of Gerona April 17, 1348," trans. John Abeth in his *The Black Death: The Great Mortality of 1348–1350: A Brief History with Documents*, 2nd ed. (Boston: Bedford-St. Martin's, 2017), pp. 113–114.

25. Abeth, *The Black Death*, p. 175.

26. Nirenberg, *Communities of Violence*, pp. 93–124; Abeth, *The Black Death*, pp. 176–180.

27. "Examination of the Jews Captured in Savoy," trans. Rosemary Horrox in her *The Black Death: Selected Sources Translated and Annotated* (Manchester: Manchester University Press, 1994), pp. 212–214.

28. Heinrich Truchess von Diessenhoven, [Continuation of Ptolemy of Lucca's] *Historia Ecclesiastica nova*, ed. Johann Friedrich Böhmer in his *Fontes rerum Germanicarum* 4 (Stuttgart: J. G. Cotta'scher, 1868), 1348–1349, pp. 68–71, and trans. Rosemary Horrox in her *The Black Death: Selected Sources Translated and Annotated* (Manchester: Manchester University Press, 1994), pp. 208–210.

29. Abeth, *The Black Death*, p. 185; Samuel K. Cohn Jr., "The Black Death and the Burning of the Jews," *Past and Present* 196 (2007): 3–36.

30. Gilles li Muisis, *Chronicle*, trans. John Abeth in his *The Black Death: The Great Mortality of 1348–1350: A Brief History with Documents*, 2nd ed. (Boston: Bedford-St. Martin's, 2017), pp. 128–129, and trans. Rosemary Horrox in her *The*

Black Death: Selected Sources Translated and Annotated (Manchester: Manchester University Press, 1994), pp. 50–51.

31. Clement VI, *Sicut Judeis*, trans. Shlomo Simonsohn in his *The Apostolic See and the Jews: Documents, I: 492–1404* (Toronto: Pontifical Institute of Medieval Studies, 1988), no. 373, pp. 397–398.

32. Susan L. Einbinder, *After the Black Death: Plague and Commemoration Among Iberian Jews* (Philadelphia: University of Pennsylvania Press, 2018), p. 150.

33. Abeth, *The Black Death*, p. 145–155.

34. "A Middle Dutch Flagellant Scroll 1349," trans. John Abeth in his *The Black Death: The Great Mortality of 1348–1350: A Brief History with Documents*, 2nd ed. (Boston: Bedford-St. Martin's, 2017), pp. 94–100.

35. Abeth, *The Black Death*, pp. 166–168.

36. Gabriele de Mussis, *Historia*, pp. 15–17.

37. Giovanni Boccaccio, *Decameron*, pp. 15–16 [McWilliam, pp. 8–9].

38. Francesco Petrarch, "Letter 7," ed. Joseph Fracassetti in his *Francisci Petrarcae epistolae de rebus familiaribus et variae*, vol. 1 (Florence: Felicis Le Monnier, 1859), pp. 437–454, esp. pp. 444–445, and partially trans. Rosemary Horrox in her *The Black Death: Selected Sources Translated and Annotated* (Manchester: Manchester University Press, 1994), p. 249.

39. The classic study is William Chester Jordan, *The Great Famine: Northern Europe in the Early Fourteenth Century* (Princeton, NJ: Princeton University Press, 1996).

40. "Ralph of Shrewsbury, Bishop of Bath and Wells, to the Clergy of His Diocese January 10, 1349," trans. Rosemary Horrox in her *The Black Death: Selected Sources Translated and Annotated* (Manchester: Manchester University Press, 1994), pp. 271–273.

41. Howard Kaminsky, "The Great Schism," in *The New Cambridge Medieval History. Vol. 6: c. 1300-c. 1415*, ed. Michael Jones (Cambridge: Cambridge University Press, 2000), pp. 674–696.

42. Justine Firnhaber-Baker, *The Jacquerie of 1358: A Peasant's Revolt* (Oxford: Oxford University Press, 2021).

43. Nicolau Eymeric, *Directorium inquisitorium*, trans. Edward Peters, in *Witchcraft in Europe 400–1700: A Documentary History*, ed. Edward Peters and Alan Charles Kors, 2nd ed. (Philadelphia: University of Pennsylvania Press, 2001), p. 122.

44. Michael D. Bailey, "From Sorcery to Witchcraft: Clerical Conceptions of Magic in the Later Middle Ages," *Speculum* 76 (2001): 960–990, esp. 972–978.

45. Heinrich Kramer and Jacob Sprenger, *Malleus Maleficarum*, ed. and trans. Christopher S. Mackay, 2 vols. (Cambridge: Cambridge University Press, 2006).

46. Michael D. Bailey, "A Late-Medieval Crisis of Superstition," *Speculum* 84 (2009): 633–661.

47. David Nirenberg, "Mass Conversion and Genealogical Mentalities: Jews and Christians in Fifteenth-Century Spain," *Past and Present* 174 (2002): 9.

48. Nirenberg, "Mass Conversion and Genealogical Mentalities," 3–41.

49. Geoffrey Chaucer, *The Norton Chaucer: The Canterbury Tales*, ed. David Lawton (New York: W. W. Norton, 2020), pp. 440–455.

50. Geoffrey Chaucer, *The Canterbury Tales*, pp. 57–76.

51. Paul Strohm, *Chaucer's Tale: 1386 and the Road to Canterbury* (New York: Penguin Books, 2014), pp. 218–219.

52. Strohm, *Chaucer's Tale*, pp. 206–207, 210–211, 219–221, 229–230.

53. Geoffrey Chaucer, *The Canterbury Tales*, p. 454.

54. Christine de Pizan, "Letter to Pierre Col (October 2, 1402)," ed. and trans. David F. Hult, in Christine de Pizan et al., *Debate of the Romance of the Rose* (Chicago: University of Chicago Press, 2010), pp. 159–193.

55. Christine de Pizan, *Le livre de la mutacion de Fortune*, trans. Kevin Brownlee, in *The Selected Writings of Christine de Pizan*, ed. Renate Blumenfeld-Kosinski (New York: W. W. Norton, 1997), p. 90.

56. Christine de Pizan, *Le livre de la mutacion de Fortune*, p. 95.

57. Christine de Pizan, *L'avision*, trans. Renate Blumenfeld-Kosinski in her *The Selected Writings of Christine de Pizan* (New York: W. W. Norton, 1997), p. 194.

58. Christine de Pizan, *Le livre de la cité des dames*, trans. Earl Jeffrey Richards as *The Book of the City of Ladies*, rev. ed. (New York: Persea Books, 1998), pp. 3–24, 217, 22, 254–255, and passim.

59. Christine de Pizan, "Letter to Pierre Col (October 2, 1402)," p. 189.

60. Christopher Allmand, *The Hundred Years War: England and France at War, c. 1300–c. 1400*, rev. ed. (Cambridge: Cambridge University Press, 2001), pp. 32–35.

61. Christine de Pizan, *Le ditié de Jehanne d'Arc*, ed. Angus J. Kennedy and Kenneth Varty (Oxford: Society for the Study of Mediaeval Literatures and Languages, 1977), trans. Renate Blumenfeld-Kosinski in her *The Selected Writings of Christine de Pizan* (New York: W. W. Norton, 1997), pp. 252–262, and Craig Taylor in his *Joan of Arc: La Pucelle: Selected Sources Translated and Annotated* (Manchester: Manchester University Press, 2006), pp. 98–108.

62. *Procès de condamnation de Jeanne d'Arc*, ed. Pierre Tisset and Yvonne Lanhers, vol. 1 (Paris: C. Klincksieck, 1960), pp. 57–68, 69–70 [and trans. Craig Taylor in his *Joan of Arc: La Pucelle: Selected Sources Translated and Annotated* (Manchester: Manchester University Press, 2006), pp. 145–151, 152; references to page numbers in this translation are in square brackets].

63. *Procès de condamnation de Jeanne d'Arc*, pp. 35–42, 84 [Taylor, pp. 137–145, 162].

64. *Procès de condamnation de Jeanne d'Arc*, pp. 123–126 [Taylor, pp. 179–180].

65. *Procès de condamnation de Jeanne d'Arc*, p. 75 [Taylor, p. 154].

66. *Procès de condamnation de Jeanne d'Arc*, pp. 361–364 [Taylor, pp. 213–216].

67. *Procès de condamnation de Jeanne d'Arc*, pp. 390–392 [Taylor, pp. 216–219].

68. *Procès de condamnation de Jeanne d'Arc*, pp. 395–399 [Taylor, pp. 220–224].

69. Clément de Fauquembergue, *Journal de Clément de Fauquembergue, greffier du Parlement du Paris, 1417–1435*, ed. Alexandre Tuetey and Henri Lacaille, vol. 3 (Paris: H. Laurens, 1915), pp. 13–14; *Journal d'un bourgeois de Paris, 1405–1449*, ed. Alexandre Tuetey (Paris: H. Champion, 1881), pp. 266–272; "Massieu [May

12, 1456]," in *Procès en nullité de la condamnation de Jeanne d'Arc*, ed. Pierre Duparc, vol. 1 (Paris: C. Klincksieck, 1977), pp. 434–435. All translated by Craig Taylor in his *Joan of Arc: La Pucelle: Selected Sources Translated and Annotated* (Manchester: Manchester University Press, 2006), pp. 228, 233–234, 336.

70. *Procès de condamnation de Jeanne d'Arc*, p. 139 [Taylor, p. 185].

Select Bibliography

PRIMARY SOURCES

Abeth, John, ed. and trans. *The Black Death: The Great Mortality of 1348–1350: A Brief History with Documents*. 2nd edition. Boston: Bedford-St. Martin's, 2017.

Acta et symbola conciliorum quae quarto saecula habita sunt. Edited by E. J. Jonkers. Leiden: Brill, 1954.

Adalbero of Laon. *Carmen ad Rotbertum regem*. Edited and translated by Claude Carozzi. Paris: Les Belles Lettres, 1979.

Die Admonitio generalis Karls des Grossen. Edited by Hubert Mordek, Klaus Zechiel-Eckes, and Michael Glatthaar. Monumenta Germaniae historica, Fontes iuris germanici antiqui 16. Hanover: Hahn, 2012.

Adomnán. *Life of Columba*. Edited and translated by Alan Orr Anderson and Marjorie Ogilvie Anderson. Oxford: Clarendon Press, 1991.

Aeschylus. *Agamemnon*. In *Oresteia: Agamemnon. Libation-Bearers. Eumenides*. Edited and translated by Alan H. Sommerstein. Cambridge, MA: Harvard University Press, 2008.

Agobard of Lyon. *De Grandine et Tonitruis*. In *Agobardi Lugdunensis: Opera Omnia*, edited by Lieven van Acker. Corpus Christianorum: Continuatio Mediaevalis 52. Turnhout: Brepols 1981.

Agobard of Lyon. *De Insolentia Iudeorum (ad Ludovicum)*. In *Agobardi Lugdunensis: Opera Omnia*, edited by Lieven van Acker. Corpus Christianorum: Continuatio Mediaevalis 52. Turnhout: Brepols, 1981.

Ahmad ibn Fadlan. *Ibn Fadlan and the Land of Darkness: Arab Travellers in the Far North*. Translated by Paul Lunde and Caroline Stone. London: Penguin Books, 2012.

Albert of Aachen. *Historia Ierosolimitana [History of the Journey to Jerusalem]*. Edited and translated by Susan B. Edgington. Oxford: Clarendon Press, 2007.

Alcuin. *Disputatio de rhetorica et de virtutibus*. Edited and translated by Wilbur Samuel Howell in *The Rhetoric of Alcuin and Charlemagne*. Princeton, NJ: Princeton University, 1941.

Alexander, Michael, ed. and trans. *The First Poems in English*. London: Penguin Books, 2008.

Ambrose. *De officiis*. Edited and translated by Ivor J. Davidson. 2 volumes. Oxford: Oxford University Press, 2001.

Ammianus Marcellinus. *History I Books 14–19*. Edited and translated by J. C. Rolfe. Cambridge, MA: Harvard University Press, 1950.

Ammianus Marcellinus. *The Later Roman Empire (A.D. 354–378)*. Translated by Walter Hamilton. Harmondsworth, UK: Penguin Books, 1986.

Ammianus Marcellinus. *Res Gestae*. Edited and translated by J. C. Rolfe. Cambridge, MA.: Harvard University Press, 1939.

Andrea da Strumi. "Passion of Arialdo." Translated by William North in *Medieval Italy: Texts in Translation*, edited by Katherine L. Jansen, Joanna Dell, and Frances Andrews, 337–350. Philadelphia: University of Pennsylvania Press, 2009.

The Anglo-Saxon Chronicle. Translated by G. N. Garmonsway. London: J. M. Dent, 1960.

Anna Komnene. *The Alexiad*. Translated by E. R. A Sewter and revised by Peter Frankopan. London: Penguin Books, 2009.

Annales Herbipolenses. Edited by Georg Heinrich Pertz. Monumenta Germaniae historica, Scriptores 16. Hanover: Hahn, 1859.

Annales regni Francorum. Edited by Georg Heinrich Pertz and Friedrich Kurz. Monumenta Germaniae historica, Scriptores rerum Germanicarum in usum scholarum separatim editi 6. Hanover: Hahn, 1895.

The Annals of Fulda: Ninth-Century Histories II. Translated by Timothy Reuter. Manchester: Manchester University Press, 1992.

The Annals of St-Bertin: Ninth-Century Histories I. Translated by Janet L. Nelson. Manchester: Manchester University Press, 1991.

Anonymi Valesiani pars posterior. Edited by Theodor Mommsen. Monumenta Germaniae historica, Auctorum antiquissimorum 9. Berlin: Weidmann, 1892.

Arnold, John H., and Peter Biller, eds. *Heresy and Inquisition in France, 1200–1300: Sources Translated and Annotated*. Manchester: Manchester University Press, 2016.

Asser. *Asser's Life of King Alfred*. Edited by William Henry Stevenson. Oxford: Clarendon Press, 1959.

Asser. *Asser's Life of King Alfred*. Translated by Simon Keynes and Michael Lapidge. In *Alfred the Great: Asser's Life of King Alfred and Other Contemporary Sources*. London: Penguin Books, 1983.

Athanasius of Alexandria. *Athanasius Werke Band III/Teil 1: Urkunden zur Geschichte des arianischen Streites 318–328*, Lieferung 1–2. Edited by Hans-Georg Opitz. Berlin: W. de Gruyter, 1934–1935.

Athanasius of Alexandria. *Historical Tracts of S. Athanasius*. Translated by Miles Atkinson et al. Library of Fathers of the Holy Catholic Church 13. Oxford: John Henry Parker, 1848.

Athanasius of Alexandria. *Vie d'Antoine: Introduction, Texte Critique, Traduction, Notes and Index*. Edited and translated by G. J. M. Bartelink. Paris: Cerf, 2011.

Attenborough, Frederick Levi, ed. and trans. *The Laws of the Earliest English Kings*. Cambridge: Cambridge University Press, 1922.

Audradus Modicus. *Liber Revelationum*. Edited by Ludwig Traube. In "O Roma nobilis. Philologische Untersuchungen aus dem Mittelalter," *Abhandlungen der philosophisch philologischen Classe der königlich Bayerischen Akademie der Wissenschaften* 19 (1982): 378–387.

Augustine. *Concerning the City of God Against the Pagans*. Translated by Henry Bettenson. London: Penguin Books, 1972.

Augustine. *Confessions.* Translated by Henry Chadwick. Oxford: Oxford University Press, 1992.

Augustine. *Selected Letters*. Translated by James Houston Baxter. Cambridge, MA: Harvard University Press, 1953.

Augustine. *Letters 1*–29* [New Letters]*. Edited by Johannes Divjak in *Epistolae ex duobus codicibus nuper in lucem prolatae. Sancti Aurelii Augustini opera* 2:6. Corpus scriptorum ecclesiasticorum Latinorum 88. Vienna: Tempskey, 1981.

Barber, Malcolm, and Keith Bate, eds. and trans. *Letters from the East: Crusaders, Pilgrims, and Settlers in* the *12th–13th Centuries*. Farnham, UK: Ashgate, 2013.

Barber, Malcolm, and Keith Bate, eds. and trans. *The Templars: Selected Sources Translated and Annotated*. Manchester: Manchester University Press, 2002.

Bardaisan of Edessa. *The Book of the Laws of Countries: Dialogue on Fate of Bardaisan of Edessa*. Edited and translated by H. J. W. Drijvers. Piscataway, NJ: Gorgias Press, 2006.

Bede. *The Ecclesiastical History of the English People*. Edited and translated by Bertram Colgrave and R. A. B. Mynors. Oxford: Clarendon Press, 1969.

Bede. *The Ecclesiastical History of the English People*. Translated by Judith McClure and Roger Collins. Oxford: Oxford University Press, 1999.

Bede. *The Ecclesiastical History of the English People*. Translated by Leo Sherley-Price and revised by Ronald Latham. London: Penguin Books, 1991.

Bede. *On Genesis*. Translated by Calvin B. Kendall. Liverpool: Liverpool University Press, 2008.

Benedict. *The Rule of Saint Benedict*. Edited and translated by Bruce Venarde. Cambridge, MA: Harvard University Press, 2011.

Beowulf: A New Verse Translation. Translated by Seamus Heaney. New York: Farrar, Straus and Giroux, 1999.

Bernard of Clairvaux. *Sancti Bernardi opera II: Sermones super Cantica Canticorum 36–38*. Edited by Jean Leclercq, Charles Talbot, and Henri Rochais. Rome: Éditions cistercienses, 1958.

Bernard of Clairvaux. *Sancti Bernardi opera V: Sermones* II. Edited by Jean Leclercq and Henri Rochais Rome: Éditions cistercienses, 1972.

Bernard of Clairvaux. *Sancti Bernardi Opera VIII: Epistolae*. Edited by Jean Leclercq and Henri Rochais. Rome: Éditions cistercienses, 1977.

Blumenfeld-Kosinski, Renate, and Kevin Brownlee, eds. and trans. *The Selected Writings of Christine de Pizan*. New York: W. W. Norton, 1997.

Boethius. *The Consolation of Philosophy*. Translated by P. G. Walsh. Oxford: Oxford University Press, 2008.

Boethius. *The Old English Boethius: With Verse Prologues and Epilogues Associated with King Alfred*. Edited and translated by Susan Irvine and Malcolm R. Godden. Cambridge, MA: Harvard University Press, 2012.

Boniface. *The Letters of Saint Boniface*. Translated by Ephraim Emerton. New York: W. W. Norton, 1976.

The Book of the Pontiffs (Liber pontificalis). Translated by Raymond Davis in *The Lives of the Eighth-Century Popes AD 715–817*. 2nd edition. Liverpool: Liverpool University Press, 2007.

Brown, R. Allen, ed. and trans. *The Norman Conquest: Sources and Documents*. Woodbridge, UK: Boydell, 1984.

Caesarius of Arles. *Sermons (1–80)*. Translated by Peggy Meuller. Washington, DC: Catholic University of America Press, 1956.

Caesarius of Arles. *Sermons (187–238)*. Translated by Mary Meuller. Washington, DC: Catholic University of America Press, 2004.

Caesarius of Heisterbach. *The Dialogue on Miracles*. Translated by H. von E. Scott and C. C. Swinton Bland. 2 volumes. London: George Routledge & Sons, 1929.

Caesarius of Heisterbach. *Dialogus Miraculorum*. Edited by J. Strange. 2 volumes. Cologne: H. Lempertz, 1851.

Cassiodorus. *Selected Variae of Magnus Aurelius Cassiodorus Senator*. Translated by S. J. B. Barnish. Liverpool: Liverpool University Press, 1992.

Christine de Pizan. *The Book of the City of Ladies*. Translated by Earl Jeffrey Richards. Revised edition. New York: Persea Books, 1998,

Christine de Pizan. *Le Ditié de Jehanne d'Arc*. Edited by Angus J. Kennedy and Kenneth Varty. Oxford: Society for the Study of Mediaeval Literatures and Languages, 1977.

Christine de Pizan et al. *Debate of the Romance of the Rose*. Edited and translated by David F. Hult. Chicago: University of Chicago Press, 2010.

Chronicle of 452. Edited by Theodor Mommsen in *Chronica Minora, saec. IV. V. VI. VII*, volume 1. Monumenta Germaniae historica, Auctores antiquissimi 9. Berlin: Weidmann, 1892.

Chronicon universale anonymi Laudunensis. Edited by Georg Waitz, 442–457. Monumenta Germaniae historica, Scriptores 26. Hanover: Hahn, 1882.

Clément de Fauquembergue. *Journal de Clément de Fauquembergue, greffier du Parlement du Paris, 1417–1435*. Edited by Alexandre Tuetey and Henri Lacaille. 3 volumes. Paris: H. Laurens, 1903–1915.

Coleman-Norton, P. R., ed. and trans. *Roman State and Christian Church: A Collection of Legal Documents to A.D. 535*. London: SPCK, 1966.

Concilia aevi Karolini. Edited by Albery Werminghoff. Monumenta Germaniae historica. 2 volumes. Hanover: Hahn, 1906.

Constable, Olivia R., ed. *Medieval Iberia: Readings from Christian, Muslim, and Jewish Sources*. 2nd edition. Philadelphia: University of Pennsylvania Press, 2011.

Das Constitutum Constantini (Konstantinische Schenkung). Edited by Horst Fuhrman. Monumenta Germaniae historica, Fontes iuris Germanici antiqui. Hanover: Hahn, 1968.

Corpus Iuris Canonici. Edited by Aemilius Friedberg. 2 volumes. Leipzig: B. Tauchnitz, 1879; reprint, Graz: Akademische Druck-u. Verlagsanstalt, 1959.

Cunliffe, Barry, ed. *The Temple of Sulis Minerva at Bath, Volume 2, The Finds from the Sacred Spring*. Oxford: Oxford University Press, 1988.

Dante Alighieri. *Dante Alighieri's* Commedia: *A Digital Edition.* 2nd edition. Edited by Prue Shaw. 2021. www.dantecommedia.it.

Dante Alighieri. *The Divine Comedy.* Translated by Clive James. New York: Liveright, 2013.

Dante Alighieri. *The Portable Dante.* Translated by Mark Musa. New York: Penguin Books, 2003.

Dante Alighieri. *Purgatorio.* Translated by D. M. Black. New York: New York Review of Books, 2021.

Dante Alighieri. *Vita Nuova: A Dual Language Edition.* Translated by Virginia Jewiss. New York: Penguin Books, 2022.

Delisle, Léopold, ed. *Recueil des historiens des Gaules et de la France.* 24 volumes. Imprint varies, 1869–1904.

Dhuoda. *Liber Manualis: Handbook for Her Warrior Son.* Edited and translated by Marcelle Thiébaux. Cambridge: Cambridge University Press, 1998.

Dio Cassius. *Roman History.* Edited and translated by Earnest Cary and Herbert B. Foster. Cambridge, MA: Harvard University Press, 1927.

Dodgeon, Michael H., and Samuel N. C. Lieu, eds. and trans. *The Roman Frontier and the Persian War (AD 226–363).* London: Routledge, 1991.

Dutton, Paul Edward, ed. and trans. *Carolingian Civilization: A Reader.* 2nd edition. Toronto: University of Toronto Press, 2009.

Einhard. *Life of Charlemagne.* Translated by Paul Edward Dutton in *Charlemagne's Courtier: The Complete Einhard.* Peterborough, ON: Broadview Press, 1998.

Eulogius. *The Eulogius Corpus.* Translated by Kenneth Baxter Wolf. Liverpool: Liverpool University Press, 2019.

Eusebius. *Historia Ecclesiastica* [*The History of the Church from Christ to Constantine*]. Translated by G. A. Williamson. New York: New York University Press, 1966.

Eusebius. *Life of Constantine.* Translated by Averil Cameron and Stuart G. Hall. Oxford: Oxford University Press, 1999.

Eusebius. *A New Eusebius: Documents Illustrating the History of the Church to AD 337.* Revised by W. H. Frend. London: SPCK, 1987.

Ex Ermentarii miraculis sancti Filiberti. Edited by Oswald Holder-Egger, 298–303. Monumenta Germaniae historica, Scriptores 15.1. Hanover: Hahn, 1887.

Francesco Petrarch. *Francisci Petrarcae Epistolae de Rebus Familiaribus et variae.* Edited by Joseph Fracassetti. 3 volumes. Florence: Felicis Le Monnier, 1859-1863.

Fulbert of Chartres. *The Letters and Poems of Fulbert of Chartres.* Edited and translated by Frederick Behrends. Oxford: Clarendon Press, 1976.

Fulcher of Chartres. *Historia Hierosolymitana.* Edited by Heinrich Hagenmeyer. Heidelberg: Carl Winters, 1913.

Fulcher of Chartres. *Historia Hierosolymitana.* Translated by Martha McGinty in *The First Crusade: The Chronicle of Fulcher of Chartres and Other Source Materials,* edited by Edward Peters, 47–101. 2nd edition. Philadelphia: University of Pennsylvania Press, 1998.

Gardner, Iain, and Samuel N. C. Lieu, eds. *Manichaean Texts from the Roman Empire.* Cambridge: Cambridge University Press, 2004.

Gervase of Tilbury. *Otia Imperialia* [*Recreation for an Emperor*]. Edited and translated by S. E. Banks and J. W. Binns. Oxford: Clarendon Press, 2002.

Geoffrey Chaucer. *The Norton Chaucer: The Canterbury Tales*. Edited by David Lawton. New York: W. W. Norton, 2020.

Gildas. *The Ruin of Britain* [*De excidio et conquestu Britanniae*]. Translated by Michael Winterbottom. London: Phillimore, 1978.

Giovanni Boccaccio. *Decameron*. Edited by Vittore Branca. Milan: Mondadori, 1989.

Giovanni Boccaccio. *The Decameron*. Translated by G. H. McWilliam. 2nd edition. London: Penguin Books, 1995.

Goodman, Peter, ed. and trans. *Poetry of the Carolingian Renaissance*. Norman: University of Oklahoma Press, 1985.

Gottschalk. *Confessio prolixior*. In *Oeuvres théologiques et grammaticales de Godescalc d'Orbais*, edited by Cyrille Lambot. Louvain: Spicilegium Sacrum Lovaniense, 1945.

Gottschalk. *Fragmentum* 15. In *Oeuvres théologiques et grammaticales de Godescalc d'Orbais*, edited by Cyrille Lambot. Louvain: Spicilegium Sacrum Lovaniense, 1945.

Gregory I. *Moralia in Job*. Edited by Marc Adriaen. Corpus Christianorum 143, 143A, 143B. Turnhout: Brepols, 1979–1985.

Gregory I. *Pastoral Care* [*Regula Pastoralis*]. Translated by Henry Davis. London: Longmans, 1950.

Gregory I. *Registrum epistularum*. Edited by Dag Norberg. Corpus Christianorum 140–140A. Turnhout: Brepols, 1982.

Gregory of Tours. *The History of the Franks*. Translated by Lewis Thorpe. London: Penguin Books, 1974.

Gregory of Tours. *The Lives of the Fathers*. In *Lives and Miracles*. Edited and translated by Giselle de Nie. Cambridge, MA: Harvard University Press, 2015.

Gregory of Tours. *The Miracles of Bishop Martin*. In *Lives and Miracles*. Edited and translated by Giselle de Nie. Cambridge, MA: Harvard University Press, 2015.

Guilhem de Montanhagol. *Les poésies de Guilhem de Montanhagol: Troubadour provençal du XIIIe siècle*. Edited and translated by Peter T. Ricketts. Toronto: Pontifical Institute of Medieval Studies, 1964.

Guilhem de Puylaurens. *Chronica Magistri Guillelmi de Podio Laurentii*. Edited and translated by Jean Duvernoy. Paris: Éditions du Centre National de la Recherche Scientifique, 1976.

Guilhem de Puylaurens. *The Chronicle of William of Puylaurens: The Albigensian Crusade and Its Aftermath*. Translated by W. A and M. D. Sibly. Woodbridge, UK: Boydell Press, 2003.

Guilhem de Tudela. *La chanson de la croisade albigeoise* [*La Canso de la Crozada*]. Edited and translated by E. Martin-Chabot. 2nd edition. 3 volumes. Paris: Les Belles Lettres, 1960.

Guillaume de Lorris and Jean de Meun. *The Romance of the Rose*. Translated by Frances Horgan. Oxford: Oxford University Press, 1994.

Guillaume de Rubruck. *Itinerarium*. Edited by Anastasius van den Wyngaert. Sinica Franciscana, I. Itinera et relationes Fratrum Minorum saeculi XIII et XIV. Florence-Quaracchi: Apud Collegium S. Bonaventurae, 1929.

Guillaume de Rubruck. *The Mission of Friar William of Rubruck: His Journey to the Court of the Great Khan Möngke, 1253–1255.* Translated by Peter Jackson and David Morgan. Indianapolis, IN: Hackett, 2000.

Heinrich Kramer and Jacob Sprenger. *Malleus Maleficarum.* Edited and translated by Christopher S. Mackay. 2 volumes. Cambridge: Cambridge University Press, 2006.

Heinrich Truchess von Diessenhoven. [Continuation of Ptolemy of Lucca's] *Historia Ecclesiastica nova.* Edited by Johann Friedrich Böhmer, 16–126. Fontes rerum Germanicarum 4. Stuttgart: J G. Cotta'scher, 1868.

Heito. *Visio Wettini.* Edited by Ernst Dümmler. In *Poetae Latini aevi Carolini,* 267–271. Monumenta Germaniae historica, Poetae Latini medii aevi 2. Berlin: Weidmann, 1884.

Heito. *Visio Wettini.* Translated by Eileen Gardiner in *Visions of Heaven and Hell Before Dante,* edited by Eileen Gardiner, 62–71. New York: Italica Press, 2019.

Heloise. "Lettre I." Edited by J. Monfrin, Appendix, 111–114. In Peter Abelard, *Historia calamitatum,* edited by J. Monfrin. Paris: J.Vrin, 1959.

Heloise. "Letter 2." Translated by Betty Radice with revisions by M. T. Clanchy, 47–50. In *The Letters of Abelard and Heloise.* London. Penguin Books, 2003.

Herlihy, David, ed. and trans. *The History of Feudalism.* Atlantic Highlands, NJ: Humanities Press, 1979.

Herman-Judah. *Short Work on His Conversion* [or *Short Account of His Own Conversion*]. Translated by Karl F. Morrison in *Conversion and Text: The Cases of Augustine of Hippo, Herman-Judah, and Constantine Tsatsos,* 76–113. Charlottesville: University Press of Virginia, 1992.

Hillgarth, J. N., ed. and trans. *Christianity and Paganism, 350–750: The Conversion of Western Europe.* Philadelphia: University of Pennsylvania Press, 1986.

Horrox, Rosemary, ed. and trans. *The Black Death: Selected Sources Translated and Annotated.* Manchester: Manchester University Press, 1994.

Humbert de Romans. *Opusculum tripartitum.* In Ortuin Gratius, *Fasciculus rerum expetendarum et fugiendarum,* edited by Edward Brown. London: Richard Chiswell, 1690.

Huneberc. "The *Hodoeporicon* of Saint Willibald." Translated by Thomas Head in *Soldiers of Christ: Saints and Saints' Lives from Late Antiquity and the Early Middle Ages,* edited by Thomas F. X. Noble and Thomas Head, 141–164. University Park: Pennsylvania State University Press, 1995.

Huneberc. *Vita Willibaldi episcopi Eichstetensis et vita Wynnebaldi abbatis Heidenheimensis auctore sanctimonale Heidenheimensis.* Edited by Oswald Holder-Egger, 86–106. Monumenta Germaniae historica, Scriptores 15.1, Hanover: Hahn, 1887.

In Praise of Later Roman Emperors: The Panegyrici Latini. Edited and translated by C. E. V. Nixon and Barbara Saylor Rodgers. Berkeley: University of California Press, 1994.

Irwin, Robert, ed. *Night and Horses and the Desert: An Anthology of Classical Arabic Literature.* New York: Anchor Books, 2002.

Isidore of Seville. *The Etymologies.* Translated by Stephen A. Barney et al. Cambridge: Cambridge University Press, 2007.

Jacques de Vitry. *Lettres de Jacques de Vitry (1160/70), évêque de Saint-Jean d'Acre*. Edited by R. B. C. Huygens. Leiden: Brill, 1960.

Jacques de Vitry. *Vita Mariae Oigniacensis*. Edited by Daniel von Papenbroeck. Acta Sanctorum . . . edition novissima 23 June 5. Paris: Palmé, 1867.

Jansen, Katherine L., Joanna Dell, and Frances Andrews, eds. *Medieval Italy: Texts in Translation*. Philadelphia: University of Pennsylvania Press, 2009.

Jerome. *Selected Letters*. Translated by F. A. Wright. Cambridge, MA: Harvard University Press, 1933.

John Cassian. *Jean Cassian: Institutions Cénobitiques*. Edited and translated by Jean-Claude Guy. Sources Chrétiennes 109. Paris: Le Cerf, 1965.

John Chrysostom. *In epistulam I ad Corinthios*. Edited by Jacques-Paul Migne. In *Patrologiae cursus completus: Series Graeca* 61, 9–382. Paris: Garnier, 1862.

John Chrysostom. *In epistulam ad Ephesios*. Edited by Jacques-Paul Migne. In *Patrologiae cursus completus: Series Graeca* 62, 9–172. Paris: Garnier, 1862.

John of Damascus. *Die Schriften des Johannes von Damaskos*, volume 5, *Opera homiletica et hagiographica*. Edited by Bonifatius Kotter. Berlin: de Gruyter, 1988.

Jonas of Bobbio. *Life of Columbanus, Life of John of Réomé, and Life of Vedast*. Translated by Alexander O'Hara and Ian Wood. Liverpool: Liverpool University Press, 2017.

Jordanes. *Romana and Getica*. Translated by Peter Van Nuffelen and Lieve Van Hoof. Liverpool: Liverpool University Press, 2020.

Jordanes. *Romana et Getica*. Edited by Theodor Mommsen. Monumenta Germaniae historica, Auctores antiquissimi 5. Berlin: Weidmann, 1882.

Journal d'un Bourgeois de Paris, 1405–1449. Edited by Alexandre Tuetey. Paris: H. Champion, 1881.

Julian. *Orations 1–5*. Edited and translated by Wilmer C. Wright. Cambridge, MA: Harvard University Press, 1913.

Justinian. *Novellae*. Edited by Rudolf Schoell and Wilhelm Kroll in *Corpus Iuris Civilis* 3. Berlin: Weidmann, 1904.

Kephalaia. Edited by Alexander Böhlig and Hans Jacob Polotsky. Stuttgart: Kohlhammer, 1940.

Kirschner, Julius, and Karl F. Morrison, eds. *Medieval Europe: Readings in Western Civilization*. Chicago: University of Chicago Press, 1986.

Der Kölner Mani-Kodex (Über das Werden seines Leibes). Edited and translated by Ludwig Koenen and Cornelia Römer. Opladen: Westdeutscher Verlag, 1988.

Lactantius. *De mortibus persecutorum*. Edited and translated by J. L. Creed. Oxford: Clarendon Press, 1984.

Landulf Senior. *Historia Mediolanensis*. Edited by Ludwig Conrad Bethmann and Wilhelm Wattenbach, 32–100. Monumenta Germaniae historica, Scriptores 8. Hanover: Hahn, 1848.

Lex Salica. Edited by Karl August Eckhardt. Monumenta Germaniae historica, Leges nationum Germanicarum 4.1. Hanover: Hahn, 1962.

Lothar I and Lothar II. *Die Urkunden Lothars I und Lothars II*. Edited by Theodor Schieffer. Monumenta Germaniae historica, Diplomata Karolinorum 3. Berlin: Weidmann, 1966.

Marcabru. *Marcabru:A Critical Edition*. Edited and translated by Simon Gaunt, Ruth Harvey, and Linda Paterson. Cambridge: D. S. Brewer, 2000.

Marcus Aurelius. *Meditations*. Edited and translated by C. R. Haines. Cambridge, MA: Harvard University Press, 1994.

Marcus Aurelius. *Meditations*. Translated by Maxwell Staniforth. New York: Penguin Books, 2005.

Matarasso, Pauline, ed. and trans. *The Cistercian World: Monastic Writings of the Twelfth Century*. Harmondsworth, UK: Penguin Books, 1993.

McCormick, Michael. *Charlemagne's Survey of the Holy Land: Wealth, Personnel, and Buildings of a Mediterranean Church Between Antiquity and the Middle Ages*. Washington, DC: Dumbarton Oaks, 2011.

McNeill, John T., and Helena Gamer, eds. *Medieval Handbooks of Penance: A Translation of the Principal Libri Poenitentiales*. New York: Columbia University Press, 1938 [repr. 1990].

Miller, Maureen C., ed. and trans. *Power and the Holy in the Age of the Investiture Controversy: A Brief History with Documents*. Boston: Bedford–St. Martin's, 2005.

Muirchú. *Vita*. In *St Patrick: His Writings and Muirchu's Life*, edited and translated by A. B. E Hood, 81–98. London: Phillimore, 1978.

Narratio de aedificatione templi Sanctae Sophiae. Edited by Theodor Preger, 74–108. *Scriptores originum Constantinopolitanarum*. Leipzig: B. G. Teubner, 1901.

The Old English History of the World: An Anglo-Saxon Rewriting of Orosius. Edited and translated by Malcolm R. Godden. Cambridge, MA: Harvard University Press, 2016.

Ovid. *Ex Ponto*. In *Tristia. Ex Ponto*, translated by A. L. Wheeler and revised by G. P. Goold. Cambridge, MA: Harvard University Press, 1924.

Paden, William D., and Frances Freeman Paden, eds. and trans. *Troubadour Poems from the South of France*. Cambridge: D. S. Brewer, 2007.

Passio Sanctarum Perpetuae et Felicitatis. Edited and translated by Joseph Farrell and Craig Williams. In *Perpetua's Passions: Multidisciplinary Approaches to the* Passio Perpetuae et Felicitatis, edited by Jan N. Bremmer and Marco Formisano. Oxford: Oxford University Press, 2012.

Passio Sanctorum Scilitanorum. Translated by Herbert Musurillo. In *The Acts of the Christian Martyrs*. Oxford: Oxford University Press, 1972.

Patricius. *Confessio*. In *St. Patrick: His Writings and Muirchu's Life*, edited and translated by A. B. E. Hood, 41–54. London: Phillimore, 1978.

Paulus Orosius. *Seven Books of History Against the Pagans* [*Historiarum adversus paganos libri VII*]: *The Apology of Paulus Orosius*. Translated by Irving Woodworth Raymond. New York: Columbia University Press, 1936.

Penn, Michael Philip, ed. and trans. *When Christians First Met Muslims: A Sourcebook of the Earliest Syriac Writings on Islam*. Berkeley: University of California Press, 2015.

Peter Abelard. *Historia calamitatum* [*Story of His Misfortunes*]. Translated by Betty Radice with revisions by M. T. Clanchy, 3-46. In *The Letters of Abelard and Heloise*. London: Penguin Books, 2003.

Peter Abelard. *Historia calamitatum*. Edited by Jacques Monfrin. Paris: J. Vrin, 1959.

Peter Damiani. *Vita Dominici Loricati*. Edited by Jacques-Paul Migne. In *Patrologiae cursus completus: Series Latina* 144, 1007–1024. Paris: Garnier, 1867.

Peters, Edward, and Alan Charles Kors, eds. and trans. *Witchcraft in Europe 400–1700. A Documentary History*. Philadelphia: University of Pennsylvania Press, 2001.

Pharr, Clyde, comp. and trans. *The Theodosian Code and Novels and The Sirmondian Constitutions*. Princeton, NJ: Princeton University Press, 1952.

Pierre des Vaux-de-Cernay. *Historia Albigensis*. Edited by P. Guébin and E. Lyon. 2 volumes. Société de l'Histoire de France. Paris: Librairie Ancienne Honoré Champion, 1926.

Pierre des Vaux-de-Cernay. *The History of the Albigensian Crusade*. Translated by W. A. Sibly and M. D. Sibly. Woodbridge, UK: Boydell Press, 1998.

Porphyry. *On the Life of Plotinus and the Order of His Books. Ennead I*. Translated by A. H. Armstrong. Cambridge, MA: Harvard University Press, 1969.

Possidius. *Vita S. Augustini*. Edited by Jacques-Paul Migne. In *Patrologiae cursus completus: Series Latina* 32, 33–66. Paris: Garnier, 1877.

Prévot, Françoise, ed. *Recueil des inscriptions chrétiennes de la Gaule*, volume 8. Paris: Éditions du Centre National de la Recherche Scientifique, 1991.

Procès de condamnation de Jeanne d'Arc. Edited by Pierre Tisset and Yvonne Lanhers. 3 volumes. Paris: C. Klincksieck, 1960–1971.

Procès en nullité de la condamnation de Jeanne d'Arc. Edited by Pierre Duparc. 3 volumes. Paris: C. Klincksieck, 1977–1983.

Proclus of Constantinople and the Cult of the Virgin in Late Antiquity: Homilies 1– 5, Texts and Translations. Edited and translated by Nicholas Constas. Leiden: Brill, 2003.

Procopius. *Buildings*. Translated by H. B. Dewing. Cambridge, MA: Harvard University Press, 1940 [repr. 1996].

Procopius. *The Secret History*. Edited and translated by Anthony Kaldellis. Indianapolis, IN: Hackett, 2010.

Procopius. *The Wars of Justinian*. Translated by H. B. Dewing and revised by Anthony Kaldellis. Indianapolis, IN: Hackett, 2014.

The Qur'an. Translated by Rudi Paret in *Der Koran*. Kohlhammer: Stuttgart, 1996.

The Qur'an. Translated by A. J. Arberry in *The Koran Interpreted*. 2 volumes. New York: Macmillan, 1955.

The Qur'an. Translated by Ahmed Ali in *Al-Qur'an: A Contemporary Translation*. Princeton, NJ: Princeton University Press, 1993.

The Qur'an. Translated by 'Abdullah Yusuf 'Ali in *The Meaning of the Holy Qur'an*. Beltsville, MD: Amana, 1997.

Le registre d'inquisition de Jacques Fournier, évêque de Pamiers (1318–1325). 3 volumes. Edited by Jean Duvernoy. Toulouse: Édouard Privat, 1965.

Riley-Smith, Louise, and Jonathan Riley-Smith, eds. and trans. *The Crusades: Idea and Reality 1095–1274*. London: Edward Arnold, 1981.

Rimbert. *Vita Anskarii*. Edited by Georg Waitz. Monumenta Germaniae historica, Scriptores rerum Germanicarum in usum scholarum. Hanover: Hahn 1884.

Rodulfus Glaber. *Historiarum libri quinque*. Edited by Neithard Bulst and translated by John France and Paul Reynolds. Oxford: Clarendon Press, 1989.

Rubenstein, Jay, ed. and trans. *The First Crusade: A Brief History with Documents*. Boston: Bedford-St. Martin's, 2015.

Shatzmiller, Joseph, ed. *La Deuxième Controverse de Paris: Un chapitre dans la polémique entre chrétiens et juifs au Moyen Âge*. Paris: E. Peeters, 1994.

Sidonius Apollinaris. *Poems and Letters*. Translated by W. B. Anderson. Cambridge, MA: Harvard University Press, 1965 [repr. 1984].

Simonsohn, Shlomo, ed. and trans. *The Apostolic See and the Jews: Documents, I: 492–1404*. Toronto: Pontifical Institute of Medieval Studies, 1988.

Snorri Sturluson. *The Prose Edda*. Translated by Jesse Byock. London: Penguin Books, 2005.

Solomon Ben Simson. *Chronicle*. Translated by Robert Chazan in *European Jewry and the First Crusade*. Berkeley: University of California Press, 1987.

Somerville, Angus A., and R. Andrew McDonald, eds. *The Viking Age: A Reader*. Toronto: University of Toronto Press, 2020.

The Song of Roland. Translated by Glyn Burgess. London: Penguin Books, 1990.

Suger. *De rebus in administratione sua gestis* [*On What Was Done Under His Administration*]. Translated and edited by Erwin Panofsky as *Abbot Suger on the Abbey Church of St.-Denis and Its Art Treasures*. 2nd edition. Revised by Gerda Panofsky-Soergel. Princeton, NJ: Princeton University Press, 1979.

Symmachus. *Relationes*. Edited and translated by R. H. Barrow in *Prefect and Emperor: The* Relationes *of Symmachus, A.D. 384*. Oxford: Clarendon Press, 1973.

Tanner, Norman P., ed. and trans. *Decrees of the Ecumenical Councils*. 2 volumes. London: Sheed and Ward, 1990.

Taylor, Craig, ed. and trans. *Joan of Arc: La Pucelle. Selected Sources Translated and Annotated*. Manchester: Manchester University Press, 2006.

Theodore. *Penitential*. Translated by John T. McNeill and Helena Gamer in *Medieval Handbooks of Penance: A Translation of the Principal Libri Poenitentiales*, edited by John T. McNeill and Helena Gamer, 182–215. New York: Columbia University Press, 1938 [repr. 1990].

Theodulf. *Opus Karoli contra synodum*. Edited by Ann Freeman with Paul Meyvaert. Monumenta Germaniae historica, Concilia 2, supplementum I. Hanover: Hahn, 1998.

Theophanes the Confessor. *The Chronicle of Theophanes the Confessor: Byzantine and Near Eastern History AD 284–813*. Translated by Cyril Mango and Roger Scott. Oxford: Clarendon Press, 1997.

Theophilus of Edessa. *Theophilus of Edessa's Chronicle, and the Circulation of Historical Knowledge in Late Antiquity and Early Islam*. Translated by Robert G. Hoyland. Liverpool: Liverpool University Press, 2011.

Theophylakt Simokatta. *The History of Theophylakt Simokatta*. Translated by Michael Whitby and Mary Whitby. Oxford: Clarendon Press, 1986.

Thomas Aquinas. *Thomas Aquinas: Selected Writings.* Translated by Ralph McInerny. London: Penguin Books, 1998.

The Trial of the Talmud, Paris, 1240. Edited and translated by John Friedman, Jean Connell Hoff, and Robert Chazan. Toronto: Pontifical Institute of Mediaeval Studies, 2012.

Usama ibn Munqidh. *The Book of Contemplation. Islam and the Crusades.* Translated by Paul Cobb. London: Penguin Books, 2008.

Venantius Fortunatus. *Poems.* Edited and translated by Michael Roberts. Cambridge, MA: Harvard University Press, 2017.

Visio Baronti monachi Longoretensis. Edited by Wilhelm Levison, 377–394. *Passiones vitaeque sanctorum aevi Merovingici.* Monumenta Germaniae historica, Scriptores rerum Merovingicarum 5. Hanover: Hahn, 1910.

Vita Findani. Edited by Oswald Holder-Egger, 502–506. Monumenta Germaniae historica, Scriptores 15.1. Hanover; Hahn, 1887.

Wakefield, Walter Leggett, and Austin P. Evans, eds. and trans. *Heresies of the High Middle Ages. Selected Sources Translated and Annotated.* New York: Columbia University Press, 1991 [orig. 1969].

Walter Map. *De nugis curialium.* Edited by Montague R. James. Oxford, 1914.

White, Carolinne, ed and trans. *Early Christian Lives.* Harmondsworth, UK: Penguin Books, 1998.

William of Tyre. *Chronicon.* Edited by R. B. C. Huygens. Corpus Christianorum: Continuatio Mediaevalis 63. Turnhout: Brepols, 1986.

Wolf, Kenneth Baxter, ed. and trans. *Conquerors and Chroniclers of Early Medieval Spain.* 2nd edition. Liverpool: Liverpool University Press, 2011.

Wolfram von Eschenbach. *Parzival (with Titurel and the Love-lyrics).* Translated by Cyril Edwards. Woodbridge: D. S. Brewer, 2004.

SECONDARY SOURCES

Abeth, John. *The Black Death: A New History of the Great Mortality in Europe, 1347–1500.* New York: Oxford University Press, 2021.

Adams, Anthony, and A. G. Rigg. "A Verse Translation of Abbo of St. Germain's 'Bella Parisiacae urbis.'" *Journal of Medieval Latin* 14 (2004): 22–23.

Adams, Colin. *Land Transport in Roman Egypt.* Oxford: Oxford University Press, 2007.

Allmand, Christopher. *The Hundred Years War. England and France at War, c. 1300–c.1400.* Revised edition. Cambridge: Cambridge University Press, 2001.

Angold, Michael. "After the Fourth Crusade: The Greek Rump States and the Recovery of Byzantium." In *The Cambridge History of the Byzantine Empire c. 500–1492,* edited by Jonathan Shepard, 731–778. Cambridge: Cambridge University Press, 2008.

Anthony, Sean W. *Muhammad and the Empires of Faith: The Making of the Prophet of Islam.* Oakland: University of California Press, 2020.

Bailey, Michael D. "A Late-Medieval Crisis of Superstition." *Speculum* 84 (2009): 633–661.

Bailey, Michael D. "From Sorcery to Witchcraft: Clerical Conceptions of Magic in the Later Middle Ages." *Speculum* 76 (2001): 960–990.

Barber, Malcolm. *The New Knighthood: A History of the Order of the Temple*. Cambridge: Cambridge University Press, 1994.

Barry, Fabio. "Walking on Water: Cosmic Floors in Antiquity and the Middle Ages." *The Art Bulletin* 89 (2007): 627–656.

Bartlett, Robert. *The Making of Europe: Conquest, Colonization and Cultural Change 950–1350*. Princeton, NJ: Princeton University Press, 1993.

Baumgarten, Elisheva. *Mothers and Children: Jewish Family Life in Medieval Europe*. Princeton, NJ: Princeton University Press, 2007.

Beard, Mary. *SPQR: A History of Ancient Rome*. New York: Liveright, 2015.

Benedictow, Ole J. *The Complete History of the Black Death*. Woodbridge, UK: Boydell Press, 2021.

Berend, Nora. *At the Gate of Christendom: Jews, Muslims, and "Pagans" in Medieval Hungary, c. 1000–c. 1300*. Cambridge: Cambridge University Press, 2001.

Bischoff, Vibeke. "Viking-Age Sails: Form and Proportion." *Journal of Maritime Archaeology* 12 (2017): 1–24.

Bjornlie, M. Shane. *Politics and Tradition Between Rome, Ravenna, and Constantinople: A Study of Cassiodorus and the Variae, 527–554*. Cambridge: Cambridge University Press, 2013.

Blessing, Patricia. *Rebuilding Anatolia After the Mongol Conquest: Islamic Architecture in the Lands of Rum, 1240–1330*. Farnham, UK: Ashgate, 2014.

Bloch, Marc. "Pour une histoire comparée des sociétés européenes" [orig. 1928]. In *Mélanges Historiques*, volume 1, edited by Charles-Edmond Perrin, 16–40. Paris: SEVPEN, 1963.

Bolton, Brenda. *Innocent III: Studies on Papal Authority and Pastoral Care*. Aldershot, UK: Ashgate, 1995.

Bomgardner, David L. "The Carthage Amphitheatre: A Reappraisal." *American Journal of Archaeology* 93 (1989): 85–103.

Borges, Jorge Luis. "Beatrice's Last Smile." Translated by Esther Allen in *Jorge Luis Borges: Selected Non-Fictions*, edited by Eliot Weinberger, 302–305. New York: Penguin Books, 1999.

Borges, Jorge Luis. "La última sonrisa de Beatriz." In *Nueve ensayos dantescos*, 155–161. Madrid: Espasa-Calpe, 1982.

Bowles, Kim. *Private Worship, Public Values, and Religious Change in Late Antiquity*. Cambridge: Cambridge University Press, 2008.

Brett, Edward Tracy. *Humbert of Romans: His Life and Views of Thirteenth-Century Society*. Toronto: Pontifical Institute of Mediaeval Studies, 1984.

Brown, Peter. *Augustine of Hippo: A Biography*. Berkeley: University of California Press, 2013 [orig. 1967].

Brown, Peter. "Christianization and Religious Conflict." In *The Cambridge Ancient History. Vol. 13: The Late Empire, A.D. 337–425*, edited by Averil Cameron and Peter Garnsey, 632–664. Cambridge: Cambridge University Press, 1997.

Brown, Peter. *The Cult of the Saints: Its Rise and Function in Latin Christianity*. 2nd edition. Chicago: University of Chicago Press, 2014.

Brown, Peter. *Power and Persuasion in Late Antiquity: Towards a Christian Empire*. Madison: University of Wisconsin Press, 1992.

Brown, Peter. *The Ransom of the Soul: Afterlife and Wealth in Early Western Christianity*. Cambridge, MA: Harvard University Press, 2015.

Brown, Peter. *The Rise of Western Christendom: Triumph and Diversity, AD 200–1000*. Oxford: Wiley-Blackwell, 2013.

Brown, Peter. *Through the Eye of a Needle: Wealth, the Fall of Rome, and the Making of Christianity in the West, 350–550 AD*. Princeton, NJ: Princeton University Press, 2012.

Brown, Peter. *Treasure in Heaven: The Holy Poor in Early Christianity*. Charlottesville: University of Virginia Press, 2016.

Brown, Peter. *The World of Late Antiquity: From Marcus Aurelius to Muhammad*. London: Thames and Hudson, 1971.

Bruce-Mitford, S. L. "The Art of the Codex Amiatinus: Jarrow Lecture, 1967." *Journal of the British Archaeological Association* 32 (1969): 1–25.

Burman, Thomas E. *Reading the Qur'an in Latin Christendom, 1140–1560*. Philadelphia: University of Pennsylvania Press, 2007.

Bynum, Caroline. *Holy Fast and Holy Feast: The Religious Significance of Food to Medieval Women*. Berkeley: University of California Press, 1987.

Cabaniss, Allen. *Son of Charlemagne: A Contemporary Life of Louis the Pious*. Syracuse, NY: Syracuse University Press, 1961.

Caldwell Ames, Christine. *Righteous Persecution: Inquisition, Dominicans, and Christianity in the Middle Ages*. Philadelphia: University of Pennsylvania Press, 2009.

Cameron, Alan. *The Last Pagans of Rome*. Oxford: Oxford University Press, 2011.

Canepa, Matthew P. *The Two Eyes of the Earth: Art and Ritual of Kingship Between Rome and Sasanian Iran*. Berkeley: University of California Press, 2009.

Caner, Daniel. *The Rich and the Pure: Philanthropy and the Making of Christian Society in Early Byzantium*. Oakland: University of California Press, 2021.

Carpenter, David. *The Struggle for Mastery: The Penguin History of Britain, 1066–1284*. London: Penguin Books, 2003.

Catlos, Brian A. *Infidel Kings and Unholy Warriors: Faith, Power, and Violence in the Age of Crusade and Jihad*. New York: Farrar, Straus and Giroux, 2014.

Catlos, Brian A. *Kingdoms of Faith: A New History of Islamic Spain*. New York: Basic Books, 2018.

Chazelle, Celia M. "Pictures, Books, and the Illiterate: Pope Gregory I's Letters to Serenus of Marseilles." *Word and Image* 2 (1990): 138–153.

Clanchy, M. T. *Abelard: A Medieval Life*. Oxford: Blackwell, 1999.

Clanchy, M. T. *From Memory to Written Record: England, 1066–1307*. 3rd edition. Oxford: Wiley-Blackwell, 2013.

Cobb, Paul M. "The Empire in Syria, 705–763." In *The New Cambridge History of Islam. Vol. 1: The Formation of the Islamic World, Sixth to Eleventh Centuries*, edited by Chase F. Robinson, 226–268. Cambridge: Cambridge University Press, 2010.

Cobb, Paul M. *The Race for Paradise: An Islamic History of the Crusades*. Oxford: Oxford University Press, 2014.

Cobb, Paul. *Usama ibn Munqidh: Warrior Poet of the Age of the Crusades*. Oxford: Oneworld, 2005.

Cohen, Jeremy. *Living Letters of the Law: Ideas of the Jew in Medieval Christianity*. Berkeley: University of California Press, 1999.

Cohn, Samuel K., Jr. "The Black Death and the Burning of the Jews." *Past and Present* 196 (2007): 3–36.

Colville, Alfred. *Recherches sur l'histoire de Lyon du Ve siècle au IXe siècle (450–800)*. Paris: Picard, 1928.

Constable, Giles. *The Reformation of the Twelfth Century*. Cambridge: Cambridge University Press, 1996.

Constable, Giles. "The Second Crusade as Seen by Contemporaries." *Traditio* 9 (1953): 213–279.

Constable, Giles. *Three Studies in Medieval Religious and Social Thought: The Interpretation of Mary and Martha, The Ideal of the Imitation of Christ, and The Orders of Society*. Cambridge: Cambridge University Press, 1995.

Cowdrey, H. E. J. "Bishop Ermenfrid of Sion and the Penitential Ordinance Following the Battle of Hastings." *Journal of Ecclesiastical History* 20 (1969): 225–242.

Cowdrey, H. E. J. "The Paterenes and the Church of Milan." *Transactions of the Royal Historical Society* 18 (1968): 25–38.

Cribiore, Raffaella. "A Hymn to the Nile." *Zeitschrift für Papyrologie und Epigraphik* 106 (1995): 97–116.

Crone, Patricia. "The Religion of the Qur'anic Pagans: God and the Lesser Deities." *Arabica* 57 (2010): 151–200.

Davis, Jennifer R., and Michael McCormick, eds. *The Long Morning of Medieval Europe: New Directions in Medieval Studies*. Aldershot, UK: Ashgate, 2008.

De Jong, Mayke. *The Penitential State. Authority and Atonement in the Age of Louis the Pious, 814–840*. Cambridge: Cambridge University Press, 2009.

Devroey, Jean-Pierre. *La nature et le roi: Environnement, pouvoir et société à l'âge de Charlemagne (740–820)*. Paris: Albin Michel, 2019.

DeVun, Leah. *The Shape of Sex: Nonbinary Gender from Genesis to the Renaissance*. New York: Columbia University Presss, 2021.

Dewitte, Sharon N., and Maryanne Kowaleski. "Black Death Bodies." *Fragments* 6 (2017): 1–37.

Diefenbach, Steffen. *Römische Erinnerungsräume: Heiligenmemoria und kollektive Identitäten im Rom des 3. bis 5. Jahrhunderts n. Chr.* Millennium-Studien 11. Berlin: de Gruyter, 2007.

Dignas, Beate, and Engelbert Winter. *Rome and Persia in Late Antiquity: Neighbours and Rivals* Cambridge: Cambridge University Press, 2007.

Dod, Bernard G. "Aristoteles latinus." In *The Cambridge History of Later Medieval Philosophy*, edited by Norman Kretzmann, Anthony Kenny, and Jan Pinborg, 45–79. Cambridge: Cambridge University Press, 1982.

Dols, Michael W. "Ibn al-Wardi's Risalah al-naba' 'an al-waba', a Translation of a Major Source for the History of the Black Death in the Middle East." In *Near Eastern Numismatics, Iconography, Epigraphy and History: Studies in Honor of George C. Miles*, edited by Dickran K. Kouymjian, 443–455. Beirut: American University of Beirut, 1974.

Dutton, Paul Edward. "Observations on Early Medieval Weather in General, Bloody Rain in Particular." In *The Long Morning of Medieval Europe: New Directions in Medieval Studies*, edited by Jennifer R. Davis and Michael McCormick, 167–180. Aldershot, UK: Ashgate, 2008.

Eddé, Anne-Marie. *Saladin*. Translated by Jane Marie Todd. Cambridge, MA: Belknap Press of Harvard University Press, 2011.

Edwards, Nancy. "Early Medieval Inscribed Stones and Stone Sculpture in Wales: Context and Function." *Medieval Archeology* 45 (2001): 15–39.

Effros, Bonnie, and Isabel Moreira, eds. *The Oxford Handbook of the Merovingian World*. Oxford: Oxford University Press, 2020.

Einbinder, Susan L. *After the Black Death: Plague and Commemoration Among Iberian Jews* Philadelphia: University of Pennsylvania Press, 2018.

Fancy, Hussein. *The Mercenary Mediterranean: Sovereignty, Religion, and Violence in the Medieval Crown of Aragon*. Chicago: University of Chicago Press, 2016.

Favereau, Marie. *The Horde: How the Mongols Changed the World*. Cambridge, MA: Belknap Press of Harvard University Press, 2021.

Fernie, Eric. *Romanesque Architecture*. New Haven, CT: Yale University Press, 2014.

Firnhaber-Baker, Justine. *The Jacquerie of 1358: A Peasant's Revolt*. Oxford: Oxford University Press, 2021.

Fleming, Robin. *Britain After Rome: The Fall and Rise, 400–1070*. London: Penguin Books, 2011.

Flood, Finbarr B. "Faith, Religion, and the Material Culture of Early Islam." In *Byzantium and Islam: Age of Transition 7th–9th Century*, edited by Helen C. Evans with Brandie Ratliff, 244–258. New Haven, CT: Yale University Press, 2012.

Flower, Richard. "'The Insanity of Heretics Must Be Restrained': Heresiology in the Theodosian Code." In *Theodosius II: Rethinking the Roman Empire in Late Antiquity*, edited by Christopher Kelly, 172–194. Cambridge: Cambridge University Press, 2013.

Frier, Bruce. "Demography." In *The Cambridge Ancient History. Vol. 11: The High Empire, A.D. 70–192*, edited by A. K. Bowman, Peter Garnesey, and Dominic Rathbone, 787–816. Cambridge: Cambridge University Press, 2000.

Gibbon, Edward. *The History of the Decline and Fall of the Roman Empire*. Edited by J. B. Bury. 12 volumes. New York: Fred De Fau, 1906.

Gillis, Mathew Bryan. *Heresy and Dissent in the Carolingian Empire: The Case of Gottschalk of Orbais*. Oxford: Oxford University Press, 2017.

Goffart, Walter. *Barbarian Tides: The Migration Age and the Later Roman Empire*. Philadelphia: University of Pennsylvania Press, 2006.

Grant, Edward. "The Effect of the Condemnation of 1277." In *The Cambridge History of Later Medieval Philosophy*, edited by Norman Kretzmann, Anthony Kenny, and Jan Pinborg, 537–539. Cambridge: Cambridge University Press, 1982.

Green, Monica H. "The Four Black Deaths." *American Historical Review* 125 (2020): 1601–1631.

Green, Monica H., ed. *Pandemic Disease in the Medieval World: Rethinking the Black Death*. Medieval Globe 1. Kalamazoo, MI: Arc Medieval Press, 2015.

Green, Peter. *Alexander to Actium: The Historical Evolution of the Hellenistic Age*. Berkeley: University of California Press, 1990.

Guidetti, Mattia. "The Contiguity Between Churches and Mosques in Early Islamic Bilad al-Sham." *Bulletin of SOAS* 76 (2013): 229–258.

Guitton, Laurent. *La fabrique de la morale au Moyen Âge. Vices, normes et identités (Bretagne, XIIe–XVe siècles)*. Rennes: Presses Universitaires de Rennes, 2022.

Hakenbeck, Susanne. "Roman or Barbarian? Shifting Identities in Early Medieval Cemeteries in Bavaria." *Post-Classical Archeologies* 1 (2011): 37–66.

Haldon, John. *The Empire That Would Not Die: The Paradox of Eastern Roman Survival, 640–740*. Cambridge, MA: Harvard University Press, 2016.

Haldon, John. "'Greek Fire' Revisted: Recent and Current Research." In *Byzantine Style, Religion and Civilization: In Honour of Sir Steven Runciman*, edited by Elizabeth Jeffreys, 290–325. Cambridge: Cambridge Unversity Press, 2006.

Halsall, Guy. *Barbarian Migrations and the Roman West, 376–568*. Cambridge: Cambridge University Press, 2007.

Härke, Heinrich. "'Warrior Graves'? The Background of the Anglo-Saxon Weapon Burial Rite." *Past and Present* 126 (1990): 22–43.

Harper, Kyle. *The Fate of Rome: Climate, Disease, and the End of an Empire*. Princeton, NJ: Princeton University Press, 2017.

Harper, Kyle. *Plagues upon the Earth: Disease and the Course of Human History*. Princeton, NJ: Princeton University Press, 2021.

Harper, Kyle. *Slavery in the Late Roman World, AD 275–425*. Cambridge: Cambridge University Press, 2011.

Harries, Jill. *Sidonius Apollinaris and the Fall of Rome*. Oxford: Clarendon Press, 1995.

Head, Thomas, and Richard Landes, eds. *The Peace of God: Social Violence and Religious Response in France Around the Year 1000*. Ithaca, NY: Cornell University Press, 1992.

Heather, Peter. *The Fall of the Roman Empire: A New History of Rome and the Barbarians*. Oxford: Oxford University Press, 2007.

Heng, Geraldine. *The Invention of Race in the European Middle Ages*. Cambridge: Cambridge University Press, 2018.

Herrin, Judith. *The Formation of Christendom*. Princeton, NJ: Princeton University Press, 2021 [orig. 1987].

Herrin, Judith. *Ravenna: Capital of Empire, Crucible of Europe*. Princeton, NJ: Princeton University Press, 2020.

Hodgson, Marshall G. S. *The Venture of Islam: Conscience and History in a World Civilization, volume 1, The Classical Age of Islam*. Chicago: University of Chicago Press, 1974.

Hoffmann, Richard. *An Environmental History of Medieval Europe*. Cambridge: Cambridge University Press, 2014.

Hopkins, Keith. "Rome, Taxes, Rent and Trade." *Kodai: Journal of Ancient History* 6–7 (1995–1996): 41–75.

Huizinga, Johan. *The Waning of the Middle Ages: A Study of the Forms of Life, Thought and Art in France and the Netherlands in the XIVth and the XVth Centuries*. Translated and abridged by Fritz Hopman. London: Edward Arnold, 1924 [orig. 1919].

Jackson, Peter. *The Mongols and the Islamic World: From Conquest to Conversion*. New Haven, CT: Yale University Press, 2017.

Jordan, William Chester. *The Apple of His Eye: Converts from Islam in the Reign of Louis IX*. Princeton, NJ: Princeton University Press, 2019.

Jordan, William Chester. *Europe in the High Middle Ages*. London: Viking-Penguin Books, 2001.

Jordan, William Chester. *The French Monarchy and the Jews: From Philip Augustus to the Last Capetians*. Philadelphia: University of Pennsylvania Press, 1989.

Jordan, William Chester. *The Great Famine: Northern Europe in the Early Fourteenth Century*. Princeton, NJ: Princeton University Press, 1996.

Kaldellis, Anthony. *Romanland: Ethnicity and Empire in Byzantium*. Cambridge, MA: Belknap Press of Harvard University Press, 2019.

Kaminsky, Howard. "The Great Schism." In *The New Cambridge Medieval History. Vol. 6: c. 1300-c. 1415*, vol. 6, edited by Michael Jones, 674–696. Cambridge: Cambridge University Press, 2000.

Kelly, Christopher, ed. *Theodosius II: Rethinking the Roman Empire in Late Antiquity*. Cambridge: Cambridge University Press, 2013.

Kennedy, Hugh. "The Muslims in Europe." In *The New Cambridge Medieval History. Vol 2: c. 700-c. 900*, edited by Rosamond McKitterick, 249–271. Cambridge: Cambridge University Press, 1995.

Klingshirn, William E. *Caesarius of Arles: The Making of a Christian Community in Late Antique Gaul*. Cambridge: Cambridge University Press, 2004.

Kreiner, Jamie. *Legions of Pigs in the Early Medieval West*. New Haven, CT: Yale University Press, 2020.

Kreiner, Jamie. *The Social Life of Historiography in the Merovingian Kingdom*. Cambridge: Cambridge University Press, 2014.

Kulikowski, Michael. *Rome's Gothic Wars from the Third Century to Alaric*. Cambridge: Cambridge University Press, 2007.

Kuttner, Stephan, and Antonio García y García. "A New Eyewitness Account of the Fourth Lateran Council." *Traditio* 20 (1964): 115–178.

La Rocca, Cristina. "An Arena of Abuses and Competing Powers: Rome on Cassiodorus's *Variae*." In *Italy and Early Medieval Europe: Papers for Chris Wickham*, edited by Ross Balzaretti, Julia Barrow, and Patricia Skinner, 201–212. Oxford: Oxford University Press, 2018.

Lavan, Myles. "The Spread of Roman Citizenship, 14–212 CE: Quantification in the Face of High Uncertainty." *Past and Present* 230 (2016): 3–46.

Lower, Michael. *The Tunis Crusade of 1270: A Mediterranean History*. Oxford: Oxford University Press, 2018.

MacCulloch, Diarmaid. *Christianity: The First Three Thousand Years*. Harmondsworth, UK: Penguin Books, 2011.

MacMullen, Ramsay. *Changes in the Roman Empire: Essays in the Ordinary*. Princeton, NJ: Princeton University Press, 1990.

Maas, Michael. "Roman Questions, Byzantine Answers: Contours of the Age of Justinian." In *The Cambridge Companion to the Age of Justinian*, edited by Michael Maas, 3–27. Cambridge: Cambridge University Press, 2005.

Mathisen, Ralph. "Dating the Letters of Sidonius." In *New Approaches to Sidonius Apollinaris*, edited by Johannes A. van Waarden and Gavin Kelly, 221–247. Leuven: Peeters, 2013.

Mazzarino, Santo. *Aspetti sociali del quarto secolo*. Rome: Bretschneider, 1951.

McClendon, Charles B. *The Origins of Medieval Architecture: Building in Europe, A.D. 600–900*. New Haven, CT: Yale University Press, 2005.

McCormick, Michael. "Gregory of Tours on Sixth-Century Plague and Other Epidemics." *Speculum* 96 (2021): 38–96.

McCormick, Michael. "New Light on the 'Dark Ages': How the Slave Trade Fuelled the Carolingian Economy." *Past and Present* 177 (2002): 17–54.

McCormick, Michael. *Origins of the European Economy: Communications and Commerce AD 300–900*. Cambridge: Cambridge University Press, 2001.

McCormick, Michael, et al. "Climate Change During and After the Roman Empire: Reconstructing the Past from Scientific and Historical Evidence." *Journal of Interdisciplinary History* 43 (2012): 169–220.

McKitterick, Rosamond. *Charlemagne: The Formation of a European Identity*. Cambridge: Cambridge University Press, 2008.

Molyneaux, George. "Did the English Really Think They Were God's Elect in the Anglo-Saxon Period?" *Journal of Ecclesiastical History* 65 (2014): 721–737.

Montgomery, James E. "Ibn Fadlan and the Rusiyyah." *Journal of Arabic and Islamic Studies* 3 (2000): 1–25.

Moore, R. I. *The First European Revolution, c. 970–1215*. Oxford: Blackwell, 2000.

Moore, R. I. *The Formation of a Persecuting Society: Authority and Deviance in Western Europe, 950–1250*. 2nd edition. Oxford: Blackwell, 2007.

Moore, R. I. *The War on Heresy*. Cambridge, MA: Belknap Press of Harvard University Press, 2014.

Mordechai, Lee, and Merle Eisenberg. "Rejecting Catastrophe: The Case of the Justinianic Plague." *Past and Present* 244 (2019): 3–50.

Morgan, David. *The Mongols*. Oxford: Blackwell, 1990.

Morlet, S., ed. *Le traité de Porphyre contre les chrétiens. Un siècle de recherches, nouvelles questions. Actes de colloque international organisé les 8 et 9 septembre 2009 à l'Université de Paris IV-Sorbonne*. Paris: Institut d'Études Augustiniennes, 2011.

Naismith, Rory. "The Social Significance of Monetization in the Early Middle Ages." *Past and Present* 223 (2014): 14–17.

Nelson, Janet L. *King and Emperor: A New Life of Charlemagne*. Berkeley: University of California Press, 2019.

Nicholson, Helen J. *The Knights Templar*. Leeds, UK: Arc Humanities Press, 2021.

Nicholson, Helen, Paul F. Crawford, and Jochen Burgtorf, eds. *The Debate on the Trial of the Templars*. Farnham, UK: Routledge, 2010.

Nirenberg, David. *Communities of Violence: Persecution of Minorities in the Middle Ages*. 2nd edition. Princeton, NJ: Princeton University Press, 2015.

Nirenberg, David. "Mass Conversion and Genealogical Mentalities: Jews and Christians in Fifteenth-Century Spain." *Past and Present* 174 (2002): 3–41.

Pegg, Mark Gregory. "The Albigensian Crusade and the Early Inquisitions into Heretical Depravity." In *The Cambridge World History of Genocide. Vol 1: Genocide in the Ancient, Medieval, and Premodern Worlds*, edited by Ben Kiernan, T. M. Lemon, and Tristan Taylor, 470–497. Cambridge: Cambridge University Press, 2022.

Pegg, Mark Gregory. *The Corruption of Angels: The Great Inquisition of 1245–1246*. Princeton, NJ: Princeton University Press, 2001.

Pegg, Mark Gregory. *A Most Holy War: The Albigensian Crusade and the Battle for Christendom*. New York: Oxford University Press, 2008.

Potter, David. *Constantine the Emperor*. Oxford: Oxford University Press, 2013.

Power, Amanda. *Roger Bacon and the Defence of Christendom*. Cambridge: Cambridge University Press, 2013.

Power, Daniel. "The Albigensian Crusade After Simon of Montfort (1218–1224)." In *Simon de Montfort (c. 1170–1218): Le croisé, son lignage et son temps*, edited by Martin Aurell, Gregory Lippiatt, and Laurent Macé, 161–178. Turnhout: Brepols, 2020.

Price, Neil. *Children of Ash and Elm: A History of the Vikings*. New York: Basic Books, 2020.

Pryor, John H. *Geography, Technology, and War: Studies in the Maritime History of the Mediterranean 649–571*. Cambridge: Cambridge University Press, 1992.

Rebillard, Eric. "Popular Hatred Against Christians: The Case of North Africa in the Second and Third Centuries." *Archiv für Religionsgeschichte* 16 (2015): 283–310.

Reuter, Timothy. "The End of Carolingian Military Expansion." In *Charlemagne's Heir: New Perspectives on the Reign of Louis the Pious (814–840)*, edited by Peter Godman and Roger Collins, 391–405. Oxford: Oxford University Press, 1990.

Reimitz, Helmut. *History, Frankish Identity and the Framing of Western Ethnicity*. Cambridge: Cambridge University Press, 2015.

Rio, Alice. *Slavery After Rome, 500–1100*. Oxford: Oxford University Press, 2017.

Rives, J. B. "The Decree of Decius and the Religion of Empire." *Journal of Roman Studies* 89 (1999): 135–154.

Robinson, Chase F. "Reconstructing Early Islam: Truth and Consequences." In *Method and Theory in the Study of Islamic Origins*, edited by Herbert Berg, 101–123. Leiden: Brill, 2003.

Rubenstein, Jay. *Armies of Heaven: The First Crusade and the Quest for Apocalypse*. New York: Basic Books, 2011.

Rubenstein, Jay. *Nebuchadnezzar's Dream: The Crusades, Apocalyptic Prophecy, and the End of History*. Oxford: Oxford University Press, 2019.

Rubin, Miri. *Gentile Tales: The Narrative Assault on Late Medieval Jews*. Philadelphia: University of Pennsylvania Press, 1999.

Rustow, Maria. *The Lost Archive: Traces of a Caliphate in a Cairo Synagogue*. Princeton, NJ: Princeton University Press, 2020.

Sahner, Christian C. "The First Iconoclasm in Islam: A New History of the Edict of Yazid II (AH 104/AD 723)." *Der Islam* 94 (2017): 5–56.

Santagata, Marco. *Dante: The Story of His Life*. Translated by Richard Dixon. Cambridge, MA: Belknap Press of Harvard University Press, 2018.

Scheidel, Walter. "Demography." In *The Cambridge Economic History of the Greco-Roman World*, edited by Walter Scheidel, Ian Morris, and Richard P. Saller, 38–86. Cambridge: Cambridge University Press, 2007.

Scheidel, Walter, and S. J. Friesen. "The Size of the Economy and the Distribution of Income in the Roman Empire." *Journal of Roman Studies* 99 (2009): 61–99.

Schmidt, Jean-Claude. *The Conversion of Herman the Jew: Autobiography, History, and Fiction in the Twelfth Century*. Translated by Alex J. Novikoff. Philadelphia: University of Pennsylvania Press, 2010.

Shaw, Brent. "The Passion of Perpetua." *Past and Present* 139 (1993): 3–45.

Smith, Katherine Allen. "Saints in Shining Armor: Martial Asceticism and Masculine Models of Sanctity, ca. 1050–1250." *Speculum* 83 (2008): 572–602.

Southern, Richard. *The Making of the Middle Ages*. New Haven, CT: Yale University Press, 1953.

Stevenson, Jane Barbara. "The Monastic Rules of Columbanus." In *Columbanus: Studies on the Latin Writings*, edited by Michael Lapidge, 203–216. Woodbridge, UK: Boydell Press, 1997.

Strohm, Paul. *Chaucer's Tale: 1386 and the Road to Canterbury*. New York: Penguin Books, 2014.

Tannous, Jack. *The Making of the Medieval Middle East: Religion, Society, and Simple Believers*. Princeton, NJ: Princeton University Press, 2018.

Tardieu, Michel. "La diffusion du Bouddhisme dans l'empire kouchan, l'Iran et la Chine d'après un Kepahalaion manichéen inédit." *Studia Iranica* 17 (1988): 153–182.

Taylor, Alice. "Homage in the Latin Chronicles of Eleventh- and Twelfth-Century Normandy." In *People, Texts and Artefacts: Cultural Transmission in the Medieval Norman Worlds*, edited by David Bates, Edoardo D'Angelo, and Elisabeth van Houts, 231–252. London: Institute of Historical Research, 2018.

Théry, Julien. "A Heresy of State: Philip the Fair, the Trial of the 'Perfidious Templars,' and the Pontificalization of the French Monarchy." *Journal of Medieval Religious Cultures* 39 (2013): 117–148.

Thompson, Augustine. *Francis of Assisi: The Life.* Ithaca, NY: Cornell University Press, 2013.

Thurmond, David L. "Some Roman Slave Collars in *CIL.*" *Athenaeum* 82 (1994): 460–492.

Tolan, John. *Saint Francis and the Sultan: The Curious History of a Christian-Muslim Encounter.* Oxford: Oxford University Press, 2009.

Tolan, John. *Saracens: Islam in the Medieval European Imagination.* New York: Columbia University Press, 2002.

Torell, Jean-Pierre. "Life and Work." In *The Oxford Handbook of Aquinas,* edited by Brian Davies, 5–28. Oxford: Oxford University Press, 2012.

Torell, Jean-Pierre. *Saint Thomas Aquinas, vol. 1, The Person and His Work.* Translated by Robert Royal. Washington, DC: Catholic University Press, 1996.

Trivellone, Alessia. *L'hérétique imaginé. Hétérodoxie et iconographie dans l'Occident Médiéval, de l'époque carolingienne à l'Inquisition.* Turnhout: Brepols, 2009.

Verhulst, Adriaan E. "Karolingische Agrarpolitik. Das *Capitulare de villis* und die Hungersnöte von 792/93 und 805/6." *Zeitschrift für Agrargeschichte une Agrarsoziologie* 13 (1965): 175–189.

Von Rummel, Philipp. *Habitus barbarus: Kleidung und Repräsentation spätantiker Eliten im 4. und 5. Jarhundert.* Berlin: de Gruyter, 2007.

Ward-Perkins, Bryan, and Carlos Machado. "410 and the End of the New Statuary in Italy." In *The Sack of Rome in 410 AD: The Event, Its Context and Its Impact,* edited by Johannes Lipps, Carlos Machado, and Philipp von Rummel, 353–364. Wiesbaden: Dr. Ludwig Reichert Verlag, 2013.

Wei, Ian P. *Intellectual Culture in Medieval Paris: Theologians and the University, c. 1100–1330.* Cambridge: Cambridge University Press, 2012.

Whalen, Brett Edward. *Dominion of God: Christendom and Apocalypse in the Middle Ages.* Cambridge, MA: Harvard University Press, 2009.

Whittow, Mark. "Sources of Knowledge: Cultures of Recording." *Past and Present supp.* 13 (2018): 45–87.

Wickham, Chris. *Framing the Early Middle Ages: Europe and the Mediterranean, 400–800.* Oxford: Oxford University Press, 2005.

Wickham, Chris. *The Inheritance of Rome: A History of Europe from 400 to 1000.* New York: Viking Penguin Books, 2009.

Wickham, Chris. *Medieval Europe.* New Haven, CT: Yale University Press, 2017.

Wickham, Chris. *Medieval Rome: Stability and Crisis of a City, 900–1150.* Oxford: Oxford University Press, 2015.

Wickham, Chris. *Sleepwalking into a New World: The Emergence of Italian City Communes in the Twelfth Century.* Princeton, NJ: Princeton University Press, 2015.

Wilberg, Christian. "Philosophy in the Age of Justinian." In *The Cambridge Companion to the Age of Justinian,* edited by Michael Maas, 316–340. Cambridge: Cambridge University Press, 2005).

Wilkinson, Kevin W. "Palladas and the Age of Constantine," *Journal of Roman Studies* 99 (2009): 3–60.

Williams, Megan Hale. *The Monk and the Book: Jerome and the Making of Christian Scholarship*. Chicago: University of Chicago Press, 2006.

Winroth, Anders. *The Age of the Vikings*. Princeton, NJ: Princeton University Press, 2014.

Winroth, Anders. *The Conversion of Scandinavia: Vikings, Merchants, and Missionaries in the Remaking of Northern Europe*. New Haven, CT: Yale University Press, 2012.

Winroth, Anders. *The Making of Gratian's Decretum*. Cambridge: Cambridge University Press, 2000.

Wood, Ian. "Entrusting Western Europe to the Church, 400–750." *Transactions of the Royal Historical Society* 23 (2013): 37–73.

Wood, Ian. *The Christian Economy in the Early Medieval West: Towards a Temple Economy*. Binghamton, NY: Punctum, 2022.

Wood, Ian. *The Transformation of the Roman West*. Leeds, UK: Arc Humanities Press, 2018.

Index